TOM MASTERS
STEVE FALLON
VESNA MARIC

LONDON
C I T Y   G U I D E

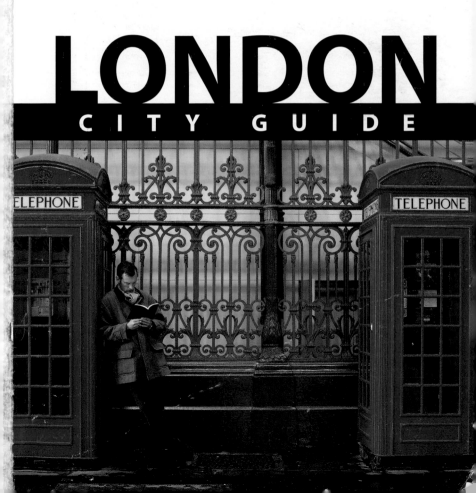

INTRODUCING LONDON

Tower Bridge (p121) *and* Timepiece *sundial sculpture by Wendy Taylor*

From its Roman core to its Olympic edges, its ancient abbeys to its iconic skyscrapers, London is an extraordinary time capsule of human history and a cross-section of all human life.

Having worked very hard to break down the many negative stereotypes it has enjoyed over the years, London now confidently assumes the mantle of Europe's cultural capital and that of one of the world's great cities, crowning itself Napoleon-style by hosting its third Olympic Games in 2012. It's safe to say that London has not exuded so much confidence since the heady days of empire in the late 19th century, despite the recent economic crisis that has seen the city's status as the world's pre-eminent financial centre take a wobble.

London has been called a 'world in one city' and that's not just empty rhetoric. The brilliant feat carried off here is that while immigrants, the city's lifeblood, continue to flow in and contribute their energy and cultures to the capital's already-spicy melting pot, London nevertheless feels quintessentially British, whether it's those boxy black cabs, the red double-deckers or those grand symbols of Britain – the mother of all parliaments at Westminster, the silhouette of Tower Bridge above the muddy Thames or the now world-famous London Eye, barely a decade old.

Don't miss these essential sights of course, but equally ensure you partake in what really makes London great: a pint and a plate of fish 'n' chips by the river, a day in the park or a night out in Soho or Shoreditch. Take a deep breath and prepare to fall in love with the British capital.

LONDON LIFE

Famous for its urban sprawl, overcrowding and expensive public transport system dating in part from the Victorian era, London life may not sound instantly attractive to outsiders. 'Dealing with London is the price you pay to live in London' is how one friend put it to us recently – and there's more than a nugget of truth in this statement as until you get here, it's not always clear what makes people love the city so much. Spend a few days in London, though, and you'll probably come to understand that living in a city as exciting, fast-changing, surprising and fascinating makes it (almost) worth the sky-high cost of living, surviving the Circle line and learning a new definition of the word 'crowded' during the rush hour.

Moreover, London has been tackling its problems with impressive zeal in the past decade. Denied self-rule by the Conservatives for 14 years because of the leftist tendencies of the leaders it invariably elected, London finally got its own mayor and Assembly in 2000. Mayor Ken Livingstone (2000–08) introduced a punishing but popular congestion charge on cars entering the city centre, massively increased bike lanes and the provision of buses, and made serious progress in sorting out the tube. When Londoners voted in the Conservative Boris Johnson in 2008 – perhaps a surprising choice politically, but London has always loved a maverick – many feared the gaffe-prone Tory would be a disaster, yet Boris (as he's known to one and all) arguably acquitted himself rather well in his first year of office, in many spheres actually building on, rather than tearing down, achievements made under his predecessor.

Another recent boon has been a food revolution that has seen London's eating scene go from international joke to one of the best in the world. Add to that newly liberalised drinking laws, a roundly welcomed smoking ban and a fantastic music scene, and London makes for one of the best places on the planet for a night out.

Big Ben (p92) and London Underground sign at night

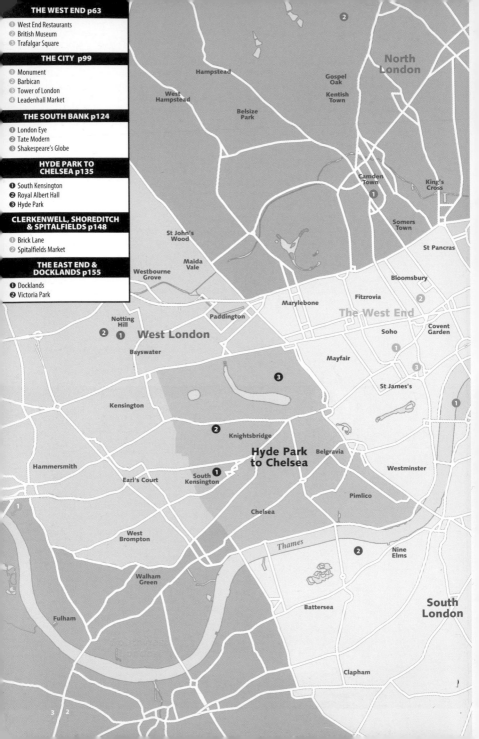

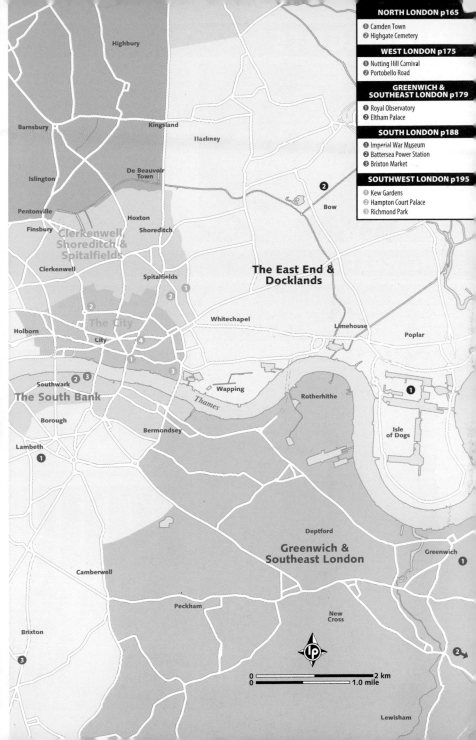

Highbury

Barnsbury

Kingsland

Hackney

Islington

De Beauvoir Town

❷

Bow

Pentonville

Hoxton

Finsbury

Shoreditch

Clerkenwell, Shoreditch & Spitalfields

Clerkenwell

Spitalfields

❶

The East End & Docklands

❷

Holborn

The City

Whitechapel

Limehouse

Poplar

City

❹

❶

❸

Wapping

Southwark

❷ ❸

❸

The South Bank

Thames

Rotherhithe

❶

Borough

Isle of Dogs

Bermondsey

Lambeth

❶

Camberwell

Deptford

Greenwich & Southeast London

Greenwich

❶

Peckham

New Cross

Brixton

❸

❷

0 ————— 2 km
0 ————— 1.0 mile

Lewisham

HIGHLIGHTS

1 **West End Restaurants** Try out the world's cuisine at one of the West End's fabulous restaurants (p236)

2 **British Museum** See the world's history at this impressive museum (p79)

3 **Trafalgar Square** Take in the great square and one of the city's best art galleries (p69)

THE WEST END

At turns exciting, glitzy, busy and chaotic, the West End is London's beating heart with far more than its fair share of the best shops, pubs, bars and restaurants in the capital.

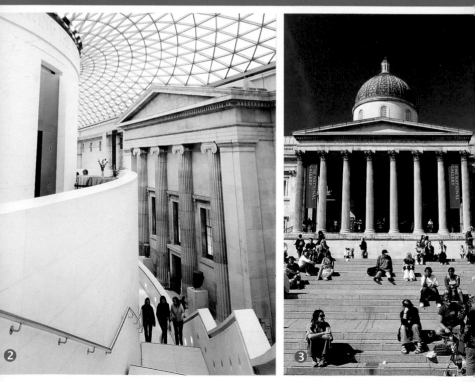

1 Monument Climb the Monument for a stunning view of the city's skyscrapers and the river (p107)

2 Barbican Catch world-famous names at the incredible Barbican cultural centre (p311)

3 Tower of London Be king or queen for a day at London's most historic castle (p117)

4 Leadenhall Market Join the city workers for a pint at lunchtime in the pubs (p259)

THE CITY

The ancient centre of London, and home to London's financial district, the City is jam-packed full of fascinating historic sights and is a delight to explore, particularly at weekends when it's almost all yours.

THE SOUTH BANK

Redevelopment and investment have turned this once rather bleak area of London into something of a cultural hub. From international galleries and street performances to cutting-edge classical-music concerts and theatre, you'll find it all here.

❶ **London Eye** Take in sweeping views of the capital from the city's top icon (p124)

❷ **Tate Modern** Drop into this prize-winning structure to discover London's most exciting (and often participatory) exhibitions (p128)

❸ **Shakespeare's Globe** Be bowled over by the Bard at the South Bank's re-created open-air theatre (p312)

HYDE PARK TO CHELSEA

The Royal Borough, home to Her Majesty, really is fit for a queen. With some of the most beautiful buildings, prestigious museums and superb outdoor spaces, this is how the other half live.

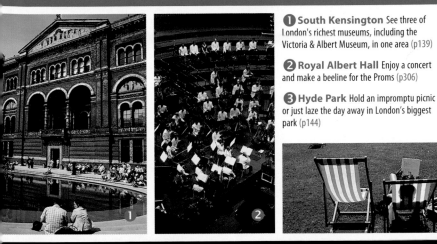

❶ South Kensington See three of London's richest museums, including the Victoria & Albert Museum, in one area (p139)

❷ Royal Albert Hall Enjoy a concert and make a beeline for the Proms (p306)

❸ Hyde Park Hold an impromptu picnic or just laze the day away in London's biggest park (p144)

CLERKENWELL, SHOREDITCH & SPITALFIELDS

The new life in London, these three ancient parishes now collectively house the city's most creative talents, its best clubs, bars and coolest shops. Even if you've never heard of them, you'll most likely find your local friends heading here time and time again.

❶ Brick Lane Shop till you drop on and around Brick Lane with its great markets and boutiques (p152)

❷ Spitalfields Market Browse the beautiful remaining sections of this historic market on a Sunday morning (p227)

THE EAST END & DOCKLANDS

The heart and soul of London-as-it-was, the East End is gearing up for massive change for the 2012 Olympics. The Docklands is London's future – a financial district to rival the City, with plenty of interesting architecture gazing out on the Thames.

❶ Docklands Join an architectural tour of this forest of skyscrapers with Open House London (p208)

❷ Victoria Park Stroll through one of London's most beautiful (and used) parks (p160)

NORTH LONDON

A glorious agglomeration of hilltop villages, leafy parks and charming high streets, each with its own long-standing identity, North London should be savoured and enjoyed at a slow pace.

❶ Camden Town Drink and dance the night away in this indie-rock nexus (p284)

❷ Highgate Cemetery Discover London's most wonderful place to be dead: fantastic, Gothic Highgate Cemetery (p169)

WEST LONDON

Old-money tradition meets multicultural fun-fest in the sprawling urban jungle of West London. The centre of gravity here is bustling Notting Hill, where great shopping, eating and drinking all combine to make any day out memorable.

❶ Notting Hill Carnival Join in the fun at Europe's biggest (and most crowded) street festival (p17)

❷ Portobello Road Rummage through the great clothing and bric-a-brac market stalls (p226)

GREENWICH & SOUTHEAST LONDON

With its fascinating naval, geographic and architectural heritage on display for all to enjoy, Greenwich is a must for any visitor to the capital. And be sure to make time for some of Southeast London's more offbeat sights as well.

❶ Royal Observatory Straddle the meridian line and two hemispheres at the spot where time really does stand still (p180)

❷ Eltham Palace Visit Britain's most extravagant art deco mansion and get a grand medieval hall to boot (p185)

SOUTH LONDON

Residential, multicultural and always surprising, South London covers a vast swath of the city, including rough and ready Brixton, suburban Clapham and often-overlooked Battersea.

❶ Imperial War Museum Once Bedlam, and now the Imperial War Museum (p188)

❷ Battersea Power Station Check out one of London's most unique pieces of architectural heritage (p192)

❸ Brixton Market Head down to Brixton Market for an exciting multicultural atmosphere and plenty of choice (p259)

SOUTHWEST LONDON

Southwest London is home to some of the city's most famous sights, which radiate from Richmond, the famously posh London village known as much for its antiques shopping and celebrity residents as it is for its rich history and royal connections.

❶ Kew Gardens Marvel at the vast collection of endlessly fascinating Kew Gardens, the largest botanic gardens in the world (p199)

❷ Hampton Court Palace Explore the incredible complex at London's superb Tudor palace – and be sure to get lost in the maze (p201)

❸ Richmond Park See the red deer and enjoy the urban wilderness in this enormous park (p198)

London is a very straightforward destination and little forward planning is required, with the glaring exception of accommodation, which is always best booked in advance, and even then will take up way more of your budget than you'd ideally like. The city is a year-round destination where you'll always find more things to do than your time will ever allow.

WHEN TO GO

You might imagine that in a country with such a temperate and mild climate as England, the weather is not much of a topic for conversation, and yet, like their middle-England cousins, Londoners are relentless weather-watchers and every rise or fall of the mercury will provoke smiles or gloom respectively. It's good, therefore, that London is not a city where fun depends on the weather – do as Londoners do, expect overcast skies and rain (even in summer) and then be elated when the sun comes out.

While summer is a great time to visit (and recent years have seen some very Continental heatwaves), spring and autumn are also good times to come, when the crowds are far thinner and sights less crowded. Winter's all cold, wet and dark, although if you're after outdoor pleasures, you'll have them largely to yourself.

For a full list of events in and around London, look out for Visit London's bimonthly *Events in London* and its *Annual Events* pamphlet. You can also check the website at www .visitlondon.com.

FESTIVALS & EVENTS

London is a vibrant city year-round, with no end of annual events, both traditional and modern. Some of our very favourites are below, and prove that from New Year's Day to New Year's Eve there will be festivities and activities aplenty in the British capital.

JANUARY

NEW YEAR'S CELEBRATIONS
On 31 December there's the famous countdown to midnight on Trafalgar Sq – London's biggest bash, but one worth avoiding unless you love crowds.

LONDON ART FAIR
www.londonartfair.co.uk; Business Design Centre, Islington

Over 100 major galleries participate in this contemporary art fair, now one of the largest in Europe, with thematic exhibitions, special events and the best emerging artists.

CHINESE NEW YEAR
Chinatown, Soho
In late January/early February, Chinatown fizzes, crackles and pops in this colourful street festival, which includes a Golden Dragon parade, and eating and partying aplenty.

FEBRUARY
PANCAKE RACES
Spitalfields Market, Covent Garden & Lincoln's Inn Fields
On Shrove Tuesday, in late February/early March, you can catch pancake races and associated silliness at various venues around town.

MARCH
HEAD OF THE RIVER RACE
www.horr.co.uk; Thames, from Mortlake to Putney
Some 400 crews participate in this colourful annual boat race, held over a 7km course.

APRIL
LONDON LESBIAN & GAY FILM FESTIVAL
www.bfi.org.uk/llgff
This vibrant event is one of the best of its kind in the world with hundreds of independent gay-themed films from around the world shown over a fun, party-intensive fortnight at the National Film Theatre.

LONDON MARATHON
www.virginlondonmarathon.com; Greenwich Park to the Mall
Some 35,000 masochists cross London in the world's biggest road race.

CONTENTS

CONTENTS

THE AUTHORS

Tom Masters

Tom has lived, studied and worked in London for over a decade, calling both Stoke Newington and Clerkenwell home in the past five years, before that being geographically scattered all over the city. Despite now residing in Berlin, London will always be home, and it was a great pleasure coming back home and seeing the capital from the perspective of a visitor for this update in 2009. You can see more of Tom's work at www.mastersmafia.com.

Tom was the coordinating author and wrote the Introducing London, Getting Started, Background, Gay & Lesbian London and Directory chapters. He also cowrote the Highlights, Neighbourhoods, Shopping, Eating, Drinking, Sleeping and Excursions chapters.

Steve Fallon

After almost a decade of living in the centre of the known universe – East London – Steve rhymes in his sleep, eats jellied eel for brekkie, drinks lager by the bucketful and dances round the occasional handbag. As always, for this edition of *London* he did everything the hard (read: fun) way: walking the walks, seeing the sights, taking (some) advice from friends, colleagues and the odd taxi driver, and digesting everything in sight.

Steve wrote the Architecture, River Thames, The Arts and Transport chapters. He also cowrote the Highlights, Neighbourhoods, Shopping, Eating, Drinking, Sleeping and Excursions chapters.

Vesna Maric

In this picture, I am standing next to the Serpentine Lake in Hyde Park, one of my favourite areas in London, on a winter's day. I'm a passionate Londoner and even after 12 years in this incredible city, my love for it grows every season – in fact I've come to the conclusion that the longer you spend here, the more you'll love it. London's parks are one of the best things about the place, though the museums, galleries, restaurants and nightlife are equally irresistible.

Vesna wrote the Nightlife and Sports & Activities chapters. She also cowrote the Highlights, Neighbourhoods, Shopping, Eating, Drinking, Sleeping and Excursions chapters.

London is a very straightforward destination and little forward planning is required, with the glaring exception of accommodation, which is always best booked in advance, and even then will take up way more of your budget than you'd ideally like. The city is a year-round destination where you'll always find more things to do than your time will ever allow.

WHEN TO GO

You might imagine that in a country with such a temperate and mild climate as England, the weather is not much of a topic for conversation, and yet, like their middle-England cousins, Londoners are relentless weather-watchers and every rise or fall of the mercury will provoke smiles or gloom respectively. It's good, therefore, that London is not a city where fun depends on the weather – do as Londoners do, expect overcast skies and rain (even in summer) and then be elated when the sun comes out.

While summer is a great time to visit (and recent years have seen some very Continental heatwaves), spring and autumn are also good times to come, when the crowds are far thinner and sights less crowded. Winter's all cold, wet and dark, although if you're after outdoor pleasures, you'll have them largely to yourself.

For a full list of events in and around London, look out for Visit London's bimonthly *Events in London* and its *Annual Events* pamphlet. You can also check the website at www .visitlondon.com.

FESTIVALS & EVENTS

London is a vibrant city year-round, with no end of annual events, both traditional and modern. Some of our very favourites are below, and prove that from New Year's Day to New Year's Eve there will be festivities and activities aplenty in the British capital.

JANUARY

NEW YEAR'S CELEBRATIONS
On 31 December there's the famous countdown to midnight on Trafalgar Sq – London's biggest bash, but one worth avoiding unless you love crowds.

LONDON ART FAIR
www.londonartfair.co.uk; Business Design Centre, Islington

Over 100 major galleries participate in this contemporary art fair, now one of the largest in Europe, with thematic exhibitions, special events and the best emerging artists.

CHINESE NEW YEAR
Chinatown, Soho
In late January/early February, Chinatown fizzes, crackles and pops in this colourful street festival, which includes a Golden Dragon parade, and eating and partying aplenty.

FEBRUARY

PANCAKE RACES
Spitalfields Market, Covent Garden & Lincoln's Inn Fields
On Shrove Tuesday, in late February/early March, you can catch pancake races and associated silliness at various venues around town.

MARCH

HEAD OF THE RIVER RACE
www.horr.co.uk; Thames, from Mortlake to Putney
Some 400 crews participate in this colourful annual boat race, held over a 7km course.

APRIL

LONDON LESBIAN & GAY FILM FESTIVAL
www.bfi.org.uk/llgff
This vibrant event is one of the best of its kind in the world with hundreds of independent gay-themed films from around the world shown over a fun, party-intensive fortnight at the National Film Theatre.

LONDON MARATHON
www.virginlondonmarathon.com; Greenwich Park to the Mall
Some 35,000 masochists cross London in the world's biggest road race.

OXFORD & CAMBRIDGE BOAT RACE
www.theboatrace.org; from Putney to Mortlake
Big crowds line the banks of the Thames for this annual event, where the country's two most famous universities go oar-to-oar. Dates vary each due to the universities' Easter breaks, so check the website.

MAY
CHELSEA FLOWER SHOW
www.rhs.org.uk; Royal Hospital Chelsea
The world's most renowned horticultural show attracts the cream of West London society and is never far from controversy – the ban on garden gnomes was, shock horror, broken by exhibitor Jekka McVicar in 2009, making national headlines. Only in Britain…

JUNE
ROYAL ACADEMY SUMMER EXHIBITION
www.royalacademy.org.uk; Royal Academy of Arts
Beginning in June and running through August, this is an annual showcase of works submitted by artists from all over Britain, distilled to a thousand or so pieces.

TROOPING THE COLOUR
www.trooping-the-colour.co.uk; Horse Guards Parade, Whitehall
The Queen's official birthday (she was born in April but the weather's better in June) is celebrated with much flag-waving, parades, pageantry and noisy flyovers.

WIMBLEDON LAWN TENNIS CHAMPIONSHIPS
www.wimbledon.com
For two weeks the quiet south London village of Wimbledon is the centre of the sporting universe as the best players on earth gather to fight for the championship. While it's as much about strawberries, cream and tradition as smashing balls for those in attendance, the rest of the capital is riveted by the women and men's finals that take place on the final weekend of the tournament.

JULY
PRIDE LONDON
www.pridelondon.org
The gay community in all its many fabulous guises paints the town pink in this annual extravaganza, featuring a morning parade and a huge afternoon event on Trafalgar Sq (although the location changes frequently).

BBC PROMENADE CONCERTS (THE PROMS)
www.bbc.co.uk/proms
Two months of outstanding classical concerts at various prestigious venues, centred on the Royal Albert Hall (p144) in Kensington.

AUGUST
NOTTING HILL CARNIVAL
www.thecarnival.tv
Europe's biggest – and London's most vibrant – outdoor carnival is a celebration of Caribbean London, featuring music, dancing and costumes over the summer bank holiday weekend. Beware of street crime.

SEPTEMBER
THAMES FESTIVAL
www.thamesfestival.org
Celebrating London's greatest natural asset, the River Thames, this cosmopolitan festival provides fun for all the family with fairs, street theatre, music, food stalls, fireworks, river races and culminating in the superb Night Procession.

LONDON OPEN HOUSE
www.londonopenhouse.org
One of London's biggest treats, for a weekend in late September, the public is invited in to see over 700 heritage buildings throughout the capital that are normally off-limits. A unique chance that has Londoners and visitors alike heading to their favourite places in droves; see the boxed text p208.

OCTOBER
DANCE UMBRELLA
www.danceumbrella.co.uk
London's annual festival of contemporary dance features five weeks of performances by British and international dance companies at venues across London.

LONDON FILM FESTIVAL
www.lff.org.uk; National Film Theatre & various venues
The city's premier film event attracts big overseas names and is an opportunity to see

over 100 British and international films before their cinema release. There are masterclasses given by world-famous directors and Q&A sessions with the cream of Hollywood and independent moviemakers too.

NOVEMBER

GUY FAWKES NIGHT (BONFIRE NIGHT)

One of Britain's best-loved traditions, Bonfire Night commemorates Guy Fawkes' foiled attempt to blow up Parliament in 1605. Bonfires and fireworks light up the night on 5 November and effigies of Fawkes are burned, while young kids run around asking for 'a penny for the guy'. Primrose Hill, Highbury Fields, Alexander Palace, Clapham Common and Crystal Palace Park are the places to aim for to see the best firework displays.

LORD MAYOR'S SHOW

www.lordmayorsshow.org

In accordance with the Magna Carta of 1215, the newly elected Lord Mayor of the City of London travels in a state coach from Mansion House to the Royal Courts of Justice to seek their approval. The floats, bands and fireworks that accompany him were added later.

DECEMBER

LIGHTING OF THE CHRISTMAS TREE & LIGHTS

A Heat-magazine favoured celebrity is normally carted in to switch on all the festive lights that line Oxford, Regent and Bonds streets, and a huge Norwegian spruce is set up in Trafalgar Sq.

COSTS & MONEY

London can be a wincingly expensive experience, but doesn't necessarily have to be. The main expense any visitor will have to bear is that of accommodation (see p332). To make your life easier, try hard to befriend a Londoner who has a spare room, otherwise you'll need to budget an absolute minimum of £25 per night for a hostel dorm, rising sharply to at least £60 for a room of your own almost anywhere, and further to somewhere around £100 for a room you're actually likely to want to spend any time in. Booking in advance is

always a good plan, and most hotels will offer reductions on the room prices if you're staying for more than a few days. Most hotels also do excellent web deals that dramatically undercut their rack rates, and, if you haven't booked in advance, websites such as www.lastminute .com and www.laterooms.com often have some fantastic deals suitable for most budgets.

Money is an issue in other aspects as well, with the general cost of living in London being far higher than anywhere else in Britain and, unless you're Norwegian or Japanese, probably higher than where you've arrived from. While prices have been tamed slightly by both the economic crisis and the fall in the value of the pound, London is never going to be a bargain city.

Eating out can be done on a budget, with plenty of good cheap eats to be had in every neighbourhood (see p234). However, even at the cheapest of the cheap, it's no trifle – a decent sandwich will cost you around £3.50, and you're unlikely to get much change from a tenner for a sit-down meal. London's fashionable eating scene is a huge draw in itself, and it's not cheap. A good meal for two with a bottle of wine is usually around the £60 to £80 mark, rising quickly to over £100 for some of the city's more fashionable tables.

Getting around London can also be expensive. One obvious step to save cash is to get yourself an Oyster card immediately upon arrival as this gives you access to lower fares across the system and will dramatically decrease the cost of using the public transport; see p379.

Entertainment is likewise not cheap: cinema tickets in the West End have long since crossed the £10 threshold and many cinemas in further

HOW MUCH?

Admission to a big-name club on a Friday £15

Adult football ticket £20 to £40

Bus ticket £2

Cinema ticket £10

DVD £10

Guardian newspaper 90p

Pint of lager £3.50

Three-course meal with wine/beer from £30

Tube ride within zone 1 £4

Tube ride within zone 1 with an Oyster card £1.60

West End theatre ticket £50

ADVANCE PLANNING

The trick in London is either to book very early, or to try at the last minute and hope you get lucky.

Three to six months before you go For big-name restaurants, such as Gordon Ramsay in Chelsea (p247), you need to get organised six months ahead. Saturday-night performances of big West End shows usually sell out three to six months ahead.

Two to three months before you go Check out sites such as www.ticketmaster.co.uk and www.seetickets.com, and think about bigger rock-music gigs. Also read www.guardian.co.uk/reviews, www.whatsonstage.com or www.time out.com before booking good Saturday-night tickets for serious theatre (eg Kevin Spacey performing at the Old Vic).

Two weeks before you go Sign up for an email newsletter, such as Urban Junkies (www.urbanjunkies.com), and double-check review sites. Two weeks is also usually ample time to get into trendy, interesting restaurants such as Hakkasan (p241).

A few days before you go The latest blockbuster exhibition at the Royal Academy of Arts (p68), Tates Modern and Britain (p128 and p93) or the Victoria & Albert Museum (p139) can usually be booked a few days beforehand, or even chanced on the day.

out areas are following, meaning seeing a film for under a tenner is becoming a bargain, although art-house and independent cinemas do still offer much more competitive prices. The big-name gigs are also fairly expensive, usually starting at around £20 and going up to £150 for a superstar at Wembley or Earl's Court. Clubbing is a mixed bag: a Saturday night at Fabric (p296) will set you back £20 just for entry, while some of the best clubs in town are free or very cheap – it's just a question of research. Flyers with discounted entry rates are available all over the West End in music and fashion stores.

One surprising boon for such an expensive city is that all state-funded museums are free, meaning you can quite happily spend days in some of the world's best exhibition spaces and galleries for absolutely nothing, although it's always good to make a donation to each space to help keep them free (£3 is usually the standard suggested amount). This also means you don't have to tackle a behemoth such as the V&A (p139) or the British Museum (p79) in one go – drop in for a couple of hours and then come back fresh another day! Other sights are variably priced: some may baulk at paying £16 for the Tower of London (p117), but you can spend the most part of a day there and see one of the UK's top attractions, while a big commercial attraction such as Madame Tussauds (p95) is just plain overpriced at £25 per person.

INTERNET RESOURCES

Unsurprisingly London is big on the web. Wifi covers much of the city now, although sadly you'll usually need to pay for it; some great exceptions are all along Upper St in Islington and on Leicester Sq. The whole of the City is covered by 'the Cloud', a service that is free for the first month you use it, after which you have to pay. The following websites are useful when wanting to learn more about London:

Flavorpill London (www.flavorpill.com/london) A weekly email magazine profiling the best of London's cultural and entertainment possibilities.

Le Cool Magazine (www.lecool.com/london) A great free graphic email sent to subscribers detailing the better clubs, bars, music and other events in the capital.

London Underground Guide (www.goingunderground.net) Annie Mole's cultishly popular tube blog, a must for anyone fascinated by the world's oldest underground system.

London Unlike (www.london.unlike.net) This 'city guide for the mobile generation' gives great insider tips on everything from the hottest new restaurants to club nights and cultural goings on.

Londonist (www.londonist.com) Our favourite London blog takes a wry look at the odder aspects of London life, with a large pool of contributors writing about their various interests.

MayorWatch (www.mayorwatch.co.uk) A politically neutral site documenting the actions of the mayor of London and the London Assembly, with discussions and regular news updates.

Streetmap.co.uk (www.streetmap.co.uk) A website many Londoners use daily, Streetmap is simply a map of London upon which you can look up any street or postcode. Vital.

Transport for London (www.tfl.gov.uk) An invaluable website from London Transport with a great journey planner to help you navigate your way across the city.

Visit London (www.visitlondon.com) The city's official tourism website is a great resource, with cheap hotel booking, listings of all sorts and links galore.

HISTORY

London's history has been a long and turbulent two millennia in which many different settlements and long-established villages slowly grew together to form the immense city around the Roman core that still marks London's heart today.

LONDINIUM

The Romans are the real fathers of London, despite there being a settlement of some form or another along the Thames for several thousand years before their arrival. Amazingly, the Roman wall built around the settlement of Londinium still more or less demarcates the City of London from neighbouring London boroughs today.

The Romans first visited in the 1st century BC, traded with the Celts and had a browse around. In AD 43 they returned with an army led by Emperor Claudius and decided to stay, establishing the port of Londinium. They built a wooden bridge across the Thames (near the site of today's London Bridge) and used the settlement as a base from which to capture other tribal centres, which at the time provided much bigger prizes. The bridge became the focal point for a network of roads fanning out around the region, and for a few years the settlement prospered from trade.

This growth was nipped in the bud around AD 60 when an army led by Boudicca, queen of the Celtic Iceni tribe based in East Anglia, took violent retribution on the Roman soldiers, who had attacked her kingdom and seized her land. The Iceni overran Camulodunum (Colchester) – which had become capital of Roman Britannia – and then turned on Londinium, massacring its inhabitants and razing the settlement. Boudicca was eventually defeated (and according to legend is buried under platform 10 of King's Cross station), and the Romans rebuilt Londinium around Cornhill.

A century later the Romans built the defensive wall around the city, fragments of which survive. The original gates – Aldgate, Ludgate, Newgate and Bishopsgate – are remembered as place names in contemporary London. Excavations in the City suggest that Londinium, a centre for business and trade although not a fully fledged *colonia* (settlement), was an imposing metropolis whose massive buildings included a basilica, an amphitheatre, a forum and the governor's palace.

By the middle of the 3rd century AD Londinium was home to some 30,000 people of various ethnic groups, and there were temples dedicated to a large number of cults. When Emperor Constantine converted to Christianity in 312, this became the official religion of the entire empire, although the remains of the Temple of Mithras (p106) survive in the City, a testament to London's pagan past.

Overstretched and worn down by ever-increasing barbarian invasions, the Roman Empire fell into decline, as did Londinium. When the embattled Emperor Honorius withdrew the last soldiers in 410, the remaining Romans scarpered and the settlement was reduced to a sparsely populated backwater.

TIMELINE

AD 43	47–50	122
The Romans invade Britain, led by Emperor Claudius himself. Before this time the Britons paid tribute to Rome following an early incursion here by Julius Caesar in 55 and 54 BC.	The defensive fort at Londinium is built. The name Londinium is probably pre-Celtic and there is no evidence as to what it means, although 'settlement on the wide river' is one suggestion.	Emperor Hadrian pays a visit to Londinium and a large number of impressive municipal buildings are constructed. This is the height of Roman London and the settlement features temples, bathhouses, a fortress and a port.

LUNDENWIC

What happened to London after the Roman withdrawal is still the subject of much historical debate. While the Dark Ages have become considerably better illuminated in the past two decades with archaeological finds and improved technology, there remain several key unknowns, including whether or not the Roman walled city was ever entirely abandoned. Most historians now think that some form of Romano-British continuity survived even as Saxon settlers, Germanic tribes that colonised the southeast of England from the 5th century onwards, established themselves in the wake of the Roman abandonment of Londinium.

Lundenwic (or London marketplace) was established due west of Londinium (around present-day Aldwych and Charing Cross) as a Saxon trade settlement and by the early 7th century the Saxons were converted from paganism to Christianity. Rome designated Lundenwic as a diocese and the first St Paul's Cathedral was established at the top of Ludgate Hill.

The settlement became the victim of its own success when it attracted the Vikings of Denmark, who raided the city in 842 and burned it to the ground 10 years later. Under the leadership of King Alfred the Great of Wessex, the Saxon population fought back, drove the Danes out in 886 and re-established what soon became Lundunburg as the major centre of trade.

Saxon London grew into a prosperous and well-organised town divided into 20 wards, each with its own alderman, and resident colonies of German merchants and French vintners. But the Danes wouldn't let it lie, and Viking raids finally broke the weakening Saxon leadership, which was forced to accept the Danish leader Canute as king of England in 1016.

With the death of Canute's son Harthacanute in 1042, the throne passed to the Saxon Edward the Confessor, who went on to found an abbey and palace at Westminster on what was then an island at the mouth of the River Tyburn (which now flows underground). When Edward moved his court to Westminster, he established divisions that would – geographically, at least – dominate the future of London. The port became the trading and mercantile centre (the area now known as the City), while Westminster became the seat of politics and administration.

THE NORMANS

The most famous date in English history, 1066 marks the real birth of England as a unified nation state. After the death of Edward the Confessor in 1066 a dispute over who would take the English throne spelled disaster for the Saxon kings. Harold Godwinson, the Earl of Wessex, was anointed successor by Edward on his deathbed, but this enraged William, the Duke of Normandy, who believed Edward had promised him the throne. William mounted a massive invasion of England from France and on 14 October defeated Harold at the Battle of Hastings, before marching on London to claim his prize. William the Conqueror was crowned king of England in Westminster Abbey on 25 December 1066, ensuring the Norman conquest was complete. He subsequently found himself in control of what was by then the richest and largest city in the kingdom.

William distrusted 'the fierce populace' of London and built several strongholds, including the White Tower, the core of the Tower of London. Cleverly, he kept the prosperous merchants on side by confirming the City's independence in exchange for taxes. Sometime following the Norman conquest, London became the principal town of England, overtaking Winchester, the ancient capital of Wessex.

190–225	410	852
London Wall is constructed around Londinium to defend the settlement from outsiders, who had breached Hadrian's Wall. The wall encloses an area of just 132 hectares and is 5m high.	The Emperor Honorius decrees that the colony of Britannia should take care of its own defences, thus effectively ending the Roman presence in Londinium; while many Romans leave, many also stay.	Vikings settle in London, having attacked the city a decade previously. This is a period of great struggle between Wessex and Denmark for control of the Thames.

MEDIEVAL LONDON

Successive medieval kings were happy to let the City of London keep its independence as long as its merchants continued to finance their wars and building projects. When Richard I (known as 'the Lionheart') needed funds for his crusade to the Holy Land, he recognised the City as a self-governing commune, and the appreciative merchants duly coughed up. The City's first mayor, Henry Fitz Aylwin, was elected sometime around 1190. A city built on money and commerce, London would always guard its independence fiercely, as Richard's successor, King John, learned the hard way. In 1215 John was forced to cede to the powerful barons, and to curb his excessive demands for pay-offs from the City. Among those pressing him to seal the Magna Carta of 1215 (which effectively diluted royal power) was the by then powerful mayor of the City of London. Amazingly, two copies of this document can be seen in the British Library (p168).

Trade and commerce boomed, and the noblemen, barons and bishops built lavish houses for themselves along the prime real estate of the Strand, which connected the City with the Palace of Westminster, the new seat of royal power. The first stone London Bridge was built in 1176, although it was frequently too crowded to cross, and most people traversed the river with waterboatmen (who plied their trade until the 18th century). Their touting shouts of 'Oars? Oars?' are said to have confused many a country visitor tempted by more carnal services.

Though fire was a constant threat in the cramped and narrow houses and lanes of 14th-century London, disease caused by unsanitary living conditions and impure drinking water from the Thames was the greatest threat to the burgeoning city. In 1348 rats on ships from Europe brought the Black Death, a bubonic plague that wiped out almost two-thirds of the population (of 100,000) over the following decades.

With their numbers subsequently down, there was growing unrest among labourers, for whom violence became a way of life, and rioting was commonplace. In 1381, miscalculating – or just disregarding – the mood of the nation, Richard II tried to impose a poll tax on everyone in the realm. Tens of thousands of peasants, led by the soldier Wat Tyler and the priest Jack Straw, marched in protest on London. The Archbishop of Canterbury was dragged from the Tower and beheaded, several ministers were murdered and many buildings were razed before the Peasants' Revolt ran its course. Tyler died at the end of the mayor's blade, while Straw and the other ringleaders were executed at Smithfield. However, there was no more mention of poll tax (until Margaret Thatcher, not heeding the lessons of history, tried to introduce one in the 1980s – see p30).

London gained wealth and stature under the Houses of Lancaster and York in the 15th century, also the era of the charitable mayor Dick Whittington, immortalised for many children in the fairy tale of his rise to power from poverty. William Caxton set up the first printing press at Westminster in 1476.

The century's greatest episode of political intrigue occurred in 1483. The 12-year-old Edward V, of the House of York, reigned for only two months before vanishing with his younger brother into the Tower of London, never to be seen again. Whether or not their uncle Richard III – who became the next king – murdered the boys has been the subject of much conjecture over the centuries. (In 1674 workers found a chest containing the skeletons of two children near the White Tower, which were assumed to be the princes' remains and were reburied in Innocents' Corner in Westminster Abbey.) Richard III didn't have long to enjoy the hot seat, however, as he was deposed within a couple of years by Henry Tudor, the first monarch of the dynasty of that name.

886	1016	1066
King Alfred the Great, first king of England, reclaims London for the Saxons and founds a new settlement within the walls of the old Roman town.	After more than a century of English rule, the Danes return to London and Canute is crowned king of England. Most famous in English folklore for failing to command the waves, Canute ushered in two decades of peace.	After his great victory over King Harold at the Battle of Hastings, William, Duke of Normandy, evermore known as William the Conqueror, is crowned in Westminster Abbey.

TUDOR LONDON

London became one of the largest and most important cities in Europe during the reign of the Tudors, which coincided with the discovery of the Americas and thriving world trade.

Henry's son and successor, Henry VIII, was the most ostentatious of the clan. Terribly fond of palaces, he had new ones built at Whitehall and St James's, and bullied his lord chancellor, Cardinal Thomas Wolsey, into gifting him Hampton Court.

His most significant contribution, however, was the split with the Catholic Church in 1534 after the Pope refused to annul his marriage to the non-heir-producing Catherine of Aragon. Thumbing his nose at Rome, he made himself the supreme head of the Church of England and married Anne Boleyn, the second of his six wives. He 'dissolved' London's monasteries and seized the church's vast wealth and property. The face of the medieval city was transformed: much of the land requisitioned for hunting later became Hyde, Regent's and Richmond Parks, while many of the religious houses disappeared, leaving only their names in particular areas, such as Whitefriars and Blackfriars (after the colour of the monks' habits).

Despite his penchant for settling differences with the axe (two of his six wives and Wolsey's replacement as lord chancellor, Thomas More, were beheaded) and his persecution of both Catholics and fellow Protestants who didn't toe the line, Henry VIII remained a popular monarch until his death in 1547. The reign of Mary I, his daughter by Catherine of Aragon, saw a brief return to Catholicism, during which the queen sanctioned the burning to death of hundreds of Protestants at Smithfield and earned herself the nickname 'Bloody Mary'. By the time Elizabeth I, Henry VIII's daughter by Anne Boleyn, took the throne, Catholicism was a waning force, and hundreds of people who dared to suggest otherwise were carted off to the gallows at Tyburn (p145).

ELIZABETHAN LONDON

The 45-year reign (1558–1603) of Elizabeth I is still looked upon as one of the most extraordinary periods in English history, and it was just as significant for London. During these four decades English literature reached new and still unbeaten heights, and religious tolerance gradually became accepted doctrine, although Catholics and some Protestants still faced persecution. England became a naval superpower, having defeated the Spanish Armada in 1588, and the city established itself as the premier world trade market with the opening of the Royal Exchange in 1566.

London was blooming economically and physically; in the second half of the 16th century the population doubled to 200,000. The first recorded map of London was published in 1558, and John Stow produced *A Survey of London,* the first history of the city, in 1598.

This was also the golden era of English drama, and the works of William Shakespeare, Christopher Marlowe and Ben Jonson packed them in at new playhouses, such as the Rose (built in 1587) and the Globe (1599). Both of these were built in Southwark, a notoriously 'naughty' place at the time, teeming with brothels, bawdy taverns and illicit sports such as bear baiting. Most importantly, they were outside the jurisdiction of the City, which frowned upon and even banned theatre as a waste of time.

When Elizabeth died without an heir in 1603, she was succeeded by her second cousin, who was crowned James I. Although the son of Catholic Mary, Queen of Scots, James was slow to improve conditions for England's Catholics and drew their wrath. He narrowly escaped death

1176	1215	1348
The first stone London Bridge was built, although it was frequently too crowded to cross, and most people traversed the river with waterboatmen (who plied their trade until the 18th century).	In a meadow in Runnymede, outside London, King John signs the Magna Carta (literally 'the Great Charter'), an agreement with England's barons forming the basis of constitutional law in England.	Rats on ships from Europe brought the Black Death, a bubonic plague that wiped out almost two-thirds of the population (of 100,000) over the following decades.

when Guy Fawkes' plot to blow up the Houses of Parliament on 5 November 1605 was uncovered. The discovery of the audacious plan is commemorated on this date each year with bonfires, fireworks and the burning of Guy Fawkes effigies throughout England.

THE ENGLISH CIVIL WARS

When Charles I came to the throne in 1625 his intransigent personality and total belief in the 'divine right of kings' set the monarchy on a collision course with an increasingly confident parliament at Westminster and a City of London tiring of extortionate taxes. The crunch came when Charles tried to arrest five antagonistic members of parliament, who fled to the City, and in 1642 the country slid into civil war.

The Puritans (extremist Protestants) and the City's expanding merchant class threw their support behind General Oliver Cromwell, leader of the Parliamentarians (the Roundheads), who battled against the Royalist troops (the Cavaliers). London was firmly with the Roundheads, and Charles I was defeated in 1646, although a Second Civil War (1648–49) and a Third Civil War (1649–51) continued to wreak havoc on what had been a stable and prosperous nation.

Charles I was beheaded for treason outside Banqueting House (p95) in Whitehall on 30 January 1649, famously wearing two shirts on the cold morning of his execution so as not to shiver and appear cowardly. Cromwell ruled the country as a republic for the next 11 years, during which time Charles I's son, Charles II, continued fighting for the restoration of the monarchy. During the Commonwealth of England, as the English republic was known, Cromwell banned theatre, dancing, Christmas and just about anything remotely fun.

THE RESTORATION: PLAGUE & FIRE

After Cromwell's death, parliament decided that the royals weren't so bad after all and restored the exiled Charles II in 1660. Death was deemed too good for Cromwell, whose exhumed body was hung, drawn and quartered at Tyburn. His rotting head was displayed on a spike at Westminster Hall for two decades.

Despite the immense wealth that London experienced during the reign of the Tudors, the capital remained a crowded and filthy place where most of the population lived below the poverty line. A lack of basic sanitation (urine and faeces were routinely poured into the streets from the slop bucket), dirty water and overcrowding had all contributed to recurrent outbreaks of deadly illnesses and fevers. The city had suffered from outbreaks of bubonic plague since the 14th century, but all previous incidences were dwarfed by the Great Plague of 1665.

As the plague spread, the panicked population retreated behind closed doors, only venturing out for supplies and to dispose of their dead. Previously crowded streets were deserted, the churches and markets were closed, and an eerie silence descended on the city. To make matters worse, the mayor believed that dogs and cats were the spreaders of the plague and ordered them all killed, thus in one stroke ridding the disease-carrying rats of their natural predators. By the time the winter cold arrested the epidemic, 100,000 people had perished; the corpses were collected and thrown into vast 'plague pits', many of which stand empty of buildings to this day.

The plague finally began to wane in late 1665, leaving the city's population decimated and a general superstition that the deaths had been a punishment from God for London's

1397	1483	1534
Richard Whittington is elected mayor of London, and instantly negotiates buying the city's liberties back from Richard II for £10,000. He goes on to be four times mayor of London and a much-loved character in London folklore.	The 12-year-old Edward V, of the House of York, reigned for only two months before vanishing with his younger brother into the Tower of London, never to be seen again. Whether or not their uncle Richard III – who became the next king – murdered the boys has been the subject of much conjecture over the centuries.	After being denied a divorce from Catherine of Aragon by the Pope, Henry VIII splits with the Catholic Church, dissolves the monasteries and brings about the English Reformation.

moral squalor. Just as Londoners breathed a sigh of relief, another disaster struck. The city had for centuries been prone to fire, as nearly all buildings were constructed from wood, but the mother of all blazes broke out on 2 September 1666 in a bakery in Pudding Lane in the City.

It didn't seem like much to begin with – the mayor himself dismissed it as 'something a woman might pisse out' before going back to bed – but the unusual September heat combined with rising winds created a tinderbox effect, and the fire raged out of control for days, razing some 80% of London. Only eight people died (officially at least), but most of London's medieval, Tudor and Jacobean architecture was destroyed. The fire was finally stopped at Fetter Lane, on the very edge of London, by blowing up all the buildings in the inferno's path. It is hard to overstate the scale of the destruction – 89 churches and more than 13,000 houses were razed, leaving tens of thousands of people homeless. Many Londoners left for the countryside, or to seek their fortunes in the New World.

WREN'S LONDON

One positive aspect of the inferno was that it created a blank canvas upon which master architect Christopher Wren could build his magnificent churches. Wren's plan for rebuilding the entire city was unfortunately deemed too expensive, and the familiar pattern of streets that had grown up over the centuries since the time of the Romans quickly reappeared (by law, brick and stone designs replaced the old timber-framed, overhanging Tudor houses, to avoid a repeat of 1666; many roads were widened for the same reason). At this time, Charles II moved to St James's Palace, and the surrounding area was taken over by the gentry, who built the grand squares and town houses of modern-day Mayfair and St James's in order to be close to the court.

By way of memorialising the blaze – and symbolising the restoration and resurgence of the subsequent years – the Monument (p107), designed by Wren, was erected in 1677 near the site of the fire's outbreak. At the time it was by far the highest structure in the city, visible from everywhere in the capital.

In 1685 some 1500 Huguenot refugees arrived in London, fleeing persecution in Catholic France. Many turned their hands to the manufacture of luxury goods such as silks and silverware in and around Spitalfields and Clerkenwell, which were already populated with Irish, Jewish and Italian immigrants and artisans. London was fast becoming one of the world's most cosmopolitan places.

The Glorious (ie bloodless) Revolution in 1688 brought the Dutch king William of Orange to the English throne. He relocated from Whitehall Palace to a new palace in Kensington Gardens, and the surrounding area smartened itself up accordingly. In order to raise finances for his war with France – and as a result of the City's transformation into a centre of finance rather than manufacturing – William III established the Bank of England in 1694.

London's growth continued unabated, and by 1700 it was Europe's largest city, with 600,000 people. The influx of foreign workers brought expansion to the east and south, while those who could afford it headed to the more salubrious environs of the north and west. London today is still, more or less, divided along these lines.

The crowning glory of the 'Great Rebuilding', Wren's St Paul's Cathedral (p99), was completed in 1710 – one of the largest cathedrals in Europe, it remains one of the city's most prominent and visible landmarks.

1558	1599	1605
The first detailed map of London is commissioned by a group of German merchants. In the same year the Elizabethan age begins when Queen Elizabeth I takes the throne.	The Globe Theatre opens in Southwark alongside other London stages, including the Rose, the Swan and the Hope. Most of Shakespeare's plays written after 1599 are staged here, including Macbeth, King Lear and Hamlet.	A Catholic plot to blow up James I by hiding gunpowder in the cellars under the House of Commons is foiled. Guy Fawkes, just one of the plotters, is executed in 1606.

GEORGIAN LONDON

When Queen Anne died without an heir in 1714, the search began for a Protestant relative (the 1701 Act of Settlement forbade Roman Catholics to occupy the throne). Eventually George of Hanover, the great-grandson of James I, arrived from Germany and was crowned king of England, though he never learned to speak English. Meanwhile, the increasingly literate population got their first newspapers, which began to cluster around Fleet St.

Robert Walpole's Whig Party controlled parliament during much of George I's reign, and Walpole effectively became Britain's first prime minister. He was presented with 10 Downing St, which has been the official residence of nearly every prime minister since.

London grew at a phenomenal pace during this time, and measures were taken to make the city more accessible. When Westminster Bridge opened in 1750 it was only the second spanning of the Thames after London Bridge, first built by the Romans. The old crossing itself was cleared of many of its buildings, and the Roman wall surrounding the City torn down.

Georgian London saw a great creative surge in music, art and architecture. Court composer George Frederick Handel wrote his *Water Music* (1717) and *Messiah* (1741) while living here, and in 1755 Dr Johnson produced the first English dictionary. William Hogarth (see boxed text, p44), Thomas Gainsborough and Joshua Reynolds produced some of their finest engravings and paintings, and many of London's most elegant buildings, streets and squares were erected or laid out by the likes of John Soane and the incomparable John Nash (see p208).

All the while, though, London was becoming ever more segregated and lawless. George II himself was relieved of 'purse, watch and buckles' during a stroll through Kensington Gardens. This was Hogarth's London, in which the wealthy built fine mansions in attractive squares and gathered in fashionable new coffee houses while the poor huddled together in appalling slums and drowned their sorrows with cheap gin. To curb rising crime, two magistrates established the 'Bow Street Runners' in 1749, a voluntary group – effectively a forerunner to the Metropolitan Police Force (set up in 1829) – that challenged the official marshals (thief-takers), who were suspected (often correctly) of colluding with the criminals themselves.

In 1780 parliament proposed to lift the law preventing Catholics from buying or inheriting property. One demented MP, Lord George Gordon, led a 'No Popery' demonstration that turned into the Gordon Riots. A mob of 30,000 went on a rampage, attacking Irish labourers, and burning prisons, 'Papishe dens' (chapels) and several law courts. At least 300 people died during the riots, including some who drank themselves to death after breaking into a Holborn distillery, and the army managed to restore order only after five days of rioting.

As the 18th century drew to a close, London's population had mushroomed to almost a million.

VICTORIAN LONDON

While the growth and achievements of the previous century were impressive, they paled in comparison with the Victorian era, which began when the 19-year-old Victoria was crowned in 1838. During the Industrial Revolution, when small 'cottage' industries were suddenly overtaken by the advance of the great factories, spurring the creation of the first industrialised society on earth, London became the nerve centre of the largest and richest empire the world has ever known, one that covered a quarter of the earth's surface area and ruled more than 500 million people.

1665	1666	1707
The Great Plague ravages London and wipes out a fifth of the capital's population. Although it had a far smaller effect than the Black Death of the 14th century, it is remembered as one of Europe's last outbreaks.	The Great Fire of London burns for five days, destroying the city Shakespeare had known and loved and changing London forever, leaving four-fifths of the metropolis in ruins.	The first ever sitting of the Parliament of the Kingdom of Great Britain occurs in London as the 1707 Acts of Union bring England and Scotland together under one parliament.

New docks in East London were built to facilitate the booming trade with the colonies, and railways began to fan out from the capital. The world's first underground railway opened between Paddington and Farringdon Rd in 1863 and was such a success that other lines quickly followed. Many of London's most famous buildings and landmarks were also built at this time: the Clock Tower (popularly known as 'Big Ben', 1859; p92), Royal Albert Hall (1871; p144) and the magnificent Tower Bridge (1894; p121).

The city, however, heaved under the burden of its vast size, and in 1858 London was in the grip of the 'Great Stink', when the population explosion so overtook the city's sanitation facilities that raw sewage seeped in through the floorboards of wealthy merchants' houses. Leading engineer Joseph Bazalgette tackled the problem by creating in the late 1850s an underground network of sewers, which was copied around the world. London had truly become the first modern metropolis.

Though the Victorian age is chiefly seen as one of great imperial power founded on industry, trade and commerce, intellectual achievement in the arts and sciences was enormous. The greatest chronicler of the times was Charles Dickens, whose *Oliver Twist* (1837) and other works explored the themes of poverty, hopelessness and squalor among the working classes. In 1859 Charles Darwin published the immensely controversial *On the Origin of Species* here, in which he outlined his epoch-making theory of evolution.

This was also the era of some of Britain's most capable and progressive prime ministers, most notably William Gladstone (four terms between 1868 and 1894) and Benjamin Disraeli (who served in 1868 and again from 1874 to 1880).

Waves of immigrants, from Chinese to Eastern European, arrived in London during the 19th century, when the population exploded from one million to six million people. This breakneck expansion was not beneficial to all – inner-city slums housed the poor in atrocious conditions of disease and overcrowding, while the affluent expanded out to leafy suburbs, where new and comfortable housing was built. The suburbs of London are still predominantly made up of Victorian terraced housing.

Queen Victoria lived to celebrate her Diamond Jubilee in 1897, but died four years later aged 81 and was laid to rest in Windsor. Her reign is seen as the climax of Britain's world supremacy, when London was the de facto capital of the world.

FROM EMPIRE TO WORLD WAR

Victoria's self-indulgent son Edward, the Prince of Wales, was already 60 by the time he was crowned Edward VII in 1901. London's belle époque was marked with the introduction of the first motorised buses, which replaced the horse-drawn versions that had plodded their trade since 1829, and a touch of glamour came in the form of luxury hotels such as the Ritz in 1906 and department stores such as Selfridges in 1909. The Olympics were held at White City Stadium in 1908 – a rather different spectacle to those planned for just over a century later. The stadium was demolished in 1985 to make way for a new British Broadcasting Corporation (BBC) building.

What became known as the Great War (WWI) broke out in August 1914, and the first German bombs fell from zeppelins near the Guildhall a year later, killing 39 people. Planes were soon dropping bombs on the capital, killing in all some 650 Londoners (half the national total of civilian casualties).

While the young, moneyed set kicked up their heels after the relative hardships of the war, the 'roaring '20s' brought only more hardship for most Londoners, with an economic slump increasing the cost of living.

1749	1807	1838
The Bow Street Runners are established by the novelist and magistrate Henry Fielding to replace the previous 'thief-takers', who would arrest criminals for a small fee.	The Houses of Parliament finally abolish the slave trade, on which much Georgian wealth has been built, after a long and hard-fought campaign led by politician and philanthropist William Wilberforce.	The coronation of Queen Victoria at Westminster Abbey ushers in the greatest period in London's history, during which the British capital becomes the economic and political centre of the world.

The population continued to rise, reaching nearly 7.5 million in 1921. The London County Council (LCC) busied itself clearing slums and building new housing estates, while the suburbs encroached ever deeper into the countryside.

Unemployment rose steadily as the world descended into recession. In May 1926 a wage dispute in the coal industry escalated into a nine-day general strike, in which so many workers downed tools that London virtually ground to a halt. The army was called in to maintain order and to keep the city functioning, but the stage was set for more than half a century of industrial strife.

Despite the economic woes, the era brought a wealth of intellectual success. The 1920s were the heyday of the Bloomsbury Group, which counted writer Virginia Woolf and economist John Maynard Keynes in its ranks. The spotlight shifted westwards to Fitzrovia in the following decade, when George Orwell and Dylan Thomas clinked glasses with contemporaries at the Fitzroy Tavern on Charlotte St.

Cinema, TV and radio arrived. The BBC aired its first radio broadcast from the roof of Marconi House on the Strand in 1922, and the first TV program from Alexandra Palace 14 years later.

The Royal Family took a knock when Edward VIII abdicated in 1936 to marry a woman who was not only twice divorced but, heaven save us, an American. The same year Oswald Mosley attempted to lead the British Union of Fascists on an anti-Jewish march through the East End but was repelled by a mob of around half a million at the famous Battle of Cable St.

WWII & THE BLITZ

Prime Minister Neville Chamberlain's policy of appeasing Adolf Hitler during the 1930s eventually proved misguided as the Führer's lust for expansion could not ultimately be sated. When Germany invaded Poland on 1 September 1939, Britain declared war, having signed a mutual-assistance pact with the Poles a few days beforehand. WWII (1939–45), Europe's darkest hour, had begun.

The first year of the war was one of anxious waiting for London; although more than 600,000 women and children had been evacuated to the countryside, no bombs fell to disturb the blackout. On 7 September 1940 this 'phoney war' came to a swift and brutal end when the German Air Force, the Luftwaffe, dropped hundreds of bombs on the East End, killing 430 people.

The Blitz (from the German 'blitzkrieg' or 'lightning war') lasted for 57 nights, and then continued intermittently until May 1941. The Underground was turned into a giant bomb shelter, although one bomb rolled down the escalator at Bank station and exploded on the platform, killing more than 100 people. Londoners responded with legendary resilience and stoicism. The Royal Family – still immensely popular and enormously respected – were also to play their role, refusing to leave London during the bombing. Begged to allow her children to leave the capital, Queen Elizabeth (the present monarch's late mother) apparently replied, 'the children could not possibly go without me, I wouldn't leave without the King, and the King won't leave'. The king's younger brother, the Duke of Kent, was killed in active service in 1942, while Buckingham Palace took a direct hit during a bombing raid, famously prompting the Queen to announce that 'now we can look the East End in the face'. Winston Churchill, prime minister from 1940, orchestrated much of the nation's war strategy from the Cabinet War Rooms (p94) deep below Whitehall, and it was from here that he made his stirring wartime speeches.

1884	1901	1908
Greenwich Mean Time is established, making Greenwich Observatory the centre of world time, against which all clocks around the globe are set.	Queen Victoria dies after a reign of more than 63 years – the longest (so far) in British history. As Victoria was averse to black funerals, London is instead festooned in purple and white.	London hosts its first Olympic Games, in the now demolished White City Stadium. A total of 22 teams take part and the entire budget is £15,000.

INVASION OF THE BODY SNATCHERS

During the 18th and 19th centuries, as the understanding of anatomy and surgery advanced, there was a huge shortage of bodies on which doctors and students could experiment. Legally, only the corpses of executed criminals were fair game for the scalpel, but the demand for specimens far outstripped supply, leading to the rise of the notorious body snatchers, or resurrectionists. Gangs of men would surreptitiously remove recently interred bodies from their graves, replacing everything as they found it, so in many cases the relatives never found out. The area around St Bart's hospital was notorious for this practice, with local gangs emptying local graveyards. Though horrific, the practice was not illegal, as by law the human body was not a possession and thus taking it could not be deemed stealing. However, the strongly held belief that the human body had to be intact to enter heaven meant that when body snatchers were discovered they were often on the receiving end of mob justice and torn to pieces on the streets. This macabre practice ended only after the Anatomy Act of 1832, which relaxed conditions for the medical uses of corpses.

London's spirit was tested again in January 1944, when Germany launched pilotless V-1 bombers (known as doodlebugs) over the city. By the time Nazi Germany capitulated in May 1945, up to a third of the East End and the City had been flattened, 32,000 Londoners had been killed and a further 50,000 had been seriously wounded. The scale of the destruction can only really be felt by taking a walk around the City – where postwar buildings (many of them monstrous) have been erected, this is usually where German bombs hit.

POSTWAR LONDON

Once the celebrations of Victory in Europe (VE) day had died down, the nation faced the huge toll that the war had taken. The years of austerity had begun, with much rationing of essential items and high-rise residences being built on bomb sites in Pimlico and the East End to solve the capital's chronic housing problem. Hosting the 1948 Olympics and the Festival of Britain in 1951 boosted morale. The festival recalled the Great Exhibition of a century earlier, with a new complex of arts buildings, the Southbank Centre (p125), built on the site of the festival.

The gloom returned, quite literally, on 6 December 1952 in the form of the Great Smog, the latest disaster to beset the city. A lethal combination of fog, smoke and pollution descended, and some 4000 people died of smog-related illnesses. This led to the 1956 Clean Air Act, which introduced zones to central London where only smokeless fuels could be burned.

Rationing of most goods ended in 1953, the year the current queen, Elizabeth II, was crowned following the death of her much-loved father King George VI the year before.

Immigrants from around the world – particularly the former British colonies – flocked to postwar London, where a dwindling population had led to labour shortages, and the city's character changed forever. However, as the Notting Hill race riots of 1958 attest, despite being officially encouraged to come, new immigrants weren't always welcomed on the streets.

Some economic prosperity returned in the late 1950s, and Prime Minister Harold Macmillan told Britons they'd 'never had it so good'. London was the place to be during the 1960s, when the creative energy that had been bottled up in the postwar era was spectacularly uncorked. London became the epicentre of cool in fashion and music, and the streets were awash with colour and vitality. The introduction of the contraceptive pill, the legalisation of homosexuality, and the popularisation of drugs such as marijuana and LSD through the hippy movement created an

1936	1940–41	1953
George VI becomes king following the abdication of his brother, Edward VIII, who chooses to give up his throne for Wallis Simpson, an American divorcée who will never be acceptable to the British establishment.	London is devastated by the Blitz, although miraculously St Paul's Cathedral and the Tower of London escape the bombing unscathed.	Queen Elizabeth II's coronation is held at Westminster Abbey, the first major live event to be broadcast around the world on TV, and one for which many English families bought their first TV sets.

unprecedentedly permissive and liberal climate, outraging the conservative older generations and delighting the young. Two seminal events were the Beatles recording at Abbey Road and the Rolling Stones performing free in front of half a million people in Hyde Park. Carnaby St was the most fashionable place on earth, and pop-culture figures from Twiggy and David Bailey to Marianne Faithfull and Christine Keeler became the icons of the new era.

top picks

HISTORICAL READS

- London: The Biography – Peter Ackroyd
- London at War – Philip Ziegler
- London in the Twentieth Century – Jerry White
- The Newgate Calender – Clive Emsley
- Restoration London, Elizabethan London and Dr Johnson's London – Liza Picard

PUNK LONDON

The party didn't last long, however, and London returned to the doldrums in the harsh economic climate of the 1970s, a decade marked by unemployment and Irish Republican Army (IRA) bombs. But, ever thriving on adversity, London ensured it was at the centre of the world's attention when in the mid-1970s a new aesthetic, punk, came vomiting and swearing into sight.

Despite the sexual liberation of the swinging '60s, London had remained a relatively conservative place, and the generation that had witnessed flower power as kids suddenly took things a step further, horrifying *Daily Mail* readers with strategically placed safety pins, dyed hair, mohawks and foul language. Punk was born – Vivienne Westwood shocked and awed the city with the wares from her clothing shop, Sex, on King's Rd, while the Sex Pistols' alternative national anthem, 'God Save the Queen', released during the national celebrations for Queen Elizabeth's Silver Jubilee in 1977, was more outrageous than anything the '60s had come up with.

While the music and fashion scene was in overdrive, torpor had set into Britain's body politic, as demonstrated by the brief and unremarkable Labour premiership of James Callaghan (1976–79). He was seen as weak and in thrall to the all-powerful trade unions, who crippled the UK with strikes in the late 1970s, most significantly during the 'Winter of Discontent' in 1978–79.

THE THATCHER & MAJOR YEARS

Recovery began – at least for the business community – under the iron fist of Margaret Thatcher, the leader of the Conservative Party, who was elected Britain's first female prime minister in 1979. Ruling for the whole of the 1980s and embarking on an unprecedented program of privatisation, Margaret Thatcher is easily the most significant of Britain's post-war leaders and opinions about her remain polarised in Britain today. While her critics decry her approach to social justice and the large gulf that developed between the haves and have nots during her time in power, her defenders point to the massive modernisation of Britain's lumbering trade-union-dominated infrastructure that went on under her leadership and the vast wealth creation her policies generated.

The Greater London Council (GLC), under the leadership of 'Red' Ken Livingstone, proved to be a thorn in Thatcher's side and fought a strong campaign to bring down the price of public transport. Thatcher responded in 1986 by abolishing the GLC, leaving London as the only

1956	1959	1966
Red Routemaster double-decker buses make their first appearance in London and instantly become an iconic symbol of the city.	The Notting Hill Carnival is started by Claudia Jones to promote good race relations in West London following the race riots of 1958 in which the local white and African Caribbean communities clashed violently.	England beats Germany to win the World Cup at Wembley – possibly the greatest day in the history of British sport and one seared into the consciousness of every schoolboy.

THE WORLD IN ONE CITY

London is historically made up of immigrants – whether Roman, Viking, Anglo-Saxon, Norman, Huguenot or Jamaican, the city has always assimilated large numbers of ethnically diverse people. While Africans are well documented to have served in the Roman army, they first came to England in significant numbers as slaves in Elizabethan times. The first truly large influx of foreigners was in the late 17th century, when Huguenots, French Protestant refugees fleeing religious persecution at home, settled in Spitalfields and Soho.

Wave upon wave followed. Jews have arrived throughout the past four centuries; their traditional areas have been the East End (particularly Spitalfields and Stamford Hill) and northwest London. The last large group of Jews arrived from India as late as the 1960s. During the potato famine in the mid-19th century there was massive migration from Ireland; Londoners with Irish ancestry remain concentrated in Kilburn today. WWII brought Poles, Ukrainians and other Eastern Europeans to London, and today the Poles are a long-established community in Hammersmith and Shepherd's Bush.

The single biggest wave of immigration came in the 1950s, when, facing a labour shortage, the government allowed anyone born in a UK colony to have British citizenship. This brought a huge black population from the Caribbean and a large Asian diaspora from India, Bangladesh and Pakistan. The black population settled in West London and South London, while Asians were concentrated in the East End. Other less noticeable waves include Italians to Clerkenwell in the early 20th century, Vietnamese refugees to Hackney in the 1980s and the Iraqi diaspora that has grown in northwest London since the 1990s.

Whoever you are, wherever you're from, you'll feel at home in London.

European capital without a unified local government, a bizarre situation that would continue for 14 years until Ken Livingstone re-emerged as a thorn in Tony Blair's side in 2000.

While poorer Londoners suffered under Thatcher's significant trimming back of the welfare state, things had rarely looked better for the wealthy. Riding on a wave of confidence partly engendered by the deregulation of the stock exchange in 1986, London underwent explosive economic growth. New property developers proved to be only marginally more discriminating than the Luftwaffe, though some outstanding modern structures, including the Lloyd's of London building (p107), went up amid other far less accomplished structures.

Like previous booms, the one of the late 1980s proved unsustainable. As unemployment started to rise and people found themselves living in houses worth much less than they had paid for them, Thatcher introduced a flat-rate poll tax. Protests around the country culminated in a 1990 march on Trafalgar Sq that ended in a fully fledged riot. Thatcher's subsequent forced resignation brought to an end a divisive era in modern British history, and her successor, the former Chancellor of the Exchequer, John Major, employed a far more collective form of government.

In 1992, to the amazement of most Londoners, the Conservatives were elected for a fourth successive term in government, even though the inspiring leadership of Thatcher was gone. The economy went into a tailspin shortly after, and Britain was forced to withdraw from the European Exchange Rate Mechanism (ERM), a humiliation from which it was impossible for the government to recover. To add to the government's troubles, the IRA detonated two huge bombs, one in the City in 1992 and another in the Docklands four years later, killing several people and damaging millions of pounds' worth of property. By 1995 the writing was on the wall for the Conservatives, as the Labour Party, apparently unelectable for a decade, came back with a new face.

1979	1981	1987
Margaret Thatcher is elected prime minister. Her contentious policies will transform Britain beyond recognition – part much-needed modernisation, part radical right-wing social policy.	Brixton sees the worst race riots in London's history. Lord Scarman, delivering his report on the events, puts the blame squarely on 'racial disadvantage that is a fact of British life'.	A fire, probably started by a dropped match, at King's Cross underground station causes the death of 31 people. While smoking was banned on tube carriages and platforms in 1985, smokers still lit up on escalators.

BLAIR'S BRITAIN

Invigorated by its sheer desperation to return to power, the Labour Party elected the thoroughly telegenic Tony Blair to lead it, who in turn managed to ditch some of the more socialist-sounding clauses in its party credo and, in a stroke of genius, reinvent the brand as New Labour, finally leading to a huge landslide win in the May 1997 general election. The Conservatives were atomised throughout the country, and the Blair era had begun.

Most importantly for London, Labour recognised the legitimate demand the city had for local government, and created the London Assembly and the post of mayor. Despite this laudable attempt to give Londoners back the much-needed representation stolen by Thatcher, Blair quickly discredited himself by attempting to turn the Labour mayoral selection process against New Labour's then bête noire Ken Livingstone, former leader of the GLC. Londoners were incensed at Blair's attempts to parachute his close ally Frank Dobson into the position, and when Livingstone stood as an independent candidate he stormed the contest. However, realising that this was a man too significant to have outside the tent, Blair's savvy and pragmatic Labour machine quickly brought Livingstone into the party fold. For London, this meant great change. Livingstone introduced a very successful congestion charge and began tackling the mammoth task of bringing London's chronically backward public transport network into the 21st century.

London's resurgence as a great world city seemed to be going from strength to strength, culminating with the announcement on 6 July 2005 that the International Olympic Committee had awarded London the 2012 games, making it the first triple Olympic city in history. However, London's buoyant mood was shattered the very next morning when terrorists detonated a series of bombs on the city's public transport network, killing 52 innocent people. Triumph turned to terror, followed quickly by anger and then defiance. Just two weeks later the attempted detonation of several more home-made bombs on London's public transport system sent the city into a state of severe unease, which culminated in the tragic and shocking shooting by the Metropolitan Police of an innocent Brazilian electrician Jean Charles de Menezes, mistaken for Hussain Osman, one of the failed bombers from the previous day. Summer 2005 definitely marked London's lowest ebb for some time.

THE ERA OF BORIS

Ken Livingstone's campaign to get a third term as London mayor in 2008 was fatally undermined when the Conservative Party fielded maverick MP and popular TV personality Boris Johnson as its candidate. Even more of a populist than Livingstone, Johnson, portrayed by the media as a gaffe-prone toff, actually proved himself to be a deft political operator. Employing his 'zone 5 strategy' (campaigning in suburban London and largely ignoring the inner city where Livingstone's traditional support lay), amassing a £1.5 million campaign fund and exploiting fears about Livingstone's rumoured cronyism, Johnson shocked everyone by sailing past the incumbent to become the first Conservative mayor of London.

While many left-wing Londoners were worried about Johnson as mayor, the disastrous scenarios they predicted have not come true. While disagreeing with Livingstone on many things, Johnson has actually continued to support several of his predecessor's policies, including the congestion charge and the expansion of bicycle lanes, albeit with a cut budget for the latter. Johnson, a keen cyclist himself, has pledged to replace Livingstone's beloved 'bendy buses', though this is proving a more problematic campaign promise to keep for financial reasons.

1990	1997	2000
Britain erupts in civil unrest, culminating in the poll tax riots in Trafalgar Sq. Thatcher's deeply unpopular poll tax is ultimately the iron lady's undoing and she is forced to resign in November.	Labour sweeps to victory after almost two decades of Tory power. Tony Blair's radical relaunch of the once left-wing Labour Party as centrist 'New Labour' gives him a huge landslide with a majority of 179.	Ken Livingstone is elected mayor of London, despite the government's attempts to shoehorn its own man into the job. Elected as an independent, Livingstone is soon welcomed back into the Labour Party.

THE BORIS PHENOMENON

When Boris Johnson, the Conservative MP then best known for a high-profile extramarital affair and regular appearances on the popular news quiz *Have I Got News For You,* was elected mayor of London in 2008 the country at large was stunned. Johnson became the most senior Tory office holder in the country, and it was at once suggested that he and his old Eton pal David Cameron, the leader of the Conservative Party, would soon find themselves rivals. Moreover, people couldn't believe that Johnson, the clownish figure with the shock of white-blond hair, the accent so ridiculously upper class that it had almost transcended the British class system and a track record for gaffes that would make Prince Phillip embarrassed, would be running one of Europe's largest cities.

Johnson was born in New York in 1964 to a supremely well-connected and cosmopolitan family. Educated in Brussels and then England, where he attended Eton and Balliol College, Oxford, along with many future leading members of the Conservative Party, Johnson became a journalist after graduating, working for both the *Times* and the *Telegraph,* and becoming deputy editor at the latter. He went on to edit the influential right-wing magazine the *Spectator,* while simultaneously beginning his political career, taking former Tory bigwig Michael Heseltine's safe Henley seat in parliament in 2001. During this time he held small posts in the Conservative Party and the Shadow Cabinet, though was sacked from them both after apparently lying to then Conservative Party leader Michael Howard over an affair he was having with Petronella Wyatt, his colleague at the *Spectator.*

Johnson became best known to the British public for his shambolic but comedy gold appearances on the weekly BBC1 news quiz *Have I Got News For You,* where he was a panellist and later a guest presenter. Despite making a fool of himself in nearly every appearance, Johnson became much loved for his unpredictability and self-deprecation.

With Ken Livingstone looking set to breeze into a third four-year term as mayor in 2008, the Tories desperately looked for a candidate who could unseat him, apparently even approaching former prime minister and life-long Londoner John Major to stand (a task Major wisely turned down). Rumours about a Johnson candidature had been circulating for some time, but they were largely taken as a joke until Johnson put himself forward in July 2007, being confirmed by a Conservative primary later that year with 75% of the votes.

Ken Livingstone fatally dismissed Johnson as a 'joke' – and while he was indeed every bit the nonconventional candidate (not least for the straight-laced Tories), on the campaign stump Johnson turned populism into an art form, had a shrewd campaign team and quickly proved his doubters wrong. A vicious anti-Livingstone campaign by the *Evening Standard* certainly didn't help the incumbent, nor did a high-profile corruption case at City Hall or a slew of typically controversial comments from the mayor that had him accused of everything from anti-Semitism to racism. In the end, Johnson soundly beat Livingstone to become London's mayor until 2012; the capital reeled, gasped and joked before carrying on as normal.

London's successful bagging of the 2012 Olympic Games meant that a vast building program in East London was rolled into action. Most importantly for Londoners, the Olympics will release money for much-promised new transport routes – including the Crossrail scheme that will see the construction of two brand-new underground train lines linking London's east to its west – and produce much-needed affordable housing after the games.

The global financial crisis has taken its toll on London, too, of course. Many of the more ambitious construction schemes were being cancelled or postponed at the time of writing, and there are likely to be far fewer iconic city skyscrapers going up in the next decade. Yet despite this, London remains buoyant, confident and as exciting a place as ever. And with so much to play for in the next mayoral election, it's likely that Ken vs Boris, round two, in 2012 will be even more of a spectacle.

2003	2005	2008
London's congestion charge is introduced by Livingstone, creating an outcry that soon disappears as traffic in London's streets begins to flow smoothly again.	A day after London is awarded the 2012 Olympics, 52 people are killed by Muslim extremist suicide bombers attacking the London transport network on 7 July.	Boris Johnson, a Conservative MP and journalist famed for his gaffes and rather eccentric appearance, beats Ken Livingstone to become London's mayor.

ARTS

When a disused power station in a run-down part of London was transformed into the Tate Modern back at the turn of the century, few had any idea what a runaway success the gallery would be. A decade later it's London's most visited sight and has inspired a city already laden with artistic merit to even greater heights of ambition. The Tate Modern is just another phase in the artistic and cultural renaissance that began in London during the 1990s with Britpop and the Young British Artists, an unleashing of cultural power into a post-Thatcher vacuum that flourished in Blair's Britain. Whether it be in art, literature, music, fashion, stage or screen, London has always been the artistic centre of the UK and, in many ways, of Europe as a whole, particularly throughout the 20th century, when it led the way in music and fashion.

The arts make an important contribution to London's economic success, but it's the quality of life they contribute to that make them so significant – London's staggeringly rich cultural life brings many people here, while for others it's what keeps them in a city that's notoriously expensive and tough to get a break in.

Hollywood stars queue up to tread the boards of the capital's theatres, while London continues to be the heart of English literature, housing both the most innovative publishers in the country and some of writing's greatest stars. While the dust is still settling after the storm of Britart, a generation of less obviously shocking artists is emerging – not to mention a host of new galleries and museums that have opened in the past decade – ensuring that Londoners are still art crazy.

London's actors are known the world over, and the British film industry still throws out some notable productions, from Oscar-winning Kate Winslet's portrayal of a former concentration camp guard in *The Reader,* to the multi-award-winning magic realism of *Slumdog Millionaire* and blockbusters such as the Harry Potter and James Bond series. Musically, the city has not looked better for over a decade, and remains one of the best places to see live bands anywhere on earth. London is also a capital of comedy, and its dance companies cut a splendid dash across the world stage.

LITERATURE
Old Literary London

In English literature, London has been portrayed in countless ways over six centuries, from Chaucer to Monica Ali, making a history of London writing a history of the city itself. London has been the inspiration for such timeless masters as Shakespeare, Defoe, Dickens, Thackeray, Wells, Orwell, Conrad, Greene and Woolf, to name but a few. It's hard to reconcile the bawdy portrayal of the city in the *Canterbury Tales* with Dickens' bleak hellhole in *Oliver Twist,* let alone Defoe's plague-ravaged metropolis in *Journal of the Plague Year* with Zadie Smith's multiethnic romp in *White Teeth.* Ever changing, yet somehow eerily consistent – something brilliantly illustrated in Peter Ackroyd's *London: The Biography* – the capital has left its mark on some of the most influential writing in the English language. What follows is a small selection of seminal moments. In most cases these are easy to find in any London bookshop, many of which have a London Writing section.

The first literary reference to the city comes in Chaucer's *Canterbury Tales,* written between 1387 and 1400, where the pilgrims gather for their trip to Canterbury at the Tabard Inn in Southwark. Sadly the inn burned down in 1676; a blue plaque marks the site of the building today.

William Shakespeare spent most of his life as an actor and playwright in London around the turn of the 17th century, when book publishing was beginning to take off here. He trod the boards of several Southwark theatres and wrote his greatest tragedies – among them *Hamlet, Othello, Macbeth* and *King Lear* – for the original Globe theatre on the South Bank. However, although London was his home for most of his life, Shakespeare was an ardent fantasist and set nearly all his plays in foreign or make-believe lands. Even his English historical plays are hardly ever set in the capital; only *Henry IV: Part II* includes a London setting – a tavern called the Boar's Head in Eastcheap.

Daniel Defoe was perhaps the first true London writer, both living in and writing about the city during the early 18th century. He is most famous for *Robinson Crusoe* (1720) and *Moll Flanders* (1722), which he wrote while living in Church St in Stoke Newington. Defoe's *Journal of the Plague Year* is his most interesting account of London life, documenting the horrors of

GRUB STREET

Grub St was the original name of a London street (now Milton St, located behind the Barbican) inhabited by impoverished writers and literary hacks. In the 18th century, any inferior book or work of literature was known as 'Grubstreet', but these days – and you shouldn't read anything into this – the term seems to be used for the whole London publishing industry. The London publishing world takes itself extremely seriously, and that's why publications such as *Private Eye* (see boxed text, p54) are so refreshing, always on the lookout for individuals or organisations that are getting too big for their boots.

the Great Plague in London during the summer and autumn of 1665, when the author was a child.

Two early-19th-century poets found inspiration here. John Keats wrote his *Ode to a Nightingale* while living near Hampstead Heath in 1819 and his *Ode on a Grecian Urn* after inspecting the Portland Vase in the British Museum. William Wordsworth visited in 1802 and was inspired to write the poem *On Westminster Bridge*.

Charles Dickens (1812–70) was the definitive London author. When his father and family were imprisoned for not paying their debts, the 12-year-old Charles was forced to fend for himself on the streets of Regency London. Although his family was released three months later, those grim months were seared into the boy's memory and provided a font of experiences on which he would later draw. His novels most closely associated with the city are *Oliver Twist*, with its story of a gang of boy thieves organised by Fagin in Clerkenwell, and *Little Dorrit*, whose heroine was born in the Marshalsea – the same Southwark prison where his family was interned. His later *Our Mutual Friend* is a scathing criticism of contemporary London values – both monetary and social – and a spirited attack on the corruption, complacency and superficiality of 'respectable' London. The Old Curiosity Shop, made famous by the book of the same name, can still be seen standing just off Lincoln's Inn today.

Sir Arthur Conan Doyle (1858–1930) portrayed a very different London, and his pipe-smoking, cocaine-snorting sleuth, Sherlock Holmes, came to exemplify a cool and unflappable Englishness the world over. Letters to the mythical hero still arrive at 221b Baker St, where there's now a museum to everyone's favourite Victorian detective.

London at the end of the 19th century is described in a number of books. HG Wells' *The War of the Worlds* wonderfully captures the sense and mood of the times. W Somerset Maugham's first novel, *Liza of Lambeth*, was based on his experiences as an intern in the slums of South London, while *Of Human Bondage*, so English and of its time, provides an engaging portrait of late-Victorian London.

20th-Century Writing

Of the Americans writing about London at the end of the 19th century and start of the 20th century, Henry James, who settled and died here, stands supreme with *Daisy Miller* and *The Europeans. The People of the Abyss*, by American socialist writer Jack London, is a sensitive portrait of the poverty and despair of life in the East End. And we couldn't forget Mark Twain's *The Innocents Abroad*, in which the inimitable humorist skewers both the Old and New Worlds. St Louis–born TS Eliot settled in London in 1915, where he published his poem *The Love Song of J Alfred Prufrock* almost immediately and moved on to his ground-breaking epic *The Waste Land*.

Between the wars, PG Wodehouse (1881–1975), the most quintessentially British writer of the early 20th century, depicted the London high life with his hilarious lampooning of the English upper classes in the Jeeves stories. Quentin Crisp, the self-proclaimed 'stately homo of England', provided the flipside, recounting what it was like to be openly gay in the sexually repressed London of the 1920s in his ribald and witty memoir, *The Naked Civil Servant*. George Orwell's experience of living as a beggar in London's East End coloured his book *Down and Out in Paris and London* (1933), while sternly modernist Senate House on Malet St, Bloomsbury, was the inspiration for the Ministry of Truth in his classic dystopian 1949 novel *1984*.

The End of the Affair, Graham Greene's novel chronicling a passionate and doomed romance, takes place in and around Clapham Common just after WWII, while *The Heat of the Day* is Elizabeth Bowen's sensitive, if melodramatic, account of living through the Blitz.

RECOMMENDED READING

- *Londonstani* (2006; Gautam Malkani) This celebrated debut novel takes a thrilling look at race and identity in contemporary London and gives a great insight into youth culture in the capital.
- *Brick Lane* (2003; Monica Ali) This debut novel tells the story of Nazneen, a Muslim Bangladeshi woman who comes to London after an arranged marriage and initially accepts her circumscribed life, before embarking on her own voyage of self-discovery. The author writes with wit and gentle irony.
- *The Buddha of Suburbia* (1990; Hanif Kureishi) This winner of the 1990 Whitbread prize for a first novel is a raunchy, funny and insightful trawl of the hopes and fears of a group of Asian suburbanites in 1970s London, from the pre-eminent Anglo-Asian voice of his generation.
- *The End of the Affair* (1951; Graham Greene) Set in battle-scarred London at the end of WWII, this intensely emotional classic deals with a three-way collision between love of self, love of another and love of God (coloured by the tension felt by the author between his Roman Catholic faith and the compulsion of sexual passion).
- *Grey Area* (1994; Will Self) Piercing wit, narrative virtuosity and incisive social commentary characterise the writing of Self. In these nine short stories – or 'comic nightmares' – he lays into contemporary London and evokes the most disturbing failings of society.
- *Journal of the Plague Year* (1722; Daniel Defoe) Defoe's classic reconstruction of the Great Plague of 1665 scans the streets and alleyways of stricken London to record the extreme suffering of plague victims. At once grisly and movingly compassionate.
- *The Line of Beauty* (2003; Alan Hollinghurst) A surprise Booker Prize winner in 2004, this account of high society as seen through the eyes of a young gay man in Thatcher's London paints a portrait of a divisive period in modern British history and brings West London society into sharp critical focus.
- *London Fields* (1989; Martin Amis) By using a constantly shifting narrative voice, Amis makes the reader work damn hard for the prize in this middle-class-fear-of-the-mob epic. Dark and postmodern, it is a gripping study of London lowlife.
- *London Observed* (1992; Doris Lessing) A collection of stories from the Iranian-born (and Rhodesian-raised) author, who observes London and its inhabitants with the shrewd and compassionate eye of an artist in 18 sketches of the city.
- *London Orbital* (2002; Iain Sinclair) Sinclair, Hackney's irrepressible voice of dissent, sets off to circumnavigate the capital on foot within the 'acoustic footprints' of the M25. Hilarious and insightful.
- *The Shoreditch Tales* (2009; Carolyn Clark & Linda Wilkinson) An excellent picture – both real and remembered – of what Shoreditch looked and felt like before its regeneration.
- *The Long Firm* (2000; Jake Arnott) The first – and best – of a London trilogy set in the seedy world of 1960s Soho. Brutal but often hilarious reading that was made into a BBC drama series, too.
- *Mother London* (2000; Michael Moorcock) This engaging, rambling novel follows three mentally disturbed characters who hear voices from the heart of London, providing for an episodic romp through the history of the capital from the Blitz to the end of the 2nd millennium. The city itself becomes a character, along with its outcasts and marginals, all treated with great compassion.
- *Mrs Dalloway* (1925; Virginia Woolf) Bloomsbury Group stalwart Woolf goes full throttle with her stream-of-consciousness style in this story, which follows a day in the life of various people trying to cope in 1923 London. It is beautifully crafted, and as brief as it is exhilarating.
- *The Naked Civil Servant* (1968; Quentin Crisp) This story of an openly gay man in London in the 1920s, a world of brutality and comedy, is told in Crisp's characteristically sarcastic, self-derogatory, bitchy and very funny way.
- *Oliver Twist* (1837; Charles Dickens) Although not necessarily Dickens' best, this moving story of an orphan who runs away to London and falls in with a gang of thieves is beautifully told, with unforgettable characters and a vivid portrayal of Victorian London.
- *White Teeth* (2000; Zadie Smith) Smith's hugely hyped novel is a funny, poignant, big-hearted and affectionate book about friendship and cultural differences, as seen through the eyes of three unassimilated families in North London.

Colin MacInnes described the bohemian, multicultural world of 1950s Notting Hill in *City of Spades* and *Absolute Beginners*, while Doris Lessing captured the political mood of 1960s London in *The Four-Gated City*, the last of her five-book *Children of Violence* series, and provided some of the funniest and most vicious portrayals of 1990s London in *London Observed*. Nick Hornby has found himself the voice of a generation, nostalgic about his days as a young football fan in *Fever Pitch* and obsessive about vinyl in *High Fidelity*.

Before it became fashionable, Hanif Kureishi explored London from the perspective of ethnic minorities, specifically young Pakistanis in his best-known novels *The Black Album* and *The Buddha of Suburbia*. He also wrote the screenplay for the ground-breaking film *My Beautiful Laundrette*. Author and playwright Caryl Phillips won plaudits for his description of the Caribbean immigrant's experience in *The Final Passage*, while Timothy Mo's *Sour Sweet* is a poignant and funny account of a Chinese family in the 1960s trying to adjust to English life.

The late 1970s and 1980s were a great time for British literature, seeing a dazzling new generation of writers coming to the fore, many of whom remain the presiding gods of the scene today. Martin Amis (*Money, London Fields*), Julian Barnes (*Metroland, Talking it Over*), Ian McEwan (*Atonement, Enduring Love*), Salman Rushdie (*Midnight's Children, The Satanic Verses*), AS Byatt (*Posession, Angels & Insects*), Alan Hollinghurst (*The Swimming Pool Library, The Line of Beauty*) and Hanif Kureishi all need little introduction to keen readers, their novels have sold millions and have been awarded all the great literary prizes collectively, and all are still writing today.

The astronomical success of Helen Fielding's *Bridget Jones's Diary* effectively founded the genre known as 'chick lit', one that has far transcended the travails of a young single Londoner to become a worldwide phenomenon. Will Self – enfant terrible and incisive social commentator – has been the toast of London for the last decade and a half. His *Grey Area* is a superb collection of short stories focusing on skewed and surreal aspects of the city, while his more recent *The Book of Dave* is the hilarious, surreal story of a bitter, present-day London cabbie (recognisable to anyone who's spent half an hour listening to a rant in transit) burying a book of his own observations only to have it discovered in the future and regarded as scripture by the people on the island of Ham (Britain is an archipelago now due to rising sea levels).

Peter Ackroyd is regarded as the quintessential London author and names the city as the love of his life. *London: The Biography* is his inexhaustible paean to the capital, while his most recent book, *The Clerkenwell Tales*, brings to life the 14th-century London of Chaucer.

Finally, Iain Sinclair is the bard of Hackney, who, like Ackroyd, has spent his life obsessed with and fascinated by the capital. His acclaimed and ambitious *London Orbital*, a journey on foot around the M25, London's mammoth motorway bypass, is required London reading, while his latest work, *Hackney, That Rose Red Empire*, is an exploration of London's most notorious borough, one undergoing enormous changes as the Olympics come to town.

The Current Scene

London remains an exciting place for writers and readers alike and is the home of most of the UK's major publishers and its best bookshops. The frustrating predominance of several powerful corporations within publishing, however, is very limiting and there's almost no will within the literary scene to throw off the hegemony of companies far more interested in turning a profit than pioneering good writing.

The frankly sad desperation with which agents and publishers are seeking 'the next big thing' is a total sign of the times. The shape of the industry is best exemplified by the 2000 runaway success *White Teeth*, a dazzling debut novel by Zadie Smith about multiethnic assimilation in North London. This novel propelled Smith, pretty much overnight, from obscurity to being the poster girl for young, hip literary London. *White Teeth* was fresh and original, making the publisher a handsome profit from the almost unheard of size of the enormous advance it paid an unknown writer on an unfinished manuscript. Publishers on a quest for the jackpot are shelling out bigger and bigger advances for new books by unknown authors in the hope that they'll uncover 'the next Zadie Smith'. In many cases, of course, they don't, but large fees on a few gambles make it harder for other writers with less marketable qualities to get into print. This now-familiar phenomenon has been seen to a lesser extent with books such as Monica Ali's 2003 *Brick Lane* and Gautam Malkani's *Londonstani*, though the latter has become known as an example of a much-hyped first novel, bought for a large advance, not selling nearly as well as expected.

This sad state of affairs has, however, created an exciting literary fringe, which, although tiny, is very active and passionate about good writing. London still has many small presses where quality and innovation are prized over public relations skills and box ticking, and events fizzle away at bookshops and in back rooms of pubs throughout the week.

PRIZE WRITERS

The Man Booker Prize is the most important literary-fiction prize in Britain. Since its foundation in 1969, the Booker Prize has identified some of the greatest novels of the day, including awarding Salman Rushdie the 'Booker of Bookers' in 2008 – the greatest of all prize winners over the award's history. Any well-read Londoner will have an opinion about the Booker Prize – some rubbish it as a self-promotional tool of publishing houses, while others slavishly read not only the winner but any book to make the short list. Either way, few are indifferent to the prize, and the winner is usually highly indicative of contemporary literary trends in Britain. Recent winners have included Aravind Adiga's *The White Tiger* in 2008 and Anne Enright's *The Gathering* in 2007.

Back in the mainstream, the big guns of the 1980s such as Martin Amis, Ian McEwan, Salman Rushdie and Julian Barnes are still going strong, although none has produced anything much to get excited about since the late 1990s. Even McEwan's Booker-winning *Saturday* was a fairly underwhelming affair. Rushdie was awarded a knighthood in 2007 for services to literature, which outraged many Muslims who consider his book *The Satanic Verses* to be blasphemous. The award was widely cheered in Britain as a mark of support for freedom of speech. Many feel, though, that Rushdie has been distancing himself from the UK in recent years, despite being a British citizen and having enjoyed police protection for years at the cost of millions to the British taxpayer.

That's not to say that new voices haven't broken through in the last decade – indeed, there have been some outstanding new London writers in recent years, from Monica Ali, who brought the East End to life in *Brick Lane*, to Jake Arnott's intelligent Soho-based gangster yarn *The Long Firm* and Gautam Malkani's much-hyped *Londonstani*.

The current scene is most notable for the wealth of superb children's literature being produced. JK Rowling and Philip Pullman have between them totally revolutionised the concept of what children's books can be and the reach they can have. When Rowling's final Harry Potter book came out in summer 2007, people queued for copies for two days in a manner befitting ticket sales for a supergroup's world tour. With Rowling famously richer than the Queen, it's safe to say that she won't be worrying about her pension.

See boxed text, p312, for details of readings and spoken-word events around the city.

THEATRE

London has more theatrical history than almost anywhere else in the world, and it's still being made nightly on the stages of the West End, the South Bank and the vast London fringe. No visit to the city is complete without taking in a show, and just a walk through 'theatreland' in the West End any evening of the week is an electrifying experience as thousands of people make their way to one of the many venerable dramatic institutions.

Dramatic History

Very little is known about London theatre before the Elizabethan period, when a series of 'playhouses', including the Globe, were built on the south bank of the Thames and in Shoreditch. Although the playwrights of the time – Shakespeare, Christopher Marlowe *(Dr Faustus, Edward II)* and Shakespeare's great rival, Ben Johnson *(Volpone, The Alchemist)* – are now considered timeless geniuses, theatre then was more about raucous popular entertainment, where the crowd drank and heckled the actors. As venues for such, the playhouses were promptly shut down by the Puritans after the Civil War in 1642.

Three years after the return of the monarchy in 1660, the first famous Drury Lane Theatre was built and the period of 'restoration theatre' began, under the patronage of the rakish Charles II. Borrowing influences from Italian and French theatre, restoration theatre incorporated drama, including John Dryden's 1677 *All for Love*, and comedy. It's the latter, known for its burlesque humour and sexual explicitness, that most holds the attention of today's audiences. During the restoration period the first female actors appeared on stage (in Elizabethan times men played female roles), and Charles II is recorded as having had an affair with at least one, Nell Gwyn.

Despite the success of John Gay's 1728 *Beggar's Opera*, Oliver Goldsmith's 1773 farce *She Stoops to Conquer* and Richard Sheridan's *The Rivals* and *School for Scandal* (also in the 1770s) at Drury Lane, popular music halls replaced serious theatre during the Victorian era. Light comic operetta, as defined by Gilbert and Sullivan (*HMS Pinafore, The Pirates of Penzance, The Mikado* etc), was all the rage. A sea change was only brought about by the emergence at the end of the 19th century of such compelling playwrights as Oscar Wilde (*An Ideal Husband, The Importance of Being Earnest*) and George Bernard Shaw (*Pygmalion*).

Comic wits such as Noel Coward (*Private Lives, Brief Encounter*) and earnest dramatists such as Terence Ratigan (*The Winslow Boy, The Browning Version*) and JB Priestley (*An Inspector Calls*) followed. However, it wasn't until the 1950s and 1960s that English drama yet again experienced such a fertile period as the Elizabethan era.

Perfectly encapsulating the social upheaval of the period, John Osborne's *Look Back in Anger* at the Royal Court in 1956 has gone down as generation defining. In the following decade, a rash of new writing appeared, including Harold Pinter's *Homecoming*, Joe Orton's *Loot*, Tom Stoppard's *Rosencrantz and Guildenstern are Dead* and Alan Ayckbourn's *How the Other Half Loves*. During the same period many of today's leading theatre companies were formed, including the National Theatre under the directorship of Laurence Olivier in 1963.

Although somewhat eclipsed by the National Theatre in the cyclical world of London theatre, today's Royal Court retains a fine tradition of new writing. In the past decade it has nurtured such talented playwrights as Jez Butterworth (*Mojo, The Night Heron*), Ayub Khan-Din (*East Is East*), Conor McPherson (*The Weir, Shining City*) and Joe Penhall (*Dumb Show*).

The Current Scene

London remains a thrilling place to be for anyone who loves theatre. Nowhere else on earth, with the possible exception of New York, offers such a huge range of high-quality drama, excellent musical theatre and such a sizzling fringe. Whether it's to see Hollywood A-listers gracing tiny stages and earning Equity minimum for their efforts or lavish West End musicals that you'll remember for years afterwards, London remains an undisputed world leader and innovator in the field.

After several terrible years from late 2001, the mainstream West End has re-established its credentials, putting on a series of extraordinary hits, while the smarter end of the fringe continues to impress with risky, controversial productions that make sure theatre often makes the news. The hottest tickets in town remain those for the National Theatre, which under Nicholas Hytner has gone from strength to strength, with productions such as *History Boys, Jerry Springer – The Opera, Elmina's Kitchen* and *Coram Boy* enjoying huge box-office success coupled with critical acclaim.

Other venues leading the way in innovation are off–West End venues such as the Arcola (the world's first carbon-neutral theatre and home to an alternative opera season called grimebourne), the Almeida, the Royal Court, the Soho Theatre and the Donmar Warehouse. At the Donmar, artistic director Michael Grandage recently staged a new production of *Hamlet* with Jude Law as the Dane – just another example of the big names it's easy to see any night of the week on London's stages, whether it be Ethan Hawke playing Treplev in Tom Stoppard's new translation of Chekhov's *The Seagull* at the Old Vic, or Dame Judi Dench in top form in Mishima's *Madame de Sade* at the Wyndham's Theatre.

Perhaps the most significant trend of the past few years, with the Blair administration limping off stage left in 2007, has been the rediscovery of political satire and serious political content in many productions, equally in the West End and on the fringe. David Hare's *Stuff Happens*, about the run-up to the Iraq War, was staged at the National, as was a highly political new production of *Henry V* set in occupied Iraq. Elsewhere, the Tricycle Theatre put on *Called to Account*, about the internal wrangling at Westminster in the lead-up to the war, and the whole British political and media establishment was sent up in *Who's the Daddy*, a play set amid the sex scandals at the *Spectator* magazine, the beating heart of the UK establishment. Other productions, such as *A Weapons Inspector Calls* and *Guantanamo*, prove that satire is firmly back on the capital's theatrical agenda.

Satire aside, there's something for all tastes in London's theatreland, and even the revivified West End juggles the serious with the frivolous. Recent productions attracting critical acclaim have included *A Streetcar Named Desire* at the Donmar Warehouse, *Arcadia* at the Duke of York's Theatre and *As You Like It* at the Globe. At the time of writing the musicals causing the most excitement in town were *Oliver!*, with Rowan Atkinson providing a wonderful Fagin in its opening six months, although he's now stepped down from that role, and *La Cage Aux Folles* at the Playhouse Theatre. A slew of superb musicals in recent years, from *Sister Act* to *Spamalot,* have revitalised the West End and ensure that London is one of the best places on earth to catch a show.

Shakespeare's legacy is generously attended to on the city's stages, most notably by the Royal Shakespeare Company (RSC) and at the Globe Theatre. The RSC stages one or two of the bard's plays in London each year, although it currently has no London home (its productions are based in Stratford-upon-Avon and usually transfer to the capital later on in the run), while the open-air Globe on the South Bank attempts to re-create the Elizabethan theatre experience. A faithful reconstruction of the original Globe, the building places audiences unusually close to the actors, and the management is quite happy to let them heckle each other. Since it opened in 1997 the Globe has enjoyed considerable success as a working theatre (as opposed to a mere curiosity). Artistic director Dominic Dromgoole, having taken over the reins at the start of 2006, has ensured that Shakespeare's plays remain at the core of the theatre's program but at the same time has produced a wider range of European and British classics, as well as originating new material, something of which the Bard himself would no doubt approve.

Finally, if all this innovation and change is too much for you, drop by St Martin's Theatre, where the same production of *The Mousetrap* has been running since 1952!

For theatre listings, see p311.

MUSIC

Modern music, from the Kinks to Lily Allen, is perhaps London's single greatest contribution to the world of arts, and after more than four decades at the top, it is still a creative hotbed and a magnet for bands and hopefuls from all over the world. Complementing the home-grown talent is the continuous influx of styles and cultures that keeps the music scene here so fresh.

The Swinging '60s

London's prolific output began with the Kinks and their North London songwriter Ray Davies, whose lyrics read like a guide to the city. 'You Really Got Me', 'All Day and All of the Night' and 'Dedicated Follower of Fashion' brilliantly capture the antiestablishment mood of the '60s, while 'Waterloo Sunset' is the ultimate feel-good London song.

Another London band, the Rolling Stones, got their first paying gig at the old Bull & Bush in Richmond in 1963. Originally an R&B outfit, they went on to define rock and roll, and success and teen mayhem quickly followed. Their second single, 'I Wanna Be Your Man', came to them via a chance encounter on the street with John Lennon and Paul McCartney, two blokes down from Liverpool recording in Abbey Road and on their way to making their band, the Beatles, the biggest the world has ever known. The Stones, no slouches in the fame stakes themselves, released 'Not Fade Away' in 1964, and they're doggedly sticking to their word after 40 years of swaggering, swilling and swearing. The Beatles themselves, while of course famously being from Liverpool, recorded most of their best-known songs in London and even performed their final concert on the roof of the Apple building in Mayfair.

Struggling to be heard above the din was inspirational mod band the Small Faces, formed in 1965 and remembered long afterwards. The Who, from West London, got attention by thrashing guitars on stage and chucking TVs out of hotel windows. The band is also remembered for rock operas and hanging around far too long flogging their back catalogue. Jimi Hendrix came to London and took guitar playing to levels not seen before or since, even tragically dying in a West London hotel under somewhat mysterious circumstances in 1970. In some ways, the swinging '60s ended in July 1969 when the Stones played a free concert in Hyde Park in front of more than a quarter of a million liberated fans.

The '70s

A local band called Tyrannosaurus Rex had enjoyed moderate success. In 1970 they changed their name to T Rex, frontman Marc Bolan donned a bit of glitter and the world's first 'glam' band had arrived. Glam encouraged the youth of uptight Britain to come out of the closet and be whatever they wanted to be. Brixton boy and self-proclaimed 'chameleon of pop' David Bowie began to steal the limelight, sealing his international fame with *The Rise and Fall of Ziggy Stardust and the Spiders from Mars* in 1972, one of the best albums of the decade. Roxy Music, incorporating art rock and synth pop, sang 'Love Is the Drug' in 1975.

Meanwhile, a little band called Led Zeppelin formed in London in 1968 and created the roots of heavy metal. Seventeen-year-old Farok Bulsara came to London from India (via Zanzibar) in the '60s and in 1970 changed his name to Freddie Mercury; the consummate showman formed Queen with a few local lads and went on to become one of the greatest rock-and-roll stars of all time. Fleetwood Mac stormed the US as much as Britain; their *Rumours* became the fifth-highest-selling album in history (one behind Cambridge boys Pink Floyd's *Dark Side of the Moon*). Bob Marley recorded his *Live* album at the Lyceum Theatre in 1975.

top picks

A MUSICAL JOURNEY THROUGH LONDON

- Zebra crossing on Abbey Road, St John's Wood – the Beatles' most famous album cover
- Heddon Street, Soho – where the cover for *Ziggy Stardust* was photographed
- 23 Brook Street, Mayfair – former home to composers Handel and Hendrix
- St Martins College, Mayfair – first Sex Pistols gig
- Tree on Queen's Ride, Barnes – where Marc Bolan died in his Mini in 1977
- 3 Savile Row, Mayfair – site of the last Beatles performance on the roof of the Apple building in 1969

While glam and rock opened the door for British youth, punk came along and kicked the bloody thing down, and set about turning the whole British establishment on its head. The Sex Pistols were the most outrageous of a wave of bands, including the Clash and the Damned, which started playing around London in 1976. The Pistols' first single was, appropriately enough, 'Anarchy in the UK'. 'God Save the Queen' and 'Pretty Vacant' followed and were brilliant. The album *Never Mind the Bollocks Here's the Sex Pistols* was released a year later to critical acclaim.

Fortunately, fellow Londoners the Clash had harnessed the raw anger of the time and worked it into a collar-grabbing brand of political protest that would see them outlast all of their peers. They trod the fine line between being pissed-off punks and great songwriters. The Clash were protesters who raged against racism, social injustice, police brutality and disenfranchisement. The disillusioned generation finally had a plan and a leader; *London Calling* is a spirited call to arms.

The Sex Pistols' ranting and raving John Lydon (formerly Johnny Rotten) became an embarrassment to a generation weaned on punk, but the dismayed reaction to the death of Clash frontman Joe Strummer in late 2002 showed that there was still lots to be proud of.

In 1977 the Jam, punk pioneers *and* mod revivalists, went on tour opening for the Clash (what days!). Lead singer and bristling live performer Paul Weller followed up with a hugely successful solo career.

The '80s

Out of the ashes of punk came, God knows how, the New Wave and new romantics. Guitars were chucked away and replaced with keyboard synthesizers and drum machines. Fashion and image became as important as the music, and it's the seriousness with which the new romantics took themselves that gives the '80s such a bad rap. Overpriced, oversexed and way overdone, '80s London produced such unforgettables as Spandau Ballet, Culture Club, Bananarama, Wham! and Howard Jones' haircut. Wham!'s Georgios Panayiotou shaved his back, changed his name to George Michael and gained great success as a solo artist.

Depeche Mode broke new ground in neo-synth pop, while American London adoptee Chrissie Hynde formed the Pretenders and became the first bad-ass rock-and-roll chick. Northern-lads-turned-Londoners the Pet Shop Boys managed to avoid the '80s-pop path to oblivion, redeeming themselves with synth innovation and still having hits almost three decades on. Neneh Cherry started rapping, and Madness came up with a winning ska-pop combo and featured London in many of their hits and videos.

BACKGROUND ARTS

While the late '80s brought blond boy band Bros and the anodyne starlets and one-hit wonders of the Stock/Aitken/Waterman Hit Factory, relief had already been coming from up north with the Smiths, and at the end of the decade the Stone Roses and the Happy Mondays broke through with a new sound that had grown out of the recent acid-house raves, with jangly guitars, psychedelic twists and a beat you just couldn't resist. Dance exploded onto the scene, with dilated pupils and Chupa Chups, in 1988's summer of love. A generation was gripped by dance music and a new lexicon had to be learned: techno, electronica, hip hop, garage, house, trance and so on. Although the E generation that launched the rave/dance culture has grown up and moved on, London still ranks among the best club cities in the world (see p294).

top picks

LONDON ALBUMS

- Abbey Road – The Beatles
- Exile on Main Street – The Rolling Stones
- The Good The Bad and The Queen – Damon Albarn et al
- London Calling – The Clash
- Modern Life Is Rubbish – Blur
- Alright, Still – Lily Allen
- The Rise and Fall of Ziggy Stardust and the Spiders from Mars – David Bowie
- Silent Alarm – Bloc Party
- Something Else – The Kinks
- Sound Affects – The Jam

Britpop

The early 1990s saw the explosion of yet another scene: Britpop, a genre broadly defined as back to (Beatles) basics, familiar old-fashioned three chords and all that jazz, with loads of slang and in-references which, frankly, made it so 'British'. There was a very public battle between two of the biggest bands, Blur from London and Oasis from Manchester, and the public loved the tit-for-tat between the cocky geezers from the capital and the swaggering, belligerent Mancs. When it came down to the line and both bands released a single on the same day, Blur overcame the northerners and got the number one slot; Blur bassist Alex James wore an Oasis T-shirt on *Top of the Pops* in a moment of utter brilliance to be remembered by a generation.

Also weighing in for the London side were the brilliant and erratic Suede (who finally disbanded in 2003) and Elastica (who disbanded in 2001), fronted by the punky, poppy Justine Frischmann, not to mention Sheffield defectors to the capital, Jarvis Cocker's Pulp. Skirting around the edges, doing their own thing without the hullabaloo, were Radiohead (from Oxford, close enough to London), one of the most iconic and ground-breaking groups of the 1990s.

As the Britpop bands and fans became more sophisticated, the genre died around 1997. Groups such as Coldplay enjoyed massive commercial and critical success, but the zeitgeist had well and truly disappeared around the start of the new millennium, leaving London's music scene looking washed up and unexciting.

21st-Century Music

At the beginning of the 21st century multicultural London pushed things forward, to bend the words of Mike Skinner (aka the Streets), whose debut album, *Original Pirate Material,* took London by storm in 2002 and whose follow-up *A Grand Don't Come for Free* saw equal success, with everyday tales from the life of a modern lad. It's a genre-straddling classic from a young white rapper originally from Birmingham and now living in Brixton, a cross-cultural gem that lit the way for London's music scene in the 21st century.

London's Asian community also made a big splash in the early 21st century, with Talvin Singh and Nitin Sawhney fusing dance with traditional Indian music to stunning effect, and Asian Dub Foundation bringing their unique brand of jungle techno and political comment to an ever-widening audience, despite being dropped by the major British record labels.

Pete Doherty and Carl Barat single-handedly renewed interest in guitar music following its post-Britpop malaise. The Libertines, formed in a Stoke Newington flat, created a huge splash with their 2002 debut single 'What a Waster', which made it into the top 40 despite no mainstream radio play, and their first album went platinum. However, despite such huge success, the duo split up after Doherty broke into Barat's Marylebone flat to steal money for heroin. Kicked out, Doherty went on to form Babyshambles, who also enjoyed moderate success, though they were much better known for Doherty's never-dull private life and his problems with drugs.

Other London talents that came to the fore at this time include art rockers Bloc Party, Anglo-Swedish group Razorlight, quirky West London singer-songwriter Lily Allen and troubled but extraordinary Southgate chanteuse Amy Winehouse.

London Music Today

The London scene has fought its way back from being an overhyped late-'90s destination for those seeking cool by association and is again one of the major creative musical hubs on earth. Whether it's home-grown capital talent or refugees from the provinces seeking fame and fortune, London's music scene is throwing up plenty of exciting and ground-breaking music, particularly on the synth pop and electropop scene. La Roux, Florence and the Machine, Little Boots, Hot Chip, MIA and the Klaxons all back up London's claim to be a world centre for musical innovation.

Grime and its successor genre dubstep, two real indigenous London musical forms born in the East End out of a fusion of hip hop and Asian influences, are currently at the cutting edge of London music. Dizzee Rascal, Lady Sovereign, Lethal Bizzle, Roll Deep, GoldieLocks and Kano are perhaps the best-known singers and groups working in the genre – for a true East End night out track them down playing a local gig while you're in town.

For a list of venues, see p302.

VISUAL ARTS

London has attracted many of the greatest artists in the world, from Monet to Van Gogh, even if Britain's contribution to the visual arts has historically not measured up to that of its European neighbours. Today, London is the art capital of Europe, with an exciting gallery scene and some of the world's best modern art collections.

Holbein to Turner

It wasn't until the rule of the Tudors that art took off in London at all. The German Hans Holbein the Younger (1497–1543) was court painter to Henry VIII, and one of his finest works, *The Ambassadors* (1533), hangs in the National Gallery (p73). A batch of great portrait artists worked at court during the 17th century. The best of them was Anthony Van Dyck (1599–1641), a Belgian who spent the last nine years of his life in London and painted some hauntingly beautiful portraits of Charles I, including *Charles I on Horseback* (1638), now in the National Gallery. Charles I was a keen collector and it was during his reign that the Raphael Cartoons, now in the Victoria & Albert Museum (p139), came to London.

Local artists began to emerge in the 18th century. Thomas Gainsborough (1727–88) extended portraiture to include the gentry and is regarded as the first great British landscapist, even though most of his landscapes are actually backgrounds. William Hogarth (1697–1764), by contrast, is best known for his satirical prints of 18th-century London lowlife (see boxed text, p44).

England has a fine tradition of watercolourists, beginning with the poet and engraver William Blake (1757–1827), some of whose romantic paintings and illustrations (he illustrated Milton's *Paradise Lost,* for example) hang in the Tate Britain (p93). John Constable (1776–1837) was a much more skilful and important visual artist than Blake. He studied the clouds and skies above Hampstead Heath, sketching hundreds of scenes that he'd later match with subjects in his landscapes.

JMW Turner (1775–1851), equally at home with oils and watercolours, represented the pinnacle of 19th-century British art. Through innovative use of colour and gradations of light he created a new atmosphere that seemed to capture the wonder, sublimity and terror of nature. His later works – including *Snow Storm – Steam-boat off a Harbour's Mouth* (1842), *Peace – Burial at Sea* (1842) and *Rain, Steam, Speed* (1844), now in the Tate Britain and the National Gallery – were increasingly abstract, and although widely vilified at the time, later inspired the likes of Claude Monet.

The Pre-Raphaelites to Hockney

The Pre-Raphaelite Brotherhood (1848–54), founded in London, burst briefly onto the scene. Taking their inspiration from the works of the Romantic poets, they ditched the pastel-coloured rusticity of the day in favour of big, bright and bold depictions of medieval legends and female beauty.

Two of Britain's leading 20th-century painters emerged next. In 1945 the tortured, Irish-born painter Francis Bacon (1909–92) caused a stir when he exhibited his *Three Studies for Figures at the Base of a Crucifixion* – now on display at the Tate Britain – and afterwards carried on unsettling the world with his distorted, repulsive and fascinating forms. The chaos in Bacon's studio was almost as legendary as his Picasso-meets-Velázquez-meets-Van Gogh-meets-Scarfe paintings. He famously worked knee-deep in scraps of paper, paint rags, newspaper cuttings and other general litter. As he was largely homosexual, it was considered a rare find in the art world when a painting of one of his female lovers went on sale in 2004, and he was also in the news when a forgotten triptych of his was found in an Iranian gallery.

Australian art critic Robert Hughes has described Bacon's contemporary Lucian Freud (b 1922) as 'the greatest living realist painter', and indeed, in 2008 Freud's 1995 *Benefits Supervisor Sleeping* sold at Christie's in New York for US$33.6 million, a world record for a painting by a living painter. From the 1950s the bohemian Freud has concentrated on pale, muted portraits – often nudes, and frequently of friends and family, although he has also painted the Queen. Twice married and rumoured to have up to 40 illegitimate children, Freud's recent self-portrait *The Painter Is Surprised by a Naked Admirer* fuelled a press frenzy, as journalists tried to guess the identity of the naked woman clinging to his leg.

After the initial shock of Bacon and Freud during the 1940s and '50s, pop art perfectly encapsulated the image of London in the swinging '60s. The brilliant David Hockney (b 1937) gained a reputation as one of the leading pop artists through his early use of magazine-style images (although he rejected the label). After a move to California, his work became increasingly naturalistic as he took inspiration from the sea, the sun, swimmers and swimming pools. Two of his most famous works, *Mr and Mrs Clark and Percy* (1971) and *A Bigger Splash* (1974), are displayed at the Tate Britain.

The Origins of Britart

Gilbert and George were the quintessential English conceptual artists of the 1960s. They, at the very least, paved the way for the shock and celebrity of Britart; they themselves were as much a part of the art as their works were. The Spitalfields odd couple are still at the heart of the British art world, having now become a part of the establishment themselves by representing Britain at the 2005 Venice Biennale, and having a very successful retrospective at the Tate Modern in 2007.

Despite its incredibly rich collections, Britain had never led, dominated or even really participated in a particular epoch or style. That all changed in the twilight of the 20th century, when Britart burst onto the scene with its sliced cows, elephant dung and piles of bricks. It's questionable whether the movement will leave a lasting impression, but one thing's for sure: during the 1990s London was the beating heart of the art world.

Britart sprang from a show called Freeze that was staged in a Docklands warehouse in 1988. It was organised by showman Damien Hirst and largely featured his fellow graduates from Goldsmiths College. Influenced by pop culture and punk, this loose movement was soon catapulted to notoriety by the advertising guru Charles Saatchi, who came to dominate the scene and bought an extraordinary number of works. Indeed, you could almost say he created the genre with his free spending

OF RAKES & HARLOTS: HOGARTH'S WORLD

William Hogarth (1697–1764) was an artist and engraver who specialised in satire and what these days might be considered heavy-handed moralising on the wages of sin. His plates were so popular in his day that they were pirated, leading parliament to pass the Hogarth Act of 1735 to protect copyright. His works provide invaluable insights into the life – particularly the poor variety – of Georgian London. Hogarth's works can be seen in Sir John Soane's Museum (p77) in Holborn, Hogarth's House (p197) in Chiswick, the Tate Britain (p93) and the National Gallery (p73).

and commissioning. From 1992 Saatchi held a series of seven exhibitions entitled Young British Artists (YBAs), which burst onto the national stage with 1997's seminal Sensation exhibition at the Royal Academy.

The work was brash, decadent, ironic, easy to grasp and eminently marketable. To shock seemed the impulse, and the artists did just that. Hirst chipped in with a cow sliced into sections and preserved in formaldehyde; flies buzzed around another cow's head and were zapped in his early work *A Thousand Years*. Chris Ofili provoked with the *Holy Virgin Mary*, a black Madonna made partly with elephant poo; the Chapman brothers produced mannequins of children with genitalia on their heads; and Marcus Harvey created a portrait of notorious child-killer Myra Hindley, made entirely with children's hand-prints, whose value skyrocketed when it was repeatedly vandalised by ink and eggs from the general public.

The areas of Shoreditch, Hoxton and Whitechapel – where many artists lived, worked and hung out – became the epicentre of the movement and a rash of galleries moved in. Among these was White Cube (p149), owned by one of the most important patrons of early Britart, Jay Jopling.

The exhibitions sent shockwaves around the world, as sections of society took turns to be outraged. Liberals were drawn into defending the works, the media went positively gaga, promoting some of the artists like pop stars, and Britart became the talk of the world. For the 10 years or so that it rode the wave of this publicity, its defining characteristics were celebrity and shock value. Damien Hirst and Tracey Emin became the inevitable celebrities – people the media knew they could sell to the mainstream.

One critic said the hugely hyped movement was the product of a 'cultural vacuum' and had become like the emperor's new clothes, which everyone was afraid to criticise for fear they'd look stupid. 'Cold, mechanical, conceptual bullshit', was how the culture minister described the nominations for the Turner Prize one year. Hirst finally admitted in 2005 that some of his own work irritated even him.

Tracey Emin (b 1963) went on to become the most famous artist-behaving-badly. She was short-listed for the Turner Prize with an installation, *My Bed*, her unmade messy bed, strewn with blood-stained underwear and used condoms. For another installation, *Everyone I Have Ever Slept with 1963–1995*, she sewed the names of all the relevant people on a tent. She was perfect for Britart because she pandered to the public's darkest levels of voyeurism *and* their love of celebrity. When her cat went missing, people tore down the notices she put up and kept them as objets d'art.

After Britart

But while the world was focusing on the stars, there were a lot of great artists hammering away on the fringes. A highlight of the era has to be Richard Wilson's iconic installation *20:50* (1987). It's a room filled waist-high with recycled oil, where you walk in and feel you've just been shot out into space. In his most famous work, *24 Hour Psycho*, Scottish video artist Douglas Gordon slowed Alfred Hitchcock's masterpiece down so much it was stripped of its narrative and viewed more like a moving sculpture, while Gary Hume quietly went about his work, the less-fashionable painting. Hume first came to prominence with his *Doors* series of full-size paintings of hospital doors, powerful allegorical descriptions of despair – or just perfect reproductions of doors.

Rachel Whiteread won the Turner Prize in 1993 for *House*, a concrete cast of an East End terrace dwelling that the council controversially knocked down shortly afterwards. In the same week she won £40,000 in the doubly lucrative prize for Worst British Artist of the year, an award set up by former disco funsters KLF, who out-shocked the Britartists by burning £1 million in cash in front of assembled journalists.

The biggest date on the current calendar is now the Turner Prize at the Tate Britain, won in 2007 by Mark Wallinger for his re-creation of Brian Haw's Parliament Sq anti-war demonstration and in 2008 by Mark Lecky for his solo exhibit Industrial Light & Magic, the winner among a field much derided by the media.

The biggest-name artists working in London today are Banksy, the anonymous street artist whose work has become a worldwide phenomenon and can still (although increasingly rarely) be seen on the streets of London; sculptor Antony Gormley, who in 2009 began putting 'ordinary' people on the fifth plinth in Trafalgar Sq to rather a mixed critical reception, but who is best known for the 22m-high *Angel of the North*, beside the A1 trunk road near Gateshead in northern England; and Anish Kapoor, an Indian sculptor working in London since the 1970s, whose fantastic installations and sculpture are extremely popular with Londoners and who is well represented in the Tate Modern (p128).

Even Emin has gone from enfant terrible of the scene to pillar of the art establishment. In 2007 she was made a Royal Academician, admitting her to the true elite of British art and allowing her to exhibit six pieces at the annual Summer Exhibition. As if this wasn't enough to confirm her position, in the same year she also represented Britain at the Venice Biennale, only the second lone female ever to have done so.

CINEMA & TELEVISION

TV was born in London and is ageing well. Although locals complain about the constant dumbing down of the BBC and ever-falling standards as producers chase an ever-lower common denominator, most countries would give their eye teeth to have TV this good, from the extraordinary BBC natural history unit films to the cutting-edge comedy and drama across the channels. However, although the UK punches well above its weight in terms of presence on the international film scene, London is far from the centre of the film industry that it might be.

London on Film

Londoners are proud of their city, but few claim London to be at the forefront of the film industry, with British film in general being massively hit and miss. Certainly, there have been some individual commercial triumphs, including recent Oscar-winner *The Queen* and the newly ripped and metrosexual James Bond sporting tight Speedos in *Casino Royale*, not to mention '90s smash hits such as *Four Weddings and a Funeral* and *Shakespeare in Love*. But there's an underlying frustration that the local film industry is not as strong as it should be, especially given the disproportionate influence of the Brits in Hollywood.

However, London is one of the most popular places to make films in the world. Recent converts have included that most die-hard of New Yorkers, Woody Allen, who has made *Match Point, Scoop* and *Cassandra's Dream* in the capital in recent years before moving on to Barcelona.

Naturally, the eponymous West London neighbourhood pops up in 1999's *Notting Hill*. The Dickensian backstreets of Borough feature in such polar opposites as chick-flick *Bridget Jones's Diary* and Guy Ritchie's gangster romp *Lock, Stock and Two Smoking Barrels*, while Smithfield is given a certain bleak glamour in *Closer*.

The city's combination of historic and ultramodern architecture certainly works to its advantage in this respect. Ang Lee's *Sense and Sensibility*, for example, could retreat to historic Greenwich for its wonderful parkland and neoclassical architecture. Inigo Jones' Queen's House, in particular, features in interior scenes. Merchant Ivory's costume drama *Howard's End* and the biopic *Chaplin* feature the neo-Gothic St Pancras Chambers, while the early 1980s film *The Elephant Man* took advantage of the moody atmosphere around the then-undeveloped Shad Thames (the site of today's Butler's Wharf).

There are some films that Londoners find heart-warming just because they feature ordinary shots of the contemporary city. Danny Boyle's *28 Days Later* (2002) has amazing opening scenes of central London and Docklands lying abandoned after a monkey virus wipes out the population. Blockbuster *Mission: Impossible* features Liverpool St station, and John Landis' irrepressibly entertaining *An American Werewolf in London* finishes with a mad chase in Piccadilly Circus.

Fans often nostalgically refer back to the golden – but honestly rather brief – era of Ealing comedies, when the London-based Ealing Studios turned out a steady stream of hits. Between 1947 and 1955, when the studios were sold to the BBC, they produced enduring classics such as *Passport to Pimlico, Kind Hearts and Coronets, Whisky Galore, The Man in the White Suit, The Lavender Hill Mob* and *The Ladykillers*. This was also the time of legendary film-makers Michael Powell and Emeric Pressburger, the men behind *The Life and Death of Colonel Blimp* and *The Red Shoes*.

Today, such halcyon days seem far distant, as the industry is stuck in a rut of romantic comedies (see Richard Curtis' horribly saccharine *Love Actually*), costume dramas (the usual adaptations of classic novels starring Keira Knightley in a corset) and increasingly dirc gangster pics. Producers, directors and actors complain about a lack of adventurousness in those who hold the purse strings, while film investors claim there are not enough scripts worth backing.

A system of public funding through the UK Film Council exists alongside private investment, and although in 2002 it only accounted for a minority of the £570 million spent on film in the UK, some critics object to the scheme. The *Evening Standard's* late, lamented former film critic Alexander Walker was one of those who suggested that it led to poor projects being made, simply because the money was there.

Meanwhile, well-known British actors such as Ewan McGregor, Ian McKellen, Ralph Fiennes, Jude Law, Liam Neeson, Hugh Grant, Rhys Ifans, Kristin Scott Thomas and Emily Watson spend time working abroad, as do many British directors, such as Tony Scott *(Top Gun, True Romance)*, Ridley Scott *(Bladerunner, Alien, Thelma & Louise, Gladiator)*, Michael Winterbottom *(The Claim)* and Sam Mendes *(American Beauty, Revolutionary Road)*.

Television

London is the home of TV; it was born and bred here, with John Logie Baird first demonstrating it in Soho to a select group of scientists in 1926, and then to the public a few years later. Perhaps more significantly, the world's first public broadcaster, the BBC, began here, too, and has originated some of the world's most recognised TV formats and personalities.

When it comes to televisual output, London plays with a somewhat stronger hand than in film: a huge amount of global TV content originates in Britain, from *Planet Earth* to *Who Wants to be a Millionaire*. There are five free-to-air national TV stations: BBC1, BBC2 (established 1964), ITV1 (1955), Channel 4 (1982) and Five (1997). Even though cable is now available and digital services were introduced in 1998 (and are due to totally replace analogue broadcasts by 2012), the BBC derives funding from a system of TV licences paid for by viewers. Ever since the BBC began broadcasts in 1932 (regularly from 1936), there's been a public service ethic driving British TV. John Reith, the first director-general of the BBC, took quite a paternalistic view of the audience, seeing the role of TV as to inform and educate as much as to entertain, and insisted on quality.

A complete history of English TV is obviously not possible here, but anyone familiar with the subject will be aware of an enormously long roll call of classic series, from comedies such as *Fawlty Towers* and *Rising Damp* and cop shows such as *The Sweeney* and *The Professionals* to cult series such as *The Prisoner, The Avengers* and *Minder;* from 1970s comedies *(The Good Life)* to heritage offerings in the 1980s *(Brideshead Revisited);* from thrillers *(Edge of Darkness)* to dramas *(The Singing Detective)* – the list could go on endlessly. However, undoubtedly the two most famous TV serials associated with London itself are the long-running soap opera *EastEnders* and the police drama *The Bill*. Ironically, the first of these is actually filmed at the BBC studios in Elstree, Hertfordshire, although Albert Sq is said to be modelled on Fassett Sq in Dalston. *The Bill* is shot around the East End.

In recent years Britain, like elsewhere, has been in the grip of reality-TV fever. While *Big Brother* and its ilk have somewhat faded from prominence a decade after they exploded and changed TV forever, talent shows have continued to capture the public imagination. This is exemplified by the worldwide success of *Britain's Got Talent,* the ITV1 show that turned Susan Boyle into an overnight success when she blew the audience away with her rendition of 'I Dreamed a Dream' from *Les Misérables* in a 2008 series of the show.

Comedy has always been something that Britain does particularly well, with Slough-set *The Office* and, um, Britain-set *Little Britain* now remade in the US (the ultimate benchmark of success). Two utter comic gems far more directly associated with London are the almost forgotten 2005 *Nathan Barley,* the Chris Morris–penned, much-needed comedic response to the Shoreditch scene, and the wonderfully spot-on political satire *The Thick of It,* a fictional behind-the-scenes look at life in the Westminster village in the age of spin, which also spawned its own hilarious 2009 movie *In the Loop*.

DANCE

Whether you're into contemporary, classical or crossover, London has the right moves for you. Recently in the danc throes of renewed *Billy Elliot* fever, thanks to the enduring success of the musical, London is up there with New York and Paris as one of the world's great dance capitals and has been the crucible of one of the most significant developments in modern choreographic history. Although it's 15 years since classical ballet was mixed with old-fashioned musical and contemporary dance in Matthew Bourne's all-male *Swan Lake,* that piece is seen as a watershed that catapulted dance from the back of the arts pages into the popular global mainstream.

Even today, Bourne's *Swan Lake* still tours the world, while the man himself produces newer pieces, from the Scottish-influenced *Highland Fling* to *The Car Man* (a *West Side Story*–style reworking of Bizet's *Carmen*). Having presented his own take on Tchaikovsky in *Nutcracker!,* Bourne crossed over into theatre in 2004, with his superlative *Play Without Words,* a two-part drama told solely through graceful movement. He has subsequently won awards for his choreography of *Edward Scissorhands* and most recently dazzled the West End with his choreography of *Oliver!* at the Theatre Royal Drury Lane. Other leading London-based talents have helped take the dance message to the wider world, with Rafael Bonachela scripting Kylie Minogue's Showgirl tour, and Wayne McGregor working on *Harry Potter and the Goblet of Fire.*

However, it's not just Bourne, Bonachela and McGregor in the vanguard. The Place (p308), in Euston, was where contemporary dance emerged in London in the 1960s, and it's recently been joined by Laban (p307) as a place to catch cutting-edge performances. Meanwhile, the revamped Sadler's Wells (p308) – the birthplace of English classical ballet in the 19th century – continues to stage an exciting program of various styles from leading national ballets and international troupes, such as Carlos Acosta, Twyla Tharp, Dance Theatre of Harlem and Alvin Ailey.

At Covent Garden's Royal Opera House (p311) principal ballerina Darcy Bussell bid goodbye to her adoring public in 2007 as she retired from the house's most prestigious position aged just 38. Going out at the height of her powers (her appearance in George Balanchine's *Apollo* the same year was considered by many to be her finest achievement to date) proved another canny move by the most famous English dancer since Margot Fonteyn; unlike Dame Margot, she will be remembered at her peak rather than for her long decline.

Despite a slight flirtation with newly commissioned pieces, including one with a Jimi Hendrix soundtrack, the capital's leading classical-dance troupe, the Royal Ballet, has largely been sticking to the traditional. Several back-to-back anniversaries have meant retrospectives devoted to choreographers Balanchine and Frederick Ashton, as well as to dancers Sergei Diaghilev and Dame Ninette de Valois (the latter was the ballet's founder). All the same, the Royal Ballet has made itself more accessible during this period by dropping some ticket prices to £10 (as at the National Theatre).

One troupe always worth keeping an eye out for is the innovative Rambert Dance Company, based in Chiswick and considered to be the UK's foremost contemporary dance troupe. Another is that of former Royal Ballet dancers Michael Nunn and William Levitt. Having made their name, via a Channel 4 TV documentary, as the Ballet Boyz, and then the George Piper Dances, they have recently teamed up with London-based French superstar Sylvie Guillem to perform works by acclaimed modern choreographer Russell Maliphant. Guillem, still a principal guest artist at the Royal Ballet, also reached out to London's strong South Asian dance tradition when she teamed up with contemporary choreographer and Kathak dance specialist Akram Khan.

The main London dance festival is Dance Umbrella (☎ 8741 4040; www.danceumbrella.co.uk). Running for six weeks from early October, it's one of the world's leading dance festivals of its kind. Otherwise, for the latest on what's on, check www.londondance.com. For more information on specific venues and companies, see p307.

ENVIRONMENT & PLANNING

THE LAND

Greater London comprises 1572 sq km enclosed by the M25 ring road. As well as being essential to the trade upon which London was built, the River Thames divided the city into north and south, a partition that had much more than geographical implications. The Romans designated the southern bank as a seedy London of gaming and debauchery, and for almost two millennia since, respectable and cultured folk settled on the northern side while the outcasts lived in the insalubrious south. The potential of the South Bank has only been realised in the last decade.

Although London grew from the area known as the City, it doesn't have a single focal point. Its expansion was never really planned; rather, the burgeoning city just consumed outlying settlements. Thus – as any reader of Dickens will appreciate – London today is more a patchwork of villages than a single city. Although the city can feel like a never-ending concrete jungle, there are actually huge swaths of green on its outskirts – take Richmond Park and Hampstead Heath, for example – and large green lungs such as Regent's Park and Hyde Park in the city centre.

GREEN LONDON

The most serious environmental problem facing the centre of London, the pollution and chronic congestion caused by heavy traffic, has been partially alleviated since 2003, when former mayor Ken Livingstone's congestion charge was introduced, whereby every car entering the city centre had to pay £5 (now £8) for the privilege. Livingstone's other environmental achievements include introducing buses running on hydrogen fuel cells (admittedly only in their trial stages) and introducing a Low Emissions Zone in February 2008 that sees additional charges levied on heavy-polluting vehicles entering Greater London. New mayor Boris Johnson worried many when campaigning for the job as his environmental program formed only a small part of his manifesto. Green groups have been disappointed by several of his actions so far, such as scrapping the third phase of London's Low Emissions Zone and cancelling the Western extension of the congestion charge zone, though at the time of writing it was still too early to judge Johnson's overall environmental record as mayor.

Local councils have also stepped up their efforts to be green, with Richmond council the first to introduce higher parking fees for 'gas-guzzlers' and Hackney the first to introduce compulsory recycling in 2007. Recycling has been available in London for many years but mainly in the form of community bins rather than separate household ones, and the mainstream hasn't really been encouraged to go green. Attitudes have changed recently and most people are doing their bit, but on the whole the UK has a poor record in this respect.

To look at the Thames' murky waters, you'd assume it was another pollution black spot, but below the surface, its health has improved dramatically in recent years and the river is playing an increasingly important role in recreation. By 1962 the combined impact of untreated sewage and industrial pollution had killed off virtually every sign of life in the river, but thanks to a massive clean-up it's now home to some 115 species of fish, including shad, sea lamprey and even salmon (for which special ladders have been built over the weirs). With them have come 10,000 herons, cormorants and other waterfowl that feed on the fish; even otters have been spotted on the river's upper reaches.

London boasts more parks and open spaces than any city of its size in the world – from the neatly manicured (Holland Park, St James's Park) to the semiwild (Richmond Park, Bushy Park). Between them they provide suitable habitats for a wide range of animals and birds.

The mammal you're most likely to spot on land is the grey squirrel, a North American import that has colonised every big park and decimated the indigenous red squirrel population. Hedgehogs also live here, though their numbers are dwindling, perhaps due to the increased use of slug pellets. Outside the very centre of town you're quite likely to see foxes if you go for a stroll after dark – their numbers are massively on the rise and most people either love or hate them. Richmond Park (p198) hosts badgers as well as herds of red and fallow deer. The oddest mammal yet was spotted in the capital in 2006 when a lost bottlenose whale swam up the Thames through central London. Sadly, the whale died after a long attempt to rescue her and release her back into the North Sea, and her skeleton can now be seen in the Natural History Museum (p140).

Birdwatchers, especially those keen on waterfowl, will love London. There are ducks, pelicans and the Queen's swans in St James's Park (p87), and more ducks and beautiful, chestnut-headed great-crested grebes in Hyde Park's Serpentine (p144). London canals are also happy hunting grounds for spotting waterfowl.

Garden birds, such as long-tailed and great tits, sparrows, robins and blackbirds, roost in all the parks, but some parks attract more interesting migrants. In Holland Park in spring you might glimpse flocks of tiny goldcrests. Kestrels nest around the Tower of London (p117), as do the better-known captive ravens. The open stretches of the commons in Barnes and Wimbledon also harbour a rich assortment of birds and mammals.

Most unusual of all, brightly coloured parrots and parakeets can be seen living wild around Richmond, Kew and many other parts of Southwest London along the Thames. Their origins are still debated, but they have been multiplying in recent years and seem to be able to survive in London thanks to global warming.

The London Wildlife Trust (LWT; ☎ 7261 0447; www.wildlondon.org.uk) maintains more than 50 nature reserves in the city, which offer the chance to see a range of birds and occasionally small mammals. Battersea Park Nature Reserve has several nature trails, while the Trent Country Park even boasts a Braille trail through the woodlands. Parts of Hampstead Heath have been designated a Site of Special Scientific Interest (SSSI) for their wealth of natural history.

Green fingers won't want to miss the exotic plants in the exceedingly lovely Kew Gardens (p199), while London's parks boast a variety of common or garden trees, shrubs and flowers. Many Londoners also take pride in their private gardens, which range from handkerchief-sized backyards to sprawling mini-estates, some of which open for a few days each summer through the National Gardens Scheme (NGS; ☎ 01483-211535; www.ngs.org.uk; Hatchlands Park, East Clandon, Guildford GU4 7RT). Admission usually costs £3, which goes to charity.

URBAN PLANNING & DEVELOPMENT

Central London has been considerably smartened up in recent years, and former mayor Ken Livingstone spearheaded many bold and imaginative schemes to make the city a more pleasant place to live and visit. Olympic Village development in East London is currently seeing the concentration of efforts, and the communities living in pockets of the Lea River Valley have succumbed to the inevitable and been moved on (the area included several large Roma camps that had been there for decades).

The biggest challenge facing London is how to house its growing population without encroaching on the green belt surrounding the city. Previously run-down central areas such as Hoxton and Clerkenwell were dolled up in the 1990s, with young populations moving in and converting warehouses. The repopulation of Docklands continues, but London is quickly running out of space. Development work, which was booming until the economic crisis of 2008, has now inevitably slowed, though large areas of Hackney and Tower Hamlets were still being redeveloped at the time of writing.

In what is perhaps a sign of things to come, the government is facing an inevitable conflict with environmentalists over the proposed regeneration of the Thames Gateway, the 60km on each side of the Thames from East London to the North Sea. The plan is to build 200,000 homes and provide 300,000 jobs, but in an area that contains some of Britain's most valuable wildlife sites and a 25km stretch of shore that is designated as an EU high-priority special protection area. The government's response has been to designate the area the UK's first 'eco-region', theoretically meaning that the development here will have to be environmentally sustainable, low-carbon producing and ecologically viable, though environmental groups are continuing to campaign against the plans.

GOVERNMENT & POLITICS
LOCAL GOVERNMENT

When 12th-century King Richard the Lionheart gave London the right to self-government in exchange for a little pocket money, supporters cheered 'Londoners shall have no king but their mayor'. That's still true for the City of London today, but Greater London, where the vast majority of the population lives and works, has had a trickier time of it.

Some form of the Greater London Council (GLC) was going about its business quietly for a few centuries, looking after local interests and acquiescently toeing the national government's line. That all changed when Labour man Ken Livingstone took over as boss of the council in the early 1980s, when Margaret Thatcher was prime minister. These two couldn't have been more different and a clash was inevitable. Livingstone campaigned for cheaper public transport in the capital and generally became a thorn in Thatcher's side. She got so fed up with him that in

1986 she abolished the GLC altogether, and London became the only European capital in the world without a self-governing authority. Fourteen years later the Labour government brought back a new version, the Greater London Assembly (GLA), and arranged elections for London's first-ever popularly elected mayor in 2000.

The 25-member GLA has limited authority over transport, economic development, strategic planning, the environment, the police, fire brigades, civil defence and cultural matters. It is elected from GLA constituencies and by London as a whole. It is not a conventional opposition, but can reject the mayor's budget, form special investigation committees and hold the mayor to public account. It currently comprises 11 Conservatives, eight Labour Party members, three Liberal Democrats, two members of the Green Party and, controversially, one member of the far-right British National Party, who reached the 5% threshold to gain their first seat in the GLA in 2008. It has its headquarters in the futuristic GLA building in Southwark, beside Tower Bridge.

The City of London has its own government in the form of the Corporation of London, headed by the Lord Mayor (only the City mayor gets to be Lord; even though the Mayor of London is a far more powerful political figure, he remains a mere pleb) and an assortment of oddly named and peculiarly dressed aldermen, beadles and sheriffs. It sits at the Guildhall. These men – and they usually *are* male – are elected by the City of London's freemen and liverymen (honorary and full members of the City of London respectively). Though its government may appear obsolete in the 3rd millennium, the Corporation of London still owns roughly a third of the supremely wealthy 'Square Mile' and has a good record for patronage of the arts.

London is further divided into 33 widely differing boroughs (13 of which are in central London), run by democratically elected councils with significant autonomy. These deal with education and matters such as road sweeping and rubbish collection. The richest borough in terms of per capita income is Richmond in the west; the poorest is Barking in the east.

NATIONAL GOVERNMENT

London is, of course, the seat of the national government of the United Kingdom of Great Britain and Northern Ireland. The UK is a constitutional monarchy with no written constitution and operates under a combination of parliamentary statutes, common law (a body of legal principles based on precedents, often dating back centuries) and convention.

Parliament is made up of the monarch, the House of Commons (the lower house) and the House of Lords (the upper house). The monarch is essentially a figurehead with no real power, while the House of Commons is where the real power lies. It comprises a national assembly of 646 seats directly elected every four to five years. Each seat represents a constituency somewhere in the country. London is made up of 72 constituencies and thus has 72 representatives in the House of Commons.

The leader of the biggest party in the House of Commons is the prime minister, who appoints a cabinet of 20 or so ministers to run government departments. At the time of writing Prime Minister Gordon Brown's Labour Party held a comfortable majority of 63 MPs over the rest of the house. This majority he inherited from Tony Blair, who won the 2005 general election but then stood down as prime minister in June 2007. The next general election will be held in mid-2010.

The Conservatives have been reinvigorated in the past few years after a decade of disarray. Their defenestration of Margaret Thatcher in 1990 tore the party to pieces and only since the arrival of Tony Blair–alike David Cameron as leader in 2005 has the party regained any sense of unity. Cameron has liberalised the Tories, a political force that the British people often consider to be, in the words of one Tory grandee, 'the nasty party'. By embracing the environment, supporting single mothers and being pro gay, the Tories are in many ways unrecognisable compared with their 1980s selves under Thatcher. Critics point out, though, that despite the veneer of ecofriendly, liberal policies, the party remains utterly that of the establishment, with Cameron and much of his cabinet a product of Eton and Oxbridge.

The only other major political party in the UK is the Liberal Democrats, who currently hold just 63 seats. Led by the young Nick Clegg, the Lib Dems are the established third party that always loses out to the first-past-the-post electoral system. While many see them as a credible alternative to the Tory–Labour double act (who have held power between them since 1922!), the reality of British electoral number crunching means that it's extremely difficult for a third party to make a national impact. Despite this the Lib Dems wield much power in local government throughout the country.

The House of Lords has a little power but these days it's largely limited to delaying legislation – even then, it's only a question of time before it goes to the Queen for royal assent, which is a formality as the Queen has never refused to sign a bill and there is no constitutional precedent for her to do so. For centuries the House of Lords consisted of some 900 'hereditary peers' (whose titles passed from one generation to the next), 25 Church of England bishops and 12 Law Lords (who also act as Britain's highest court). But Tony Blair 'modernised' the institution in 1999 and all but a few of the hereditary peers were shuffled out. Ninety-two of them have been allowed to stay, for the time being. A new system of 'life peerage' was introduced, which, critics say, allowed the prime minister to hand out plum jobs to loyal MPs who wouldn't have to go through the bother of getting elected in the future. In the second stage of Lords reform (for which there is no time frame and on which there has been not insignificant heel dragging on the part of the government in recent years), elected members will enter the upper house for the first time and hereditary peers will be swept away altogether.

MEDIA

London is in the eye of the British media, an industry comprising some of the best and worst of the world's TV, radio and print media.

NEWSPAPERS

The main London newspaper is the centre-right *Evening Standard,* a tabloid that comes out in early and late editions throughout the day. After fighting a long battle with former mayor Ken Livingstone and becoming something of a joke to Londoners for its love of dramatic headlines for the most banal stories, it was bought in 2009 by Russian tycoon Alexander Lebedev, who promised to rebrand the paper, and began with a large advertising campaign in which the paper apologised to its readers for its past mistakes. Foodies should check out the restaurant reviews of London's most influential critic, Fay Maschler, while style aficionados shouldn't miss Friday's *ES* magazine, a useful guide to the city's cutting edge. *Metro Life* is a useful listings supplement on Thursday.

Free newspapers, distributed at tube stations and on the streets wherever commuters can be stopped and a paper shoved in their face, also vie for the attentions of Londoners – *London Lite* and *Metro* (both owned by the *Daily Mail* parent group Associated Newspapers) are light-weight, easy-to-digest reads with a firm focus on celebrity, and can be found littering buses or tube carriages all over London.

National newspapers in England are almost always financially independent of any political party, although their political leanings are easily discerned. Rupert Murdoch is the most influential man in British media and his News Corp owns the *Sun,* the *News of the World,* the *Times* and the *Sunday Times.* The industry is self-regulating, having set up the Press Complaints Commission (PCC) in 1991 to handle public grievances, although many complain that the PCC is unable to really maintain any level of discipline among the unruly tabloids, being a 'toothless guard dog'.

There are many national daily newspapers, and competition for readers is incredibly stiff; although some papers are printed outside the capital, they are all pretty London-centric. There are two broad categories of newspapers, most commonly distinguished as broadsheets (or 'qualities') and tabloids, although the distinction is becoming more about content than physical size as most of the major broadsheets are now published in a smaller, easier-to-use tabloid size.

Readers of the broadsheets are extremely loyal to their paper and rarely switch from one to another. The right-wing *Daily Telegraph* is sometimes considered old-fogeyish, but nonetheless the writing and world coverage are very good. The *Times* is traditionally the newspaper of record; it's particularly good for sports. On the left side of the political spectrum, the *Guardian* features lively writing and an extremely progressive agenda, is very strong in its coverage of the arts and has some excellent supplements, particularly Monday's *Media Guardian,* a bible for anyone in the industry. It's also the best paper for white-collar job seeking. Another good read is the left-field *Independent,* which rejoices in highlighting stories or issues that other papers have ignored. Its writing can be excellent and it's the paper of choice for nonpolitically aligned centrists and free thinkers.

The Sunday papers are as important as Sunday mornings in London. Most dailies have Sunday stablemates, and predictably the tabloids have bumper editions of trashy gossip, star-struck adulation, fashion extras and mean-spirited diatribes directed at whomever they've decided to hunt for sport on that particular weekend. The qualities have so many sections and supplements that two hands are required to carry even one paper from the shop. The *Observer,* established in 1791, is the oldest Sunday paper and sister of the *Guardian;* there's a brilliant *Sports* supplement with the first issue of the month. Even people who normally only buy broadsheets sometimes slip a copy of the best-selling *News of the World* (sister paper to the *Sun*) under their arm for some Sunday light relief.

See p388 for a list of the major daily and Sunday newspapers.

MAGAZINES

There is an astonishing range of magazines published and consumed here, from celebrity gossip to political heavyweights. London loves celebrities (especially when they are overweight, underweight or out of control) and *Heat, Closer* and *Grazia* are the most popular purveyors of the genre. US import *Glamour* is the queen of the women's glossies, having toppled traditional favourite *Cosmopolitan,* which is beginning to look a little wrinkled in comparison with its younger, funkier rival – maybe it's time for a nip and tuck. *Marie Claire, Elle* and *Vogue* are regarded as the thinking woman's glossies. The smarter men's magazines include *GQ* and *Esquire,* while less edifying reads are the so-called 'lads mags': *FHM, Loaded, Maxim, Nuts* and *Zoo.* A slew of style magazines are published here – *i-D, Dazed & Confused* and *Vice* – and all maintain a loyal following.

Political magazines are particularly strong in London. The satirical *Private Eye* (see boxed text, p54) has no political bias and takes the mickey out of everyone equally, although anyone in a position of power is preferred. You can keep in touch with what's happening internationally with the *Week,* a useful round-up of the British and foreign press, and the excellent *Economist* cannot be beaten for international political and business analysis.

Time Out is the listings guide par excellence and great for taking the city's pulse, with strong arts coverage, while the *Big Issue,* sold on the streets by the homeless, is not just an honourable project but a damned fine read.

London is a publishing hub for magazines and produces hundreds of internationally renowned publications specialising in music, visual arts, literature, sport, architecture and so on. See p389 for a list of the city's main magazines.

NEW MEDIA

There's a thriving alternative media scene catering to the many who feel marginalised by the mainstream media. Some websites worth checking out include the outstanding and original Urban 75 (www.urban75.com), the global network of alternative news at Indymedia (www.uk.indymedia.org), the weekly activists' newsletter from SchNews (www.schnews.org.uk), London-centric blog Londonist (www.londonist.com) and the video activists' Undercurrents (www.undercurrents.org).

Online gossip sites have also gained notoriety in recent years by knocking spin on its arse and breaking some big stories about celebrities misbehaving. Check out Popbitch (www.popbitch .com) for a rude laugh.

BROADCASTING

The BBC, the owners of Lonely Planet, is probably the most famous broadcasting corporation in the world and one of the standard bearers of radio and TV journalism and programming (see p177). Its independence frequently irks the establishment and it incurred the very significant wrath of the British Government in 2003 because of its probing of the events leading to the invasion of Iraq. When BBC journalist Andrew Gilligan alleged that Tony Blair's then press secretary Alistair Campbell had 'sexed up' a dossier of evidence against the Iraqi regime in order

PRIVATE EYE LASHES ESTABLISHMENT

'Parliament's Shame', screams the headline of the magazine in the wake of the MPs' expenses scandal of 2009, above a picture of the Houses of Parliament from which a speech bubble emerges saying 'Shame we got caught!' This is a typical cover of London's best-known satirical magazine, *Private Eye*, a barometer of what's going on politically and culturally in the country.

It was founded in 1961 by a group of clever clogs that included the late comedian and writer Peter Cook and still retains the low-tech, cut-and-paste charm of the original. It specialises in gossip mongering about the misdeeds of public figures and in the giddy lampooning of anyone who takes themselves too seriously. There are lots of running jokes (the Queen is always referred to as Brenda, for example, and Rupert Murdoch as the Dirty Digger), wicked cartoons and regular features such as an editorial from Lord Gnome, a composite of media magnates. There's also a serious investigative side to the mag and its reports have contributed to the downfall of several high-fliers, including Jeffrey Archer and Robert Maxwell. This means that the magazine is loathed by many in high office, although it's also much loved – after all, your enemy's enemy is your friend...

That *Private Eye* still exists at all is astonishing. It has regularly been sued by its targets and only remains afloat thanks to the charity of its readers. Its future is looking brighter these days, with circulation above 600,000 and at its highest level in a decade. *Private Eye* is now far and away the most popular current affairs magazine in the land. Essential reading, even if you don't follow much more than the cartoons.

to generate public support for going to war, there was a huge outcry and mutual recriminations between Westminster and White City began. The country's chief weapons expert, Dr David Kelly, committed suicide after being named by the government as the source of the BBC's report, and when the government-appointed Hutton inquiry came down on the BBC as the wrongdoers, almost everybody in the media dismissed it as a whitewash. The BBC's director general resigned the same day and, chastened, the BBC has since been taking a far more careful line when it comes to reporting on the government. But just four years later the corporation found itself in trouble again, when doctored footage was shown in a fly-on-the-wall documentary about the Queen. The BBC faced backlash from the public and the rest of the media, and despite an abject apology from Director General Mark Thompson, 2007 was definitely a new low for faith in the corporation. This was followed by a phone lines scandal that affected many UK broadcasters when it was revealed that many telephone votes were not counted in several high-profile shows. Since then the BBC, as well as other UK channels, have tightened their production guidelines to ensure that such scandals don't get repeated.

Britain still turns out some of the world's best TV programs, padding out the decent home-grown output with American imports, Australian soaps, inept sitcoms, and trashy chat and game shows of its own. There are five regular TV channels. BBC1 and BBC2 are publicly funded by a TV licensing system and, like BBC radio stations, don't carry advertising; ITV1, Channel 4 and Five are commercial channels and do. These regular channels are now competing with the satellite channels of Rupert Murdoch's BSkyB – which offers a variety of channels with less-than-inspiring programs – and assorted cable channels.

Many viewers feel that the investment in new technology is damaging to the core channels and that the BBC is spreading itself too thinly, trying to chase ratings and compete with the commercial channels rather than concentrating on its public-service responsibilities. The entire country is gradually switching over to digital TV, and analogue broadcasting will end by 2012.

The BBC broadcasts several radio stations, including BBC 1, 2, 3, 4, 5, 6 and 7, catering to young, mature, classical, intellectual, talkback, mixed and comedy/drama audiences respectively. XFM is your best chance of hearing interesting music these days. In 2007 the government announced Channel 4 was to be awarded a licence to broadcast 10 more national digital radio channels, a huge shake-up for an industry in need of winning back loyal audiences.

FASHION

London has weathered a tough few years that saw its status as an international fashion centre drop, but the city is now back at the heart of the fashion universe, boasting a new firmament of young stars who have caught the collective eye of the fashion pack.

Giles Deacon is the undisputed figurehead for the new London, and with his witty designs and eclectic references the St Martins graduate has taken London by storm with his own label,

Giles. Alongside Deacon are other Brit stars with a buzz around them, such as Henry Holland, Jonathan Saunders, Christopher Kane and Greek-Austrian import Marios Schwab, who shows in London and attended the hallowed St Martins as well. Nu-rave darling Gareth Pugh is also someone to look out for, another St Martins alumnus (can you see a pattern emerging? – see boxed text, p56) who has taken the underground club fashions of Shoreditch and transposed them to the shop floor, putting himself on the global fashion map at the same time.

The influence of London's designers continues to spread well beyond the capital. The 'British Fashion Pack' still work at, or run, the major Continental fashion houses such as Chanel, Givenchy and Chloé. Meanwhile, regardless of whether they send models down the catwalks here, designers such as Alexander McQueen retain design studios in London, and erstwhile defectors to foreign catwalks, such as Luella Bartley and Matthew Williamson, have returned to London to show their collections.

London has always been about eccentricity when compared with the classic feel of the major Parisian and Milanese houses or the cool street-cred of New York designers. Nobody summed up that spirit better than Isabella Blow, the legendary stylist who discovered – among many others – Alexander McQueen, Stella Tennant and Sophie Dahl during her career at *Vogue* and *Tatler*. Blow sadly committed suicide in 2007 and, although she wasn't widely known outside of the fashion world, her tragic loss was deeply felt in the fashion industry of the city she worked in. Never seen in public without an extraordinary Philip Treacy hat, Blow's sheer force of personality was a great generator of enthusiasm and excitement about London's changing fashion fates, and the scene has been far less interesting without her.

A trend that has come out of London over the past couple of years is the celebrity lines being sold in bargain chains. Karl Lagerfeld and Stella McCartney have designed lines for H&M, Kate Moss and Beth Ditto for Top Shop, and Lily Allen for New Look, each one generating huge excitement and – in the case of Kate Moss' collections – a virtual stampede from shoppers.

The British fashion industry has always been more on the edge of younger, directional stuff, and never really established that very polished 'Gucci Slick'; the London equivalent is the bespoke men's tailoring of Savile Row. London has no history of real couture like Paris or Milan, where tastes in styles and fabrics are much more classic and refined. The market also shapes British fashion to a large extent; customers here are more likely to spend £100 on a few different bargains – hence the boom in outlet malls – while their counterparts in Paris and Italy will blow the lot on one piece, which they'll wear regularly and well.

So London fashion has always been about street wear and 'wow', with a few old reliables keeping the frame in place and mingling with hot new designers who are often unpolished through lack of experience, but bursting with talent and creativity. As a result London is definitely exciting on a global scale and nobody with an interest in street fashion will be disappointed by what they find here.

LANGUAGE

The English language is the country's greatest contribution to the modern world. It is an astonishingly rich language, containing an estimated 600,000 uninflected words (compared with, for example, Indonesian's or Malay's 60,000). It's actually a magpie tongue – just as England plundered treasure for its museums, so too the English language dipped into the world's vocabulary, even when it already had several words of the same meaning. Dr Johnson, compiler of the first English dictionary, tried to have the language protected from foreign imports (possibly to reduce his own workload) but failed. As far as English goes, all foreigners are welcome.

English speakers are spoilt for choice when they go looking for descriptive words such as nouns and adjectives, as you'll discover pretty quickly (fast, swiftly, speedily, rapidly, promptly) by looking in a thesaurus. Some 50 years ago linguists came up with Basic

LONDON'S LANGUAGES

These days you'll encounter a veritable Babel of some 300 languages being spoken in London, and there are pockets of the capital where English is effectively the second language. Head to Southall if you want to see train station signs in Hindi, Gerrard St in Soho for telephone boxes with Chinese instructions, Golders Green or Stamford Hill for shop signs in Hebrew and Yiddish, and Kingsland Rd for *everything* written in Turkish.

ST MARTINS

Most of the stars of the British fashion industry have passed through the rather shabby doors of St Martins on Charing Cross Rd, the world's most famous fashion college. Founded in 1854, Central St Martins School of Art & Design – to give its rather cumbersome and correct title – began life as a place where cultured young people went to learn to draw and paint. In the 1940s a fashion course was created and within a few decades aspiring designers from around the world were scrambling to get in. Courses are more than 100 times oversubscribed these days and the college has faced some criticism for admitting names over talent (a famous Beatle's daughter, to name just one). St Martins graduate shows – for which Stella had friends Naomi Campbell and Kate Moss model – are one of the highlights of the fashion calendar and are *always* shocking, making huge statements, be they good, bad or ridiculous.

The less-conspicuous Royal College of Art only takes postgraduates and its fashion course is just as old and almost as successful as St Martins. Its alumni are said to provide the backbone of some of the world's most prestigious fashion houses.

English, a stripped-down version with a vocabulary of 850 words, which was all one needed to say just about anything. But where's the fun in that? Shakespeare himself is said to have contributed more than 2000 words, along with hundreds of common idioms such as 'poisoned chalice', 'one fell swoop', 'cold comfort' and 'cruel to be kind'.

Be grateful if English is your mother tongue because it's a bitch to learn, and has possibly the most illogical and eccentric approach to spelling and pronunciation of any language. Take the different pronunciation of rough, cough, through, though and bough. Attempts to rationalise English spelling are passionately resisted by people who see themselves as the guardians of proper English and rail against the American decision to drop the 'u' from words such as colour and glamour.

In terms of accent, Standard English or Received Pronunciation (RP) centres on London and, traditionally, was perceived to be that spoken by the upper classes and those educated at public schools. It is by no means the easiest form to understand; in fact, sometimes it's near impossible ('oh, eye nare' apparently means 'yes, I know'). Those 'what talk posh' despair at the perceived butchering of their language by most ordinary Londoners, who speak what's come to be known as 'Estuary English', so called because it's a sort of subcockney that spread along the estuary in postwar London. And so a common language divides the city.

The BBC is considered the arbitrator on the issue, and by comparing the contrived – and frankly hilarious – tone of old newsreels from WWII with today's bulletins, it's obvious that Standard English has gone from posh to a more neutral middle register. Even the Queen, claim Australian linguistic researchers, has allowed elements of Estuary pronunciation to sully her clipped RP.

Some say that Estuary English – which can now be heard within a 100-mile radius of the capital – is quickly becoming the standard. Its chief features, according to Stephen Burgen in Lonely Planet's *British phrasebook,* are rising inflection; constant use of 'innit'; a glottal 't', rendering the double 't' in 'butter' almost silent and making 'alright' sound like 'orwhy'; and, in general, a slack-jawed, floppy-tongued way of speaking that knocks the corners off consonants and lets the vowels whine to themselves. The lack of speech rhythm that can result from blowing away your consonants is made good by the insertion of copious quantities of 'fuck' and 'fucking', whose consonants are always given the full nine yards. In London it's not rare to hear people whose speech is so dependent on the word 'fuck' they are virtually dumbstruck without it.

But like just about everything in London, the language is constantly changing, absorbing new influences, producing new slang and altering the meaning of words. The city's ethnic communities are only beginning to have an influence and many young Londoners these days are mimicking Caribbean expressions and what they perceive to be hip-hop speak from black urban America.

As England has absorbed wave after wave of immigrants, so too will the insatiable English language continue to take in all comers. Meanwhile, as class distinctions exist, the linguistic battle for London will rage on.

NEIGHBOURHOODS

top picks

- **Tower of London** (p117)
  Historic fortress and home to the Crown Jewels.
- **St Paul's Cathedral** (p99)
  Wren's masterpiece soars with its incredible dome.
- **Westminster Abbey** (p89)
  Impressive and iconic, with a fascinating royal history.
- **Tate Modern** (p128)
  Join the crowds digesting this fantastic collection.
- **National Gallery** (p73)
  Superb national art collection that's one of Europe's best.
- **British Museum** (p79)
  A truly great (and controversial) museum collection.
- **Shakespeare's Globe** (p128)
  See the Bard performed as the Elizabethans saw it.
- **Hampton Court Palace** (p201)
  The capital's greatest Tudor palace opens its doors daily.
- **London Eye** (p124)
  Take a 'flight' on the iconic Eye for unbeatable city views.

What's your recommendation? www.lonelyplanet.com/london

Look at a map of London in all its vastness and you may feel slightly overwhelmed. This is totally normal – the agglomeration of villages and towns that have slowly merged to form the tapestry that is modern London still confounds seasoned residents of the capital. No matter how much time you spend here, you'll always find brand new areas you've never heard of before.

'London takes years to get to know and even Londoners never entirely agree on what to call certain areas'

London is also a tough city to divide, with its divergent councils, ancient parishes and haphazard postcodes, none of which take into account the borders of any of the others. But the very centre of the city is the commercial West End, with its kernel Soho and Covent Garden surrounded by academic Bloomsbury, bohemian Fitzrovia, chic Marylebone, super-rich Mayfair, royal St James's and the political village of Westminster. Here you'll find many of the best shopping, eating and entertainment options in London – as well as most of the other visitors to the city.

The South Bank, facing the West End and the City across the Thames, offers theatre, art, film and music, and features two of London's most iconic modern sights, Tate Modern and the London Eye, and the South Bank Centre. The wealthy neighbourhoods from Hyde Park to Chelsea include exclusive Belgravia, shopping mecca Knightsbridge, posh Kensington and the large village of Chelsea, famed for the King's Rd. No visit to London is complete without visiting South Ken's museums, Harrods and Harvey Nichols in Knightsbridge, or wandering the open spaces of Hyde Park.

To the east of the West End lie both the City (once the ancient Roman walled city of Londinium, now the financial hub of London) and the once shabby neighbourhoods of Clerkenwell, Shoreditch and Spitalfields, now London's most creative and exciting districts. Here you'll find supercool Hoxton Sq with its clubs and bars, Spitalfields Market and fantastic Brick Lane, longtime curry hub of Banglatown and now one of the best clothes-shopping areas in London.

Further east lie the East End and Docklands: the East End is 'real' London, a multi-ethnic yet strangely traditional stretch of the city that's the home of the famous cockney. It's currently being transformed for the 2012 Olympics, which are centred around the valley of the River Lea in and around Stratford at the East End's furthest edge. Docklands is another, albeit government- and financial-sector–driven, example of urban renewal – now seriously rivalling the City as the home of money men and London's tallest skyscrapers. The future belongs to the east, due not only to the Olympics but also to the Thames Gateway, a huge development of the Thames estuary.

North London is a hilly collection of charming villages, which often seem to exist as worlds within themselves, such as old-money Hampstead and Highgate, celebrity-filled Primrose Hill, fashionable Islington, hippie Stoke Newington and well-heeled Crouch End. In between are urban centres such as Finchley Rd, Camden Town, Holloway and Finsbury Park.

West London is grand, moneyed and home to traditional must-sees: Buckingham Palace, the Houses of Parliament and Kensington Palace. It has its cooler side, too, in Notting Hill and Portobello Rd, with its street market, superb shopping and many of the city's better pubs and bars.

South of the river, Greenwich enchants with its huge historic importance as a centre of maritime activity, and, of course, time. Neighbouring Southeast London areas of Deptford, New Cross and Woolwich are showing signs of becoming South London's long-awaited answer to Shoreditch.

Vast, residential South London has multiple flavours, from leafy Blackheath, Clapham, Putney and Richmond to edgier, rougher Brixton, Kennington and Vauxhall, now the area's gay enclave. Southwest London includes urban villages of Putney, Barnes, Richmond, Wimbledon and Kew that, between them, attract huge visitor numbers for the lovely botanical gardens, the world-famous tennis tournament and the almost perfectly preserved Tudor palace of Henry VIII at Hampton Court.

London takes years to get to know and even Londoners never entirely agree on what to call certain areas – so take things easy and always have a good map – although much of London's charm rests in what you'll discover when you leave the beaten track and explore on your own.

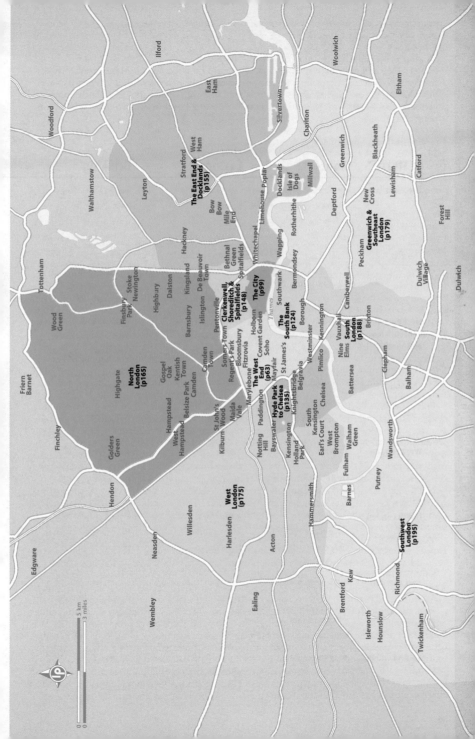

The East End & Docklands (p155)

The City (p99)

Clerkenwell, Shoreditch & Spitalfields (p148)

The West End (p63)

The South Bank (p124)

Hyde Park to Chelsea (p135)

North London (p165)

West London (p175)

South London (p188)

Greenwich & Southeast London (p179)

Southwest London (p195)

Thames

5 km
3 miles

ITINERARY BUILDER

London is best approached in small, easy-to-digest chunks – its sheer size and variety of things to see and do (not to mention eat, drink and buy) may result in heart failure or at the very least severe exhaustion. For the purposes of our Itinerary Builder, West London includes our Hyde Park to Chelsea and West London neighbourhoods. South London includes the Greenwich & Southeast London, South London and Southwest London neighbourhoods.

ACTIVITIES	Sights	Eating	Drinking
The West End	National Gallery (p73) National Portrait Gallery (p74) Sir John Soane's Museum (p77)	Gay Hussar (p236) Busaba Eathai (p241) Portrait (p238)	Gordon's Wine Bar (p276) French House (p275) Seven Stars (p276)
The City	Tower of London (p117) St Paul's Cathedral (p99) Temple Church (p103)	Paternoster Chop House (p245) Place Below (p245) Sweeting's (p245)	Ye Olde Watling (p278) Counting House (p278) Black Friar (p278)
Clerkenwell, Shoreditch & Spitalfields	Geffrye Museum (p149) Dennis Severs' House (p152) Spitalfields Market (p153)	St John (p252) Moro (p252) Modern Pantry (p252)	Foundry (p282) George & Dragon (p282) Jerusalem Tavern (p281)
The South Bank	Tate Modern (p128) London Eye (p124) Southwark Cathedral (p130)	Skylon (p246) Anchor & Hope (p246) Applebee's Fish Café (p247)	George Inn (p280) King's Arms (p279) Baltic (p279)
West London	Victoria & Albert Museum (p139) Kensington Place (p264) Leighton House (p175)	Awana (p249) Daquise (p250) Olivo (p250)	Windsor Castle (p288) Earl of Lonsdale (p288) Churchill Arms (p288)
North London	London Zoo (p167) Hampstead Heath (p169) Highgate Cemetery (p169)	Manna (p258) Afghan Kitchen (p262) Wells Tavern (p261)	Holly Bush (p286) Elk in the Woods (p286) Edinboro Castle (p285)
East London	V&A Museum of Childhood (p158) Museum of London Docklands (p161) Ragged School Museum (p159)	Café Spice Namaste (p255) El Faro (p257) Tayyabs (p255)	Bistrotheque (p283) Prospect of Whitby (p284) Grapes (p284)
South London	Royal Observatory (p180) Hampton Court Palace (p201) Imperial War Museum (p188)	Inside (p266) Rosie's Deli Cafe (p267) Lobster Pot (p270)	Trafalgar Tavern (p290) Barmy Arms (p292) So.uk (p291)

AREA

HOW TO USE THIS TABLE

The table below allows you to plan a day's worth of activities in any area of the city. Simply select which area you wish to explore, and then mix and match from the corresponding listings to build your day. The first item in each cell represents a well-known highlight of the area, while the other items are more off-the-beaten-track gems.

Shopping	Entertainment	Nightlife
Selfridges (p218)	Royal Opera House (p311)	Black Gardenia (p296)
Liberty (p218)	Curzon Soho (p309)	Madame Jo Jo's (p297)
Habitat (p222)	Donmar Warehouse (p314)	Bar Rumba (p295)
Leadenhall Market (p108)	Barbican (p306)	
	Rhythm Factory (p304)	
Hoxton Boutique (p228)	Sadler's Wells (p308)	Fabric (p296)
Tatty Devine (p228)	93 Feet East (p294)	333 (p295)
Labour & Wait (p229)	Macbeth (p282)	Herbal (p297)
Konditor & Cook (p224)	BFI Southbank (p309)	Ministry of Sound (p298)
Black + Blum (p224)	National Theatre (p311)	
	Royal Festival Hall (p308)	
Harvey Nichols (p225)	Royal Albert Hall (p306)	Notting Hill Arts Club (p298)
Portobello Road market (p226)	Electric Cinema (p309)	
Fortnum & Mason (p217)	Coronet (p309)	
Camden Market (p226)	Hampstead Heath Ponds (p319)	Scala (p298)
Housmans (p229)	Everyman Hampstead (p309)	Egg (p296)
Camden Passage (p227)	Almeida Theatre (p313)	Koko (p297)
Broadway Market (p229)	Arcola Theatre (p313)	Bethnal Green Working Men's Club (p295)
Fabrications (p229)	Whitechapel Art Gallery (p155)	Passing Clouds (p298)
Burberry Factory Shop (p229)	Café Oto (p303)	Dalston Superstore (p287)
Brixton Market (p226)	Ritzy Picturehouse (p310)	Matter (p297)
Joy (p231)	Battersea Arts Centre (p313)	O2 Academy Brixton (p303)
		Dogstar (p296)

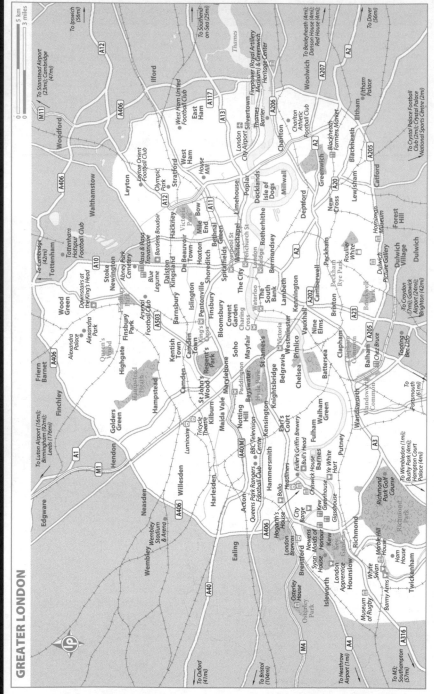

GREATER LONDON

Drinking p274; Eating p236; Shopping p214; Sleeping p334

London has always turned people on. Samuel Johnson raved about the city's 'wonderful immensity', and Henry James famously claimed that for him the British capital offered 'the most possible form of life'. Much of the complexity, chaos and vivacity that they found so enticing is centred on the West End, London's physical, cultural and social heart and where, whether you are a first-time visitor, regular or resident, you'll be gawping, rushing or strolling much of the time. The West End is a vague term (any Londoner you meet will give you their own take on which neighbourhoods it does and doesn't include), and its component areas are often startlingly unlike one another. Londoners might complain about the notorious crowds in the West End, but most find it irresistible. It's monumental and majestic, packed with sights and splattered with a gritty urbanity.

At its centre is Soho (below), famed for its history and loved for its rampant nightlife and excellent restaurants and bars. The nearby leafy area of Bloomsbury hides the British Museum (p79) and counters Soho's sauciness with its high-brow reputation – this is where university campuses abound and where Virginia Woolf and her posse lived and loved. Shoppers and tourists flock to Covent Garden (p69) for its street performers, boutiques and busy theatres. Aromatic Chinatown (p65) oozes authentic culture but its restaurants need careful choosing, while cinema-central and tourist-trap Leicester Sq (p75) clogs up with tourists, inebriated weekend revellers and discount-ticket touts. Holborn and The Strand (p76) is where London's legal business gets sorted out and the city starts to dip its toes into the River Thames. Piccadilly Circus (p67) flashes its illuminated adverts and – even though it's busy with traffic, shoppers and tourists – most Londoners can't help but love it. Magnificent Trafalgar Sq (p69) is home to celebrations, protests and the city's best galleries, while Westminster (p89), Britain's political heart, is where many important decisions are made before breakfast, yet Westminster Abbey offers a calming influence. Soothing St James's Park (p87) leads to Buckingham Palace (p86), a place that needs no introduction, though it's safe to say that you won't find many Londoners gawping through its gates. If you fancy seeing an area of the West End that isn't heaving with human and vehicle traffic, stroll around the aristocratic neighbourhoods of Mayfair (p89) and St James's (p83), or try Marylebone (p95), a real London 'village' with a quaint High Street that's stacked with independent shops and small (but posh) eateries.

The best way to get to know the West End, and indeed the whole of London, is on foot. Most sights are within walking distance from one another; though, if it gets too much, you're best resting your feet on a bus. While the tube will take you to most sights, sometimes it's quicker to walk the short distances between two areas (eg Covent Garden and Leicester Sq or Piccadilly). Do arm yourself with an Oyster card (see p379) if you intend to use public transport at all, otherwise you may have to come up with a small fortune to cover the cost of a couple of tube rides.

top picks

THE WEST END

- British Museum (p79)
- National Gallery & National Portrait Gallery (p73 & p74)
- Somerset House (p76)
- Soho (left)
- Wallace Collection (p96)

SOHO & CHINATOWN

Even though Soho doesn't have a single 'proper' sight, it's still one of London's most popular hangouts thanks to the contagious energy it exudes. Soho's name is a hunting cry from Tudor times: the neighbourhood was the aristocratic hunting ground during the reign of Henry VIII. Its privileged status was knocked down considerably when the homeless victims of the Great Fire moved here, followed by many waves of immigrants, which gave Soho the infamous anarchic, bad-boy image that it still retains (though in a much diluted form). It's home to a 5000-strong community, the traditional heart of London's gay scene, numerous media companies, a red-light district, shops, restaurants, theatres, boozers, nightclubs and, of course, tourists, who can easily take part in the action.

Soho is besieged by the four Circuses – Oxford, Piccadilly, Cambridge and St Giles's.

Wardour St divides Soho neatly in two halves; high Soho to the east, and low or West Soho opposite. Old Compton St is the de facto main High Street and the gayest street in London. The West End's only fruit 'n' veg market is on atmospheric Berwick St. The epicentre of 1960s fashion, Carnaby and Newburgh Sts have recovered from a decade of tourist tat shops and are home to some of Soho's hippest shops once again.

SOHO SQUARE & AROUND Map p66

At Soho's northern end, leafy Soho Sq is the area's back garden. This is where people come to laze in the sun on spring and summer days, and where office workers have their lunch or gather for a picnic. It was laid out in 1681, and originally named King's Sq, which is why the statue of Charles II stands in its northern half. In the centre is a tiny mock-Tudor–style

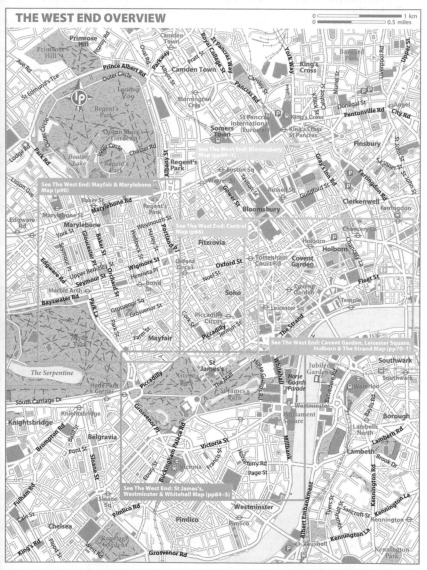

THE WEST END OVERVIEW

SEX & DRUGS & ROCK'N'ROLL – THE HISTORY OF SOHO

Soho's character was formed by the many waves of immigration, and residential development started in the 17th century, after the Great Fire had levelled much of the city. An influx of Greek and Huguenot refugees and, later, the 18th-century influx of Italian, Chinese and other artisans and radicals into Soho replaced the bourgeois residents, who moved out of the area and into Mayfair. During the following century Soho was no more than a slum, with cholera frequently attacking the impoverished residents. But despite its difficulties, the cosmopolitan vibe attracted writers and artists, and the overcrowded area became a centre for entertainment, with restaurants, taverns and coffee houses springing up.

The 20th century was even more raucous, when a fresh wave of European immigrants settled in, making Soho a bona fide bohemian enclave for two decades after WWII. Ronnie Scott's famous club, originally on Gerrard St, provided Soho's jazz soundtrack from the 1950s, while the likes of Jimi Hendrix, the Rolling Stones and Pink Floyd did their early gigs at the legendary Marquee club, which used to be on Wardour St. Soho had long been known for its seediness but when the hundreds of prostitutes who served the Square Mile were forced off the streets and into shop windows, it became the city's red-light district and a centre for porn, strip joints and bawdy drinking clubs. Gay liberation soon followed, and by the 1980s Soho was the hub of London's gay scene, as it remains today. The neighbourhood has a real sense of community, best absorbed on a weekend morning when Soho is at its most villagelike.

house – the gardener's shed – whose lift was a passage to underground shelters during WWII. Apart from being a relaxing green space, Soho Sq (along with the rest of Soho) is media central: 20th Century Fox and the British Board of Film Classification have their offices here.

Heading south of Soho Sq, down Dean Street, you'll come upon No 28, the home of Karl Marx and his family from 1851 to 1856. Marx, his wife Jenny and their four children lived in extreme poverty, without a toilet or running water, and three of their children died of pneumonia in this flat. While the father of communism spent his days researching *Das Kapital* in the British Museum, his main sources of income were from writing articles for newspapers and financial help from his friend and colleague Friedrich Engels. The Marx family was eventually saved by a huge inheritance from Mrs Marx' relatives, after which they upped sticks and moved to the more salubrious surroundings of Primrose Hill. Today it's a lively street lined with shops, bars and many other consumer outlets that no doubt would have given Marx indigestion.

Seducer and heart-breaker Casanova and opium-addicted writer Thomas de Quincey lived on Greek Street, whereas the parallel Frith Street (No 20) housed Mozart for a year from 1764.

CHINATOWN Map p66

Immediately north of Leicester Sq – but a world away in atmosphere – are Lisle and Gerrard Sts, the focal point for London's Chinese community. Although not as big as Chinatowns in many other cities – it's just two streets really – this is a lively quarter with fake oriental gates, Chinese street signs, red lanterns, many, many restaurants and great Asian supermarkets. London's original Chinatown was further east, near Limehouse, but moved here after heavy bombardments in WWII. To see it at its effervescent best, time your visit for Chinese New Year in late January/early February (see p16). Do be aware that the quality of food here varies enormously – many places are mediocre establishments aimed squarely at the tourist market but several good-quality restaurants have opened up in recent years. For the best of the lot see Eating, p236.

PHOTOGRAPHERS' GALLERY
Map p66

☎ 0845 262 1618; www.photonet.org.uk; 16-18 Ramillies St W1; admission free; ☷ 11am-6pm Tue, Wed & Sat, 11am-8pm Thu & Fri, noon-6pm Sun; ⊖ Oxford Circus; ♿

Moved from its two-part gallery space off Leicester Sq in December 2008, this fantastic institution has massively benefited from the new premises. Designed by O'Donnell + Tuomey Architects, the gallery now consists of two floors of exhibition space, a lovely cafe and well-stocked bookshop, plus a top-floor shop where you can buy original prints. The prestigious Deutsche Börse Photography Competition (annually 9 February to 8 April) is of major importance for contemporary photographers; past winners include Richard Billingham, Luc Delahaye, Andreas Gursky, Boris Mikhailov and

THE WEST END: CENTRAL

0 ————————— 200 m
0 ————————— 0.12 miles

Bloomsbury

Bedford Square

Bedford Sq

Gower St

Store St

Fitzrovia

New Cavendish St

Great Titchfield St

Foley St

Riding House St

Goodge St

Scala St

Charlotte St

Whitfield St

Tottenham Court Rd

Alfred St

Bedford Ave

Langham St

Cleveland St

Great Portland St

Hanson St

Ogle St

Goodge St

Windmill St

Percy St

Great Russell St

Bayley St

Morwell St

Langham St

Mortimer St

Little Portland St

Margaret St

Great Titchfield St

Eastcastle St

Riding House St

Berners St

Wells Mews

Berners Mews

Newman St

Rathbone St

Rathbone Pl

Gresse St

Morwell St

Tottenham Court Rd

Portland Pl

Mortimer St

Regent St

Great Portland St

Oxford St

Winsley St

Poland St

Berwick St

Newman St

Perry's Pl

Oxford St

Soho St

Falconberg Ct

Charing Cross Rd

Sutton Row

Soho Square

Oxford Circus

Noel St

D'Arblay St

Wardour St

Richmond Mews

Dean St

Frith St

Greek St

Manette St

Hanover St

Princes St

Carnaby St

Kingly St

Ganton St

Marshall St

Broadwick St

Beak St

Lexington St

Great Windmill St

Brewer St

Peter St

Meard St

Dean St

Berwick Street Market

Soho

Shaftesbury Ave

Gerrard St

Lisle St

Leicester Square

Maddox St

St George St

Conduit St

Regent St

Golden Sq

Bridle Ln

Denman St

Rupert St

Wardour St

Mayfair

New Bond St

Boyle St

Clifford St

Old Burlington St

New Burlington St

Savile Row

Heddon St

Warwick St

Vigo St

Glasshouse St

Regent St

Grafton St

Albemarle St

Cork St

New Bond St

Burlington Gdns

Burlington Arc

Sackville St

Swallow St

Piccadilly Circus

Haymarket

Lower Regent St

Jermyn St

Eagle Pl

Panton St

Irving St

Orange St

St Martin's St

Whitcomb St

Hay Hill

Royal Arcade

Dover St

Stafford St

Old Bond St

Albemarle St

Piccadilly

Jermyn St

Duke St

Duke of York St

Charles II St

St James's

Pall Mall

Cockspur St

Berkeley St

Stratton St

Mayfair Pl

Piccadilly

Arlington St

St James's St

Bury St

Ryder St

King St

St James's Sq

St James's Square

Pall Mall

Waterloo Pl

Carlton House Tce

Green Park

Bolton St

Park Pl

Leicester Square

Juergen Teller. The gallery always exhibits excellent and thought-provoking work.

PICCADILLY CIRCUS Map p66
⊖ Piccadilly Circus
Together with Big Ben and Trafalgar Sq, this is postcard London. And despite the stifling crowds and racing midday traffic, the flashing ads and buzzing liveliness of

Piccadilly Circus always make it exciting to be in London. The circus looks its best at night, when the flashing advertisement panels really shine against the dark sky.

Designed by John Nash in the 1820s, the hub was named after the street Piccadilly, which earned its name in the 17th century from the stiff collars (picadils) that were the sartorial staple of the time (and were

THE WEST END: CENTRAL

the making of a nearby tailor's fortune). At the centre of the circus is the famous lead statue, the Angel of Christian Charity, dedicated to the philanthropist and child-labour abolitionist Lord Shaftesbury, and derided when unveiled in 1893, sending the sculptor into early retirement. The sculpture was at first cast in gold, but it was later replaced by the present-day one. Down the years the angel has been mistaken for Eros, the God of Love, and the misnomer has stuck (you'll even see signs for 'Eros' from the Underground). It's a handy meeting place for tourists, though if you don't like the crowds, meet at the charging Horses of Helios statue at the edge of Piccadilly and Haymarket – apparently a much cooler place to convene.

John Nash had originally designed Regent St and Piccadilly to be the two most elegant streets in town (see below) but, curbed by city planners, Nash couldn't realise his dream to the full. In the many years since his noble plans, Piccadilly Circus has become swamped with tourists, with streets such as Coventry St flogging astronomically priced cheap tat to unsuspecting visitors. Coventry St leads to Leicester Sq, while Shaftesbury Ave takes you to the heart of the West End's theatreland. Piccadilly itself leads to the sanctuary of Green Park. On Haymarket, check out New Zealand House (built in 1959 on the site of the Carlton Hotel, which was bombed during the war), where the Vietnamese revolutionary leader Ho Chi Minh (1890–1969) worked as a waiter in 1913. Have a look down Lower Regent St for a glimpse of glorious Westminster.

Just east of the circus is London Trocadero (Map p66; ☎ 0906 888 1100; www.troc.co.uk; 1 Piccadilly Circus W1; admission free; ☑ 10am-1am), a huge and soulless indoor amusement arcade that has six levels of hi-tech, high-cost fun for youngsters, along with cinemas, US-themed restaurants and bowling alleys.

REGENT STREET Map p66
Regent St is the border separating the hoi polloi of Soho and the high-society residents of Mayfair. Designed by John Nash as a ceremonial route, it was meant to link the Prince Regent's long-demolished city dwelling with the 'wilds' of Regent's Park, and was conceived by the architect as a grand thoroughfare that would be the centrepiece of a new grid for this part of town. Alas, it was never to be – too many toes were

being stepped on and Nash had to downscale his plan. There are some elegant shop fronts that look older than their 1920s origins (when the street was remodelled) but, as in the rest of London, the chain stores have almost completely taken over. Two distinguished retail outlets are Hamleys (p223), London's premier toy and game store, and the upmarket department store Liberty (p218).

ROYAL ACADEMY OF ARTS Map p66
☎ 7300 8000; www.royalacademy.org.uk; Burlington House, Piccadilly W1; admission varies; ☑ 10am-6pm, to 10pm Fri; ⊖ Green Park; ⌖ Britain's first art school was founded in 1768, though it only moved here in the following century. It's a great place to come for some free art, thanks to the John Madejski's Fine Rooms, where drawings ranging from Constable, Reynolds, Gainsborough and Turner to Hockney are displayed for now. The Academy's galleries have sprung back to life in recent years with mega successful exhibitions such as the great Byzantium and Kuniyoshi shows. The famous Summer Exhibition (early June to mid-August), which has showcased art submitted by the general public for nearly 250 years, is the Academy's biggest event.

The Academy's Annenberg Courtyard features a dashing stone-paved piazza with choreographed lights and fountains flanking a statue of founder Joshua Reynolds, though he's often replaced or joined by various (and dubious) art pieces.

BURLINGTON ARCADE Map p66
51 Piccadilly W1; ⊖ Green Park
Flanking Burlington House – home of the Royal Academy of Arts – on its western side is the curious Burlington Arcade, built in 1819 and evocative of a bygone era. Today it is a shopping precinct for the very wealthy and is most famous for the Burlington Berties, uniformed guards who patrol the area keeping an eye out for punishable offences such as running, chewing gum or whatever else might lower the arcade's tone. The fact that the arcade once served as a brothel isn't mentioned.

ST JAMES'S PICCADILLY Map p66
☎ 7734 4511; 197 Piccadilly W1; ☑ 8am-7pm; ⊖ Green Park or Piccadilly Circus
The only church Christopher Wren built from scratch and on a new site (most of the

others were replacements for ones razed in the Great Fire), this simple building is exceedingly easy on the eye and substitutes what some might call the pompous flourishes of his most famous churches with a warm and elegant user-friendliness. The spire, although designed by Wren, was added only in 1968. This is a particularly sociable church: it houses a counselling service, stages lunchtime and evening concerts, provides shelter for an antiques market (10am to 6pm Tuesday) and an arts and crafts fair (10am to 6pm Wednesday to Sunday), has Caffé Nero attached on the side, as well as, what was the last thing... oh, yeah, teaching the word of God.

WHITE CUBE GALLERY Map p66
☎ 7930 5373; www.whitecube.com; 25-26 Mason's Yard SW1; admission free; ☷ 10am-6pm Tue-Sat; ⊖ Piccadilly Circus

This central sister to the Hoxton original (p149) hosted Tracey Emin's first exhibition in five years, 'Those who suffer Love', in 2009, thus, together with the massively publicised Damien Hirst 'For the Love of God' exhibition two years before, bringing back some of the publicity for the (now not-so-young) Young British Artists (YBAs). Housed in Mason's Yard, a traditional courtyard with brick houses and an old pub, the White Cube looks like an ice block – white, straight-lined and angular. The two contrasting styles work well together and the courtyard often serves as a garden for the gallery on popular opening nights.

COVENT GARDEN & LEICESTER SQUARE

Covent Garden, though the throbbing heart of tourist London, is as beautiful and pleasant as tourist areas can get. Located east of Soho, the area is dominated by the piazza, which draws thousands of tourists into its elegant arched belly with boutiques, stalls, open-air cafes and pubs, and street entertainers who mostly perform outside St Paul's Church. Most Londoners avoid the human traffic jam of the area, but you should see it at least once. If you can, try to walk through the piazza after 11pm: it's calmer and almost totally empty, save for a busker or two, and you can appreciate its old-world beauty and Inigo Jones's design without the crowds. Additionally, there is an excellent antiques market on Monday that's worth a wander.

To the north of the piazza is the Royal Opera House, ruthlessly yet brilliantly rebuilt in the late 1990s to make it one of the world's most superb singing venues. The wider area of Covent Garden is a honeypot for shoppers who revel in the high-street outlets on Long Acre and independent boutiques along the little side streets. Neal St is no longer the grooviest strip, although the little roads cutting across it maintain its legendary style. Neal's Yard is a strange and charming little courtyard featuring overpriced vegetarian eateries. Floral St is where swanky designers such as Paul Smith have stores.

Covent Garden's history is quite different from its present-day character: it was the site of a convent (hence, 'covent') and its garden in the 13th century, owned by Westminster Abbey, which became the property of John Russell, the first Earl of Bedford, in 1552. The area developed thanks to his descendants, who employed Inigo Jones to convert a vegetable field into a piazza in the 17th century. He built the elegant Italian-style piazza, flanked by St Paul's Church to the west, and its tall terraced houses soon started to draw rich socialites who coveted the central living quarters. The bustling fruit and veg market – immortalised in *My Fair Lady* where it was a flower market – dominated the piazza. London society, including writers such as Pepys, Fielding and Boswell, gathered here in the evenings looking for some action among the coffee houses, theatres, gambling dens and brothels. Lawlessness became commonplace, leading to the formation of a volunteer police force known as the Bow Street Runners (see Georgian London, p26). In 1897 Oscar Wilde was charged with gross indecency in the now-closed Bow St magistrate's court. A flower market designed by Charles Fowler was added at the spot where London's Transport Museum now stands.

During the 1970s the city traffic made it increasingly difficult to maintain the fruit and veg market so it was moved in 1974. Property developers loomed over the space and there was even talk of the market being demolished for a road but, thanks to the area's dedicated residential community who demonstrated and picketed for weeks, the piazza was saved and transformed into what you see today.

TRAFALGAR SQUARE Map pp70-1
⊖ Charing Cross

In many ways this is the centre of London, where rallies and marches take place, tens of thousands of revellers usher in the New

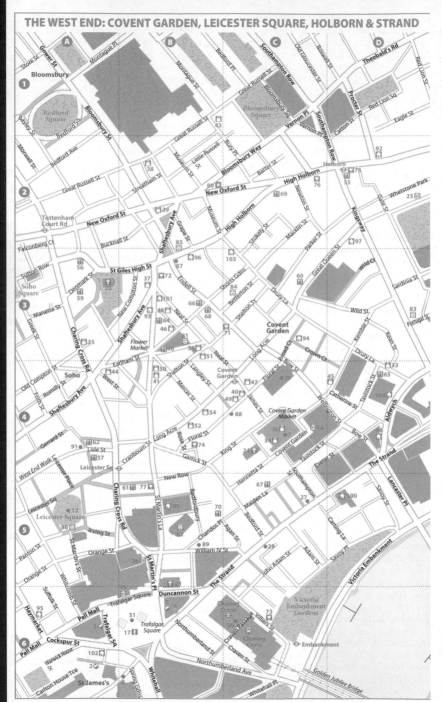

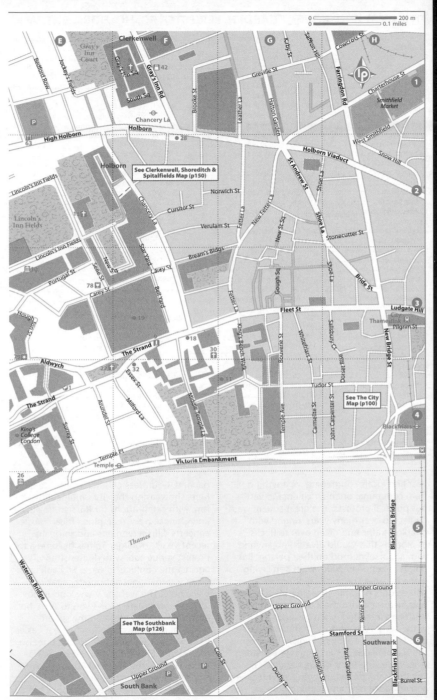

0 ———————— 200 m
0 ———————— 0.1 miles

E **F** **G** **H**

Gray's Inn Court

Clerkenwell

Kirby St
Saffron Hill
Cowcross St

Greville St
Charterhouse St

Farringdon Rd

Smithfield Market

42

Brooke St
Leather La
Hatton Garden

St Andrew St
Shoe La

Holborn Viaduct
West Smithfield
Snow Hill

Chancery La

High Holborn
63

Holborn

28

Holborn

See Clerkenwell, Shoreditch & Spitalfields Map (p150)

Norwich St

Cursitor St
Fetter La
New Fetter La
New St Sq
Shoe La
Stonecutter St

Lincoln's Inn Fields

Chancery La

Verulam St

Bream's Bldgs

Gough Sq
Shoe La
Bride St

Lincoln's Inn Fields

15

Portugal St
Star Yard
New Sq
Seale St

Carey St

78

Carey St
Bell Yard

19

Fleet St

Ludgate Hill
City Thameslink
Pilgrim St

Hough St
79

The Strand

18

30

King's Bench Walk

Bowerie St
Whitefriars St
St Bride's Ave
Dorset Rise
New Bridge St

Aldwych

22
Essex St
32

11

Temple Ave
Tudor St
Carmelite St
John Carpenter St

See The City Map (p100)

The Strand

Arundel St
Surrey St
Millford La
Middle Temple La

Blackfriars

King's College London

Temple Pl

Temple
26

Victoria Embankment

Waterloo Bridge

Thames

Blackfriars Bridge

Upper Ground
Rennie St

Upper Ground

Stamford St
Southwark

See The Southbank Map (p126)

Upper Ground
Coin St
Duchy St
Hatfields St
Paris Garden
Blackfriars Rd
Burrel St

South Bank

71

Year and locals congregate for anything
from communal open-air cinema to various political protests. The great square was
neglected over many years, ringed with
gnarling traffic and given over to flocks
of pigeons that would dive-bomb anyone
with a morsel of food on their person. But
things changed in 2000 when Ken Livingstone became London Mayor and em-
barked on a bold and imaginative scheme
to transform it into the kind of space John
Nash had intended when he designed it
in the early 19th century. Traffic was ban-
ished from the northern flank in front of
the National Gallery, and a new pedestrian
plaza built. The front of the National Gallery itself was dolled up with a new facade
and entrance hall, and feeding pigeons was

banned. Countless cultural events are held
here, showcasing the city's multiculturalism, with celebrations for Russian, Jewish
and Chinese New Year, plus African music
concerts, film screenings and so on. In
recent years, Trafalgar Sq has become a top
protest venue too, with demonstrations
against the conflicts in Gaza, Sri Lanka and
other international hot potatoes taking
place here. The website www.london.gov
.uk/trafalgarsquare allows you to see what
events are taking place on the square.

The pedestrianisation has made it easier
to appreciate not only the square but also
the splendid buildings around it: the National Gallery, the National Portrait Gallery
and the newly renovated church of St
Martin-in-the-Fields. The ceremonial Pall Mall

runs southwest from the top of the square. To the southwest stands Admiralty Arch (p75), with The Mall leading to Buckingham Palace beyond it. To the west is Canada House (1827), designed by Robert Smirke. Standing in the centre of the square since 1843, the 52m-high Nelson's Column (upon which the admiral surveys his fleet of ships to the southwest) commemorates Nelson's victory over Napoleon off Cape Trafalgar in Spain in 1805.

NATIONAL GALLERY Map pp70-1

☎ 7747 2885; www.nationalgallery.org.uk; Trafalgar Sq WC2; admission free, prices vary for temporary exhibitions; ⏰ 10am-6pm Thu-Tue, to 9pm Wed; ⊖ Charing Cross; ♿
With more than 2000 Western European paintings on display, this is one of the largest galleries in the world. But it's the quality of the works, and not the quantity, that impresses most. Almost five million people visit each year, keen to see seminal paintings from every important epoch in the history of art, including works by Giotto, Leonardo da Vinci, Michelangelo, Titian, Velázquez, Van Gogh and Renoir, just to name a few. Although it can get ridiculously busy in here, the galleries are spacious, sometimes even sedate, and it's never so bad that you can't appreciate the works. That said, weekday mornings and Wednesday evenings (after 6pm) are the best times to visit, as the crowds are small. If you have the time to make multiple visits, focus on one section at a time to fully appreciate the astonishing collection.

The size and layout can be confusing, so make sure you pick up a free gallery plan at the entrance. To see the art in chronological order, start with the Sainsbury Wing on the gallery's western side, which houses paintings from 1260 to 1510. In these 16 rooms you can explore the Renaissance through paintings by Giotto, Leonardo da Vinci, Botticelli, Raphael and Titian, among others. This is where you'll also find the Micro gallery, a dozen computer terminals on which you can explore the pictorial database, find the location of your favourite works or create your own personalised tour.

The High Renaissance (1510–1600) is covered in the West Wing, where Michelangelo, Titian, Correggio, El Greco and Bronzino hold court, while Rubens, Rembrandt and Caravaggio can be found in the North Wing (1600–1700). The most crowded part of the gallery – and for good reason – is likely to be the East Wing (1700–1900) and particularly the many works of the impressionists and postimpressionists, including Van Gogh, Gauguin, Cézanne, Monet, Degas and Renoir. Although it hardly stands out in such exalted company, the impressive display featuring 18th-century British landscape artists Gainsborough, Constable and Turner is also well worth checking out.

The gallery's collection cuts off at 1900; to see 20th-century art you need to head to Tate Modern (p128) and, for British art, Tate Britain (p93).

Temporary exhibitions – for which you normally have to pay, and often book in

THE FOURTH PLINTH

Three of the four plinths located at Trafalgar Sq's corners are occupied by notables, King George IV on horseback, and military men General Sir Charles Napier and Major General Sir Henry Havelock. One, originally intended for a statue of William IV, has largely remained vacant for the past 150 years. The Royal Society of Arts conceived the unimaginatively titled Fourth Plinth Project (www.london.gov.uk/fourthplinth) in 1999, deciding to use the empty space for works by contemporary artists. The stunning Ecce Homo by Mark Wallinger (1999) was the first one, a life-size statue of Jesus which appeared tiny in contrast to the enormous plinth, commenting on the human illusions of grandeur; it was followed by Bill Woodrow's Regardless of History (2000) and Rachel Whiteread's Monument (2001), a resin copy of the plinth, turned upside down.

The Mayor's office has since taken over the Fourth Plinth Project, continuing with the contemporary-art theme, with Marc Quinn's Alison Lapper Pregnant (2005), a statue of thalidomide-affected artist Lapper, being replaced by Tomas Schütte's Model for a Hotel 2007 (2007). Possibly the most interesting so far has been Anthony Gormley's One & Other (2009) which featured no inanimate object but simply a space for individuals to occupy – each person spent an hour on the plinth, addressing the crowds on any chosen subject, performing or simply sitting quietly. The project ran 24 hours a day, every day for 100 days and the rules specified that the participants spent their hour on the plinth alone, could do what they wanted as long as it wasn't illegal and were allowed to take with them anything they could carry.

NATIONAL GALLERY HIGHLIGHTS

- *Pentecost* – Giotto
- *Virgin and Child with St Anne and St John the Baptist* – Leonardo da Vinci
- *Arnolfini Wedding* – Van Eyck
- *Venus and Mars* – Botticelli
- *The Ansidei Madonna* – Raphael
- *The Madonna of the Pinks* – Raphael
- *Le Chapeau de Paille* – Rubens
- *Charles I* – Van Dyck
- *Bacchus and Ariadne* – Titian
- *The Entombment* – Michelangelo
- *Rokeby Venus* – Velásquez
- *The Supper at Emmaus* – Caravaggio
- *Bathers* – Cézanne
- *Sunflowers* – Van Gogh
- *The Water Lily Pond* – Monet
- *Miss La La* – Degas
- *The Hay Wain* – Constable
- *The Fighting Temeraire* – Turner

advance – go on show in the basement of the Sainsbury Wing and are often outstanding.

The highlights listed in the boxed text (above) include many of the most important works, but if you want to immerse yourself in this pool of riches rather than just skim across the surface, borrow a themed or comprehensive audioguide (£3.50 donation recommended) from the Central Hall. Free one-hour introductory guided tours leave from the information desk in the Sainsbury Wing daily at 11.30am and 2.30pm, with an extra tour at 6.30pm on Wednesday. There are also special trails and activity sheets for children.

The new National Dining Rooms (☎ 7747 2525; www.thenationaldiningrooms.co.uk; ☽ 10am-5pm Sun-Tue, to 8.30pm Wed), in the Sainsbury Wing, is a wonderful recent addition to the gallery. Run by Oliver Peyton (the man behind Inn the Park in St James's Park; see p242), this is an excellent, well-lit space, with quality British food in the restaurant, and pastries and cakes in the bakery.

NATIONAL PORTRAIT GALLERY
Map pp70-1

☎ 7306 0055; www.npg.org.uk; St Martin's Pl WC2; admission free, prices vary for temporary exhibitions; ☽ 10am-6pm, to 9pm Thu & Fri; ⊖ Charing Cross or Leicester Sq; ㉖
Excellent for putting faces to names over the last five centuries of British history, the gallery houses a primary collection of some

10,000 works, which are regularly rotated, among them the museum's first acquisition, the famous Chandos portrait of Shakespeare. Despite the recent discovery that the Royal Shakespeare Company's Flower portrait of the Bard was a 19th-century forgery, the National Portrait Gallery still believes this one to have been painted during Shakespeare's lifetime.

To follow the paintings chronologically you should take the huge escalator to the top floor and work your way down. The 1st floor is dedicated to the Royal Family, but the most fun is seeing one of the two portraits of the Queen made by Andy Warhol. The ground floor is most interesting with portraits of contemporary figures using a variety of media, including sculpture and photography. Among the most popular of these is Sam Taylor-Wood's *David*, a video-portrait of David Beckham asleep after football training, which caused a lot of women to suddenly take an interest in this part of the gallery. There's an annual Photographic Portrait Prize exhibition, featuring some of the best contemporary photographers.

Audioguides (a £3.50 donation is suggested) highlight some 200 portraits and allow you to hear the voices of some of the people portrayed. The Portrait Café and bookshop are in the basement and the Portrait (p238) restaurant is on the top floor, offering some superb views towards Westminster.

ST MARTIN-IN-THE-FIELDS Map pp70-1
☎ general info/box office 7766 1100, for brass-rubbing 7766 1122; www.stmartin-in-the-fields.org; Trafalgar Sq WC2; admission free, brass-rubbing from £4.50; ☽ 8am-6.30pm, brass-rubbing centre 10am-7pm Mon-Wed, 10am-9pm Thu-Sat, 11.30am-6pm Sun, evening concerts 7.30pm; ⊖ Charing Cross
The 'royal parish church' is a delightful fusion of classical and baroque styles that was completed by James Gibbs (1682–1754) in 1726. A £36-million refurbishment project, completed at the end of 2007, provided a new entrance pavilion and foyer, and several new areas at the rear of the church, including spaces offering social care to London's Chinese community and the many homeless people who rely on the church's help. These are in addition to the main hall, where Mass and musical concerts are held in English, Mandarin and Cantonese, and the famous crypt cafe, where over 150 classical and jazz concerts are held each year, in candlelight.

Refurbishment excavations unearthed a 1.5-tonne limestone Roman sarcophagus containing a human skeleton in the churchyard; the yard also holds the graves of 18th-century artists Reynolds and Hogarth.

COVENT GARDEN PIAZZA Map pp70-1
↔ Covent Garden
London's first planned square is now the exclusive reserve of tourists who flock here to shop in the quaint old arcades, be entertained by buskers, pay through the nose for refreshments at outdoor cafes and bars, and watch men and women pretend to be statues.

On its western flank is St Paul's Church (☎ 7836 5221; www.actorschurch.org; Bedford St WC2; admission free; ☼ 8.30am-5.30pm Mon-Fri, 9am-1pm Sun). The Earl of Bedford, the man who had commissioned Inigo Jones to design the piazza, asked for the simplest possible church, basically no more than a barn. The architect responded by producing 'the handsomest barn in England'. It has long been regarded as the actors' church for its associations with the theatre, and contains memorials to the likes of Charlie Chaplin and Vivien Leigh. The first Punch and Judy show took place in front of it in 1662.

Check out the lovely courtyard at the back, perfect for a picnic.

LONDON TRANSPORT MUSEUM
Map pp70-1
☎ 7379 6344; www.ltmuseum.co.uk; Covent Garden Piazza WC2; adult/senior/student/concession/under 16s £10/8/6/5/free; ☼ 10am-6pm Sat-Thu, 11am-6pm Fri; ↔ Covent Garden; ⑤
The museum reopened in late 2007, after a £22-million refurbishment and redesign. You can now see the revitalised existing collection (consisting of buses from the horse age until today, plus taxis, trains and all other modes of transport) and new collections that feature other major cities' transport systems, as well as tons of great original poster art and a 120-seat lecture theatre for educational purposes. Check out the poster collection (ranging from £10) for original and interesting souvenirs.

ADMIRALTY ARCH Map pp70-1
↔ Charing Cross
From Trafalgar Sq, The Mall passes under this grand Edwardian monument, a triple-arched stone entrance designed by Aston

Webb in honour of Queen Victoria in 1910. The large central gate is opened only for royal processions and state visits.

ROYAL OPERA HOUSE Map pp70-1
☎ 7304 4000; www.roh.org.uk; Bow St WC2; adult/concession/student £9/8/7; ☼ tours 10.30am, 12.30pm & 2.30pm Mon-Fri, 10.30am, 11.30am, 12.30pm & 1.30pm Sat; ↔ Covent Garden; ⑤
On the northeastern flank of Covent Garden piazza is the gleaming, redeveloped – and practically new – Royal Opera House. Unique 'behind the scenes' tours take you through the venue, and let you experience the planning, excitement and hissy fits that take place before a performance at one of the world's busiest opera houses. As it's a working theatre, plans can change so you'd best call ahead. Of course, the best way to enjoy it is by seeing a performance (see p311).

LEICESTER SQUARE Map pp70-1
↔ Leicester Sq
Enormous cinemas and nightclubs dominate this 'aesthetically challenged' square, which could really do with a makeover. It heaves with crowds on weekends and becomes the playground of the inebriated at night. There was a serious pickpocketing problem here some years ago, until a heavy police presence improved matters, but still keep an eye on your bag/wallet, especially when the square is very crowded. Britain's glitzy film premieres take place here, as well as the majority of London Film Festival screenings. The major Odeon cinema boasts the biggest screen in the country, and definitely the highest ticket prices (a whopping £18!).

It's been on a major comedown since the 19th century, when the square was so fashionable that artists Joshua Reynolds and William Hogarth chose to hang their hats here. Inside the little park stands a small statue of Charlie Chaplin, which is there mainly because of Leicester Sq's cinematic importance rather than any historical connection between the comedian and the area.

ST GILES-IN-THE-FIELDS Map pp70-1
☎ 7240 2532; 60 St Giles High St; ☼ 9am-4pm Mon-Fri; ↔ Tottenham Court Rd
Built in what used to be countryside between the City and Westminster, St Giles

church isn't much to look at but has an interesting history, while the area around St Giles High St had perhaps the worst reputation of any London quarter. The current structure is the third to stand on the site of an original chapel built in the 12th century to serve the leprosy hospital. Until 1547, when the hospital closed, prisoners on their way to be executed at Tyburn (p145) stopped at the church gate and sipped a large cup of soporific ale – their last refreshment – from St Giles's Bowl. From 1650 the prisoners were buried in the church grounds. It was also within the boundaries of St Giles that the Great Plague of 1665 took hold (this is cheerful, isn't it?). In Victorian times it was London's worst slum, oft namechecked by Dickens. Today the forbidding streets and drug-users who hang out around the area make you feel like things haven't changed much.

An interesting relic in the church is the pulpit that was used for 40 years by John Wesley, the founder of Methodism.

HOLBORN & THE STRAND

This area – compacted here for convenience's sake – comprises the rough square wedged between the City to the east, Covent Garden to the west, High Holborn to the north and the Thames to the south. Past glory and prominence are its key characteristics: The Strand, connecting Westminster with the City, used to be one of the most important streets in London and was lined with fabulous town houses built by local luminaries and aristocrats. This rich history is only vaguely evident today but, while much of this pocket is soulless and commercial, it is saved by some architectural gems, a few splendid galleries and the calm, green recesses of the charming Inns of Court, the cradle of English law. Behind The Strand runs the Victoria Embankment

Gardens, a lovely place for a picnic, a stroll and splendid views across the Thames to the recharged South Bank.

Fleet St was the former home of British journalism. It was named after the River Fleet, which in the 17th and 18th centuries was a virtual sewer filled with entrails and other grisly bits from Smithfield Market (p105) upriver. Holborn was named after one of its tributaries. Both were filled in the late 18th century, with the River Fleet now running underground. The area was a notorious slum in Victorian times and although efforts were made to smarten it up in the early 20th century, it was probably no great loss when the Germans flattened much of it during WWII, after which the current business moved in.

SOMERSET HOUSE Map pp70-1

☎ 7845 4600; www.somerset-house.org.uk; The Strand WC2; admission free; ☯ house 10am-6pm, Great Court 7.30am-11pm; ☻ Temple or Covent Garden

Passing beneath the arch towards this splendid Palladian masterpiece, it's hard to believe that the magnificent courtyard in front of you, with its 55 dancing fountains, was in recent times a car park for tax collectors until a spectacular refurbishment in 2000. William Chambers designed the house in 1775 for royal societies and it now contains three fabulous museums. The courtyard is transformed into a popular ice rink in winter and used for concerts in summer, as well as an improvised fountain-bathing area for toddlers. Behind the house, there's a sunny terrace and cafe overlooking the embankment.

Immediately to your right as you enter the grounds of Somerset House from The Strand, you'll find the Courtauld Institute of Art (☎ 7848 2526; www.courtauld.ac.uk; adult/concession/UK student £5/4/free, 10am-2pm Mon free; ☯ 10am-6pm), a

---

PICK OF THE STYX: LONDON'S UNDERGROUND RIVERS

The Thames is not London's only river. Many others have been culverted over the centuries and now course unseen underground. Some survive only in place names: Hole Bourne, Wells, Tyburn, Walbrook and Westbourne, which was dammed up in 1730 to form the Serpentine in Hyde Park. The most famous of these Rivers Styx is the Fleet, which rises in Hampstead and Kenwood ponds and flows south through Camden Town, King's Cross, Farringdon Rd and New Bridge St, where it empties into the Thames at Blackfriars Bridge. For centuries it had been used as an open sewer and as a dumping area by butchers; the Elizabethan playwright Ben Jonson describes a voyage on the Fleet on a hot summer's night in which every stroke of the oars 'belch'd forth an ayre as hot as the muster of all your night-tubs discharging their merd-urinous load'. After the Great Fire of 1666 Christopher Wren oversaw the deepening and widening of a section of the Fleet into a canal, but this was covered over in 1733, as was the rest of the river three decades later.

superb gallery connected to the Courtauld Institute of Arts, Britain's foremost academy of art history. Have an uncrowded stroll between the walls of this wonderful place, and see work by Rubens, Botticelli, Cranach, Cézanne, Degas, Renoir, Manet, Monet, Matisse, Gauguin, Van Gogh and Toulouse-Lautrec, to mention but a few. There are lunchtime talks on specific works or themes from the collection at 1.15pm every Monday and Friday. A little cafe and the plush Admiral 2 restaurant provide sustenance.

ROYAL COURTS OF JUSTICE Map pp70-1

☎ 7936 6000; 460 The Strand; admission free; ⊙ 9am-4.30pm Mon-Fri; ⊖ Temple

Where The Strand joins Fleet St, you'll see the entrance to this gargantuan melange of Gothic spires, pinnacles and burnished Portland stone, designed by aspiring cathedral builder GE Street in 1874. (It took so much out of the architect that he died of a stroke shortly before its completion.) Inside the Great Hall there's an exhibition of legal costumes, as well as a list of cases to be heard in court that day; if you're interested in 'the criminal mind' and decide to watch, leave your camera behind and expect airportlike security.

THE STRAND Map pp70-1

⊖ Charing Cross

From the time it was built, at the end of the 12th century, The Strand (from the Old English and German word for beach) ran by the Thames. Its grandiose stone houses, built by the nobility, counted as some of the most prestigious places to live, sitting as they did on a street that connected the City and Westminster, the two centres of power; indeed, its appeal lasted for seven centuries, with the 19th-century prime minister Benjamin Disraeli pronouncing it 'the finest street in Europe'. Buildings included the now-no-more Cecil Hotel, the Savoy hotel, Simpson's, King's College and Somerset House.

But modern times haven't treated The Strand with the same sort of respect and awe: the street is now overrun by offices, cheap restaurants and odd souvenir shops, and despite the fact that the Savoy (which is mid-refurbishment at the time of writing), the building formerly Simpson's and the wonderful Somerset House still grace the street, it is hardly seen as the fine drag

it once was. Still, there are some lovely things to see here, such as Twinings at No 216, a teashop opened by Thomas Twining in 1706 and believed to be the oldest company in the capital still trading on the same site and owned by the same family. It's also the centre of London philatelic life, with stamp- and coin-collector's mecca Stanley Gibbons at No 339.

SIR JOHN SOANE'S MUSEUM
Map pp70-1

☎ 7405 2107; www.soane.org; 13 Lincoln's Inn Fields WC2; admission free, suggested donation £3; ⊙ 10am-5pm Tue-Sat & 6-9pm 1st Tue of month; ⊖ Holborn

This little museum is one of the most atmospheric and fascinating sights in London. The building is the beautiful, bewitching home of architect Sir John Soane (1753–1837), which he left brimming with surprising personal effects and curiosities, and the museum represents his exquisite and eccentric taste.

Soane was a country bricklayer's son, most famous for designing the Bank of England. In his work and life, he drew on ideas picked up while on an 18th-century grand tour of Italy. He married a rich woman and used the wealth to build this house and the one next door, which was opened as an exhibition and education space in late 2007.

The heritage-listed house is largely as it was when Sir John was carted out in a box, and is itself a main part of the attraction. It has a glass dome that brings light right down to the basement, a lantern room filled with statuary, rooms within rooms, and a picture gallery where paintings are stowed behind each other on folding wooden panes. You can see Soane's choice paintings, including Canalettos and Turners, drawings by Christopher Wren and Robert Adam, and the original *Rake's Progress*, William Hogarth's set of cartoon caricatures of late-18th-century London lowlife (see boxed text, p44). You'll have to ask a guard to open the panes so that you can view all the paintings. Among Soane's more unusual acquisitions are an Egyptian hieroglyphic sarcophagus, an imitation monk's parlour, and slaves' chains.

Note that groups of seven or more need to book ahead and are not admitted on Saturday, which is by far the museum's busiest day. Evenings of the first Tuesday of each month are a choice time to visit as the house is lit by candles and the atmosphere is even more magical.

HUNTERIAN MUSEUM Map pp70-1

☎ 7869 6560; www.rcseng.ac.uk/museums; Royal College of Surgeons, 35-43 Lincoln's Inn Fields WC2; admission free; ⏰ 10am-5pm Tue-Sat; ⊖ Holborn

The collection of anatomical specimens of pioneering surgeon John Hunter (1728–93) inspired this fascinating, slightly morbid, little-known, yet fantastic London museum. Among the more bizarre items on display are the skeleton of a 2.3m giant, half of mathematician Charles Babbage's brain and, hilariously, Winston Churchill's dentures. Thanks to a massive refurbishment some years back, the atmosphere is less gory and allows decent viewing of things such as animal digestive systems, forensically documented in formaldehyde, and wonders such as the 'hearing organ' of a blue whale. Upstairs includes a display on plastic surgery techniques, which will impress and disgust in equal measure. There's a free guided tour every Wednesday at 1pm.

ST CLEMENT DANES Map pp70-1

☎ 7242 8282; The Strand WC2; ⏰ 8.30am-4.30pm Mon-Fri, 9am-3.30pm Sat, 9am-12.30pm Sun; ⊖ Temple

An 18th-century English nursery rhyme that incorporates the names of London churches goes: 'Oranges and lemons, say the bells of St Clements', with the soothing final lines: 'Here comes a chopper to chop off your head/Chop, chop, chop, chop, the last man's dead!' Isn't that nice? Well, even though the bells of this church chime that nursery tune every day at 9am, noon and 3pm, this *isn't* the St Clements referred to in the first line the verse – that's St Clements Eastcheap, in the City. But we all know that historical fact needn't get in the way of a good story.

Sir Christopher Wren designed the original building in 1682 but only the walls and a steeple added by James Gibbs in 1719 survived the Luftwaffe, and the church was rebuilt after the war as a memorial to Allied airmen. Today it is the chapel of the Royal Air Force (RAF), and there are some 800 slate badges of different squadrons set

INNS OF COURT

For all of the West End's urban mania, the area hides some unexpected pockets of Zenlike calm. Clustered around Holborn and Fleet St are the Inns of Court, with quiet alleys, open spaces and a serene atmosphere. All London barristers work from within one of these four inns, and a roll call of former members ranges from Oliver Cromwell and Charles Dickens to Mahatma Gandhi, to Margaret Thatcher. It would take a lifetime working here to grasp the intricacies of the protocols of the inns – they're similar to the Freemasons, and both are 13th-century creations with centuries of tradition – and it's best to just soak in the dreamy atmosphere and relax.

Gray's Inn (Map pp70–1; ☎ 7458 7800; Gray's Inn Rd WC1; ⏰ grounds 10am-4pm Mon-Fri, chapel 10am-6pm Mon-Fri; ⊖ Holborn or Chancery Lane) This inn – destroyed during WWII, rebuilt and expanded – is less interesting than Lincoln's Inn although the peaceful gardens are still something of a treat. The walls of the original hall absorbed the first ever performance of Shakespeare's *Comedy of Errors*.

Inner Temple (Map pp70–1; ☎ 7353 8559; King's Bench Walk EC4; ⊖ Temple or Blackfriars) Duck under the archway next to Prince Henry's Room and you'll find yourself in the Inner Temple, a sprawling complex of some of the finest buildings on the river. The church (see p103) was originally planned and built by the secretive Knights Templar between 1161 and 1185. At the weekend you'll usually have to enter from the Victoria Embankment.

Lincoln's Inn (Map pp70–1; ☎ 7405 1393; Lincoln's Inn Fields WC2; ⏰ grounds 9am-6pm Mon-Fri, chapel 12.30-2.30pm Mon-Fri; ⊖ Holborn) Lincoln's Inn is the most attractive of the four inns and has a chapel, pleasant square and picturesque gardens that invite a stroll, especially early or late in the day when the legal eagles aren't flapping about. The court itself, although closed to the public, is visible through the gates and is relatively intact, with original 15th-century buildings, including the Tudor Lincoln's Inn Gatehouse on Chancery Lane. Inigo Jones helped plan the well-preserved chapel which was built in 1623.

Staple Inn (Map pp70–1; Holborn; ⊖ Chancery Lane) The 16th-century shop-front facade is the main interest at Staple Inn (1589), the last of eight Inns of Chancery whose functions were superseded by the Inns of Court in the 18th century. The buildings, mostly postwar reconstructions, are now occupied by the Institute of Actuaries and aren't actually open to the public, although nobody seems to mind a discreet and considerate look around. On the same side of Holborn but closer to Fetter Lane stood Barnard's Inn, redeveloped in 1991. Pip lived here with Herbert Pocket in Dickens' *Great Expectations*.

into the pavement of the nave. The statue in front of the church quietly and contentiously commemorates the RAF's Sir Arthur 'Bomber' Harris, who led the bombing raids that obliterated Dresden and killed some 10,000 civilians during WWII.

BLOOMSBURY

Immediately north of Covent Garden – though worlds away in look and atmosphere – is Bloomsbury, a leafy quarter and the academic and intellectual heart of London. Here you will find the University of London and its many faculties and campuses scattered along the streets. And shaded by many trees and surrounded by Georgian and Victorian town houses is what must be one of the world's best museums: the British Museum. The beautiful squares were once colonised by the 'Bloomsbury Group', a group of artists and writers who included Virginia Woolf and EM Forster, and the stories of their many intricate love affairs are as fascinating as their books. Charles Dickens, Charles Darwin, William Butler Yeats and George Bernard Shaw also lived here or hereabouts, as attested by the many blue plaques dotted around. Today Bloomsbury continues to teem with students, bookshops and cafes, while remaining relatively uncommercial. At its heart London's largest green square, Russell Sq, is looking better than ever with an excellent refit and tidy up a few years ago. It remains a wonderful place for lunch and people-watching.

BRITISH MUSEUM Map pp80-1

☎ 7323 8000, tours 7323 8181; www.thebritish museum.ac.uk; Great Russell St WC1; admission free, £3 donation suggested; ◷ galleries 10am-5.30pm Sat-Wed, to 8.30pm Thu & Fri, Great Court 9am-6pm Sun-Wed, to 11pm Thu-Sat; ✆ Tottenham Court Rd or Russell Sq; &

One of London's most visited attractions (see also p83), this museum draws an average of five million punters each year through its marvellous porticoed main gate on Great Russell St (a few go through the quieter Montague Pl entrance). One of the world's oldest and finest museums, the British Museum started in 1749 in the form of royal physician Hans Sloane's 'cabinet of curiosities' – which he later bequeathed to the country – and carried on expanding its collection (which now numbers some seven million items) through judicious acquisition and the controversial plundering of empire. It's an exhaustive and exhilarating stampede through world cultures, with galleries devoted to Egypt, Western Asia, Greece, the Orient, Africa, Italy, the Etruscans, the Romans, prehistoric and Roman Britain and medieval antiquities.

The museum is huge, so make a few focused visits if you have time, and consider the choice of tours. There are nine free 50-minute eyeOpener tours of individual galleries throughout the day, and 20-minute eyeOpener spotlight talks at 1.15pm focusing on different themes from the collection. Ninety-minute highlights tours (adult/concession £8/5) leave at 10.30am, 1pm and 3pm. If you want to go it alone, audioguide tours (£3.50) are available at the information desk, including a family-oriented one narrated by comedian, writer and TV presenter Stephen Fry. One specific to the Parthenon Sculptures (aka the Parthenon Marbles or Elgin Marbles) is available in that gallery. You could also check out Compass, a multimedia public access system with 50 computer terminals that lets you take a virtual tour of the museum, plan your own circuit or get information on specific exhibits.

The British Museum is planning to build a major new extension in its north-western corner, to be completed in 2012. The new building will have, among other things, a gallery dedicated to special exhibitions and a conservation and science centre.

BRUNSWICK CENTRE Map pp80-1

www.brunswick.co.uk; The Brunswick WC1, ✆ Russell Sq

This now wonderful 1960s complex consists of apartments, restaurants, shops and a cinema. A £24-million project transformed it from a dreary, stern space to a lovely, cream-coloured airy square in 2006, and the centre is now packed with people seven days a week. The original architect, Patrick Hodginson, worked on the renovations and claimed that the centre now looks like what he'd planned in the '60s, but that the design was stunted by the local council. For more, see the website.

DICKENS HOUSE MUSEUM Map pp80-1

☎ 7405 2127; www.dickensmuseum.com; 48 Doughty St WC1; adult/under 16yr/concession £5/3/4; ◷ 10am-5pm Mon-Sat, 11am-5pm Sun; ✆ Russell Sq

The great Victorian novelist lived a nomadic life in the big city, moving around London

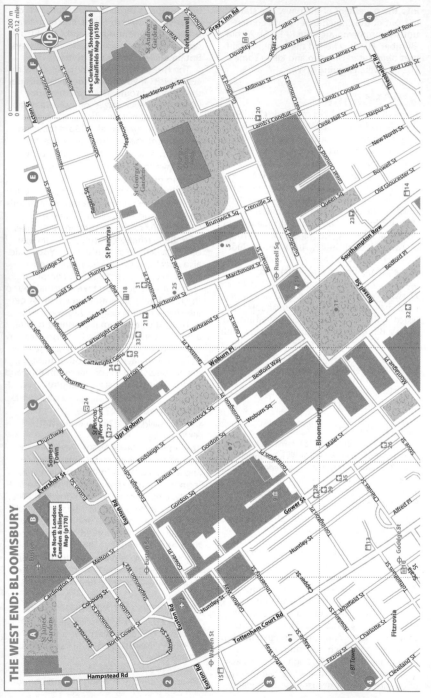

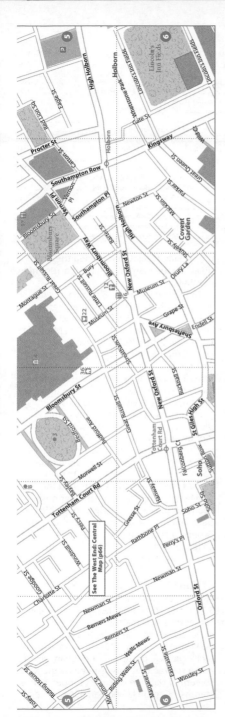

so often that he left behind an unrivalled trail of blue plaques. This handsome four-storey house is his sole surviving residence before he upped and moved to Kent. Not that he stayed here for very long – he lasted a mere 2½ years (1837–39) – but this is where his work really flourished: he dashed off *The Pickwick Papers, Nicholas Nickleby* and *Oliver Twist* despite worry over debts, deaths and his ever-growing family. The house was saved from demolition and the fascinating museum opened in 1925, showcasing the family drawing room (restored to its original condition) and 10 rooms chock-a-block with memorabilia. In the dressing room you can see texts Dickens had prepared for his reading tours, which include funny notes-to-self such as 'slapping the desk'. The said slapped desk is on display, a velvet-topped bureau purpose-made for his public readings.

NEW LONDON ARCHITECTURE
Map pp80-1

☎ 7636 4044; www.newlondonarchitecture.org; Building Centre, 26 Store St WC1; admission free; 9am-6pm Mon-Fri, 10am-5pm Sat, closed Sun; ⊖ Goodge St

An excellent way to see which way London's architectural development is going, this is a frequently changing exhibition that will capture the imagination and interest of anyone who loves London. A large model of the capital highlights the new building areas, showing the extent of the 2012 Olympics plans and various neighbourhood regeneration programs. Photographs and details of individual buildings make it easy to locate each new structure, so that you can either go and see it in real life or spot it as you go along. There is a good architecture bookshop in the basement.

PETRIE MUSEUM OF EGYPTIAN ARCHAEOLOGY Map pp80-1

UCL; ☎ 7679 2884; www.petrie.ucl.ac.uk; University College London, Malet Pl WC1; admission free; 1-5pm Tue-Fri, 11am-2pm Sat; ⊖ Goodge St

If you've got any interest in things Egyptian, you'll love this quiet and oft-overlooked museum, where some 80,000 objects make up one of the most impressive collections of Egyptian and Sudanese archaeology in the world. Behind glass – and amid an atmosphere of academia – are exhibits ranging from fragments of pottery to the

THE WEST END: BLOOMSBURY

world's oldest dress (2800 BC). The museum is named after Professor William Flinders Petrie (1853–1942), who uncovered many of the items during his excavations and donated the collection to the university in 1933. The entrance is through the University's Science Library.

POLLOCK'S TOY MUSEUM Map pp80-1

☎ 7639 3452; www.pollockstoymuseum.com; 1 Scala St W1; adult/child £3/1.50; ☺ 10am-5pm Mon-Sat; ⊖ Goodge St

Aimed at both kids and adults, this museum is simultaneously creepy and mesmerising. You walk in through its shop, laden with excellent wooden toys and various games, and start your exploration by climbing up a rickety narrow staircase, where displays begin with framed dolls from Latin America, Africa, India and Europe. Upstairs is the museum's collection of toy theatres, many made by Benjamin Pollock himself, the leading Victorian manufacturer of the popular sets. Up another set of stairs and you see tin toys and weird-looking dolls in cotton nighties. As you continue on the higgledy-piggledy trail of creaking stairs and floorboards, the dolls follow you with their glazed eyes. After you've climbed three flights of stairs, you'll descend four and, as if by magic, be led back to the shop.

THE SQUARES OF BLOOMSBURY
Map pp80-1 & Map p66

At the very heart of Bloomsbury is Russell Square. Originally laid out in 1800 by Humphrey Repton, it was dark and bushy until

the striking facelift that pruned the trees, tidied up the plants and gave it a 10m-high fountain.

The centre of literary Bloomsbury was Gordon Square where, at various times, Bertrand Russell lived at No 57, Lytton Strachey at No 51 and Vanessa and Clive Bell, Maynard Keynes and the Woolf family at No 46. Strachey, Dora Carrington and Lydia Lopokova (the future wife of Maynard Keynes) all took turns living at No 41. Not all the buildings, many of which now belong to the university, are marked with blue plaques.

Lovely Bedford Square, the only completely Georgian square still surviving in Bloomsbury, was home to many London publishing houses until the 1990s, when they were swallowed up by multinational conglomerates and relocated. They included Jonathan Cape, Chatto and the Bodley Head (set up by Woolf and her husband Leonard), and were largely responsible for perpetuating the legend of the Bloomsbury Group by churning out seemingly endless collections of associated letters, memoirs and biographies.

ST GEORGE'S BLOOMSBURY Map pp80-1

☎ 7405 3044; Bloomsbury Way WC1; ☺ 9.30am-5.30pm Mon-Fri, 10.30am-12.30pm Sun; ⊖ Holborn or Tottenham Court Rd

Superbly restored in 2005, this Nicholas Hawksmoor church (1731) is distinguished by its classical portico of Corinthian capitals and a steeple that was inspired by the Mausoleum of Halicarnassus. It is topped with a statue of George I in Roman dress.

BRITISH MUSEUM HIGHLIGHTS (AND CONTROVERSIES)

The first and most impressive thing you'll see is the museum's Great Court, covered with a spectacular glass-and-steel roof designed by Norman Foster in 2000; it is the largest covered public square in Europe. In its centre is the world-famous Reading Room, formerly the British Library, which has been frequented by all the big brains of history: George Bernard Shaw, Mahatma Gandhi, Oscar Wilde, William Butler Yeats, Karl Marx, Vladimir Lenin, Charles Dickens and Thomas Hardy.

The northern end of the courtyard's lower level houses the terrific new Sainsbury African Galleries, a romp through the art and cultures of historic and contemporary African societies.

Check out the 1820 King's Library, the most stunning neoclassical space in London, which hosts a permanent exhibition 'Enlightenment: Discovering the World in the 18th Century'.

One of the museum's major stars is the Rosetta Stone (room 4), discovered in 1799. It is written in two forms of ancient Egyptian and Greek and was the key to deciphering Egyptian hieroglyphics.

A major star is the Parthenon Sculptures (aka Parthenon Marbles; room 18). The marble works are thought to show the great procession to the temple that took place during the Panathenaic Festival, on the birthday of Athena, one of the grandest events in the Greek world.

They are better known as the Elgin Marbles (after Lord Elgin, the British ambassador who shipped them to England in 1806), though this name is fraught with controversy due to the British Museum's dispute with the Greek government, who want to see the pieces back in Athens. The New Acropolis Museum in Athens was built especially to house the works in 2009, after objections that there was no suitable venue for them to be displayed in Greece. The British Museum has since offered to lend the marbles to Athens for a period of three or four months, as is customary with loaned objects. The Greek government rejected the idea. The majority of voters in a *Guardian* newspaper online survey in June 2009 thought the marbles should go back to Greece – but the final outcome is anyone's guess.

Prepare for a bit of gore in the Mexican Gallery (room 27), at the foot of the eastern staircase. The room features the 15th-century Aztec Mosaic Mask of Tezcatlipoca (The Skull of the Smoking Mirror), which has a turquoise mosaic laid over a human skull.

On a calmer note, rooms 33 and 34 host the Asian collections with the wonderful Amaravati Sculptures (room 33a), Indian goddesses, dancing Shivas and serene cross-legged Buddhas in copper and stone.

The story goes that bandits tried to steal the 7th- to 4th-century BC pieces of Persian gold known as the Oxus Treasure (room 52), which originated in the ancient Persian capital of Persepolis, but the British rescued the impressive collection and brought it to the museum.

The Lindow Man (room 50) is a 1st-century unfortunate who appears to have been smacked on the head with an axe and then garrotted. His remains were preserved in a peat bog until 1984 when a peat-cutting machine sliced him in half.

The old Percival David Foundation of Chinese Art (room 95) is now housed in the museum. With some 1700 pieces, it's the largest collection of Chinese ceramics from the 10th to 18th centuries outside China. Sir Percival David donated it to the University of London in 1950 on the condition that every single piece be displayed at all times, and the collection was moved to the British Museum from its own space nearby in 2009. Among the highlights are the David Vases (1351), the earliest dated and inscribed blue-and-white Chinese porcelain, named after Sir Percival himself.

FITZROVIA

In the years following the war, Fitzrovia – located to the west of Bloomsbury – was a forerunner to Soho as a bohemian enclave populated by struggling artists and writers who frequented its numerous pubs, particularly the Fitzroy Tavern. It's now the home to hundreds of media offices, with tons of bars and restaurants along Charlotte St heaving after office hours. It tends to be a bit of a tourist blind spot due to the fact that its one main sight, the 1960s BT Tower (which was once the highest structure in London), closed many years ago as a result of terrorist threats.

ST JAMES'S

St James's is where the aristocrats are entertained in exclusive gentlemen's clubs (the Army and Navy sort, as opposed to lap-dancing), and whose refined tastes are catered to in the many galleries, historic shops and elegant buildings. Despite much commercial development, its matter-of-fact elitism remains intact, and as you enter the seat of royal London along the grand, processional Mall that sweeps alongside the gorgeous St James's Park, up to Buckingham Palace and the Queen's driveway, you'll see why.

The district took shape when Charles II moved his court to St James's Palace in the

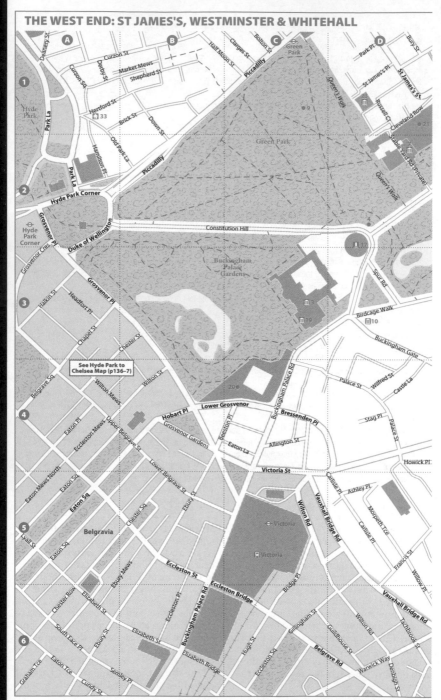

See Hyde Park to
Chelsea Map (p136–7)

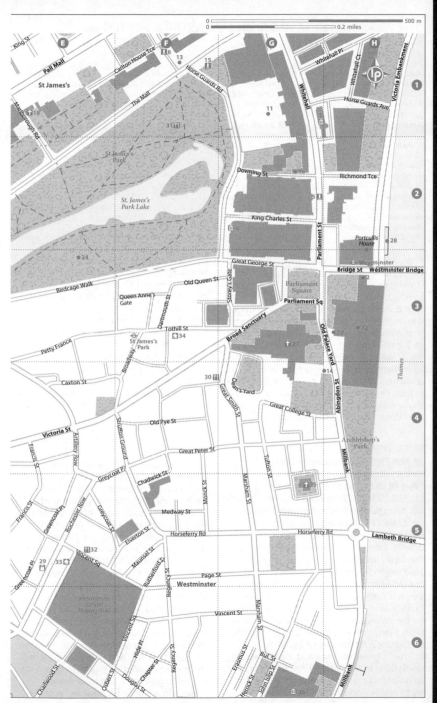

lonelyplanet.com

THE WEST END: ST JAMES'S, WESTMINSTER & WHITEHALL

17th century, and the toffs followed. The great Georgian squares – Berkeley, Hanover and Grosvenor – were built in the next century, by which time St James's was largely filled. By 1900 it was the most fashionable part of London, teeming with theatres, restaurants and boutiques. Savile Row is still where gentlemen go for tailoring, Bond Sts (old and new) are where ladies go for jewellery, and Cork St is where they go together for expensive art. Some residents couldn't keep up with the Joneses of St James's and moved out, to be replaced by businesses, offices and embassies. Grosvenor Sq is dominated by the US embassy.

BUCKINGHAM PALACE Map pp84–5

☎ 7766 7300, for disabled access 7766 7324; www.royalcollection.org.uk; Buckingham Palace Rd SW1; adult/child/concession/family £15.50/8.75/14/39.75; ☼ 9.30am-4.30pm 28 Jul-25 Sep, timed ticket with admission every 15min; ⊖ St James's Park, Victoria or Green Park; ☐
Built in 1705 as Buckingham House for the duke of the same name, this palace has been the royal family's London lodgings since 1837, when St James's Palace was judged too old-fashioned and insufficiently impressive. It is dominated by the 25m-high Queen Victoria Memorial at the end of The Mall. Tickets for the palace are on sale from the Ticket Office (☼ 9.15am to 5pm, summer only) at the Visitor Entrance, Buckingham Palace Rd.

After a series of crises and embarrassing revelations in the early 1990s, the royal spin doctors cranked things up a gear to try to revive popular support, and it was

decided to swing open the doors of Buck House to the public for the first time. Well, to 19 of the 661 rooms, at least. And only during August and September, when HRH is holidaying in Scotland. And for a veritable king's ransom, but still, we mustn't quibble – no price is too great for an opportunity to see the Windsors' polaroids plastered all over the fridge door.

The 'working rooms' are stripped down each summer for the arrival of the commoners, and the usual carpet is replaced with industrial-strength rugs, so the rooms don't look all that lavish. The tour starts in the Guard Room (too small for the Ceremonial Guard, who actual use adjoining quarters); allows a peek inside the State Dining Room (all red damask and Regency furnishings); then moves on to the Blue Drawing Room, with a gorgeous fluted ceiling by John Nash; to the White Drawing Room, where foreign ambassadors are received; and to the Ballroom, where official receptions and state banquets are held. The Throne Room is pretty hilarious with kitschy his-and-hers pink chairs initialled 'ER' and 'P', sitting smugly under what looks like a theatre arch.

The most interesting part of the tour (for all but royal sycophants) is the 76.5m-long Picture Gallery, featuring splendid works by artists such as Van Dyck, Rembrandt, Canaletto, Poussin, Canova and Vermeer, although the likes of these and much more are yours for free at the National Gallery. Wandering the gardens is another highlight here – it's bound to give you a real royal feeling.

Book in advance for disabled access.

CHANGING OF THE GUARD Map pp84-5

☎ 7766 7300; Buckingham Palace, Buckingham Palace Rd SW1; ☺ 11.30am daily Apr-Jul & alternate days, weather permitting Aug-Mar; ⊖ St James's Park or Victoria

This is a London 'must see' – if you actually get to see anything from among the crowds. The old guard (Foot Guards of the Household Regiment) comes off duty to be replaced by the new guard on the forecourt of Buckingham Palace, and tourists gape – sometimes from behind as many as 10 people – at the bright red uniforms and bearskin hats of shouting and marching soldiers for just over half an hour. The official name for the ceremony is Guard Mounting, which, dare we say, sounds more interesting.

QUEEN'S GALLERY Map pp84-5

☎ 7766 7300; www.the-royal-collection.com; southern wing, Buckingham Palace, Buckingham Palace Rd SW1; adult/child/concession £8.50/4.25/7.50; ☺ 10am-5.30pm; ⊖ St James's Park or Victoria; ♿

Paintings, sculpture, ceramics, furniture and jewellery are among the items displayed in the collection of art amassed by the royals over 500 years. The splendid gallery was originally designed by John Nash as a conservatory. It was converted into a chapel for Queen Victoria in 1843, destroyed in a 1940 air raid and reopened as a gallery in 1962. A £20-million renovation for Elizabeth II's Golden Jubilee in 2002 enlarged the entrance and added a Greek Doric portico, a multimedia centre and three times as much display space. Entrance to the gallery is through Buckingham Gate.

ROYAL MEWS Map pp84-5

☎ 7766 7302; www.the-royal-collection.com; Buckingham Palace Rd SW1; adult/child/concession £7.50/4.80/6.75; ☺ 11am-4pm Mar-Jul, 10am-5pm Aug & Sep; ⊖ Victoria; ♿

South of the palace, the Royal Mews started life as a falconry but is now a working stable looking after the royals' immaculately groomed horses, along with the opulent vehicles the monarchy uses for getting from A to B. Highlights include the stunning gold coach of 1762, which has been used for every coronation since that of George III, and the Glass Coach of 1910, used for royal weddings. The Mews is closed in June during the four-day racing carnival of Royal Ascot, when the royal heads try to win some money on the horses.

ST JAMES'S PARK Map pp84-5

☎ 7930 1793; The Mall SW1; ☺ 5am-dusk; ⊖ St James's Park

This is one of the smallest but most gorgeous of London's parks. It has brilliant views of the London Eye, Westminster, St James's Palace, Carlton Terrace and Horse Guards Parade, and the view of Buckingham Palace from the footbridge spanning St James's Park Lake is the best you'll find (get those cameras out). The central lake is full of different types of ducks, geese, swans and general fowl, and its southern side's rocks serve as a rest stop for pelicans (fed at 3pm daily). Some of the technicolour flowerbeds were modelled on John Nash's original 'floriferous' beds of mixed shrubs, flowers and trees, and old-aged squirrel-feeders congregate under the trees daily, with bags of nuts and bread. Spring and summer days see Londoners and tourists alike sunbathing, picnicking and generally enjoying the sunshine, though sometimes in annoyingly large numbers.

Near the popular cafe and restaurant Inn the Park (p242) stands the National Police Memorial, one column of marble and another of glass. Conceived by film director Michael (Death Wish) Winner and designed by architect Norman Foster and artist Per Arnoldi, it pays tribute to 1600 'bobbies' who have lost their lives in the line of duty.

There is also a wonderful allotment in the park, close to the Pall Mall entrance to the park and the Inn the Park restaurant and cafe, open in spring and summer only (May to October); it was initially modelled as a showcase for WWII allotments that flourished in London and the rest of the UK. It grows a number of fruit and veg, has a herb garden and is a lovely place to wander about, especially with children.

ST JAMES'S PALACE Map pp84-5

Cleveland Row SW1; closed to the public; ⊖ Green Park

The striking Tudor gatehouse of St James's Palace, the only surviving part of a building initiated by the palace-mad Henry VIII in 1530, is best approached from St James's St to the north of the park. This was the official residence of kings and queens for more than three centuries. Foreign ambassadors are still formally accredited to the Court of St James, although the tea and biscuits are actually served at Buckingham Palace. Princess Diana, who hated this place, lived here until her divorce from Charles in 1996, when she moved to Kensington Palace. Prince Charles and his sons stayed on at St James's until 2004, before decamping next door to Clarence House, leaving St James's Palace to a brace of minor royals including Charles's famously tetchy sister, Princess Anne. Don't get too close in case she sends out a footman to tell you to naff off.

CLARENCE HOUSE Map pp84-5

☎ 7766 7303, for disabled access 7766 7324; Cleveland Row SW1; guided tour adult/concession £7.50/4; ☺ 9.30am-5pm Aug-Oct; ☻ Green Park; &

After his beloved granny the Queen Mum died in 2002, Prince Charles got the tradesmen into her former home and spent £4.6 million of taxpayers' money reshaping Clarence House to his own design. The 'royal residences are held in trust for future generations', but the current generation has to pay to have a look at five official rooms when the Prince, his sons and Camilla are away on their summer hols. The highlight is the late Queen Mother's small art collection, including one painting by playwright Noël Coward and others by WS Sickert and Sir James Gunn. Admission is by tour only, which must be booked (far in advance); book also for disabled access. The house was originally designed by John Nash in the early 19th century, but – as Prince Charles wasn't the first royal to call in the redecorators – has been modified much since.

SPENCER HOUSE Map pp84-5

☎ 7499 8620; www.spencerhouse.co.uk; 27 St James's Pl SW1; admission & tour adult/concession £9/7; ☺ 10.30am-5.45pm Sun, last entry 4.45pm, closed Jan & Aug; ☻ Green Park; &

Just outside the park, Spencer House was built in the Palladian style between 1756 and 1766, for the first Earl Spencer, an ancestor of Princess Diana. The Spencers moved out in 1927 and their grand family home was used as an office, until Lord Rothschild stepped in and returned it to its former glory in 1987 with an £18-million restoration. Visits to the eight lavishly furnished rooms of the house are by guided tour only.

The gardens, returned to their 18th-century design, are open only between 2pm and 5pm on a couple of Sundays in summer. They were closed completely during 2009, so check the website for prices from 2010 onwards.

QUEEN'S CHAPEL Map pp84-5

Marlborough Rd SW1; ☺ services only, 8.30am & 11.15am Sun Apr-Jul; ☻ St James's Park

The royal sights generally don't leave people breathless, but this one may touch your heartstrings: it's where all the contemporary royals from Princess Diana to the Queen Mother have lain in their coffins in the run-up to their funerals. The church was originally built by Inigo Jones in the Palladian style and was the first post-Reformation church in England built for Roman Catholic worship. It was once part of St James's Palace but was separated after a fire. The simple interior has exquisite 17th-century fittings and is atmospherically illuminated by light streaming in through the large windows above the altar.

GREEN PARK Map pp84-5

Piccadilly W1; ☺ 5am-dusk; ☻ Green Park

Less manicured than the adjoining St James's, this park has wonderful huge oaks and hilly meadows, and it's never as crowded as St James's. It was once a duelling ground and served as a vegetable garden during WWII.

GUARDS MUSEUM Map pp84-5

☎ 7976 0850; www.theguardsmuseum.com; Wellington Barracks, Birdcage Walk SW1; adult/child/concession £3/free/2; ☺ 10am-4pm Feb-Dec, last entry 3.30pm; ☻ St James's Park; &

If you found the crowds at the Changing of the Guards tiresome and didn't see a thing, get here for 10.50am on any day from April to August to see the guards getting into formation outside the museum, for their march up to Buckingham Palace. In addition, check out the history of the five regiments of foot guards and their role in military campaigns from Waterloo on, in this little museum established in the 17th century during the reign of Charles II. There are uniforms, oil paintings, medals, curios and memorabilia that belonged to the soldiers. Perhaps the biggest draw here is the huge collection of toy soldiers in the shop.

INSTITUTE OF CONTEMPORARY ARTS Map pp84-5

ICA; ☎ 7930 3647; www.ica.org.uk; The Mall SW1; admission free, exhibition admission prices vary; ☽ noon-10.30pm Mon, to 2am Tue-Sat, to 11pm Sun; ⊖ Charing Cross or Piccadilly Circus; ♿

Housed in a traditional building along The Mall, the ICA (as it's locally known) is as untraditional as you can possibly get. This was where Picasso and Henry Moore had their first UK shows, and ever since then the institute has sat comfortably on the cutting and controversial edge of the British arts world, with an excellent range of experimental/progressive/radical/obscure films, music and club nights, photography, art, theatre, lectures, multimedia works and book readings. Sure, you may see an exhibition here and come out none the wiser – we often do – and the place has been known to award a £26,000 prestigious sculpture prize for what was essentially a wonky shed, but the institute's program is generally fantastic. Plus there's the licensed ICA Bar & Restaurant (☽ noon-1am Tue-Sat, noon-11pm Mon, noon-10.30pm Sun). The complex also includes an excellent bookshop, gallery, cinema and theatre.

The Duke of York Column, up the steps beside the ICA into Waterloo Pl, commemorates a son of George III. It was erected in 1834, but never quite caught the public imagination like Nelson's Column in Trafalgar Sq, although it's only 6m shorter.

MAYFAIR

London has many well-heeled neighbourhoods but none is so frightfully Jimmy Chooed up as this. Just wander up Old Bond St and you'll understand that this is a path walked by those with blue blood, old money and designer shoes. It's fascinating to witness the unabated flow of wealth and power stretching between Mayfair (the highest step on London's property ladder) and Chelsea.

Mayfair is west of Regent St and is where high society gives high-fives to one another; defining features are silver spoons and old-fashioned razzamatazz. But in its southwestern corner, nudging Hyde Park, Shepherd Market is near the site of a rowdy and debauched fair that gave the area its name. The fair was banned in 1730 and today 'the old village centre of Mayfair' is a tiny enclave of pubs and bistros.

HANDEL HOUSE MUSEUM Map p90

☎ 7495 1685; www.handelhouse.org; 25 Brook St W1; adult/child/concession £5/2/4.50; ☽ 10am-6pm Tue-Sat, to 8pm Thu, noon-6pm Sun; ⊖ Bond St; ♿

George Frederick Handel lived in this 18th-century Mayfair building for 36 years until his death in 1759, and the house opened as a museum in late 2001. It has been restored to how it would have looked when the great German-born composer was in residence, complete with artworks borrowed from several museums. Exhibits include early editions of Handel's operas and oratorios, although being in the hallowed space where he composed and first rehearsed pieces such as *Water Music, Messiah, Zadok the Priest* and *Fireworks Music* is ample attraction for any enthusiast. The museum celebrated the 250th anniversary of Handel's death with numerous events. Entrance to the museum is on Lancashire Ct.

Funnily enough, the house at No 23 (now part of the museum) was home to a musician as different from Handel as could be imagined: American guitarist Jimi Hendrix (1942–69) lived there from 1968 until his death.

WESTMINSTER

WESTMINSTER ABBEY Map pp84-5

☎ 7222 5152; www.westminster-abbey.org; Dean's Yard SW1; adult/under 11yr/11-17yr/concession £15/free/6/12; ☽ 9.30am-3.45pm Mon-Fri, to 6pm Wed, to 1.45pm Sat, last entry 1hr before closing; ⊖ Westminster; ♿

Westminster Abbey is such an important commemoration site for both the British royalty and the nation's political and artistic idols, it's difficult to overstress its symbolic value or imagine its equivalent anywhere else in the world. With the exception of Edward V and Edward VIII, every English sovereign has been crowned here since William the Conqueror in 1066, and most of the monarchs from Henry III (died 1272) to George II (died 1760) were also buried here.

There is an extraordinary amount to see here but, unless you enjoy feeling like part of a herd, come very early or very late.

The abbey is a magnificent sight. Though a mixture of architectural styles, it is considered the finest example of Early English Gothic (1180–1280). The original church was built in the 11th century by King (later St) Edward the Confessor, who

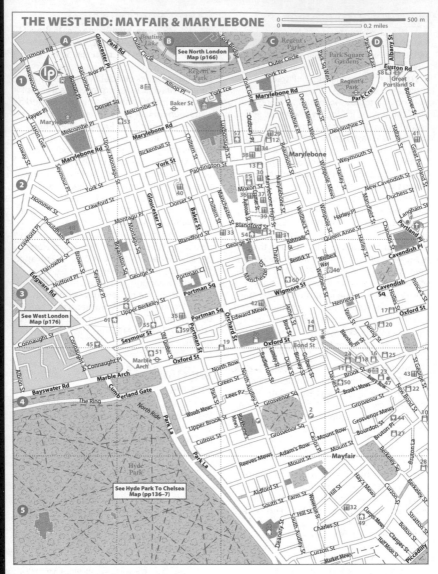

THE WEST END: MAYFAIR & MARYLEBONE

is buried in the chapel behind the main altar. Henry III (r 1216–72) began work on the new building but didn't complete it; the French Gothic nave was finished in 1388. Henry VII's huge and magnificent chapel was added in 1519. Unlike St Paul's, Westminster Abbey has never been a cathedral – it is what is called a 'royal peculiar' and is administered directly by the Crown.

It is perhaps more impressive from outside than within. The interior is chock-a-block with small chapels, elaborate tombs of the monarchy, and monuments to various luminaries down through the ages. And, as you might expect for one of the most visited churches in Christendom, it can get intolerably busy.

Immediately past the barrier through the north door is what's known as Statesmen's

THE WEST END: MAYFAIR & MARYLEBONE

Aisle, where politicians and eminent public figures are commemorated mostly by staggeringly large marble statues. The Whig and Tory prime ministers who dominated late Victorian politics, Gladstone (who is buried here) and Disraeli (who is not), have their monuments uncomfortably close to one another. Nearby is a monument to Robert Peel, who, as home secretary in 1829, created the Metropolitan Police. Robert's policemen became known as 'Bobby's boys' and later, simply, 'bobbies'.

At the eastern end of the sanctuary, opposite the entrance to the Henry VII Chapel, is the rather ordinary-looking Coronation Chair, upon which almost every monarch since the late 13th century is said to have been crowned. Up the steps in front of you and to your left is the narrow Queen Elizabeth Chapel, where Elizabeth I and her half-sister 'Bloody Mary' share an elaborate tomb.

The Henry VII Chapel, in the easternmost part of the abbey, has spectacular circular vaulting on the ceiling. Behind the chapel's altar is the elaborate sarcophagus of Henry VII and his queen, Elizabeth of York.

Beyond the chapel's altar is the Royal Air Force (RAF) Chapel, with a stained-glass window commemorating the force's finest hour, the Battle of Britain. Next to it, a plaque marks the spot where Oliver Cromwell's body lay for two years until the Restoration, when it was disinterred, hanged and beheaded. The bodies believed to be those of the two child princes (allegedly) murdered in the Tower of London in 1483 are buried here. The chapel's southern aisle contains the tomb of Mary Queen of Scots, beheaded on the orders of her cousin Elizabeth and with the acquiescence of her son, the future James I.

The Chapel of St Edward the Confessor, the most sacred spot in the abbey, lies just east of the sanctuary and behind the high altar; access may be restricted to protect the 13th-century floor. St Edward was the founder of the abbey and the original building was consecrated a few weeks before his death. His tomb was slightly altered after the original was destroyed during the Reformation.

The south transept contains Poets' Corner, where many of England's finest writers are buried and/or commemorated; a memorial here is the highest honour the Queen can bestow. Just north is the Lantern, the heart of the abbey, where coronations take place. If you face eastwards while standing in the centre, the sanctuary is in front of you. George Gilbert Scott designed the ornate high altar in 1897. Behind you, Edward Blore's chancel, dating from the mid-19th century, is a breathtaking structure of gold, blue and red Victorian Gothic. Where monks once worshipped, boys from the

Choir School and lay vicars now sing the daily services.

The entrance to the Cloister is 13th century, while the cloister itself dates from the 14th. Eastwards down a passageway off the Cloister are three museums run by English Heritage. The octagonal Chapter House (9.30am-5pm Apr-Sep, 10am-5pm Oct, 10am-4pm Nov-Mar) has one of Europe's best-preserved medieval tile floors and retains traces of religious murals. It was used as a meeting place by the House of Commons in the second half of the 14th century. To the right of the entrance to Chapel House is what is claimed to be the oldest door in the UK – it's been there 950 years. The adjacent Pyx Chamber (10am-4.30pm) is one of the few remaining relics of the original abbey and contains the abbey's treasures and liturgical objects. The Abbey Museum (10.30am-4pm) exhibits the death masks of generations of royalty, wax effigies representing Charles II and William III (who is on a stool to make him as tall as his wife Mary), as well as armour and stained glass.

To reach the 900-year-old College Garden (10am-6pm Tue-Thu Apr-Sep, to 4pm Tue-Thu Oct-Mar), enter Dean's Yard and the Little Cloisters off Great College St.

On the western side of the cloister is Scientists' Corner, where you will find Sir Isaac Newton's tomb; a nearby section of the northern aisle of the nave is known as Musicians' Aisle.

The two towers above the west door are the ones through which you exit. These were designed by Nicholas Hawksmoor and completed in 1745. Just above the door, perched in 15th-century niches, are the latest sacred additions to the abbey: 10 stone statues of international 20th-century martyrs. These were unveiled in 1998 and they include the likes of Martin Luther King and the Polish priest St Maximilian Kolbe, who was murdered by the Nazis at Auschwitz.

To the right as you exit is a memorial to innocent victims of oppression, violence and war around the world. 'All you who pass by, is it nothing to you?' it asks poignantly.

The 90-minute guided tours (7222 7110; tours £3) leave several times during the day (Monday to Saturday). One of the best ways to visit the abbey is to attend a service, particularly evensong (5pm weekdays, 3pm at weekends). Sunday Eucharist is at 11am.

HOUSES OF PARLIAMENT Map pp84-5

7219 4272; www.parliament.uk; St Stephen's Entrance, St Margaret St SW1; admission free; during Parliamentary sessions 2.30-10.30pm Mon, 11.30am-7pm Tue & Wed, 11.30am-6.30pm Thu, 9.30am-3pm Fri; Westminster;

The House of Commons and House of Lords are housed here in the sumptuous Palace of Westminster. Charles Barry, assisted by interior designer Augustus Pugin, built it between 1840 and 1860, when the extravagant neo-Gothic style was all the rage. The most famous feature outside the palace is the Clock Tower, commonly known as Big Ben. Ben is the bell hanging inside and is named after Benjamin Hall, the commissioner of works when the tower was completed in 1858. If you're very keen (and a UK resident) you can apply in writing for a free tour of the Clock Tower (see the website). Thirteen-tonne Ben has rung in the New Year since 1924, and the clock gets its hands and face washed by abseiling cleaners once every five years. The best view of the whole complex is from the eastern side of Lambeth Bridge. At the opposite end of the building is Victoria Tower, completed in 1860.

The House of Commons is where Members of Parliament (MPs) meet to propose and discuss new legislation, and to grill the prime minister and other ministers. The huge expenses scandal of 2009 has made those very MPs (or at least those remaining in parliament) more famous than they had ever hoped to be – for all the wrong reasons. The best time to watch a debate is during Prime Minister's Question Time, for which you will have to book advance tickets through your MP or local British embassy.

The layout of the Commons Chamber is based on that of St Stephen's Chapel in the original Palace of Westminster. The current chamber, designed by Giles Gilbert Scott, replaced the earlier one destroyed by a 1941 bomb. Although the Commons is a national assembly of 646 MPs, the chamber has seating for only 437. Government members sit to the right of the Speaker and Opposition members to the left. The Speaker presides over business from a chair given by Australia, while ministers speak from a despatch box donated by New Zealand.

When Parliament is in session, visitors are admitted to the House of Commons Visitors' Gallery via St Stephen's Entrance. Expect to queue for an hour or two if you haven't already organised a ticket. Parliamentary recesses last for three months over the summer and a couple of weeks over Easter and Christmas, so it's best to ring in advance. To find out what's being debated on a particular day, check the notice board beside the entrance, or look in the *Daily Telegraph* or the freebie *Metro* newspaper under 'Today in Parliament', though it has to be said that the debates leave a lot to be desired both in terms of attendance and enthusiasm. Bags and cameras must be checked at a cloakroom before you enter the gallery and no large suitcases or backpacks are allowed through the airport-style security gate.

After campaign group 'Fathers 4 Justice' lobbed a condom full of purple powder at Tony Blair in May 2004 and prohunt campaigners broke into the Commons that September, security was further tightened, and a bulletproof screen now sits between members of the public and the debating chamber.

As you're waiting for your bags to go through the X-ray machines, look left at the stunning roof of Westminster Hall, originally built in 1099 and today the oldest surviving part of the Palace of Westminster, the seat of the English monarchy from the 11th to the early 16th centuries. Added between 1394 and 1401, it is the earliest known example of a hammer-beam roof and has been described as 'the greatest surviving achievement of medieval English carpentry'. Westminster Hall was used for coronation banquets in medieval times, and also served as a courthouse until the 19th century. The trials of William Wallace (1305), Thomas More (1535), Guy Fawkes (1606) and Charles I (1649) all took place here. In the 20th century, monarchs and Winston Churchill lay in state here.

The House of Lords Visitors' Gallery (☎ 7219 3107; admission free; ☼ 2.30-10pm Mon-Wed, 11am-1.30pm & 3-7.30pm Thu, 11am-3pm Fri) is also open for visits. Against a backdrop of peers' gentle snoring, you can view the intricate Gothic interior that led poor Pugin (1812–52) to an early death from overwork and nervous strain.

When Parliament is in recess, there are 75-minute guided summer tours (☎ 0870 906 3773; St Stephen's Entrance, St Margaret St; adult/child/concession £12/5/8) of both chambers and other historic buildings. Times change, so telephone or check www.parliament.uk for latest details.

TATE BRITAIN Map pp84-5
☎ 7887 8000, 7887 8888; www.tate.org.uk; Millbank SW1; admission free, prices vary for temporary exhibitions; ☼ 10am-5.50pm; ⊖ Pimlico; ☖
You'd think that Tate Britain might have suffered since its lavish, sexy sibling, Tate Modern (p128), took half its collection and all of the limelight upriver when it opened in 2000, but on the contrary, things have worked out perfectly for both galleries. The venerable Tate Britain, built in 1897, stretched out splendidly to fill the increased space with its definitive collection of British art from the 16th to the late 20th centuries, while the Modern sister devoted its space to, well, modern art.

The permanent galleries are broadly chronological in order, and you can expect to see some of the most important works by artists such as Constable and Gainsborough – who have entire galleries devoted to them – and Hogarth, Reynolds, Stubbs, Blake and Henry Moore, among others. Adjoining the main building is the Clore Gallery, which houses the superb JMW Turner, including the two recovered classics *Shade and Darkness* and *Light and Colour*, which were nicked in 1994 and found nine years later.

Just as you are thinking that all the moderns and contemporaries were up at the Modern, Tate Britain's got work by Lucian Freud, Francis Bacon, David Hockney and Howard Hodgkin, as well as Anthony Gormley and bad-girl Tracey Emin. Tate Britain also hosts the prestigious and often controversial Turner Prize for contemporary art from October to early December every year.

There are several free one-hour thematic tours each day, mostly on the hour (last tour at 3pm), along with free 15-minute talks on paintings, painters and styles at 1.15pm Tuesday to Thursday in the Rotunda. Audioguide tours (adult/concession £3.50/3) for the collection are available. A good time to visit the gallery is Late at Tate night, on the first Friday of every month, when the gallery stays open until 10pm. The best way to see both Tates and have a fabulous art day is to catch the boat that connects the two galleries; see p128.

HORSE GUARDS PARADE Map pp84–5

☎ 0906 866 3344; ◷ Changing of the Guard 11am Mon-Sat, 10am Sun; ⊖ Westminster

In a more accessible version of Buckingham Palace's Changing of the Guard, the mounted troopers of the Household Cavalry change guard here daily, at the official entrance to the royal palaces (opposite the Banqueting House). A lite-pomp version takes place at 4pm when the dismounted guards are changed. On the Queen's official birthday in June, the Trooping of the Colour is also staged here.

Fittingly, as the parade ground and its buildings were built in 1745 to house the Queen's so-called 'Life Guards', this will be the pitch for the beach volleyball during the London 2012 Olympics (see www .london2012.org).

ST JOHN'S, SMITH SQUARE Map pp84–5

☎ 7222 1061; www.sjss.org.uk; Smith Sq, Westminster SW1; ⊖ Westminster or St James's Park

In the heart of Westminster, this eye-catching church was built by Thomas Archer in 1728 under the Fifty New Churches Act (1711), which aimed to build 50 new churches for London's rapidly growing metropolitan area. Though they never did build all 50 churches, St John's, along with a dozen others, saw the light of day. Unfortunately, with its four corner towers and monumental facades, the structure was much maligned for the first century of its existence thanks to rumours that Queen Anne likened it to a footstool, though it's also said that she actually requested a church built in the shape of a footstool. Whatever the case, it's generally agreed now that the church is a masterpiece of English baroque, although it no longer serves as a church. After receiving a direct hit during WWII, it was rebuilt in the 1960s as a classical music venue (p308), and is renowned for its crisp acoustics.

The brick-vaulted restaurant in the crypt is called, predictably, the Footstool, and is open for lunch Monday to Friday, as well as for pre- and postconcert dinner.

WHITEHALL

Whitehall and its extension, Parliament St, is the wide avenue that links Trafalgar and Parliament Sqs, and it is lined with many government buildings, statues, monuments and other historical bits and pieces.

CHURCHILL MUSEUM & CABINET WAR ROOMS Map pp84–5

☎ 7930 6961; www.iwm.org.uk; Clive Steps, King Charles St SW1; adult/under 16yr/senior & student £13/free/10.40; ◷ 9.30am-6pm, last admission 5pm; ⊖ Charing Cross or Westminster; ♿

Down in the bunker where Prime Minister Winston Churchill, his cabinet and generals met during WWII, £6 million has been spent on a huge exhibition devoted to 'the greatest Briton'. This whizz-bang multimedia Churchill Museum joins the highly evocative Cabinet War Rooms, where chiefs of staff slept, ate and plotted Hitler's downfall, blissfully believing they were protected from Luftwaffe bombs by the 3m slab of concrete overhead. (Turns out it would have crumpled like paper had the area taken a hit.) Together, these two sections make you forget the Churchill who was a maverick and lousy peacetime politician, and drive home how much the cigar-chewing, wartime PM was a case of right man, right time.

The Churchill Museum contains all sorts of posters, trivia and personal effects, from the man's cigars to a 'British bulldog' vase in his image, and from his formal Privy Council uniform to his shockingly tasteless red velvet 'romper' outfit. Even though the museum doesn't shy away from its hero's fallibilities, it does begin with his strongest suit – his stirring speeches, replayed for each goosebumped visitor who steps in front of the screen. 'I have nothing to offer but blood, toil, tears and sweat', 'We will fight them on the beaches', 'Never in the course of human history has so much been owed by so many to so few'. Elsewhere, silver-tongued Winnie even gets credit for inspiring Orson Welles' famous rant about Switzerland and cuckoo clocks, with a speech he made to Parliament several years before The Third Man was filmed.

There's fantastically edited footage of Churchill's 1965 state funeral, making the April 2005 burial of Pope John Paul II look like a low-key family affair, and you can check on what the PM was doing nearly every day beforehand via the huge tabletop interactive lifeline. Touch on a particular year on the screen and it will open up into months and days for you to choose.

In stark contrast, the old Cabinet War Rooms have been left much as they were when the lights were turned off on VJ Day in August 1945 and everyone headed off for a well-earned drink. The room where the Cabinet held more than 100 meetings, the Telegraph Room with a hotline to Roosevelt, the cramped typing pool, the converted broom cupboard that was Churchill's office and scores of bedrooms have all been preserved.

You will pass the broadcast niche where Churchill made four of his rousing speeches to the nation, including one about Germany fuelling 'a fire in British hearts' by launching the London Blitz. In the Chief of Staff's Conference Room, the walls are covered with huge, original maps that were only discovered in 2002. If you squint two-thirds of the way down the right wall, somebody (Churchill himself?) drew a little doodle depicting a cross-eyed and bandy-legged Hitler knocked on his arse.

The free audioguide is very informative and entertaining and features plenty of anecdotes, including some from people who worked here in the nerve centre of Britain's war effort – and weren't even allowed by their irritable boss to relieve the tension by whistling.

BANQUETING HOUSE Map pp84-5
☎ 0870 751 5178; www.hrp.org.uk; Whitehall SW1; adult/under 16yr/concession £4.80/free/4; 🕑 10am-5pm Mon-Sat; ⊖ Westminster or Charing Cross; 🚻

This is the only surviving part of the Tudor Whitehall Palace, which once stretched most of the way down Whitehall and burned down in 1698. It was designed as England's first purely Renaissance building by Inigo Jones after he returned from Italy, and looked like no other structure in the country at the time. Apparently, the English hated it for more than a century.

A bust outside commemorates 30 January 1649 when Charles I, accused of treason by Cromwell after the Civil War, was executed on a scaffold built against a 1st-floor window here. When the monarchy was reinstated with Charles II, it inevitably became something of a royalist shrine. In a huge, virtually unfurnished hall on the 1st floor there are nine ceiling panels painted by Rubens in 1635. They were commissioned by Charles I and depict the 'divine right' of kings.

It is still occasionally used for state banquets and concerts, but fortunately you don't have to be on the royal A-list to visit, though if the house is rented for an event it will be closed to the public, so phone in advance to check.

Book in advance for disabled access.

CENOTAPH Map pp84-5
Whitehall SW1; ⊖ Westminster or Charing Cross
The Cenotaph (Greek for 'empty tomb'), built in 1920 by Edwin Lutyens, is Britain's main memorial to the British and Commonwealth victims who were killed during the two world wars. The Queen and other public figures lay poppies at its base on the second Sunday in November (Remembrance Sunday).

NO 10 DOWNING STREET Map pp84-5
www.number10.gov.uk; 10 Downing St SW1; ⊖ Westminster or Charing Cross
This has been the official office of British leaders since 1732, when George II presented No 10 to Robert Walpole, and since refurbishment in 1902 it's also been the PM's official London residence. As Margaret Thatcher, a grocer's daughter, famously put it, the PM 'lives above the shop' here.

For such a famous address, however, No 10 is a small-looking building on a plain-looking street, hardly warranting comparison to the White House, for example. A stoic bobby stands guard outside, but you can't get too close; the street was cordoned off with a rather large iron gate during Margaret Thatcher's times.

Breaking with tradition when he came to power, Tony Blair and his family swapped houses with the then-unmarried Chancellor, who traditionally occupied the rather larger flat at No 11. His successor, Gordon Brown, went back to traditional ways and moved into No 10.

MARYLEBONE

MADAME TUSSAUDS Map p90
☎ 0870 400 3000; www.madame-tussauds.com; Marylebone Rd NW1; adult/under 16yr £25/21; 🕑 9.30am-5.30pm Mon-Fri, 9am-6pm Sat & Sun; ⊖ Baker St; 🚻

What can one say about Madame Tussauds? It's unbelievably kitsch and terribly overpriced, yet it draws more than three million people every year and sits high on the 'must-do' list of any visitor to London. Different strokes for different folks, as they say, but if you like the idea of wax celebrities, movie stars and fantastically lifelike figures of the Windsors, you're in for a treat.

Madame Tussauds dates back more than two centuries when the eponymous Swiss model-maker started making death masks of the people killed during the French Revolution. She came to London in 1803 and exhibited around 30 wax models in Baker St, on a site not far from this building, which has housed the waxworks since 1885. The models were an enormous hit in Victorian times, when they provided visitors with their only glimpse of the famous and infamous before photography was widespread and long before the advent of TV.

Madame Tussauds is very keen on public surveys telling it who the punters would like to see most, resulting in such highlights as a photo op with the Kate Moss figure (a poor likeness), an eco Prince Charles statue, the Blush Room where A-listers stand listlessly and where the J-Lo figure blushes if you whisper in her ear. Bollywood fans are treated with a smiling Shahrukh Khan and 'Big Bruvva' lovers can get into the Diary Room and take the video home. The latest addition to the collection is of London Mayor Boris Johnson, smiling cheekily at the visitors, and the website features a YouTube video of the live Boris Johnson next to his waxen doppelganger, telling a bunch of journalists that Madame Tussauds is 'one of those London attractions that will pull this city out of the recession'. All for a good cause, then.

Permanent photo opportunities include the political leaders in World Stage and the array of celebrities in Premiere Room. The famous Chamber of Horrors details the gory exploits of Jack the Ripper and is usually a huge hit with children. Finally you can take a ride in the Spirit of London 'time taxi', where you sit in a mock-up of a London black cab and are whipped through a five-minute historical summary of London, a mercifully short time to endure the god-awful scripts and hackneyed commentary. The old Planetarium is now the Stardome, which screens an entertaining and educational animation by Nick Park, creator of *Wallace and Gromit* (it involves aliens and celebrities).

In case you were wondering what happens to the models of those people whose 15 minutes have passed, contrary to popular belief, they are never melted down, but simply rest in storage.

If you want to avoid the queues (particularly in summer) book your tickets online and get a timed entry slot. They are cheaper this way too.

WALLACE COLLECTION Map p90

☎ 7563 9500; www.wallacecollection.org; Hertford House, Manchester Sq W1; admission free; ☽ 10am-5pm; ⊖ Bond St; ♿

Arguably London's finest small gallery (relatively unknown even to Londoners), the Wallace Collection is an enthralling glimpse into 18th-century aristocratic life. The sumptuously restored Italianate mansion houses a treasure-trove of 17th- and 18th-century paintings, porcelain, artefacts and furniture collected by generations of the same family and bequeathed to the nation by the widow of Sir Richard Wallace (1818–90) on condition it should always be on display in the centre of London.

Among the many highlights here – besides the warm and friendly staff – are paintings by Rembrandt, Hals, Delacroix, Titian, Rubens, Poussin, Van Dyck, Velàzquez, Reynolds and Gainsborough in the stunning Great Gallery. There's a spectacular array of medieval and Renaissance armour (including some to try on), a Minton-tiled smoking room, stunning chandeliers and a sweeping staircase that is reckoned to be one of the best examples of French interior architecture (including in France) in existence. There are also temporary exhibitions (admission payable) and very popular themed events involving Marie Antoinette and other French aristocrats, costumes and ballroom dancing (check the website for what's on when you're here).

Have lunch at the excellent glass-roofed restaurant, Café Bagatelle – which occupies the central courtyard and feels like something in southern Spain – and you'll have spent one of the most outstanding days in London.

SHERLOCK HOLMES MUSEUM Map p90

☎ 7935 8866; www.sherlock-holmes.co.uk; 221b Baker St; adult/child £6/4; ☽ 9.30am-6pm; ⊖ Baker St

Though the museum gives its address as 221b Baker St, the actual fictional abode of Sherlock Holmes is the Abbey National building a bit further south. Fans of the books will enjoy examining the three floors of reconstructed Victoriana, deerstalkers, burning candles and flickering grates, but may baulk at the dodgy waxworks of

Professor Moriarty and 'the Man with the Twisted Lip'. The only disappointment is the lack of material and information on Arthur Conan Doyle.

BROADCASTING HOUSE Map p90

☎ 0870 603 0304; www.bbc.co.uk; Portland Pl;
☽ shop 9.30am-6pm Mon-Sat, 10am-5.30pm Sun;
⊖ Oxford Circus

This is the iconic building from which the BBC began radio broadcasting in 1932, and from where much of its radio output still comes. There's a shop stocking any number of products relating to BBC programs, even though the majority of the Beeb's output is produced in the corporation's glassy complex in Shepherd's Bush (hop on the website if you want to get tickets to a recording). The vast extension that was under construction at the time of writing is intended to be the new location of the World Service.

ALL SOULS CHURCH Map p90

☎ 7580 3522; www.allsouls.org; Langham Pl W1;
☽ 9am-6pm, closed Sat; ⊖ Oxford Circus

A Nash solution for the curving, northern sweep of Regent St was this delightful church, which features a circular columned porch and distinctive needlelike spire, reminiscent of an ancient Greek temple. Built from Bath stone, the church was very unpopular when completed in 1824 – a contemporary cartoon by George Cruikshank shows Nash rather painfully impaled on the spire through the bottom with the words 'Nashional Taste!!!' below it. It was bombed during the Blitz and renovated in 1951, and is now one of the most distinctive churches in central London.

THE WEST END WALK
Walking Tour

1 Covent Garden Piazza Yes it's touristy, but it's worth seeing this wonderful Inigo Jones Piazza (p75) and some of the street performers who make a living buffooning around in front of St Paul's Church.

2 Chinatown Avoid Leicester Sq and walk down Lisle St under the ersatz Oriental gates of Chinatown (p63). Breathe in the aromatic spices, pick one of the restaurants – try Jen Café (p239) or Baozi Inn (p239) for some delicious Chinese food.

3 Shaftesbury Ave This is theatreland and some of the West End's most prestigious theatres are on Shaftesbury Ave. Hollywood stars such as Juliette Lewis, Jessica Lange and Christian Slater have performed here, along with London's own Daniel Radcliffe.

4 Piccadilly Circus Hectic and traffic-choked, but still lovely, Piccadilly Circus (p67) is like London's Times Sq, full of flashing ads, tons of shops and tourists.

5 Piccadilly An elegant stretch away from the Circus, Piccadilly gives a whiff of the nearby aristocratic St James's and Mayfair. Pop into St James's Piccadilly (p68), the only church Sir Christopher built from scratch. Check out the market stalls selling crafts and antiques outside, and sit down for a coffee while the pigeons fight for the breadcrumbs left behind. Or you could visit Minamoto Kitchoan (p220) Japanese sweet shop for a green tea and some sweeties.

Free art and exhibitions with entry fees abound at the brilliant Royal Academy of Arts (p68), where the courtyard installations can often be quite bizarre.

6 Green Park Walk past the Ritz and turn left into Green Park (p88), a quiet green space with some stunning oak trees and olde-worlde street lamps.

7 Buckingham Palace Admire the Queen's abode (p86), though if you're keen on seeing some of the rooms (public access summer only), you're better off buying a ticket in advance. Walk down the grandiose Mall, where processions often take place and the Queen's limousine is escorted by her guards.

8 St James's Park One of London's smaller but definitely one of its most beautiful parks, St James's (p87) is wonderful in summer and winter. Feed the ducks, squirrels or swans, and take a look at the pelicans. Have a break in the stylish wooden Inn the Park (p242), where you can have some modern British food too. It's one of the more atmospheric places for dinner.

9 Institute of Contemporary Arts Pop into the edgy ICA (p89) and have a look at whatever exhibition is taking place – you'll come out feeling something, good or bad.

10 Trafalgar Square Another tourist magnet, but worth it all the way, Trafalgar Square (p69)

THE WEST END WALK

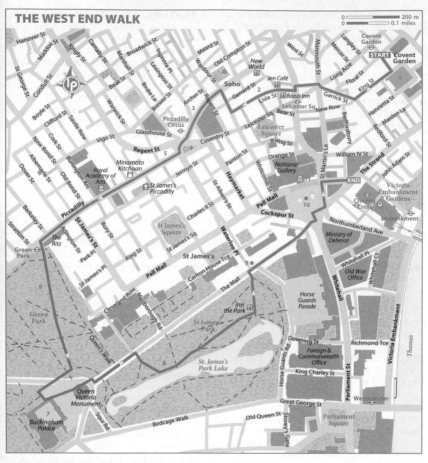

0 ————— 200 m
0 ————— 0.1 miles

WALK FACTS

Start Covent Garden tube station
End Trafalgar Sq (Charing Cross tube station)
Distance 2.5 miles
Duration One hour 15 minutes
Fuel stops Jen Café (p239), Baozi Inn (p239), Inn the
Park (p242), National Dining Rooms (p74)

is a magnificent beauty of a square. Check out
the views of Big Ben from its southern side.

11 The National Gallery Take a few hours
to admire the artwork at the National Gallery (p73).
Sit down for a well-deserved lunch or dinner in the new and stylish National Dining
Rooms, where you can enjoy British cuisine
in its finest form

Drinking p278; Eating p245; Sleeping p340

The ancient, hallowed streets of the City are some of London's most fascinating. The Square Mile occupies pretty much exactly the same patch of land around which the Romans first constructed a defensive wall almost two millennia ago and probably contains more history within it than the rest of the city put together.

The tiny backstreets and ancient churches are today juxtaposed with skyscrapers and office blocks as this is the home of London's stock exchange, the Bank of England and countless other financial institutions. Very few people now live in the City (which was badly bombed during the Blitz) and so, while it's very animated Monday to Friday, you can hear a pin drop at the weekend and even on a weeknight after 9pm once the commuters are all safely on their way home.

top picks

THE CITY

- St Paul's Cathedral (left)
- Tower of London (p117)
- Museum of London (p103)
- 30 St Mary Axe (p106)
- Temple Church (p103)

The centre of gravity for the City is Wren's masterpiece and London's great survivor, St Paul's Cathedral (below), still a must for all visitors to the capital. To the north of here is Smithfield, home for centuries to the notorious St Bartholomew's fair and a favoured spot for witch burnings and other gory public executions. East of Smithfield is the area now known as the Barbican (p107), a vast arts complex and a visual statement that will either make your heart sing or your eyes ache depending what side of the architectural debate you bat for. Personally we love it, but there you go.

Further east is Bank, the prosaically named district home to many of the major financial institutions of the country including the titular Bank of England. This is where the City can justly be called a bit sterile – pubs often only open Monday to Friday and eating choices split between Marks & Spencer sandwiches or five-course *haute cuisine* meals for those with expense accounts – yet beauties such as Lloyd's of London, the Gherkin (30 St Mary Axe, p106) and wonderful Leadenhall Market (p108) more than compensate for the lack of life at street level.

Further to the east still is Tower Hill, home to the world-famous Tower of London (p117) and iconic Tower Bridge (p121). This is an area dominated by faceless office blocks, although pockets of colour do spill over from the neighbouring multicultural areas of Aldgate and Whitechapel and well-heeled Wapping. However, what the City lacks in great hangouts and community it more than makes up for with a wealth of historic sights and fascinating museums.

SMITHFIELD & ST PAUL'S

ST PAUL'S CATHEDRAL Map p100 & p102

☎ 7236 4128; www.stpauls.co.uk; St Paul's Churchyard EC4; adult/7-16yr/senior/student £11/3.50/10/8.50; ☒ 8.30am-4pm (last entry) Mon-Sat; ⊖ St Paul's; ☒

Occupying a superb position atop Ludgate Hill, one of London's most recognisable buildings is Sir Christopher Wren's masterwork, completed in 1710 after the previous building was destroyed in the Great Fire of 1666. The proud bearer of the capital's largest church dome, St Paul's Cathedral has seen a lot in its 300-plus years, although Ludgate Hill has been a place of worship for almost 1400 years, the current incarnation being the fifth to stand on this site. St Paul's almost didn't make it off the draw-

ing board, as Wren's initial designs were rejected. However, since its first service in 1697, it's held funerals for Lord Nelson, the Duke of Wellington and Winston Churchill, and has played host to Martin Luther King as well as the ill-fated wedding of Charles and Diana. For Londoners the vast dome, which still manages to loom amid the far higher skyscrapers in the Square Mile, is a symbol of resilience and pride – miraculously surviving the Blitz unscathed. Having undergone a huge restoration project to coincide with its 300th anniversary in 2010, the cathedral is today looking better than it has done for decades, though parts of its facade were still covered in scaffolding at the time of writing.

Despite all the fascinating history and its impressive interior, people are usually most

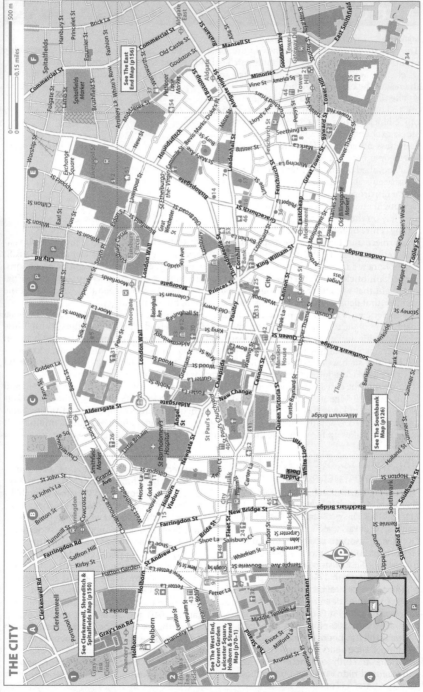

0 500 m
0 0.15 miles

See The East
End Map (p156)

See Clerkenwell, Shoreditch &
Spitalfields Map (p150)

See The West End,
Covent Garden,
Leicester Square,
Holborn & Strand
Map (p70–1)

See The Southbank
Map (p126)

Thames

THE CITY

interested in climbing the dome for one of the best views of London imaginable. It actually consists of three domes, one inside the other, but it made the cathedral Wren's *tour de force* and only a handful of others throughout the world (mostly in Italy) outdo it in size. Exactly 530 stairs take you to the top, but it's a three-stage journey. The cathedral is built in the shape of a cross, with the dome at its intersection. So first find the circular paved area between the eight massive columns supporting the dome, then head to the door on the western side of the southern transept. Some 30m and precisely 259 steps above, you reach the interior walkway around the dome's base. This is the Whispering Gallery, so called because if you talk close to the wall it really does carry your words around to the opposite side, 32m away.

Climbing even more steps (another 119) you reach the Stone Gallery, which is an exterior viewing platform, with 360-degree views of London, all of which are rather obscured by pillars and other suicide-preventing measures.

The further 152 iron steps to the Golden Gallery are steeper and narrower than below but are really worth the effort as long as you don't suffer from claustrophobia. From here, 111m above London, the city opens up to you, the view unspoilt by superfluous railings; you'll be hard pushed to see anything better.

Of course, back on the ground floor, St Paul's offers plenty of riches for those who like to keep their feet firmly on its black-and-white tiled floor – and the interior has been stunningly restored in recent years. Just beneath the dome, for starters, is a compass and an epitaph written for Wren by his son: *Lector, si monumentum requiris, circumspice* (Reader, if you seek his monument, look around you).

In the northern aisle you'll find the All Souls' Chapel and the Chapel of St Dunstan, dedicated to the 10th-century archbishop of Canterbury, and the grandiose Duke of Wellington Memorial (1875). In the north transept chapel is Holman Hunt's celebrated painting The Light of the World, which depicts Christ knocking at an overgrown door that, symbolically, can only be opened from the inside. Beyond, in the cathedral's heart, are the particularly spectacular quire (or chancel) – its ceilings and arches dazzling with green, blue, red and gold mosaics – and the high altar. The ornately carved choir stalls by Grinling Gibbons on either side of the quire are exquisite, as are the ornamental wrought-iron gates, separating the aisles from the altar, by Jean Tijou (both men also

ST PAUL'S CATHEDRAL

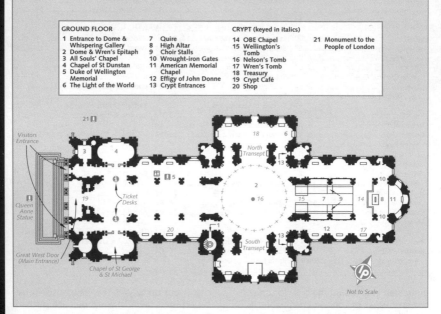

GROUND FLOOR
1 Entrance to Dome &
  Whispering Gallery
2 Dome & Wren's Epitaph
3 All Souls' Chapel
4 Chapel of St Dunstan
5 Duke of Wellington
  Memorial
6 The Light of the World
7 Quire
8 High Altar
9 Choir Stalls
10 Wrought-iron Gates
11 American Memorial
   Chapel
12 Effigy of John Donne
13 Crypt Entrances

CRYPT (keyed in italics)
14 OBE Chapel
15 Wellington's
   Tomb
16 Nelson's Tomb
17 Wren's Tomb
18 Treasury
19 Crypt Café
20 Shop
21 Monument to the
   People of London

worked on Hampton Court Palace). Walk around the altar, with its massive gilded oak canopy, to the American Memorial Chapel, a memorial to the 28,000 Americans based in Britain who lost their lives during WWII.

Around the southern side of the ambulatory is the effigy of John Donne (1573–1631). The one-time dean of St Paul's, Donne was also a metaphysical poet, most famous for the immortal lines 'No man is an island' and 'Ask not for whom the bell tolls, it tolls for thee' (both in the same poem!).

On the eastern side of both the north and south transepts are stairs leading down to the crypt, treasury and OBE Chapel, where weddings, funerals and other services are held for members of the Order of the British Empire. The crypt has memorials to some 300 military demigods, including Florence Nightingale and Lord Kitchener, while both the Duke of Wellington and Admiral Nelson are actually buried here, Nelson having been placed in a black sarcophagus that is directly under the centre of the dome. On the surrounding walls are plaques in memory of those from the Commonwealth who died in various conflicts during the 20th century.

Wren's tomb is in the crypt, while architect Edwin Lutyens, painter Joshua Reynolds and poet William Blake are also remembered here. In a niche, there is also an exhibition of Wren's controversial plans for St Paul's and his actual working model. St Paul's was one of the 50 commissions the great architect was given after the Great Fire of London wiped out most of the City.

The treasury hosts temporary exhibitions and is not always open, but it's worth a look when it is, depending on what's on. Elsewhere in the crypt is the Crypt Café (🕐 9am-5pm Mon-Sat, 10.30am-5pm Sun) and the restaurant Refectory (🕐 9am-5.30pm Mon-Sat, 10.30am-5.30pm Sun), in addition to a shop (🕐 9am-5pm Mon-Sat, 10.30am-5pm Sun).

Just outside the north transept, there's a simple monument to the people of London, honouring the 32,000 civilians killed (and another 50,000 seriously injured) in the City during WWII. Also to the left as you face the entrance stairway is Temple Bar, one of the original gateways to the City of London. This medieval stone archway once straddled Fleet St at a site marked by a griffin (Map pp70–1) but was removed to Middlesex in 1878. Temple Bar was restored and made a triumphal return to London (albeit in a totally new place) alongside the redevelopment of Paternoster Sq in 2003.

Audioguide tours (adult/senior & student £4/3.50) in multiple languages last 45 minutes; guided tours (adult/6-12yr/senior & student/child aged six to 16 years £3/1/2.50) lasting 1½ to two hours leave the tour desk at 10.45am, 11.15am, 1.30pm and 2pm. There are free organ recitals at St Paul's at 5pm most Sundays, as well as regular celebrity recitals, which are listed on the website. Evensong takes place at 5pm Monday to Saturday and at 3.15pm on Sunday.

There is limited disabled access. Call ahead for further information.

MUSEUM OF LONDON Map p100

☎ 7001 9844; www.museumoflondon.org.uk; London Wall EC2; admission free; ⏰ 10am-6pm; ⊖ Barbican or St Paul's; ♿

The Museum of London is one of the capital's best museums but remains largely off the radar for most visitors. That's not surprising when you consider that it's encased in concrete and located above a roundabout in the Barbican. Despite this, once you're inside it's a fascinating walk through the various incarnations of the capital from Anglo-Saxon village to global financial centre. At the time of writing the lower floor of the museum, covering the period 1666 to the present day, was shut for a total revamp, but it was due to reopen in early 2010.

The first gallery here, London Before London, outlines the development of the Thames Valley from 450 million years ago. Harnessing computer technology to enliven its exhibits and presenting impressive fossils and stone axe heads in shiny new cases, it does a good job of bringing to life the ancient settlements that pre-dated the capital. Next up is the city's Roman era, a far more interactive experience, full of interesting displays and models of how the city would have looked at the height of Roman influence. The rest of the floor takes you through the Saxon, medieval, Tudor and Stuart periods, culminating in the Great Fire of 1666.

You can pause for a breather in the pleasant garden in the building's central courtyard or head for the adjoining Museum Café, which serves light meals from 10am to 5.30pm (from 11.30am on Sunday). Alternatively, on a sunny day, pack some sand-

wiches and lunch in the next-door Barber Surgeon's Herb Garden.

When arriving, look for the Barbican's gate 7; before leaving, don't forget to have a browse through the well-stocked bookshop and check in on the temporary exhibits also held here.

TEMPLE CHURCH Map p100

☎ 7353 3470; www.templechurch.com; Temple EC4; admission free; ⏰ approx 2-4pm Wed-Sun, call or email to check; ⊖ Temple or Chancery Lane

This magnificent church lies within the walls of the Temple, built by the legendary Knights Templar, an order of crusading monks founded in the 12th century to protect pilgrims travelling to and from Jerusalem. The order moved here around 1160, abandoning its older headquarters in Holborn. Today the sprawling oasis of fine buildings and pleasant traffic-free green space is home to two Inns of Court (housing the chambers of lawyers practising in the City, the Middle and the Lesser Temple.

The Temple Church has a distinctive design: the Round (consecrated in 1185 and designed to recall the Church of the Holy Sepulchre in Jerusalem) adjoins the Chancel (built in 1240), which is the heart of the modern church. Both parts were severely damaged by a bomb in 1941 and have been lovingly reconstructed. Its most obvious points of interest are the life-size stone effigies of nine knights that lie on the floor of the Round. These include the Earl of Pembroke, who acted as the go-between for King John and the rebel barons, eventually leading to the signing of the Magna Carta in 1215. In recent years the church has become a must-see for readers of The Da Vinci Code, in which a key scene was set here.

Check opening times in advance as they change frequently. During the week, the easiest access to the church is via Inner Temple Lane, off Fleet St. At the weekends, you'll need to enter via the Victoria Embankment.

CENTRAL CRIMINAL COURT (OLD BAILEY) Map p100

☎ 7248 3277; cnr Newgate & Old Bailey Sts; admission free; ⏰ approx 10am-1pm & 2-5pm Mon-Fri; ⊖ St Paul's

Just as fact is often better than fiction, taking in a trial in the 'Old Bailey' leaves watching a TV courtroom drama for dust. Of course, it's too late to see author Jeffrey Archer being found guilty of perjury here, watch the Guildford Four's convictions being quashed after their wrongful imprisonment for IRA terrorist attacks or view the Yorkshire Ripper Peter Sutcliffe being sent down. However, the Old Bailey is a byword for crime and notoriety. So even if you sit in on a fairly run-of-the-mill trial, simply being in the court where such people as the Kray twins and Oscar Wilde (in an earlier building on this site) once appeared is memorable in itself.

Choose from 18 courts, of which the oldest – courts 1, 2 and 3 – usually have the most interesting cases. As cameras, video equipment, mobile phones, large bags and food and drink are all forbidden inside, and there are no cloakrooms or lockers, it's important not to take these with you. Take a cardigan or something to cushion the hard seats though, and if you're interested in a high-profile trial, get there early.

The Central Criminal Court gets its nickname from the street on which it stands: *baillie* was Norman French for 'enclosed courtyard'. The current building opened in 1907 on the combined site of a previous Old Bailey and Newgate Prison. Intriguingly, the figure of justice holding a sword and scales in her hands above the building's copper dome is *not* blindfolded (against undue influence, as is traditionally the case). That's a situation that has sparked many a sarcastic comment from those being charged here.

DR JOHNSON'S HOUSE Map p100
☎ 7353 3745; www.drjohnsonshouse.org; 17 Gough Sq EC4; adult/child/concession/family £4.50/1.50/3.50/10; ☑ 11am-5.30pm Mon-Sat May-Sep, to 5pm Mon-Sat Oct-Apr; ⊖ Chancery Lane or Blackfriars
This wonderful house, built in 1700, is a rare surviving example of a Georgian city mansion. All around it today huge office blocks loom and tiny Gough Sq can be quite hard to find as a result. The house has been preserved, of course, as it was the home of the great Georgian wit Samuel Johnson, the author of the first serious dictionary of the English language (transcribed by a team of six clerks in the attic) and the man who proclaimed 'When a man is tired of London, he is tired of life'.

The museum doesn't exactly crackle with Dr Johnson's immortal wit, yet it's still an atmospheric and worthy place to visit, with its antique furniture and artefacts from Johnson's life (his brick from the Great Wall of China must surely be the oddest of these). The numerous paintings of Dr Johnson and his associates, including his black manservant Francis Barber and his clerk and biographer James Boswell, are, sadly, not particularly revealing of the great minds who would have considered the building a home from home. A more revealing object is a chair from Johnson's local pub, the Old Cock Tavern on Fleet St.

There's a rather ponderous video, plus leaflets telling how the lexicographer and six clerks (Boswell wasn't among them, yet) developed the first English dictionary in the house's attic during the period he lived here from 1748 to 1759. Children will love the Georgian dressing-up clothes on the top floor, and the temporary exhibits in the attic look at other aspects of 18th-century life.

Across Gough Sq is a statue of Johnson's cat, Hodge, sitting above the full quote explaining why when a man is tired of London, he is tired of life: 'For there is in London all that life can afford.'

ST BARTHOLOMEW-THE-GREAT
Map p100
☎ 7606 5171; www.greatstbarts.com; West Smithfield EC1; adult/concession £4/3; ☑ 8.30am-5pm Mon-Fri, to 4pm mid-Nov–mid-Feb, plus 10.30am-4pm Sat & 8.30am-8pm Sun year-round; ⊖ Farringdon or Barbican
This spectacular Norman church dates from 1123, originally a part of the monastery of Augustinian Canons, but becoming the parish church of Smithfield in 1539 when King Henry VIII dissolved the monasteries. The authentic Norman arches, the weathered and blackened stone, the dark wood carvings and the low lighting lend this space an ancient calm – especially as you'll often be the only visitor. There are historical associations with William Hogarth, who was baptised here, and with politician Benjamin Franklin, who worked on site as an apprentice printer. The church sits on the corner of the grounds of St Bart's Hospital, on the side closest to Smithfield Market. Another selling point for modern audiences is that scenes from *Shakespeare in Love* and *Four Weddings and a Funeral* were filmed here. The location managers for

those movies knew what they were doing: St Bartholomew-the-Great is indeed one of the capital's most atmospheric places of worship.

ST BRIDE'S, FLEET STREET Map p100

☎ 7427 0133; www.stbrides.com; St Bride's Lane EC4; ☒ 8am-4.45pm Mon-Fri, 11am-3pm Sat, 10am-1pm & 5-7.30pm Sun; ⊖ St Paul's or Blackfriars

Rupert Murdoch might have frogmarched the newspaper industry out to Wapping in the 1980s, but this small church off Fleet St remains 'the journalists' church'. Candles were kept burning here for reporters John McCarthy and Terry Anderson during their years as hostages in Lebanon during the 1990s, and a memorial plaque keeps tab of the growing number of journalists killed in Iraq.

There's a brief, well-presented history of the printing industry in the crypt, dating from 1500 when William Caxton's first printing press was relocated next to the church after Caxton's death, though the crypt was closed indefinitely at the time of writing. St Bride's is also of architectural interest. Designed by Sir Christopher Wren in 1671, its add-on spire (1703) reputedly inspired the first tiered wedding cake.

ST ANDREW HOLBORN Map p100

☎ 7353 3544; Holborn Viaduct EC4; ☒ 9am-4.30pm Mon-Fri; ⊖ Chancery Lane

This church on the southeastern corner of Holborn Circus, first mentioned in the 10th century, was rebuilt by Wren in 1686 and was the largest of his parish churches. Even though the interior was bombed to smithereens during WWII, much of what you see inside today is original 17th century as it was brought from other churches.

GOLDEN BOY OF PYE CORNER Map p100

Cnr Cock Lane & Giltspur St, ⊖ St Paul's or Farringdon

This small statue of a corpulent boy opposite St Bartholomew's Hospital, at the corner of Cock Lane and Giltspur St, has a somewhat odd dedication: 'In memory put up for the fire of London occasioned by the sin of gluttony 1666'. All becomes clear, however, when you realise the Great Fire started in a busy bakery on Pudding Lane and finally burned itself out in what was once called Pye (Pie) Corner, where

the statue now stands. This was interpreted by many as a sign that the fire was an act of God as punishment for the gluttony of Londoners.

SMITHFIELD MARKET Map p100

West Smithfield EC1; ☒ 4am-noon Mon-Fri; ⊖ Farringdon

Smithfield is central London's last surviving meat market. Its name derives from it being a smooth field where animals could be grazed, although its history is far from pastoral. Built on the site of the notorious St Bartholomew's fair, where witches were traditionally burned at the stake, this is where Scottish Independence leader William Wallace was executed in 1305 (there's a large plaque on the wall of St Bart's Hospital south of the market) as well as the place where the leader of the Peasants' Revolt, Wat Tyler, met his end in 1381. Described in terms of pure horror by Dickens in *Oliver Twist*, this was once the armpit of London, where animal excrement and entrails created a sea of filth. Today it's a very smart annexe of Clerkenwell and full of bars and restaurants, while the market itself is a wonderful building, although one constantly under threat of destruction and redevelopment into office blocks.

HOLBORN VIADUCT Map p100

⊖ St Paul's or Farringdon

This fine iron bridge was built in 1869 in an effort to smarten up the area, as well as to link Holborn and Newgate St above what had been a valley created by the River Fleet. The four bronze statues represent Commerce and Agriculture (on the northern side) and Science and Fine Arts (on the south).

BANK

By its very nature, much of the work of the City goes on behind closed doors. However, a short exploration of the streets around Bank tube station will take you to the door of many financial, as well as political and religious, landmarks. Here, at the tube station's main exit, seven bank-filled streets converge. Take Princes St northwestwards to get to the Guildhall or head northeastwards along Threadneedle St for the Bank of England Museum. (All the following sights are on the City map, p100.)

The Royal Exchange (founded by Thomas Gresham) is the imposing, colonnaded building you see at the juncture of Threadneedle St and Cornhill to the east. It's the third building on a site originally chosen in 1564 by Gresham. It has not had a role as a financial institution since the 1980s and now houses a posh shopping centre.

In the angle between Lombard St and King William St further south you'll see the twin towers of Nicholas Hawksmoor's St Mary Woolnoth (☎ 7626 9701; ⏱ 8am-5pm Mon-Fri), built in 1717. The architect's only City church, its interior Corinthian columns are a foretaste of his Christ Church in Spitalfields.

Between King William St and Walbrook stands the grand, porticoed Mansion House (☎ 7626 2500; www.cityoflondon.gov.uk; guided tour adult/ concession £6/4), the official residence of the Lord Mayor of London, which was built in the mid-18th century by George Dance the Elder. It's not open to the public save on the weekly tour, which leaves at 2pm on Tuesday from outside St Stephen Walbrook, with a maximum of 40 participants; tickets are sold on a first-come-first-served basis. Inside there are magnificent interiors, an impressive art collection and a very impressive banqueting hall.

Along Walbrook, past the City of London Magistrates Court, is St Stephen Walbrook (☎ 7626 9000; www.ststephenwalbrook.net; 39 Walbrook EC4; ⏱ 11am-4pm Mon-Thu, to 3pm Fri), built in 1672. Widely considered to be the finest of Wren's City churches and a forerunner to St Paul's Cathedral, this light and airy building is indisputably impressive. Some 16 pillars with Corinthian capitals rise up to support its dome and ceiling, while a large cream-coloured boulder lies at the heart of its roomy central space. There is a modern altar by sculptor Henry Moore, cheekily dubbed 'the Camembert' by critics.

Queen Victoria St runs southwestwards from Bank. A short way along it on the left, in front of Temple Court at No 11, you'll find the remains of the 3rd-century AD Temple of Mithras. This potentially fascinating site was uncovered in the 1950s during the construction of Bucklersbury House, an office block on Walbrook St. The entire site was moved to its current location shortly afterwards for display. Truth be told, however, there's little to see here. If you're interested in this Persian God and the religion worshipping him, you're better off checking out the Museum of London (p103), where sculptures and silver incense boxes found in the temple are on display. There is a plan to move the remains of the Temple back to Walbrook as part of a Sir Norman Foster–designed redevelopment of the area, where hopefully these extraordinary remains will get a rather more sympathetic display.

Due west of Bank is Poultry. The modern building at the corner, with striped layers of blond and rose stone, is by Stirling Wilford (the Wilford in question is also behind the much-acclaimed Lowry centre in Salford Quays near Manchester). Behind this, Poultry runs into Cheapside, site of a great medieval market. On the left you'll see another of Wren's great churches, St Mary-le-Bow (☎ 7248 5139; www.stmarylebow.co.uk; Cheapside EC2; ⏱ 7am-6pm Mon-Wed, to 6.30 Thu, to 4pm Fri), built in 1673. It's famous as the church whose bells dictate who is – and who isn't – a cockney; it's said that a true cockney has to have been born within earshot of Bow Bells, although before the advent of motor traffic this would have been a far greater area than it is today. The church's delicate steeple is one of Wren's finest works and the modern stained glass is striking.

30 ST MARY AXE Map p100

Gherkin; ☎ 7071 5008; www.30stmaryaxe.com; St Mary Axe EC3; ⊖ Aldgate or Bank

Known to one and all as 'the Gherkin' (for obvious reasons when you see its incredible shape), 30 St Mary Axe – as it is officially and far more prosaically named – remains London's most distinctive skyscraper, dominating the city despite actually being slightly smaller than the neighbouring Nat-West Tower. The phallic Gherkin's futuristic, sci-fi exterior has become an emblem of modern London as recognisable as Big Ben or the London Eye.

Built in 2002–03 to a multi-award-winning design by Norman Foster, this is London's first ecofriendly skyscraper: Foster laid out the offices so they spiral around internal 'sky gardens'. The windows can be opened and the gardens are used to re-process stale air, so air-conditioning is kept to a minimum. Its primary fuel source is gas, low-energy lighting is used throughout the building and the design maximises the amount of natural light let into the building, meaning that less electricity is used.

Its 41 floors mainly house the reinsurance giant Swiss Re's London offices, and tours are not currently possible. The gorgeous top-floor restaurant is usually open only to staff and their guests, but it's possible to gain access by booking one of the private dining rooms, although this will need to be done well in advance. In some years mere mortals are granted access when the Gherkin participates in the superb Open House Weekend (www.openhouse .org.uk), an annual September event. When included, the Gherkin is always one of the most popular venues.

MONUMENT Map p100

☎ 7626 2717; www.themonument.info; Monument St EC3; adult/5-15yr/concession £3/1/2; ⏲ 9.30am-5.30pm; ⊖ Monument

Sir Christopher Wren's vast 1677 column, known simply as the Monument, is definitely one of the best vantage points over London due to its centrality as much as to its height: with the river, St Paul's and the City surrounding it, you truly feel at London's bustling heart. The column itself is a memorial to the Great Fire of London in 1666, whose impact on London's history cannot be overstated. Slightly southeast of King William St, near London Bridge, the Monument is exactly 60.6m from the bakery in Pudding Lane where the fire started and exactly 60.6m high. To reach the viewing platform, just below a gilded bronze urn of flames that some call a big gold pincushion, you will need to climb 311 steps on the impressive circular staircase. On descent, you're given a certificate to say you did it.

BARBICAN Map p100

☎ information 7638 8891, switchboard 7638 4141; www.barbican.org.uk; Silk St EC2; ⏲ 9am-11pm Mon-Sat, noon-11pm Sun; ⊖ Barbican or Moorgate

Londoners remain fairly divided about the architectural legacy of this vast housing and cultural complex in the heart of the City. While the Barbican is named after a Roman fortification protecting ancient Londinium that may once have stood here, what you see here today is very much a product of the 1960s and '70s. Built on a huge bombsite abandoned since WWII and opened progressively between 1969 and 1982, it's fair to say that its brutalist concrete isn't everyone's cup of tea. Yet, although it topped several recent polls as London's ugliest building, many Londoners see something very beautiful about its cohesion and ambition – incorporating

Shakespeare's local church, St Giles Cripplegate, into its brave-new-world design and embellishing its public areas with lakes and ponds. With a £7-million refit bringing the complex a much-needed facelift in 2005, the Barbican is much better loved than London's other modernist colossus, the South Bank Centre. Trendy urban architects have long prized apartments here, and the residences in the three high-rise towers that ring the cultural centre are some of the city's most sought-after living spaces.

Home of the London Symphony Orchestra and one of the best places to see dance in the capital, the Barbican is still London's pre-eminent cultural centre, boasting three cinemas that show a combination of commercial and independent films, two theatres, which feature touring drama as well as dance performances, and the highly regarded Barbican Gallery (⏲ 11am-8pm, to 6pm Tue & Thu), which stages excellent temporary exhibitions.

See The Arts chapter for details of the theatres (p311), cinemas (p309) and concert halls (p306).

LLOYD'S OF LONDON Map p100

1 Lime St EC3; ⊖ Aldgate or Bank

While the world's leading insurance brokers are inside underwriting everything from trains, planes and ships to cosmonauts' lives and film stars' legs, people outside still stop to gawp at the stainless-steel external ducting and staircases of the Lloyd's of London building. French free climber, or 'spiderman', Alain Robert even felt moved to scale the exterior with his bare hands in 2003.

Lloyd's is the work of Richard Rogers, one of the architects of the Pompidou Centre in Paris, and although it was a watershed for London when it was built in 1986, it's since been overtaken by plenty of other stunning architecture throughout the capital and looks rather tiny next to the giant Gherkin across the road. However, its brave-new-world postmodernism still strikes a particular contrast with the olde-worlde Leadenhall Market next door.

While you can watch people whizzing up and down the outside of the building in its all-glass lifts, sadly you can't experience it yourself. Access to the elevators and the rest of the interior is restricted to employees or professional groups, who must book in advance. Some years the Lloyd's building takes part in Open House Weekend (www.open house.org.uk), which gives the public very rare access to the inside of the building.

LEADENHALL MARKET Map p100

www.leadenhallmarket.co.uk; Whittington Ave EC3; ☯ public areas 24hr, shop opening times vary; ⊖ Bank

Like stepping into a small slice of Victorian London, a visit to this dimly lit, covered mall off Gracechurch St is a minor time-travelling experience. There's been a market on this site since the Roman era, but the architecture that survives is all cobblestones and late-19th-century ironwork; even modern restaurants and chain stores decorate their facades in period style here. The market also appears as Diagon Alley in *Harry Potter and the Philosopher's Stone*. For details of what's on sale, see p227.

BANK OF ENGLAND MUSEUM Map p100

☎ 7601 5545; www.bankofengland.co.uk; Bartholomew Lane EC2; admission free, audioguides £1; ☯ 10am-5pm Mon-Fri; ⊖ Bank

When James II declared war against France in the 17th century, he looked over his shoulder and soon realised he didn't have the funds to finance his armed forces. A Scottish merchant by the name of William Paterson came up with the idea of forming a joint-stock bank that could lend the government money and, in 1694, so began the Bank of England and the notion of national debt. The bank rapidly expanded in size and stature and moved to this site in 1734. During a financial crisis at the end of the 18th century, a cartoon appeared depicting the bank as a haggard old woman, and this is probably the origin of its nickname 'the Old Lady of Threadneedle St', which has stuck ever since. The institution is now in charge of maintaining the integrity of the British currency and financial system – and, since Gordon Brown, as Chancellor of the Exchequer, gave it the power in 1997, even sets interest rates. The gifted Sir John Soane built the original structure, although the governors saw fit to demolish most of his splendid bank in the early 20th century and replace it with a utilitarian, no-frills model that they would soon regret.

The centrepiece of the museum – which explores the evolution of money and the history of this venerable institution, and

which is not *nearly* as dull as it sounds, even if it's no substitute for some of London's more essential museums – is a post-war reconstruction of Soane's original stock office complete with mannequins in period dress behind original mahogany counters. A series of rooms leading off the office are packed with exhibits ranging from photographs and coins to a gold bar you can lift up (it's amazingly heavy) and the muskets once used to defend the bank.

GUILDHALL Map p100

☎ 7606 3030; www.cityoflondon.gov.uk; Gresham St EC2; admission free; ☯ 9am-5pm unless closed for events; ⊖ Bank or St Paul's; ☒

Bang in the centre of the Square Mile, the Guildhall has been the City's seat of government for nearly 800 years. The present building dates from the early 15th century, making it the only secular stone structure to have survived the Great Fire of 1666, although it was severely damaged both then and during the Blitz of 1940.

Most visitors' first port of call is the impressive Great Hall, where you can see the banners and shields of London's 12 guilds (principal livery companies), which used to wield absolute power throughout the City. The lord mayor and sheriffs are still elected annually in the vast open hall, with its chunky chandeliers and its church-style monuments. It is often closed for various other formal functions, so it's best to ring ahead. Meetings of the Common Council are held here on the third Thursday of each month (except August) at 1pm, and the Guildhall hosts the awards dinner for the Man Booker Prize, the leading British literary award.

Among the monuments to look out for (if the hall is open) are statues of Winston Churchill, Admiral Nelson, the Duke of Wellington and the two prime ministers Pitt the Elder and Younger. In the minstrels' gallery at the western end are statues of the biblical giants Gog and Magog, traditionally considered to be guardians of the City; today's figures replaced similar 18th-century statues destroyed in the Blitz. The Guildhall's stained glass was also blown out during the Blitz but a modern window in the southwestern corner depicts the city's history; look out for a picture of London's first lord mayor, Richard 'Dick' Whittington, and his famous cat.

(Continued on page 117)

RIVER THAMES

For two thousand years the Thames has been the constant in London's ever-changing cityscape and the focus of the capital's life. For all its importance and global renown, though, 'Father Thames' is a relatively short stretch of water; but size doesn't matter for Londoners who've always held the river in deep affection. The best way to appreciate the Thames – and the many iconic buildings along its banks – is from a front-row seat in a boat (p380) cruising down this watery highway. In this section we've picked out some of the highlights of the trip.

Crossing the Hungerford Foot Bridge (p124) while the London Eye watches on

Heading north from Pimlico, you'll leave rural Thames behind. Locks turn into piers, tree-lined banks become concrete embankments. Father Thames puts on his work clothes.

6

❶ Swans
The Queen and two City livery companies own all the swans on the Thames and in July they are 'upped' (herded), 'nicked' (tagged) and their particulars entered on a swan roll.

❷ Church of St Mary-at-Lambeth
This 14th-century church contains a Museum of Garden History (p191) and lovely stained glass, including *The Peddler of Lambeth,* whose donor left the parish an acre of land provided he (and his dog) were immortalised in a church window.

❸ Big Ben
The hands of the world's most famous clock (p92), standing head and shoulders above the Houses of Parliament, have seized up with snow and under the weight of roosting starlings, but otherwise the clock has kept near perfect time for some 170 years.

❹ Queen Boudicca Statue
Near Westminster Pier is a majestic bronze (1905) of the queen of the Celtic Iceni tribe (p20) and her three daughters, all of whom gave the Romans a run for their money in 60 AD.

❺ County Hall
Home to London County Council and then the renamed (in 1965) Greater London Council until its final disagreement with Margaret Thatcher in 1986, this grand curved building (p125) houses museums and hotels.

❻ London Eye
This giant Ferris wheel (p124) that went up to mark the millennium and was meant to be temporary has, like the Eiffel Tower in Paris, stayed put and become a city landmark.

❼ Golden Jubilee Bridge
Opened in 2002 to mark the 50th anniversary of the Queen's coronation, these two sailboat-like footbridges stayed by cables cling to the sides of the existing Hungerford rail bridge.

❽ Charing Cross Station
Looking not unlike a Viking helmet, the railway station was covered in 1990 by Embankment Place, a postmodern office and shopping complex designed by Terry Farrell that created 32,000 sq metres of office space.

GOLDEN JUBILEE BRIDGE TO MILLENNIUM BRIDGE

This bend is Entertainment Central, with the Southbank Centre, National Theatre and British Film Institute all anchored here. From Waterloo Bridge, see the best river views.

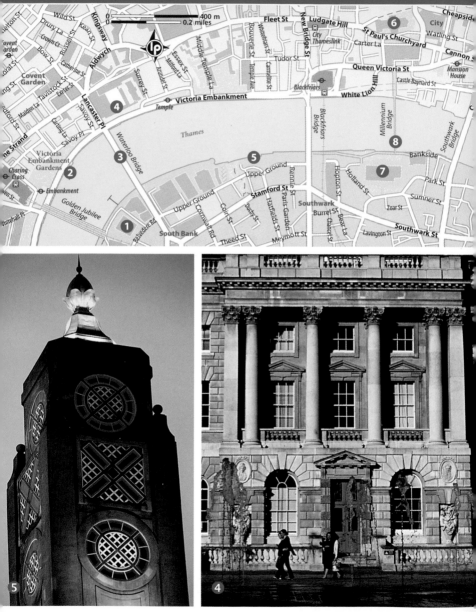

1 Royal Festival Hall

The brutalist Royal Festival Hall (p304), a building that helped shape the face of the river-facing Southbank Centre for decades, has had a facelift and now looks as modern as tomorrow.

2 Cleopatra's Needle

Carved under the pharaohs 3500 years ago in Alexandria, this 20m-tall obelisk was presented to London by the viceroy of Egypt in 1819 and erected here six decades later.

3 Waterloo Bridge

Opening just as WWII broke out in 1939, this bridge's lofty views have inspired musicians from the Kinks ('Waterloo Sunset') to Jools Holland ('Waterloo Bridge').

4 Somerset House

Standing on the site of a Renaissance palace, this handsome Palladian building (1770s; see p76), until recently the home of several public registers and the Inland Revenue, now contains museums.

5 Oxo Tower

The neon-lit windows of this art deco tower (restored in 1996) spell out O-X-O vertically; it's a graphic designer's dream. The tower and its restaurant (p246) single-handedly helped to bring people to 'the other side'.

6 St Paul's Cathedral

Christopher Wren had to be sneaky to get it built according to his plans, but the dome of his masterpiece lords over London. Some 28 incendiary bombs bounced off the cathedral during the Blitz, but it held fast. See p99.

7 Tate Modern

The most visited sight in London, the Tate's innards attract the hordes but it's the two-storey glass box Herzog & de Meuron (2000) added to the roof and illuminated at night that creates the magic. See p128.

8 Millennium Bridge

Among the most beautiful (and certainly the most useful) of the so-called millennium projects to open in 2000, this 'blade of light' links the Tate Modern with St Paul's Cathedral.

MILLENNIUM BRIDGE TO TOWER BRIDGE

Here is the lion's share of London's historical sights, including two of its most famous bridges. From between the bridges, the working and seafaring Thames starts to flow.

8

1 Shakespeare's Globe
With the Tate Modern, this painstakingly re-created copy of Shakespeare's original theatre (p312), which opened to considerable acclaim in 1997, is the jewel in the crown of the south bank of the Thames.

2 Southwark Cathedral
There was already a church on this site almost a millennium ago and it was rebuilt several times over the centuries, but much of what you see today is actually Victorian. See p130.

3 London Bridge
London's only river crossing from Roman times until 1750, the span (p131) 'fell down' most dramatically in 1014 when the Vikings yanked out the supporting posts (the words to that grating children's ditty refers to the incident).

4 Monument
This tall column (p107) topped with a flaming urn commemorates the Great Fire of 1666, a conflagration that the mayor, woken up with the news at night, derided with: 'Pish! A woman might piss it out'.

5 HMS Belfast
This large cruiser (p132), which took its name from the Belfast shipyard where it was built, saw action in two wars and was almost broken up before the Imperial War Museum bought it in 1972.

6 City Hall
Glass-clad City Hall, designed by Sir Norman Foster and nicknamed both 'the Egg' and 'the Testicle', is transparent in both the figurative and literal senses. It's now closed to visitors for security reasons.

7 Tower of London
The tower's most famous residents are the ravens whose clipped wings prevent them from flying the coop. According to legend, should the ravens leave it, the White Tower will crumble and a great disaster will befall England. See p117.

8 Tower Bridge
This Victorian span (p121), often mistaken for London Bridge by tourists, is as much a London icon as the Tower and the Eye. And it remains a working bridge, lifting as often as 1000 times a year.

View of O2 (p303; formerly the Millenium Dome) from the Thames

Beneath the Great Hall is London's largest medieval crypt, with 19 stained-glass windows showing the livery companies' coats of arms. The crypt can be seen only as part of a free guided tour (☎ 7606 1463).

The buildings to the west house Corporation of London offices and the Guildhall Library (☎ 7606 1461; Aldermanbury EC2; ☼ 9.30am-5pm Mon-Sat), founded in about 1420 under the terms of Dick Whittington's will. It is divided into three sections for research: printed books; manuscripts; and prints, maps and drawings. Also here is the Clockmakers' Museum (☎ 7332 1868; Guildhall Library, Aldermanbury EC2; admission free; ☼ 9.30am-4.45pm Mon-Sat), which have a collection of more than 700 clocks and watches dating back some 500 years. The clock museum sometimes closes for an hour or two on Monday to wind the clocks.

GUILDHALL ART GALLERY & ROMAN LONDON AMPHITHEATRE Map p100
☎ 7332 3700; www.guildhall-art-gallery.org.uk; Guildhall Yard EC2; adult/senior & student £2.50/1, all day Fri & daily after 3.30pm free; ☼ 10am-5pm Mon-Sat, noon-4pm Sun; ⊖ Bank
The gallery of the City of London provides a fascinating look at the politics of the Square Mile over the past few centuries, with a great collection of paintings of London in the 18th and 19th centuries, as well as the vast frieze entitled *The Defeat of the Floating Batteries* (1791), depicting the British victory at the Siege of Gibraltar in 1782. This huge painting was removed to safety just a month before the gallery was hit by a German bomb in 1941 – it spent 50 years rolled up before a spectacular restoration in 1999.

An even more recent arrival is a sculpture of former prime minister Margaret Thatcher, which has to be housed in a protective glass case as the iron lady was decapitated here by an angry punter with a cricket bat soon after its installation in 2002. Today, following some tricky neck surgery, Maggie has finally rejoined the gallery's collection, but her contentious legacy lives on.

The real highlight of the museum is deep in the darkened basement, where the archaeological remains of Roman London's amphitheatre (coliseum) lie. Discovered only in 1988 when work finally began on a new gallery following the original's destruc-

tion in the Blitz, they were immediately declared an Ancient Monument, and the new gallery was built around them. While only a few remnants of the stone walls lining the eastern entrance still stand, they're imaginatively fleshed out with a black-and-fluorescent-green trompe l'oeil of the missing seating, and computer-meshed outlines of spectators and gladiators. The roar of the crowd goes up as you reach the end of the entrance tunnel and hit the central stage, giving a real sense of how Roman London might have felt. Markings on the square outside the Guildhall indicate the original extent of the amphitheatre, allowing people to visualise its scale.

ST LAWRENCE JEWRY Map p100
☎ 7600 9478; Gresham St EC2; admission free; ☼ 7.30am-2.15pm; ⊖ Bank; ♿
To look at the Corporation of London's extremely well preserved official church, you'd barely realise that it was almost completely destroyed during WWII. Instead, it does Sir Christopher Wren, who built it in 1678, and its subsequent restorers proud, with its immaculate alabaster walls and gilt trimmings. The arms of the City of London adorn the organ above the door at the western end. The Commonwealth Chapel is bedecked with the flags of member nations. Free piano recitals are held each Monday at 1pm; organ recitals at the same time on Tuesday.

As the church name suggests, this was once part of the Jewish quarter – the centre being Old Jewry, the street to the southeast. The district was sadly not without its pogroms. After some 500 Jews were killed in 1262 in mob 'retaliation' against a Jewish moneylender, Edward I expelled the entire community from London to Flanders in 1290. They did not return until the late 17th century.

TOWER HILL

TOWER OF LONDON Map p100 & Map p118
☎ 0844 482 7777; www.hrp.org.uk; Tower Hill EC3; adult/5-15yr/senior & student/family £17/9.50/14.50/47; ☼ 9am-5.30pm Tue-Sat, 10am-5.30pm Sun & Mon Mar-Oct, closes 4.30pm daily Nov-Feb, last admission 30min before closing time; ⊖ Tower Hill; ♿
The absolute kernel of London with a history as bleak and bloody as it is fascinating,

TOWER OF LONDON

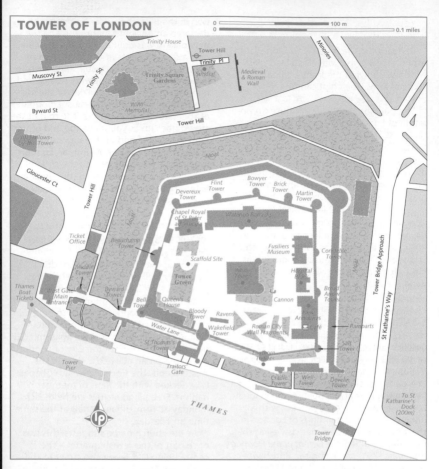

the Tower of London should be first on anyone's list of London's sights. Despite ever-growing ticket prices and the hordes of tourists that descend here in the summer months, this is one of those rare pleasures: somewhere worth the hype. Throughout the ages, murder and political skulduggery have reigned as much as kings and queens, so tales of imprisonment and executions will pepper your trail.

The Tower is in fact a castle, and not towerlike at all (although in the Middle Ages it's easy to imagine how the White Tower would have dwarfed the huts of the peasantry surrounding the castle walls) and has been the property (and sometime London residence) of the monarch since it was begun during the reign of William the Conqueror (1066–87). By far the best pre-

served medieval castle in London, it's one of the capital's four Unesco World Heritage Sites (the others are Westminster Abbey, Kew Gardens and Maritime Greenwich), and will fascinate anyone with any interest at all in history, the monarchy and warfare.

With more than two million visitors a year, this place is seriously crowded in the high season so it's best to buy a ticket in advance, and to visit later in the day. You can buy Tower tickets online (for a £1 discount), or at any tube station up to a week beforehand, which can save you a lot of time when you arrive. Also, after 3pm the groups have usually left and the place is a lot more pleasant to stroll around. During the winter months it's far less crowded, so there's no need to take either of these precautions.

Your best bet is to start with a free hour-long tour given by the Yeoman Warders, which is a great way to bring the various parts of the tower to life. The Yeoman Warders have been guarding the tower since 1485, and have all served a minimum of 22 years in the British Armed Forces. Known affectionately as 'beefeaters' by the public (due to the large rations of beef given to them in the past), there are 35 Yeoman Warders today, including Moira Cameron, the first ever female beefeater, who began serving in 2007. While officially they guard the tower and Crown Jewels at night, their main role today is as tour guides (and to pose for photographs with curious foreigners). These tours leave from the Middle Tower every 30 minutes from 9.30am (10am on Sunday) to 3.30pm (2.30pm in winter) daily. The warders also conduct about eight different short talks (35 minutes) and tours (45 minutes) on specific themes. The first is at 9.30am Monday to Saturday (10.15am on Sunday in summer, 11.30am in winter), the last at 5.15pm (3pm in winter). Less theatrical are the self-paced audioguides available in nine languages for £4 from the information point on Water Lane.

You enter the tower via the West Gate and proceed across the walkway over the dry moat between the Middle Tower and Byward Tower. The original moat was finally drained of centuries of festering sewage in the 19th century, necessitated by persistent cholera outbreaks, and a superbly manicured lawn now takes its place. Before you stands the Bell Tower, housing the curfew bells and one-time home to Thomas More. The politician and author of *Utopia* was imprisoned here in 1534 before his execution for refusing to recognise King Henry VIII as head of the Church of England in place of the Pope. To your left are the casements of the former Royal Mint, which were moved from this site to new buildings northeast of the castle in 1812.

Continuing past the Bell Tower along Water Lane between the walls you come to the famous Traitors' Gate, the gateway through which prisoners being brought by river entered the tower. Above the gate, rooms inside St Thomas's Tower show what the hall and bedchamber of Edward I (1272–1307) might once have looked like. Here also archaeologists have peeled back the layers of newer buildings to find what

went before. Opposite St Thomas's Tower is Wakefield Tower, built by Henry III between 1220 and 1240. Its upper floor is actually entered via St Thomas's Tower and has been even more enticingly furnished with a replica throne and huge candelabra to give an impression of how, as an anteroom in a medieval palace, it might have once looked in Edward I's day. During the 15th-century War of the Roses between the Houses of Lancaster and York, Henry VI was almost certainly murdered in this tower.

Below, in the basement of Wakefield Tower, there's a Torture at the Tower exhibition. However, torture wasn't practised as much in England as it was on the Continent apparently, and the display is pretty perfunctory, limiting itself to a rack, a pair of manacles and an instrument for keeping prisoners doubled up called a Scavenger's Daughter. Frankly, you'd see scarier gear at any London S&M club (or the London Dungeon, across the river near London Bridge; p131). To get to this exhibition and the basement level of Wakefield Tower, enter the tower courtyard through the arch opposite Traitors' Gate.

As you do so, you'll also observe at the centre of the courtyard the Norman White Tower with a turret on each of its four corners and a golden weather vane spinning atop each. This tower has a couple of remnants of Norman architecture, including a fireplace and garderobe (lavatory). However, most of its interior is given over to a collection of cannons, guns and suits of armour for men and horses, which come from the Royal Armouries in Leeds. Among the most remarkable exhibits are the 2m suit of armour made for John of Gaunt (to see that coming towards you on a battlefield must have been terrifying) and alongside it a tiny child's suit of armour designed for James I's young son, Henry. Another unmissable suit is that of Henry VIII, a virtually cuboid shape to match the monarch's bloated body in his 40s, and featuring what must have been the most impressive posing pouch in the kingdom.

The stretch of green between the Wakefield and White Towers is where the Tower's famous ravens are found. According to legend, if these birds leave the Tower it would presage the fall of the kingdom, so their wings are clipped to ensure this will never happen. Watching them being fed chunks of meat is a fascinating sight.

Opposite Wakefield Tower and the White Tower is the Bloody Tower, with an exhibition on Elizabethan adventurer Sir Walter Raleigh, who was imprisoned here three times by the capricious Elizabeth I, most significantly from 1605 to 1616.

The Bloody Tower acquired its nickname from the story that the 'princes in the tower', Edward V and his younger brother, were murdered here to annul their claims to the throne. The blame is usually laid at the door of their uncle Richard III, although Henry VII might also have been responsible for the crime.

Beside the Bloody Tower sits a collection of black-and-white half-timbered Tudor houses that are home to Tower of London staff. The Queen's House, where Anne Boleyn lived out her final days in 1536, now houses the resident governor and is closed to the public.

North of the Queen's House, across Tower Green, is the scaffold site, where seven people were executed by beheading in Tudor times: two of Henry VIII's six wives, the alleged adulterers Anne Boleyn and Catherine Howard; the latter's lady-in-waiting, Jane Rochford; Margaret Pole, countess of Salisbury, descended from the House of York; 16-year-old Lady Jane Grey, who fell foul of Henry's daughter Mary I by being her rival for the throne; William, Lord Hastings; and Robert Devereux, Earl of Essex, once a favourite of Elizabeth I. These people were executed within the tower precincts largely to spare the monarch the embarrassment of the usual public execution on Tower Hill, an event that was usually attended by thousands of spectators. In the case of Robert Devereux, the authorities perhaps also feared a popular uprising in his support.

Behind the scaffold site is the Beauchamp Tower, where high-ranking prisoners including Anne Boleyn and Lady Jane Grey were jailed and where fascinating, unhappy inscriptions from the condemned are on display today.

Behind the scaffold site lies the Chapel Royal of St Peter ad Vincula (St Peter in Chains), a rare example of ecclesiastical Tudor architecture and the burial place of those beheaded on the scaffold outside or at nearby Tower Hill. Unfortunately, it can only be visited on a group tour or after 4.30pm, so if you aren't already part of a group hang

around until one shows up and then tag along. Alternatively, attend a service, which takes place at 9am on Sunday.

To the east of the chapel and north of the White Tower is the building most visitors want to see: Waterloo Barracks, the home of the Crown Jewels. You file past footage of Queen Elizabeth II's coronation backed by stirring patriotic music before you reach the vault itself (check out the doors as you go in – they look like they'd survive a nuclear attack). Once inside you'll be confronted with ornate sceptres, plates, orbs and, naturally, crowns. A very slow-moving travelator takes you past the dozen or so crowns that are the centrepiece, including the £27.5 million Imperial State Crown, set with diamonds (2868 of them to be exact), sapphires, emeralds, rubies and pearls, and the platinum crown of the late Queen Mother, Elizabeth, which is famously set with the 105-carat Koh-i-Noor (Mountain of Light) diamond. Surrounded by myth and legend, the 14th-century diamond has been claimed by both India and Afghanistan. It reputedly confers enormous power on its owner, but male owners are destined to die a tormented death. The Crown Jewels display will be redesigned in time for the Queen's Diamond Jubilee in 2012, although exactly when this will happen was unclear at the time of writing.

Behind the Waterloo Barracks is the Bowyer Tower, where George, Duke of Clarence, brother and rival of Edward IV, was imprisoned and, according to a long-standing legend that has never been proved, was drowned in a barrel of malmsey (sweet Madeira wine).

The Fusiliers Museum to the east of Waterloo Barracks is run by the Royal Regiment of Fusiliers. It covers the history of the Royal Fusiliers dating back to 1685, and has models of several battles. A 10-minute video gives details of the modern regiment.

The red-brick New Armouries in the southeastern corner of the inner courtyard houses the New Armouries Café where you can grab a pricey sandwich or soup lunch.

There are plenty of other attractions, as well as churches, shops and toilets within the tower complex, but before you leave you should walk along the inner ramparts. This Wall Walk begins with the 13th-century Salt Tower, probably used to store saltpetre for gunpowder, and takes in Broad Arrow Tower, which houses an exhibit about the gunpowder plotters imprisoned here, many of their original inscriptions having been discovered on the walls. The walk ends at the Martin Tower, which houses an exhibition about the original coronation regalia. Here you can see some of the older crowns, whose jewels have been removed. The oldest surviving crown is that of George I, which is topped with the ball and cross from James II's crown. It was from the Martin Tower that Colonel Thomas Blood attempted to steal the Crown Jewels in 1671, disguised as a clergyman.

Finally, for those interested in the obscure ritual and ceremony of the British monarchy, the Key Ceremony takes place every evening at 9.30pm. This elaborate locking of the main gates makes the changing of the guard at Buckingham Palace look like a recently invented tourist trick – the guards have been performing the ceremony every day without fail for more than 600 years. Even when a bomb hit the Tower of London during the Blitz, the ceremony was only delayed by 30 minutes, which everyone agrees is the essence of the famed stiff upper lip. Entry to the ceremony is free but, in a suitably antiquated style, you have to apply for tickets by post as demand is so high. See the website for details.

There is limited disabled access to the tower. Call ahead for more information.

AROUND THE TOWER OF LONDON
Map p118

Despite the Tower's World Heritage Site status, the area immediately to the north is fairly disappointing, especially as in recent years much of it has been a construction site. Just outside Tower Hill tube station, a giant bronze sundial depicts the history of London from AD 43 to 1982. It stands on a platform offering a view of the neighbouring Trinity Square Gardens, once the site of the Tower Hill scaffold and now home to Edwin Lutyens' memorial to the marines and merchant sailors who lost their lives during WWI. A grassy area, off the steps leading to a subway under the main road, lets you inspect a stretch of the medieval wall built on Roman foundations, with a modern statue of Emperor Trajan (r AD 98–117) standing in front of it. At the other end of the tunnel is a postern (gate) dating from the 13th century.

TOWER BRIDGE Map p100
⊖ Tower Hill

Perhaps second only to Big Ben as London's most recognisable symbol, Tower Bridge doesn't disappoint up close. There's something about its neo-Gothic towers and blue suspension struts that make it quite enthralling to look at. Built in 1894 as a much-needed crossing point in the east, it was equipped with a then revolutionary bascule (seesaw) mechanism that could clear the way for oncoming ships in three minutes. Although London's days as a thriving port are long over, the bridge still does its stuff, lifting around 1000 times per year and as many as 10 times per day in summer. (For information on the next lifting ring ☎ 7940 3984 or check the bridge's website.)

The Tower Bridge Exhibition (☎ 7940 3985; www .towerbridge.org.uk; adult/under 5yr/5-15yr/senior & student/family £7/free/3/5/from 10.50; ☺ 10am-6.30pm Apr-Oct, 9.30am-6pm Nov-Mar, last admission 1hr before closing) explains the nuts and bolts of it all. If you're not particularly technically minded, however, it's still interesting to get inside the bridge and look out its windows along the Thames. At the time of writing, the bridge was undergoing a gradual three-year renovation, which should be complete in 2011. Until then, parts may be obscured by scaffolding, but both the bridge and exhibition will remain open to the public.

ALL HALLOWS-BY-THE-TOWER Map p100
☎ 7481 2928; www.ahbtt.org.uk; Byward St EC3; admission free; ☺ 8am-6pm Mon-Fri, 10am-5pm Sat & Sun; ⊖ Tower Hill

All Hallows is the parish where famous diarist Samuel Pepys recorded his observations of the nearby Great Fire of London in 1666. Above ground it's a pleasant enough church, rebuilt after WWII. There's a copper spire (added in 1957 to make the church stand out more), a pulpit from a Wren church in Cannon St that was destroyed in the WWII, a beautiful 17th-century font cover by the master woodcarver Grinling Gibbons, and some interesting modern banners. Free 20-minute church tours leave at 2pm each day.

However, a church by the name All Hallows (meaning 'All Saints') has stood on this site since AD 675, and the best bit of the building today is undoubtedly its atmospheric Saxon undercroft (crypt). There you'll find a pavement of reused Roman tiles and walls of the 7th-century Saxon church, as well as coins and bits of local history.

William Penn, founder of Pennsylvania, was baptised here in 1644 and there's a memorial to him in the undercroft. John Quincy Adams, sixth president of the USA, was also married at All Hallows in 1797.

THE CITY WALK
Walking Tour

1 Dr Johnson's House Find your way to this miraculously well-preserved Georgian mansion (p104) in the heart of the City and explore the story of Dr Johnson's amazing life and wit within, perhaps even dropping by to his local, Ye Olde Cheshire Cheese on Fleet St (see p278).

2 St Paul's Cathedral Wren's masterpiece, this cathedral (p99) is an unlikely survivor of the Blitz and one of the London skyline's best-loved features. Join the crowds to see the dazzling interior, the fascinating crypt, the whispering gallery and the breathtaking views over the capital from the cupola.

3 Museum of London This wonderful museum (p103) may not look like much from the outside, but it's one of the city's best, totally devoted to documenting the multifaceted history of the capital through its many stages of development from Saxon village to three-time Olympic city.

4 Barbican Built on the site of an old Roman watchtower whence its name, the modern Barbican (p107) is the City's fabulous arts centre and an architectural wonder all of its own – love it or hate it, it's worth a visit; check out the greenhouse, the lakes and Shakespeare's parish Church, St Giles' Cripplegate.

5 Guildhall Once the very heart of the City, seat of power and influence, the Guildhall (p108) is today still the home to the Corporation of London, which runs not only the City but many of the capital's biggest parks. Here delve into the bizarre ritual of the guilds, see the excellent art gallery and go back in time two millennia to see the remains of London's Roman amphitheatre.

6 Monument This column (p107) commemorates the Great Fire of London, and – while not for the vertiginous – is a superb way to see the City up close. Despite the number of high-rises all around, the Monument still feels extremely high, giving you an idea of how massive it would have looked in the 17th century!

WALK FACTS

Start **Chancery Lane tube station**
End **Tower Bridge (Tower Hill tube station)**
Distance **1.5 miles**
Duration **Two hours**
Fuel stop **Place Below (p245)**

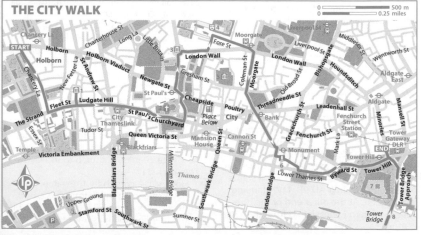

THE CITY WALK

7 Tower of London The sheer amount of history within the massive stone walls of the Tower of London (p117) is hard to fathom. The White Tower, the Crown Jewels, the Yeoman Warders, the Scaffold Site and Traitor's Gate all have fascinating stories associated with them and the Tower of London deserves at least a half-day's visit at the end of the walk.

8 Tower Bridge A wonderful icon of Victorian engineering, Tower Bridge (p121) has been a symbol of London since the day it was built, when it was the largest bascule bridge in the world. A walk across it (and visit to the interesting exhibition, from which the views are spectacular) is a must to appreciate old Father Thames at its widest and most spectacular.

THE SOUTH BANK

Drinking p279; Eating p245; Shopping p223; Sleeping p341

Until the late 1990s the southern part of central London was the city's forgotten underside – rundown, neglected and offering little to visitors once they'd been to the Southbank arts venues. That's all changed now, and the transformation of the so-called South Bank has been nothing short of astonishing. This is where new London faces off old London, and both come out winners. Indeed, two of the city's newer landmarks are located here, and they stare a pair of its oldest icons straight in the face across the Thames. The London Eye 'wheel of good fortune' (below) has been raised across the water from the neo-Gothic Parliament at Westminster, while the disused Bankside Power Station has morphed into Tate Modern (p128), London's most visited sight, opposite august St Paul's Cathedral.

The South Bank is made up of five contiguous areas, which tend to blend into one another without much warning. From west to east they are: the area around Waterloo railway station and the renovated Southbank Centre (opposite) complex of theatres, concert halls and museums; Bankside and, to the south, Southwark, with the stunning Millennium Bridge (p129) pushing off from between Tate Modern and Shakespeare's Globe; Borough, with London's most popular food market; and Bermondsey, boasting a slew of popular museums, including the London Dungeon (p131) and the Design Museum (p133).

top picks

THE SOUTH BANK

- London Eye (below)
- Shakespeare's Globe (p129)
- Tate Modern (p128)
- London Bridge Experience & London Tombs (p131)
- Borough Market (p130)

The best way to see this neighbourhood is on foot. And if you follow the Silver Jubilee Walkway and the South Bank section of the Thames Path (p198) along the southern riverbank – one of the most pleasant strolls in town – you're in the perfect position to see it all. And always in sight is Father Thames himself.

WATERLOO

In 1951 the British government attempted to raise the spirits of a nation still digging through rubble and on restricted rations six years after the end of WWII, by holding a national celebration called the Festival of Britain. Its permanent legacy in London was the Royal Festival Hall.

A cluster of concrete buildings known as the Southbank Centre still stands but has undergone a remarkable makeover in recent years. Though it will never compete with the impressive County Hall or iconic London Eye in a beauty or popularity contest, the remodelled centre is now a lot easier on the eyes and continues to be the capital's most important cultural complex.

Waterloo, named after a field in Belgium where the Duke of Wellington contained Napoleon's advance through Europe, was nearly all marshland until the 18th century. Bridges from the northern bank of the Thames at Westminster and Waterloo changed all that and the massive Waterloo train station opened in 1848.

LONDON EYE Map p126

☎ 0870 500 0600; www.londoneye.com; Jubilee Gardens SE1; adult/4-15yr/senior £17/8.50/14; ⏰ 10am-8pm Oct-Apr, to 9pm May, Jun & Sep, to 9.30pm Jul & Aug, closed 1 week in Jan; ⊖ Waterloo; ♿

It's difficult to remember what London looked like before the landmark London Eye began twirling at the southwestern end of Jubilee Gardens in 2000. Not only has it fundamentally altered the skyline of the South Bank but, standing 135m tall in a fairly flat city, it is visible from many surprising parts of the city (eg Kennington and Mayfair). A ride – or 'flight', as it is called here – in one of the wheel's 32 glass-enclosed gondolas holding up to 28 people is something you really can't miss if you want to say you've 'done' London; 3.5 million people a year give it a go. It takes a gracefully slow 30 minutes and, weather permitting, you can see 25 miles in every direction from the top of what is the world's tallest Ferris wheel. Save money and avoid the queues by buying online.

COUNTY HALL Map p126
Riverside Bldg, Westminster Bridge Rd SE1;
Westminster or Waterloo;
Begun in 1909 but not completed until 1922, this grand building with its curved, colonnaded facade contains an art museum and gallery, a vast aquarium, a museum devoted to the local film industry and two hotels.

It seems that no major European city's list of attractions is complete these days without a museum devoted to the work of Salvador Dalí, and the Dalí Universe (0870 744 7485; www.thedaliuniverse.com; adult/7-15yr/15-18yr/senior & student/family £14/7/9/12/38; 9.30am-6pm Mon-Thu, to 7pm Fri-Sun) is the world's largest, with 500 of the prolific surrealist artist's twisted paintings, etchings, sculptures and other works on display in a series of low-lit galleries arranged by theme: Sensuality and Femininity, Religion and Mythology, and Dreams and Fantasy. Keep an eye out for Dalí's famous melting pocket watch (*Persistence of Memory*), Mae West Lips Sofa, the Lobster Telephone and the long-legged Space Elephant. The adjacent Fine Art Gallery contains 100 works by Picasso. It keeps the same hours as the Dalí Universe and entry is included in the general admission price.

The London Sea Life Aquarium (7967 8000; www.sealife.co.uk; adult/3-14yr/senior & student/family £15.25/11.75/13.25/50; 10am-6pm Mon-Fri, to 7pm Sat & Sun;) is one of the largest in Europe and, with its new owner and branding, has got even better. Fish and other creatures from the briny deep are grouped in some 15 zones according to their geographic origin, from the Pacific to the Atlantic Oceans and from temperate waters to tropical seas. The coral caves (zone 8) and tropical rainforest (zone 10) displays are particularly impressive, and there's a shark walkway at the end. Things get localised with The River Thames Story (zone 11).

The Movieum (7202 7040; www.themovieum.com; adult/5-16yr/senior & student £17/13/15; 10am-5pm Mon-Fri, to 6pm Sat & Sun;) may cost a bomb but this awkwardly named attraction devoted to the British film industry is surprisingly well done. It's divided into various genres – fantasy, musicals, costume drama, horror, science fiction and so on – and because it looks at the industry and not just British films; it includes things like the sets for *Star Wars* and *Superman* (filmed at Elstree Studios in Hertfordshire). There's lots of participatory stuff – you can film yourself driving though London in an open-top vintage car or flying with Superman; and the large circular room at the finish – which examines all aspects of film production, from makeup and sound to animation and animatronics – is fascinating.

TOPOLSKI CENTURY Map p126
 7620 1275; www.topolskicentury.org.uk; 150-152 Hungerford Arches, Concert Hall Approach SE1; admission free; 11am-7pm Mon-Sat, noon-6pm Sun; Waterloo;
Within the arches below Hungerford Bridge is the lifework of one Feliks Topolski (1907–89), a Polish-born British artist who painted mural after mural on board and canvas (with Dulux paint, no less) more than 180m long, which trace the history of the 20th century from the artist's early life in bohemian Warsaw to his death in 1989. The murals may not be everyone's cup of tea and the artistic merits of much of the work is questionable, but it's interesting to see how one man viewed the world during a lifetime of more than eight decades.

SOUTHBANK CENTRE Map p126
 0871 663 2500; www.southbankcentre.co.uk; Belvedere Rd SE1; Waterloo;
The flagship venue of the Southbank Centre, the collection of concrete buildings and walkways shoehorned between Hungerford and Waterloo Bridges, is the Royal Festival Hall. It is the oldest building of the centre still standing, having been erected to cheer up a glum postwar populace as part of the 1951 Festival of Britain. Its slightly curved facade of glass and Portland stone always won it more public approbation than its 1970s neighbours, but a recent £90-million refit added new pedestrian walkways, bookshops, music stores and food outlets below it, including a restaurant called Skylon (p246).

Just north, Queen Elizabeth Hall is the second-largest concert venue in the centre and hosts chamber orchestras, quartets, choirs, dance performances and sometimes opera. It also contains the smaller Purcell Room. Underneath its elevated floor you'll find a real skateboarders' hang-out, suitably decorated with masterful graffiti tagging.

The Hayward Gallery (0871 663 2509; www.southbankcentre.co.uk/visual-arts; admission £7-9; 10am-6pm, to 10pm Fri) is one of London's

THE SOUTH BANK

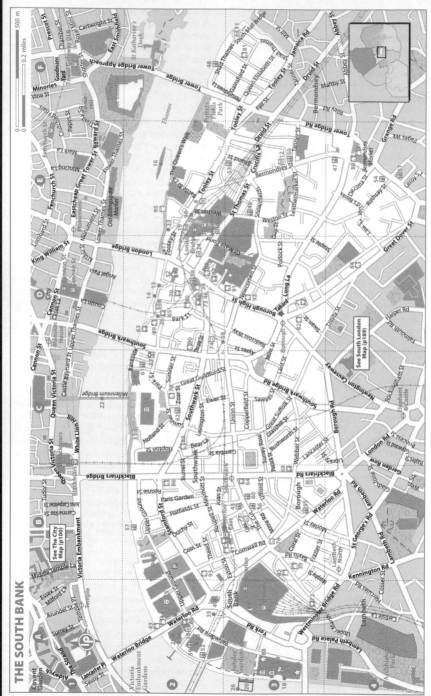

premier exhibition spaces for major international art shows. The grey fortresslike building dating from 1968 makes an excellent hanging space for the blockbuster temporary exhibitions it puts on.

The South Bank Book Market (🕐 11am-7pm), with prints and second-hand books, takes place daily immediately in front of the BFI Southbank (p309) under the arches of Waterloo Bridge.

BFI IMAX CINEMA Map p126

☎ information & bookings 0870 787 2525; www
.bfi.org.uk/imax; 1 Charlie Chaplin Walk SE1;
adult/4-14yr/senior & student from £9/5.75/6.25;
🕐 6 screenings 11am-9pm, additional screening
11.30pm Sat; ⊖ Waterloo; &

The British Film Institute IMAX Cinema is located in the centre of a busy roundabout (there are plans to pedestrianise it in the not-too-distant future). The cinema screens the predictable mix of 2-D and IMAX 3-D documentaries about travel, space and wildlife, lasting anywhere from 40 minutes to 1½ hours, as well as recently released blockbusters like *Star Trek* à la IMAX (DMR and digital titles cost £13.50/8.75/9.75). The drum-shaped building sits on 'springs' to reduce vibrations and traffic noise from the traffic circle and subways beneath it, and the exterior changes colour at night. And size does matter here: the 477-seat cinema is the largest in the UK, with a screen that's 20m high and 26m wide.

THE SOUTH BANK

NATIONAL THEATRE Map p126

☎ 7452 3000; www.nationaltheatre.org.uk; South Bank SE1; ⊖ Waterloo; ♿

This is the nation's flagship theatre complex, comprising three auditoriums: the Olivier, the Lyttelton and the Cottesloe. Opened in 1976 and modernised to the tune of £42 million a decade back, it's been undergoing an artistic renaissance under the directorship of Nicholas Hytner. Backstage tours (adult/concession/family £5.90/4.90/12.70), lasting 1¼ hours, are also available. There are six daily Monday to Friday, two on Saturday and one on Sunday. Consult the website for exact times.

BANKSIDE & SOUTHWARK

Outside the jurisdiction of the City and notorious for its 'stews' (bathhouses-cum-brothels), bear-baiting pits and prisons, Bankside was London's very own Sodom and Gomorrah during Elizabethan times. And because playhouses were banned in the City, the Globe and nearby Rose Theatres were built here. Today the area's entertainments are somewhat more highbrow. The Globe has gone respectable and a disused power station has become the world's leading modern art gallery (and London's most visited sight).

TATE MODERN Map p126

☎ information & bookings 7887 8000; www.tate .org.uk/modern; Queen's Walk SE1; admission free, special exhibitions £8-10; ⏰ 10am-6pm Sun-Thu, to 10pm Fri & Sat; ⊖ St Paul's, Southwark or London Bridge; ♿

The public's love affair with this phenomenally successful modern art gallery shows no sign of waning a decade after it opened. Serious art critics have occasionally swiped at its populism, particularly the 'participatory art' exhibited in the Turbine Hall (Carl Höller's funfair-like slides called *Test Site;* Olafur Eliasson's arm-flapping *The Weather Project;* Doris Salcedo's enormous crack in the floor called *Shibboleth* and *Bodyspacemotionthing;* and Robert Morris' climbable geometric sculpture first exhibited in London in 1971 and recreated here in 2009). But an average five million visitors a year appear to disagree, making it the world's most popular contemporary art gallery and – almost unbelievably – the most visited sight in London, just ahead of the British Museum.

The critics are right in one sense, though: this 'Tate Modern effect' is really more about the building and its location than about the mostly 20th-century art inside. Swiss architects Herzog & de Meuron won the prestigious Pritzker Prize for their transformation of the empty Bankside Power Station, which was built between 1947 and 1963 and closed in 1981. Leaving the building's single central chimney, adding a two-storey glass box onto the roof and using the vast Turbine Hall as a dramatic entrance space were three strokes of genius. Then, of course, there are the wonderful views of the Thames and St Paul's, particularly from the restaurant-bar on the 7th level and the espresso bar on the 4th. There's also a cafe on the 2nd level, plus places to relax overlooking the Turbine Hall. An 11-storey sloping brick extension to the southwest corner, by the same architects, will be completed in 2012.

Tate Modern's permanent collection on levels 3 and 5 is now arranged by both theme and chronology. States of Flux is devoted to early-20th-century avant-garde movements, including cubism and futurism. Poetry and Dream examines surrealism through various themes and techniques. Material Gestures features European and American painting and sculpture of the 1940s and '50s. The new Energy and Process gallery will have Arte Povera, revolutionary art of the 1960s, as its main focus.

More than 60,000 works are on constant rotation here, and the curators have at their disposal paintings by Georges Braque, Henri Matisse, Piet Mondrian, Andy Warhol, Mark Rothko, Roy Lichtenstein and Jackson Pollock, as well as pieces by Joseph Beuys, Marcel Duchamp, Damien Hirst, Rebecca Horn, Claes Oldenburg and Auguste Rodin. Special exhibitions (level 4) in the past have included retrospectives on Edward Hopper, Frida Kahlo, August Strindberg, Nazism and 'Degenerate' Art, local 'bad boys' Gilbert & George and the Russian constructivists Aleksandr Rodchenko and Liubov Popova. Audioguides, with four different tours, are available for £2. Free guided highlights tours depart at 11am, noon, 2pm and 3pm daily.

The Tate Boat (www.tate.org.uk/tatetotate; one way adult/5-16yr/student £5/2.50/3.35; ⏰ every 40min 10.10am-4.50pm) operates between the Bankside Pier at Tate Modern and the Millbank Pier at its sister-museum Tate Britain. Services from the latter depart from 10.30am to 5.10pm daily also at 40-minute intervals. Discounts are available for Travelcard holders.

SHAKESPEARE'S GLOBE Map p126

☎ 7902 1400, bookings 7401 9919; www.shake
speares-globe.org; 21 New Globe Walk SE1; exhibition incl guided tour of theatre adult £7.50-10.50,
5-15yr £4.50-6.50, senior & student £6.50-8.50,
family £20-28; ⏱ 9am-12.30 & 1-5pm Mon-Sat,
9am-11.30am & noon-5pm Sun late Apr–mid-Oct,
9am-5pm mid-Oct-late Apr; ⊖ St Paul's or London
Bridge; ♿

Shakespeare's Globe consists of the reconstructed Globe Theatre and, beneath it, an
exhibition hall, entry to which includes a
tour (departing every 15–30 minutes) of the
Globe Theatre, except when matinées are
being staged in season. Then the tour shifts
to the nearby Rose Theatre (right) and costs
less. The exhibition focuses on Elizabethan
London and stagecraft and the struggle to
get the theatre rebuilt in the 20th century.
The exhibits devoted to Elizabethan special
effects and costumes are especially interesting as are the recordings of some of the
greatest Shakespearean performances ever.

The original Globe – known as the
'Wooden O' after its circular shape and
roofless centre – was erected in 1599 with
timber taken from the demolished Theatre
(1576) on Curtain Rd in Shoreditch. The
Globe was closed in 1642 after the English
Civil War was won by the Puritans, who
regarded the theatre as the devil's workshop, and it was dismantled two years later.
Despite the worldwide popularity of Shakespeare over the centuries, the Globe was
barely a distant memory when American
actor (and later film director) Sam Wanamaker came searching for it in 1949. Un-
deterred by the fact that the foundations
of the theatre had vanished beneath a row
of listed Georgian houses, Wanamaker set
up the Globe Playhouse Trust in 1970 and
began fundraising for a memorial theatre.
Work started only 200m from the original
Globe site in 1987, but Wanamaker died
four years before it opened in 1997.

The new Globe was painstakingly constructed with 600 oak pegs (there's not a
nail or a screw in the house), specially fired
Tudor bricks and thatching reeds from
Norfolk that pigeons supposedly don't like;
even the plaster contains goat hair, lime
and sand as it did in Shakespeare's time.
Unlike other venues for Shakespearean
plays, this theatre has been designed to
resemble the original as closely as
possible – even if that means leaving the
arena open to the fickle London skies and

roar of passing aircraft, expecting the 700
'groundlings' to stand even in the rain, and
obstructing much of the view from the
seats closest to the stage with two enormous 'original' Corinthian pillars in faux
marble. The Swan at the Globe runs a pub-bar
at the Piazza level and a brasserie open for
lunch and dinner (lunch only on Sunday)
with glorious views of the Thames and the
City on the 1st floor.

ROSE THEATRE Map p126

☎ 7902 1400; www.rosetheatre.org.uk; 56 Park
St SE1; adult/5-15yr/senior & student/family
£7.50/4.50/6.50/20; ⏱ 1-5pm Mon-Sat, noon-5pm
Sun late Apr–mid-Oct; ⊖ London Bridge; ♿

The Rose, for which Christopher Marlowe
and Ben Jonson wrote their greatest plays
and in which Shakespeare learned his craft,
is unique in that its original 16th-century
foundations have been unearthed. They
were discovered in 1989 beneath an office
building at Southwark Bridge and given a
protective concrete cover. Administered by
the nearby Globe Theatre, the Rose is open
to the public only when matinées are being
performed at the Globe Theatre and can
only be visited as part of a group.

MILLENNIUM BRIDGE Map p126

The Millennium Bridge pushes off from
the south bank of the Thames in front of
Tate Modern and berths on the north bank
at the steps of Peter's Hill below St Paul's
Cathedral. The low-slung frame designed
by Sir Norman Foster and Antony Caro
looks pretty spectacular, particularly lit up
at night with fibre optics, and the view of
St Paul's from the South Bank has swiftly
become one of London's iconic images. The
bridge got off on the wrong, err, footing
when it had to be closed just three days
after opening in June 2000 because of the
alarming way it swayed under the weight
of pedestrians. An 18-month refit costing
£5 million eventually saw it right.

GOLDEN HINDE Map p126

☎ 7403 0123, bookings 0870 011 8700; www
.goldenhinde.org; St Mary Overie Dock, Cathedral
St SE1; adult/concession/family £7/5/20; ⏱ 10am-
5.30pm; ⊖ London Bridge

Okay, it looks like a dinky theme-park ride
and kids do love it, but stepping aboard
this replica of Sir Francis Drake's famous
Tudor ship will inspire genuine admiration

for the admiral and his rather short – average height: 1.6m – crew, which counted between 40 and 60. A tiny five-deck galleon just like this was home to Drake and his crew from 1577 to 1580 as they became the first sailors to circumnavigate the globe. Adult visitors wandering around stooped must also marvel at how the taller, modern-day crew managed to spend 20 years at sea on this 37m-long replica, after it was launched in 1973.

Tickets are available from the Golden Hinde Shop (Pickfords Wharf, 1 Clink St SE1). You can also spend the night aboard for £39.95 per person, including a supper of stew and bread and a breakfast of bread and cheese.

VINOPOLIS Map p126

☎ 0870 241 4040, bookings 7940 8300; www
.vinopolis.co.uk; 1 Bank End SE1; tours £19.50-
32.50; ☽ noon-10pm Mon, Thu & Fri, 11am-9pm
Sat, noon-6pm Sun; ✪ London Bridge; ☖
Vinopolis, spread over a hectare of Victorian railway vaults in Bankside, cashes in on Londoners' love affair with things red and white and rosé. Vinopolis provides a pretty sketchy tour of the world of wine and it's very popular with hen parties (need we say more?). However, those with time and patience who want to know a little more about wine production and regional varieties from France to South Africa and California to Australia (and a few lesser-known areas like Thailand and Georgia) will find it interesting enough. Be advised, though, that you need to follow the audioguide to make sense of the exhibits, which introduce visitors to the history of wine-making, vineyards and grape varietals, regional characteristics and which wine goes with which food. All tours, including the Vinopolis Grapevine (£19.50), involve sampling at least five wines at various tasting stops along the way. The Vinopolis Vineyard (£25), the Spirit of Vinopolis (£27.50) and the Vinopolis Celebration (£32.50) tours include additional wine tastings as well as sampling other alcoholic libations.

CLINK PRISON MUSEUM Map p126

☎ 7403 0900; www.clink.co.uk; 1 Clink St SE1;
adult/concession/family £5/3.50/12; ☽ 10am-6pm
Mon-Fri, to 9pm Sat & Sun; ✪ London Bridge
This one-time private jail in the park of Winchester Palace, a 32-hectare area known as the Liberty of the Clink and under the ju-

risdiction of the bishops of Winchester and not the City, was used to detain debtors, prostitutes, thieves and even actors. This was the notorious address that gave us the expression 'in the clink' (in jail). The poky little museum inside, which was getting a much needed refit at the time of research, reveals the wretched life of the prisoners who were forced to pay for their own food and accommodation and sometimes had to resort to catching and eating mice. There's a nice little collection of instruments of torture, too.

BANKSIDE GALLERY Map p126

☎ 7928 7521; www.banksidegallery.com;
48 Hopton St SE1; admission free; ☽ 11am-6pm;
✪ St Paul's, Southwark or London Bridge; ☖
Home of the Royal Watercolour Society and the Royal Society of Painter-Printmakers, this friendly upbeat place has no permanent collection, but there are frequently changing exhibitions of watercolours, prints and engravings. Call ahead or visit the website for details of events, such as evenings on which artists talk about their work.

BOROUGH & BERMONDSEY

Although parts are still pretty rundown and derelict, this area is very much on the up and up and trend-followers like to bill it as 'the new Hoxton'. Indeed, all the prerequisites are already in place here: a trendy market, a community of creative types living in loft buildings such as the former Hartley jam factory, and a growing cluster of gastropubs, restaurants and hip cafes in and around popular Bermondsey St. The HMS *Belfast*, the London Bridge Experience and the neighbourhood's several museums, including designer Zandra Rhodes' Fashion & Textile Museum, are all worth exploring.

SOUTHWARK CATHEDRAL Map p126

☎ 7367 6700; www.southwark.anglican.org/
cathedral; Montague Close SE1; admission free,
requested donation £4; ☽ 8am-6pm Mon-Fri, from
9am Sat & Sun; ✪ London Bridge; ☖
The earliest surviving part of this relatively small cathedral is the retrochoir at the eastern end, which contains four chapels and was part of the 13th-century Priory of St Mary Overie (from 'St Mary over the Water'). However, most of the cathedral is Victorian, including the nave (1897).

You enter via the southwest door and immediately to the left is the Marchioness memorial to the 51 people who died when a pleasure cruiser on the Thames hit a dredger and sank near Southwark Bridge in 1989. Walk up the north aisle of the nave and on the left you'll see the brightly coloured and canopied tomb of John Gower, the 14th-century poet who was the first to write in English. In the north transept you'll see a memorial tablet to Lionel Lockyer, a quack doctor celebrated for his patent medicines; note its humorous epitaph. On the eastern side of the north transept is the Harvard Chapel, named after John Harvard, founder of the namesake University in Cambridge, Massachusetts, who was baptised here in 1607.

Cross into the choir to admire the 16th-century Great Screen separating the choir from the retrochoir, a gift of the bishop of Winchester in 1520. On the choir floor below the organ is a tablet marking the tomb of Edmond Shakespeare, actor-brother of the Bard, who died in 1607.

In the south aisle of the nave have a look at the green alabaster monument to William Shakespeare with depictions of the original Globe Theatre and Southwark Cathedral; the stained-glass window above shows characters from *A Midsummer Night's Dream*, *Hamlet* and *The Tempest*. Beside the monument is a plaque to Sam Wanamaker (1919–93), the American film director and actor who was the force behind the rebuilt Globe Theatre.

LONDON BRIDGE EXPERIENCE & LONDON TOMBS Map p126

☎ 0800 043 4666; www.londonbridgeexperience .com; 2-4 Tooley St SE1; adult/under 16/concession/ family £21.95/16.95/17.95/64.95; ⏰ 10am-6pm; ⊖ London Bridge

London's latest attraction marrying history with hysteria – 'edutainment' as it's (unfortunately) becoming known in these parts – is far and away its scariest. Located in the vaults beneath so-called New London Bridge (dating back to 1831), the history part takes you on a whistle-stop tour of London's most famous span – from the Romans to the Vikings, from Peter de Colechurch's 'Old London Bridge' (1209) with all the shops, to the American Robert McCulloch, who paid US$2.5 in 1967 for the privilege of transporting the dismantled bridge to Arizona. This is essentially a kids' show so there's much focus on such personalities

as 'the Keeper of the Heads' whose job it was to preserve (mummified) the severed heads of the executed that were displayed on the bridge. At the end of this rather painless history lesson you descend into a series of tombs and plague pits dating as far back as the 14th century, which play on every fear known to man, woman and German Shepherd – darkness, rodents (animatronics), claustrophobia (you have to wiggle your way through an inflated tunnel) and shock (zombies – actors – who jump out in front, beside and behind you, scaring the bejesus out of you every time). We are still shaking. Save up to 50% by buying online.

LONDON DUNGEON Map p126

☎ 7403 7221, bookings 0871 423 2240; www .thedungeons.com; 28-34 Tooley St SE1; adult/ 5-15yr/concessions £21.95/15.95/19.95; ⏰ 10.30am-5pm; ⊖ London Bridge

Under the arches of the Tooley St railway bridge, the London Dungeon was supposedly developed after somebody's kid didn't find Madame Tussauds Chamber of Horrors frightening enough. Well, it failed in that endeavour but the place has been minting money ever since.

It all starts with a stagger through a mirror maze (the Labyrinth of the Lost); followed by a waltz through Bedlam; a push through a torture chamber; a run 'through' the Great Fire of London (where wafting fabric makes up the 'flames'); a close shave with Sweeney Todd, the demon barber of Fleet St; and an encounter with Jack the Ripper: the Victorian serial killer is shown with the five prostitutes he sliced and diced, their entrails hanging out in full gory display. A new attraction called Surgery: Blood & Guts takes its cue from the Old Operating Theatre Museum just around the corner.

The best bits are the vaudevillian delights of being sentenced by a mad, bewigged judge on trumped-up charges, the fairground-ride boat to Traitor's Gate and the Extremis Drop Ride to Doom that has you 'plummeting' to your death by hanging from the gallows.

It's a good idea to buy tickets online for this camped-up 90-minute gore-fest to avoid the mammoth queues. Depending on the time slot you choose the cost of tickets can drop to as low as £16.95/10.95/13.95 for adults/children

5–15 years/concessions. Hours vary according to season, check the website.

HMS BELFAST Map p126

☎ 7940 6300; www.hmsbelfast.iwm.org.uk; Morgan's Lane, Tooley St SE1; adult/under 16yr/concession £10.70/free/8.60; ⏰ 10am-6pm Mar-Oct, to 5pm Nov-Feb; ⊖ London Bridge; ♿ Moored on the Thames opposite Potters Fields Park, HMS *Belfast* is a big toy that kids of all ages generally love. Of course, for most of its commissioned life this large, light cruiser had a rather more serious purpose. Launched in 1938 she served in WWII, most noticeably in the Normandy landings, and during the Korean War.

It probably helps to be keen on things naval, but the HMS *Belfast*, spread over five decks and four platforms, is surprisingly interesting for what it shows of the way of life on board a cruiser, from boiler room to living quarters. The operations room has been reconstructed to show its role in the 1943 Battle of North Cape off Norway, which ended in the sinking of the German battleship *Scharnhorst*. On the bridge you can visit the admiral's cabin and sit in his chair, and you can peer through the sights of the 4in HA/LA guns on the open deck.

BRITAIN AT WAR EXPERIENCE Map p126

☎ 7403 3171; www.britainatwar.co.uk; 64-66 Tooley St SE1; adult/5-15yr/concession/family £11.45/5.50/6.50/29; ⏰ 10am-5pm Apr-Oct, to 4.30pm Nov-Mar; ⊖ London Bridge
Under another Tooley St railway arch, the Britain at War Experience aims to educate the younger generation about the effect WWII had on daily life, while simultaneously playing on the nostalgia of the war generation. In general it's a tribute to ordinary people and comes off fairly well – though the rather musty displays make it feel like you're on a low-budget TV stage-set.

You descend by lift to a reproduction of an Underground station fitted with bunks, tea urns, gas masks and even a lending library (as some stations were, for use as air-raid shelters) and then progress through rooms that display wartime newspaper front pages, posters and Ministry of Food ration books. The BBC Radio Studio allows you to hear domestic and international broadcasts by everyone from Winston Churchill and Edward Murrow to Hitler and Lord Haw Haw. The Rainbow Corner is a

mock-up of a club frequented by American GIs 'overpaid, oversexed and over here'. Finally, you emerge amid the wreckage of a shop hit by a bomb during the Blitz, with the smoke still eddying around and the injured – or dead – being carried from the rubble.

OLD OPERATING THEATRE MUSEUM & HERB GARRET Map p126

☎ 7188 2679; www.thegarret.org.uk; 9a St Thomas St SE1; adult/under 16yr/concession/family £5.60/3.25/4.60/13.75; ⏰ 10.30am-5pm; ⊖ London Bridge
This unique museum, at the top of the narrow and rickety 32-step tower of St Thomas Church (1703), focuses on the nastiness of 19th-century hospital treatment. The garret was used by the apothecary of St Thomas's Hospital to store medicinal herbs and now houses an atmospheric medical museum delightfully hung with bunches of herbs that soften the impact of the horrible devices on display.

Even more interesting is the 19th-century operating theatre attached to the garret. Here you'll see the sharp, vicious-looking instruments 19th-century doctors used, and you'll view the rough-and-ready conditions under which they operated – without antiseptic or anaesthetic on a wooden table in what looks like a modern lecture hall. Surgeons had to perform quickly on patients; one minute to complete an amputation was reckoned about right. A box of sawdust was placed beneath the table to catch the blood and guts and contemporary accounts record the surgeons wearing frock coats 'stiff and stinking with pus and blood'. There's a lecture and demonstration on this Victorian speed surgery at 2pm on Saturday and one on how drugs were made at the same time on Sunday.

FASHION & TEXTILE MUSEUM Map p126

☎ 7407 8664; www.ftmlondon.org; 83 Bermondsey St SE1; adult/under 12yr/concession £5/free/3; ⏰ 11am-6pm Wed-Sun; ⊖ London Bridge; ♿ London, with its cutting-edge street style and designers like Stella McCartney, Matthew Williamson and Vivienne Westwood, is one of the hot centres of fashion, so this brainchild of pink-haired designer Zandra Rhodes is particularly fitting. The plain concrete interior of the striking orange and magenta building doesn't detract from the displays, which are on the ground floor and upper mezzanine. There is no permanent collection; just quarterly temporary exhibitions, which have included retrospectives on Swedish fashion and the evolution of underwear.

DESIGN MUSEUM Map p126

☎ 7403 6933, recorded information 0870 833 9955; www.designmuseum.org; 28 Shad Thames SE1; adult/under 12/student/concession £8.50/free/5/6.50; ⏱ 10am-5.45pm; ⊖ Tower Hill or London Bridge; ♿

Founded by Sir Terence Conran and housed in a 1930s-era warehouse, the Design Museum has a revolving program of special exhibitions devoted to contemporary design. Both populist and popular, past shows have dealt with everything from Manolo Blahnik shoes to Formula One racing cars, the Model T Ford in its centenary year and that miracle material, Velcro. The informal White Café (⏱ 10am-5.30pm) is on the ground floor; go upstairs for the more formal Blue Print Café (p246). The museum is scheduled to move to a new site in the former Commonwealth Institute (Map p178; Kensington High St W8; ⊖ High Street Kensington) in Holland Park over the next couple of years.

BOROUGH MARKET Map p126

☎ 7407 1002; www.boroughmarket.org.uk; cnr Southwark & Stoney Sts SE1; ⏱ 11am-5pm Thu, noon-6pm Fri, 9am-4pm Sat; ⊖ London Bridge

On this spot in some form or another since the 13th century, 'London's Larder' has enjoyed an enormous renaissance in recent years, overflowing with food-lovers, both experienced and wannabes, and has become quite a tourist destination. See p259).

THE SOUTH BANK WALK
Walking Tour

1 County Hall Across Westminster Bridge from the Houses of Parliament, this monumental building (p125) was the seat of London's local government from 1922 until Prime Minister Margaret Thatcher dissolved the Greater London Council in 1986. It now houses museums and hotels.

2 BFI Southbank The flashy headquarters of the British Film Institute (p309) in South Bank is a mecca for film buffs and historians alike. It screens thousands of films in four theatres each year, and archived films are available for watching in the new Mediatheque.

3 Millennium Bridge This pedestrian bridge (p129) linking the north and south banks of the Thames, a slender 'blade of light' designed by Sir Norman Foster, is everything contempo-

WALK FACTS

Start **Waterloo tube station**
End **London Bridge tube station**
Distance **1.5 miles**
Duration **Two hours**
Fuel stop **Le Pain Quotidien** (p268)

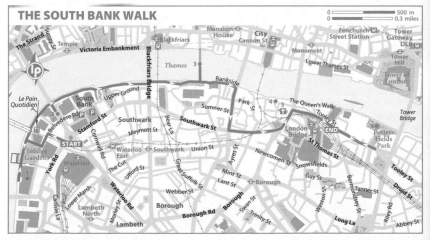

THE SOUTH BANK WALK

rary architecture should be: modern, beautiful and useful. It carries up to 10,000 pedestrians each day.

4 Golden Hinde Now that the *Cutty Sark* (p181) is on sick leave, this barge (p128) is the only masted ship open to visitors in a city that was once the largest and richest port in the world. It's tiny but fascinating and well worth a visit.

5 Southwark Cathedral Sometimes referred to as the 'Cinderella of English cathedrals', this house of worship (p130) is often overlooked but well worth a visit, especially for its historical associations. A monument to Shakespeare, whose great works were originally written for the Bankside playhouses nearby, takes pride of place here.

6 City Hall Nicknamed 'the egg' (or, more cheekily, 'the testicle' because of its shape), this glass-clad building (☎ 7983 4100; www.london.gov .uk; The Queen's Walk SE1; admission free; ⏲ 8.30am-6pm Mon-Thu, to 5.30pm Fri; ✪ Tower Hill or London Bridge; ♿) could also be likened to a spaceman wearing a helmet. It has an interior spiral ramp ascending above the assembly chamber to the building's roof, which has now been fitted with energy-saving solar panels.

Drinking p280; Eating p247; Shopping p224; Sleeping p342

The area stretching from Hyde Park – the largest of London's so-called Royal Parks – to Chelsea is high-class territory; indeed, Kensington & Chelsea enjoys the highest average gross income of all central London boroughs. But it's not all about multimillion-pound properties and glitzy shopping here. This area can boast some of the capital's most important attractions, particularly museums, and its communities are among the most cosmopolitan.

Chelsea has been one of London's most fashionable districts ever since chancellor Thomas More moved here in the early 16th century. The 'village of palaces' became one of London's most desirable neighbourhoods, as it was close to the bustle of the City and to Westminster yet still concealed behind a big bend in the river. Even when it was consumed by Greater London in the 20th century, it retained its aristocratic edge and managed to mix it with a bohemian vibe, with the swinging '60s scene starting at its main artery, King's Rd (below). Chelsea didn't miss out on a big slice of punk cred in the following decade, either.

Belgravia has had a reputation for elitism ever since it was laid out by builder Thomas Cubitt in the 19th century, with its white stucco-ed squares and charming, mainly residential streets and quaint cobbled mews. It's also home to numerous embassies and a few wonderfully old-fashioned pubs.

top picks

OBJECTS IN SOUTH KEN'S MUSEUMS

- Diplodocus dinosaur skeleton (p140), Natural History Museum
- Morris, Gamble and Poynter Refreshment Rooms (p139), Victoria & Albert Museum
- Fashion Room (p139), Victoria & Albert Museum
- Apollo 10 Command Module (p141), Science Museum
- Raphael Cartoons (p139), Victoria & Albert Museum

Knightsbridge, once famous for highwaymen and raucous drinking, is where you'll find some of London's best-known department stores, including Harrods (p224) and Harvey Nichols (p225). To the west and northwest is Kensington, another thoroughly desirable London neighbourhood. Its main thoroughfare, Kensington High St, is a lively blend of upmarket boutiques and chain stores. North of here is Holland Park, a residential district of elegant town houses built around a wooded park.

Thanks to Prince Albert and the 1851 Great Exhibition, South Kensington is first and foremost museumland, boasting three of London's richest all on the same street: the Natural History Museum (p140), the Science Museum (p140) and the Victoria & Albert Museum (p139). Albert's fabulously renovated memorial (p144) is due north of this admirable trio.

Splendid Hyde Park and Kensington Gardens – just one big sprawling green mass – separate the glitz of Knightsbridge and Kensington from the noise and havoc of the West End, shooing the hoi polloi away with exclusive hotels and expensive shopping.

Apart from Westminster Cathedral, Victoria is best known as a transit area, via its huge train and coach stations and predominantly cheerless accommodation. Still it retains a smidgen of character. Pimlico, on the other hand, while being posh in appearance, is as flat as a pancake in terms of personality. It does, however, have some wonderful early 19th-century housing stock and excellent views across the river to the Battersea Power Station.

CHELSEA & BELGRAVIA

KING'S ROAD Map pp136-7

⊖ Sloane Sq or South Kensington

In the 17th century, Charles II set up a love nest here for himself and his mistress Nell Gwyn, an orange-seller turned actress at the Drury Lane Theatre. Heading back to Hampton Court Palace of an evening, Charles would make use of a farmer's track that inevitably came to be known as the King's Rd. The street was at the forefront of London fashion during the technicolour '60s and anarchic '70s, and continues to be trendy now, albeit in a more self-conscious way.

Close to the start is the new Saatchi Gallery (☎ 7823 2363; www.saatchi-gallery.co.uk; Duke of York's HQ, King's Rd SW3 4SQ; admission free; ☯ 10am-6pm) funded by the eponymous Charles, patron of such Brit Artists as Damien Hirst and

Tracey Emin, and offering some 6500 sq metres of space for temporary exhibitions.

CHELSEA OLD CHURCH Map pp136-7

☎ 7795 1019; cnr Cheyne Walk & Old Church St SW3; ⏱ 2-4pm Tue, Wed & Thu, 1.30-5.30pm Sun; ⊖ Sloane Sq; ♿

This church stands behind a bronze monument to Thomas More (1477–1535), the former chancellor (and now Roman Catho-

lic saint) who lost both his property and his head for refusing to go along with Henry VIII's plan to establish himself as supreme head of the Church of England. Original features in the church include the Tudor More Chapel. More's body is thought to be buried somewhere within the church; his head, having been hung out on London Bridge, is now at rest a long way away in St Dunstan's Church, Canterbury. At the

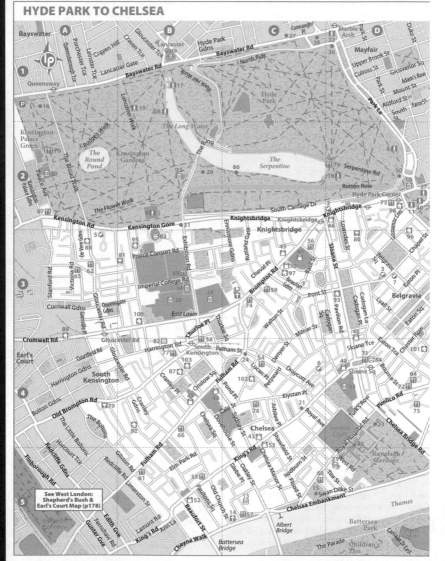

HYDE PARK TO CHELSEA

western end of the south aisle don't miss the only chained books in a London church (chained, of course, to stop anyone making off with them), including two volumes of Foxe's *Book of Martyrs* dating from 1684 and the so-called Vinegar Bible (1717).

CARLYLE'S HOUSE Map pp136-7
☎ 7352 7087; www.nationaltrust.org.uk; 24 Cheyne Row; adult/child/family £4.90/2.50/12.30;

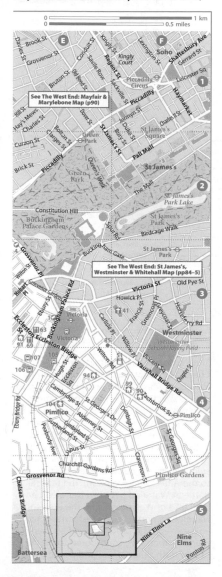

2-5pm Wed-Fri, 11am-5pm Sat & Sun mid-Mar–Oct; ⊖ Sloane Sq

From 1834 until his death in 1881, the great Victorian essayist and historian Thomas Carlyle lived in this three-storey terrace house, which became London's first literary shrine in 1895. Here in his soundproofed attic study he wrote his famous history of the French Revolution; legend has it that, when the manuscript was complete, a maid accidentally threw it on the fire, whereupon the diligent Thomas duly wrote it all again.

While it's not particularly large – you'll also get to see the kitchen, dining room, drawing room and bedroom – this charming house, built in 1708, has been left much as it was when Carlyle was living here and Chopin, Tennyson and Dickens came to call. There's a small garden at the rear.

CHELSEA PHYSIC GARDEN Map pp136-7
☎ 7352 5646; www.chelseaphysicgarden.co.uk; 66 Royal Hospital Rd SW3; adult/5-15yr & student £8/5; noon-5pm Wed-Fri (to 10pm Wed Jul & Aug), noon-6pm Sun Apr-Oct, noon-5pm daily during the Chelsea Flower Show, 10am-4pm on Snowdrop Days (1st & 2nd Sat & Sun in Feb), 9-11am Sat & Sun during Open Garden Squares Weekend (mid-Jun); ⊖ Sloane Sq;

Established by the Apothecaries' Society in 1676 for students working on medicinal plants and healing, this garden is one of the oldest of its kind in Europe and contains many rare trees, shrubs and plants. The fascinating pharmaceutical garden grows plants used in contemporary Western medicine; the world medicine garden has a selection of plants used by tribal peoples in Australia, China, India, New Zealand and North America; and there's a heady perfume and aromatherapy garden. Enter from Swan Walk.

ROYAL HOSPITAL CHELSEA Map pp136-7
☎ 7881 5200; www.chelsea-pensioners.co.uk; Royal Hospital Rd SW3; admission free; 10am-noon & 2-4pm Apr-Sep, 10am-noon & 2-4pm Mon-Sat Oct-Mar; ⊖ Sloane Sq;

Designed by Christopher Wren, this superb structure was built in 1692 to provide shelter for ex-servicemen. Since the reign of Charles II it has housed hundreds of war veterans, known as Chelsea Pensioners. They're fondly regarded as national treasures, and cut striking figures in the dark-blue greatcoats (in winter) or scarlet frock coats (in summer) that they wear on ceremonial occasions. In 2009

137

HYDE PARK TO CHELSEA

the new Margaret Thatcher Infirmary opened, partly as a result of donations collected over the years by the Chelsea Pensioners Appeal.

The museum contains a huge collection of war medals bequeathed by former residents and you'll get to peek at the hospital's Great Hall refectory, Octagon Porch, Chapel and courtyards. Opening times of the grounds vary wildly through the year but are usually open from 10am to between 4.30pm and 8.30pm Monday to Saturday and from 2pm on Sunday.

NATIONAL ARMY MUSEUM Map pp136-7
☎ 7881 2455, 7730 0717; www.national-army
-museum.ac.uk; Royal Hospital Rd SW3; admission
free; ☷ 10am-5.30pm; ◉ Sloane Sq; ☷

Suitably located next door to the Royal Chelsea Hospital, this museum on four levels tells the history of the British army from the perspective of the men and women who put their lives on the line for king and country, conveying both the horrors and perceived glories of war. The best pieces in the exhibition feature the life and times of the 'Redcoat' (the term for the British soldier from the Battle of Agincourt in 1415 to the American Revolution), the tactical battle at Waterloo between Napoleon and the Duke of Wellington, and the skeleton of Napoleon's horse. Several exhibits focus on animals – our heroic furred and feathered friends – that have contributed to the nation in both times of war and peace.

KNIGHTSBRIDGE, KENSINGTON & HYDE PARK

VICTORIA & ALBERT MUSEUM
Map pp136-7

☎ 7942 2000; www.vam.ac.uk; Cromwell Rd SW7; admission free; ☻ 10am-5.45pm, to 10pm Fri; ⊖ South Kensington; ⑤

The Museum of Manufactures, as the V&A was originally known when it opened in 1852, specialises in decorative art and design, with some 4.5 million objects reaching back as far as 3000 years, from Britain and around the globe. It was part of Prince Albert's legacy to the nation in the aftermath of the successful Great Exhibition of 1851, and its original aims – which still hold today – were the 'improvement of public taste in design' and 'applications of fine art to objects of utility'. It's done a fine job so far.

As you enter under the stunning blue-and-yellow blown glass chandelier by Dale Chihuly you can pick up a museum map (free; £1 donation requested) at the information desk. (If the 'Grand Entrance' on Cromwell Rd is too busy, there's another around the corner on Exhibition Rd.) Consider one of the free introductory guided tours, which last 45 minutes to an hour and leave the main reception area every hour from 10.30am to 3.30pm.

Spread over 145 galleries, the museum houses the world's greatest collection of decorative arts, including ancient Chinese ceramics, modernist architectural drawings, Korean bronze and Japanese swords, cartoons by Raphael, spellbinding Asian and Islamic art, Rodin sculptures, gowns from the Elizabethan era, dresses straight from this year's Paris fashion shows, ancient jewellery, a 1930s wireless set – and a lot more. Choose the section(s) you want to visit and stick to that plan.

Level 1 – the floor at street level – is mostly devoted to art and design from India, China, Japan, Korea and Southeast Asia, as well as European art. The museum has the best collection of Italian Renaissance sculpture outside Italy, as well as excellent French, German and Spanish pieces. One of the museum's highlights are the Cast Courts in room 46a, containing plaster casts collected in the Victorian era, such as Michelangelo's David, which was acquired in 1858. The museum's then director, Henry Cole, commissioned casts of Europe's finest works to be used by art students.

The Photography collection (room 38a) is one of the country's best, with more than 500,000 images collected since 1852. Among the highlights are the 19th-century photographs of London by Lady Clementina Hawarden. Room 40, the museum's Fashion Room, is among the most popular, with displays ranging from Elizabethan costumes to Vivienne Westwood gowns, dated 1980s Armani outfits and designs from this year's catwalks. A fascinating display of women's undergarments shows the 'progress' from the stifling and life-endangering corsets from Victorian times to present-day Agent Provocateur's sexy (and comfortable) versions.

The Jameel Gallery (room 42) contains more than 400 objects from the Islamic Middle East, including ceramics, textiles, carpets, glass and woodwork from the 8th-century caliphate up to the years before WWI. The pieces were collected from Spain to Afghanistan, though the exhibition's highlight is the gorgeous mid-16th-century Ardabil Carpet, the world's oldest (and one of the largest) dated carpet, from Iran.

The landscaped John Madejski Garden is a lovely shaded inner courtyard where you can collect your thoughts. Cross it to reach the original Refreshment Rooms dating from the 1860s (Morris, Gamble and Poynter Rooms) and redesigned by McInnes Usher McKnight Architects (MUMA) in 2006. MUMA has also renovated the V&A's Medieval and Renaissance galleries which are now located to the right of the Grand Entrance.

The British Galleries, featuring every aspect of British design from 1500 to 1900, are on levels 2 and 4. They include Henry VIII's writing desk and the so-called Great Bed of Ware from the late 16th century, big enough to sleep five and designed as an early advertising gimmick for an inn in Hertfordshire. Shakespeare mentions it in *Twelfth Night*. The Architecture gallery (rooms 127 to 128a) is also on level 4, with descriptions of architectural styles, videos, models and plans. In rooms 70 to 73 on level 4 is part of the Gilbert Collection of gold, silver, mosaics, gold boxes and enamel miniatures, which was housed in Somerset House until 2008.

The V&A's temporary exhibitions – such as 2007's Kylie (as in Minogue), 2008's Cold War Modern Design: 1945–70 and 2009's

Hats by mad milliner Stephen Jones – are compelling, fun and bring lots of visitors (note that admission fees apply), so check the website to find out what's on. The V&A also has an excellent program of talks, workshops and events, plus one of the best museum shops around.

NATURAL HISTORY MUSEUM
Map pp136-7

☎ 7942 5000; www.nhm.ac.uk; Cromwell Rd SW7; admission free; ☼ 10am-5.50pm; ⊖ South Kensington; ♿

This mammoth institution is dedicated to the Victorian pursuit of collecting and cataloguing. Walking into the Life galleries (Blue Zone) in the 1880 Gothic Revival building off Cromwell Rd evokes the musty moth-eaten era of the Victorian gentleman scientist. The main museum building, with its blue and sand-coloured brick and terracotta, was designed by Alfred Waterhouse and is as impressive as the towering diplodocus dinosaur skeleton in the Central Hall just ahead of the main entrance. It's hard to match any of the exhibits with this initial sight, except perhaps the huge blue whale just beyond it.

Children, who are the main fans of this museum, are primed for more primeval wildlife by the dinosaur skeleton, and yank their parents to the dinosaur gallery to the left of the Central Hall to see the roaring and tail-flicking animatronics T-rex dinosaur, the museum's star attraction.

The Life galleries to the right of the Central Hall (Green Zone) are full of fossils and glass cases of taxidermied birds, and the antiquated atmosphere is mesmerising. There is also a stunning Creepy Crawlies room, the Ecology gallery's video wall and the vast Darwin Centre (Orange Zone) which focuses on taxonomy (the study of the natural world), with some 450,000 jars of pickled specimens, including an 8.6m-long giant squid called Archie, shown off during free guided tours every half-hour (book in advance). The centre's new feature showcases some 28 million insects and six million plants in 'a giant cocoon'.

The second part of the museum, the Earth galleries (Red Zone) can be reached most easily from the Exhibition Rd entrance. Here Victorian fustiness is exchanged for sleek, modern design and the black walls of its Earth Hall are lined with crystals, gems and precious rocks. An escalator slithers up

through a hollowed-out globe into displays about earth's geological make-up.

Volcanoes, earthquakes and storms are all featured on the upper floors, but the star attraction inside the Restless Surface gallery, is the mock-up of the Kobe earthquake, a facsimile of a small Japanese grocery shop that trembles in a manner meant to replicate the 1995 earthquake that killed 6000 people. Exhibitions on the lower floors focus on ecology, look at gems and other precious stones and explore how planets are formed.

The Wildlife Garden (open April to September) displays a range of British lowland habitats. A stunning temporary exhibit that may become permanent is the Butterfly Jungle (adult/child & senior/family £6/4/17; ☼ 10am-6pm May-late Sep), a tunnel tent on the East Lawn swarming with what must originally have been called 'flutter-bys'.

SCIENCE MUSEUM Map pp136-7

☎ 0870 870 4868; www.sciencemuseum.org.uk; Exhibition Rd SW7; admission free, adult/concession IMAX Cinema £8/6.25, Motionride simulator £2.50/1.50; ☼ 10am-6pm; ⊖ South Kensington; ♿

With seven floors of interactive and educational exhibits, the Science Museum is informative, entertaining and comprehensive. Be advised that it is slated to undergo a massive modernisation costing £150 million. Parts or all of the museum may be closed when you visit so call or check the website beforehand.

The Energy Hall, on the ground floor as you enter, concentrates on full-sized machines of the Industrial Revolution, showing how the first steam engines such as Puffing Billy, a steam locomotive dating from 1813, helped Britain become 'the workshop of the world' in the early 19th century. Animations show how the machines worked and are accompanied by detailed overall explanations, including a section on the Luddites who opposed the march of technology.

Of course, it's impossible to miss the Energy Ring, a huge interactive sculpture that hangs in the space next to the gallery called Energy: Fuelling the Future on the 2nd floor. Kids can enter their names then ask energy questions: the answers appear like electronic tickertape messages, running around the inside of the ring. On the same level you will also find a re-creation of

Charles Babbage's Analytical Engine (1834), now considered the forerunner to the computer.

The 3rd-floor Flight and Launchpad galleries are favourite places for children, with its gliders, hot-air balloon and varied aircraft, including the *Gipsy Moth,* in which Amy Johnson flew to Australia in 1930. This floor also features an adapted flight simulator that's been turned into a 'Motionride' (admission fees apply). The 1st floor has displays on food and time, while the 4th and 5th floors offer exhibits on medical and veterinary history.

Nostalgic parents will delight in the old cars and the Apollo 10 command module in the Making the Modern World gallery on the ground floor. However, both they and their children will probably most enjoy the hi-tech Wellcome Wing, which is spread over several floors at the back of the building. IMAX Cinema here shows the usual crop of travelogues, space adventures and dinosaur attacks in stunning 3-D. There's a superlative exploration of identity on the 1st floor entitled Who am I? as well as other hands-on displays for children.

APSLEY HOUSE Map pp136-7
☎ 7499 5676; www.english-heritage.org.uk; 149 Piccadilly W1; adult/5-15yr/concession/family £5.70/2.90/4.80/17.50, with Wellington Arch £7/3.50/6/17.50; ⏰ 11am-5pm Wed-Sun Apr-Oct, 11am-4pm Wed-Sun Nov-Mar; ⊖ Hyde Park Corner
This stunning house, which contains exhibits devoted to the life and times of the Duke of Wellington, was once the first building to come into view when entering the city from the west and was therefore known as 'No 1 London'. Still one of London's finest but overlooking the nightmarish Hyde Park Corner roundabout, Apsley House was designed by Robert Adam for Baron Apsley in the late 18th century, but was later sold to the first Duke of Wellington, who cut Napoleon down to size in the Battle of Waterloo and lived here for 35 years until his death in 1852.

In 1947 the house was given to the nation, which must have come as a surprise to the duke's descendants who still live in a flat here; 10 of its rooms are open to the public and visited on a self-guided audio-guide tour. Wellington memorabilia, including the Iron Duke's medals, some entertaining old cartoons and his death mask, fill the basement gallery, while there's an astonishing collection of china, including

some of his personal silverware, on the ground floor. The stairwell is dominated by Antonio Canova's staggering 3.4m-high statue of a fig-leafed Napoleon, adjudged by the subject as 'too athletic'. The 1st-floor Wellington Gallery contains paintings by Velasquez, Rubens, Van Dyck, Brueghel and Murillo, but the most interesting is Goya's portrait of the duke, which some years ago was discovered to have the face of Napoleon's brother, Joseph Bonaparte, beneath the duke's. Apparently, the artist had taken a punt on Napoleon winning the Battle of Waterloo and had to do a quick 'about face' when news of Wellington's victory arrived.

WELLINGTON ARCH Map pp136-7
☎ 7930 2726; www.english-heritage.org.uk; Hyde Park Corner W1; adult/5-15yr/concession/family £3.50/1.80/3/17.50, with Apsley House £7/3.50/6/17.50; ⏰ 10am-5pm Wed-Sun Apr-Oct, 10am-4pm Wed-Sun Nov-Mar; ⊖ Hyde Park Corner; ♿
Opposite Apsley House in the little bit of green space being strangled by the Hyde Park Corner roundabout is England's answer to the Arc de Triomphe (except this one commemorates France's *defeat* – specifically, Napoleon's at the hands of the Duke of Wellington). The neoclassical arch, erected in 1826, used to be topped by a disproportionately large equestrian statue of the duke, but this was removed in 1883 and replaced some years later with the biggest bronze sculpture in Britain, *Peace Descending on the Quadriga of War* (1912).

For years part of the monument served as the capital's smallest police station, but was restored and opened up to the public as a three-floor exhibition space, with exhibits on the blue plaque scheme (p142) of historical markers (on the 1st floor), the nearby Australian and New Zealand war memorials (2nd floor; see below) and triumphal arches around the world (3rd floor). The open-air balconies (accessible by lift) afford unforgettable views of Hyde Park, Buckingham Palace and the Houses of Parliament.

AUSTRALIAN & NEW ZEALAND WAR MEMORIALS Map pp136-7
Hyde Park Corner W1; ⊖ Hyde Park Corner
Just southwest of Wellington Arch is the grey-green granite sweep of the Australian War Memorial (www.awmlondon.gov.au), erected in

2004, which commemorates the men and women of Australia who served in WWI and WWII. The names of four-dozen battle sites from both world wars are etched onto the blocks of the monolithic upper wall.

In the opposite direction (northeast) is the simpler yet more evocative New Zealand Monument (Southern Stand; www.mch.govt.nz/projects/memorials/london.html), erected in 2006, which consists of 16 cross-shaped bronze 'stand-ards' set out on a grassy slope. Standards 1 to 10 are adorned with text and reliefs and each has a theme (flag bearer, army, Maori at war, the forest); standards 11 to 16 form the Southern Cross constellation.

MICHELIN HOUSE Map pp136-7
81 Fulham Rd SW3; ⊖ South Kensington
Even if you're not up for dinner at the Bibendum (p248) restaurant in Michelin House,

LOCAL VOICES: EMILY COLE

Raised in Palmers Green in West London and now a resident of Walthamstow, Emily Cole is in charge of English Heritage's Blue Plaques Scheme, which has for almost a century-and-a-half memorialised the link between a building and a famous person with its distinctive 'cook's blue' ceramic roundel. She is also editor of the lavishly illustrated *Lived in London: Blue Plaques and the Stories Behind Them*, the most ambitious book on the scheme to date.

Bluer than blue too. But why? Brown plaques were used before the war but they weren't very noticeable. Blue stands out best against London's building materials – red brick, yellow brick, stucco. They've been developed specifically for London, though. They'd look dreadful on buildings in, say, Bath. They use bronze plaques there.

The scheme seems to have more rules than a Victorian grammar school. The most important is the '20/100-year rule'. The proposed person must have been dead 20 years or have passed the centenary of their birth. In the '60s, the 20 years was reduced to 10 for a short time. Perhaps it wasn't long enough to ensure that the person's fame was long-lasting.

Speaking of 15 minutes of fame, will every building one day have a plaque? At present there are 800 blue plaques here with a maximum 15 added each year. London is huge and expanding – people live in areas where there are almost none of our plaques at all. That's not counting plaques put up under different schemes, though, like those run by Westminster City Council, the Corporation of London and the Ealing Civic Society.

Some parts of town – Chelsea springs to mind – seem to be chock-a-block with plaques while others are deserts. Is this a classic 'have/have not' situation? The focus of the scheme was inner London until the Greater London Council took over in 1965. As a result there's high concentration in places like Bloomsbury (p79), a favourite of writers, painters and architects. Covent Garden (p75) has a huge percentage of plaques to foreigners (Benjamin Franklin, Herman Melville, Heinrich Heine) because of all the boarding houses that once stood there.

But aren't there gaps? Stalin lived on Jubilee St in Stepney Green for a couple of years but most people would never know that. Stalin definitely does not fit our 'contributed to human happiness or welfare' criteria! We'd get real grief if we put plaques up to people like him! The GLC was on slightly dodgy ground even when they put up a plaque to Lenin as 'Founder of USSR'. Even a plaque to Karl Marx in Chalk Farm was so seriously vandalised it was eventually moved to another Marx-associated location in Soho in the 1960s.

The public proposes, the panel sometimes disposes. Why are proposals rejected? It might be that the street has been renumbered and the person didn't actually live in the house in question. More likely, though, it has to do with the person's time in London not being long enough or having had little or no impact on them or their work.

A kind of 'Washington Slept Here' situation then. And as pithy as that. It's hard to summarise a person's achievements in 19 words, the maximum we're allowed on a plaque. Gandhi's plaque in Bow in East London has no description at all; his name stands for itself. Some are poetic. One of our favourites is scientist Luke Howard's in Tottenham. It says 'Namer of Clouds'.

Where can we find you when you're not creating posterity? I love London's open spaces and much of my life revolves around buildings. Ideally I'd merge the two and spent the day in a place like Hampton Court. In the evening it would be a gig at a place like the Luminaire (p303) in Kilburn, the 12 Bar Club (☎ 7240 2622; www.12barclub.com; 22-23 Denmark St WC2; ⊖ Tottenham Court Rd) in Soho or the Green Note (☎ 7485 9899; www.greennote.co.uk; 106 Parkway, London, NW1; ⊖ Camden Town) in Camden. I'm a musician's daughter and we have such a great music scene in this city. But I need to escape too. When life is dominated by London as much as mine is, it's nice to get away.

Emily Cole was interviewed by Steve Fallon.

mosey past and have a look at the superb art nouveau architecture. It was built for Michelin between 1905 and 1911 by François Espinasse, and completely restored in 1985. The famous roly-poly Michelin Man appears in the modern stained glass while the lobby is decorated with tiles showing early-20th-century cars.

KENSINGTON PALACE Map pp136-7

☎ 0844 482 5170; www.hrp.org.uk; Kensington Gardens W8; adult/5-16yr/concession/family £12.50/6.25/11/34, park & gardens free; ☉ 10am-6pm Mar-Oct, to 5pm Nov-Feb; ⊖ Queensway, Notting Hill Gate or High St Kensington
Kensington Palace already had a long history when Diana moved in with the Queen's sister, Princess Margaret, after her separation (and 1996 divorce) from Prince Charles. Built in 1605, the palace became the favourite royal residence under William and Mary of Orange in 1689, and remained so until George III became king and relocated to Buckingham Palace. Even after that the royal family stayed here occasionally, with Queen Victoria being born here in 1819.

In the 17th and 18th centuries, Kensington Palace was variously renovated by Sir Christopher Wren and William Kent. A self-paced audio tour leads you through the surprisingly small, wood-panelled State Apartments dating from William's time and then the grander apartments by Kent. For most visitors, however, the highlight is the Royal Ceremonial Dress Collection, which contains costumes and outfits dating from the 18th century to the present day, including some of Diana's most impressive frocks.

Most beautiful of all the quarters is the Cupola Room, where the ceremony initiating men into the exclusive Order of the Garter took place and where Victoria was christened; you can see the order's crest painted on the trompe l'œil 'domed' ceiling, which is actually flat. The Queen's Apartments nearby is where Queen Mary entertained her visitors.

The King's Gallery, the largest and longest of the State Apartments displays some of the royal art collection, including the only known painting of a classical subject by Van Dyck. On the ceiling William Kent painted the story of Odysseus but slipped up by giving the Cyclops two eyes.

The King's Drawing Room is dominated by a monumentally ugly painting of Cupid and Venus by Giorgio Vasari (1511–74), an Italian mannerist painter who used to brag about the speed at which he worked and was better known for his historical record of the Renaissance. There are splendid views of the park and gardens from here; you can also see the Round Pond, once full of turtles for turtle soup but now popular for sailing model boats.

The King's Staircase is decorated with striking murals by William Kent, who painted himself in a turban on the fake dome.

The Sunken Garden near the palace is at its prettiest in summer; the nearby Orangery (p249) designed by Vanbrugh and Hawksmoor as a free-standing conservatory in 1704, is a bright, rather formal, place for tea.

KENSINGTON GARDENS Map pp136-7

☎ 7298 2000; www.royalparks.org.uk; ☉ 6am-dusk; ⊖ Queensway, High St Kensington or Lancaster Gate
Immediately west of Hyde Park and across the Serpentine lake, these gardens are technically part of Kensington Palace. The palace and the gardens have become something of a shrine to the memory of Princess Diana since her death in 1997. If you have kids, visit the Diana, Princess of Wales Memorial Playground, in the northwest corner of the gardens, which has some pretty ambitious attractions for children including tepees and a pirate ship.

Art is also characteristic of these gardens. George Frampton's celebrated Peter Pan statue is close to the lake. On the opposite side is a statue of Edward Jenner, who developed a vaccine for smallpox. To the west of the Serpentine is a sculpture of John Hanning Speke, the explorer who discovered the Nile.

SERPENTINE GALLERY Map pp136-7

☎ 7402 6075, recorded information 7298 1515; www.serpentinegallery.org; Kensington Gardens W2; admission free; ☉ 10am-6pm; ⊖ Knightsbridge; ♿
What looks like an unprepossessing 1930s-style tearoom in the midst of the leafy Kensington Gardens is one of London's most important contemporary art galleries. Artists including Damien Hirst, Andreas Gursky, Louise Bourgeois, Gabriel Orozco, Tomoko Takahashi and Jeff Koons have all exhibited at the Serpentine Gallery, and the gallery's huge windows beam natural light onto the pieces, making the space perfect for sculpture and interactive displays.

Every year a leading architect (who has never built in the UK) is commissioned to build a new 'Summer Pavilion' nearby, which is open from May to October. Past architects have included Alvaro Siza, Oscar Niemeyer, Daniel Libeskind, Zaha Hadid and SANAA partners Kazuyo Sejima and Ryue Nishizawa, who did the stunning New Museum in New York's Bowery district. Reading, talks and open-air cinema screenings take place here as well.

ALBERT MEMORIAL Map pp136-7
☎ 7495 0916; www.royalparks.org.uk/parks/kensington_gardens; 45min tours adult/concession £5/4.50; ☼ tours 2pm & 3pm 1st Sun of the month Mar-Dec; ✆ Knightsbridge or Gloucester Rd

On the southern edge of Kensington Gardens and facing the Royal Albert Hall on Kensington Gore, this memorial is as ostentatious as the subject, Queen Victoria's German husband Albert (1819–61), was purportedly humble. Albert explicitly said he did not want a monument and 'if (as is very likely) it became an artistic monstrosity like most of our monuments, it would upset my equanimity to be permanently ridiculed and laughed at in effigy'. Ignoring the good prince's wishes, the Lord Mayor (with Victoria's consent) got George Gilbert Scott to build the 53m-high, gaudy Gothic monument in 1872; the 4.25m-tall gilded statue of the prince, thumbing through a catalogue for his Great Exhibition and surrounded by 187 figures representing the continents (Asia, Europe, Africa and America), the arts, industry and science, was erected in 1876. The monument was unveiled again in 1998 after undergoing an £11.2-million renovation.

ROYAL ALBERT HALL Map pp136-7
☎ 7589 3203, tour bookings 0845 401 5045; www.royalalberthall.com; Kensington Gore SW7; ✆ South Kensington; ♿

This huge, domed, red-brick amphitheatre adorned with a frieze of Minton tiles is Britain's most famous concert venue and home to the BBC's Promenade Concerts (the Proms; see p306) every summer. The hall, built in 1871, was never intended as a concert venue but as a 'Hall of Arts and Sciences'; Queen Victoria added the 'Royal Albert' when she laid the foundation stone, much to the surprise of those attending. Consequently it spent the first 133 years

of its existence tormenting concert performers and audiences with its terrible acoustics. It was said that a piece played here was assured of an immediate second hearing, so bad was the reverberation around the oval structure. A massive refurbishment was completed in 2004, however, installing air-conditioning, modernising the backstage areas, moving the entrance to the south of the building and fixing the acoustics. You can take a 45-minute guided tour (☎ 7959 0558; adult/concession £8/7; ☼ tours hourly 10am-3.30pm Fri-Tue) of the hall from the box office at Door 12.

ROYAL GEOGRAPHICAL SOCIETY Map pp136-7
☎ 7591 3000; www.rgs.org; 1 Kensington Gore SW7; admission free; ☼ 10am-6.30pm Mon-Fri; ✆ South Kensington; ♿

Just east of the Royal Albert Hall is the headquarters of the Royal Geographical Society, founded in 1830 and housed in a Queen Anne–style red-brick edifice (1874) easily identified by the statues of explorers David Livingstone and Ernest Shackleton outside. The society holds a regular talks program (especially on Monday evenings) and photography exhibitions, while the Foyle Reading Room (☎ 7591 3044; adult/student per day £10/free; ☼ 10am-6.30 Mon,10am-5pm Tue-Fri) offers access to the society's collection of more than half a million maps, photographs, books and manuscripts. Enter from Exhibition Rd.

HYDE PARK Map pp136-7
☎ 7298 2000; www.royalparks.org.uk; ☼ 5.30am-midnight; ✆ Hyde Park Corner, Marble Arch, Knightsbridge or Lancaster Gate

London's largest royal park spreads itself over a whopping 142 hectares of neatly manicured gardens and wild, deserted expanses of overgrown grass. Spring prompts the gorgeous Rose Gardens, added in 1994, into vivacious bloom, and summers are full of sunbathers, picnickers, frisbee-throwers and general London populace who drape themselves across the green. It is also a magnificent backdrop for open-air concerts, demonstrations and royal occasions. Gun salutes are fired here and soldiers ride through the park each morning on their way to Horse Guards Parade in Whitehall.

Hyde Park is separated from Kensington Gardens by the L-shaped Serpentine, a small lake created by the damming of the Westbourne River in the 1730s; it's a good spot for pleasure boating in summer. Henry VIII expropriated the park from the Church in 1536, after which it became a hunting ground for kings and aristocrats; later it became a popular venue for duels, executions and horse racing. It became the first royal park to open to the public in the early 17th century, and famously hosted the Great Exhibition in 1851. During WWII it became an enormous potato bed.

You'll either love or hate the ornate Queen Elizabeth Gate designed by Giuseppe Lund and David Wynne in 1993 to honour the late Queen Mother, which leads onto Park Lane near Hyde Park Corner. West of the gate is the Holocaust Memorial Garden (1983), a simple stone marker in a grove of trees with a quote from Lamentations: 'For thee I weep, streams of tears flow from my eyes because of the destruction of my people.' North of the gate is the new 7 July Memorial of 52 square stainless steel pillars dedicated to the victims of the terrorist bombings in London in July 2005.

PRINCESS DIANA MEMORIAL FOUNTAIN Map pp136-7
Kensington Gardens W2; ⊖ Knightsbridge
Opposite the Kensington Gardens' Serpentine Gallery and across West Carriage Drive is this memorial fountain dedicated to the late Princess of Wales in 2004. Envisaged by the designer Kathryn Gustafson as a 'moat without a castle' and draped 'like a necklace' around the southwestern edge of Hyde Park near the Serpentine Bridge, this circular double stream initially invited visitors, especially children, to wade in the fountain. But when several people slipped on the smooth granite basin and injured themselves, a gravel path was built around it. Visitors still flock here to be mesmerised by the water's flow both left and right from the fountain's highest point, or to sun themselves around it in fine weather, but guards prevent them jumping into the water.

SPEAKERS' CORNER Map pp136-7
⊖ Marble Arch
The northeastern corner of Hyde Park is traditionally the spot for oratorical acrobatics and soapbox ranting. It's the only place in Britain where demonstrators can assemble without police permission, a con-cession granted in 1872 as a response to serious riots 17 years before when 150,000 people gathered to demonstrate against the Sunday Trading Bill before Parliament. Speakers' Corner was frequented by Karl Marx, Vladimir Lenin, George Orwell and William Morris; if you've got something to get off your chest, you can get rid of it here on Sunday, although it'll be largely loonies, religious fanatics and hecklers you'll have for company.

MARBLE ARCH Map pp136-7
⊖ Marble Arch
John Nash designed this huge arch in 1827. It was moved here, to the northeastern corner of Hyde Park, from its original spot in front of Buckingham Palace in 1851, when it was adjudged too small and unimposing to be the entrance to the royal manor. If you're feeling anarchic, walk through the central portal, a privilege reserved by (unenforced) law for the royal family and the ceremonial King's Troop Royal Horse Artillery. A plaque on the traffic island at Marble Arch indicates the spot where the infamous Tyburn Tree, a three-legged gallows, once stood. An estimated 50,000 people were executed here between 1571 and 1783, many having been dragged from the Tower of London. During the 16th century many Catholics were executed for their faith and it later became a place of Catholic pilgrimage.

TYBURN CONVENT Map pp136-7
☎ 7723 7262; www.tyburnconvent.org.uk; 8 Hyde Park Pl W2; admission free; ⊙ 6.30am-8.30pm, crypt tours 10.30am, 3.30pm & 5.30pm daily; ⊖ Marble Arch
A convent was established here in 1903, close to the site of the Tyburn Tree gallows (above). The crypt contains the relics of some 105 martyrs, along with paintings commemorating their lives and recording their deaths. A closed order of Benedictine sisters still form a community here.

BROMPTON ORATORY Map pp136-7
☎ 7808 0900; www.bromptonoratory.com; 215 Brompton Rd SW7; ⊙ 7am-8pm; ⊖ South Kensington
Also known as the London Oratory and the Oratory of St Philip Neri, this Roman Catholic church was built in the Italian baroque

style in 1884. It has marble and statues galore, and counts Tony and Cherie Blair, Britain's former 'First Couple', among its celebrity parishioners. There are five daily Masses on weekdays (including a Latin one at 6pm), four on Saturday, and nine between 7am and 7pm on Sunday.

VICTORIA & PIMLICO

WESTMINSTER CATHEDRAL
Map pp136-7

☎ 7798 9055; www.westminstercathedral.org.uk; Victoria St SW1; cathedral admission free, tower adult/concession/family £5/2.50/11; ☉ cathedral 7am-7pm, tower 9.30am-12.30pm & 1-5pm daily Apr-Nov, Thu-Sun Dec-Mar; ☻ Victoria; ☒ John Francis Bentley's 19th-century cathedral, mother church of Roman Catholicism in England and Wales, is a superb example of neo-Byzantine architecture with its distinctive candy-striped red-brick and white-stone tower features. Although construction started here in 1896 and worshippers began attending services seven years later, the church ran out of money and the interior has never been completed.

Some parts of the interior are ablaze with mosaics and ornamented with 100 types of marble; other areas are just bare brick. The highly regarded stone bas-reliefs of the Stations of the Cross (1918) by Eric Gill and the marvellously sombre atmosphere make this a welcome haven from the traffic outside. The views from the 83m-tall bell tower – thankfully, accessible by lift – are

impressive. Six Masses are said daily from Sunday to Friday and five on Saturday.

THE HYDE PARK WALK
Walking Tour

1 Hyde Park Corner Climb monumental Wellington Arch (p141) for great views and, in the same small square of grass, you will find the rather tasteful wall of eucalypt-green granite of the Australian War Memorial (p141) and the 16 'standards' of the New Zealand Monument (p142).

2 The Serpentine Keep to the lake's northern side and interrupt your walk by renting a paddle boat from the Serpentine boathouse (☎ 7262 1330; adult/child per 30min £6/2, per 1hr £8/3; ☉ 10am-4pm Feb & Mar, 10am-6pm Apr-Jun, 10am-7pm Jul & Aug, 10am-5pm Sep & Oct, 10am-5pm Sat & Sun Nov). The Serpentine solar shuttle boat (single/return adult £2.50/4.50, child £1/1.50, family £6/10; ☉ every 30min noon-5pm), uses only solar power to get you from the boathouse to the Princess Diana Memorial Fountain.

3 Princess Diana Memorial Fountain Despite early teething problems, this con-

WALK FACTS
Start Hyde Park Corner tube station
End Lancaster Gate tube station
Distance 2 miles
Duration About 1½ hours
Fuel stops Coffee and cake at the Lido Café (opposite), end-of-walk drink at the Swan (opposite)

THE HYDE PARK WALK

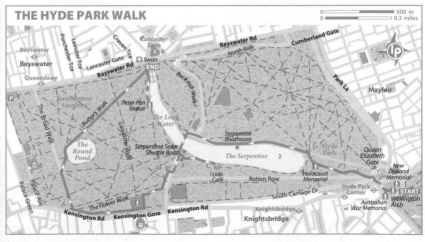

crete memorial fountain (p139) sitting on a perfectly manicured lawn is a popular chill-out spot today. Water flows from the highest point in both directions, into a small pool at the bottom. Bathing is forbidden, although you are allowed to dip your feet. From here you can walk over to the Lido Café (☎ 7706 7098; ☽ 9am-8pm Apr-Oct, 10am-4pm Nov-Mar).

4 Serpentine Gallery This former teahouse is now one of the city's best contemporary art galleries (p143) and houses interesting exhibitions and summer pavilions designed by the world's leading architects.

5 Albert Memorial Gilded and enormous, the Albert Memorial (p144) is in stark contrast with the humility of the real Prince Albert, Queen Victoria's much-loved husband.

6 Royal Albert Hall Another memorial to Queen Victoria's beloved husband, this is Britain's most famous concert hall (p144). It has seen more big names and significant performances in its time than most others, including the choral version of Blake's *Jerusalem*, held to celebrate the granting of the vote to women in 1928.

7 Kensington Palace Princes Diana's former home and a long-standing royal residence (p143), this is where you can stop off and take a look at the permanent and temporary exhibitions and the stunning interior, before surrendering to one of the park's many stretches of grass.

8 Lancaster Gate There's plenty more to see in the park, if you have time, stamina and the strength of will to resist merely having a snooze on the grass or stopping in at the

CLERKENWELL, SHOREDITCH & SPITALFIELDS

Drinking p281; Eating p251; Shopping p225; Sleeping p345

These three redeveloped post-industrial areas northeast of the city remain London's creative engine room and, for many visitors, its current throbbing heart. Whatever you may think of that, these are undoubtedly good areas for some of London's best nightlife, shopping, eating and cultural distractions. The three adjoining but very different districts are Clerkenwell, just north of the City; Shoreditch and its northern extension Hoxton, an area (roughly) between Old St tube station and just east of Shoreditch High St; and Spitalfields, centred around the market of that name and Brick Lane (p152), Banglatown's main thoroughfare (the nickname Banglatown refers to the Bengali community in this area).

The Shoreditch phenomenon began in the late 1990s, when creative types chased out of the West End by prohibitive rents began buying warehouses in this then urban wasteland, abandoned after the collapse of the fabrics industry. Within a few years the area was seriously cool, boasting superslick bars, cutting-edge clubs, galleries and restaurants that catered to the new media-creative-freelance squad. The fact that it was in walking distance of the City and its high-spending, heavy-drinking denizens didn't hurt.

Yet despite the general expectation that the Shoreditch scene would collapse under the weight of its own trucker hats, the regenerated

top picks

CLERKENWELL, SHOREDITCH & SPITALFIELDS

- Dennis Severs' House (p152)
- Geffrye Museum (opposite)
- Spitalfields Market (p153)
- St John's Gate (opposite)
- White Cube Gallery (opposite)

area is flourishing stronger than ever, with new developments bringing life to some of London's poorest corners, and even spilling over into nearby Hackney and Bethnal Green.

Clerkenwell and Spitalfields, either side of Shoreditch, have also profited from the resurgence of the area. Historic Clerkenwell is now the most wealthy of the three, with many once-empty warehouses that have been converted into expensive flats and work spaces. While a great place to see historic landmarks, it is also home to London superclub Fabric (p296) and enjoys a superb eating scene. Spitalfields, a diverse area that has seen wave after wave of immigration spanning centuries, is centred on its once historic market, which was recently redeveloped and now sadly feels a shadow of its former self, stuffed to the rafters with chain restaurants. Despite this, the neighbourhood remains one of London's edgiest and most exciting – as any stroll around Brick Lane will tell you.

CLERKENWELL

CHARTERHOUSE Map p150

☎ 7251 5002; Charterhouse Sq EC1; admission £10; ⏰ guided tours 2.15pm Wed Apr-Aug; ⊖ Barbican or Farringdon

You need to book nearly a year in advance to see inside this former Carthusian monastery, whose centrepiece is a Tudor hall with a restored hammer-beam roof. Its incredibly popular two-hour guided tours, held from April to August, begin at the 14th-century gatehouse on Charterhouse Sq, before going through to the Preachers' Court (with three original monks' cells in the western wall), the Master's Court, the Great Hall and the Great Chamber, where Queen Elizabeth I stayed on numerous occasions.

The monastery was founded in 1371 by the Carthusians, the strictest of all Roman Catholic monastic orders, who refrained from eating meat and took vows of silence, broken only for three hours on Sunday. During the Reformation the monastery was oppressed, with at least three priors hanged at Tyburn (p145) and a dozen monks sent to Newgate, where they were chained upright and died of starvation. King Henry VIII confiscated the monastery in 1537, and it was purchased in 1611 by Thomas Sutton, known at the time as the 'richest commoner in England'. Sutton – of Sutton House (p158) fame – opened an almshouse for destitute gentlemen; some three dozen pensioners (known as 'brothers') live here today and lead the tours.

For tickets, send a stamped self-addressed envelope, a covering letter giving the dates of three Wednesdays between April and August when you would like to visit, and a cheque made payable to 'Charterhouse', to Tour Bookings, Charterhouse, Charterhouse Sq, London EC1M 6AN. A slightly less antediluvian way to visit is simply by coming during Open House weekend (www.openhouse.org.uk).

ST JOHN'S GATE Map p150
➌ Farringdon

This surprisingly out-of-place medieval gate cutting across St John's Lane is no modern folly, but the real deal. It dates from the early 16th century and was heavily restored 300 years later. During the Crusades, the Knights of St John of Jerusalem, soldiers who took on a nursing role, established a priory in Clerkenwell that originally covered around 4 hectares. The gate was built in 1504 as a grand entrance to their church, St John's Clerkenwell in St John's Sq.

Although most of the buildings were destroyed when Henry VIII dissolved every priory in the country between 1536 and 1540, the gate lived on. It had a varied afterlife, not least as a Latin-speaking coffee house run, without much success, by William Hogarth's father during Queen Anne's reign. The restoration dates from the period when it housed the Old Jerusalem Tavern in the 19th century. A pub of (almost) that name can now be found round the corner on Britton St (see p281).

Inside St John's Gate is the small Order of St John Museum (☎ 7324 4005; www.sja.org.uk/museum; St John's Lane EC1), which was closed for a full refit at the time of writing and should reopen in 2010. Definitely try to time your visit for one of the guided tours (adult/senior £5/4; ☼ tours 11am & 2.30pm Tue, Fri & Sat) of the gate and the restored church remains, though. This includes the fine Norman crypt with a sturdy alabaster monument commemorating a Castilian knight (1575); a battered monument portraying the last prior, William Weston, as a skeleton in a shroud; and stained-glass windows showing the main figures in the story. You'll also be shown the sumptuous Chapter Hall where the Chapter General of the Order meets every three months.

BUNHILL FIELDS Map p150
Bunhill Row EC1; ☼ 8am-7pm Mon-Fri, 9.30am-7pm Sat & Sun Apr-Sep, closes 4pm Oct-Mar; ➌ Old St

This cemetery just outside the City walls has been a burial ground for over 1000 years (indeed 'Bunhill' supposedly comes from the rather macabre historical name for the area – 'Bone Hill'). It's probably the best-known 'dissenters' (ie non–Church of England) cemetery in the country. Here you can see the graves of such literary giants as Daniel Defoe, John Bunyan and William Blake. It's a lovely place for a stroll, and a rare green space in this built-up area. Across City Rd to the east of the cemetery is Wesley's Chapel, built in 1778. It was home and place of work and worship for John Wesley, the founder of Methodism.

KARL MARX MEMORIAL LIBRARY
Map p150

☎ 7253 1485; www.marx-memorial-library.org; 37a Clerkenwell Green EC1; admission free; ☼ 1-6pm Mon-Thu; ➌ Farringdon

Clerkenwell has quite a radical history. An area of Victorian-era slums (the so-called Rookery), it was settled by mainly Italian immigrants in the 19th century. Modern Italy's founding father, Garibaldi, dropped by in 1836. During his European exile, Lenin edited 17 editions of the Russian-language Bolshevik newspaper *Iskra* (Spark) from here in 1902–03, while he lived in nearby Finsbury. Copies of the newspaper have been preserved in today's library, along with a host of other socialist literature. Nonmembers are free to look around between 1pm and 2pm.

SHOREDITCH & HOXTON

WHITE CUBE GALLERY Map p150

☎ 7930 5373; www.whitecube.com; 48 Hoxton Sq N1; admission free; ☼ 10am-6pm Tue-Sat; ➌ Old St

Jay Jopling, dealer to the stars of the Brit Art firmament, made his reputation in the 1990s by exhibiting then-unknown artists such as Damien Hirst, Antony Gormley and Tracey Emin. This Hoxton Sq cube is aptly named and, while the gallery is now part of Britain's 'new establishment', it's always worth a visit just to have a look at the latest shows. There's another White Cube (p69) in St James's.

GEFFRYE MUSEUM Map p150

☎ 7739 9893; www.geffrye-museum.org.uk; 136 Kingsland Rd E2; admission by donation; ☼ 10am-5pm Tue-Sat, noon-5pm Sun; ➌ Old St or Liverpool St; ♿

Definitely Shoreditch's most accessible sight, this 18th-century ivy-clad series of

CLERKENWELL, SHOREDITCH & SPITALFIELDS

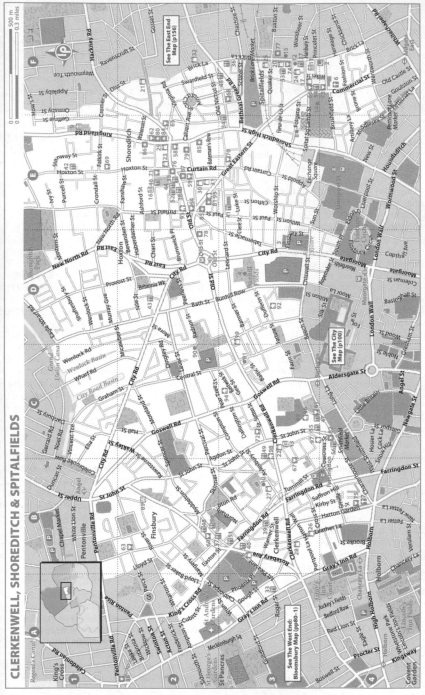

CLERKENWELL, SHOREDITCH & SPITALFIELDS

almshouses with a herb garden draws you in immediately. The museum inside is devoted to domestic interiors, with each room of the main building furnished to show how the homes of the relatively affluent middle class would have looked from Elizabethan times right through to the end of the 19th century. A postmodernist extension completed in 1998 contains several 20th-century rooms (a flat from the 1930s, a room in the contemporary style of the 1950s and a 1990s converted warehouse complete with Ikea furniture) as well as a lovely herb garden, gallery for temporary exhibits, a design centre with works from the local community, a shop and restaurant.

Another development has been the exquisite restoration of a historic almshouse interior (adult/under 16yr £2/free). It's the absolute attention to detail that impresses, right down to the vintage newspaper left open on the breakfast table. The setting is so fragile, however, that this small almshouse is only open twice a month (usually on a Wednesday and Saturday).

SPITALFIELDS

Crowded around its eponymous market and the marvellous Hawksmoor Christ Church, Spitalfields, this wedge of the capital between the city and Shoreditch is a layer cake of immigration from all over the world. Waves of Huguenots (French Protestants persecuted in France), Jews, Irish and, more recently, Indian and Bangladeshi immigrants have made Spitalfields home and it remains one of the capital's most multicultural areas. Don't miss Spitalfields Market, the beautiful Victorian landmark that is one of the city's most vibrant weekend shopping experiences (see p227).

BRICK LANE Map p150

Brick Lane is the centrepiece of a thriving Bengali community in an area nicknamed Banglatown. The lane itself, south of the Old Truman Brewery is one long procession of curry and balti houses intermingled with fabric shops and Indian supermarkets. Sadly, the once-high standard of cooking in the curry houses is a distant memory, so you're probably better off trying subcontinental cuisine in Whitechapel (p255).

Just past Hanbury St is the converted Old Truman Brewery. This was once London's largest brewery. The Director's House on the left harks back to 1740, the old Vat House across the road with its hexagonal bell tower is early 19th century, and the Engineer's House next to it dates from 1830. The brewery stopped producing beer in 1989, and in the 1990s became home to a host of independent music businesses, small shops and hip clubs and bars. North of here Brick Lane is a very different place, stuffed with great clothing, book and record stores, some of London's best bagel bakeries and plenty of cafes and bars.

DENNIS SEVERS' HOUSE Map p150

☎ 7247 4013; www.dennissevershouse.co.uk; 18 Folgate St E1; Sun/Mon/Mon evening £8/5/12; ☒ noon-4pm Sun, noon-2pm Mon following 1st & 3rd Sun of the month plus evening (times vary seasonally) every Mon; ⊖ Liverpool St
This quirky hotchpotch of a cluttered house is named after the late American eccentric who restored and turned it into what he called a 'still-life drama'. Visitors find they have entered the home of a 'family' of Huguenot silk weavers, who were common to the Spitalfields area in the 18th century. However, while they see the fabulous restored Georgian interiors, with meals and drinks half-abandoned and rumpled sheets, and while they smell cooking and hear creaking floorboards, their 'hosts' always remain tantalisingly just out of reach. It's a unique and intriguing proposition by day, but 'Silent Night' tours by candlelight every Monday evening (bookings essential) are even more memorable.

Dennis Severs' House is not the only fine Georgian house in Folgate St, north of Spitalfields market: the street is lined with them, and they too were once occupied by the Huguenots who fled religious persecution in France to settle here in the late 17th century, bringing with them their skills as silk weavers. Their presence is still recalled by such street names as Fleur-de-Lis St and Nantes Passage. There are yet more restored Georgian houses along Fournier St.

BRICK LANE GREAT MOSQUE Map p150

Brick Lane Jamme Mosjid; www.bricklanemosque .com; 59 Brick Lane E1; ☒ Sat-Thu; ⊖ Liverpool St
The best example of the changes in population that this area has experienced over the past several centuries is this house of worship on Brick Lane. Built in 1743 as the New French Church for the Huguenots, it served as a Methodist chapel from 1819 until it was transformed into the Great Synagogue for Jewish refugees from Russia and central Europe in 1898. In 1976 it changed faiths yet again, becoming the Great Mosque. Visits allowed outside prayer times.

CHRIST CHURCH, SPITALFIELDS Map p150

☎ 7859 3035; www.christchurchspitalfields.org; Commercial St E1; ☒ 11am-4pm Tue, 1-4pm Sun; ⊖ Liverpool St
Diagonally opposite Spitalfields market, on the corner of Commercial and Fournier Sts, is this restored church, where many of the weavers worshipped. The magnificent English baroque structure, with a tall spire sitting on a portico of four great Tuscan columns, was designed by Nicholas Hawksmoor and completed in 1729.

MUSEUM OF IMMIGRATION & DIVERSITY Map p150

☎ 7247 5352; www.19princeletstreet.org.uk; 19 Princelet St E1; admission free, donations gratefully accepted; ⊖ Liverpool St
This unique Huguenot town house was built in 1719 and housed a prosperous family of weavers, before becoming home to waves of immigrants including Polish, Irish and Jewish families, the last of which built a synagogue in the back garden in 1869. In keeping with the house's multicultural past, it now houses a Museum of Immigration & Diversity, whose carefully considered exhibits are aimed at both adults and

children. Unfortunately the house is in urgent need of repair and as such opens only infrequently (usually no more than a dozen times a year). Check the website for dates.

SUNDAYS AT SPITALFIELDS & SHOREDITCH
Walking Tour

1 Spitalfields Market This is one of London's best markets (p227), and a great weekend treat for clothing, records and food. As you approach from Liverpool St, you'll see the new development, which, although trying to maintain an independent spirit, lacks the old market's rugged and spontaneous atmosphere. Enter the old market building and get lost among the many stalls.

2 Absolute Vintage Check out the tons of vintage shoes in this excellent shop (p219). There are colours and sizes for all, with shoes ranging from designer vintage to something out of your grandma's storage. Clothes for men and women line the back of the shop.

WALK FACTS

Best time Sunday mornings
Start Liverpool St tube station
End Old St tube station
Distance 2 miles
Duration One hour
Fuel Stops Food stalls at the back of Sunday UpMarket (p227), Brick Lane Beigel Bake (p255), drink at Hoxton Sq

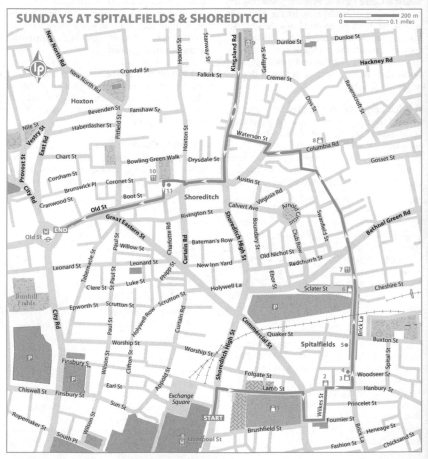

SUNDAYS AT SPITALFIELDS & SHOREDITCH

3 Sunday UpMarket Having lost valuable stall space with the new development, the young designers moved their market (p227) inside the Old Truman Brewery. The new space is brilliant – not as crowded, with wonderful clothes, music and crafts, and the excellent food hall (on the Brick Lane end) has worldwide grub, from Ethiopian veggie dishes to Japanese delicacies.

4 Old Truman Brewery This was the biggest brewery (p152) in London by the mid-18th century, and the Director's House on the left dates from 1740. Next to the 19th-century Vat House is the 1830 Engineer's House and a row of former stables. The brewery shut down in 1989 and is now part of Sunday UpMarket.

5 Brick Lane In 1550 this was just a country road leading to brickyards; by the 18th century it had been paved and lined with houses and cottages inhabited by the Spitalfields weavers. Today the southern part of this vibrant street (p152) is taken up by touristy curry houses and all the street names are in Bengali as well as English.

6 Brick Lane Market Sundays at Brick Lane around the soon-to-be-reopened Shoreditch tube station are the best place to find good bargains for clothes, but the market (p227) is particularly good for furniture. Saunter down Cheshire St for little boutiques featuring new designers and vintage collections.

7 Brick Lane Beigel Bake At the far end of Brick Lane, this excellent bagel business (p255) was started by some of the Jewish families who originally settled in the neighbourhood and still live here. It operates 24 hours a day and is always busy: with market shoppers on Sunday and Shoreditch clubbers by night.

8 Columbia Road Flower Market Every Sunday from dawn market stalls sell freshly cut flowers, plants and orchids for Londoners' gardens and window sills. The earlier you arrive, the better the market (p227), though the best bargains are to be had later on (around noon) as things wrap up. Make a beeline for the food stalls behind the main flower sellers for a mid-morning snack.

9 Geffrye Museum A small estate of Victorian houses, this fascinating museum (p149) is devoted to English interiors through the ages. End your walk in the lovely glass cafe in the back, and have a look at the museum's aromatic herb garden.

10 Hoxton Square Pop into Hoxton Sq on the way. Check out the small park where there's always something going on and join the crowds having a drink outside if the weather is good.

11 White Cube Gallery The first (of the two) creations of Brit Art pioneer Jay Jopling, this gallery (p149) always has something fun or controversial hanging on its pristine white walls.

THE EAST END & DOCKLANDS

Drinking p283; Eating p255; Shopping p229; Sleeping p346

The East End district of Whitechapel may lie within easy walking distance east of the City, and neighbourhoods to the northeast such as Bethnal Green and Mile End may be just one and two tube stops away, but the change of style and visuals is nothing short of extraordinary. Traditionally this was working-class London, an area settled by wave upon wave of immigrants, giving it a curious mixture of French Huguenot, Irish, Jewish and Bangladeshi cultures, which can still be felt to varying degrees today. Rundown and neglected in the early 1980s, the East End is starting to look up in many areas. Signs of wealth have started to trickle into the areas around Whitechapel and Aldgate, property prices have risen meteorically in Mile End, Bethnal Green and Bow, and there's increased development in down-at-the-heel Hackney and Dalston.

Anyone interested in modern multicultural London should visit the East End. Alongside some interesting, well-endowed museums you'll find some of London's best-value Asian cuisine, as well as some of its most colourful markets. You may also want to pop into the newly extended Whitechapel Art Gallery (below) or cycle through Victoria Park (p160), which is among London's most beautiful.

top picks

THE EAST END & DOCKLANDS

- Whitechapel Gallery (left)
- Museum of London Docklands (p161)
- Canary Wharf Tower (p162)
- Ragged School Museum (p159)
- Victoria Park (p160)

Cobbled from the warehouses, docks and basins that made London so fabulously wealthy from the 18th century onward, Docklands, the East End's southern extension, is a world of contrasts. Eye-catching bridges across docks and futuristic buildings dominate the skyline; it really is today's view of London tomorrow. But it is an area rich in history, too, and the Museum of London Docklands (p161) helps bring it all to life.

THE EAST END

Whitechapel

The East End's main thoroughfare, Whitechapel High St, hums with a cacophony of Asian, African and Middle Eastern languages, its busy shops selling everything from Indian snacks to Nigerian fabrics and Turkish jewellery, as the East End's multitudinous ethnic groupings rub up against each other more or less comfortably. It's still a chaotic and poor place, but it's full of life and should not be missed.

WHITECHAPEL GALLERY Map p156

☎ 7522 7888; www.whitechapelgallery.org; 77-82 Whitechapel High St E1; admission free; ⏰ 11am-6pm Tue-Sun, to 9pm Thu; ⊖ Aldgate East; ♿
This ground-breaking gallery, which moved into its main art nouveau building in 1899, has now extended into the library next door, bringing its total number of galleries to 10 and doubling its exhibition space. Founded by the Victorian philanthropist Canon Samuel Barnett at the end of the 19th century to bring art to the people of East London, it has made its name by putting on exhibitions

by both established and emerging artists, cartoonists and architects, including Jackson Pollock (his first UK show), Gary Hume, Robert Crumb and Mies van der Rohe. Picasso's *Guernica* was first shown here in 1939; and a tapestry of the painting, on loan from the UN building in New York, went on display in 2009, to mark the reopening. The gallery's ambitiously themed shows change every couple of months – check the program online – and there's also live music, poetry readings, talks and films till late on Thursday and sometimes on Friday. And don't miss the phenomenal 'social sculptures' in various (and ephemeral) spaces throughout. Other features are an excellent bookshop, the Whitechapel Gallery Dining Room (p155) and an überdesigned cafe on the 1st floor.

WHITECHAPEL BELL FOUNDRY Map p156

☎ 7247 2599; www.whitechapelbellfoundry.co.uk; 32-34 Whitechapel Rd E1; tours per person £10; ⏰ tours 10am & 2pm Sat, shop 9.30am-4.15pm Mon-Fri; ⊖ Aldgate East
The Whitechapel Bell Foundry has been standing on this site since 1738, although

an earlier foundry nearby is known to have been in business in 1570. Both Big Ben (1858; p92) and the Liberty Bell (1752) in Philadelphia were cast here, and the foundry also cast a new bell for New York City's Trinity Church, damaged in the terrorist attacks of 11 September 2001. The 1½-hour guided tours on Saturday (maximum 25 people) are often booked out a year in advance. During weekday trading hours you can view a few small exhibits in the foyer or buy bell-related items from the shop.

WHITECHAPEL ROAD Map p156

Within a few minutes' walk of Whitechapel tube station you'll find the large East London Mosque (46-92 Whitechapel Rd E1) and behind it on Fieldgate St the Great Synagogue built in 1899.

On Cable St, just south of Commercial Rd and heading towards Wapping, you'll find

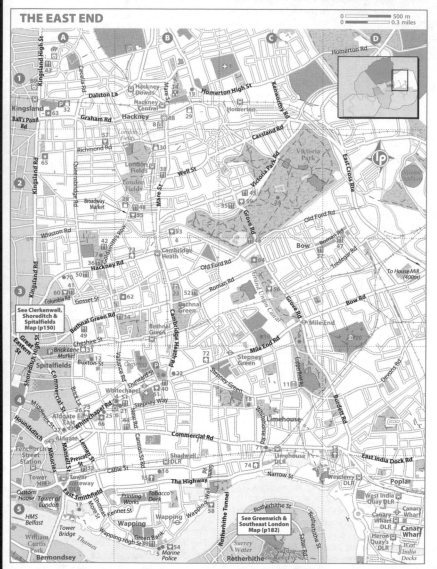

THE EAST END

the former St George's Town Hall building (236 Cable St E1), now a council library on the corner with Library Place. On the east wall of the building is a large mural commemorating the riots that took place here in October 1936 when the British fascist Oswald Mosley led a bunch of his Blackshirt thugs into the area to intimidate the local Jewish population. They were repelled by local people – Jews and non-Jews alike.

You're now also deep in Jack the Ripper territory. In fact, Mary Ann Nichols, first of the serial killer's five victims, was hacked to death on 31 August 1888 on what is now Durward St, north of (and just behind) Whitechapel tube station.

Along Whitechapel Rd itself, the criminal connections continue through the centuries. Just before the intersection with Cambridge Heath Rd sits a pub called the Blind Beggar (☎ 7247 6195; 337 Whitechapel Rd E1), where the notorious gangster Ronnie Kray shot George Cornell dead in 1966, in a turf war over control of the East End's organised crime. He was jailed for life and died in 1995.

After the intersection with Cambridge Heath Rd, this traditionally poor area's history takes a more philanthropic turn, with a statue of William Booth (1829–1912) who established his Salvation Army Christian Mission here in 1865, and the Trinity Green Almshouses, poorhouses built for injured or retired sailors in 1695. The two rows of almshouses run at right angles away from the street, facing a village-type green and a chapel with a clock tower.

WOMEN'S LIBRARY Map p156

☎ 7320 2222; www.thewomenslibrary.ac.uk; Old Castle St E1; admission free; ⏰ 9.30am-5.30pm Mon-Wed & Fri, to 8pm Thu, 10am-4pm Sat; ⊖ Aldgate East; ♿

Just round the corner from the Whitechapel Gallery, the Women's Library, part of the London Metropolitan University, is a unique repository for all manner of books and documents related to women's history. It contains a reading room open to the public, as well as archive and museum collections, and organises talks and special

THE EAST END

exhibitions (last seen – Between the Covers: Women's Magazines and Their Reader). The building is a modern take on the former Goulston Square Wash House, one of the oldest public baths in London.

Bethnal Green & Hackney

Bethnal Green, the poorest district of London during Victorian times, and sprawling Hackney – whose Saxon name, from *haccan* (to kill with an axe or sword) and *ey* (river), indicates a place of battle – make up the 'proper' East End and can lay claim to being among the most ethnically diverse areas of the capital, with sizable populations of Afro-Caribbeans, Bangladeshis, Turks and Kurds. While neither district is on the tourist trail, both amply repay a visit.

V&A MUSEUM OF CHILDHOOD
Map p156

☎ 8983 5200, recorded information 8983 5235; www.vam.ac.uk/moc; cnr Cambridge Heath & Old Ford Rds E2; admission free; ✆ 10am-5.45pm; ⊖ Bethnal Green; ♿

Housed in a renovated Victorian-era building moved from South Kensington in 1866, this branch of the Victoria & Albert Museum (p139) is aimed at both kids – with its activity rooms and corners of child-friendly, interactive exhibits, games and toys, including a dressing-up box and a 'beach' with sand – and nostalgic grown-ups who come to admire the antique toys. From carved ivory figures (one, a 'paddle doll', dates back to 1300 BC) to teddy bears, from Meccano to Lego and from peep shows to computer games, childhood artefacts from around the world are on display in this cheery museum.

SUTTON HOUSE Map p156

☎ 8986 2264; www.nationaltrust.org.uk; 2 & 4 Homerton High St E9; adult/child/family £2.90/80p/£6.60; ✆ 12.30-4.30pm Thu-Sun Feb-late Dec; ⊛ Hackney Central, ⊞ 38, 106, 277 or 394

Abandoned and taken over by squatters in the 1980s, what was originally known as Bryk Place when built in 1535 by a prominent courtier of Henry VIII, Sir Ralph Sadleir, could have been tragically lost to history, but it's since been put under the care of the National Trust and magnificently restored.

The first historic room you enter, the Linenfold Parlour, is the highlight, where the Tudor oak panelling on the walls has

been carved to resemble draped cloth. Other notable rooms include the panelled Great Chamber, the Victorian study, the Georgian parlour and the intriguing mock-up of a Tudor kitchen. There's a shop and pleasant cafe on site.

West of Sutton House in the restored St John's Churchyard Gardens is 13th-century St Augustine's Tower (☎ 8986 0029; www.hhbt.org.uk; Mare St E8), all that remains of a church that was demolished in 1798. The tower and its 135 steps can be climbed on special open days. See the website for details.

HACKNEY MUSEUM Map p156

☎ 8356 3500; www.hackney.gov.uk/cm-museum; Hackney Learning & Technology Centre, 1 Reading Lane E8; admission free; ✆ 9.30am-5.30pm Tue, Wed & Fri, to 8pm Thu, 10am-5pm Sat; ⊛ Hackney Central, ⊞ 38, 106, 277 or 394; ♿

This small museum tracing the history of one of the most ethnically diverse neighbourhoods in the country is particularly stylish, with display boards featuring translucent squares of the same colour and one case showing single mementos and effects from diverse ethnic communities – Jews, Chinese, Indians etc – behind square panes of glass. Even the 1000-year-old Saxon log boat, discovered on the marshes of Springfield Park in 1987, has been placed in the floor under glass squares.

Yet the design is not so flashy as to interfere with what's on show, from zoetropes and an early-20th-century (and very confusing) locality map to a pie 'n' mash shop and a dream kitchen of the 1950s. There's a copy of the genre-defining London crime novel *Yardie*, which was published locally, and recorded oral histories can be listened to by picking up phone handsets.

Mile End & Victoria Park

A busy junction where Docklands meet Hackney and the inner city meets Bow and Stratford Marsh, Mile End and vicinity is an increasingly popular residential area with some decent bars and restaurants, a unique Lottery Fund–supported park and a more traditional one in the enormous and gorgeous expanse of Victoria Park, the East End's biggest and most attractive green lung. A short distance to the west of Mile End Station is the campus of Queen Mary, University of London (Map p156; ☎ 7882 5555; www.qmul.ac.uk; Mile End Rd E1; ⊖ Mile End). It contains Novo Sephardic Cemetery, founded in 1733

OLD MACDONALD'S LONDON FARMS

To demonstrate to young Londoners that cows' udders are not shaped like milk bottles, farms have been set up all over the city in the past few decades with real, live bovines (as well as ovines and porcines) on display, chewing and mooing and doing what barnyard animals are supposed to do. The farms are more popular with local people than visitors so they also offer a way of getting off the beaten track. Admission is always free, many have an educational centre and most are closed on Tuesday.

Freightliners Farm (Map p170; ☎ 7609 0467; www.freightlinersfarm.org.uk; Sheringham Rd N7; ⏱ 10am-4.45pm Tue-Sun summer, 10am-4pm Tue-Sun winter; ⊖ Highbury & Islington)

Hackney City Farm (Map p156; ☎ 7729 6381; www.hackneycityfarm.co.uk; 1a Goldsmith's Row E2; ⏱ 10am-4.30pm Tue-Sun; ⊖ Bethnal Green)

Kentish Town City Farm (Map p166; ☎ 7916 5421; www.ktcityfarm.org.uk; 1 Cressfield Close, off Grafton Rd NW5; ⏱ 9am-5pm daily; ⊖ Kentish Town)

Mudchute Park & Farm (Map p162; ☎ 7515 5901; www.mudchute.org; Pier St E14; ⏱ 9am-5pm daily summer, 10am-4pm daily winter; DLR Mudchute)

Spitalfields City Farm (Map p156; ☎ 7247 8762; www.spitalfieldscityfarm.org; Weaver St E1; ⏱ 10am-4.30pm Tue-Sun; ⊖ Shoreditch)

Stepping Stones Farm (Map p156; ☎ 7790 8204; Stepney Way E1; ⏱ 10am-4pm Tue-Sun; ⊖ Stepney Green, DLR Limehouse)

Surrey Docks Farm (Map p182; ☎ 7231 1010; www.surreydocksfarm.org.uk; South Wharf, Rotherhithe St SE16; ⏱ 10am-5pm Tue-Sun; ⊖ Rotherhithe)

Vauxhall City Farm (Map p189; ☎ 7582 4204; www.vauxhallcityfarm.info; Tyers St, off Kennington Lane SE11; ⏱ 10am-2.30pm Thu-Sun; ⊖ Vauxhall)

by Spanish and Portuguese Jews. In the mid-1970s, when the college was expanding, some 7500 graves were emptied and the remains reburied in unmarked sites in Brentwood. These included the bones of the celebrated pugilist Daniel Mendoza (p160). Just east, over the busy A12 motorway, is Stratford and Olympic Park (Map p62; www.london2012.org), now busily under construction behind a perimeter fence but due to be the focus of the known world through the summer of 2012, when the London Olympics will take place here. For a preview of what it will become, take a Blue Badge (☎ 7495 5504; www.toursof2012sites.com; adult/child £8/5; ⏱ 11am Sat & Sun) tour of the site lasting about 1½ hours. It departs from outside the Bromley-By-Bow tube station and ends at the Pudding Mill Lane DLR station, but consult the website for any changes to the schedule.

MILE END PARK Map p156
www.towerhamlets.gov.uk; ⊖ Mile End
The 36-hectare Mile End Park is a long, narrow series of interconnected green spaces wedged between Burdett and Grove Rds and the Grand Union Canal. Landscaped to great effect during the millennium year, it now incorporates a go-kart track, a children's centre

for under-10s, areas for public art, an ecology area, an indoor climbing wall and a sports stadium under renovation. The centrepiece, though, is architect Piers Gough's 'green bridge' linking the northern and southern sections of the park over busy Mile End Rd and planted with trees and shrubs.

RAGGED SCHOOL MUSEUM Map p156
☎ 8980 6405; www.raggedschoolmuseum.org.uk; 46-50 Copperfield Rd E3; admission free, suggested donation £2; ⏱ 10am-5pm Wed & Thu, 2 5pm 1st Sun of month; ⊖ Mile End
Both adults and children are inevitably charmed by this combination of mock Victorian schoolroom – with hard wooden benches and desks, slates, chalk, inkwells and abacuses – on the 1st floor, and social history museum below. 'Ragged' was a Victorian term used to refer to pupils' usually torn, dirty and dishevelled clothes, and the museum celebrates the legacy of Dr Joseph Barnardo, who founded the first free school for destitute East End children in this building in the 1860s. On the first Sunday of the month, a Victorian lesson in which 'pupils' are taught reading, writing and 'rithmetic by a strict school ma'am in full Victorian

159

A HERO RISES IN THE EAST

Daniel Mendoza (1764–1836), the father of 'scientific boxing' who billed himself as 'Mendoza the Jew', was the first bare-knuckle boxer to employ strategy and speed in the ring. Mendoza was born in Aldgate and left school at age 13, taking odd jobs as a porter, being taunted as an 'outsider' and getting into scrapes. He was eventually discovered by 'gentleman boxer' Richard Humphreys, 20 years his senior, who took him under his wing and started him training. Mendoza developed a style of fighting in direct opposition to the norm of the day, where two fighters would stand face to face and slug it out until one collapsed.

Mendoza began a highly successful career in the ring, but eventually fell out with his mentor. His most infamous fight came during a 'grudge match' in 1788 with Humphreys. Just as Mendoza was about to administer the *coup de grâce*, Humphreys' second grabbed Mendoza's arm, a moment caught in a contemporary print called *Foul Play* on display in the National Portrait Gallery (p74). Mendoza went on to fight Humphreys fairly two more times, emerging the victor and moral superior.

Mendoza was the first sportsman in Britain to achieve cult status – a veritable David Beckham of 18th-century London. He made (and lost) a fortune, wrote his memoirs and also a how-to book called *The Art of Boxing*, mixed with the high and mighty (including royalty) and sold branded trinkets and images of himself. Most importantly, he advanced the cause of Jews in a country that had only allowed them back the century before. People learned for the first time that Jew could and would fight back – and win.

regalia called Miss Perkins, takes place at 2.15pm and 3.30pm.

TOWER HAMLETS CEMETERY PARK
Map p156

☎ 07904 186 981; www.towerhamletscemetery .org; Southern Grove E3; admission free; ☺ 7am-dusk; ⊖ Mile End or Bow Rd

Opened in 1841, this 13-hectare cemetery was the last of the 'Magnificent Seven', then-suburban cemeteries – including Highgate (p169) and Stoke Newington's Abney Park (p173) – created by an act of Parliament in response to London's rapid population growth and overcrowded burial grounds. Some 270,000 souls were laid to rest here until the cemetery was closed for burials in 1966 and turned into a park and local nature reserve in 2001. Today it is a quiet, restful site, its Victorian monuments slowly being consumed by vines. There are usually two-hour guided tours from 2pm on the 3rd Sunday of the month.

HOUSE MILL Map p62

☎ 8980 4626; www.housemill.org.uk; Three Mill Lane, Three Mills Island E3; adult/concession £3/1.50; ☺ 11am-4pm 1st Sun Mar-Dec, 1-4pm 2nd, 3rd & 4th Sun May-Oct; ⊖ Bromley-by-Bow

The only remaining one of a trio of mills that once stood on this small island in the River Lea, the House Mill (1776) operated as a sluice tidal mill, grinding grain for a nearby distillery, until 1940. Tours, which run according to demand and last about 45 minutes, take visitors to all four floors

of the mill and offer a fascinating look at traditional East End industry. There's a small cafe and shop on site.

VICTORIA PARK Map p156

☎ 8985 1957; www.towerhamlets.gov.uk; ☺ dawn-dusk; ⊖ Mile End, ◻ 277 or 425

If you want a little more green than Mile End Park affords, head north from Mile End tube along Grove Rd, until you reach 88-hectare Victoria Park, the 'Regent's Park of the East End'. This leafy expanse has lakes, fountains, a bowling green, tennis courts, a deer park and much more. It was the East End's first public park when it opened in 1845 and came about after a local MP presented Queen Victoria with a petition of 30,000 signatures. In the early 20th century it was known as the Speaker's Corner of the East End. During WWII the park was largely closed to the public and was used as an anti-aircraft shelling site as well as an internment camp for Italian and then German prisoners of war.

Wapping & Limehouse

The gateway to the warehouse district of Wapping is St Katharine's Dock (Map p156; www.skdocks .co.uk; ⊖ Tower Hill), built in 1828 after 1250 'insanitary' houses were razed and 11,300 people made homeless and shut some 140 years later. Its current incarnation, a marina for luxury yachts surrounded by cafes, restaurants and twee shops, dates from the 1980s.

Wapping was traditionally home to sailors and dock workers. One of the most important historic sites is Execution Dock (Map p156; Wapping New Stairs; ⊙ 100 ⊖ Wapping) near the marine police station at 94 Wapping High St E1. This is where convicted pirates were hanged and their bodies chained to a post at low tide, to be left until three tides had washed over their heads.

There isn't much to Limehouse, although it became the centre of London's Chinese community – its first Chinatown – after some 300 sailors settled here in 1890. It gets a mention in Oscar Wilde's *The Picture of Dorian Gray* (1891), when the protagonist passes by this way in search of opium. The most notable attraction here is St Anne's, Limehouse (Map p156; ☎ 7515 0977; www.stanneslimehouse.org; cnr Commercial Rd & Three Colt St E1; DLR Westferry). This was Nicholas Hawksmoor's earliest church (1725) and still boasts the highest church clock in the city. In fact, the 60m-high tower is still a 'Trinity House mark' for identifying shipping lanes on the Thames (thus it flies the Royal Navy's white ensign).

DOCKLANDS

You'd probably never guess it while gazing up at the ultramodern skyscrapers that dominate the Isle of Dogs and Canary Wharf, but from the 16th century until the mid-20th century this area was the centre of the world's greatest port, the hub of the British Empire and its enormous global trade. At the docks here cargo from global trade was landed, bringing jobs to a tight-knit working-class community. Even up to the start of WWII this community still thrived, but then the docks were badly firebombed during the Blitz.

After WWII the docks were in no condition to cope with the postwar technological and political changes as the British Empire evaporated. At the same time, enormous new bulk carriers and container ships demanded deep-water ports and new loading and un-loading techniques. From the mid-1960s dock closures followed one another as fast as they had opened, and the number of dock workers dropped from as many as 50,000 in 1960 to about 3000 by 1980.

The financial metropolis that exists today was begun by the London Docklands Development Corporation (LDDC), a body established by the Thatcher government in the free-wheeling 1980s to take pressure for office space off the City. This rather artificial community had a shaky start. The low-rise toytown buildings had trouble attracting tenants, the Docklands Light Railway – the main transport link – had teething troubles

and the landmark Canary Wharf Tower itself had to be rescued from bankruptcy twice. Now, however, news media people and financial behemoths have moved in – with Citigroup and HSBC boasting their own buildings.

The Docklands today is a world of contrasts. Eye-catching bridges across docks and futuristic buildings dominate the skyline; it really is today's view of London's future. But it is also an area rich in history.

MUSEUM OF LONDON DOCKLANDS
Map p162

☎ 7001 9844; www.museumindocklands.org.uk; No 1 Warehouse, West India Quay E14; adult/concession/after 4.30pm £5/3/free; ⏱ 10am-6pm; ⊖ Canary Wharf or DLR West India Quay; ☒

Housed in a converted 200-year-old warehouse once used to store sugar, rum and coffee, this museum offers a comprehensive overview of the entire history of the Thames from the arrival of the Romans in AD 43. But it's at its best when dealing with specifics close by such as the controversial transformation of the decrepit docks into Docklands in the 1980s.

The tour begins on the 3rd floor (take the lift to the top) with the Roman settlement of Londinium – don't miss the delightful Roman blue-glass bowl discovered in pieces at a building site in Prescot St E1 in 2008 – and works its way downwards through the ages. Keep an eye open for the scale mode of the old London Bridge and the *Rhinebeck Panorama* (1805–10), a huge mural of the upper Pool of London. An excellent new gallery called London, Sugar & Slavery examines the capital's role in the transatlantic slave trade.

Kids adore such exhibits as Sailortown (an excellent re-creation of the cobbled streets, bars and lodging houses of a mid-19th-century dockside community and nearby Chinatown) and the hands-on Mudlarks gallery, where five- to 12-year-olds can explore the history of the Thames, tipping the clipper, trying on old-fashioned diving helmets, learning to use winches and even constructing a simple model of Canary Wharf.

ISLE OF DOGS Map p162
DLR Westferry, West India Quay, Canary Wharf
Pundits can't even really agree on whether this is an island, let alone where its name

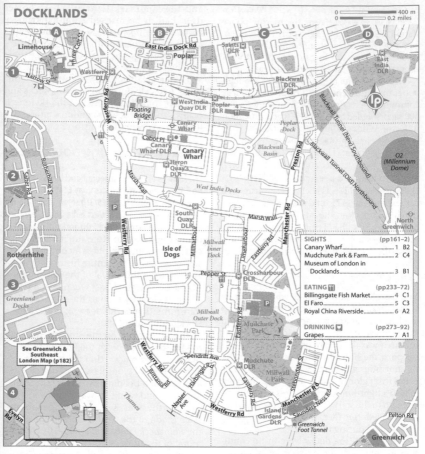

DOCKLANDS

```
0 ————————————— 400 m
0 ————————————— 0.2 miles
```

Limehouse

East India Dock Rd
Poplar

All Saints DLR

Blackwall DLR

East India DLR

Narrow St

Westferry DLR

West India Quay DLR

Poplar DLR 4

Floating Bridge

Canary Wharf

Poplar Dock

Cabot Pl

Blackwall Tunnel (New Southbound)

O2 (Millennium Dome)

Canary Wharf DLR

Canary Wharf

Blackwall Basin

Heron Quay's DLR

West India Docks

South Quay DLR

Marsh Wall

North Greenwich

Isle of Dogs

Millwall Inner Dock

Rotherhithe

Pepper St

Crossharbour DLR

Greenland Docks

Millwall Outer Dock

Mudchute Park

See Greenwich & Southeast London Map (p182)

Spendrift Ave

Mudchute DLR

Millwall Park

Thames

Napier Ave

Westferry Rd

Island Gardens DLR

Greenwich Foot Tunnel

Pelton Rd

Greenwich

SIGHTS	(pp161–2)	
Canary Wharf	1	B2
Mudchute Park & Farm	2	C4
Museum of London in Docklands	3	B1

EATING	(pp233–72)	
Billingsgate Fish Market	4	C1
El Faro	5	C3
Royal China Riverside	6	A2

DRINKING	(pp273–92)	
Grapes	7	A1

actually came from originally. Strictly speaking it's a peninsula of land on the northern shore of the Thames, though without modern road and transport links it would *almost* be separated from the mainland at West India Docks. And etymologists are still out to lunch over the origin of the island's name. Some believe it's because the royal kennels were located here during the reign of Henry VIII's. Others maintain it's a corruption of the Flemish word *dijk* (dyke), recalling the Flemish engineers who shored up the area's muddy banks.

It can be agreed, however, that the centrepiece of the Isle of Dogs is Canary Wharf. If you want to see how the isle once looked, check out Mudchute Park & Farm (p159).

CANARY WHARF Map p162
⊖ Canary Wharf or DLR Canary Wharf

Cesar Pelli's 244m-high Canary Wharf Tower, which was built in 1991 at 1 Canada Sq and has been described as a 'square prism with a pyramidal top', presides over a veritable array of venues including a toytown and financial theme park. It's surrounded by more recent towers housing HSBC and Citigroup, and offices for Bank of America, Barclays, Morgan Stanley, Credit Suisse and more. It took a long time for the place to come this far. Canary Wharf Tower, still the tallest building in the UK and one of the largest property developments in Europe, had to be saved from bankruptcy twice before it reached today's levels of occupancy.

NEIGHBOURHOODS THE EAST END & DOCKLANDS

WAPPING & WHITECHAPEL WALK
Walking Tour

1 St Katharine's Dock If you pass under Tower Bridge from the Tower of London you'll soon come to this symbolic 'entrance' to Docklands. St Katharine's (p160) was the first of the docks to be renovated following its closure in 1968.

2 Execution Dock Among the more famous people who died at this notorious site (p161) just off Wapping High St is one Captain William Kidd, hanged here in 1701 for piracy. A nearby landmark is the Captain Kidd pub (p284).

3 St George-in-the-East This church (☎ 7481 1345; www.stgite.org.uk; 16 Canon St Rd E1) was erected by Nicholas Hawksmoor in 1729 and badly damaged in the Blitz of WWII. All that now remains is a shell enclosing a smaller modern core. It was closed for a time in the 1850s when the vicar introduced what was considered 'Romish' (Roman Catholic) liturgy.

4 Cable Street In the late 18th century ropes were manufactured in this street (p156) – it was once as long as the standard English measure for cable (180m or 600ft). This was

WAPPING & WHITECHAPEL WALK

COCKNEY RHYMING SLANG

Some visitors arrive in London expecting to find a city populated by people conversing in cockney à la Dick Van Dyke in the film *Mary Poppins*. Traditionally the cockneys were people born within earshot of the Bow Bells – the church bells of St Mary-le-Bow in Cheapside. Since few people live in the City, that means most cockneys are East Enders.

The term cockney is often used to describe anyone speaking what is also called estuarine English (in which 't' and 'h' are routinely dropped and glottal stops – what the two 't's' sound like in 'bottle' – abound). In fact the true cockney language also uses something called rhyming slang, which may have developed among London's costermongers (street traders) as a code to avoid police attention. This code replaced common nouns and verbs with rhyming phrases. So 'going up the apples and pears' meant going up the stairs, the 'trouble and strife' was the wife, 'telling porky pies' was telling lies and 'would you Adam and Eve it?' was would you believe it? Over time the second of the two words tended to be dropped so the rhyme vanished. Few – if any – people still use pure cockney but a good many still understand it. You're more likely to come across it in residual phrases like 'use your loaf' ('loaf of bread' for head), 'ooh, me plates of meat' (feet) or "'e's me best china' ('china plate' for mate). Most Londoners would have understood – not to mention believed – the newspaper headline, announcing the results of the British Soap Awards, which read: 'East Enders is TV we can Adam and Eve in'.

the site of the celebrated Cable St riots that evicted British fascists from the East End. Shorter and narrower Twine Ct runs south off Cable St.

5 Tower House This enormous building (41 Fieldgate St E1) now redeveloped as an apartment block was once a hostel and then a dosshouse. Past residents include Joseph Stalin and au-

thors Jack London and George Orwell. The latter describes it in detail in his *Down and Out in Paris and London* (1933).

6 Whitechapel Bell Foundry In business for nigh on 450 years, this bell foundry (p155) can lay claim to producing some of the most recognisable bells in history, including Big Ben and the Liberty Bell in Philadelphia.

Drinking p284; Eating p257; Shopping p229; Sleeping p346

North London is a nebulous term for an area made up of many smaller neighbourhoods, most of which are ancient villages that have slowly been drawn into London's dark matter over the centuries as the metropolis has expanded.

Starting north of Euston Rd, this region of the capital includes King's Cross and Camden Town – two names both likely to elicit a response from Londoners. King's Cross has historically been one of the capital's nastiest urban blights, but a redevelopment of the tube station, the opening of the beautiful St Pancras International train terminal and the slow but thorough urban renewal going on elsewhere is making King's Cross more and more desirable, although it's fair to say it'll be a while before we're all meeting there for drinks. Camden is an even stranger beast – much reviled among Londoners for its touristy market (p168) and 'crusty' locals, outside of the Lock and away from Camden High St the area is actually a wonderful place full of great bars, restaurants and some architectural gems.

Reactions are nearly always universally positive to the posh neighbourhoods of Primrose Hill, Belsize Park and Hampstead, in as much as very few of us can afford these lovely, leafy slices of urban village life, although many of us would like to. With their quiet, unpretentious gentility there's little surprise that these are the preferred neighbourhoods for the superstar classes. Luckily we can all visit Primrose Hill and Hampstead Heath (just don't try going for a walk in Belsize Park as there is no actual parkland there!).

top picks

NORTH LONDON

- Hampstead Heath (p169)
- British Library (p168)
- Highgate Cemetery (p169)
- Camden Market (p168)
- Kenwood House (p172)

Highgate, on the other side of massive Hampstead Heath, is London's highest point and possibly its most gorgeous urban village. Seriously posh, it's a charming place where locals have developed freakishly large calf muscles from all that uphill walking. Nearby Crouch End and Muswell Hill are less expensive but retain a very well-off middle-class feel, while scruffier Stoke Newington in Hackney is a wonderful blend of hippies, yummy mummies (and daddies), gay and lesbian couples and pockets of Orthodox Jews and Turkish Muslims, all living in the most unlikely of harmonies.

Hampstead and Highgate should be everyone's first choice for the sheer breadth of things to see and do. North London also includes one of the city's largest and most wonderful outdoor spaces, genteel Regent's Park (below), which features famous London Zoo and has the beautiful Regent's Canal running along its northern edge.

REGENT'S PARK

REGENT'S PARK Map p166

☎ 7486 7905; ☽ 5am-dusk; ⊖ Baker St or Regent's Park

The most elaborate and ordered of London's many parks, this one was created around 1820 by John Nash, who planned to use it as an estate to build palaces for the aristocracy. Although the plan never quite came off – like so many at the time – you can get some idea of what Nash might have achieved from the buildings along the Outer Circle, and in particular from the stuccoed Palladian mansions he built on Cumberland Tce.

Like many of the city's parks, this one was used as a royal hunting ground, and then as farmland, before it was used as a place for fun and leisure during the 18th century. These days it's a well-organised but relaxed, lively but serene, local but cosmopolitan haven in the heart of the city. Among its many attractions are the London Zoo, the Grand Union Canal along its northern side, an ornamental lake, an open-air theatre in Queen Mary's Gardens where Shakespeare is performed during the summer months, ponds and colourful flowerbeds, rose gardens that look spectacular in June, football pitches and summer games of softball.

On the western side of the park is the impressive London Central Islamic Centre & Mosque (☎ 7725 2213; www.iccuk.org; 146 Park Rd NW8;

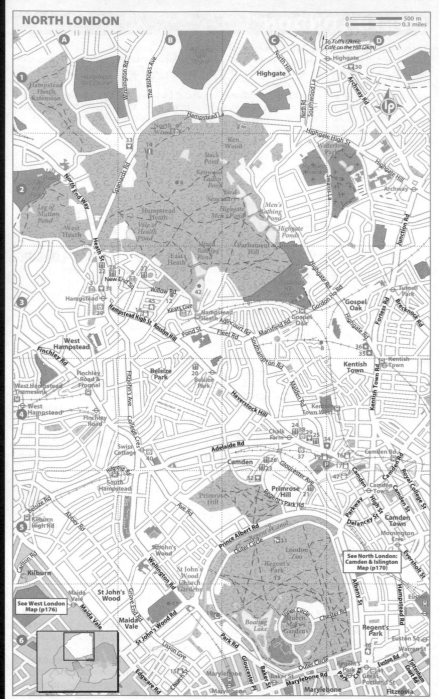

0   500 m
0   0.3 miles

A   **B**   **C**   **D**

To Toff's (2km);
Café on the Hill (2km)

Highgate

30

Highgate

Hampstead
Heath
Extension

Highbarrow
Golf Course

North Hill

Archway Rd

Hampstead La

The Bishops Ave

Wildwood Rd

North
Wood

Highgate High St

Waterlow
Park

North Rd

Southwood La

Highgate Hill

Highgate Hill

Archway

Stock
Pond

Ken
Wood

Kenwood
Ladies
Pond

Bird
Sanctuary

Highgate
Men's Pond

Men's
Bathing
Pond

Highgate
Ponds

Archway Rd

North End Way

Golders
Hill
Pond

Leg of
Mutton
Pond

West
Heath

Hampstead
Heath

Vale of
Health
Pond

Parliament Hill

4

East
Heath

Mixed
Bathing
Pond

Parliament
Hill Fields

Tufnell
Park

Heath St

Spaniards Rd

33

14

Gospel
Oak

Gordon Hse Rd

Highgate Rd

Fortess Rd

Brecknock Rd

28
3
27
New End Sq
31
45
12
Willow Rd
42
Keats Gve
7

Hampstead

Hampstead
Heath

Agincourt Rd

Mansfield Rd

Gospel
Oak

39

Hampstead High St
Rosslyn Hill
18

Pond St

Fleet Rd

Southampton Rd

8

36
35

Kentish
Town

West
Hampstead

Finchley Rd

Belsize
Park

20
Belsize
Park

Kentish
Town West

Kentish Town Rd

West Hampstead
Thameslink

Fitzjohn's Ave

Haverstock Hill

Maiden Rd

West
Hampstead

Finchley
Road

College Cres

Chalk
Farm

24
29
25

34

Camden Rd

16

Royal College St

Finchley Rd

Swiss
Cottage

40

Adelaide Rd

37

19
17

Camden High St

Camden
Town

Camden

26
23

Gloucester Ave

21
47

Camden Rd

Parkway

Delancey St

Camden
Town

Mornington
Cres

Eversholt St

Hillgrove Rd

South
Hampstead

Belsize Rd

Abbey Rd

St John's
Wood

32

Primrose
Hill

Primrose
Hill

Regent's Park Rd

London
Zoo

11

See North London:
Camden & Islington
Map (p170)

5

Kilburn
High Rd

Carlton Rd

Kilburn

Ave Rd

Prince Albert Rd

Outer Circle

Regent's
Canal

Regent's
Park

13

Albany St

Hampstead Rd

Euston

Wellington Rd

St John's
Wood
Church
Gardens

St John's
Wood

Grove End Rd

43

Maida
Vale

St John's
Wood Rd

Inner Circle

Queen
Mary's
Gardens

Chester Rd

Regent's
Park

See West London
Map (p176)

6

Maida
Vale

Maida Vale

Lisson Gve

Edgware Rd

Church St

15
16

St John's Wood Rd

Park Rd

Gloucester Pl

Boating
Lake

Outer Circle

Regent's
Park

46

Euston Sq

Warren St

Baker St

Baker St

Marylebone Rd

Regent's
Park
Cres

44

Great
Portland St

Euston Rd

Tottenham Court Rd

Marylebone

Marylebone

Marylebone

Fitzrovia

NORTH LONDON

↔ Marylebone), a huge white edifice with a glistening dome. Provided you take your shoes off and dress modestly you're welcome to go inside, although the interior is fairly stark.

LONDON ZOO Map p166

☎ 7722 3333; www.zsl.org/london-zoo; Outer Circle, Regent's Park NW1; adult/child/concession £16.80/13.30/15.30 plus optional £1.70 donation to protect endangered species; ☿ 10am-5.30pm mid-Mar–Oct, to 4pm Nov-Jan, to 4.30pm Feb–mid-Mar; ↔ Baker St or Camden Town

Established in 1828, these zoological gardens are among the oldest in the world. This is where the word 'zoo' originated and after a patchy period in the 1990s, London Zoo has become one of the most progressive in the world. It is in the process of implementing a long-term modernisation plan and the emphasis is now firmly placed on conservation, education and breeding, with fewer species and more spacious conditions.

The newest developments have brought Gorilla Kingdom, a project that involves a gorilla conservation program in Gabon with the aim of providing habitat for Western gorillas and protecting them by providing the local communities and former poachers with work in the program. The zoo has three gorillas – Zaire, Effie and Mjukuu –

who live on their own island; their space measures 1600 sq metres.

The Clore Rainforest Lookout and Nightzone is another excellent installation – a slice of the South American rainforest complete with marmosets, monkeys, fruit bats and other creatures wandering and flying freely among the visitors inside the humid, tropical-climate room. The monkeys are especially happy to roam – they see it as their territory, so watch out!

The elegant and cheerful Penguin Pool, designed by Berthold Lubetkin in 1934, is one of London's foremost modernist structures, although the penguins didn't like it and are now bathing at a more ordinary round pool.

Other highlights include Butterfly Paradise, Into Africa and Meet the Monkeys. In 2008 the Mappin Terrace (which was formerly home to London Zoo's polar bears) reopened as the Outback exhibit, a slice of Australia, home to wallabies and emus, and focusing on the challenges that climate change will present to animals living in already hot climates.

A great way to visit the zoo is by canal boat from Little Venice or Camden, but you can also reach it by walking along the canal towpath. There's a delightful children's zoo, which is built almost entirely from sustainable materials, and busy programs of events and attractions (such as elephant bathing and penguin feeding) throughout the year.

LORD'S CRICKET GROUND Map p166

☎ 7616 8595; bookings 7432 1000; www.lords .org; St John's Wood Rd NW8; tours adult/child & concession/family £14/8/38; ☒ tours when no play 10am, noon & 2pm Apr-Sep, noon & 2pm Oct-Mar; ⊖ St John's Wood; ☒

The 'home of cricket' is a must for any devotee of this peculiarly English game: book early for the test matches here, but it's also worth taking the absorbing and anecdotal 90-minute tour of the ground and facilities. This interesting tour takes in the famous Long Room, where members watch the games surrounded by portraits of cricket's great and good, and a museum featuring evocative memorabilia that will appeal to fans old and new. The famous little urn containing the Ashes, the prize of the most fiercely contested competition in cricket, resides here when in English hands.

The ground itself is dominated by a striking media centre that looks like a clock radio, but you should also keep an eye out for the famous weather vane in the shape of Father Time and the remarkable tentlike modern Mound Stand.

CAMDEN

CAMDEN MARKET Map p170

cnr Camden High & Buck Sts NW1; ☒ 9am-5.30pm Thu-Sun; ⊖ Camden Town or Chalk Farm

Although – or perhaps because – it stopped being cutting-edge several thousand cheap leather jackets ago, Camden market gets a whopping 10 million visitors each year and is one of London's most popular attractions. What started out as a collection of attractive craft stalls by Camden Lock on the Grand Union Canal now extends in various other forms most of the way from Camden Town tube station north to Chalk Farm tube station. You'll find a bit of everything but in particular a lot of tourist-oriented tat (see p226 for more information). A bad fire in the Camden Canal Market area in 2008 has not affected the market's seemingly limitless popularity – it's completely mobbed at the weekend, and preferably avoided on those days.

KING'S CROSS & EUSTON

BRITISH LIBRARY Map p170

☎ 0870 444 1500; www.bl.uk; 96 Euston Rd NW1; admission free; ☒ 10am-6pm Mon & Wed-Fri, 9.30am-8pm Tue, 9.30am-5pm Sat, 11am-5pm Sun; ⊖ King's Cross; ☒

In 1998 the British Library moved to these spanking-new premises between King's Cross and Euston stations. At a cost of £500 million, it was Britain's most expensive building, and not one that is universally loved; Colin St John Wilson's exterior of straight lines of red brick, which Prince Charles reckoned was akin to a 'secret-police building', is certainly not to all tastes. But even people who don't like the building from the outside can't fault the spectacularly cool and spacious interior.

It is the nation's principal copyright library and stocks one copy of every British publication as well as historic manuscripts, books and maps from the British Museum. The library counts some 186 miles of shelving on four basement levels and will have some 12 million volumes when it reaches the limit of its storage capacity.

At the centre of the building is the wonderful King's Library, the 65,000-volume collection of the insane George III, which was given to the nation by his son, George IV, in 1823 and is now housed in a six-storey, 17m-high glass-walled tower. To the left as you enter are the library's excellent bookshop and exhibition galleries.

Most of the complex is devoted to storage and scholarly research, but there are also several public displays including the John Ritblat Gallery: Treasures of the British Library, which spans almost three millennia and every continent. Among the most important documents here are the Magna Carta (1215); the Codex Sinaiticus, the first complete text of the New Testament, written in Greek in the 4th century; a Gutenberg Bible (1455), the first Western book printed using movable type; Shakespeare's First Folio (1623); manuscripts by some of Britain's best-known authors (eg Lewis Carroll, Jane Austen, George Eliot and Thomas Hardy); and even some of the Beatles' earliest handwritten lyrics.

You can hear historic recordings, such as the first one ever, made by Thomas Edison in 1877, James Joyce reading from *Ulysses* and Nelson Mandela's famous speech at the Rivonia trial in 1964, at the National Sound Archive Jukeboxes, where the selections are changed regularly. The Turning the Pages exhibit allows you a 'virtual browse' through several important texts including the *Sforza Book of Hours,* the *Diamond Sutra* and a Leonardo da Vinci notebook.

The Philatelic Exhibition, next to the John Ritblat Gallery, is based on collections established in 1891 with the bequest of the Tapling Collection, and now consists of more than 80,000 items, including postage and revenue stamps, postal stationery and first-day covers from almost every country and from all periods.

The Workshop of Words, Sounds & Images documents the development of writing and communicating through the written word by carefully examining the work of early scribes, printers and bookbinders. The sound section compares recordings on different media, from early-20th-century wax cylinders to modern CDs.

Access to the reading rooms is by reader's pass only. See the website for details of how to apply for one and the conditions that need to be met.

There are guided tours (adult/child £8/6.50) of the library's public areas at 3pm Monday, Wednesday and Friday and at 10.30am and 3pm Saturday, and another that includes a visit to one of the reading rooms at 11.30am and 3pm Sunday. Call ☎ 01937-546 546 to make a booking. Further tours, including free tours of the reading rooms focusing on how books are ordered, and tours of the conservation studios, are also regularly available – see the website for details.

LONDON CANAL MUSEUM Map p170
☎ 7713 0836; www.canalmuseum.org.uk; 12-13 New Wharf Rd N1; adult/child/student £3/1.50/2; ⊗ 10am-4.30pm Tue-Sun & bank holidays; ⊖ King's Cross
This quirky but worthwhile museum is in an old ice warehouse (with a deep well where the frozen commodity was stored) dating from the 1860s. It traces the history of Regent's Canal, the ice business and the development of ice cream through models, photographs, exhibits and archive documentaries. The ice trade was huge in late Victorian London, and 35,000 tonnes of it were imported from Norway in 1899.

HAMPSTEAD & HIGHGATE

HAMPSTEAD HEATH Map p166
☎ 7485 4491; ⊖ Hampstead, ⊠ Gospel Oak or Hampstead Heath, ⊕ 214 or C2 to Parliament Hill Fields
Sprawling Hampstead Heath, with its rolling woodlands and meadows, feels a million miles away – despite being approximately four – from the City of London. It covers 320 hectares, most of it woods, hills and meadows, and is home to about 100 bird species. It's a wonderful place for a ramble, especially to the top of Parliament Hill, which offers expansive views across the city and is one of the most popular places in London to fly a kite. Alternatively head up the hill in North Wood or lose yourself in the West Heath.

If walking is too pedestrian for you, another major attraction is the bathing ponds (separate beautiful ones for men and women and a slightly less pleasant mixed pond – see p319). Sections of the heath area are also laid out for football, cricket and tennis. Those of a more artistic bent should make a beeline for Kenwood House (p172) but stop to admire the sculptures by Henry Moore and Barbara Hepworth on the way.

If you work up a thirst, there's no better place to quench it than at the atmospheric – and possibly haunted – Spaniard's Inn (p286), which has a fascinating history and a terrific beer garden.

By day and night the West Heath is a gay cruising ground that is so well established that the police often pitch up in the evenings to protect the men who spend their nights here. Continuing the theme, South Green, opposite Hampstead Heath station, is one of Britain's oldest lavatories, which was built in 1897 and restored in 2000. This was playwright Joe Orton's lavatory of choice for 'cottaging' (cruising for gay sex). George Orwell worked in a bookshop opposite the toilets and doubtless used them now and then for their originally intended purpose.

HIGHGATE CEMETERY Map p166
☎ 8340 1834; www.highgate-cemetery.org; Swain's Lane N6; adult/under 16yr £3/free; ⊗ 10am-5pm Mon-Fri, 11am-5pm Sat & Sun Apr-Oct, closes 4pm daily Nov-Mar; ⊖ Highgate
Most famous as the final resting place of Karl Marx, Christina Rosetti, George Eliot (pseudonym of Mary Ann Evans) and other

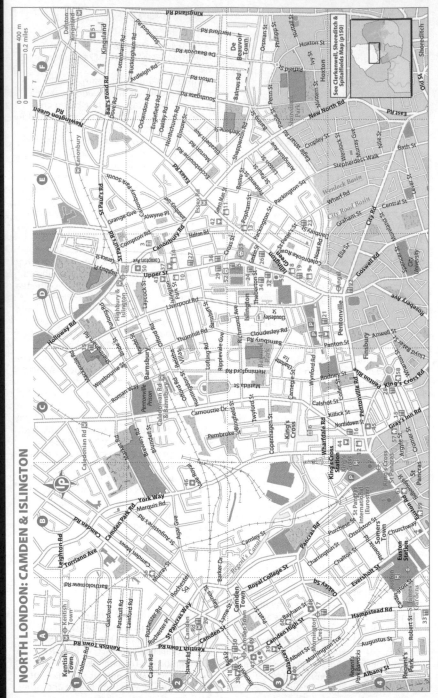

See Clerkenwell, Shoreditch &
Spitalfields Map (p150)

NORTH LONDON: CAMDEN & ISLINGTON

notable mortals, Highgate Cemetery is set in 20 wonderfully wild and atmospheric hectares, with dramatic and overdecorated Victorian family crypts. It is divided into two parts on either side of Swain's Lane. On the eastern side you can visit the grave of Karl Marx, which is regularly graced with bouquets from the few remaining communist embassies in London. This slightly overgrown and wild part of the cemetery is a very pleasant walk but it's merely the overflow area. It's the wonderfully atmospheric western section of this Victorian Valhalla that is the main draw. To visit it, you'll have to take a tour and deal directly with the brigade of sometimes stroppy silver-haired ladies who run the cemetery. It is a maze of winding paths leading to the Circle of Lebanon, rings of tombs flanking a circular path and topped with a majestic, centuries-old cedar tree. The guides are engaging and gladly point out the various symbols of the age and the eminent dead occupying the tombs, including the scientist Michael Faraday and the dog-show founder Charles Cruft. 'Dissenters' (non-Church of Englanders) were buried way off in the woods. Tours (adult/8–15yr £5/1) depart 2pm Monday to Friday except in December to February (book ahead by phone) and every hour 11am to 4pm Saturday and Sunday (last tour at 3pm December to February, no bookings). Children under the age of eight are not allowed on tours of the West Cemetery.

Highgate remains a working cemetery – the most recent well-known addition was Russian dissident Alexander Litvinenko, who was done away with under most sinister circumstances in 2006, when the radioactive isotope Polonium 210 somehow made it into his tea in a Mayfair hotel. The cemetery closes during burials, so you might want to call ahead just to be sure it will be open.

HIGHGATE WOOD Map p166
dawn-dusk; ⊖ Highgate

With more than 28 hectares of ancient woodland, this park is a wonderful spot for a walk any time of the year. It's also teeming with life, and some 70 different bird species have been recorded here, along with five types of bat, 12 types of butterfly and 80 different kinds of spider. It also has a huge clearing in the centre for sports, a popular playground and nature trail for kids and a range of activities – from falconry to bat-watching – throughout the year.

KEATS HOUSE Map p166

☎ 7435 2062; www.keatshouse.org.uk; Wentworth Pl, Keats Grove NW3; ⊖ Hampstead or ℝ Hampstead Heath

Reopened mid-2009 following redevelopment, this elegant Regency house was home to the golden boy of the Romantic poets from 1818 to 1820. Never short of generous mates, Keats was persuaded to take refuge here by Charles Armitage Brown, and it was here that he met his fiancée Fanny Brawne, who was literally the girl next door. Keats wrote his most celebrated poem, *Ode to a Nightingale*, while sitting under a plum tree in the garden (now replaced) in 1819. Original documents such as the poet's letters and the original *Bright Star* manuscript will be on display as part of the redevelopment. The house is dripping with atmosphere, thanks in part to the collection of Regency furniture amassed here in recent years.

KENWOOD HOUSE Map p166

☎ 8348 1286; www.english-heritage.org.uk; Hampstead Lane NW3; admission free; ☼ house 11am-4pm, the Suffolk Collection (upstairs) 11am-4pm Thu-Sun; ⊖ Archway or Golders Green, then 🚌 210; ♿

Hampstead's most impressive sight is this magnificent neoclassical mansion, which stands at the northern end of the heath in a glorious sweep of perfectly landscaped gardens leading down to a picturesque lake, around which classical concerts take place during the summer months (see p306). The house was remodelled by Robert Adam in the 18th century, and rescued from developers by Lord Iveagh Guinness, who donated it and the wonderful collection of art it contains to the nation in 1927. The Iveagh Bequest contains paintings by such greats as Gainsborough, Reynolds, Turner, Hals, Vermeer and Van Dyck and is one of the finest small collections in Britain.

Robert Adam's Great Stairs and the library, one of 14 rooms open to the public, are especially fine. The Suffolk Collection occupies the 1st floor. It includes Jacobean portraits by William Larkin and royal Stuart portraits by Van Dyck and Lely. There are guided tours of the house (adult/concession £2/1) daily at 2.30pm.

The Brew House Café has excellent grub, from light snacks to full meals (mains around £7.50), and plenty of room on the lovely garden terrace.

NO 2 WILLOW ROAD Map p166

☎ 7435 6166, 0149 475 5570; www.nationaltrust .org.uk; 2 Willow Rd NW3; admission incl tour adult/child £5.30/2.80; ☼ noon-5pm Thu-Sat Apr-Oct, 11am-5pm Sat Mar-Nov, guided tours noon, 1pm & 2pm daily plus 11am Sat, closed Dec-Feb; ⊖ Hampstead or ℝ Hampstead Heath

Fans of modern architecture will want to swing past this property, the central house in a block of three, designed by the 'structural rationalist' Ernö Goldfinger in 1939 as his family home. Although the architect was following Georgian principles in creating it, many people think it looks uncannily like the sort of mundane 1950s architecture you see everywhere. They may look similar now, but 2 Willow Rd was in fact a forerunner; the others were mostly bad imitations. The interior, with its cleverly designed storage space and collection of artworks by Henry Moore, Max Ernst and Bridget Riley, is certainly interesting and accessible to all. Entry is on a tour until 3pm, after which non-guided viewing is allowed.

BURGH HOUSE Map p166

☎ 7431 0144; www.burghhouse.org.uk; New End Sq NW3; admission free; ☼ noon-5pm Wed-Fri & Sun, 2-5pm bank holidays, by appointment Sat; ⊖ Hampstead

If you happen to be in the neighbourhood, this late-17th-century Queen Anne mansion houses the Hampstead Museum of local history, a small art gallery and the delightful Buttery Garden Café (☼ 11am-5.30pm Wed-Sat), where you can get a decent and reasonably priced lunch (sandwiches £5).

FENTON HOUSE Map p166

☎ 7435 3471; www.nationaltrust.org.uk; Windmill Hill, Hampstead Grove NW3; adult/child £5.70/2.80; ☼ 2-5pm Wed-Fri, 11am-5pm Sat & Sun Apr-Oct, 2-5pm Sat & Sun Mar; ⊖ Hampstead

One of the oldest houses in Hampstead, this late-17th-century merchant's residence has a charming walled garden with roses and an orchard, fine collections of porcelain and keyboard instruments – including a 1612 harpsichord played by Handel – as well as 17th-century needlework pictures and original Georgian furniture. Joint tickets with 2 Willow Rd are available.

ISLINGTON

ESTORICK COLLECTION OF MODERN ITALIAN ART Map p170

☎ 7704 9522; www.estorickcollection.com; 39a Canonbury Sq N1; adult/concession/student £5/3.50/free; ☻ 11am-6pm Wed-Sat, noon-5pm Sun; ⊖ Highbury & Islington

The only museum in Britain devoted to Italian art, and one of the leading collections of futurist painting in the world, the Estorick Collection is housed in a listed Georgian house and stuffed with works by such greats as Giacomo Balla, Umberto Boccioni, Gino Severini and Ardengo Soffici. The collection of paintings, drawings, etchings and sculpture, amassed by American writer and art dealer Eric Estorick and his wife Salome, also includes drawings and a painting by the even more famous Amedeo Modigliani. Well-conceived special exhibitions have included many 20th century art movements and lesser-known artists from Italy and beyond. The museum also encompasses an extensive library, cafe and shop. Highly recommended.

MUSWELL HILL & CROUCH END

ALEXANDRA PARK & PALACE Map p62

☎ 8365 2121; www.alexandrapalace.com; Alexandra Palace Way N22; ☒ Alexandra Palace

Built in 1873 as North London's answer to Crystal Palace, Alexandra Palace suffered the ignoble fate of burning to the ground only 16 days after opening. Encouraged by attendance figures, investors decided to rebuild and it reopened just two years later. Although it boasted a theatre, museum, lecture hall, library and Great Hall with one of the world's largest organs, it was no match for Crystal Palace. It housed German prisoners of war during WWI and in 1936 was the scene of the world's first TV transmission – a variety show called *Here's Looking at You*. The palace burned down again in 1980 but was rebuilt for the third time and opened in 1988. Today 'Ally Pally' (as it is affectionately known) is a multipurpose conference and exhibition centre with additional facilities, including an indoor ice-skating rink, the panoramic Phoenix Bar & Beer Garden and funfairs in summer. It hosts occasional club nights and concerts too.

The park in which it stands sprawls over some 196 hectares consisting of public gardens, a nature conservation area, a deer park and various sporting facilities including a boating lake, pitch-and-putt golf course and skate park, making it a great place for a family outing.

STOKE NEWINGTON

ABNEY PARK CEMETERY Map p62

www.abney-park.org.uk; Stoke Newington Church St N16; admission free; ☻ 8am-dusk; ☒ Stoke Newington, ☒ 73, 106, 149, 243, 276, 476

Unfairly dubbed 'the poor man's Highgate' by some, this magical place was bought and developed by a private firm from 1840 to provide burial grounds for central London's overflow. It was a dissenters (ie non–Church of England) cemetery and many of the most influential London Presbyterians, Quakers and Baptists are buried here, including the Salvation Army founder, William Booth, whose grand tombstone greets you as you enter from Church St. Since the 1950s the cemetery has been left to fend for itself and, these days, is as much a bird and plant sanctuary, a gay cruising ground and a hang-out for some of Hackney's least salubrious drug users, as a delightfully overgrown ruin. The derelict chapel at its centre could be right out of a horror film, and the atmosphere of the whole place is nothing short of magical.

HAMPSTEAD & HIGHGATE WALK
Walking Tour

1 No 2 Willow Rd Drop into this fascinating slice of modernism on your way to nearby Hampstead Heath. Here you'll find Ernö Goldfinger's pioneering international modernist apartment block (opposite), run by the formidable dames of the National Trust. Just don't say that it looks like any other modern building – it really was the first.

2 Hampstead Heath One of London's most lovely open spaces, the hills and woods of this gorgeous, rambling park (p169) are enough to inspire anyone to poetry (and of course Keats lived nearby; see opposite). Enjoy the view from Parliament Hill and cool off in the swimming ponds or in the fabulous Parliament Hill Lido (p319).

3 Kenwood House On the northern edge of the heath, this grand mansion (opposite) houses two superb collections of British art, features

HAMPSTEAD & HIGHGATE WALK

some gorgeous interiors and has lovely gardens to walk in, all for free.

4 Highgate Village Wandering up the hill to London's highest natural point, it's hard not to be seduced instantly by Highgate Village, with its charming shops, pubs and cafes.

5 Highgate Wood Take a stroll in the thick foliage of this charming wood (p171), where you can combine a walk with plenty of other activities including birdwatching (although look out for the butterflies and even bats at dusk). Kids will especially love the nature trail.

6 Highgate Cemetery

Wandering down Highgate Hill – and you only ever want to walk down this hill, it was,

WALK FACTS

Start **Hampstead tube station**
End **Archway tube station**
Distance **5 miles**
Duration **Three hours**
Fuel stop **Boogaloo** (p286)

after all the site of Europe's first cable car in the late 19th century – you can walk down Swain's Lane to London's most famous burial ground (p169). Here lie Karl Marx, George Eliot and Christina Rossetti in some wonderful surroundings. Be sure to take the West Cemetery tour as while it's a pain to have to visit in a group, it's only here that you understand why Highgate is London's most desirable place to be dead.

WEST LONDON

Drinking p287; Eating p263; Shopping p230; Sleeping p348

The sprawl west of Hyde Park in all directions is one of the most vibrant areas of London, and few parts of the capital can boast the area's sheer variety: its rampant multiculturalism (the Caribbean community of Notting Hill, the Poles in Hammersmith and the Australian home away from home in Earl's Court), its exciting bars (check out Portobello Rd or Westbourne Grove) and its grand parks and mansions (wander the back streets of Holland Park).

To the west of Primrose Hill are St John's Wood and Maida Vale – both leafy inner suburbs of genteel houses, a charming canal and boutique shopping.

Notting Hill has lots of highly individual shops, restaurants and pubs. Narrow Portobello Rd is its heart and soul and most well known these days for hosting one of London's best markets (p226). The neighbourhood also gives its name to the Notting Hill Carnival (p17), a highlight of London's summer. Trendy Westbourne Grove, roughly in the northeastern corner, is lined with distinctive shops, pubs, artists' galleries and studios.

Despite the shabby, incoherent architecture of Shepherd's Bush Green and the general chaos that rules here, this West London hub is a decent place to hang out and has some budget accommodation and quirky restaurants and bars. Synonymous for many with the sprawling BBC TV Centre (p177) in nearby White City that opened in 1960, the area had actually become famous 50 years earlier as the site of the 1908 London Olympics, as well as the Great Exhibition of the same year.

Earl's Court is a lively, cosmopolitan part of town, with a large, mobile population, particularly Poles (who stay) and Australians (who don't – usually). It's a funny mix of the smart and the scruffy – one minute you're on Earl's Court Rd watching tall cans of lager being swilled on the street by vowel-wringing Ockers, the next you're on Old Brompton Rd with its gay bars and chichi continental-style cafes.

West Brompton is even quieter and less remarkable, but is home to one of London's most magnificent cemeteries and is pleasant for a stroll.

Hammersmith is a different story: it's a very urban neighbourhood dominated by a huge flyover and roundabout, with little to entice the visitor save some decent restaurants and the famously arty Riverside Studios (p310).

MUSEUM OF BRANDS, PACKAGING & ADVERTISING Map p176

☎ 7908 0880; www.museumofbrands.com; 2 Colville Mews, Lonsdale Rd W11; adult/7-16yr/concession/family £5.80/2/3.50/14; 🕙 10am-6pm Tue-Sat, 11am-5pm Sun; ⊖ Notting Hill Gate

This unexpected find in the heart of Notting Hill is the brainchild of designer Robert Opie, who has been collecting advertising memorabilia since the age of 16. It's fairly low-tech, though (we spotted one TV screen on our last visit) and of most interest to nostalgia-seeking Brits, as the brands are almost entirely from the UK.

LINLEY SAMBOURNE HOUSE Map p178

☎ 7602 3316, 7938 1295; www.rbkc.gov.uk/linley sambournehouse; 18 Stafford Tce W8; adult/child/ concession £6/1/4; 🕙 tours 11.15am & 2.15pm Wed, 11.15am, 1pm, 2.15pm, 3.30pm Sat & Sun mid-Sep–mid-Jun; ⊖ High St Kensington

Tucked away behind Kensington High St, this was the home of *Punch* cartoonist and amateur photographer Linley Sambourne

and his wife Marion from 1875 to 1914. (Sambourne was the great-grandfather of Anthony Armstrong-Jones, Lord Snowdon, former husband of the late Princess Margaret.) It's one of those houses whose owners never redecorated or threw anything away. What you see is pretty much the typical home of a comfortable middle-class Victorian family, with dark wood, Turkish carpets and rich stained glass throughout. You can visit some nine rooms, by 90-minute guided tour only. (On the weekend, the guide on all but the first tour is in period costume.)

LEIGHTON HOUSE Map p178

☎ 7602 3316; www.leightonhouse.co.uk; 12 Holland Park Rd W14; 🕙 11am-5.30pm Wed-Mon; ⊖ High St Kensington

Sitting on a quiet street near Holland Park and designed in 1866 by George Aitchison, Leighton House was home to the eponymous Frederic, Lord Leighton (1830–96), a painter belonging to the Olympian

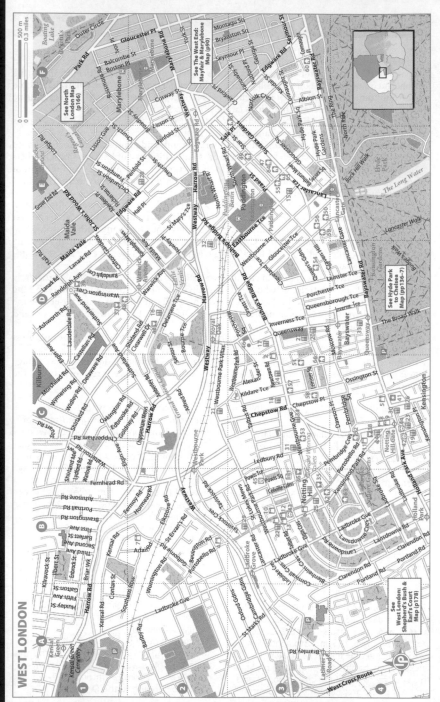

movement. The ground floor is decorated in an Orientalist style, with the exquisite Arab Hall added in 1879 and densely covered with blue and green tiles from Rhodes, Cairo, Damascus and Iznik in Turkey; a fountain trickles away in the centre. Even the wooden latticework of the windows and gallery was brought from Damascus. The house, undergoing a £1.3 million restoration at the time of research, contains notable pre-Raphaelite paintings by Burne-Jones, Watts, Millais and Lord Leighton himself.

BROMPTON CEMETERY Map p178
☎ 7352 1201; www.royalparks.gov.uk; Old Brompton Rd SW5; tours £4; ⏰ 8am-dusk daily, tours 2pm Sun; ⊖ West Brompton or Fulham Broadway
As London's vast population exploded in the 19th century, seven new cemeteries – the 'Magnificent Seven' – opened, among them Brompton Cemetery, a long expanse running between Fulham Rd and Old Brompton Rd. The chapel and colonnades at one end are modelled on St Peter's in Rome. While the most famous resident is Emmeline Pankhurst, the pioneer of women's suffrage in Britain, the cemetery is most interesting as the inspiration for many of Beatrix Potter's characters. A local

resident in her youth before she moved to the north, Potter seems to have taken many names from the deceased of Brompton Cemetery and immortalised them in her world-famous books. They include Mr Nutkin, Mr McGregor, Jeremiah Fisher, Tommy Brock – and even a Peter Rabbett.

Tours lasting two hours depart at 2pm Sunday from the South Lodge, near the Fulham Rd entrance.

BBC TELEVISION CENTRE Map p62
☎ 0370 901 1227; www.bbc.co.uk/tours; Wood Lane W12; tours adult/9-15yr & student/senior/family £9.50/7/8.50/27; ⏰ by appointment Mon-Sat; ⊖ White City; ♿
If you're interested in TV production, this is the perfect chance to visit the vast complex of studios and offices that bring the BBC's TV programs to the world. Visit is by two-hour guided tour only and bookings two days in advance are essential (no children under nine years, nine tours Monday to Saturday). You'll see the BBC News and Weather Centres as well as studios where shows are being made; keep your eyes peeled all the while as you're very likely to spot a celebrity wandering around the corridors.

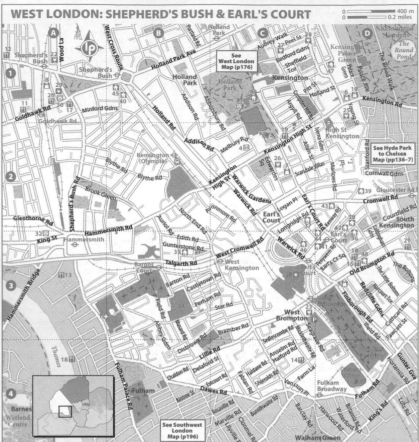

INFORMATION		
Charing Cross Hospital	1	A3

SIGHTS	(pp175–7)	
Brompton Cemetery	2	D4
Former Commonwealth Institute	3	C2
Leighton House	4	C2
Linley Sambourne House	5	C2

SHOPPING	(pp213–32)	
Miss Sixty	6	D1
Orsini	7	C2
Shepherd's Bush Market	8	A1
Troubadour Wines	9	D3
Urban Outfitters	10	D1

EATING	(pp233–272)	
Blah Blah Blah	11	A1
Esarn Kheaw	12	A1
Gate	13	A3
Harwood Arms	14	C4
Krungtap	15	D3
Mr Wing	16	D3
Patio	17	A1
River Café	18	A4
Sticky Fingers	19	C2
Tatra	20	A1
Tendido Cero	21	D3

DRINKING	(pp273–92)	
Albertine Wine Bar	22	A1
Atlas	23	C3
Churchill Arms	24	C1
Greyhound	25	D1
Scarsdale Arms	26	C2
Troubadour	(see 9)	
Windsor Castle	27	C1

NIGHTLIFE	(pp293–304)	
Earl's Court Exhibition Centre	28	C3
Shepherd's Bush Empire	29	A1

THE ARTS	(pp305–16)	
Bush Theatre	30	A1
Korn/Ferry Opera Holland Park	31	C1
Lyric Hammersmith	32	A3

SPORTS & ACTIVITIES	(pp317–22)	
Chelsea Football Club	33	D4
K Spa	(see 40)	
Queen's Club	34	B3

SLEEPING	(pp331–54)	
Ace Hotel	35	B3
Barkston Hostel	36	D3
Barmy Badger Backpackers	37	C2
base2stay	38	D2
easyHotel Earl's Court	39	D2
K West	40	B1
Mayflower	41	D3
Merlyn Court Hotel	42	D2
Rockwell	43	D2
Rushmore	44	D3
St Christopher's Shepherd's Bush	45	B1
Twenty Nevern Square	46	C3
Vicarage Hotel	47	D1
YHA Earl's Court	48	D3
YHA Holland House	49	C1

GREENWICH & SOUTHEAST LONDON

Drinking p289; Eating p266; Shopping p231; Sleeping p352

Southeast London by and large feels like a succession of small villages, and that's exactly what many of these suburbs were until as recently as the late 19th century. Although there's evidence of early prehistoric settlements in areas such as Greenwich, Woolwich and Forest Hill, for most of its history this area was merely on the fringes of the big city.

Greenwich, right on the banks of the Thames, is something of an exception. Packed with splendid architecture, it has strong connections with the sea, science, sovereigns and – of course – time. Ever since Greenwich was made the prime meridian of longitude, Greenwich Mean Time has dictated how clocks and watches around the globe are set.

Now a Unesco World Heritage Site known as Maritime Greenwich, the district's leafy green expanses and wedding-cake buildings give it an air of semirural gentility. This tranquil aura continues, although to a lesser degree, as you venture further southeast into

top picks

GREENWICH & SOUTHEAST LONDON

- National Maritime Museum (below)
- British Music Experience (p183)
- Royal Observatory (p180)
- Thames Barrier (p184)
- Eltham Palace (p185)

places like Dulwich, site of Britain's oldest public art gallery, and Eltham, which boasts an art deco palace alongside a Tudor one dating back to the 14th century.

A lot edgier are the areas of Deptford and New Cross just west of Greenwich. Here you'll find a district in transition, with recording studios opening up in what used to be garages, galleries and art centres squeezing in between pie 'n' mash shops, and pubs turning into bars.

GREENWICH

Greenwich (*gren*-itch) lies to the southeast of central London, where the Thames widens and deepens, and there's a sense of space that is rare elsewhere in the city. Quaint, villagelike and boasting the Royal Observatory and the fabulous National Maritime Museum, Greenwich has been on Unesco's list of World Heritage Sites since 1997. A trip there will be one of the highlights of any visit to London, and you should certainly allow a day to do it justice, particularly if you want to head down the river to the Thames Barrier, passing the stunning O2 (formerly the Millennium Dome) along the way.

Greenwich is home to an extraordinary interrelated cluster of classical buildings; all the great architects of the Enlightenment made their mark here, largely due to royal patronage. In the early 17th century, Inigo Jones built one of England's first classical Renaissance homes, the Queen's House, which still stands today. Charles II was particularly fond of the area and had Sir Christopher Wren build both the Royal Observatory and part of the Royal Naval College, which John Vanbrugh then completed in the early 17th century.

Virtually everything in Greenwich can be easily reached from the Cutty Sark DLR station. A quicker way to get here from central London, however, is via one of the mainline trains from Charing Cross or London Bridge to Greenwich railway station. An alternative from Docklands is to use the historic 370m-long foot tunnel running under the Thames and completed in 1902. The lifts down to the tunnel run between 7am and 7pm Monday to Saturday and 10am and 5.30pm on Sunday. Otherwise you're facing between 88 and 100 steps down and – shudder – up (open 24 hours).

NATIONAL MARITIME MUSEUM
Map p182

☎ 8858 4422, recorded information 8312 6565; www.nmm.ac.uk; Romney Rd SE10; admission free; ⏰ 10am-5pm; ⬆ Greenwich or DLR Cutty Sark; ♿ Though it hardly sounds like a crowd-pleaser, this museum designed to tell the long and convoluted history of Britain as a seafaring nation is the best attraction in Greenwich. From the moment you step through the entrance of this magnificent neoclassical building you'll be won over. And it just gets better as you progress through the glass-roofed Neptune Court into the rest of the three-storey building.

The exhibits are arranged by theme, focusing on Explorers, Maritime London, Art and Sea and so on. Visual highlights include the 19m-long golden state barge built in 1732 for Frederick, Prince of Wales, and the huge ship's propeller installed on level 1. The museum also owns the uniform coat that Britain's greatest sea-faring hero, Horatio Nelson, was wearing when he was fatally shot (including the actual bullet), plus a replica of the lifeboat *James Caird* used by explorer Ernest Shackleton and a handful of his men after the *Endurance* sank on their epic mission in Antarctica. The restored stained glass from the Baltic Exchange, blown up by the IRA in 1992, is now a memorial to the victims of WWI.

The environmentally minded are catered for with the Your Ocean exhibit on level 1, examining the science, history, health and future of the sea. Kids will love firing a cannon in the All Hands exhibit or manoeuvring a tanker into port by using the state-of-the-art Bridge Simulator on level 2. Fashionistas and stylists will be wowed on the ground floor by Rank and Style (uniforms and leisurewear worn at sea) and the Passengers exhibit (classic travel posters and the mock-up of the cocktail bar of a cruise ship).

ROYAL OBSERVATORY Map p182
☎ 8858 4422, recorded information 8312 6565; www.nmm.ac.uk/places/royal-observatory; Greenwich Park, Blackheath Ave SE10; admission free; ☼ 10am-5pm; ⓡ Greenwich or DLR Cutty Sark; ☺
Following an ambitious £15-million renovation the Royal Observatory is now divided into two sections.

The northern half deals with time and is contained in the original Observatory that Charles II had built on a hill in the middle of Greenwich Park in 1675, intending that astronomy be used to establish longitude at sea. It contains the Octagon Room, designed by Wren, and the nearby Sextant Room where John Flamsteed (1646–1719), the first astronomer royal, made his observations and calculations.

The globe is divided between east and west at the Royal Observatory, and in the Meridian Courtyard (☼ 10am-5pm Sep-Apr, to 8pm May-Aug) you can place one foot either side of the meridian line and straddle the two hemispheres. Every day at 1pm the red

time ball at the top of the Royal Observatory continues to drop as has done since 1833. You can get great views of Greenwich and spy on your fellow tourists at the same time by visiting the unique Camera Obscura.

The southern half is devoted to astronomy and includes the 120-seat state-of-the-art Peter Harrison Planetarium (☎ 8312 8565; www.nmm.ac.uk/astronomy; adult/child/family £6/4/16; ☼ hourly shows 1-4pm Mon-Fri, 11am-5pm Sat & Sun), with a digital laser projector that can show entire heavens on the inside of its bronze-clad roof and is the most advanced in Europe. Galleries here trace the history of astronomy and interactive displays focus on such subjects as meteorites, space missions and the effects of gravity.

OLD ROYAL NAVAL COLLEGE Map p182
☎ 8269 4799; www.oldroyalnavalcollege.org; King William Walk SE10; admission free; ⓡ Greenwich or DLR Cutty Sark
When Christopher Wren was commissioned by William and Mary to build a naval hospital here in 1692, he designed it in two separate halves so as not to spoil the view of the river from the Queen's House (p179), Inigo Jones' miniature masterpiece to the south. Today it also frames Canary Wharf and the skyscrapers of Docklands to the north.

Built on the site of the Old Palace of Placentia, where Henry VIII was born in 1491, the hospital was initially intended for those wounded in the victory over the French at La Hogue. In 1869 the building was converted to a Naval College. Now even the navy has left and the premises are home to the University of Greenwich and Trinity College of Music.

Two main rooms are open to the public. In the King William Building, the Painted Hall (☼ 10am-5pm daily) is one of Europe's greatest banquet rooms and is covered in decorative 'allegorical Baroque' murals by artist James Thornhill, who also painted the cupola of St Paul's Cathedral. The mural above the Lower Hall show William and Mary enthroned amid symbols of the Virtues. Beneath William's feet you can see the defeated French king Louis XIV grovelling with a furled flag in hand. Up a few steps is the Upper Hall where, on the western wall, George I is depicted with his family. In the bottom right-hand corner Thornhill drew himself into the picture, pointing towards his work.

Off the Upper Hall is the Nelson Room, originally designed by Nicholas Hawksmoor, then used as a smoking room and now open to the public. In January 1806 the brandy-soaked (for embalming purposes, of course) body of the great naval hero lay in state here before his funeral at St Paul's. Today the room contains a plaster replica of the statue atop Nelson's column in Trafalgar Sq plus other memorabilia, including lots of hospital silver. Look to the courtyard through the window; the cobbles form an outline of the Union Flag (Union Jack).

A 90-minute guided tour (☎ 8269 4791; adult/ under 16yr £5/free; ☼ tours 11.30am & 2pm) from the Painted Hall will take you to places not normally open to the public: the Jacobean undercroft of the former Placentia palace and the 140-year-old Victorian Skittle Alley, featuring enormous hand-carved wooden bowling balls and pins.

The chapel (☼ 10am-5pm Mon-Sat, 12.30-5pm Sun) in the Queen Mary Building opposite the Painted Hall is decorated in a lighter rococo style. The eastern end of the chapel is dominated by a painting by the 18th-century American artist Benjamin West showing *The Preservation of St Paul after Shipwreck at Malta*. It's certainly a beautiful room, but is more famous for its organ and acoustics. If possible come on the first Sunday of the month, when there's a free 50-minute organ recital at 3pm, or time your visit for sung Eucharist at 11am on Sunday.

QUEEN'S HOUSE Map p182
☎ 8858 4422, recorded information 8312 6565; www.nmm.ac.uk/places/queens-house; Romney Rd SE10; admission free; ☼ 10am-5pm; ⑧ Greenwich or DLR Cutty Sark; ⑤
The first Palladian building by architect Inigo Jones after he returned from Italy, what was at first called the 'House of Delight' is indeed far more enticing than the art collection it contains, even though it includes some Turners, Holbeins, Hogarths and Gainsboroughs. The house was begun in 1616 for Anne of Denmark, wife of James I, but was not completed until 1638, when it became the home of Charles I and his queen, Henrietta Maria. The Great Hall is the principal room – a lovely cube shape, with an elaborately tiled floor and the helix-shaped Tulip Staircase (named for the flowers on the wrought-iron balustrade) leading to a gallery on level 2, hung with paintings

and portraits with a sea or seafaring theme from the National Maritime Museum's fine art collection . Don't miss the paintings in the Historic Greenwich gallery on level 1.

RANGER'S HOUSE (WERNHER COLLECTION) Map p182
☎ 8853 0035; www.english-heritage.org.uk; Greenwich Park, Chesterfield Walk SE10; adult/ 5-15yr/concession £5.70/2.90/4.80; ☼ tours 11.30am & 2.30pm Mon-Wed, 11am-5pm Sun early Apr-Sep; ⑧ Greenwich or DLR Cutty Sark
This elegant Georgian villa in the southwest corner of Greenwich Park was built in 1723 and once housed the park's ranger. It now contains a collection of 700 works of art (medieval and Renaissance paintings, porcelain, silverware, tapestries etc) amassed by one Julius Wernher (1850–1912), a German-born railway engineer's son who struck it rich in the diamond fields of South Africa in the 19th century. The Spanish Renaissance jewellery collection is the best in Europe, and the rose garden fronting the house defies description.

CUTTY SARK Map p182
☎ 8858 2698; www.cuttysark.org.uk; Cutty Sark Gardens SE10; ⑧ Greenwich or DLR Cutty Sark
This Greenwich landmark, the last of the great clipper ships to sail between China and England in the 19th century, was undergoing £25-million repair work in 2007 when a fire damaged about 50% of the 'fabric' of the vessel. Luckily half of the ship's furnishings and equipment, including the mast, had been removed for conservation. At the time of writing, repairs costing an additional £10 million were under way and the *Cutty Sark* will rise, phoenix-like, from the ashes any day now.

FAN MUSEUM Map p182
☎ 8305 1441, 8858 7879; www.fan-museum.org; 12 Crooms Hill SE10; adult/7-16yr & concession/ family £4/3/10; ☼ 11am-5pm Tue-Sat, noon-5pm Sun; ⑧ Greenwich or DLR Cutty Sark; ⑤
The world's only museum entirely devoted to fans has a wonderful collection of ivory, tortoiseshell, peacock-feather and folded-fabric examples alongside kitsch battery-powered versions and huge ornamental Welsh fans. Some of the temporary exhibits on the 1st floor are wonderful and there are fan-making classes on the first Saturday of the month. The 18th-century Georgian

GREENWICH & SOUTHEAST LONDON

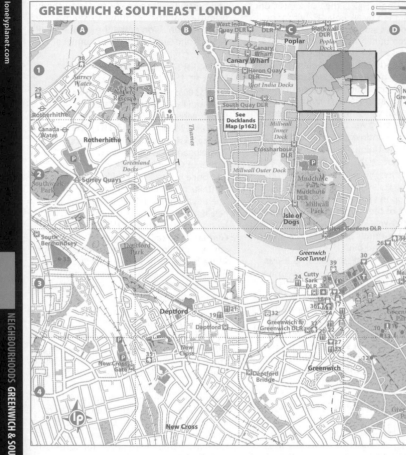

town house in which the collection resides also has a Japanese-style garden with an Orangery (half-/full tea £3.50/4.50; ☿ 3-5pm Tue & Sun) with lovely trompe l'œil murals and serving afternoon tea twice a week.

ST ALFEGE CHURCH Map p182
☎ 8691 8337; Church St SE10; admission free; ☿ 10am-4pm Mon-Sat, 1-4pm Sun; ☯ Greenwich or DLR Cutty Sark

Designed by Nicholas Hawksmoor in 1714 to replace a 12th-century building, this parish church features a restored mural by James Thornhill (whose work includes the Painted Hall at the Royal Naval College and St Paul's Cathedral). St Alfege was an archbishop of Canterbury, killed on this site by Vikings in 1012.

GREENWICH PARK Map p182
☎ 8858 2608; www.royalparks.gov.uk; ☿ dawn-dusk, cars from 7am; ☯ Greenwich or Maze Hill, DLR Cutty Sark

This is one of London's largest and loveliest parks, with a grand avenue, wide-open spaces, a rose garden, picturesque walks and impressive views across the River Thames to Docklands from the top of the hill near the statue of General Wolfe opposite the Royal Observatory. Covering a full 73 hectares, it is the oldest enclosed royal park and is partly the work of Le Nôtre, who landscaped the palace gardens of Versailles for Louis XIV. It contains several historic sights, a teahouse near the Royal Observatory, a cafe behind the National Maritime Museum and a deer park in the southeast corner.

GREENWICH & SOUTHEAST LONDON

O2 (FORMER MILLENNIUM DOME)
Map p182

☎ 8463 2000, bookings 0844 856 0202;
www.theo2.co.uk; Millennium Way SE10;
⊖ North Greenwich

The 380m-wide circular Millennium Dome (renamed O2) cost £750 million to build and more than £5 million a year just to keep it erect. It closed at the end of 2000, having failed miserably in its bid to attract 12 million visitors, and was until 2007 for the most part unemployed. Since then it has hosted big acts like Madonna, Prince, Justin Timberlake and Barbara Streisand in its 23,000-seat O2 Arena and soul, pop and jazz bands in the 2350-seat Indig02. Massive exhibitions (Tutankhamen and the Golden Age of the Pharaohs, The Human Body) and sporting events have made their temporary homes here and there's a slew of bars, clubs and restaurants sheltering under what was originally derided as 'the latest in tent technology'.

BRITISH MUSIC EXPERIENCE Map p182

☎ 0844 847 1761; www.britishmusicexperience
.com; Millennium Way SE10; adult/child &
concession/family £15/12/40; ⏰ 10am-7pm;
⊖ North Greenwich

Our favourite new attraction in the O2 'bubble' traces the history of British popular music from 1945 to the present day in a series of eight galleries filled with instruments and stage costumes, music, lights and buttons to push. And it's about as hands-on as

you can get. Film yourself playing guitar, singing or dancing and fill up your chip-impregnated entrance ticket with information and music to be downloaded onto your computer at home. The Finale, in which you stand next to holograms performing before a massive cheering (filmed) audience, has to be experienced to be believed. We're still taking our bows after a Standing Room Only concert of air guitar.

DEPTFORD & NEW CROSS Map p182

🚇 Deptford, New Cross or DLR Cutty Sark then
🚌 77 or 25

In recent years Deptford and its southern extension, New Cross, just over the Deptford Creek west of Greenwich, have been experiencing something of a renaissance with the advent of music studios and shops, art galleries, the celebrated Laban (p307) dance institute and other cultural centres and creative outlets. The Elizabethan playwright Christopher Marlowe was stabbed to death here during a drunken brawl. To see the neighbourhood up close and dirty, take a walk (p186).

CHARLTON & WOOLWICH

From early Iron Age hill forts to mammoth gates in the Thames designed to prevent flooding, humankind has been determined to leave a mark on these areas over the centuries. One of the most enduring landmarks has been the Royal Arsenal, which followed Henry VIII's royal dockyards out here in the 16th and 17th centuries. When it was finally closed in 1994, it made way for a unique museum.

THAMES BARRIER Map p62

⊖ North Greenwich, then ☐ 177 or 180, or ☒ Charlton, then ☐ 161 or 472

The sci-fi–looking Thames Barrier is in place to protect London from flooding and, with global warming increasing the city's vulnerability to rising sea levels and surge tides, the barrier is likely to be of growing importance in coming years. Under construction for a decade and completed in 1982, the barrier consists of 10 movable gates anchored to nine concrete piers, each as tall as a five-storey building. The silver roofs on the piers house the operating machinery to raise and lower the gates against excess water. They make a surreal sight, straddling the river in the lee of a giant warehouse.

The reason why London needs such a flood barrier is that the water level has been rising by as much as 60cm per century, while the river itself has been narrowing; in Roman times it was probably around 800m wide at the site of today's London Bridge while now it's barely 250m, with constant pressure to develop the foreshores. The Thames tide rises and falls quite harmlessly twice a day, and once a fortnight there's also a stronger 'spring' tide. The danger comes when the spring tide coincides with an unexpected surge, which pushes tons of extra water upriver. The barrier has been built to prevent that water pouring over the riverbanks and flooding nearby houses. Today environmentalists are already talking about a bigger, wider damming mechanism further towards the mouth of the river, before the current barrier comes to the expected end of its design life in 2030.

The barrier looks best when it's raised, and the only guaranteed time this happens is once a month, when the mechanisms are checked. For exact dates and times, ring or check the website of the Thames Barrier Information Centre (☎ 8305 4188; www.environment-agency.gov.uk/thamesbarrier; 1 Unity Way SE18; adult/5-16 yr/concession £3.50/2/3; ☽ 10.30am-4.30pm Apr-Sep, 11am-3.30pm Oct-Mar).

If you're coming from central London, take a train to Charlton from Charing Cross or London Bridge. Then walk along Woolwich Rd to Eastmoor St, which leads northward to the centre. If you're coming from Greenwich, you can pick up bus 177 or 180 along Romney Rd and get off at the Thames Barrier stop (near Holborn College on Woolwich Rd). The closest tube station is North Greenwich, from where you can pick up bus 472 or 161.

Boats also travel to and from the barrier, although they don't land here. For details see p380.

FIREPOWER (ROYAL ARTILLERY MUSEUM) Map p62

☎ 8855 7755; www.firepower.org.uk; Royal Arsenal, Woolwich SE18; adult/5-15yr/concession/family £5/2.50/4.50/12; ☽ 10.30am-5pm Wed-Sun; DLR Woolwich Arsenal, ⊖ North Greenwich then ☐ 161 or 472, DLR Cutty Sark then ☐ 177 or 180

Not a place for pacifists or those of a nervous disposition, Firepower is a shoot-'em-up display of how artillery has developed through the ages. The History Gallery traces the story of artillery from catapults to nuclear warheads, while the multimedia Field of Fire tries to convey the experience of artillery gunners from WWI to Bosnia in a 15-minute extravaganza. There's a Gunnery Hall packed with weapons and vehicles from the 20th century and a Medals Gallery with 7000 pieces. The Camo Zone includes four different activities (£1.50 each, or £4.50 for four), including a firing range and remote-control tanks. The whole place is loud and reeking of adrenaline – and the kids just can't get enough of it.

GREENWICH HERITAGE CENTRE

Map p62

☎ 8854 2452; www.greenwichheritage.org; Royal Arsenal, Artillery Sq SE18; admission free; ☽ 9am-5pm Tue-Sat; DLR Woolwich Arsenal, ⊖ North Greenwich then ☐ 161 or 472, DLR Cutty Sark then ☐ 177 or 180

If you've seen Firepower (or the kids are seeing it and you are not) and want to know more about Greenwich and its rich history, visit this well-endowed centre just next door. it traces the history of the Royal Arsenal and Woolwich Dockyards; the eye-witness televised testimonials by former employees and local residents are brilliant. Don't miss the stunning Millennium Embroideries, eight stitched panels from 1998 representing key periods in local history from the Celts and Romans to the late 20th century, at least one of which should be on display.

DULWICH & FOREST HILL

Tucked away in the wide expanse of South London that the tube fails to reach, Dulwich (*dull*-itch) and Forest Hill are leafy, quiet suburbs with some fine architecture and an air of gentility. Both boast outstanding museums well worth a trip out here.

DULWICH PICTURE GALLERY Map p62

☎ 8693 5254; www.dulwichpicturegallery.org.uk; Gallery Rd SE21; adult/child & student/concession £5/free/4; ⏲ 10am-5pm Tue-Fri, 11am-5pm Sat & Sun; ⓡ West Dulwich; ♿

The UK's oldest public art gallery, the Dulwich Picture Gallery was designed by the idiosyncratic architect Sir John Soane between 1811 and 1814 to house Dulwich College's collection of paintings by Raphael, Rembrandt, Rubens, Reynolds, Gainsborough, Poussin, Lely, Van Dyck and others. It's a wonderful, atmospheric place but, with scarcely a dozen rooms to hang the artwork, wall space is limited and it is difficult to view some of the paintings properly. Unusually, the collectors Noel Desenfans and painter Sir Peter Francis Bourgeois chose to have their mausoleums, lit by a moody *lumière mystérieuse* (mysterious light) created with tinted glass, placed among the pictures. An annexe (additional £4) contains space for what are usually cutting-edge temporary exhibitions and free guided tours of the museum depart at 3pm on Saturday and Sunday.

The museum is a 10-minute walk northwards along Gallery Rd, which starts almost opposite West Dulwich railway station. Bus P4 conveniently links the picture gallery with the Horniman Museum (below).

HORNIMAN MUSEUM Map p62

☎ 8699 1872; www.horniman.ac.uk; 100 London Rd SE23; admission free; ⏲ 10.30am-5.30pm; ⓡ Forest Hill; ♿

This museum is an extraordinary place, comprising the original collection of wealthy tea merchant Frederick John Horniman, a pack rat who had the art nouveau building with clock tower and mosaics specially designed to house it in 1901. Today it encompasses everything from a dusty stuffed walrus and voodoo altars from Haiti and Benin to a mock-up of a Fijian reef and a collection of concertinas. It's wonderful.

On the ground and 1st floors is the Natural History Gallery, the core of the Horni-man collection, with usual animal skeletons and pickled specimens. On the lower ground floor you'll find the African Worlds Gallery, the first permanent gallery of African and Afro-Caribbean art and culture in the UK. The Music Gallery next door has instruments from 3500-year-old Egyptian clappers and early English keyboards to Indonesian gamelan and Ghanaian drums, with touch screens so you can hear what they sound like and videos to see them being played in situ. The Centenary Gallery traces the history of the museum's first 100 years. The aquarium in the basement is small but state of the art. The cafe, with seating in the stunning conservatory, is a delight, as are the surrounding 6.5 hectares of hillside gardens (⏲ 7.30-dusk Mon-Sat, from 8am Sun) with views of far-flung central London.

To get here from Forest Hill station, turn left out of the station along Devonshire Rd and then right along London Rd. The museum is about 500m on the right.

ELTHAM

Eltham was the favoured home of the Plantagenet kings. But after the Tudors turned their royal attention to Greenwich, the palace here lay neglected for more than 500 years. Only when the wealthy Courtauld family arrived in the 1930s to build their fabulous home were the remains of the original 14th-century Eltham Palace restored.

ELTHAM PALACE Map p62

☎ 8794 2548; www.english-heritage.org.uk; Court Rd SE9; palace & gardens adult/5-15yr/concession/ family £8.30/4.20/7.10/20.80, gardens only adult/ child/concession £5.30/2.70/4.30; ⏲ 10am-5pm Sun-Wed Apr-Oct, 11am-4pm Sun-Wed Nov-late Dec, Feb & Mar, closed late Dec-Jan; ⓡ Eltham; ♿

The art deco house here was built between 1933 and 1937 by the well-to-do textile merchant Stephen Courtauld (of Courtauld Institute fame) and his wife Virginia; from the impressive entrance hall with its dome and huge circular carpet with geometric shapes, to the black-marble dining room with silver-foil ceiling and burlwood-veneer fireplace, it appears the couple had taste as well as money. They also, rather fashionably for the times, had a pet lemur, and the heated cage, complete with tropical murals and a bamboo ladder leading to the ground floor, for the spoiled (and vicious) 'Mah-jongg' is also on view.

A royal palace was built on this site in 1305 and was for a time the boyhood home of Henry VIII, before the Tudors decamped to Greenwich. Little of the palace remains, apart from the restored Great Medieval Hall. Its hammer-beam roof is generally rated the third best in the country, behind those at Westminster Hall (p93) and Hampton Court Palace (p201). The 8 hectares of gardens include rockery and moat with working bridge.

BEXLEYHEATH

Formerly known as Bexley New Town and dominated by an expanse of open space, this attractive suburban development east of Eltham contains two important historic houses.

DANSON HOUSE Off Map p62

☎ 8303 6699; www.dansonhouse.com; Danson Park, Bexleyheath DA6; adult/child/concession £6/free/5; ⊗ 11am-5pm Wed, Thu, Sun & bank holiday Mon late Mar-Oct, 11am-5pm Tue-Thu, Sun & bank holiday Mon Jun-Aug; ⏏ Bexleyheath, then 20min walk southwest

This Palladian villa was built by one John Boyd, an East India Company director, in 1766. A 10-year restoration to bring the house back to its original Georgian style was completed in 2005, aided by the discovery of a series of fine watercolours of the interiors by the second owner's daughter, Sarah Johnston, in 1805. Highlights include the dining room's numerous reliefs and frescoes celebrating love and romance; the library and music room, with its functioning organ; the dizzying spiral staircase accessing the upper floors; and the Victorian kitchens (open only occasionally). The English-style garden is a delight, and on the large lake in Danson Park, which is flanked by some splendid art deco houses along Danson Rd to the east, you can hire rowing boats (☎ 8303 2828; 30/60min morning £5/7.50, afternoon £7.50/10; ⊗ 10am-5pm Sat & Sun, to 8pm Jul & Aug).

RED HOUSE Off Map p62

☎ 8304 9878; www.nationaltrust.org.uk; 13 Red House Lane, Bexleyheath DA6; adult/5-15yr/family £6.90/3.45/17.25; ⊗ 11am-4.45pm Wed-Sun Mar-late Nov, 11am-4.45pm Fri-Sun late Nov–late-Dec; ⏏ Bexleyheath, then 20min walk south

From the outside, this red-brick house built by Victorian designer William Morris in

1859 conjures up a gingerbread house in stone. The nine rooms open to the public bear all the elements of the Arts and Crafts style to which Morris adhered – a bit of Gothic art here, some religious symbolism there, an art nouveau–like sunburst over there. Furniture by Morris and the house's designer Philip Webb are in evidence, as are paintings and stained glass by Edward Burne-Jones. Entry is by guided tour only, which must be prebooked. The surrounding gardens were designed by Morris 'to clothe' the house. Don't miss the well with a conical roof inspired by the oast houses of nearby Kent.

DEPTFORD & NEW CROSS WALK
Walking Tour

1 Creekside This cobbled street running parallel to Deptford Creek is lined with galleries and artists' studios that have regularly changing art exhibitions, including APT Gallery (☎ 8694 8344; www.aptstudios.org; 6 Creekside SE8) and Art Hub (☎ 8691 5140; www.arthub.org.uk; 5-9 Creekside SE8).

2 Laban What is acknowledged as the largest and best equipped contemporary dance school (p307) in Europe is housed in an award-winning £23-million plastic-clad building (2003) at the northern end of Creekside designed by the architects who designed Tate Modern. Highly innovative are the turf-covered mounds of debris cleared from the site in the forecourt.

3 Statue of Peter the Great This unusual statue (Glaisher St SE8), with the tiny head and gnome-like creature at his feet commemorates the four-month stay of Tsar Peter I of Russia, who in 1698 came to Deptford to learn more about new developments in shipbuilding. The original party dude, Peter stayed with diarist John Evelyn and his drunken parties badly damaged the writer's house.

4 St Nicholas Church This late-17th-century church (☎ 8692 2749; Deptford Green SE8; 9.30am-12.30pm Wed-Sat) contains a memorial to playwright Christopher Marlowe, who was murdered in Deptford in a tavern brawl at the age of 29 in 1593 and may be buried here. The fight supposedly broke out over who was to pay the bill but it is generally believed that Marlowe was in the employ of the Elizabethan intelligence service. The skull and crossbones over the entrance is said to have been the inspiration for the Jolly Roger pirate flag.

5 Albury Street This delightful street is lined with Georgian buildings that once housed Deptford's naval officers, including (it is said) Lord Nelson and Lady Hamilton. Notice the exquisite wood carvings decorating many of the doorways.

6 St Paul's Church To the south of Albury St is this baroque church (☎ 8692 7449; Mary Ann Gardens SE8) built in 1730. In the churchyard is the grave of Mydiddee, a native Tahitian who returned with Captain Bligh (of *Bounty* mutiny fame) on the HMS *Providence* and died in Deptford almost immediately in 1793.

7 Deptford Market This colourful market (Deptford High St SE8; 🕑 8.30am-3pm Wed, Fri & Sat) takes place in the centre of Deptford three days a week, and comprises a vibrant flea market as well as food and clothing stalls. Southwest is the Albany (☎ 8692 4446; www .thealbany.org.uk; Douglas Way SE8), a busy arts and community centre with comedy, music and theatre productions and a lovely cafe.

WALK FACTS

Start Deptford Bridge DLR station
End Deptford rail station
Distance 1.5 miles
Duration Two hours
Fuel stop AJ Goddard (p254)

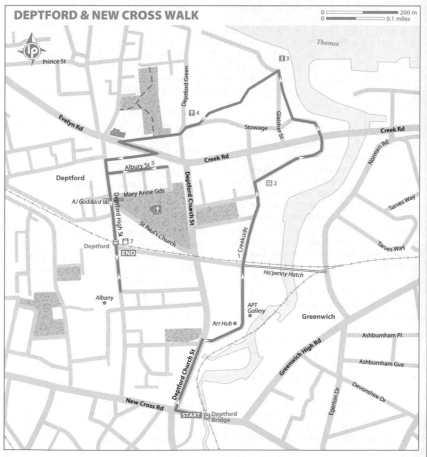

DEPTFORD & NEW CROSS WALK

SOUTH LONDON

Drinking p290; Eating p267; Shopping p231

Londoners still talk as if the Thames was the huge barrier between north and south that it was in the Middle Ages. In fact, the psychological gulf between the two banks is as wide as ever; many people in North London refuse to believe there's anything of importance across the river. But it really isn't so grim down south. In recent years even former residents of North London have discovered there's something rather pleasant about the more affordable property prices and relaxed lifestyle of what was once the river's B-list side (referring, of course, to the number of place names beginning with that letter such as Battersea, Brixton, Balham and so on).

Anarchic and artistic Brixton is without a doubt the most interesting area. Besides coming here to go clubbing, to a attend a gig at the O2 Academy Brixton (p303) or to catch a film at the historic Ritzy (p310), probably the best way to taste the area's Afro-Caribbean flavour is to visit Brixton Market (p259).

Clapham has long been the flag-bearer for South London style, with upmarket restaurants and bars lining its High Street since the

top picks

SOUTH LONDON

- Battersea Park (p192)
- Battersea Power Station (p192)
- Brixton Market (p193)
- Imperial War Museum (left)
- Lambeth Palace (opposite)

1980s. Attention has started to focus more recently on Battersea, with its magnificent park and the announced conversion of the monolithic Battersea Power Station. Kennington has some lovely streets lined with Georgian terraced houses, so it can only be a matter of time before the gentrification of 'Little Portugal' – its southern extension of Stockwell – begins.

Lambeth can boast both the episcopal seat of the Church of England and one of London's finest museums.

LAMBETH

The name Lambeth translates as 'muddy landing place', attesting to the fact that this, like nearby Waterloo, was largely marsh land and polder dams until the 18th century. Apparently, the only notables brave enough to live here earlier were archbishops of Canterbury, who began coming and going in barges from waterside Lambeth Palace in the 13th century. It was the arrival of bridges and the railways centuries later that finally connected Lambeth to London.

IMPERIAL WAR MUSEUM Map p189

☎ 7416 5320; www.iwm.org.uk; Lambeth Rd SE1; admission free; ⊙ 10am-6pm; ⊖ Lambeth North; ⭐

Despite the threatening pair of 15in naval guns outside the front entrance to what was once Bethlehem Royal Hospital, commonly known as Bedlam, this is for the most part a very sombre, thoughtful museum. Most of its exhibits are given over to exploring the human and social cost of conflict.

Although the museum's focus is officially on military action involving British

or Commonwealth troops during the 20th century, it gives 'war' a wide interpretation. So it not only has serious discussion of the two world wars, Korea and Vietnam, but also covers the Cold War, 'secret' warfare (ie spying) and even the war on apartheid in South Africa.

The core of the six-floor museum is a chronological exhibition on the two world wars on the lower ground floor. In the Trench Experience you walk through the grim day-to-day reality of life on the Somme front line in WWI, and in the more hair-raising Blitz Experience you cower inside a mock bomb shelter during a WWII air raid and then emerge through ravaged East End streets.

On the upper floors you find the two most outstanding – and moving – sections: the extensive Holocaust Exhibition (not recommended for under 14s) on the 3rd floor, and a stark gallery called Crimes against Humanity devoted to genocide in Cambodia, Yugoslavia and Rwanda (not recommended for under 16s). The 2nd floor features war paintings by the likes of Stanley Spencer and John Singer Sargent.

Audioguides to the permanent collection will cost you £4/3 adult/concession. Temporary exhibits, which charge an admission fee, cover topics ranging from war reporting, camouflage and modern warfare and – our favourite – the role of animals in conflicts from WWI to the present day.

LAMBETH PALACE Map p189
Palace Rd SE1; ⊖ Lambeth North

The red-brick Tudor gatehouse located beside the church of St Mary-at-Lambeth leads to Lambeth Palace, the London residence of the Archbishop of Canterbury. Although the palace is not usually open to the public, the gardens occasionally are;

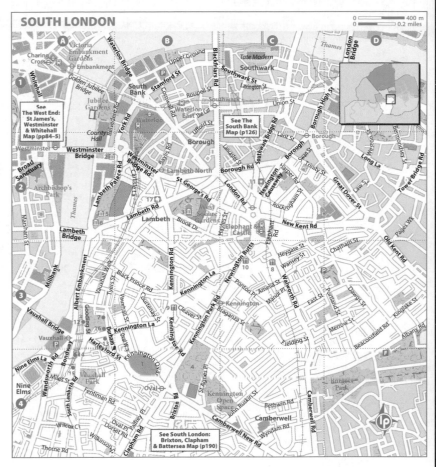

SOUTH LONDON

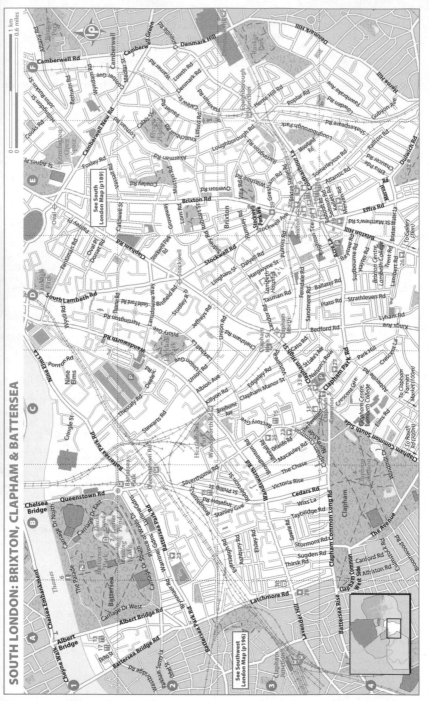

See South
London Map (p189)

See Southwest
London Map (p196)

SOUTH LONDON: BRIXTON, CLAPHAM & BATTERSEA

check with a tourist office for more details (see p392).

MUSEUM OF GARDEN HISTORY
Map p189

☎ 7401 8865; www.museumgardenhistory.org; St Mary-at-Lambeth, Lambeth Palace Rd SE1; admission free, requested donation £3; ☏ 10.30am-5pm Tue-Sun; ☺ Lambeth North

In a city that offers the broad attractions of Kew Gardens, the modest Museum of Garden History housed in the church of St Mary-at-Lambeth is mainly for the seriously green-thumbed. Its trump card is the charming knot garden, a replica of a 17th-century formal garden, with topiary hedges clipped into an intricate, twirling design. Keen gardeners will enjoy the displays on the 17th-century Tradescant *père* and *fils* – a father-and-son team who were gardeners to Charles I and Charles II, globetrotters and enthusiastic collectors of exotic plants (they introduced the pineapple to London). Nongardeners might like to pay their respects to Captain William Bligh (of mutinous *Bounty* fame), who is buried here (he lived and died nearby at 100 Lambeth Rd). The excellent cafe has vegetarian food.

FLORENCE NIGHTINGALE MUSEUM
Map p189

☎ 7620 0374; www.florence-nightingale.co.uk; St Thomas's Hospital, 2 Lambeth Palace Rd SE1; adult/senior, student & child/family £5.80/4.80/16; ☏ 10am-5pm Mon-Fri, to 4.30pm Sat & Sun; ☺ Westminster or Waterloo; ♿

Attached to St Thomas's Hospital, this small museum tells the story of feisty war heroine Florence Nightingale (1820–1910), who led a team of nurses to Turkey in 1854 during the Crimean War. There she worked to improve conditions for the soldiers before returning to London to set up a training school for nurses at St Thomas's in 1859. So popular did she become that baseball-card–style photos of the gentle 'Lady of the Lamp' were sold during her lifetime. There is no shortage of revisionist detractors who dismiss her as a 'canny administrator' and 'publicity hound'; Nightingale was, in fact, one of the world's first modern celebrities. But the fact remains she improved conditions for thousands of soldiers in the field and saved quite a few lives in the process. We can hardly think of a more glorious achievement.

BRIXTON

'We gonna rock down to Electric Avenue,' sang Eddy Grant optimistically in 1983. (This street, just to the left as you exit Brixton tube station, was one of the first in London to be lit by electricity, in 1888). In contrast, the much darker tone of the Clash's 'Guns of Brixton' (1979) depicted the community discontent with the police that soon provoked the riots of the 1980s. These are just two sides of this edgy, vibrant, multicultural neighbourhood.

There was a settlement on the site of today's Brixton as early as just one year after the Norman invasion. But Brixton remained an isolated, far-flung village until the 19th century, when the new Vauxhall Bridge (1810) and the railways (1860) linked it with central London.

The years that most shaped contemporary Brixton, however, were the post-WWII

'Windrush' years, when immigrants arrived from the West Indies in reply to the British government's call for help in solving the labour shortage of the time. (*Windrush* was the name of one of the leading ships that brought these immigrants to the UK.) A generation later the honeymoon period was over, as economic decline and hostility between the police and particularly the black community (who accounted for only 29% of the population of Brixton at the time) led to the riots in 1981, 1985 and 1995. These centred on Railton Rd and Coldharbour Lane.

Since then the mood has been decidedly more upbeat. Soaring property prices have sent house-hunters foraging in these parts, and pockets of gentrification sit alongside the more run-down streets (see opposite).

BATTERSEA & WANDSWORTH

Against the looming shell of the Battersea Power Station, this area southwest along the Thames was a site of industry until the 1970s. Now its abandoned factories and warehouses have been replaced by luxury flats. Even residents from well-heeled Chelsea are defecting across the Thames to what estate agents like to call 'Chelsea South'.

Wandsworth, the poorer working-class sibling of more affluent Battersea immediately downriver, has similarly gentrified in recent years. You'll hear the area repeatedly referred to as 'nappy valley'. Apparently Wandsworth has the highest birth rate of any borough in London.

BATTERSEA POWER STATION Map p190
www.batterseapowerstation.com;
🚇 Battersea Park
Familiar to an entire generation from Pink Floyd's 1977 *Animals* album cover, with the four smokestacks that somewhat resemble a table turned upside down, Battersea Power Station is a building both loved and reviled. It was built by Giles Gilbert Scott in 1933, with two chimneys (the other two were added in 1955). The power station ceased operations in 1983 and since then there have been innumerable proposals to give the building new life. In November 2006 it was sold to yet another group of developers; the previous ones, Parkview International, had owned it for more than a dozen years from 1993 and had wanted to demolish the chimneys and turn the 'nave' of the structure into a 24-hour entertain-

ment complex with restaurants, hotels, retail shops, cinemas etc. The power station's future seems as uncertain as ever as a new 'master plan' is redrawn, though one sensible proposal suggests that it house the government's new Energy Technologies Institute, established to research new technologies into combating climate change.

BATTERSEA PARK Map p190
☎ 8871 7530; www.batterseapark.org;
🕐 dawn-dusk; 🚇 Battersea Park
These 50 hectares of greenery stretch between Albert and Chelsea Bridges. With its Henry Moore sculptures and Peace Pagoda, erected in 1985 by a group of Japanese Buddhists to commemorate Hiroshima Day, the park's tranquil appearance belies a bloody past. It was the site of an assassination attempt on King Charles II in 1671 and of a duel in 1829 between the Duke of Wellington and an opponent who accused him of treason.

A recent refurbishment has seen the 19th-century landscaping reinstated and the grand riverside terraces spruced up. At the same time, the Festival of Britain pleasure gardens, including the spectacular Vista Fountains, have been restored. There are lakes, plenty of sporting facilities, an art space called the Pump House Gallery (☎ 8871 7572; www.wandsworth.gov.uk/gallery; Battersea Park SW11; admission free; 🕐 11am-5pm Wed-Sun) and a small Children's Zoo (☎ 7924 5826; www.battersea parkzoo.co.uk; adult/2-15yr/family £6.50/4.95/20.50; 🕐 10am-5pm Apr-Oct, to 4pm Nov-Mar).

WANDSWORTH COMMON Map p196
🚇 Wandsworth Common or Clapham Junction
Wilder and more overgrown than the nearby common in Clapham, Wandsworth Common is full of couples pushing prams on a sunny day. On the western side is a pleasant collection of streets known as the toast rack, because of their alignment. Baskerville, Dorlcote, Henderson, Nicosia, Patten and Routh Rds are lined with Georgian houses. There's a blue plaque at 3 Routh Rd, home to the former British prime minister David Lloyd George.

CLAPHAM

The so-called 'man on the Clapham omnibus' – English civil law's definition of the hypothetical reasonable person since the turn of the

20th century – has largely left this neighbourhood. Today Clapham is the home of well-heeled young professionals in their 20s and 30s, who eat in the area's many restaurants, drink in its many bars and generally drive up property prices. It was the railways that originally conferred on Clapham its status as a home for everyday commuters from the late 19th century. Clapham Junction is still the largest rail interchange in Britain, and in 1988 was the tragic site of one of Britain's worst train disasters.

The area was first settled after the Great Fire of London in 1666, when noted diarist Samuel Pepys and later explorer Captain James Cook, among others, escaped the desecration of the City to build homes here. Its name dates back much further still; it's from Anglo-Saxon for 'Clappa's farm'.

CLAPHAM COMMON Map p190
⊖ Clapham Common

This large expanse of green is the heart of the Clapham neighbourhood. Mentioned both by Graham Greene in his novel *The End of the Affair* and Ian McEwan in his brilliant *Atonement,* it's now a venue for many outdoor summer events (see http://claphamhighstreet.co.uk). The main thoroughfare, Clapham High St, starts at the common's northeastern edge and is lined with many of the bars, restaurants and shops for which people principally come to Clapham. However, for a simple stroll it's much more pleasant to explore the more upmarket streets of Clapham Old Town, a short distance northwest of the tube station, and Clapham Common North Side at the common's northwesternmost edge.

On the corner of Clapham Park Rd and Clapham Common South Side you'll find the Holy Trinity Church (1776). This was home to the Clapham Sect, a group of wealthy evangelical Christians that included William Wilberforce, a leading antislavery campaigner, active between 1790 and 1830. The sect also campaigned against child labour and for prison reform.

KENNINGTON, OVAL & STOCKWELL

Only cricket-lovers and those who set up home here will really venture into this neck of the woods. It centres on Kennington Park, which isn't that much to look at but has an interesting history. Off Kennington Lane, just west of its intersection with Kennington Rd, lies a lovely enclave of leafy streets – Cardigan St, Courtney St and Courtney Sq – with neo-Georgian houses. They're not really worth travelling to see, but make a nice diversion should rain interrupt play at the Oval just south.

KENNINGTON PARK Map p189
⊖ Oval

This unprepossessing space of green has a great rabble-rousing tradition. Originally a common, where all were permitted entry, it acted as a speakers' corner for South London. During the 18th century, Jacobite rebels trying to restore the Stuart monarchy were hanged, drawn and quartered here, and in the 18th and 19th centuries preachers used to deliver hellfire-and-brimstone speeches to large audiences; John Wesley, founder of Methodism and an antislavery advocate, is said to have attracted some 30,000 followers. After the great Chartist rally on 10 April 1848, where millions of working-class people turned out to demand the same voting rights as the middle classes, the royal family promptly fenced off the common as a park.

BRIT OVAL Map p189
☎ 0871 246 1100; www.surreycricket.com; Surrey County Cricket Club SE11; international match £15-103, county £12-20; ⏱ booking office 9.30am-12.30pm & 1.30-4pm Mon-Fri Apr-Sep; ⊖ Oval

Home to the Surrey County Cricket Club, the Brit Oval is London's second cricketing venue after Lord's (p321). As well as Surrey matches, it also regularly hosts international test matches. The season runs from April to September.

BRIXTON WALK
Walking Tour

1 Brixton Market At London's most exotic market (p259), you can drink in the heady mix of incense and the smells of the exotic fruits, vegetables, meat and fish on sale. It's also a good place to splash out on African fabrics and trinkets.

2 Ritzy London's second-oldest movie house – after the Electric Cinema in Camden (p309) – the Ritzy (p310) opened as the Electric Pavilion in 1911. Next door is the Brixton Library (☎ 7926 1056; Brixton Oval SW2), built in 1892 by

BRIXTON WALK

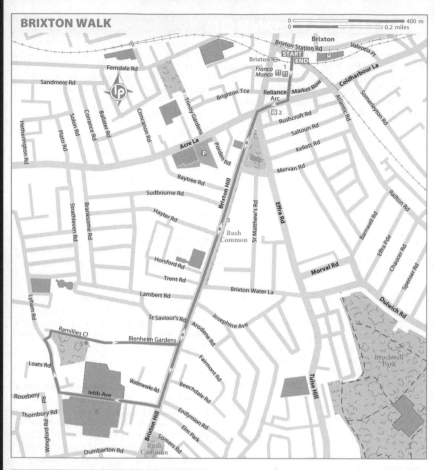

WALK FACTS

Start Brixton tube station
End Brixton tube station
Distance 2.75 miles
Duration 2½ hours
Fuel stop Franco Manca (p267)

industrialist/philanthropist Sir Henry Tate, the man who gave London the Tate Gallery and the world the sugar cube.

3 Rush Common An Act of Parliament in 1806 declared a wide strip along the eastern side of Brixton Hill to be 'proscribed land' on which nothing could be built. Over the years, however, tracts of it were illegally walled off to create private front gardens. It is now

being restored as common land (Brixton Hill SW2) but remains patchy in areas.

4 Brixton Prison Serving a number of courts in South London, Brixton Prison (☎ 8588 6000; Jebb Ave SW2) started life as the Brixton House of Correction in 1819 and has done time as everything from a jail for women to a military prison. It now houses a mixture of remand and sentenced prisoners.

5 Brixton Windmill Built for one John Ashby in 1816, this is the closest windmill (Blenheim Gardens SW2) to central London still in existence. It was later powered by gas and milled as recently as 1934. It's been refitted with sails and machinery for a wind-driven mill but is not open to the public at present.

Drinking p291; Eating p270; Shopping p231; Sleeping p353

Although Southwest London is a little far out if you're only in London for a long weekend, it's the perfect place to base yourself for a longer stay. Anyone wanting to get out of the city for the day without too much trouble or expense should take a trip here; and for people who aren't big-city fans but need to be in London it's a great place to stay.

During the day much of Southwest London is a quiet residential area; you'll see lots of young mothers out pushing prams and doing their shopping. This is the best time to enjoy the area's green spaces: walk along the Thames Path (p198) from Putney Bridge to Barnes, sup on a pint by Parson's Green or picnic on Barnes Common.

It's at night that the area comes alive. Fulham is very popular for its plethora of good pubs, bars and restaurants. Putney and Barnes like to think that they're a little more refined, though a trip to any of the pubs on the High Street on a Saturday night will put paid to that notion.

Further afield the well-to-do have been retreating from the city to the palaces and villas of London's riverside boroughs for more than 500 years, and the area's appeal to those wishing to escape the more frenetic pace of life in zones 1 and 2 is still very much apparent. Chiswick, Richmond and Kew in particular offer an

top picks

SOUTHWEST LONDON

- Buddhapadipa Temple (p203)
- Hampton Court Palace (p201)
- Kew Gardens (p199)
- The Thames (p198)
- London Wetland Centre (p196)

expensive slice of village life far removed from the crowds of central London. Twickenham is the home of English rugby while Hampton boasts what is arguable the most ambitious palace in the country. Wimbledon and its enormous common is another place for an afternoon idyll.

FULHAM

Fulham and Parson's Green merge neatly into one neighbourhood that sits comfortably in a curve of the Thames between Chelsea and Hammersmith. While the attractive Victorian terraces and riverside location have drawn a very well-to-do crowd, Fulham's blue-collar roots are still evident in the strong tradition of support for Fulham Football Club.

FULHAM PALACE Map p196

☎ 7736 8140; www.fulhampalace.org; Bishop's Ave SW6; admission free; ☼ palace & museum noon-4pm Mon & Tue, 11am-2pm Sat, 11.30am-3.30pm Sun, garden dawn-dusk daily; ⊖ Putney Bridge; ⑤ Summer home of the bishops of London from 704 to 1973, Fulham Palace is an interesting mix of architectural styles set in beautiful gardens and, until 1924, when filled with rubble, enclosed by the longest moat in England. The oldest part to survive is the little red-brick Tudor gateway, but the main building you see today is from the mid-17th century and was remodelled in the 19th century. There's a pretty walled garden and, detached from the main house, a Tudor Revival chapel designed by Butterfield in 1866.

You can learn about the history of the palace and its inhabitants in the museum. Guided tours (☎ 7736 3233; tickets £5; ☼ tours 2pm 2nd & 4th Sun, 3rd Tue of month), which depart a couple of times a month on Sunday, usually take in the Great Hall, the Victorian chapel, Bishop Sherlock's Room and the museum and last about 1¼ hours. The palace has been undergoing refurbishments in recent years so there may be changes in the tour.

The surrounding land, once totalling almost 15 hectares but now reduced to just over five, forms Bishop's Park, and consists of a shady promenade along the river, a bowling green, tennis courts, a rose garden, a cafe and even a paddling pond with fountain.

PUTNEY & BARNES

Putney is best known as the starting point of the annual Oxford and Cambridge Boat Race (p17), held each spring. There are references to the race in the pubs and restaurants in the area and along the Thames Path. Barnes is less well known and more villagey in feel. Its former residents include author Henry Fielding.

The best way to approach Putney is to follow the signs from Putney Bridge tube station for the footbridge (which runs parallel to the rail track), admiring the gorgeous riverside houses, with their gardens fronting the Thames, and thereby avoiding the tatty High Street until the last minute. Alternatively, catch the train from Vauxhall or Waterloo to Putney or Barnes stations.

LONDON WETLAND CENTRE Map p196

☎ 8409 4400; www.wwt.org.uk; Queen Elizabeth's Walk SW13; adult/under 4yr/4-16yr/senior & student/family £9.50/free/5.25/7.10/26.55; ⏰ 9.30am-6pm Mar-Oct, 9.30am-5pm Nov-Feb, to 8pm Thu Jun-late Sep; ⊖ Hammersmith then 🚌 283 (Duck Bus), 33, 72 or 209, or 🚆 Barnes; ♿

One of Europe's largest inland wetland projects, this 43-hectare centre run by the Wildfowl & Wetlands Trust was transformed from four Victorian reservoirs in 2000 and attracts some 140 species of bird as well as 300 types of moth and butterfly. From the Visitor Centre and glassed-in Observatory overlooking the ponds, meandering paths and boardwalks lead visitors around the grounds, taking in the habitats of its many residents, including ducks, swans, geese and coots and the rarer bitterns, herons and kingfishers. There's even a large colony of parakeets, which may or may not be the descendants of caged pets. By no means

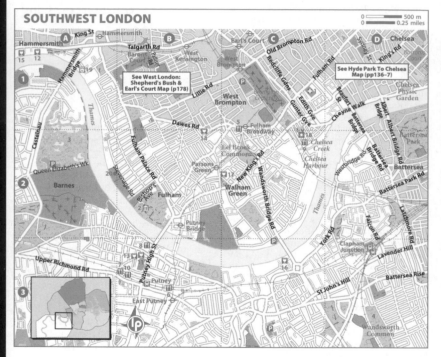

SOUTHWEST LONDON

miss the Peacock Tower, a three-storey hide on the main lake's eastern edge. Though there are half-a-dozen hides sprinkled elsewhere around the reserve, the tower is the mecca for more serious birders. Free daily tours, which are led by knowledgeable and enthusiastic staff members and are highly recommended, depart at 11am and 2pm daily.

CHISWICK

Notwithstanding the abomination of the A4 motorway, which cuts off the riverside roads from the centre, Chiswick (*chiz*-ick) is still a pleasant southwest London suburb that does not deserve the flak it gets for its well-heeled residents and unfeasibly grand mansions.

Chiswick High Rd itself is an upmarket yet uninspiring main drag, full of pubs and twee shops with the odd decent restaurant. There's little to waylay you, so best head straight over to the park and Chiswick House, up to Hogarth Lane and Hogarth House or down Church St to Chiswick Mall and the riverfront.

CHISWICK HOUSE Map p62
☎ 8995 0508; www.chgt.org.uk; Chiswick Park, Burlington Lane W4; adult/child/senior & student £4.40/2.20/3.70; ☐ 10am-5pm Wed-Fri & Sun, to 2pm Sat Apr-Oct; ☒ Chiswick or ↦ Turnham Green; ☐
This is a fine Palladian pavilion with an octagonal dome and colonnaded portico. It was designed by the third Earl of Burlington (1694–1753) when he returned from his grand tour of Italy, fired up with enthusiasm for all things Roman. Lord Burlington used it to entertain friends and to house his library and art collection.

Inside, some of the rooms are so grand as to be almost overpowering. The dome of the main salon has been left ungilded and the walls are decorated with eight enormous paintings. In the Blue Velvet Room look for the portrait of Inigo Jones, the architect much admired by Lord Burlington, over one of the doors. The ceiling paintings are by William Kent, who also decorated the Kensington Palace State Apartments.

Lord Burlington also planned the house's original gardens, now Chiswick Park surrounding the house, but they have been much altered since his time. The gardens started being restored in March 2008, followed by the restoration of the conservatory and café in 2009. The work aims to be

completed by spring 2010. The restored Cascade waterfall is bubbling again after being out of action for years.

The house is about a mile southwest of the Turnham Green tube station and 750m northeast of the Chiswick train station.

HOGARTH'S HOUSE Map p62
☎ 8994 6757; www.hounslow.info/arts/hogarthshouse; Hogarth Lane W4; admission free; ☐ 1-5pm Tue-Fri, 1-6pm Sat & Sun Apr-Oct, 1-4pm Tue-Fri, 1-5pm Sat & Sun Nov, Dec, Feb & Mar; ↦ Turnham Green
Home between 1749 and 1764 to artist and social commentator William Hogarth, this house now diplays his caricatures and engravings, with such works as the haunting *Gin Lane, Marriage-à-la-mode* and a copy of *A Rake's Progress* (see the boxed text, p44). Here you'll also find the private engravings *Before* and *After* (1730), commissioned by the Duke of Montagu and bearing Aristotle's aphorism *Omne Animal Post Coitum Triste* (Every creature is sad after intercourse). Although the house and grounds are attractive, very little original furniture remains so this is really for ardent Hogarth fans. It was closed for refurbishment until September 2009, and they promise 'new displays and a lively program of activities', so watch this space.

FULLER'S GRIFFIN BREWERY Map p62
☎ 8996 2063; www.fullers.co.uk; Chiswick Lane South W4; adult/concession (incl tasting) £10/8; ☐ tours 11am, noon, 1pm & 2pm Mon & Wed-Fri; ↦ Turnham Green or ☒ Chiswick
Of interest to anyone who enjoys bitter and/or wants to see it being made and/or would like to engage in a comprehensive tasting session (over-18s only), Fuller's is now the last working brewery in London. You can visit only on the 1½-hour guided tour, which must be booked in advance by phone.

RICHMOND

If anywhere in London could be described as a village, Richmond – with its delightful green and riverside vistas – is it. Centuries of history, some stunning Georgian architecture and the graceful curve of the Thames has made this one of London's swankiest locales, home to ageing rock stars and city high-flyers alike.

Richmond was originally named Sheen, but Henry VII, having fallen in love with the place, renamed the village after his Yorkshire

197

THAMES PATH

The Thames Path National Trail is a long-distance walk stretching from the river's source at Thames Head near Kemble in the Cotswolds to the Thames Flood Barrier, a distance of some 184 miles. It's truly magnificent, particularly in its upper reaches, but tackling the entire course is for the truly ambitious (and indefatigable). The rest of us walk sections of it, such as the 16-mile section from Battersea to the barrier, which takes about 6½ hours. A much more manageable section for afternoon strollers, taking about 1½ hours, is the 4 miles between Putney Bridge and Barnes Footbridge. The initial stretch along the Embankment that runs north from Putney Bridge on the southern bank of the river is always a hive of activity, with rowers setting off and returning to their boat clubs and punters from nearby pubs lazing by the water. The majority of the walk, though, is intensely rural – at times the only accompaniment is the call of songbirds and the gentle swish of old Father Thames (yes, we are still in London). From the footbridge Chiswick train station is about 0.75 miles to the northwest.

Full details of these and other sections of the Thames Path can be found in Lonely Planet's *Walking in Britain* (3rd edition) or visit the National Trails (www.nationaltrail.co.uk/thamespath) website. Another useful source is the River Thames Alliance's Visit Thames (www.visitthames.co.uk) site. Also see River Thames (p109) for more on London's riparian attractions.

earldom. This started centuries of royal association with the area; the most famous local, Henry VIII, acquired nearby Hampton Court Palace (p201) from Cardinal Wolsey after the latter's fall from grace in 1529, while his daughter Elizabeth I died here in 1603.

RICHMOND GREEN Map p200
⊖ / ⊛ Richmond
A short walk west of the Quadrant where you'll emerge from the tube is the enormous open space of Richmond Green with its mansions and delightful pubs. Crossing the green diagonally will take you to what remains of Richmond Palace, just the main entrance and red-brick gatehouse, built in 1501. You can see Henry VII's arms above the main gate: he built the Tudor additions to the edifice, although the palace had been in use as a royal residence since 1125.

RICHMOND PARK Map p200
☎ 8948 3209; www.royalparks.gov.uk; admission free; ☼ 7am-dusk Mar-Sep, from 7.30am Oct-Feb; ⊖ / ⊛ Richmond, then ⊟ 65 or 371
At just over 1000 hectares (the largest urban parkland in Europe), this Park offers everything from formal gardens and ancient oaks to unsurpassed views of central London 12 miles away. It's easy to escape the several roads that cut up the rambling wilderness, making the park an excellent spot for a quiet walk or picnic, even in summer when Richmond's riverside can be heaving. Such is its magic, it somehow comes as no surprise to happen upon herds of more than 600 red and fallow deer basking under the trees. Be advised that the creatures can be less than docile in rutting season (May to July) and when the does bear young (September and

October). It's a great place for birdwatchers too, with a wide range of habitats, from neat gardens to woodland and assorted ponds.

Coming from Richmond, it's easiest to enter via Richmond Gate or from Petersham Rd. Take a map with you and wander around the grounds; flower-lovers should make a special trip to Isabella Plantation, a stunning woodland garden created after WWII, in April and May when the rhododendrons and azaleas are in bloom.

Pembroke Lodge (☼ 10am-5.30pm summer, to 4.30pm winter), the childhood home of Bertrand Russell, is now a cafe set in a beautiful 13-hectare garden and affording great views of the city from the back terrace.

ST PETER'S CHURCH Map p200
☎ 8940 8435; Church Lane, Petersham TW10; admission free; ☼ 3-5pm Sun; ⊖ / ⊛ Richmond, then ⊟ 65
This Norman church has been a place of worship for 1300 years and parts of the present structure date from 1266. It's a fascinating place, not least for its curious Georgian box pews, which local landowners would rent while the serving staff and labourers sat in the open seats in the south transept. Against the north wall of the chancel is the Cole Monument, depicting barrister George Cole, his wife and child, all reclining in Elizabethan dress – an unusual design for an English church. Of interest to Canadians, St Peter's is the burial place of Captain George Vancouver, who was laid to rest here in 1798; his simple tomb is on the southern wall of the cemetery.

THE THAMES Map p200
The stretch of the river from Twickenham Bridge to Petersham and Ham is one of the

prettiest in London. The action is mostly around Richmond Bridge, built in 1777 and London's oldest surviving crossing, only widened for traffic in 1937. The lovely walk to Petersham can be crowded in nice weather; best to cut across Petersham Meadows and continue to Richmond Park for peace and quiet. There are several companies near Richmond Bridge, including Richmond Boat Hire (☎ 8948 8270), that offer skiff hire (adult/child £5/2.50 per hour, £15/7.50 per day).

HAM HOUSE Map p62

☎ 8940 1950; www.nationaltrust.org.uk; Ham St, Ham TW10; adult/5-15yr/family £9.90/5.50/25.30, gardens only £3.30/2.20/8.80; ♡ house 1-5pm Mon-Wed, Sat & Sun late Mar-Oct, gardens 11am-6pm Mon-Wed, Sat & Sun; ⊖ / ⓡ Richmond, then ⬜ 371; ⓖ
Known as 'Hampton Court in miniature', Ham House was built in 1610 and became home to the first Earl of Dysart, an unlucky individual who had been employed as 'whipping boy' to Charles I, taking the punishment for all the king's wrongdoings. Inside it's furnished with grandeur; the Great Staircase is a magnificent example of Stuart woodworking. Look out for ceiling paintings by Antonio Verrio, who also worked at Hampton Court Palace, and for a miniature of Elizabeth I by Nicholas Hilliard. Other notable paintings are by Constable and Reynolds. The grounds of Ham House slope down to the Thames, but there are also pleasant 17th-century formal gardens. Just opposite the Thames and accessible by small ferry is Marble Hill Park and its splendid mansion (p201). There is partial disabled access. Call for more information.

KEW & BRENTFORD

Kew will be forever associated with its World Heritage–listed Botanic Gardens, headquarters of the Royal Botanical Society and boasting one of the world's finest plant collections. A day at Kew Gardens will appeal even to those with no knowledge of plants and flowers. This smart Southwest London suburb is also pleasant for an idle wander; watch out for cricket matches played on central Kew Green in summer.

Across a mighty bend in the Thames is Brentford, essentially nondescript except for sprawling Syon Park and its magnificent house.

KEW GARDENS Map p62

☎ 8332 5655; www.kew.org; Kew Rd TW9; adult/under 17yr/senior & student £13/free/11; ♡ gardens 9.30am-6.30pm Mon-Fri, to 7.30pm Sat & Sun Apr-Aug, 9.30am-6pm Sep & Oct, 9.30am-4.15pm Nov-Feb, glasshouses 9.30am-5.30pm April-Oct, 9.30am-3.45pm Nov-Feb; ⊖ / ⓡ Kew Gardens; ⓖ
Royal Botanic Gardens at Kew is one of the most popular attractions in London, which means it can get very crowded during summer, especially at weekends. Spring is probably the best time to visit, but at any time of year this 120-hectare expanse of lawns, formal gardens and greenhouses has delights to offer. As well as being a public garden, Kew is an important research centre, and it maintains its reputation as the most exhaustive botanical collection in the world.

Its wonderful plants and trees aside, Kew has several specific sights within its borders. Assuming you come by tube and enter via Victoria Gate, you'll come almost immediately to a large pond overlooked by the enormous Palm House, a hothouse of metal and curved sheets of glass dating from 1848 and housing all sorts of exotic tropical greenery; the aerial walkway offers a birds'-eye view of the lush vegetation. Just northwest of the Palm House is the tiny but irresistible Water Lily House (♡ Mar-Dec), dating from 1852 and the hottest glasshouse at Kew.

Further north is the stunning Princess of Wales Conservatory, opened in 1987 and housing plants in 10 different climatic zones – everything from a desert to a mangrove swamp. In the tropical zone you'll find the most famous of Kew's 38,000-odd plant species, the 3m-tall *titan arum,* or 'corpse flower', which is overpoweringly obnoxious-smelling when it blooms in April. Just beyond the conservatory is Kew Gardens Gallery bordering Kew Green, which houses exhibitions of paintings and photos mostly of a horticultural theme.

Heading westwards from the gallery you'll arrive at the red-brick Kew Palace (adult/under 17yr/senior & student £5/free/4.50; ♡ 10am-5.30pm late Mar-late Oct), a former royal residence once known as Dutch House and built in 1631. It was the favourite home of George III and his family; his wife, Queen Charlotte, died here in 1818. The palace underwent extensive renovations for almost a decade and reopened in 2006; don't miss the Georgian rooms, restored to how they would have looked in 1804, and Princess Elizabeth's wonderful doll's house.

Other highlights include the Temperate House, the world's largest ornamental glasshouse, and nearby Evolution House, tracing plant evolution over 3500 million years; the

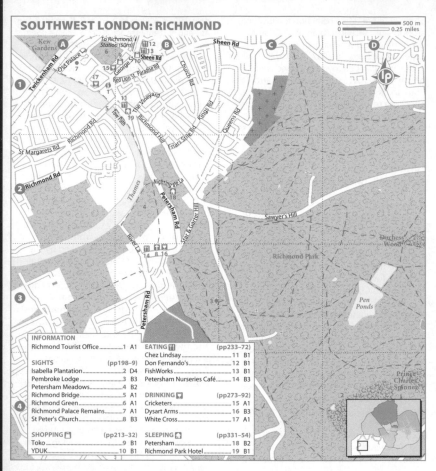

SOUTHWEST LONDON: RICHMOND

0 — 500 m
0 — 0.25 miles

INFORMATION		
Richmond Tourist Office	1	A1
SIGHTS	**(pp198–9)**	
Isabella Plantation	2	D4
Pembroke Lodge	3	B3
Petersham Meadows	4	B2
Richmond Bridge	5	A1
Richmond Green	6	A1
Richmond Palace Remains	7	A1
St Peter's Church	8	B3
SHOPPING	**(pp213–32)**	
Toko	9	B1
YDUK	10	B1

EATING	**(pp233–72)**	
Chez Lindsay	11	B1
Don Fernando's	12	B1
FishWorks	13	B1
Petersham Nurseries Café	14	B3
DRINKING	**(pp273–92)**	
Cricketers	15	A1
Dysart Arms	16	B3
White Cross	17	A1
SLEEPING	**(pp331–54)**	
Petersham	18	B2
Richmond Park Hotel	19	B1

idyllic Queen Charlotte's Cottage (🕙 10am-4pm Sat & Sun Jul & Aug) was popular with 'mad' George III and his wife. Don't forget to see the Japanese Gateway and the celebrated 10-storey Pagoda (1761), designed by William Chambers.

Just north is the Marianne North Gallery featuring paintings on a botanical theme. Marianne North was one of those indomitable Victorian female travellers who roamed the continents from 1871 to 1885, painting plants and trees along the way. The results of her labour now cover the walls of this small purpose-built gallery. The Orangery near Kew Palace contains a restaurant, cafe and shop.

If you want a good overview of the gardens, jump aboard the Kew Explorer minitrain (adult/under 17yr £3.50/1), which allows you to hop on and off at stops along the way. The full circuit takes about 40 minutes.

You can get to Kew Gardens by tube or train. Come out of the station and walk straight (west) along Station Ave, cross Kew Gardens Rd and then continue straight along Lichfield Rd. This will bring you to Victoria Gate. Alternatively, from April to October, boats run by the Westminster Passenger Services Association (☎ 7930 2062; www .wpsa.co.uk) sail from Westminster Pier to Kew Gardens up to four times a day (see p380).

There is now a Rhizotron and Xstrata Treetop Walkway which takes you underground and then 18 metres up in the air, for an alternative and new view of tree anatomy.

SYON HOUSE Map p62

☎ 8560 0881; www.syonpark.co.uk; Syon Park, Brentford TW7; adult/5-16yr/student & senior/family £8/4/7/18, gardens only adult/child/concession/family

£4/free/2.50/9; 11am-5pm Wed, Thu & Sun late Mar-Oct, gardens 10.30am-4pm or 5pm; Gunnersbury or Gunnersbury, then 237 or 267
Just across the Thames from Kew Gardens, Syon House was once a medieval abbey named after Mt Zion. In 1542 Henry VIII dissolved the order of Bridgettine nuns who were peacefully living here and had it rebuilt into a residence. (In 1547, they say, God got his revenge when Henry's coffin was brought to Syon en route to Windsor for burial and burst open during the night, leaving his body to be set upon by the estate's dogs.)

The house from where Lady Jane Grey ascended the throne for her nine-day reign in 1553 was remodelled in the neoclassical style by Robert Adam in the 18th century and has plenty of Adam furniture and oak panelling. The interior was designed on gender-specific lines, with pastel pinks and purples for the ladies' gallery, and mock Roman sculptures for the men's dining room. The estate's 16-hectare gardens, with a lake and the Great Conservatory (1820), were landscaped by Capability Brown. Syon Park is filled with attractions for children, including an adventure playground, aquatic park and trout fishery.

TWICKENHAM

As Wimbledon is to tennis, so Twickenham is to rugby, and you'll find one of the few museums in the world devoted to the sport here. Otherwise there's not much to detain you in this quiet and pretty Middlesex suburb aside from the delights of fine Marble Hill House overlooking the Thames.

MARBLE HILL HOUSE Map p62
8892 5115; www.english-heritage.org.uk; Richmond Rd TW1; adult/under 15yr/senior & student £4.20/2.10/3.20; 10am-2pm Sat, to 5pm Sun, guided tours noon & 3pm Tue & Wed Apr-Oct; St Margaret's, Richmond;
This is an 18th-century Palladian love nest, originally built for George II's mistress Henrietta Howard and later occupied by Mrs Fitzherbert, the secret wife of George IV. The poet Alexander Pope had a hand in designing the park, which stretches down to the Thames. Inside you'll find an exhibition about the life and times of Henrietta, and a collection of early-Georgian furniture.

To get there from St Margaret's station, turn right along St Margaret's Rd. Then take the right fork along Crown Rd and turn left along Richmond Rd. Turn right along Beaufort Rd and walk across Marble Hill Park to the house. It is also easily accessible by pedestrian ferry from Ham House (p199). It's a 25-minute walk from Richmond station.

There is partial disabled access. Call for more information.

HAMPTON

Out in London's southwestern outskirts, the wonderful Hampton Court Palace is pressed up against 445-hectare Bushy Park (www.royalparks .gov.uk), a semiwild expanse with herds of red and fallow deer.

HAMPTON COURT PALACE Off Map p62
0870 751 5175; www.hrp.org.uk/Hampton CourtPalace; Hampton Court Rd, East Molesey KT8; all-inclusive ticket adult/5-15yr/senior & student/family £13.30/6.65/11.30/37; 10am-6pm late March-Oct, to 4.30pm Nov-late Mar; Hampton Court;
London's most spectacular Tudor palace is the 16th-century Hampton Court Palace in the city's suburbs, easily reached by train from Waterloo Station. Here history is palpable, from the kitchens where you see food being prepared and the grand living quarters of Henry VIII to the spectacular gardens complete with a 300-year-old maze. This is one of the best days out London has to offer and should not be missed by anyone with any interest in British history. Set aside plenty of time to do it justice, bearing in mind that if you come by boat from central London the trip will have already eaten up half the day.

Like so many royal residences, Hampton Court Palace was not built for the monarchy at all. In 1515 Cardinal Thomas Wolsey, Lord Chancellor of England, built himself a palace in keeping with his sense of self-importance. Unfortunately, even Wolsey couldn't persuade the pope to grant Henry VIII a divorce from Catherine of Aragon and relations between king and chancellor soured. Against that background, you only need to take one look at the palace to understand why Wolsey felt obliged to present it to Henry, a monarch not too fond of anyone trying to muscle in on his mastery. The hapless Wolsey was charged with high treason but died before he could come to trial, in 1530.

As soon as he acquired the palace, Henry set to work expanding it, adding the Great Hall, the exquisite Chapel Royal and the sprawling kitchens. By 1540 this was one of the grandest and most sophisticated palaces in Europe, but Henry only spent an average three weeks a year here. In the late 17th century, William and Mary employed Sir Christopher Wren to build extensions. The result is a beautiful blend of Tudor and 'restrained baroque' architecture.

Tickets are on sale in the shop to the left as you walk up the path towards the main Trophy Gate. Be sure to pick up a leaflet listing the daily program, which will help you plan your visit. This is important as some of the free guided tours require advance booking.

Passing through the main gate you arrive first in the Base Court and then the Clock Court, named after the 16th-century astronomical clock that still shows the sun revolving round the earth. The second court is your starting point; from here you can follow any or all of the six sets of rooms in the complex. Here behind the colonnade you'll also find the useful Introductory Exhibition, explaining what's where and how the compound functions.

The stairs inside Anne Boleyn's Gateway lead up to Henry VIII's State Apartments, including the Great Hall, the largest single room in the palace, decorated with tapestries and what is considered the country's best hammer-beam roof. The Horn Room, hung with impressive antlers, leads to the Great Watching Chamber where guards controlled access to the king. Leading off from the chamber is the smaller Pages' Chamber and the Haunted Gallery. Arrested for adultery and detained in the palace in 1542, Henry's fifth wife, Catherine Howard, managed to evade her guards and ran screaming down the corridor in search of the king. Her woeful ghost is said to do the same thing to this day.

Further along the corridor is the beautiful Chapel Royal, built in just nine months and still a place of worship after 450 years. The blue-and-gold vaulted ceiling was originally intended for Christ Church, Oxford, but was installed here instead; the 18th-century reredos was carved by Grinling Gibbons.

Also dating from Henry's day are the delightful Tudor kitchens, again accessible from Anne Boleyn's Gateway and originally able to rustle up meals for a royal household of some 1200 people. The kitchens have been fitted out to look as they might have done in Tudor days and palace 'servants' turn the spits, stuff the peacocks and frost the marzipan with real gold leaf. Don't miss the Great Wine Cellar, which handled the 300 barrels each of ale and wine consumed here annually in the mid-16th century.

West of the colonnade in the Clock Court is the entrance to the Wolsey Rooms and the Young Henry VIII Exhibition. East of the colonnade you'll find the stairs to the King's Apartments, completed by Wren for William III in 1702. A tour of the apartments takes you up the grand King's Staircase, painted by Antonio Verrio in about 1700 and flattering the king by comparing him to Alexander the Great. Highlights include the King's Presence Chamber, dominated by a throne backed with scarlet hangings. The King's Great Bedchamber, with a bed topped with ostrich plumes, and the King's Closet (where His Majesty's toilet has a velvet seat) should not be missed.

William's wife, Mary II, had her own Queen's State Apartments, accessible up the Queen's Staircase, decorated by William Kent. When Mary died in 1694, work on these was incomplete; they were finished during the reign of George II. The rooms are shown as they might have been when Queen Caroline used them for entertaining between 1716 and 1737. Compared with the King's Apartments, those for the queen seem austere, although the Queen's Audience Chamber has a throne as imposing as that of the king.

Also worth seeing are the Georgian Rooms used by George II and Queen Caroline on the court's last visit to the palace in 1737. The first rooms were designed to accommodate George's second son, the Duke of Cumberland, whose bed is woefully tiny for its grand surroundings. In the Cartoon Gallery, the real Raphael Cartoons (now in the Victoria & Albert Museum; p139) used to hang; nowadays it's just the late-17th-century copies.

Beyond the Cartoon Gallery are the Queen's Private Apartments: her drawing room and bedchamber, where she and the king would sleep if they wanted to be alone. Particularly interesting are the Queen's Bathroom, with its tub set on a floor cloth to soak up any spillage, and the Oratory, an attractive room with its exquisite 16th-century Persian carpet.

Once you're finished with the palace interior there are still the gardens to appreciate. Carriage rides for up to five people around the gardens cost £10 and last 20 minutes. Look out for the Real Tennis Court, dating from the 1620s and designed for real tennis, a rather different version of the game from that played today. In the restored 24-hectare Riverside Gardens, you'll find the Great Vine. Planted in 1768, it's still producing just under 320kg of grapes per year; it's an old vine, no doubt about it, but not the world's oldest, as they say it is here (that one is in Slovenia). The Lower Orangery in the gardens houses Andrea Mantegna's nine *Triumphs of Caesar* paintings, bought by Charles I in 1629; the Banqueting House was designed for William III and painted by Antonio Verrio. Look out for the iron screens designed by Jean Tijou.

No-one should leave Hampton Court without losing themselves in the famous 800m-long maze, made of hornbeam and yew and planted in 1690. The average visitor takes 20 minutes to reach the centre. The maze is included in entry, although those not visiting the palace can enter for £3.50 (£2.50/10 for children/families). Last admission is 5.15pm in summer and 3.45pm in winter.

There are trains every half-hour from Waterloo direct to Hampton Court station (30 minutes); it's a three-minute walk to the palace entrance. The palace can also be reached from Westminster Pier in central London twice daily on riverboats operated by Westminster Passenger Services Association (p380) from April to October. This is a great trip if the weather is good, but it takes three hours.

WIMBLEDON

For a few weeks each June and July the sporting world's attention is fixed on the quiet southern suburb of Wimbledon, as it has been since 1877 (see p322). Then the circus leaves town and Wimbledon returns to unremarkable normality. That said, it's a pleasant little place, and the Wimbledon Lawn Tennis Museum will excite any tennis fan, even in darkest December.

WIMBLEDON COMMON
www.wpcc.org.uk; ⊖ / ⓡ Wimbledon, then ⓑ 93
Running on into Putney Heath, Wimbledon Common covers 460 hectares of South London and is a wonderful expanse of open space for walking, nature trailing and picnicking. There are a few specific sights on Wimbledon Common, including Wimbledon Windmill (☎ 8947 2825; www.wimbledonwindmill museum.org.uk; Windmill Rd SW19; adult/child £2/1; ⓨ 2-5pm Sat, 11am-5pm Sun late Mar-Oct; ⊖ Wimbledon), a fine smock mill (ie octagonal-shaped with sloping weatherboarded sides) dating from 1817 which now contains a museum with working models on the history of windmills and milling. It was during a stay in the mill in 1908 that Robert Baden-Powell was inspired to write parts of his *Scouting for Boys*.

On the southern side of the common, the misnamed Caesar's Camp is what's left of a roughly circular earthen fort built in the 5th century BC, which proves that Wimbledon was settled before Roman times.

WIMBLEDON LAWN TENNIS MUSEUM
☎ 8946 6131; www.wimbledon.org; Gate 3, Church Rd SW19; adult/child/concession £8.50/4.75/7.50, museum & tour £15.50/11/13.75; ⓨ 10.30am-5pm; ⊖ / ⓡ Wimbledon, then ⓑ 93
This museum is of specialist interest, dwelling as it does on the minutiae of the history of tennis playing, traced back here to the invention of the all-important lawnmower in 1830 and of the India-rubber ball in the 1850s. It's a state-of-the-art presentation, with plenty of video clips to let fans of the game relive their favourite moments. The museum is open to spectators only during the championships; it houses a tearoom and a shop selling all kinds of tennis memorabilia.

BUDDHAPADIPA TEMPLE
☎ 8946 1357; www.buddhapadipa.org; 14 Calonne Rd SW19; admission free; ⓨ temple 1-6pm Sat, 8.30-10.30am & 12.30-6pm Sun, grounds 8am-9.30pm summer, to 6pm winter; ⊖ Wimbledon, then ⓑ 93
A surprising sight in a residential neighbourhood half a mile from Wimbledon Village, this is as authentic a Thai temple as ever graced this side of Bangkok. The Buddhapadipa Temple was built by an association of young Buddhists in Britain and opened in 1982. The *wat* (temple) boasts a *bot* (consecrated chapel) decorated with traditional scenes by two leading Thai artists. Remember to take your shoes off before entering.

To get to the temple take the tube or train to Wimbledon and then bus 93 up to Wimbledon Parkside. Calonne Rd leads off it on the right.

RICHMOND WALK
Walking Tour
1 Richmond Green With its lovely houses and crowds of families playing ball games, it's easy to imagine this beautiful stretch of grass as the site of jousting contests during the Middle Ages. The path across the green (p198) takes you to the meagre remains of Richmond Palace, where Queen Elizabeth I spent her final years.

2 Richmond Bridge London's oldest river crossing still in use and dating back to 1777, this five-span masonry bridge (p198) gracefully curves over the Thames towards Twickenham. Just

lonelyplanet.com

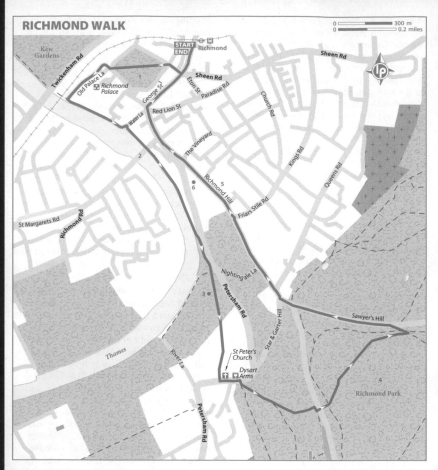

RICHMOND WALK

NEIGHBOURHOODS SOUTHWEST LONDON

WALK FACTS

Start Richmond tube station
End Richmond tube station
Distance 2.5 miles
Duration About two hours
Fuel stop Dysart Arms (p292)

before it, along one of the loveliest stretches of the Thames, is tiny Corporation Island, which has been colonised by flocks of feral parakeets.

3 Petersham Meadows These meadows fronting the Thames and at the foot of Richmond Hill are still grazed by cows. At the southern end is St Peter's Church (p198), a Saxon place of worship since the 8th century, which contains an unusually laid out Georgian interior.

4 Richmond Park Petersham Gate leads to London's most sumptuous green space. Established by Edward I in the 13th century, this royal park (p198) has changed little. There are uninterrupted views to the centre of London.

5 Richmond Hill The view from here has inspired painters and poets for centuries and still beguiles. It's the only view (which includes St Paul's Cathedral 10 miles away) in the country to be protected by an act of Parliament.

6 Royal British Legion Poppy Factory This unusual factory (☎ 8940 3305; www.britishlegion.org.uk; 20 Petersham Rd TW10; admission free; ☒ tours 10am Mon-Fri, 1.30pm Mon-Thu) creates 34 million artificial poppies and 107,000 wreaths for Remembrance Day (11 November) each year. Admission is on a guided tour only, which takes about two hours.

204

ARCHITECTURE

Ornate choir stalls and mosaic ceiling in St Paul's Cathedral (p99)

Westminster Abbey (p89), London's finest example of Early English Gothic architecture

Unlike other world-class cities, London has never been methodically planned. Rather, it has developed in an organic (read: haphazard) fashion. London retains architectural reminders from every period of its long history, but they are often hidden: part of a Roman wall enclosed in the lobby of a postmodern building near St Paul's, say, or a galleried coaching inn dating from the Restoration tucked away in a courtyard off a high street in Borough. This is a city for explorers. Bear that in mind and you'll make discoveries at virtually every turn.

LAYING THE FOUNDATIONS

London's roots lie in the walled Roman settlement of Londinium, established in AD 43 on the northern banks of the River Thames, roughly on the site of today's City. Few traces of it survive outside museums, though you can see the relocated Temple of Mithras (p106), built in AD 240, at the eastern end of Queen Victoria St in the City. Stretches of the Roman wall (Map p100; ⊖ Tower Hill) remain as foundations to a medieval wall outside Tower Hill tube station and in a few sections below Bastion Highwalk, next to the Museum of London.

The Saxons, who moved into the area after the decline of the Roman Empire, found Londinium too small and built their communities further up the Thames. Excavations carried out by archaeologists from the Museum of London during renovations at the Royal Opera House (p75) in the late 1990s uncovered extensive traces of the Saxon settlement of Lundenwic, including some wattle-and-daub housing. But the best place to see in situ what the Saxons left behind is the church of All Hallows-by-the-Tower (p121), northwest of the Tower of London, which boasts an important archway and the walls of a 7th-century Saxon church.

With the arrival of William the Conqueror in 1066, the country got its first example of Norman architecture in the shape of the White Tower (p119), the sturdy keep at the heart of the Tower of London. The church of St Bartholomew-the-Great (p104) at Smithfield also has Norman arches and columns marching down its nave. The west door and elaborately moulded porch at the Temple Church (p103) in Inner Temple are other outstanding details of Norman architecture.

The neo-Gothic towers of Tower Bridge (p121)

Plastic-clad exterior of Laban dance institute (p307)

MEDIEVAL LONDON

Westminster Abbey (p89), enlarged and refurbished between the 12th and 14th centuries, is a splendid reminder of what the master masons of the Middle Ages could produce. Perhaps the finest surviving medieval church in the City is the 13th-century Church of St Ethelburga-the-Virgin (Map p100; 78 Bishopsgate EC2; ⊖ Aldgate) near Liverpool St station, which was restored after Irish Republican Army (IRA) bombings in 1993. The 15th-century Church of St Olave (Map p100; Hart St EC3; ⊖ Tower Hill), northwest of Tower Hill, is one of the City's few remaining Gothic parish churches, while the crypt at the largely restored church of St Ethelreda (Map p150; Ely Pl EC1; ⊖ Chancery Lane), north of Holborn Circus, dates from about 1250.

Secular medieval buildings are even scarcer, although the ragstone Jewel Tower (Map pp84–5; Abingdon St SW1; ⊖ St James's Park) opposite the Houses of Parliament dates from 1365, and most of the Tower of London (p117) goes back to the Middle Ages. Staple Inn (Map pp70–1; High Holborn WC1; ⊖ Chancery Lane) in Holborn dates from 1378, but the half-timbered shopfront facade (1589) is mostly Elizabethan, heavily restored in the mid-20th century.

A TRINITY OF ARCHITECTS

The finest London architect of the first half of the 17th century was Inigo Jones (1573–1652), who spent a year and a half in Italy and became a convert to Palladian Renaissance architecture. His *chefs-d'œuvre* include Banqueting House (1622; p95) in Whitehall and Queen's House (1635; p181) in Greenwich. Often overlooked is the much plainer church of St Paul's (Map pp70–1; ⊖ Covent Garden) in Covent Garden, which Jones designed in the 1630s and described as 'the handsomest barn in England'.

The greatest architect ever to leave his mark on London was Sir Christopher Wren (1632–1723), responsible not just for his masterpiece and monument St Paul's Cathedral (1710; p99) but also for many of central London's finest churches. He oversaw the building of dozens of them, many replacing medieval churches lost in the Great Fire, as well as the Royal Hospital Chelsea (1692; p137) and the Old Royal Naval College (p180), begun in 1694 at Greenwich. His neoclassical buildings and churches are taller, lighter and generally more graceful than their medieval predecessors.

Nicholas Hawksmoor (1661–1736) was a pupil of Wren who worked with him on several churches before going on to design his own

Painted Hall detail, Old Royal Naval College (p180)

207

masterpieces. The restored Christ Church (1729; p152) in Spitalfields and the 1731 St George's Bloomsbury (Map pp80–1; Bloomsbury Way WC1; ⊖ Holborn), as well as St Anne's, Limehouse (1725; p161) and St George-in-the-East (1726; p163) at Wapping, are among his finest works, which are usually defined as English baroque.

GEORGIAN MANNERS

The Georgian period saw the return of classicism (or neo-Palladianism). Among the greatest exponents of this revived style was Robert Adam (1728–92). Much of his work was demolished by the Victorians, but an excellent example that managed to survive is Kenwood House (1773; p172) on Hampstead Heath.

Adam's fame has been eclipsed by that of John Nash (1752–1835), whose contribution to London's architecture compares to that of Wren. Nash was responsible for the layout of Regent's Park and its surrounding elegant crescents. To give London a 'spine', he created Regent Street (Map p66; ⊖ Piccadilly Circus) as a straight north–south axis from St James's Park in the south to the new Regent's Park in the north. This grand scheme also involved the formation of Trafalgar Sq, and the development of the Mall and the western end of the Strand.

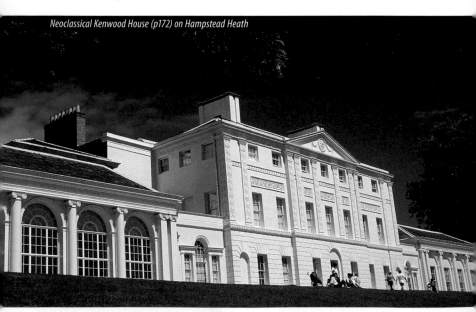

Neoclassical Kenwood House (p172) on Hampstead Heath

Central Hall of the Gothic Revival Natural History Museum (p140)

Nash's contemporary, John Soane (1753–1837), was the architect of the Bank of England (Map p100; Threadneedle St EC2; ⊖ Bank), completed in 1833 (though much of his work was lost during the bank's rebuilding by Herbert Baker, 1925–39), as well as the Dulwich Picture Gallery (1814; p185). Robert Smirke (1780–1867) designed the British Museum (p79) in 1823, one of the finest expressions anywhere of the Greek Revivalist style.

A 'GOTHICK' RETHINK

In the 19th century a reaction emerged in the form of the highly decorative neo-Gothic style, also known as Victorian High Gothic or 'Gothick'. Champions were George Gilbert Scott (1811–78), Alfred Waterhouse (1830–1905), Augustus Pugin (1812–52) and Charles Barry (1795–1860). Scott was responsible for the elaborate Albert Memorial (1872; p144) in Kensington Gardens and the 1874 St Pancras Chambers (Map p170; ⊖ Kings Cross St Pancras). Waterhouse designed the flamboyant Natural History Museum (1880; p140), while Pugin and Barry worked together from 1840 on the Houses of Parliament (p92) after the Palace of Westminster burned down in 1834. The last great neo-Gothic public building to go up in London was the Royal Courts of Justice (1882; p77), designed by George Edmund Street.

The emphasis on the artisanship and materials necessary to create these elaborate neo-Gothic buildings led to the so-called Arts and Crafts movement – 'British art nouveau', for lack of a better term – of which William Morris (1834–96) was the leading exponent. Morris' work can be best enjoyed in the Green Dining Room of the Victoria & Albert Museum (p139) and at his Bexley-heath residence, Red House (1860; p186). The 1902 Euston Fire Station (Map p170; 172 Euston Rd NW1; ⊖ Euston) opposite St Pancras New Church is a wonderful example of Arts and Crafts architecture.

FLIRTING WITH MODERNISM

Not many public buildings of note were built during the first 15 years of the 20th century, apart from Admiralty Arch (1910; p75) in the Edwardian baroque style of Aston Webb (1849–1930), who also designed the 1911 Queen Victoria Memorial (Map pp84–5; ⊖ St James's Park) opposite Buckingham Palace (p86) and worked on the front facade of the palace itself. County Hall (p125), designed by Ralph Knott in 1909, was not completed until 1922.

In the period between the two world wars, English architecture was hardly more creative, though Edwin Lutyens (1869–1944), whose work is sometimes classified as British art deco,

Spire of early-18th-century St Martin-in-the-Fields (p74)   *Heritage-listed BT Tower (below)*

designed the Cenotaph (1920; p95) in Whitehall as well as the impressive 1927 Britannic House (Map p150; Finsbury Sq EC2), now Triton Court, in Moorgate.

European architects introduced the modernist style, but the works they left are generally on a small scale. Russian architect Berthold Lubetkin (1901–90) is perhaps the best remembered, principally because of his Penguin Pool at the London Zoo (p167), with its concrete spiral ramp. Built in 1934, it is considered to be London's earliest modernist structure. St Olaf House (Map p126; Tooley St SW1; ⊖ London Bridge), a diminutive office block fronting the Thames, was designed by HS Goodhart-Rendel in 1928 and is one of London's finest art deco buildings.

POSTWAR RECONSTRUCTION

Hitler's bombs during WWII wrought the worst destruction on London since the Great Fire and the immediate postwar problem was a chronic housing shortage. Low-cost developments and ugly high-rise housing were thrown up on bomb sites and many of these blocks still contribute to London's urban blight today.

The Royal Festival Hall (p125), designed by Robert Matthew and J Leslie Martin for the 1951 Festival of Britain and overhauled more than half a century later, attracted as many accolades as brickbats when it opened as London's first major public building in the modernist style. Hardly anyone seems to have a good word to say about Denys Lasdun's brutalist National Theatre (p128), however, begun in 1966 and finished a decade later.

The 1960s saw the ascendancy of the workaday glass-and-concrete high-rises exemplified by the mostly unloved 1967 Centre Point (Map p66; New Oxford St WC1; ⊖ Tottenham Court Rd) by Richard Seifert. But one person's muck is another's jewel; the once-vilified modernist tower has been listed by English Heritage, meaning that it represents a particular style, is of great value to the patrimony and largely cannot be altered outside (and in some cases inside as well). The 1964 BT Tower (Map pp80–1; 60 Cleveland St W1), formerly the Post Office Tower and designed by Eric Bedford, has also been given Heritage-listed status.

The 1970s saw very little building in London apart from roads, and the recession of the late 1980s and early 1990s brought much of the development and speculation in the Docklands and the City to a standstill. Helping to polarise traditionalists and modernists still further was a statement by 'architectural tastemaker' Prince Charles in 1984 describing a proposed extension to the National Gallery as 'a monstrous carbuncle on the face of an elegant and much loved friend'. (His Highness followed on six years later with the publication of *A Vision of Britain*, a reactionary tract that argued for a synthetic 'English tradition', and entered the fray yet again almost two decades later over the redevelopment of the Chelsea Barracks development, causing the developers to back out.) For these and other reasons, the London skyline had little to compare with that of New York or Hong Kong.

POSTMODERNISM LANDS

London's contemporary architecture was born in the City and the revitalised Docklands in the mid-1980s. The former's centrepiece was the 1986 Lloyd's of London (Map p100; ⊖ Aldgate or Bank), Sir Richard Rogers' 'inside-out' masterpiece of ducts, pipes, glass and stainless steel. Taking pride of place in the Docklands was Cesar Pelli's 244m-high 1 Canada Square (1991), commonly known as Canary Wharf (p162) and easily visible from central London.

With a youthful New Labour in power at the end of the 1990s, Britain's economy on the up and the new millennium looming, attention turned to public buildings, including several landmarks that would define London in the early 21st century.

Tate Modern (Herzog & de Meuron, 1999; p128) was a success beyond even its architects' wildest dreams. From the disused Bankside Power Station (Sir Giles Gilbert Scott, 1963) they fashioned an art gallery that went straight to first place in the top 10 London tourist attractions and then walked away with international architecture's most prestigious prize, the Pritzker. The stunning Millennium Bridge (Sir Norman Foster and Antony Caro, 2000; p129), the first bridge to be built over the Thames in central London since Tower Bridge in 1894, had a case of the wobbles when it was first opened, but it is now much loved and much used. Even the Millennium Dome (Sir Richard Rogers), the class dunce of 2000, has got a new lease of life as the 02 (p183) concert and sports hall.

The graceful British Library (Colin St John Wilson, 1998; p168), with its warm red-brick exterior, Asian-like touches and its wonderfully bright interior, met a very hostile reception. It has now become a popular and much loved London landmark.

The straight red-brick lines of the British Library (p168)

BY ANY OTHER NAME

The *Evening Standard* newspaper makes a sport of nicknaming new skyscrapers – whether built or planned – and Londoners accept them with such alacrity that one could almost mistake them for Aussies, who are always nicknaming everything. Here's a half-dozen of the popular ones inspired, of course, by the building's outline as it is now or might be in future:

Cheese Grater (Map p100; Leadenhall Bldg; 122 Leadenhall St EC3) This planned 48-storey, 224m-tall tower in the form of a stepped wedge would face architect Richard Rogers' other icon, the Lloyd's of London building. But though the site is ready, construction has yet to begin.

Flatiron (Map p90; South Molton St W1) The West End's answer to Manhattan's iconic eponymous building (1902) – though only six storeys high – is to be built along Oxford St.

Gherkin (30 St Mary Axe; p106) The bullet-shaped tower that seems to pop up at every turn has also been known as the Swiss Re Tower (after its first major tenants), Cockfosters (after its architect, Norman Foster), the exotic pickle etc.

Helter Skelter (Map p100; Bishopsgate Tower; 22-24 Bishopsgate EC2) At 288m and 63 storeys, what will be the City's tallest tower (Kohn Pedersen Fox Associates) is supposed to look like those high spiral slides at fairgrounds or amusement parks. It should be completed by the time you read this.

Shard of Glass (Map p126; London Bridge Tower; 32 London Bridge St SE) This needle-like, 310m-tall tower (by Renzo Piano) is one mother of a splinter you wouldn't want to tussle with. It should also be completed by the time you read this.

Walkie Talkie (Map p100; 20 Fenchurch St EC3) This 36-storey,160m-tall tower, expected in 2012, bulges in and bulges out, vaguely resembling an old fashioned walkie talkie.

TODAY & TOMORROW

The millennium icons and more recent structures such as the 2002 glass 'egg' of City Hall (Map p126; ⊖ London Bridge) and the ever-popular, ever-present 2003 30 St Mary Axe (Map p100; ⊖ Aldgate), or 'the Gherkin', gave the city the confidence to continue planning more heady buildings – especially of the tall variety.

The former mayor of London, Ken Livingstone, favoured 'clusters' of high-quality highrises throughout the capital, targeting not just the existing financial districts of the City and Canary Wharf, but other neighbourhoods as well, including three distinct sections of Paddington to the west, Elephant & Castle to the south, Silvertown Quays at the Docklands in the east and the Greenwich Peninsula to the southeast.

The current mayor, Boris Johnson, appeared to be suspicious of such developments while on the campaign trail but has changed his tune after taking office, throwing his support behind buildings such as a 143m tower (since cancelled) called the 'Penny Whistle' in Ealing in West London. But the so-called credit crunch that struck in October 2008 put paid to what was the most ambitious building program in London since WWII. Even buildings so iconic as to already have been given nicknames (see above) have been cancelled, delayed or shrunk considerably in size.

30 St Mary Axe, or 'the Gherkin' (p106)

Unstoppable is London's biggest urban development project, the 200-hectare Olympic Park (Map p62; www.london2012.com) in the Lea River Valley near Stratford, where most of the events of the 2012 Summer Olympiad will take place. Front and centre will be Zaha Hadid's stunning Aquatic Centre, a building that has yet to be given a moniker (it looks like a wave to us – but deserves the iconic status it will no dout win).

top picks

- **Apple Store** (p216)
- **Minamoto Kitchoan** (p220)
- **Arty Globe** (p231)
- **Harrods** (p224)
- **Start** (p229)
- **Magma** (p225)
- **Vivienne Westwood** (p220)
- **Selfridges** (p218)
- **Tatty Devine** (p228)
- **Alfie's Antiques Market** (p219)

What's your recommendation? www.lonelyplanet.com/london

Despite the bitter bite of the economic crisis, shopping remains a big part of many Londoners' lives. And while 'It bags' (read: Prada beauties with a £1000-plus price tag) are no longer publicly touted as objects of desire and ethical shopping is becoming a more acceptable way to spend (lots of) cash, at the time of writing most of the city's 30,000 shops – both chain and independent – are still going strong, or at least, not so infirm. True, some independent (and indeed chain) businesses have folded under financial pressure, but London is still a shrine to shopping and its massive variety – from the clever high-street fashion of Topshop (p220) to the luxurious delights of Harrods (p224), and the cutting-edge clothes from young designers at Spitalfields Market (p227) to the antiques of Portobello (p226) – are still here for the willing visitor and resident to enjoy.

London's main shopping attractions are its sheer variety and number of shopping opportunities. The big-name emporiums, such as Selfridges, Harvey Nichols, Hamleys, Fortnum & Mason and Liberty, are both sightseeing attractions in their own right and temples to shopping devotees; the side-street boutiques – the capital's true delights – also sell just about anything, from clothes to old-style British homewares. Despite the fact that High-Street chains are progressively taking over more and more of the city, funky street-wear outlets in places such as Hoxton, Brick Lane and Spitalfields continue to thrive, and Londoners are increasingly returning to the charm of individual design and decor. For those on a budget, charity shops, especially in the posher areas, are becoming more and more popular as shopping options, especially since big spending is increasingly frowned upon as unemployment figures soar.

If you're in the market for something a little more exclusive and expensive, New Bond St and surrounds is laden with designer shops, and a whole host of hot British designers, such as Stella McCartney and Matthew Williamson, maintain lavish outlets where admiring the setting is an integral part of the experience. You'll probably be familiar with classic British brands such as Burberry, Mulberry and Pringle, which have radically reinvented themselves and become part of high fashion.

But perhaps fashion is not your obsession? Worry not, the British capital has just about anything on sale, from handmade umbrellas to technology or exotic foodstuffs.

The fact that, at the time of writing, the pound is at an all-time low makes the once unimaginable possible: London is something of a bargain, especially for those spending the Euro.

OPENING HOURS

The good news is that you can go shopping every day of the week. The bad news is that this is not universally true throughout the city.

Generally, shops open from 9am or 10am to about 6pm or 6.30pm Monday to Saturday, at least. Shops in the West End (Oxford St, Soho and Covent Garden) open late (to 9pm) on Thursday; those in Chelsea, Knightsbridge and Kensington open late on Wednesday.

In the West End and in Chelsea, Knightsbridge and Kensington, many shops are also open on Sunday, typically from noon to 6pm but sometimes 10am to 4pm. Sunday trading is also common in Greenwich and Hampstead and along Edgware and Tottenham Court Rds.

Because the Square Mile, or the City of London, does most of its business during the week, most shops in this area open only Monday to Friday. Additionally, smaller designer stores tend to keep hours to suit their owners, opening later in the morning and often closing on a Monday or Tuesday to stay open on weekends. It's a good idea to ring ahead, as these places often have last-minute changes.

If there's a major market on a certain day – say, Columbia Road Flower Market on a Sunday morning – it's a good bet that neighbouring stores will fling their doors open too.

THE WEST END

We're not sure the West End's shopping needs introducing. This is the very area where you can spend your monthly salary on a pair of shoes or a handbag. Oxford St is heaven or hell, depending on your shopping stamina: it is *the* quintessential high street and brimming with an ocean of people most of the day. It can be a nightmare to tackle, so if you want to shop here, focus on what you want – you might find that strolling is more stressful than is warranted. Covent Garden is better thanks to its smaller-size High-Street outlets and little side-street boutiques. It throbs with shoppers on weekends, but is less hectic than Oxford St. Carnaby St and Newburgh Sts, and the independent boutique-laden Kingly Ct, are excellent for fashion – vintage and designer. Soho is superb for music stores (see the boxed text, p221), and Charing Cross Rd for books. You'll find excellent electronics and computer shops along Tottenham Court Rd (Map p66).

Just minutes from Oxford St is Marylebone 'village', whose high street is a miraculously calm and stylish strip. A weekly farmers market (Map p90; 10am-2pm Sun) is held in the nearby Cramer St car park, behind Waitrose.

BLACKWELL'S Map pp70-1   Books

☏ 7292 5100; www.bookshop.blackwell.co.uk; 100 Charing Cross Rd WC2; Tottenham Court Rd
Once a specialist in academic titles, this shop has now branched out into travel and other general-interest books. It is still, how-ever, the favourite haunt for those hunting for academic textbooks and is perfect for anyone starting a new course.

BORDERS Map p66   Books

☏ 7292 1600; www.borders.co.uk; 203 Oxford St; Oxford Circus
This is one of London's bigger bookshop chains, with five floors of books, magazines and newspapers from around the world, plus CDs and DVDs.

DAUNT BOOKS Map p90   Books

☏ 7224 2295; www.dauntbooks.co.uk; 83-84 Marylebone High St W1; Baker St
An original Edwardian bookshop, with oak panels and gorgeous skylights, Daunt is one of London's loveliest travel bookshops. It has two floors and the ground level is stacked with fiction and nonfiction titles; the lower ground is where to head if you're travel focused.

FORBIDDEN PLANET MEGASTORE
Map pp70-1   Books
☏ 7836 4179; www.forbiddenplanet.com; 179 Shaftesbury Ave WC1; Covent Gardens or Tottenham Court Rd
A massive trove of comics, sci-fi, horror and fantasy literature, this is an absolute dream for anyone into manga comics or off-beat genre titles.

FOYLE'S Map p66   Books

☏ 7437 5660; www.foyles.co.uk; 113-119 Charing Cross Rd WC2; Tottenham Court Rd
This is London's best and most legendary bookshop, where you can bet on finding even the most obscure of titles. The lovely, now extended cafe is on the 1st floor, and Ray's Jazz Shop (see the boxed text, p221) is up on the 5th floor. There are alternative, smaller branches at the Southbank Centre, St Pancras International Station and West-field Shopping Centre. Visit the website for details for more details on their range across all stores.

GOSH! Map pp70-1   Books

☏ 7636 1011; www.goshlondon.com; 39 Great Russell St WC1; Tottenham Court Rd
Draw up here for graphic novels, manga, newspaper-strip collections and children's books such as the Tin Tin and Asterix series. It's also perfect for finding presents for children and teenagers.

CLOTHING SIZES

Women's clothing

Aus/UK	8	10	12	14	16	18
Europe	36	38	40	42	44	46
Japan	5	7	9	11	13	15
USA	6	8	10	12	14	16

Women's shoes

Aus/USA	5	6	7	8	9	10
Europe	35	36	37	38	39	40
France only	35	36	38	39	40	42
Japan	22	23	24	25	26	27
UK	3½	4½	5½	6½	7½	8½

Men's clothing

Aus	92	96	100	104	108	112
Europe	46	48	50	52	54	56
Japan	S		M	M		L
UK/USA	35	36	37	38	39	40

Men's shirts (collar sizes)

Aus/Japan	38	39	40	41	42	43
Europe	38	39	40	41	42	43
UK/USA	15	15½	16	16½	17	17½

Men's shoes

Aus/UK	7	8	9	10	11	12
Europe	41	42	43	44½	46	47
Japan	26	27	27½	28	29	30
USA	7½	8½	9½	10½	11½	12½

Measurements approximate only; try before you buy

SHOPPING STRIPS

There have been talks of turning Oxford St into a traffic-free paradise, with breezy trams going up and down, but until that becomes even a remote reality, the street's ocean of consumers and stagnant traffic is likely to feel simultaneously overwhelming (in terms of its crowds) and underwhelming (regarding its offerings). This is where, however, you'll find the chain 'headquarters' with massive H&Ms, Zaras, Urban Outfitters and large department stores such as John Lewis, Debenhams and Selfridges.

Camden Market (p226) at weekends is just as likely to make you want to flee rather than spree, so try to visit during the week, unless you enjoy crowds. Better central areas to head to are listed below. (Apart from the chains listed under High St Kensington, where no address details are given for a particular store it is reviewed more fully in the relevant section of this chapter.)

Clerkenwell, Shoreditch & Spitalfields (see p225) This is London's trendiest shopping area, home to Sunday's fabulous Spitalfields Market where young cutting-edge designers display their creations; Brick Lane, Dray Walk and Cheshire St are full of quirky shops, vintage dens and cool household havens. Come here if you want to see London at its hippest and to search out small boutiques for something unique.

Covent Garden (p214) Visit, but don't shop at the touristy old market hall. Instead branch out into the little side streets for a whole lot of cool fashion, and hit Long Acre and Neil St for less hectic high-street chains. The Thomas Neal Centre on Earlham St is packed with urban/skate/surf fashions from the likes of High Jinks.

High Street Kensington (see p224) The less crowded, more salubrious alternative to Oxford St, this has all the high-street chains, plus trendy stores, such as Miss Sixty (No 63) and Urban Outfitters (No 36). Snap up antiques along Church St.

King's Road (p224) A far cry from its 1960s mod heyday, well-heeled King's Rd is now strong on household goods, with the Designer's Guild (No 269), Habitat (No 206) and Heal's (No 234). Children are well catered for at Trotters (No 34).

Knightsbridge (p224) Harrods (p224) is a national institution, so go and witness the exuberant food halls and dramatic Egyptian Hall of gifts at least once. Harvey Nichols (p225) is within easy reach, and there are many nearby stores for cashed-up fashionistas.

Marylebone High Street (p214) You'll feel like you're in a small town of its own along this quaint and elegant street, where homeware stores such as Cath Kidston (p222) are plenty. But food is the neighbourhood speciality, with London's best butcher Ginger Pig (Map p90; 8-10 Moxon St).

GRANT & CUTLER Map p66 Books
☎ 7734 2012; www.grantandcutler.com; 55-57 Great Marlborough St W1; ⊖ Oxford Circus
This is London's best-stocked foreign-language bookshop, running the gamut from Arabic to Zulu. However, sometimes staff aren't as knowledgeable as you'd hope in recommending specific books.

LONDON REVIEW BOOKSHOP
Map pp70-1 Books
☎ 7269 9030; www.lrb.co.uk; 14 Bury Pl WC1; ⊖ Russell Sq or Holborn
The bookshop of London Review of Books lit magazine doesn't believe in piles of books, taking the clever approach of stocking wide-ranging titles in one or two copies only. It often hosts high-profile author talks.

STANFORD'S Map pp70-1 Books
☎ 7836 1321; www.stanfords.co.uk; 12-14 Long Acre WC2; ⊖ Leicester Sq or Covent Garden

As a 150-year-old seller of maps, guides and literature, the grand daddy of travel bookshops is a destination in its own right. Ernest Shackleton, David Livingstone, Michael Palin and even Brad Pitt have all popped in here.

WATERSTONE'S Map p66 Books
☎ 7851 2400; www.waterstones.co.uk; 203-206 Piccadilly W1; ⊖ Piccadilly Circus
The chain's megastore is the largest bookshop in Europe, boasting knowledgeable staff and regular author readings. This is London's biggest Waterstone's, with four floors of titles, a cafe in the basement and a nice rooftop bar.

APPLE STORE Map p66 Computers
☎ 7153 9000; www.apple.com/uk/retail/regent street; 235 Regent St W1; ⏲ 10am-9pm Mon-Sat, noon-6pm Sun; ⊖ Oxford Circus
Mac geeks of the world unite! Here's your temple, your winter fireplace, so come and

warm your faces on the soft glow emanating from MacBooks and iPods, laptops and desktops, inside this white and airy two-storey emporium. Weekly workshops and talks help you get to know your computer, and the banks of iMacs are a free-for-all internet surfing base – a practice that's approved by Apple staffers. Come and worship.

DR HARRIS Map p66 Cosmetics
☎ 7930 3915; www.drharris.co.uk; 29 St James's St SW1; ⏰ 8.30am-6pm Mon-Fri, 9.30am-5pm Sat; ⊖ Green Park

Operating as chemist and perfumer since 1790, come here for your moustache wax and pick up a bottle of DR Harris Crystal Eye Drops to combat the red eyes after a late night and combine it with Dr Harris' own hangover cure: a bitter herbal concoction called DR Harris Pick-Me-Up.

MOLTON BROWN Map pp70-1 Cosmetics
☎ 7240 8383; www.moltonbrown.co.uk; 18 Russell St WC2; ⏰ 10am-7pm Mon-Fri, 10am-6pm Sat, noon-6pm Sun; ⊖ Covent Garden

A fabulously fragrant British natural beauty range, Molton Brown is *the* choice for boutique hotel and posh restaurant bathrooms. Its skin-care products offer plenty of pampering for men and women. In this store you can also have a facial, and buy make-up or even home accessories. There are branches across the city.

SPACE NK Map pp70-1 Cosmetics
☎ 7379 6384; www.spacenk.co.uk; 32 Shelton St WC2; ⏰ 10am-7pm Mon-Sat, to 7.30pm Thu, noon-5pm Sun; ⊖ Covent Garden

It's always a bit intimidating to face the glowing skin of SPACE NK's shop assistants/skin-care experts, but it's what gives people

---

TAXES & REFUNDS

In certain circumstances visitors from non-EU countries are entitled to claim back the 15% value-added tax (VAT) they have paid on purchased goods. The rebate only applies to items purchased in stores displaying a 'tax free' sign (there are plenty of these along Bond St). To claim it, visitors must be staying in the UK for less than six months.

The procedure to follow is relatively simple: don't forget to pick up the relevant form in the shop at the time of sale, and then hand it in at the airport when you leave. For details on getting your tax back, see p385.

---

top picks

BEST BOOKSHOPS

- Foyle's (p215)
- London Review Bookshop (opposite)
- Daunt Books (p215)
- Stanford's (opposite)
- Books for Cooks (p230)

the confidence in the products – the shop stocks Dr Hauschka, Eve Lom, Chantecaille, Kiehl's and Phyto, and anti-ageing ranges such as 24/7 and Dr Sebagh. Men's products range from Anthony to Kiehl's for men. There are SPACE NK branches across the city.

TAYLOR OF OLD BOND STREET
Map p66 Cosmetics
☎ 7930 5321; www.tayloroldbondst.co.uk; 74 Jermyn St SW1; ⏰ 9am-6pm Mon-Fri, 8.30am-6pm Sat; ⊖ Green Park

This shop has been plying its trade since the mid-19th century and has much contributed to the expression 'well-groomed gentleman'. It stocks every sort of razor, shaving brush and flavour of shaving soap imaginable.

FORTNUM & MASON
Map p66 Department Store
☎ 7734 8040; www.fortnumandmason.co.uk; 181 Piccadilly W1; ⏰ 10am-6.30pm Mon-Sat, noon-6pm Sun; ⊖ Piccadilly Circus

London's oldest department store celebrated its 300th birthday in 2007 by not yielding to modern times (its staff are still dressed in old-fashioned tailcoats) and keeping its glam food hall supplied with its famed food hampers, cut marmalade, speciality teas and so on. Downstairs is an elegant wine bar designed by the man behind the Wolseley (p242). Clothes, gifts and perfumes occupy the other six floors.

JOHN LEWIS Map p90 Department Store
☎ 7629 7711; www.johnlewis.co.uk; 278-306 Oxford St W1; ⏰ 9.30am-7pm Mon-Sat, to 8pm Thu; ⊖ Oxford Circus

'Never knowingly undersold' is the motto of this store, whose range of household goods, fashion and luggage is better described as reliable rather than cutting edge. Strong points include its fabrics department.

LIBERTY Map p66 — Department Store

☎ 7734 1234; www.liberty.co.uk; 210-220 Regent St W1; ☻ 10am-7pm Mon-Sat, to 8pm Thu, noon-6pm Sun; ⊖ Oxford Circus

An irresistible blend of contemporary styles in an old-fashioned mock-Tudor atmosphere, Liberty has a huge cosmetics department and an accessories floor, along with a breathtaking lingerie section. A classic London souvenir is a Liberty fabric print.

SELFRIDGES Map p90 — Department Store

☎ 7629 1234; www.selfridges.com; 400 Oxford St W1; ☻ 10am-8pm Mon-Fri, 9.30am-8pm Sat, noon-6pm Sun; ⊖ Bond St

Selfridges loves innovation – it's famed for its inventive window displays by international artists, gala shows and above all an amazing range of products. It's the funkiest and most vital of London's one-stop shops, with labels such as Boudicca, Luella Bartley, Emma Cook, Chloé and Missoni; an unparalleled food hall; and Europe's largest cosmetics department.

AQUASCUTUM Map p66 — Fashion & Designer

☎ 7675 8200; www.aquascutum.co.uk; 100 Regent St W1; ☻ 10am-6.30pm Mon-Sat, to 7pm Thu, 11am-5pm Sun; ⊖ Piccadilly Circus

Despite the store's modern look, Aquascutum's mackintoshes, scarves, bags and hats remain traditional. For men, this means classic gabardine; for women, the look is straight lines, classic fashion and natural beauty, as worn by the super-rich.

BEYOND THE VALLEY
Map p66 — Fashion & Designer

☎ 7437 7338; www.beyondthevalley.com; 2 Newburgh St W1; ☻ 11am-7pm Mon-Sat, 12.30-6pm Sun; ⊖ Oxford Circus

One of central London's best places to discover unique new fashion talent, with clothes, jewellery, accessories and artwork on display inside the lovely shop. The Side Room, at the back of the shop, is a conservatory-style gallery space with small exhibitions regularly taking place.

BURBERRY Map p90 — Fashion & Designer

☎ 7839 5222; www.burberry.com; 21-23 New Bond St SW1; ☻ 10am-7pm Mon-Sat, noon-6pm Sun; ⊖ Bond St

The first traditional British brand to reach the heights of fashion, you'll know you've reached Burberry when you see hordes of giggling Japanese girls standing outside. It's known for its innovative take on classic pieces (bright-coloured trench coats, khaki pants with large and unusual pockets), its brand check pattern and a tailored, groomed look. You'll see a lot of its catwalk pieces ripped-off by high-street shops.

KOH SAMUI Map pp70-1 — Fashion & Designer

☎ 7240 4280; www.kohsamui.co.uk; 65-67 Monmouth St WC2; ☻ 10.30am-6.30pm Mon-Sat, to 7pm Thu, 11.30am-6pm Sun; ⊖ Covent Garden

It's high-end fashion galore at this little boutique that prides itself on finding new designer talent and specialises in floaty pieces from Brit designers such as Chloé, Marc Jacobs, Clements Ribeiro and Julien MacDonald. You'll drool over the handsome Chloé bags.

MULBERRY Map p90 — Fashion & Designer

☎ 7491 3900; www.mulberry.com; 41-42 New Bond St W1; ☻ 10am-6pm Mon-Sat, to 7pm Thu; ⊖ Bond St

Is there a woman in the world who doesn't covet a Mulberry bag? They are voluptuous, soft and a massive style statement. The brand followed in the footsteps of its other British design brethren, Burberry and Pringle, and modernised itself in recent years.

PAUL SMITH Map pp70-1 — Fashion & Designer

☎ 7379 7133; www.paulsmith.co.uk; 40-44 Floral St WC2; ☻ 10am-6.30pm Mon-Sat, to 7pm Thu, noon-5pm Sun; ⊖ Covent Garden

Paul Smith represents the best of British classic with innovative twists. Super-stylish menswear, suits and tailored shirts are all laid out on open shelves in this walk-in closet of a shop. Smith also does womenswear.

PRINGLE Map p90 — Fashion & Designer

☎ 0800 360 200, 7297 4580; www.pringle scotland.com; 112 New Bond St W1; ☻ 10am-6.30pm Mon-Sat, to 7.30pm Thu; ⊖ Bond St

Fabulously classy and somehow sexy at the same time (we're talking golfers' V-necks and knitted cardies), this traditional Brit brand turned slightly hip when London rekindled its passion for knitwear. An item will set you back at least £150, however.

STELLA McCARTNEY

Map p90   Fashion & Designer

☎ 7518 3100; www.stellamccartney.co.uk; 30 Bruton St W1; ☼ 10am-6pm Mon-Sat, to 7pm Thu; ⊖ Bond St or Green Park

Does Stella McCartney need introducing? Her floaty designs send many-a-girl's heart aflutter (as do her prices), Kate Moss makes her jeans the most covetable in the UK and her 'ethical' approach to fashion is very of the moment. This three-storey terraced Victorian home is a temple to all things Stella – a ritzy glasshouse garden, an olde-worlde 'apothecary' selling perfume, vegetarian

LONDON LOVES VINTAGE

Gripped as it is by looking good and with a permanent shopping fever, London's love affair with vintage apparel seems to be a lasting one. Vintage designer pieces from Chanel, Dior, Miu Miu, Vivienne Westwood, you name it – and odd bits and pieces from the 1920s to the 1980s are all busting the rails in shops that are often as extravagant as the clothes they stock.

The rise of burlesque and cabaret club nights (see the boxed text, p295) has meant that 1920s to 1950s costume dresses and jewellery have become much coveted, and it's fascinating to see the mastery and effort that goes into dressing up for such events. Some vintage shops can be quite expensive, with designer and rare pieces costing up to £300, but you can find cheaper things (between £10 and £50) if you dig deep; if you don't feel like buying, it's fantastic to simply browse around and see what your grandma's generation used to wear (or remember your own '80s excesses). If you, however, discover the vintage king or queen inside you, check out the cabaret nights, dress up and join in!

The best areas for vintage shops are: Camden Passage at Islington; Kingly Ct, off Carnaby St; Spitalfields Market, Cheshire St and on and around Brick Lane; and Portobello Rd and Notting Hill. Try charity shops in areas such as Chelsea, Notting Hill and Kensington – they usually have cheap designer wear (the general rule is, the richer the area, the better the secondhand shops).

Vintage Shops

The following typically trade from 10am to 7pm Monday to Saturday and from noon until 6pm on Sunday.

Absolute Vintage (Map p150; ☎ 7247 3883; 15 Hanbury St E1; ⊖ Liverpool St) If you don't mind shoes that have been worn by other feet, enter this huge barn full of stilettos, peep-toes, ankle-/knee-high boots and glittery vintage Manolos. Men's shoes are stocked, too, and there are frocks and suits at the back. It's handily close to Spitalfields Market.

Alfie's Antiques Market (Map p166; ☎ 7723 6066; www.alfiesantiques.com; 13-25 Church St NW8; ⊖ Marylebone) Alfie's Market is an entire ex-department store, in an art deco building, dedicated to fab 20th-century furniture and rare 1920s to 1950s pieces. An absolute delight.

Annie's Vintage Costumes & Textiles (Map p170; ☎ 7359 0796; 12 Camden Passage N1; ⊖ Angel) One of London's most enchanting vintage shops, Annie's has costumes to make you look like Greta Garbo.

Bang Bang Exchange (Map p66; ☎ 7631 4191; www.myspace.com/bangbangexchange; 21 Goodge St W1; ⊖ Goodge St) Got some designer pieces you're tired of? Bang Bang exchanges, buys and sells vintage pieces, proving the saying 'One girl's faded Prada dress is another girl's top new wardrobe piece'.

Marshmallow Mountain (Map p66; ☎ 7434 8498; www.marshmellowmountain.com; Kingly Ct, 49 Carnaby St W1; ⊖ Oxford Circus) One of our favourites, with eccentric, well-chosen dresses and wonderful shoes.

Orsini (Map p178; ☎ 7937 2903; www.orsini-vintage.co.uk; 76 Earl's Court Rd W8; ⊖ Earl's Court) One of the best vintage designer collections in town, Orsini is small, beautiful and friendly. Alterations are available in-store.

Radio Days (Map p126; ☎ 7928 0800; 87 Lower Marsh Rd SE1; ⊖ Waterloo) Radio Days loves 1920s and '30s clothes, hats and jewellery; also has vintage electric items like phones, record players and radios, and magazines.

Rellik (Map p176; ☎ 8962 0089; 8 Golborne Rd W10; ⊖ Westbourne Park) This is a fashionista favourite retro store. It stocks the likes of Ossie Clark, Zandra Rhodes and Vivienne Westwood.

Retro Woman (Map p176; ☎ 7221 2055; 20 Pembridge Rd W11; ⊖ Notting Hill Gate) Contains an excellent collection of second-hand designer shoes. More stock is in the unmarked sister store at No 16, while Retro Man (Map p176) is at No 34.

Steinberg & Tolkien (Map pp136–7; ☎ 7376 3660; 193 King's Rd SW3; ⊖ South Kensington) London's oldest and most bizarre vintage shop, S&T has had its frocks featured in *Vogue,* among other magazines; shoppers are always taken aback by its dark and eccentric atmosphere.

shoes and not-leather bags, plus bespoke tailoring. Depending on your devotion and wallet, you'll feel right at ease or like an intruder.

TOPSHOP & TOPMAN
Map p66   Fashion & Designer
☎ 7636 7700; www.topshop.co.uk; 36-38 Great Castle St W1; ☺ 9am-8pm Mon-Sat, to 9pm Thu, noon-6pm Sun; ⊖ Oxford Circus
Topshop is the it-store when it comes to high-street shopping. Encapsulating London's supreme skill at bringing catwalk fashion to the youth market affordably and quickly, it constantly innovates by working with young designers and celebrities. It's the store that famously runs the popular Kate Moss collection. It also does manicure/pedicure and hair-styling sessions, and you can have a consultation with a personal stylist and get tips from a shopping guru.

URBAN OUTFITTERS
Map p66   Fashion & Designer
☎ 7759 6390; www.urbanoutfitters.com; 200 Oxford St W1; ☺ 10am-8pm Mon-Sat, to 9pm Thu, noon-6pm Sun; ⊖ Oxford Circus
Probably the trendiest of all chains, this cool American store serves both men and women and has the best young designer T-shirts, an excellent designer area (stocking Paul & Joe Sister, Vivienne Westwood's Red Label, Hussain Chalayan and See by Chloé, among others), 'renewed' second-hand pieces, saucy underwear, silly homewares and quirky gadgets. There is also a Covent Garden branch (Map pp70–1; Seven Dials House, 42-56 Earlham St; ⊖ Covent Garden) and a Kensington branch (Map p178; 36-38 Kensington High St; ⊖ High St Kensington).

VIVIENNE WESTWOOD
Map p66   Fashion & Designer
☎ 7439 1109; www.viviennewestwood.com; 44 Conduit St W1; ☺ 10am-6pm Mon-Sat, to 7pm Thu; ⊖ Bond St or Oxford Circus
The ex-punk who dressed the punks and created the punk look now says that 'fashion is boring' and that she disagrees with everything she used to say. Always a controversial character with a reputation for being a bit barmy (she flashed her privates to the paparazzi after receiving her OBE), Ms Westwood is, thankfully, still designing clothes as bold, innovative and provocative as ever, featuring 19th-century-inspired bustiers, wedge shoes and loads of tartan.

ALGERIAN COFFEE STORES
Map p66   Food & Drink
☎ 7437 2480; www.algocoffee.co.uk; 52 Old Compton St W1; ☺ 9am-7pm Mon-Sat; ⊖ Leicester Sq
Stop and have a shot of espresso made in-store, while you select your fresh-ground coffee beans. Choose among dozens of varieties of coffees and teas.

MINAMOTO KITCHOAN
Map p66   Food & Drink
☎ 7437 3135; www.kitchoan.com; 44 Piccadilly W1; ☺ 10am-7pm Sun-Fri, to 8pm Sat; ⊖ Piccadilly Circus
Walking into this Japanese sweet shop is a mind-blowing experience. *Wagashi* – Japanese sweets – are made out of all sorts of beans and rice and shaped into glazed red cherries, green-bean bunches or spiky kidney bean rolls. Order a couple, sit down and enjoy with a complimentary green tea, or buy a box for a sure-hit souvenir.

NEAL'S YARD DAIRY
Map pp70-1   Food & Drink
☎ 7240 5700; 17 Shorts Gardens WC2; ☺ 9am-7pm Mon-Sat; ⊖ Covent Garden
A fabulous, smelly cheese house that would fit in rural England, this place is proof that the British can do just as well as the French when it comes to big rolls of ripe cheese. There are more than 70 varieties that the shopkeepers will let you taste, including independent farmhouse brands. Condiments, pickles, jams and chutneys are also available.

VINTAGE HOUSE Map p66   Food & Drink
☎ 7437 2592; 42 Old Compton St W1; ☺ 9am-11pm Mon-Fri, 9.30am-11pm Sat, noon-10pm Sun; ⊖ Leicester Sq
A whisky connoisseur's paradise, this shop stocks more than 1000 single-malt Scotches, from smooth Macallan to peaty Lagavulin.

SHEPHERDS Map pp136-7   Gifts & Souvenirs
☎ 7620 0060; www.bookbinding.co.uk; 76 Rochester Row SW1; ☺ 10am-6pm Mon-Fri, 10.30am-5pm Sat; ⊖ Victoria or Pimlico

Suckers for fine stationery, leather boxes and that exquisite, specialised Florentine *papier* à *cuve* (paper that is hand-decorated with marbled designs), we get our fix at this wonderful bookbindery. There's also a **Holborn branch** (Map pp80–1; ☎ 7831 1151; 76 Southampton Row WC1; ⊖ Holborn or Russell Sq).

ARAM Map pp70-1   Homewares
☎ 7557 7557; www.aram.co.uk; 110 Drury Lane WC2; ◷ 10am-6pm Mon-Sat, to 7pm Thu; ⊖ Covent Garden or Holborn
Despite the fact that most of the furniture stocked by Aram is unaffordable to ordinary mortals, admiring the designer pieces in this fantastic shop is an experience to be

INDEPENDENT MUSIC STORES

It is sad that independent music stores find it difficult to keep going, especially in central London. That said, Britons buy more music per head than any other nation on earth (much of it in London), so here's hoping that little fish don't get munched by big nasty chains. Most are open 10am until 6pm Monday to Saturday and noon until 5pm on Sunday. Here's a selection of the city's best:

BM Soho (Map p66; ☎ 7437 0478; www.bm-soho.com; 25 D'Arblay St W1; ⊖ Oxford Circus) Formerly Black Market Records, this is where club DJs flock for the latest international dance music.

Haggle Vinyl (Map p170; ☎ 7354 4666; www.haggle.freeserve.co.uk; 114 Essex Rd N1; ◷ 9am-7pm Mon-Sat, 10am-5.30pm Sun; ⊖ Angel) Vinyl records from as little as £2.50 for the stuff that has spilled over into the boxes on the floor. From 1950s crooners to early hip hop.

Harold Moore's Records (Map p66; ☎ 7437 1576; www.hmrecords.co.uk; 2 Great Marlborough St W1; ⊖ Oxford Circus) London's finest classical-music store stocks an extensive range of vinyl, CDs and DVDs, plus jazz in the basement.

Honest Jon's (Map p176; ☎ 8969 9822; 276-278 Portobello Rd W10; ⊖ Ladbroke Grove) Two adjoining shops with jazz, soul and reggae.

Music & Video Exchange (Map p176; ☎ 7243 8573; 38 Notting Hill Gate W11; ⊖ Notting Hill Gate) Second-hand store *par excellence*. One of countless London branches of 'Exchange' shops. Get a leaflet and check them all out.

On the Beat (Map p66; ☎ 7637 8934; 22 Hanway St W1; ⊖ Tottenham Court Rd) Mostly '60s and '70s retro; helpful staff.

Phonica (Map p66; ☎ 7025 6070; www.phonicarecords.co.uk; 51 Poland St W1; ⊖ Tottenham Court Rd or Oxford Circus) A cool and relaxed Poland St store that stocks a lot of house, electro and hip hop, but you can find just about anything from reggae to dub, jazz and rock.

Ray's Jazz Shop (Map p66; ☎ 7440 3205; www.foyles.co.uk; 1st fl, Foyle's, 113-119 Charing Cross Rd WC2; ⊖ Tottenham Court Rd) Quiet and serene with friendly and helpful staff, this is one of the best jazz shops in London, with a fab independent cafe in tow.

Revival (Map p66; ☎ 7437 4271; 30 Berwick St W1; ⊖ Oxford Circus) The old Reckless Records store was replaced by Revival, though the outfit hasn't changed much. It's still new and second-hand records/CDs, from punk, soul, dance and independent to mainstream.

Rough Trade (Map p176; ☎ 7229 8541; 130 Talbot Rd W11; ⊖ Ladbroke Grove) With its underground, alternative and vintage rarities, this home of the eponymous punk-music label remains a haven for vinyl junkies who get misty-eyed about the days before CDs (also on sale) and MP3 players. Check out the Covent Garden branch (Map pp70–1) in Neal's Yard.

Sister Ray (Map p66; ☎ 7734 3297; www.sisterray.co.uk; 34-35 Berwick St W1; ⊖ Oxford Circus) If you were a fan of the late, great John Peel on the BBC/BBC World Service, this specialist in innovative, experimental and indie music is just right for you.

Sounds of the Universe (Map p66; ☎ 7734 3430; www.soundsoftheuniverse.com; 7 Broadwick St W1; ⊖ Oxford Circus) Outlet of Soul Jazz Records label (responsible for so many great soul, reggae, funk and dub albums), this place stocks CDs and vinyl plus some original 45s.

Sterns Music (Map pp80–1; ☎ 7387 5550; www.sternsmusic.com; 74-75 Warren St W1; ⊖ Warren St) A world-music oldie, Sterns has been around since the 1980s, lording it over London's world-music scene. Excellent website where you can listen to albums in the shop's charts.

cherished. Originally opened by Zeev Aram on King's Rd in 1964, the shop was a key player in the Conran-led furniture design revolution that saw the end of a chintz-laden Britain. The shop grew and eventually moved to this four-floor, free-standing luminous building, where the furniture is given the space it deserves, as if in a museum. Among the many accomplished designers, Aram stocks pieces by Alvar Aalto, Eileen Grey, Eames, Le Corbusier and Arne Jacobsen. The top floor is an exhibition space, where you can see new talent in fine or applied art and design.

CATH KIDSTON Map p90   Homewares
☎ 7935 6555; www.cathkidston.co.uk; 51 Marylebone High St W1; ☺ 10am-7pm Mon-Sat, 11am-5pm Sun; ☻ Baker St
Cath Kidston has single-handedly made floral patterns and pastel colours fashionable again. She splashes her homewares and handbags with funky floral designs, and is famous for her polka-dot picnic tableware and 1950s-style watering cans.

DO SHOP Map p66   Homewares
☎ 7494 9090; www.do-shop.com; 47 Beak St W1; ☻ Oxford Circus
A great collection of quirky designer furniture, kitchenware and home accessories; check out the versatile tables that double as bookshelves or scrunched-up paper cups that are made of porcelain, really. Perfect for presents (to self, as well as others).

HABITAT Map pp80-1   Homewares
☎ 7631 3880; www.habitat.net; 196 Tottenham Court Rd W1; ☺ 10am-6.30pm Mon-Sat, to 8pm Thu, noon-6pm Sun; ☻ Goodge St
Started by the visionary designer and restaurateur Terence Conran in the 1950s, Habitat still does what it originally set out to do – brighten up your home with inventive and inspiring furniture and decorations. Artists, actors, musicians and fashion designers are often employed to design something of their own. The chain is found across London.

HEAL'S Map pp80-1   Homewares
☎ 7636 1666; www.heals.co.uk; 196 Tottenham Court Rd W1; ☺ 10am-6pm Mon-Wed, to 8pm Thu, to 6.30pm Fri & Sat, noon-6pm Sun; ☻ Goodge St
Heal's is more serious, classical and expensive than Habitat, serving a more conservative,

yet practical clientele. It's a long-established furniture and homewares store. Check out the great kitchenware section.

BUTLER & WILSON
Map p90   Jewellery & Accessories
☎ 7409 2955; www.butlerandwilson.co.uk; 20 South Molton St SW1; ☺ 10am-6pm Mon-Sat, to 7pm Thu, noon-6pm Sun; ☻ Bond St
There's a sybaritic 1920s Shanghai vibe to Butler & Wilson's central branch, where costume jewellery, handbags, T-shirts and knick-knacks are sold beneath red Chinese lanterns, watched by Chinese shop dummies. The Chelsea store (Map pp136–7; ☎ 7352 3045; 189 Fulham Rd SW3) has a large collection of retro dresses, too.

JAMES SMITH & SONS
Map pp70-1   Jewellery & Accessories
☎ 7836 4731; www.james-smith.co.uk; 53 New Oxford St WC1; ☺ 9.30am-5.30pm Mon-Fri, 10am-5.30pm Sat; ☻ Tottenham Court Rd
'Outside every silver lining is a big black cloud', claim the cheerful owners of this quintessential English shop. Nobody makes and stocks such elegant umbrellas, walking sticks and canes as this traditional place, and thanks to bad English weather, they'll hopefully do great business for years to come.

MONOCLE SHOP
Map p90   Jewellery & Accessories
☎ 7486 8770; www.monocle.com; 2a George St W1; ☺ 10am-6pm Mon-Sat, to 7pm Thu, noon-6pm Sun; ☻ Bond St
Run by the people behind the design and international current affairs magazine Monocle, this shop is pure understated heaven. True, most things cost more than many spend in a year, but if you're a fan of minimalist, quality design across the board (there are bicycles, clothes, bags and so on), you won't regret dropping in. Beautifully bound first editions are on sale here, as well as stunning photography.

WRIGHT & TEAGUE
Map p90   Jewellery & Accessories
☎ 7629 2777; www.wrightandteague.com; 1a Grafton St W1; ☺ 10am-6pm Mon-Fri, to 7pm Thu, 10am-5pm Sat; ☻ Green Park
The Wright & Teague gold charm bracelets are absolutely ravishing, as are its elegant silver and gold bangles, long necklaces and

rings for men and women. What's more, many are very affordable. The couple met while studying at St Martins School of Art more than 20 years ago and have been together ever since.

AGENT PROVOCATEUR Map p66   Lingerie
☎ 7439 0229; www.agentprovocateur.com; 6 Broadwick St W1; ⏰ 11am-7pm Mon-Sat, to 8pm Thu, noon-5pm Sun; ⊖ Oxford Circus
For women's lingerie that is to be worn and seen, and certainly *not* hidden, pull up to Joseph (son of Vivienne Westwood) Corre's wonderful Agent Provocateur. Its sexy and saucy corsets, bras and nighties for all shapes and sizes exude confident and posi-tive sexuality.

RIGBY & PELLER Map p66   Lingerie
☎ 7491 2200; 22a Conduit St W1; ⏰ 9.30am-6pm Mon-Sat, to 7pm Thu; ⊖ Oxford Circus
This old-fashioned place makes the Queen's bras, but Rigby & Peller's fit-ting and alteration service – open to us plebs – is equally legendary. Get yourself measured – many a customer has been surprised to discover they've been wear-ing the wrong size for years. Off-the-peg underwear and swimwear is also available. There's also a Knightsbridge branch (Map pp136–7; 3 Hans Rd; ⊖ Knightsbridge).

KURT GEIGER Map p90   Shoes
☎ 7758 8020; www.kurtgeiger.com; 65 South Molton St W1; ⏰ 10am-7pm Mon-Sat, to 8pm Thu, noon-6pm Sun; ⊖ Bond St
Fashion, quality and affordability all come together at this superlative men's and women's shoe store, where footwear from the likes of Birkenstock, Chloé, Hugo Boss, Marc Jacobs, Paul Smith and United Nude adorns the shelves.

POSTE Map p90   Shoes
☎ 7499 8002; 10 South Molton St; ⏰ 10am-7pm Mon-Sat, noon-6pm Sun; ⊖ Bond St
Sitting on one of London's most fashion-able streets, this very cool shop is aimed at boys who like good shoes, and stocks everything from vintage street labels to razor-sharp Italian imports.

POSTE MISTRESS Map pp70-1   Shoes
☎ 7379 4040; 61-63 Monmouth St WC2; ⏰ 10am-7pm Mon-Sat, noon-6pm Sun; ⊖ Leicester Sq

This is where all shoe fetishists should head for the wonderful collection of wom-en's shoes from Emma Hope, Vivienne Westwood, Miu Miu and Dries Van Noten. Money should not be an object.

BENJAMIN POLLOCK'S TOYSHOP
Map pp70-1   Toys
☎ 7379 7866; www.pollocks-coventgarden.co.uk; 1st fl, 44 Covent Garden Market WC2; ⏰ 10am-6.30pm Mon-Sat, 11am-4pm Sun; ⊖ Covent Garden
Here's a traditional toyshop that's loved by kids of all ages. There are Victorian paper theatres, wooden marionettes and finger puppets, plus antique teddy bears that might be too fragile to play with.

HAMLEYS Map p66   Toys
☎ 0870 333 2455, 7494 2000; www.hamleys.com; 188-196 Regent St W1; ⏰ 10am-8pm Mon-Sat, noon-6pm Sun; ⊖ Oxford Circus
Reportedly the largest toy store in the world and certainly the most famous, Hamleys is a layer cake of playthings. Computer games are in the basement, the latest playground trends at ground level. Science kits are on the 1st floor, preschool toys on the 2nd, girls' playthings on the 3rd and model cars on the 4th, while the whole confection is topped off with Lego world and its cafe on the 5th.

THE CITY

SILVER VAULTS Map p100   Silver
☎ 7242 3844; www.thesilvervaults.com; 53-63 Chancery La WC2; ⊖ Chancery Lane
The shops that work out of these incred-ibly secure subterranean vaults make up collectively the largest collection of silver under one roof in the world. The different businesses tend to specialise in different types of silverware – from cutlery sets to picture frames and lots of jewellery. The quality of the goods here is guaranteed, although even if you're not buying it's well worth visiting just to have a look round this extraordinary place.

THE SOUTH BANK

The South Bank has become one of London's most popular promenades and, needless to say, business has followed on the heels of locals and tourists alike. Borough Market (p259), London's best food market, has benefited from the surge in visitors and shouldn't be missed. And if you like household and fashion design, head for Oxo Tower, home to two dozen small design studios with clothes, jewellery and quirky housewares. Gabriel's Wharf has some sweet boutiques, and curious fashionistas might appreciate a quick scout in and around Bermondsey St.

IAN ALLAN Map p126   Books

☎ 7401 2100; www.ianallanpublishing.com; 45-46 Lower Marsh SE1; ⏱ 9am-5.30pm Mon-Fri, to 5pm Sat; ✦ Waterloo

The train-spotter in you won't be able to resist this shop, which specialises in books on transport and defence: aircraft, motor vehicles, buses and, of course, those choo-choo trains.

KONDITOR & COOK Map p126   Food & Drink

☎ 7261 0456; www.konditorandcook.com; 22 Cornwall Rd SE1; ⏱ 7.30am-8.30pm Mon-Fri, 8.30am-3pm Sat; ✦ Waterloo

This elegant cake shop and bakery produces wonderful cakes – lavender and orange, and lemon and almond – massive raspberry meringues, cookies (including gingerbread men!), and loaves of warm bread with olives, nuts and spices. There are four other K&C shops, including a Borough Market branch (Map p126; ☎ 7407 5100; 10 Stoney St SE1; ✦ London Bridge) and a Holborn branch (Map pp70–1; ☎ 7404 6300; 46 Gray's Inn Rd WC1; ✦ Chancery Lane).

BLACK + BLUM Map p126   Homewares

☎ 7633 0022; www.black-blum.com; Unit 2.07, 2nd fl, Oxo Tower, Barge House St SE1; ⏱ 9am-

5pm Mon-Fri, from 11am Sat; ✦ Southwark or Waterloo

You might see 'James the doorman/bookend' (a human-shaped doorstop/bookend) and 'Mr and Mrs Hangup' (anthropomorphic coat hooks that can indicate your mood through a choice of eyes) in numerous gift shops across town, but this Anglo-Swiss partnership produces more wonderful stuff in its shop, such as the intricate wire 'bowl' called a Fruit Loop or the Spudski potato masher inspired by a ski pole.

HYDE PARK TO CHELSEA

This well-heeled part of town is all about high fashion, glam shops and groomed shoppers and is home to Chelsea's chic King's Rd. Knightsbridge draws the hordes with high-end department stores and glamorous boutiques. Among the glitz, venerable and atmospheric stores survive thanks to centuries of catering to the whims and vanities of the rich and refined folk who live here. High St Kensington has a good mix of chains and boutiques.

HARRODS Map pp136-7   Department Store

☎ 7730 1234; www.harrods.com; 87-135 Brompton Rd SW1; ⏱ 10am-8pm Mon-Sat, 11.30am-6pm Sun; ✦ Knightsbridge

It's garish and stylish at the same time, and sure to leave you reeling with a consumer-rush after you've spent a few hours within its walls. Harrods is an obligatory stop for many of London's tourists, always crowded and with more rules than an army barracks.

HELP THE SMALL ONES

London's small and independent local businesses were at the rough end of both the economic boom and the downturn – in the former they were being swamped by big chains, while in the latter they were often the first victims. Businesses that don't generate much turnover are at particular risk, such as antique shops, or those that suffer from direct competition with large chains (think small coffee shop versus Starbucks, or local record shops versus Virgin Megastores).

Areas traditionally rich in local businesses are: Old Conduit St (near Holborn tube station), Amwell St (near Angel tube), Brick Lane and Spitalfields, Chiswick and some of Richmond, Soho, Endell St (near Covent Garden tube), Camden Passage (Angel tube), Farringdon, Clerkenwell and Marylebone High St.

Seek out independent shops on your visit to London and you're guaranteed to find original products and a personal atmosphere, meet some of London's funny characters and get under the skin of the city better than in any other way.

If you're spending some time in London or are moving here, consider purchasing a Wedge Card (www.wedgecard .co.uk; per card £10), an affinity card that encourages people to shop locally by giving them a discount in shops that have signed up to be part of the Wedge initiative. The brilliant project was started in 2004 by John Bird, founder and editor-in-chief of the *Big Issue*. We're hoping that London's local and independent stores will serve their communities for decades to come.

See the boxed text on p221 for details on London's independent music stores.

And despite the tacky elements (a wax figure of proprietor Mohammad Al Fayed and a memorial fountain to Dodi and Di), you're bound to swoon over the spectacular food hall and impeccable 5th-floor perfumery. **Harrods 102** (Map pp136–7; ☎ 7730 1234; 102 Brompton Rd SW1; ☒ 9am-9pm Mon-Sat, noon-6pm Sun), across the street, contains a luxury food shop and several casual restaurants.

HARVEY NICHOLS
Map pp136-7   Department Store
☎ 7235 5000; www.harveynichols.com; 109-125 Knightsbridge SW1; ☒ 10am-8pm or 9pm Mon-Sat, 11.30am-6pm Sun; ⊖ Knightsbridge
This is London's temple of high fashion, where you'll find Chloé and Balenciaga bags, London's best denim range, a massive make-up hall with exclusive lines, great jewellery and the fantastic restaurant Fifth Floor, with a three-course set lunch from £19.50.

PETER JONES Map pp136-7   Department Store
☎ 7730 3434; www.peterjones.co.uk; Sloane Sq SW1; ☒ 9.30am-7pm Mon, Tue & Thu-Sat, to 8pm Wed, 11am-5pm Sun; ⊖ Sloane Sq
The slightly more upmarket brother of John Lewis (p217), Peter Jones is now competitive with Selfridges and Harvey Nicks. Upmarket china, furnishings and gifts are its forte, though it stocks accessories and cosmetics, too. The Top Floor (and that's where it's at) is a restaurant-cafe-bar with stunning views.

LULU GUINNESS
Map pp136-7   Fashion & Designer
☎ 7823 4828; www.luluguiness.com; 3 Ellis St SW1; ☒ 10am-6pm Mon-Fri, from 11am Sat; ⊖ Sloane Sq
Female silhouettes, dice, board games and various other playful insignia grace Lulu Guinness' range of coin purses, cosmetic bags, handbags and totes, while some of her collectable evening bags come in striking shapes, such as fans. Love those feather boas.

RIPPON CHEESE STORES
Map pp136-7   Food & Drink
☎ 7931 0628; www.ripponcheese.com; 26 Upper Tachbrook St SW1; ☒ 8.15am-5.15pm Mon-Fri, 8.30am-5pm Sat; ⊖ Victoria or Pimlico
This is the type of shop we all wish we had in the neighbourhood, a cheesemonger with some 500 varieties of (mostly) English and French cheese on offer and all ripened on site. Staff are knowledgeable and helpful and will allow you to taste before you buy.

ROCOCO CHOCOLATES
Map pp136-7   Food & Drink
☎ 7352 5857; www.rococochocolates.com; 321 King's Rd SW3; ☒ 10am-6.30pm Mon-Sat, noon-5pm Sun; ⊖ Sloane Sq
This *chocolatier* sells the type of real chocolate that comes in glorious moulds and flavours. There are truffles, Swiss chocolates, organic bars, surprising vegan varieties and bags of assorted 'broken chocolate' so you can taste different varieties.

CLERKENWELL, SHOREDITCH & SPITALFIELDS

This is the area for discovering cool boutiques or wandering market stalls for vintage clothes and up-and-coming designers. There are tonnes of shops off Brick Lane, especially burgeoning Cheshire St, Hanwell St and the Old Truman Brewery on Dray Walk. Spitalfields Market (p227) should also not be missed at the weekend for its little designer stalls and quirky shops.

Each December there's a major showcase of the latest products, clothes, jewellery and art at Shoreditch Town Hall; see www.eastlondondesignshow.co.uk.

Nearby Clerkenwell is mostly known for its jewellery. For classic settings and unmounted stones, visit London's traditional jewellery and diamond trade area, **Hatton Garden** (Map p150; www.hatton-garden.net; ⊖ Chancery Lane). **Craft Central** (Map p150; www.craftcentral.org.uk; 33-35 St John's Sq EC1; ⊖ Farringdon) is an excellent starting point for searching out crafts and design items.

MAGMA Map p150   Books
☎ 7242 9503; www.magmabooks.com; 117-119 Clerkenwell Rd EC1; ⊖ Farringdon
This much-loved shop sells books, magazines, T-shirts and almost anything on the design cutting edge. There's a smaller branch in Covent Garden (Map pp70–1; ☎ 7240 8498; 8 Earlham St, ⊖ Covent Garden), which now includes a design sale shop. Great for present shopping.

ANTONI & ALISON Map p150   Fashion & Designer
☎ 7833 2002; www.antoniandalison.co.uk; 43 Rosebery Ave EC1; ☒ 10.30am-6.30pm Mon-Fri; ⊖ Farringdon
The original independent London fashion house, A&A sell quirky tees, mad floral

MARKET FORCES

Shopping at London's markets isn't just about picking up bargains and rummaging through tonnes of knick-knacks, clothes and all sorts of mystical ephemera and earthly accoutrements – although they give you plenty of opportunity to do that. It's also about taking in the character of this vibrant city, in all its many facets and moods.

For information on farmers markets, see p251.

Borough

Here in some form since the 13th century, Borough Market (Map p126; ☎ 7407 1002; www.boroughmarket.org.uk; cnr Borough High & Stoney Sts SE1; ☯ 11am-5pm Thu, noon-6pm Fri, 9am-4pm Sat; ⊖ London Bridge) is testament to the British public's increasing interest in good food. Helped by celebrity shopper Jamie Oliver, 'London's Larder' has enjoyed an enormous renaissance in recent years, overflowing with food lovers. As well as a section devoted to quality fresh fruit, exotic vegetables and organic meat, there's a fine-foods retail market, with products such as home-grown honey and homemade bread. Throughout, takeaway stalls allow you to sample a sizzling gourmet sausage or tuck into a quality burger. Shoppers queue at the excellent Monmouth Coffee Company, Neal's Yard Dairy (p220), the Spanish deli Brindisa or Ginger Pig butcher. Plans for a new railway link threaten to cut the market in two, but the market's trustees claim 'it won't affect the market' (which seems hard to believe). Check the website for updates.

Brixton

This market (Map p190; Reliance Arcade, Market Row, Electric Lane & Electric Ave SW9; ☯ 8am-6pm Mon-Sat, 8am-3pm Wed; ⊖ Brixton) is a heady, cosmopolitan mix, ranging from silks, wigs, knock-off fashion, Halal butchers and the occasional Christian preacher on Electric Ave to the foodstuffs in the covered Brixton Village (formerly Granville Arcade; Map p190). Tilapia fish, pig's trotters, yams, mangoes, okra, plantains and Jamaican *bullah* cakes (gingerbread) are just some of the exotic products on sale.

Camden

Although this market (Map p170; www.camdenlock.net/markets; ⊖ Camden Town) remains a top attraction, its heyday is a distant memory. Commercial tat has long taken over from the truly inventive, although you might find some good retro pieces. The place is busiest at weekends, especially Sunday, when the crowds elbow each other all the way north from Camden Town tube station to Chalk Farm Rd. It's composed of several separate markets, which tend to merge.

Camden Canal Market (Map p166; cnr Chalk Farm & Castlehaven Rds NW1; ☯ 10am-6pm Sat & Sun; ⊖ Chalk Farm or Camden Town) Further north and just over the canal bridge, Camden Canal Market has bric-a-brac from around the world. If you're pushed for time, this is the bit to skip.

Camden Lock Market (Map p170; Camden Lock Pl NW1; ☯ 10am-6pm Sat & Sun, indoor stalls 10am-6pm daily) Right next to the canal lock, with diverse food, ceramics, furniture, oriental rugs, musical instruments and designer clothes.

Camden Market (Map p170; cnr Camden High & Buck Sts NW1; ☯ 9am-5.30pm Thu-Sun) This covered market houses stalls for fashion, clothing, jewellery and tourist tat.

Stables (Map p166; Chalk Farm Rd NW1; ☯ 8am-6pm Sat & Sun; ⊖ Chalk Farm) Just beyond the railway arches, opposite Hartland Rd, the Stables is the best part of the market, with antiques, Asian artefacts, rugs and carpets, pine furniture, and '50s and '60s clothing.

Portobello Road

Perhaps because it's less crowded and littered than Camden, Londoners generally prefer this market (Map p176; Portobello Rd W10; ☯ 8am-6pm Mon-Wed, 9am-1pm Thu, 7am-7pm Fri & Sat, 9am-4pm Sun; ⊖ Notting Hill Gate or Ladbroke Grove). Though shops and stalls open daily, the busiest days are Friday, Saturday and Sunday. There's an antiques market on Saturday, and a flea market on Portobello Green on Sunday morning. Fruit and veg are sold all week at the Ladbroke Grove end, with an organic market on Thursday. Antiques, jewellery, paintings and ethnic stuff are concentrated at the Notting Hill Gate end of Portobello Rd. Stalls move downmarket as you move north. Beneath the Westway a vast tent covers more stalls selling cheap clothes, shoes and CDs, while the Portobello Green Arcade is home to some cutting-edge clothing and jewellery designers.

Spitalfields

This market (Map p150; www.visitspitalfields.com; Commercial St, btwn Brushfield & Lamb Sts E1; 9.30am-5.30pm Sun; Liverpool St) was originally the place to snaffle the latest street wear at good prices, with young fashion designers joined by jewellers, furniture makers and a variety of fresh-produce stalls. Unfortunately, with big businesses wanting a piece of the action, part of the old market was converted into a new restaurant and shopping complex in 2006. The old market still stands, thankfully, and much of the young designer stalls have moved up the road to the Old Truman Brewery's Sunday UpMarket (Map p150; www.sundayupmarket.co.uk; 10am-6pm), basically a Spitalfields extension. The space is a car park during the week, but on Sunday it's filled with excellent clothes, delicious international cuisine, jewellery and music stands.

Other Markets

Bermondsey (Map p126; Bermondsey Sq; 5am-1pm Fri; Borough or Bermondsey) Reputedly, it's legal to sell stolen goods here before dawn, but late risers will find this market altogether upright and sedate, with cutlery and other old-fashioned silverware, antique porcelain, paintings and some costume jewellery.

Berwick Street (Map p66; Berwick St W1; 8am-6pm Mon-Sat; Piccadilly Circus or Oxford Circus) South of Oxford St and parallel to Wardour St, this fruit-and-veg market is a great spot to put together a picnic or shop for a prepared meal.

Brick Lane (Map p150; Brick Lane E2; 8am-1pm Sun; Aldgate East) Goods on sale range from clothes, fruit and vegetables to household goods, paintings and bric-a-brac.

Camden Passage (Map p170; Camden Passage N1; 7am-2pm Wed, 8am-4pm Sat; Angel) Not to be confused with Camden Market, this is a series of four arcades selling antiques and curios, located in Islington, at the junction of Upper St and Essex Rd. Stallholders know their stuff, so bargains are rare. Wednesday is busiest, but it's worth visiting on Sunday for the Islington Farmers Market between 10am and 2pm.

Columbia Road Flower Market (Map p150; Columbia Rd E2; 7am-1pm Sun; Bethnal Green, Cambridge Heath, 26, 48 or 55) London's most fragrant market shouldn't be missed. Merchants lay out their blooms, from everyday geraniums to rare pelargoniums, between Gosset St and the Royal Oak pub.

Covent Garden (Map pp70–1; Covent Garden) The shops in the touristy piazza are open daily, while handicrafts and curios are sold in the North Hall. Don't miss the antiques market in the Jubilee Hall on Monday before 3pm; quality crafts are sold on Saturday and Sunday inside Jubilee Hall.

Greenwich (Map p182; College Approach SE10; 9am-5pm Thu, 9.30am-5.30pm Sat & Sun; DLR Cutty Sark) Greenwich Market is ideally suited for a relaxed few hours' rummaging through its second-hand household objects, glass, rugs, prints and wooden toys. In between, you can snack on speciality foods in the food court. Thursday is the day for antiques, while the general market is open on weekends. Stores around the market open daily, but weekends are best.

Leadenhall Market (Map p100; Whittington Ave EC1; 7am-4pm Mon-Fri; Bank) As well as being a small attraction in its own right (see p108), this market, off Gracechurch St, has clothes stores and curio shops, a fishmonger, a butcher and a cheesemonger. As it serves a City clientele, prices tend to be high.

Leather Lane (Map p150; Leather Lane EC1; 10.30am-2pm Mon-Fri; Chancery Lane or Farringdon) South of Clerkenwell Rd and parallel to Hatton Garden, Leather Lane attracts local office workers with its suspiciously cheap DVDs, tapes and CDs, household goods and clothing sold by archetypal cockney stallholders.

Petticoat Lane (Map p100; Middlesex & Wentworth Sts E1; 8am-2pm Sun, Wentworth St only 9am-2pm Mon-Fri; Aldgate, Aldgate East or Liverpool St) The famous lane itself has been renamed Middlesex St. The market, however, soldiers on, selling cheap consumer items and clothes.

Ridley Road (Map p156; Ridley Rd E8; 8.30am-6pm Mon-Sat; Dalston Kingsland) Massively enjoyed by the Afro-Caribbean community it serves, this market is best for its exotic fruit and vegetables, as well as specialist cuts of meat.

Riverside Walk (Map p126; Riverside Walk SE1; 10am-5pm Sat & Sun; Waterloo or Embankment) Great for cheap second-hand books long out of print, this is held in all weather outside the National Film Theatre, under the arches of Waterloo Bridge. In summer it helps the South Bank vaguely resemble Paris' Left Bank. Occasionally, individual dealers set up during the week.

Smithfield (Map p100; West Smithfield EC1; 4am-noon Mon-Fri; Farringdon) London's last surviving meat market is still clinging on, despite nearly getting the chop for an office development in 2005. While cattle were slaughtered here once, today this is the most modern market of its kind in Europe. Note, this is a wholesale market only.

skirts, gorgeous leather purses and funky cashmere knits among other gorgeous little things in its Rosebery Ave shop. Look out for its brilliant sales.

BREAD & HONEY Map p150 Fashion & Designer
☎ 7253 4455; www.breadnhoney.com; 205 Whitecross St; ☽ 10am-6pm Mon-Sat; ⊖ Barbican
This unexpectedly located slice of retail heaven on up-and-coming Whitecross St is a great place to buy fun, bright yet accessible clothing selected by the two French owners, Laurent and Laurent. Here you'll find a selection of mens- and womenswear from Modern Amusement, Stüssy and Lee, among others.

HOXTON BOUTIQUE
Map p150 Fashion & Designer
☎ 7684 2083; www.hoxtonboutique.co.uk; 2 Hoxton St; ☽ 10.30am-6.30pm Mon-Fri, 11am-6pm Sat; ⊖ Old St
If you want to look like a true Hoxtonite, come here for your (women's) street wear – there's Isabel Marant, Hussein Chalayan, Repetto shoes and the shop's own brand, +HOBO+. The boutique is meant to resemble Studio 54, with a mirror ball, white walls and neon lights.

JUNKY STYLING Map p150 Fashion & Designer
☎ 7247 1883; www.junkystyling.co.uk; 12 Dray Walk, Old Truman Brewery, 91 Brick Lane E1; ☽ 11am-5.30pm Mon-Fri, 10.30am-6pm Sat & Sun; ⊖ Liverpool St or Aldgate East
On retail-friendly Dray Walk, Junky 'recycles' traditional suits into sleek, eye-catching fashion pieces. A man's jacket might become a woman's halterneck top, for example, or tiny shorts with heart-shaped hot-water bottles for back pockets. Menswear includes short-sleeved half-shirts/half–T-shirts, and jackets with sweatsuit-material sleeves and suit-material hoods. Bring your own clothes to be transformed.

LADEN SHOWROOMS
Map p150 Fashion & Designer
☎ 7247 2431; www.laden.co.uk; 103 Brick Lane E1; ☽ 11am-6.30pm Mon-Fri, to 7pm Sat, 10.30am-6pm Sun; ⊖ Liverpool St or Aldgate East
The unofficial flagship for the latest Hoxton street wear, Laden was once 'London's best-kept secret', though a slew of celebrity endorsements have made the showrooms' reputation soar and the 55 independent

designers it stocks much in demand. A perfect one-stop shop for both womenswear and menswear.

NO-ONE Map p150 Fashion & Designer
☎ 7613 5314; www.no-one.co.uk; 1 Kingsland Rd E2; ☽ 11am-7pm Mon-Sat, noon-6pm Sun; ⊖ Old St or Liverpool St
This boutique, brought to you by the same people as hip nearby drinkery Dreambags-jaguarshoes (p282) can be found inside the Old Shoreditch station bar. It's all ultrahip, with fashion magazines, quirky accessories and shoes, and stocks Eley Kishimoto, Peter Jensen and new labels for women and men.

START Map p150 Fashion & Designer
☎ 7739 3636; www.start-london.com; 42-44 Rivington St; ☽ 10.30am-6.30pm Mon-Fri, 11am-6pm Sat, 1-5pm Sun; ⊖ Liverpool St or Old St
'Where fashion meets rock n roll' is the appropriate tagline to this group of three boutiques brought to you by former Fall guitarist Brix Smith, a cult rocker who loves girly clothes. Designer labels such as Miu Miu and Helmut Lang dominate and Smith prides herself on her selection of flattering jeans. A similarly excellent store, Start Menswear (Map p150; 59 Rivington St), is over the road, and there is a third location, Start Made to Measure (Map p150; 40 Rivington St), showcasing formal wear.

LESLEY CRAZE GALLERY
Map p150 Jewellery & Accessories
☎ 7608 0393; www.lesleycrazegallery.co.uk; 33-35a Clerkenwell Green EC1; ☽ 10am-5.30pm Tue-Sat; ⊖ Farringdon
Considered one of Europe's leading centres for arty, contemporary jewellery, this gallery has exquisitely understated, and sometimes pricey, metal designs. There's also a smaller selection of mixed-media bangles, brooches, rings and the like (to the right of the main door), where prices start from about £20.

TATTY DEVINE Map p150 Jewellery & Accessories
☎ 7739 9191; www.tattydevine.com; 236 Brick Lane E2; ☽ 11am-6pm Tue-Sun; ⊖ Liverpool St
Duo Harriet Vine and Rosie Wolfenden make hip and witty jewellery that's become the favourite of many young Londoners. Their original designs feature record earrings and plectrum bracelets (that high-street stores have ripped off since), pea

necklaces, knitted stilettos, and key rings that look like crinkle-cut crisps. Perspex name necklaces (made to order; £25) are also a treat. There's a Soho shop (Map p66; 57b Brewer St W1; ⊖ Piccadilly Circus).

THE EAST END & DOCKLANDS

Shopping options are limited in the East End but the Burberry and Carhartt connections ensure a steady flow, while the boutiques and galleries lining Columbia Rd E2 (Map p156; www.columbiaroad.info; 🚇 Cambridge Heath, 🚌 8 or 55), which are usually open at the weekend only, and, to a lesser extent, the shops along Broadway Market (Map p156; www.broadwaymarket.co.uk; 🚇 London Fields or Cambridge Heath, 🚌 48, 55, 106 or 394) in Hackney are among London's up-and-coming retail scenes. There's a massive underground shopping mall beneath the skyscrapers around Canary Wharf, with upmarket shops, bars and restaurants.

BURBERRY FACTORY SHOP
Map p156   Fashion & Designer
☎ 8328 4287; 29-53 Chatham Pl E9; ⏰ 10am-6pm Mon- Sat, 11am-5pm Sun; ⊖ Bethnal Green then 🚌 106 or 256, 🚇 Hackney Central
This warehouse stocks seconds and samples from the reborn-as-trendy Brit brand's current collection or stuff from last season. Prices can be up to 50% to 70% lower than those on the high street, with the best deals on accessories, especially scarves.

CARHARTT Map p156   Fashion & Designer
☎ 8986 8875; www.thecarharttstore.co.uk; 18 Ellingfort Rd E8; ⏰ 11am-6pm Tue-Sat, noon-5pm Sun; 🚇 London Fields or Hackney Central
You'll find hoodies, sweats and jeans at this outlet of the street wear label of the moment under the railway arches just north of London Fields station. Prices start as low as £5. Album launches and other events take place here; check the website.

FABRICATIONS Map p156   Homewares
☎ 7275 8043; www.fabrications1.co.uk; 7 Broadway Market E8; ⏰ noon-5pm Tue-Fri, 10am-5.30pm Sat; 🚇 London Fields or Cambridge Heath, 🚌 48, 55, 106 or 394
This shop does a lot for the recycling cause, making mostly soft furnishings for the

home such as cushions, rugs and mats from unusual and unexpected material, from bicycle tyre tubes to used ribbon.

LABOUR & WAIT Map p156   Homewares
☎ 7729 6253; www.labourandwait.co.uk; 18 Cheshire St E2; ⏰ 11am-5pm Wed & Fri, 1-5pm Sat, 10am-5pm Sun; ⊖ Liverpool St or Aldgate East
Dedicated to simple and functional yet scrumptiously stylish traditional British homewares, Labour & Wait specialises in items by independent manufacturers who make their products the old-fashioned way. There are school tumblers, enamel coffee pots, luxurious lambswool blankets, elegant ostrich-feather dusters and gardening tools. Note the limited opening hours.

NORTH LONDON

Shopping in Camden is more about cheap, disposable fashion and made-for-tourist trinkets at the huge market (see the boxed text, p226), although you might occasionally be tempted to pop into one of the many clothes boutiques lining the high street.

Islington is a great area for independent shops, particularly around Camden Passage for vintage clothing and Upper St for household goods and designers. Nearby King's Cross is being regenerated and the chains are beginning to move in, but icons of independence, such as Housmans, are standing their ground.

HOUSMANS Map p170   Books
☎ 7837 4473; www.housmans.com; 5 Caledonian Rd N1; ⊖ King's Cross/St Pancras
This long-standing radical bookshop, where you'll find books unavailable on the shelves of the more mainstream stockists, is a good place to keep up to date with all sorts of political and social campaigns, and with your more radical reads. The forthcoming owner is a mine of local information.

ROSSLYN DELICATESSEN
Map p166   Food & Drink
☎ 7794 9210; www.delirosslyn.co.uk; 56 Rosslyn Hill NW3; ⏰ 8.30am-8.30pm Mon-Sat, to 8pm Sun; ⊖ Hampstead or Belsize Park
Helen Sherman's enchanting store has been voted the best local delicatessen in London several times, and rightly so. There is a fantastic meat counter, with the most aromatic pancetta you'll ever try; the jarred chutneys, terrines and marinated

vegetables are a wonder; and you'll find unusual flavours such as damson jam and mulberry salad dressing. The cakes, chocolates and Union Roasters coffee are delicious, too.

PAST CARING Map p170 Homewares
76 Essex Rd N1; ⊗ **noon-6pm Mon-Sat;** ⊖ **Angel**
Stuffed full of second-hand retro bric-a-brac from ashtrays and 1970s LPs to mannequins and loud china, this wonderful shop is so removed from the modern world that it doesn't even have a phone number.

GILL WING
Map p170 Kitchenware, Shoes, Gifts & Souvenirs
☎ **7226 8012; www.gillwing.co.uk; 190 Upper St N1;** ⊗ **10am-6pm;** ⊖ **Highbury & Islington**
Gill Wing's wonderfully individual boutiques have colonised this strip of Upper St – her shoe shop is much loved, the gift shop is full of amusing and garishly designed presents, but the real favourite is her stylish cook shop that has launched the dreams of many an aspirant Islington homemaker.

SAMPLER Map p170 Wine
☎ **7226 9500; www.thesampler.co.uk; 266 Upper St N1;** ⊗ **11.30am-9pm Mon-Sat, 1-8pm Sun;** ⊖ **Highbury & Islington**
One of London's leading wine shops, this brilliant place allows you to sample 80 different wines before buying. Just load up a smart card and use it to sample from the machines – from as little as 30p for a sample up to £20 for a good vintage wine. Staff are friendly and knowledgeable.

WEST LONDON

Portobello Rd has to be a priority for any market lover, with its wall-to-wall antique stores, funky fashion stores, knick-knack shops and weekend market (see boxed text, p236). Moneyed Notting Hill and Westbourne Grove have the best (and priciest) boutiques and designer shops.

Otherwise, shopping in the west is definitely not wild. Try Shepherd's Bush Market (Map p178; ⊗ 9.30am-5pm Mon-Wed, Fri & Sat, to 1pm Thu), stretching underneath the Hammersmith & City line between Goldhawk Rd and Shepherd's Bush tube stations. Troubadour Wines (Map p178; ☎ 7341 6341; www.troubadour.co.uk; 265 Old

Brompton Rd SW5; ⊖ Earl's Court), next to the cafe-bar-eatery of the same name, is an excellent source for wine.

AL SAQI Map p176 Books
☎ **7229 8543; www.alsaqibookshop.com; 26 Westbourne Grove W2;** ⊖ **Bayswater**
Located in a beautiful building topped with a dozen busts, this shop specialises in books in English about the Arab world and Islam, including the full catalogue of books it publishes itself.

BOOKS FOR COOKS Map p176 Books
☎ **7221 1992; www.booksforcooks.com; 4 Blenheim Cres W11;** ⊗ **10am-6pm Tue-Sat;** ⊖ **Ladbroke Grove**
All the recipe books from celeb and non-celeb chefs you can imagine are sold here. Perfect for some of the more adventurous cooks among you, or those looking for 'exotic' cookbooks. The cafe has a test kitchen where you can sample recipes at lunch and teatime.

TRAVEL BOOKSHOP Map p176 Books
☎ **7229 5260; www.thetravelbookshop.co.uk; 13 Blenheim Cres W11;** ⊗ **10am-6pm Mon-Sat, noon-5pm Sun;** ⊖ **Ladbroke Grove**
Still known as the bookshop on which Hugh Grant's was modelled in the movie *Notting Hill,* this is crammed with new guidebooks, travel literature and fiction, as well as second-hand and antiquarian books.

SHARPEYE Map p176 Fashion & Designer
☎ **7221 3898; www.sharpeye.uk.com; 15 Portobello Rd W11;** ⊗ **11am-6pm Mon-Fri, 10am-6.30pm Sat, noon-5pm;** ⊖ **Notting Hill Gate**
For durable men's street wear check out Barrie K Sharpe's collection of loose trousers, tees, shorts and boots with their 'inna city' ethos. Lasts a lifetime this stuff.

SPICE SHOP Map p176 Food & Drink
☎ **7221 4448; www.thespiceshop.co.uk; 1 Blenheim Cres W11;** ⊗ **9.30am-6pm Mon-Sat, 11am-3pm Sun;** ⊖ **Ladbroke Grove**
Can't find that Turkish sumac, Sichuan peppercorn or African ajowan that recipe you're following so desperately calls for? The Spice Shop just off Portobello Rd will have it – along with hundreds more herbs, spices and essential oils.

CERAMICA BLUE Map p176 Homewares

☎ 7727 0288; www.ceramicablue.co.uk;
10 Blenheim Cres W11; ⏰ 10am-6.30pm Mon-Sat,
noon-5pm Sun; ⊖ Ladbroke Grove

A wonderful place for original and beautiful crockery, imported from more than a dozen countries: there's Japanese eggshell-glaze teacups, serving plates with tribal South African designs and much more.

GREENWICH & SOUTHEAST LONDON

Greenwich is paradise for lovers of retro clothes stores and second-hand bookshops, which seem to surface every few steps. The vintage clothes shops are cheaper than those in the West End, and there are some retro household shops and general gift shops around DLR Cutty Sark.

EMPORIUM Map p182 Fashion & Designer

☎ 8305 1670; 330-332 Creek Rd SE10;
⏰ 10.30am-6pm Wed-Sun; DLR Cutty Sark

Each piece is individual at this lovely vintage shop (unisex), where glass cabinets are crammed with costume jewellery, old perfume bottles and straw hats, while gorgeous jackets and blazers intermingle on the clothes racks.

ARTY GLOBE Map p182 Gifts & Souvenirs

☎ 0793 912 0686; www.artyglobe.com; 2a
Greenwich Market; ⏰ 11am-6pm; DLR Cutty Sark

The unique fisheye-view drawings of various areas of London (and other cities, including New York, Paris and Berlin) by architect Hartwig Braun are works of art and appear on the shopping bags, placemats, notebooks, coasters, mugs and jigsaws available in this tiny shop. They make excellent gifts.

COMPENDIA Map p182 Gifts & Souvenirs

☎ 8293 6616; www.compendia.co.uk;
10 Greenwich Market; ⏰ 11am-5.30pm Mon-Fri,
from 10am Sat & Sun; DLR Cutty Sark

Compendia's owners are madly enthusiastic about games – board or any other kind – and they'll look for the rarest of things if you ask them to. The shop is excellent for gifts you can enjoy with your mates – backgammon, chess, Scrabble, solitaire and rarities such as Mexican Train Domino, which claims to be the world's fastest game.

ROULLIER WHITE

Map p62 Homewares, Gifts & Souvenirs

☎ 8693 5150; www.roullierwhite.com;
125 Lordship Lane SE22; ⏰ 10am-6pm Mon-Sat,
11am-5pm Sun; ☒ West Dulwich, 🚌 40 or 176

Back-to-basics shop with wooden floors and Victorian-style display cabinets flogging hard-to-find household products and gift items from often long-forgotten manufacturers (slippers, glassware, towelling, cleaning products). Worth the trip.

SOUTH LONDON

Brixton Market (see the boxed text, p226) is the best place for shopping in South London, though the area has some interesting shops such as Joy (Map p190; ☎ 7787 9616; 432 Coldharbour Lane SW11; ⏰ 10am-7.30pm Mon-Sat, 11am-7pm Sun; ⊖ Brixton), where you can pick up quirky accessories.

In Clapham there are several worthwhile stores near the common, including gift shop Oliver Bonas (Map p190; ☎ 7720 8272; www.oliverbonas .com; 23 The Pavement SW4; ⊖ Clapham Common) and shoe store Bullfrogs (Map p190; ☎ 7627 4123; 9 The Pavement SW4; ⊖ Clapham Common).

Northcote Rd in Wandsworth offers some quality food shopping.

SOUTHWEST LONDON

Fulham and Parson's Green are pretty uninspiring when it comes to shopping, but you can find a few designer furniture and fabric shops, one of the best being Mufti (☎ 7610 9123; 789 Fulham Rd SW6; ⊖ Parson's Green); for antiques head to the northern end of Munster Rd. North End Road Market (⏰ 9am-5pm Mon-Sat; ⊖ Fulham Broadway or West Brompton) is great for fresh fruit and veg, cheap clothing and household goods.

Overgentrified Putney is full of grim chains. Instead, head to Church Rd and High St in Barnes, both of which are lined with interesting shops such as Blue Door (☎ 8748 9785; www.bluedoor barnes.co.uk; 74 Church Rd; ☒ Barnes), with gorgeous Swedish and French home furnishings. Anyone wishing to indulge their ankle-biters could try children's toy shops Farmyard (☎ 8878 7338; www .thefarmyard.co.uk; 63 Barnes High St; ⏰ 9.30am-5.30pm Mon-Sat; ☒ Barnes) and Bug Circus (☎ 8741 4244; 153 Church Rd; ⏰ 9.30am-5.30pm Mon-Sat; ☒ Barnes).

Richmond High St is full of chains, but there are some independent stores around. There's YDUK (Map p200; ☎ 8940 0060; 4 The Square

ON THE HIGH STREET

Overseas retailers, such as Diesel, Gap, H&M, Mango, Muji and Zara, abound in London. The UK also has many home-grown clothing and shoe chains, some of which are listed following. Most stores are open from 10am to 8pm Monday to Wednesday, from 10am to 9pm from Thursday to Saturday and from noon to 7pm on Sunday.

French Connection UK (Map p90; ☎ 7629 7766; 396 Oxford St W1; ⊖ Bond St) This chain's clothes are more sober than the FCUK sobriquet suggests, though its advertising's always risqué.

Jigsaw (Map p90; ☎ 7491 4484; 126-127 New Bond St W1; ⊖ Bond St) Classic women's clothes, with an emphasis on tweeds and knits, plus some chiffon and glitter.

Joseph (Map pp136–7; ☎ 7823 9500; 77 Fulham Rd SW3; ⊖ South Kensington) Show them who wears the trousers, with classically smart pants and pants suits, plus a whole range of other fashion.

Karen Millen (Map pp70–1; ☎ 7836 5355; 32-33 James St WC2; ⊖ Covent Garden) An upmarket womenswear store, with glam suit-trousers, voluptuous knits, shiny trench coats and evening frocks.

Marks & Spencer (Map p90; ☎ 7935 7954; www.marksandspencer.co.uk; 458 Oxford St W1; ⊖ Bond St) Rising from the years of being synonymous with 'quality knickers' M&S has pulled its socks up with some fabulous fashion lines.

Miss Selfridge (Map p90; ☎ 7927 0188; 325 Oxford St W1; ⊖ Oxford Circus or Bond St) Fun, throwaway fashion (but is it ethical?) for female teens.

Oasis (Map pp70–1; ☎ 7240 7445; 13 James St WC2; ⊖ Covent Garden) Good catwalk rip-offs that are sure to keep you in fashion.

Office (Map pp70–1; ☎ 7379 1896; 57 Neal St WC2; ⊖ Covent Garden) Shoes that go the distance from work to after-hours drinks.

Reiss (Map p66; ☎ 7637 9111; www.reiss.co.uk; 14-17 Market Pl W1; ⊖ Oxford Circus) Its sales are constantly rising, as are its prices, and Reiss is now synonymous with quality on the high street. Men's and women's street fashion is given a mature edge with quality materials and precise tailoring.

Warehouse (Map pp70–1; ☎ 7240 8242; 24 Long Acre WC2; ⊖ Covent Garden or Leicester Sq) Somewhere between Topshop and Oasis in the fashion stakes.

TW9; ⊖ Richmond) for street wear. In an enclave of cobbled streets you'll find jewellery stores such as Toko (Map p200; ☎ 8332 6620; 18 Brewers Lane TW9; ⊖ Richmond).

In Chiswick don't miss the fantastic Mortimer & Bennett (☎ 8995 4145; www.mortimerandbennett.co.uk; 33 Turnham Green Tce W4; ☽ 8.30am-6pm Mon-Fri, 8.30am-5.30pm Sat; ⊖ Turnham Green) deli, or Sunday's Chiswick Farmers & Fine Foods Market (Masonian Bowls Hall, Duke's Meadow W4; ☽ 10am-2pm Sun; ⊖ Turnham Green). Antiques are also a local speciality; try Strand Antiques (☎ 8994 1912; 46 Devonshire Rd W4; ⊖ Turnham Green) or the Old Cinema (☎ 8995 4166; 160 Chiswick High Rd W4; ⊖ Turnham Green).

top picks

- Bocca di Lupo (p236)
- Giaconda Dining Room (p239)
- Tayyabs p255
- Pearl Liang (p263)
- Lucio (p249)
- Modern Pantry (p252)
- Café Spice Namaste (p255)
- El Faro (p257)
- Roussillon (p250)
- Fish House (p257)
- Ottolenghi (p261)
- Afghan Kitchen (p262)
- Franco Manca (p267)

London is the undisputed culinary capital of the UK and, in terms of the types of cuisines on offer, just about the best place in Europe for dining out. No matter what you fancy eating, there's bound to be a restaurant serving it here.

Yes, things have improved remarkably over the past couple of decades, and the traditional view of dining in the UK – greasy fried breakfasts, rancid-smelling fish and chips and wrestling with a chop on gingham tablecloth – is now well and truly out of date. Indeed, London has caught up with and, in many respects, overtaken its European cousins.

So what exactly happened? At some point the purveyors of stodge were lined up against the wall, stripped of their aprons and replaced by a savvy new generation of chefs (eg Gordon Ramsay, Gary Rhodes, Heston Blumenthal, Jamie Oliver). As trailblazing restaurants progressively raised the bar, the competition followed. Markets selling fresh, free-range, organic produce sprang up, staff were drilled into professional service and the designers were brought in to create some of the world's coolest and most aesthetically pleasing eating spaces. As a result, food in all its guises became the new sex, and everyone wanted a piece of the action.

That's not to say you can't still get greasy fries, overcooked vegetables and traditional British stodge (particularly in pubs, although it's less common there, too, since the 1990s trend to 'gastropubs'), but with chefs absorbing the influences of this most cosmopolitan of cultures, you're more likely to get the world on your plate.

But don't expect value for money. We can't count the number of times we've dropped more than £40 a head for refined Italian food or the ubiquitous Modern European that tasted like the last such meal we'd had and wondered why we hadn't just cooked a pasta at home. On the other hand we've had Pakistani food in Whitechapel, Turkish in Dalston and Chinese in the Docklands that has made our hearts sing, our tastebuds zing and our wallets only slightly lighter.

Eating out in London can be a real hit-or-miss affair. What we've done in this chapter is separate the wheat from the chaff. The restaurants and other eateries reviewed here range from pretty good (convenient location, cheap price, unusual cuisine) to fantabulous (worth a big splurge or a lengthy journey). Hopefully this list will lead you in the right direction and you won't walk out wondering why *you* bothered.

HISTORY & SPECIALITIES

London is the capital of a country that gave the world beans on toast, mushy peas and chip butties (French fries between two slices of buttered – and untoasted – white bread). But that's hardly the whole story. When well prepared – be it a Sunday lunch of roast beef and Yorkshire pudding (light batter baked until fluffy and eaten with gravy) or a cornet of lightly battered fish and chips eaten on the hoof – English food can have its moments. And with the emergence of the Modern British style of cooking, it is becoming a 'cuisine'.

Pubs generally serve low-cost traditional dishes of varying quality such as filled pastry – pork pies, Cornish pasties and steak-and-kidney pie. (Shepherd's pie, on the other hand, has no crust but is a baked dish of minced lamb and onions topped with mashed potatoes.) On a pub menu you'll also usually find bangers and mash (sausages served with mashed potatoes and gravy), sausage rolls and ploughman's lunch (thick slices of bread served with Cheddar or Cheshire cheese, chutney and pickled onions). The catalogue of calorific desserts includes bread-and-butter pudding, steamed pudding (a cake that contains beef suet, a key ingredient) served with treacle (molasses) or jam, and the alarmingly named spotted dick, a steamed suet pudding with currants and raisins.

The most English of dishes, though, is fish and chips: cod, plaice or haddock dipped in batter, deep-fried and served with chips (French fries) doused in vinegar and sprinkled with salt. With the arrival of American-style fast-food joints, authentic 'chippies' (fish-and-chip shops) are becoming rarer, but there are still a number of decent ones sprinkled around town.

From the middle of the 19th century until just after WWII the staple lunch for many Londoners was a pie filled with spiced eel (then abundant in the Thames) and served with mashed potatoes and liquor (a parsley sauce). Nowadays the pies are usually meat-filled and the eel served smoked or jellied as a side dish. The best places to try this are the pie 'n' mash shops listed in the boxed text, p254.

London's newest favourite, Modern British cuisine, is a lot more than 'staples like bangers and mash with the grease removed', as one philistine described it. Modern British food includes traditional ingredients such as root vegetables, smoked fish, shellfish, game and other meats, and even things like sausages and black pudding (a kind of sausage stuffed with oatmeal, spices and blood), and combines them in ways that accentuate their flavour. Dishes can be anything from game served with a traditional vegetable such as Jerusalem artichoke, or smoked Norfolk eel with little buckwheat pancakes, to seared scallops with orange-scented black pudding and roast pork with chorizo on rosemary mash.

VEGETARIANS & VEGANS

London has been one of the best places for vegetarians to dine out since the 1970s. That's mostly due to its many Indian restaurants, which always cater for people who don't eat meat for religious reasons. Most places offer at least a couple of dishes for those who don't eat meat (where there's a decent selection, it's noted in the reviews) but there are also up to a dozen dedicated vegetarian eateries. For dedicated vegetarian eateries, try Blah Blah Blah (p266), Blue Légume (p262), Eat & Two Veg (p244), Gate (p266), Manna (p258), Mildred's (p237), the Place Below (p245), Rasa (p262), Red Veg (p238) and Woodlands (p260).

PRACTICALITIES
Opening Hours
Londoners tend to eat their evening meal early by European (but not American) standards, generally between 7pm and 9.30pm. Most places serve lunch between noon and 2.30pm or 3pm and dinner from 6pm or 7pm to 11pm (last orders 10pm); many midrange restaurants stay open throughout the day. Hours can change from one neighbourhood to the next – for example, many restaurants in Soho close on Sunday, and those in the City close for the whole weekend. We've noted which venues stray from the standard, but it's always safest to call and check first.

How Much?
Eating out in London is outlandishly expensive compared with the USA, most of the rest of Europe and Australia. Go to a top-end restaurant, order three courses à la carte and wash it down with a decent European red, and a couple will be lucky to get much change out of £200. Then again, you can have an excellent meal for less than half that at the same place, if you arrive at times when set meals are offered (at lunch, pre-theatre sitting etc). If you choose carefully, it is possible to have a meal with wine that you both remember fondly for £40 per person. In this guide the range of prices for main courses is included after the establishment's address.

Booking Tables
Making reservations is virtually compulsory for restaurants in central London from Thursday to Saturday, and for the trendiest places at all times. A good internet booking service is Top-table (www.toptable.co.uk), which is reliable and offers substantial discounts on selected restaurants. Many of the top-end restaurants run the annoying system of multiple sittings, where you have the option of an early or late slot, for example 7pm to 9pm or 9pm to 11pm. It's always best to go for the latter and not be rushed.

Tipping
Most restaurants now automatically tack a 'recommended' or 'discretionary' service charge (usually 12.5%) onto the bill and this should be clearly advertised (you don't have to pay it if you feel service wasn't good enough). If they *still* leave space for a tip on the credit-card slip, just ignore it.

Self-Catering
If you're keen to self-cater, you'll find lots of great food at various markets (p259) and farmers markets (p251), Continental delis, and ethnic and organic stores sprinkled all over town. You can find mini versions of the big supermarkets (Tesco, Sainsbury, Waitrose) across the city for basic shopping requirements.

PRICE GUIDE

The symbols below indicate the average cost per main course at the restaurant in question.

£££	more than £20
££	£10-20
£	less than £10

THE WEST END

With neighbourhoods as diverse as Soho, Mayfair, Bloomsbury and Marylebone, the West End is a difficult area to encapsulate, but it's true: many of the city's most eclectic, fashionable and, quite simply, best restaurants are dotted around this area. As with most things in London, it pays to be in the know: while there's a huge concentration of mediocre places to eat along the main tourist drags, the best eating experiences are frequently tucked away on backstreets and not at all obvious. You'll find everything here, from Hungarian to Korean and from *haute cuisine* to vegetarian cafes. Chinatown, as you might guess, is a great spot for inexpensive Chinese and other Asian food.

SOHO & CHINATOWN

LA TROUVAILLE Map p66   French £££
☎ 7287 8488; www.latrouvaille.co.uk; 12a Newburgh St W1; 2-/3-course set lunch £17/20, dinner £30/35; ⊠ closed Sun; ⊖ Oxford Circus
Just what its name suggests it is, the 'Find' is perfect for a romantic dinner. Here you'll find a gorgeous, warm space perfect for candlelit canoodling and an excellent menu of rich traditional French cuisine – quail and foie gras terrine, guinea fowl hotpot – on a quiet backstreet.

BAR SHU Map p66   Chinese ££
7287 8822; www.bar-shu.co.uk; 28 Frith St W1; mains £8-28; ⊖ Leicester Sq
The story goes that a visiting businessman from Chengdu, capital of Sichuan Province in China, found London's Chinese food offerings so inauthentic that he decided to open up his own restaurant with five chefs from home. Well, it's authentic all right, with dishes redolent of smoked chillies and the all-important Sichuan peppercorn. We love the spicy *gung bao* chicken with peanuts and the *mapo doufu* (bean curd braised with minced pork and chilli).

VEERASWAMY Map p66   Indian ££
☎ 7734 1401; www.veeraswamy.com; 1st fl, 99 Regent St (enter from Swallow St) W1; mains £10-20; ⊖ Piccadilly Circus
Having opened in 1926, this upmarket curry house can lay claim to being the oldest Indian restaurant in Britain. It's now owned by the same people who run Masala

Zone (p261) and the standards are as high as ever, with the kitchen producing such crowd-pleasers as slow-cooked Hyderabad lamb biryani and Keralan-style sea bass.

ARBUTUS Map p66   Modern European ££
☎ 7734 4545; www.arbutusrestaurant.co.uk; 63-64 Frith St W1; mains £14-19; ⊖ Tottenham Court Rd
This Michelin-starred brainchild of Anthony Demetre does great British food, focuses on seasonal produce and just keeps on getting better. Try inventive dishes such as squid and mackerel 'burger', slow-cooked lamb, sweetbreads and artichokes, and don't miss the bargain £15.50 for a three-course lunch or £17.50 for a three-course pre- and post-theatre dinner. Booking in advance is essential.

BOCCA DI LUPO Map p66   Italian ££
☎ 7734 2223; www.boccadilupo.com; 12 Archer St W1; mains £8.50-17.50; ⊖ Piccadilly Circus
A new Italian restaurant that has sent ecstatic tremors down Londoners' tastebuds, Bocca di Lupo hides on a dark Soho backstreet and radiates elegant sophistication. The menu has dishes such as the *cacciucco* (fish and shellfish stew with spicy tomato), grilled lemony langoustines or pasta with chicken liver ragout, or you can go for the more straightforward grilled swordfish or parmigiana. Enjoy with an array of Italian wines and fantastic desserts.

GAY HUSSAR Map p66   Hungarian ££
☎ 7437 0973; www.gayhussar.co.uk; 2 Greek St W1; mains £10-17; ⊠ closed Sun; ⊖ Tottenham Court Rd
This is the Soho of the 1950s, when dining was still done in the grand style in wood-panelled rooms with brocade and sepia prints on the walls. And it serves portions only the Hungarians do: try the roast duck leg with all the trimmings or the 'Gypsy quick dish' of pork medallions, onions and green peppers. A two-/three-course lunch is £17/19.50.

ANDREW EDMUNDS
Map p66   Modern European ££
☎ 7437 5708; 46 Lexington St W1; mains £9-18; ⊖ Piccadilly
This cosy little place is exactly the sort of restaurant you wish you could find everywhere in Soho. Two floors of wood-panelled bohemia with a mouth-watering menu of

Soho Cafes

Soho presents the nearest thing London has to a sophisticated cafe culture to match that of its Continental neighbours. The area has been synonymous with sipping and schmoozing since Victorian times, but its heyday came with the mod hangouts of the '60s.

Bar Italia (Map p66; ☎ 7437 4520; 22 Frith St W1; sandwiches £4-7; ☼ 24hr; ✈ Leicester Sq or Tottenham Court Rd) Pop into this Soho favourite at any time of day or night and you'll see slumming celebrities lapping up reviving juices and chunky sandwiches amid retro '50s decor.

Maison Bertaux (Map p66; ☎ 7437 6007; 28 Greek St W1; cakes £3-3.50; ☼ 8.30am-10.30pm Mon-Sat, to 8pm Sun; ✈ Tottenham Court Rd) Bertaux has exquisite confections, unhurried service, a French bohemian vibe and 130 years of history on this spot. Seating is limited to a half-dozen tables.

Monmouth Coffee Company (Map pp70–1; ☎ 7836 5272, 7379 3516; www.monmouthcoffee.co.uk; 27 Monmouth St WC2; cakes from £2.50; ☼ 8am-6.30pm Mon-Sat; ✈ Tottenham Court Rd or Leicester Sq) Essentially a shop selling beans from just about every coffee-growing country in the world, Monmouth has a few wooden alcoves at the back where you can squeeze in and savour blends from around the world.

Star Café (Map p66; ☎ 7437 8778; www.thestarcafe.co.uk; 22 Great Chapel St W1; mains £6-9; ☼ 7am-4pm Mon-Fri; ✈ Tottenham Court Rd) So Soho, this wonderfully atmospheric cafe has vintage advertising and Continental decor that makes it feel like not much has changed since it opened in 1933. It's best known for its breakfast, particularly the curiously named Tim Mellor Special of smoked salmon and scrambled eggs.

French (confit of duck) and European (penne with goat's cheese) country cooking – it's a real find and reservations are essential.

YAUATCHA Map p66   Dim Sum ££
☎ 7494 8888; 15 Broadwick St W1; dim sum £3.80-15.90; ✈ Oxford Circus

This most glamorous of dim sum restaurants housed in the award-winning Ingeni building is divided into two parts. The upstairs tearoom offers an exquisite blue-bathed oasis of calm from the chaos of Berwick St Market as well as some of the most arrestingly beautiful cakes we've ever seen. The downstairs dining room has a smarter, more atmospheric feel with constellations of 'star' lights and an original offering of the three main categories of dim sum (steamed, fried and *cheung fun* – long, flat rice-flour rolls stuffed with meat, seafood or vegetables) all day.

MILDRED'S Map p66   Vegetarian £
☎ 7494 1634; www.mildreds.co.uk; 45 Lexington St W1; mains £7-9; ☼ closed Sun; ✈ Oxford Circus

Central London's most inventive veggie restaurant, Mildred's heaves at lunchtime so don't be shy about sharing a table in the sky-lit dining room. Expect the likes of roasted fennel and chickpea terrine and puy lentil casserole as well as more standard (and hugely portioned) salads and stir-fries. Drinks include juices, coffee, beer and organic wine.

PRINCI Map p66   Italian £
☎ 7478 8888; www.princi.co.uk; 135 Wardour St W1; mains £6-9; ☼ 7am-midnight Mon-Fri; ✈ Oxford Circus

Princi is a love child of Alan Yau (who's behind Wagamama, Busaba Eathai, Hakkasan and Yauatcha) and Italian Rocco Princi, owner of a similar venue in Milan. The two men have teamed up to create good quality, simple Italian fast food, presented elegantly and sold at reasonable prices. They've succeeded in all their attempts (though the hot food counter is better than their bakery) – try the bean soup, the huge lasagna, the pesto gnocchi and the good parmigiana. The salad counter has seasonal offerings, and the cakes are delicious. Princi is invariably busy thanks to its heavenly opening hours, so expect to queue and lurk around for a seat, but we're grateful for a quality pit stop that's quickly turning into the city's favourite.

FERNANDEZ & WELLS
Map p66   European, Spanish £
☎ 7734 1546; www.fernandezandwells.com; 43 Lexington St W1; mains £4-14; ✈ Oxford Circus

A wonderful Soho mini-chain, this is one of the three branches of Fernandez & Wells, each located within 200m of each other in small, friendly and elegant spaces. This branch offers simple lunches and dinners of Spanish *jamon* (ham) and cured meats and cheese platters accompanied by quality wine. Grilled chorizo sandwiches are perfect for quick lunchtime bites and there are ample breakfasts, too (until 11am). The place is usually busy, with a relaxed atmosphere and outside seating. The other two branches are the Café (☎ 7287 8124; 73 Beak St; ⊖ Oxford Circus) and the Espresso Bar (☎ 7494 4242; 16a St Anne's Court W1; ⊖ Oxford Circus) – both do sandwiches and incredibly good coffee.

NEW WORLD Map p66   Chinese £
☎ 7734 0677; 1 Gerrard Pl W1; mains £6.50-9.90; ⊖ Leicester Sq

If you hanker after dim sum, the three-storey New World can oblige. All the old favourites – from *ha gau* (prawn dumpling) to *pai gwat* (steamed pork spare rib) – are available from steaming carts wheeled around the dining room daily 11am to 6pm.

BARRAFINA Map p66   Spanish £
☎ 7813 8016; www.barrafina.co.uk; 54 Frith St W1; tapas £4.20-9.50; ⊖ Tottenham Court Rd

Tapas are always better value in Spain but the quality of the food here and the fact that its popularity just seems to rise may justify the price of what are essentially appetisers to go with your drink. Along with *gambas al ajillo* (prawns in garlic; £7.50), there are more unusual things such as tuna tartare and grilled quails with aioli. If you can't get enough, try one of the large platters of cold Spanish meats (£5 to £17.50).

NOSH BAR Map p66   Jewish £
☎ 7734 5638; 39 Great Windmill St W1; mains £4-6; ⊖ Piccadilly Circus

A famous Soho institution in the 1940s and '50s, the Nosh has been reincarnated, though now in a sleeker edition. It still serves old Jewish staples such as salt beef (tender, juicy) in bagels (filling, sturdy) and garnished with pickles (hot and sour). You can also have latkes (potato pancakes), chicken soup and Jewish cheesecakes and eat it all as you watch the (under)world of Soho through the window.

MILK BAR Map p66   Cafe £
☎ 7287 4796; 3 Bateman St W1; mains £4-6; ⊖ Tottenham Court Rd

Sister to popular Flat White (☎ 77340370; www.flat-white.co.uk; 17 Berwick St, London, W1) cafe, Milk Bar arguably has the friendliest staff, all of whom are very relaxed Kiwis (hence the emphasis is on Antipodean coffee types

such as flat white). This place has some of the best breakfasts in central London, with great big omelettes, homemade beans on toast, porridge, pancakes with fruit and honey, and so on, none of which exceed the £5 mark – just what you need on a weekend morning. The coffee is superb, too, and tea is served in mismatching flea-market bone-china cups.

NORDIC BAKERY Map p66   Scandinavian £
☎ 3230 1077; www.nordicbakery.com; 14a Golden Sq W1; mains £3-4; ⊖ Oxford Circus

The perfect place to escape the chaos that is Soho and relax in the dark-wood panelled space. Lunch on some Scandinavian smoked fish sandwiches or have an afternoon break with tea/coffee and cake. The thick, sticky cinnamon buns are a naughty breakfast favourite. You can sit on the small bench outside and enjoy the calm of Golden Sq, too.

Also recommended:

Red Veg (Map p66; ☎ 7437 3109; www.redveg.com; 95 Dean St W1; mains £2.95-4.35; ⏰ noon-9.30pm Mon-Sat, to 6.30pm Sun; ⊖ Tottenham Court Rd) Delicious vegetarian and vegan fast food (burgers, falafels, wraps).

Kulu Kulu (Map p66; ☎ 7734 7316; 76 Brewer St W1; sushi £1.50-3.60; ⊖ Piccadilly Circus) This simple, bustling place just off Piccadilly Circus has the best inexpensive conveyor-belt sushi in London.

COVENT GARDEN & LEICESTER SQUARE

J SHEEKEY Map pp70-1   Seafood £££
☎ 7240 2565; www.j-sheeky.co.uk; 28-32 St Martin's Ct WC2; mains £11.75-37.50; ⊖ Leicester Sq

A jewel of the local scene, this incredibly smart restaurant, whose pedigree stretches back to 1896, has four elegant, discreet and spacious wood-panelled rooms in which to savour the riches of the sea, cooked simply and exquisitely. The fish pie (£11.75) is justifiably legendary, though the Cornish fish stew is just as good. Three-course weekday lunch is £24.75.

PORTRAIT Map pp70-1   British £££
☎ 7312 2490; www.npg.org.uk/live/portrest.asp; 3rd fl, St Martin's Pl WC2; mains £13.95-28.95; ⏰ restaurant 11.30am-3pm daily plus 5.30-8.30pm Thu & Fri, lounge & bar 10am-5pm Sat-Wed,

10am-10pm (last food orders 8.30pm) Thu & Fri;
⊖ Charing Cross
This stunningly located restaurant above
the excellent National Portrait Gallery (p74) – with
views over Trafalgar Sq and Westminster! –
and just past the Tudors is a place for a
decent meal after the gallery; why not pop
in for brunch when the two-/three-course
menu is £19.95/24.95? Unfortunately, Portrait is restricted in its opening times by the
gallery, so it only serves (early-ish) dinner on
Thursday and Friday.

RULES Map pp70-1 Traditional British ££
☎ 7836 5314; www.rules.co.uk; 35 Maiden Lane
WC2; mains £16.95-21; ⊖ Covent Garden
Established in 1798, this very posh and very
British establishment is London's oldest
restaurant. The menu is inevitably meat-
oriented – Rules specialises in classic game
cookery, serving up tens of thousands of
birds between mid-August and January
from its own estate – but fish dishes are
also available. Puddings are traditional:
trifles, treacles and lashings of custard.

GREAT QUEEN STREET
Map pp70-1 British ££
☎ 7242 0622; 32 Great Queen St WC2; mains £9-
18; ⊖ Covent Garden or Holborn
One of Covent Garden's best places to eat,
Great Queen St is sister to the Anchor & Hope
(p246) in Waterloo. The menu is seasonal (and
changes daily), with an emphasis on quality,
hearty dishes and good ingredients – there
are always delicious stews, roasts and simple
fish dishes. The atmosphere is lively, with a
small bar downstairs, and coming here to
eat with a group of friends – when you can
indulge in slow-roast meats for five – is as
good as having a small intimate dinner for
two (or indeed, one). The staff are knowledgeable about what they serve, the wine
list is good and booking is, as you may have
guessed, essential.

GIACONDA DINING ROOM
Map pp70-1 Modern European ££
☎ 7240 3334; www.giacondadining.com; 9 Denmark St; mains £9-13; ⊖ Tottenham Court Rd
A tiny room off the Charing Cross Rd hides
some of the best food around, with simple
dishes such as half-a-chicken and chips,
good fresh fish of the day or great steak
tartare. The wine list is decent and you're

greeted with a carafe of delicious sparkling
water and friendly staff.

ROCK & SOLE PLAICE
Map pp70-1 Fish & Chips £
☎ 7836 3785; 47 Endell St WC2; mains £4.50-14;
⊖ Covent Garden
The approach at this no-nonsense fish-and-
chips shop dating back to Victorian times is
simplicity: basic wooden tables under the
trees (in summer), simple decor inside and
delicious cod, haddock or skate in batter
served with a generous portion of chips.

ASSA Map pp70-1 Korean £
☎ 7240 8256; 53 St Giles High St WC2; mains £5.50-
9; 🕑 closed lunch Sun; ⊖ Tottenham Court Rd
The best of a trio of Korean restaurants behind the unsightly (and listed) Centre Point
building, Assa attracts a crowd of friendly
young Asians who come for the cut-price
soup noodles, *bibimbab* (rice served in a
sizzling pot topped with thinly sliced beef,
preserved vegetables and chilli-laced soy
bean paste) and potent *soju* (Korean saki).

BAOZI INN Map pp70-1 Chinese £
☎ 7287 6877; 25 Newport Court WC2; mains £6-7;
⊖ Leicester Sq
The smaller sister of Bar Shu has its own
personality and a unique (and cheap) menu.
Decorated in vintage style that plays at kitsch
communist pop, with old Chinese communist songs tinkling out of the speakers, Baozi
Inn serves quality Beijing and Chengdu-style
street food, with things like dan dan noodles
(served with spicy beef) handmade daily. It's
authentic, delicious and cheap food gold in
often-unreliable Chinatown.

JEN CAFÉ Map pp70-1 Chinese £
☎ 7287 9708; 7-8 Newport Pl WC2; mains £5-7.95;
🕑 11am-8.30pm Mon-Wed, to 9.30pm Thu-Sun;
⊖ Leicester Sq
This is the best place to come for homemade
wonton soup and dumplings – bar none.
And you can be assured of their freshness
by looking through the plate glass window
where they're in the process of being made.

PRIMROSE BAKERY Map pp70-1 Cafe £
☎ 7836 3638; www.primrosebakery.org.uk; 42
Tavistock St WC2; cakes £2.70; ⊖ Covent Garden
Finally Covent Garden has a decent tea
house. True, it's tiny and has only three

tables, but people squeeze round, order in one of the many varieties of cupcakes and pots of tea, and chat away for hours while comforting wafts of baking float from the downstairs kitchen. The £1.70 breakfast of toast and jams or Marmite is the perfect bargain. The decor is of a sort of 1950s America, without being too cutesy or ersatz, and we simply love it.

SCOOP Map pp70-1 Cafe £
☎ 7240 7086; www.scoopgelato.com; 40 Shorts Gardens WC2; ice creams £2.50-5; ☼ 8am-11pm; ⊖ Covent Garden

The queue outside Scoop can stretch down the street on summer weekends, and it's no wonder: this is central London's only true *gelateria* and, boy, does it set a precedent. Storms of ice cream swell in the fridge, all the ingredients are natural and the servings are huge. Try the pistachio, coconut, mango, pure chocolate or any of the incredible flavours.

Also recommended:

Canela (Map pp70–1; ☎ 7240 6926; www.canelacafe .com; 33 Earlham St WC2; mains £7.50-8.90; ⊖ Covent Garden) Small cafe serving tasty Portuguese and Brazilian dishes.

Wahaca (Map pp70–1; ☎ 7240 1883; www.wahaca .com; 66 Chandos Pl WC2; mains £3.50-6.50; ☼ noon-3.30pm & 5.30-11pm Mon-Sat, noon-3.30pm & 5.30-10.30pm Sun; ⊖ Covent Garden) This delightful cantina styles itself as a 'Mexican market eating' experience and the food is as authentic as you'll find in central London.

HOLBORN & THE STRAND

MATSURI Map pp70-1 Japanese £££
☎ 7430 1970; www.matsuri-restaurant.com; Mid City Place, 71 High Holborn WC1; set menus £22-45; ☼ closed Sun; ⊖ Holborn

This high-quality and very authentic Japanese restaurant on the fringe of the City can sometimes feel a little sterile, although the quality of the food is extremely high. With a sushi counter and stylish dining room on the ground floor and a large *teppanyaki* (hotplate) room in the basement where the meals are prepared in all seriousness by celebrated chef Hiroshi Sudo, there's plenty of choice.

SHANGHAI BLUES Map pp70-1 Chinese ££
☎ 7404 1668; www.shanghaiblues.co.uk; 193-197 High Holborn WC1; mains £9.50-42; ⊖ Holborn

What was once the St Giles Library now houses one of London's most stylish Chinese restaurants. The dark and atmospheric interior – think black and blue tables and chairs punctuated by bright red screens – recalls imperial Shanghai with a modern twist, and the menu is just as disarming, particularly the 'new style' dim sum served as appetisers, the *pipa* duck and the twice-cooked pork belly. There's a vast selection of teas, some of them quite rare. There's a three-course weekday lunch for £15 and live jazz on Friday and Saturday nights.

ASADAL Map pp70-1 Korean £
☎ 7430 9006; www.asadal.co.uk; 227 High Holborn WC1; mains £6.50-11.50; ☼ closed lunch Sun; ⊖ Holborn

If you fancy Korean but want a bit more style thrown into the act than what you'll find at Assa (p239), head for this spacious basement restaurant next to the Holborn tube station. The *kimchi* (pickled Chinese cabbage with chillies) is searing, the barbecues (£7 to £11.50) are done on your table and the *bibimbab* – rice served in a sizzling pot topped with thinly sliced beef, preserved vegetables and chilli-laced soybean paste – the best in town.

BLOOMSBURY
NORTH SEA FISH RESTAURANT
Map pp80-1 Fish & Chips ££
☎ 7387 5892; 7-8 Leigh St WC1; mains £9-19; ☼ closed Sun; ⊖ Russell Sq

The North Sea sets out to cook fresh fish and potatoes, a simple ambition in which it succeeds admirably. Look forward to jumbo-sized plaice or halibut steaks, deep-fried or grilled, and a huge serving of chips. There's takeaway next door if you can't handle the soulless dining room.

ABENO Map pp80-1 Japanese £
☎ 7405 3211; 47 Museum St WC1; mains £6.50-12.80; ⊖ Tottenham Court Rd

This understated Japanese restaurant specialises in *okonomiyaki*, a savoury pancake from Osaka of cabbage, egg and flour combined with the ingredients of your choice (there are more than two dozen varieties, including anything from sliced meats and vegetables to egg, noodles and cheese) and cooked on the hotplate at your table. There is a range of set lunches (£7.80 to £12.80).

HUMMUS BROS Map pp80-1 Middle Eastern £
☎ 7404 7079; www.hbros.co.uk; Victoria House, 37-63 Southampton Row WC1; mains £2.50-6; ⊖ Holborn
The deal at this very popular minichain is a bowl of filling hummus with your choice of topping (beef, chicken, chickpeas etc) eaten with warm pita bread.

FITZROVIA

HAKKASAN Map p66 Chinese £££
☎ 7907 1888, 7927 7000; 8 Hanway Pl W1; mains £9.50-42; ⊖ Tottenham Court Rd
This basement restaurant – hidden down a most unlikely back alleyway – successfully combines celebrity status, stunning design, persuasive cocktails and surprisingly sophisticated Chinese food. It was the first Chinese restaurant to receive a Michelin star. The low, nightclub-style lighting (lots of red) makes it a good spot for dating, while the long, glitzy bar is a great place for truly inventive cocktails. For dinner in the formal main dining room you'll have to book far in advance and no doubt be allocated a two-hour slot. Do what savvy Londoners do and have lunch in the more informal Ling Ling lounge.

OOZE Map p66 Italian £
☎ 7436 9444; www.ooze.biz; 62 Goodge St W1; mains £5-14; ⊘ closed Sun; ⊖ Goodge St
Ooze is, in its own words 'mad keen on risotto' (and brands itself as a 'risotteria'), though there are alternatives in the shape of good pasta dishes, meat and seasonal Italian offerings, plus ice cream made in house. It's a friendly place, with a simple, tasteful decor and a good wine list, and is popular at lunchtimes with office workers in the vicinity.

ROKA Map p66 Japanese ££
☎ 7580 6464; www.rokarestaurant.com; 37 Charlotte St W1; mains £10-19; ⊖ Goodge St or Tottenham Court Rd
This stunner of a Japanese restaurant mixes casual dining (wooden benches) with savoury titbits from the *robatayaki* (grill) kitchen in the centre. It has modern decor, with the dominating materials grey steel and glass. Sushi is £5 to £9, set lunch is £37.

FINO Map p66 Spanish ££
☎ 7813 8010; www.finorestaurant.com; 33 Charlotte St (enter from Rathbone St) W1; tapas £2-17; ⊖ Goodge St or Tottenham Court Rd

Critically acclaimed (and it's easy to see why), Fino represents an example of good Spanish cuisine in a London all too dominated by dreary and uninventive tapas bars. Set in a glamorous basement, Fino is a tapas restaurant with a difference. Try the Jerusalem artichoke cooked with mint, the prawn tortilla with wild garlic or the foie gras with chilli jam for a feast of innovative and delightful Spanish cooking.

RASA SAMUDRA Map p66 Indian £
☎ 7637 0222; www.rasarestaurants.com; 5 Charlotte St W1; mains £6.25-12.95; ⊘ closed lunch Sun; ⊖ Goodge St or Tottenham Court Rd
This bubblegum-pink eatery just up from Oxford St showcases the seafood cuisine of Kerala state on India's southwest coast, supported by a host – eight out of 14 main courses – of more familiar vegetarian dishes. The fish soups are outstanding, the breads superb and the various curries devinely spiced. The same group runs the South Indian vegetarian restaurant Rasa (p262) in Stoke Newington.

BUSABA EATHAI Map p66 Thai £
☎ 7299 7900; 22 Store St WC1; mains £6.40-8.90; ⊖ Goodge St
We prefer the slightly less hectic Store St premises of this West End favourite, but there are also a couple more locations, including a Wardour St branch (Map p66; ☎ 7255 8686; 106-110 Wardour St; ⊖ Tottenham Court Rd). Here the sumptuous Thai menu greets you via an electronic screen outside and the uberstyled interior is softened by communal wooden tables. This isn't the place to come for a long and intimate dinner, but it's a superb option for an excellent and (usually) speedy meal of stir-fries and noodles.

ST JAMES'S

NOBU Map pp84-5 Japanese £££
☎ 7447 4747; www.noburestaurants.com; 1st fl, Metropolitan Hotel, 19 Old Park Lane W1; mains £7-33, set lunches/dinners from £50/70; ⊖ Hyde Park Corner
You'll have to book a month in advance to eat here, but you'll get to chew and view the greatest celebrity restaurant magnet in town. Nobu recently made headlines with its introduction of a one-line warning on its menu that its prime dish, bluefin tuna, is an

endangered species so, the menu advises, 'please ask your server for an alternative'. The restaurant's been lobbied for years to stop serving bluefin tuna altogether, but it's been to no avail. Anyway, whatever your stance, this place serves some of the best Asian food in London. It's minimalist in decor, anonymously efficient in service, and out of this world when it comes to exquisitely prepared and presented sushi and sashimi. The black cod with miso and salmon kelp roll are divine.

INN THE PARK Map pp84–5 British ££
☎ 7451 9999; www.innthepark.com; St James's Park SW1; mains £10-18; ⏰ 8am-11pm Sun-Thu, 9am-11pm Fri & Sat; ⊖ Trafalgar Sq

This stunning wooden cafe and restaurant in St James's Park (p87) is run by the Irish wonder that is Oliver Peyton and offers cakes and tea as well as substantial and quality British food. The recent addition of extra seating under the trees for the cafe part and the new roof terrace are perfect, but if you're up for a special dining experience, come here for dinner, when the park is quiet and slightly illuminated. One of London's most gorgeous structures and locations.

MAYFAIR

GORDON RAMSAY AT CLARIDGE'S
Map p90 Modern British £££
☎ 7499 0099, 7592 1373; www.gordonramsay.com; 55 Brook St W1; 3-course set lunch/dinner £30/70; ⊖ Bond St

This match made in heaven – London's most celebrated chef in arguably its grandest hotel – will make you weak at the knees. A meal in the gorgeous art deco dining room is a special occasion indeed; the Ramsay flavours will have you reeling, from the pressed foie gras marinated in white port and the cannon of salt marsh lamb with crystallised walnuts and cumin, all the way to the cheese trolley, whether you choose the one with French, British or Irish number plates. Consider the six-course tasting menu (£80).

GREENHOUSE Map p90 Modern European £££
☎ 7499 3331; www.greenhouserestaurant.com; 27a Hay's Mews W1; 2-/3-course set lunch £25/29, 3-course set dinner £65; ⏰ lunch Mon-Fri, dinner Mon-Sat; ⊖ Green Park

Located in an incongruously uninspiring building in a mews at the end of a wonderful sculpted 'garden', Greenhouse offers some of the best food in Mayfair served with none of the attitude commonly found in restaurants of this class. Try the veal sweetbreads with hazelnuts and the hare with black truffles. The tasting menu (£80) is only for the intrepid and truly hungry. Greenhouse doles out so many freebies – from *amuses-gueule* (literally 'throat amusers'; snacks or appetisers) and inter-course sorbets to petits fours at the finale – you'll never get up.

SKETCH Map p66 Modern European £££
☎ 0870 777 4488; www.sketch.uk.com; 9 Conduit St W1; Gallery mains £18-32, Lecture Room & Library mains £39-55; ⏰ closed Sun; ⊖ Oxford Circus

The stunning collection of bars and restaurants at what was once the Christian Dior headquarters in Mayfair remains a draw for fashionistas, the curious, the pretentious, and the downright loaded. The Gallery restaurant downstairs buzzes informally in shimmering white and features video art projections. The Glade on the ground floor is the place for affordable lunch (two/three courses for £20/26) and the stunning Parlour patisserie to the right of the main entrance is great for tea and cakes. The ultimate attraction is the more formal Lecture Room & Library upstairs, where the high prices and haute cuisine in sumptuous surroundings from three-Michelin-starred chef Pierre Gagnaire attract an exclusive crowd. Upstairs you'll also find the East Bar, with a dozen of London's most unusual individual loos.

WOLSELEY Map p66 Modern European £££
☎ 7499 6996; www.thewolseley.com; 160 Piccadilly W1; mains £10-36; ⏰ 7am-midnight Mon-Fri, 8am-midnight Sat, 8am-11pm Sun; ⊖ Green Park

This erstwhile Bentley car showroom has been transformed into an opulent Viennese-style brasserie, with golden chandeliers and stunning black-and-white tiled floors, and it remains a great place for spotting celebrities. That said, the Wolseley tends to work better for breakfast, brunch or tea, rather than lunch or dinner, when the dishes (choucroute à l'Alsacienne, Wiener schnitzel) are somewhat stodgy and the black-attired staff more than a bit frayed. Daily specials are £15.75.

MOMO Map p66   North African ££
☎ 7434 4040; www.momoresto.com; 25 Heddon St W1; mains £15-24, 2-/3-course set lunches £15/19; ⊖ Piccadilly Circus

Sister of the celebrated 404 in Paris' Marais district, this wonderfully atmospheric North African restaurant is stuffed with cushions and lamps, and staffed by all-dancing, tambourine-playing waiters. It's a funny old place that manages to be all things to all diners, who range from romantic couples to raucous office-party ravers. Service is very friendly and the dishes are as exciting as you dare to be, so after the meze eschew the traditional and ordinary *tajine* (stew cooked in a traditional clay pot) and tuck into the splendid Moroccan speciality *pastilla,* a scrumptious nutmeg and pigeon pie. There's outside seating in this quiet backstreet in the warmer months.

VILLANDRY Map p90   Modern European ££
☎ 7631 3131; www.villandry.com; 170 Great Portland St W1; mains £12-24; ⊙ closed dinner Sun; ⊖ Great Portland St

This excellent Modern European restaurant with a strong Gallic slant has an attractive market-delicatessen attached (not to mention a bar) so freshness and quality of ingredients is guaranteed. Try the cassoulet or one of the several daily fish dishes.

WILD HONEY Map p90   Modern European ££
☎ 7758 9160; www.wildhoneyrestaurant.co.uk; 12 St George St W1; mains £14-20, set meals £19-22; ⊖ Oxford Circus or Bond St

Wild Honey has had consistently good reviews for years now, for its food and wine, relaxed atmosphere and professional service. Sister to Arbutus (p236), Wild Honey does inventive dishes, such as salad of crab with white peach and almonds, and straightforward mains like slow-cooked pork belly or roast chicken with veg, all cooked to perfection. The desserts range from wild-honey ice cream with crushed honeycomb, to delicious English wild strawberries in the summer months. The menu is seasonal, so surprises await.

SAKURA Map p66   Japanese £
☎ 7629 2961; 9 Hanover St W1; mains £7-12; ⊖ Oxford Circus

This very authentic Japanese restaurant has something for everyone throughout the day – from sushi and sashimi (£2 to £5)

to tempura, sukiyaki and a host of sets (£9 to £24). Just opposite is a small Japanese shopping centre with a grocery store, cafe-restaurant and pub.

KERALA Map p66   Indian £
☎ 7580 2125; 15 Great Castle St W1; mains £5-10; ⊖ Oxford Circus

Oxford Circus may seem an odd place to go for Indian food, but this little gem gets consistent thumbs ups for its South Indian dishes. Try one of its distinctive biryanis or the prawns cooked in masala sauce.

WESTMINSTER

CINNAMON CLUB Map pp84-5   Indian £££
☎ 7222 2555; www.cinnamonclub.com; Old Westminster Library, 30 Great Smith St SW1; mains £11-32; ⊙ closed lunch Sat & all day Sun; ⊖ St James's Park

Domed skylights, high ceilings, parquet flooring and a book-lined mezzanine – this just had to be a library in a former life – and the hushed, efficient staff only add to the illusion. The atmosphere is colonial club and the food modern – or perhaps palace – Indian.

VINCENT ROOMS
Map pp84-5   Modern European £
☎ 7802 8391; www.westking.ac.uk; Westminster Kingsway College, Vincent Sq SW1; mains £6-9, 3-course set menu £24; ⊙ lunch noon-1pm Mon-Fri, dinner 5-7pm Tue & Thu, term time only; ⊖ Victoria

Here you're essentially offering yourself up as a guinea pig for the student chefs at Westminster Kingsway College, where celebrity chef and overall nice guy Jamie Oliver trained. Service is nervously eager to please, the atmosphere in both the Brasserie and the Escoffier Room is smarter than expected, and the food (including veggie options) ranges from well-executed to occasionally exquisite.

MARYLEBONE

LOCANDA LOCATELLI Map p90   Italian £££
☎ 7935 9088; www.locandalocatelli.com; 8 Seymour St W1; mains £20-29.50; ⊖ Marble Arch

This dark but quietly glamorous restaurant in an otherwise unremarkable Marble Arch hotel is still one of London's hottest tables, and you're likely to see some famous faces being greeted by celebrity chef Giorgio

Locatelli at some point during your meal. Locatelli is renowned for its pasta dishes, which are sublime, but still rather over-priced for what they are (£20 to £25 for a pasta main course). Still, the smart international crowd doesn't seem to mind one bit. Booking a few weeks ahead is essential.

PROVIDORES & TAPA ROOM
Map p90   Fusion £££

☎ 7935 6175; www.theprovidores.co.uk; 109 Marylebone High St W1; mains £18-26; ⊖ Baker St or Bond St

This place is split over two levels: tempting tapas (£2.80 to £15) on the ground floor; full meals along the same innovative lines – Spanish and just about everything else – in the elegant and understated dining room above. It's popular enough to be frenetic at the busiest times; don't come for quiet conversation over your plate of chorizo and chillies.

REUBENS Map p90   Jewish ££

☎ 7486 0035; www.reubensrestaurant.co.uk; 79 Baker St W1; mains £10-24; ⊗ closed after lunch Fri, all day Sat; ⊖ Baker St

This kosher central cafe-restaurant has all the Ashkenazi favourites: gefilte fish, latkes and sandwiches as well as more complicated (and filling) main courses. It's pricey for what you get, but if you answer to a higher authority, it's money well spent.

IL BARETTO Map p90   Italian ££

☎ 7486 7340; www.ilbaretto.co.uk; 43 Blandford St W1; mains £9-22; ⊗ closed dinner Sun; ⊖ Bond St

Perhaps having 'bland' in the address is one of the reasons that this Marylebone location has changed hands between one Italian restaurant and another, but Il Baretto, the latest Italian incarnation, is an unpretentious trattoria that seems to be winning over the locals. It specialises in good, wood-fired oven pizza and simple Italian dishes such as penne with tomato sauce and sausage, while sometimes venturing into exciting territory with its delicious langoustine grill. The main draw here is the buzzy atmosphere and top ingredients sourced from Italy.

WALLACE Map p90   French ££

☎ 7563 9505; www.wallacecollection.org; Hertford House, Manchester Sq W1; mains £12.50-18;

⊗ 10am-5pm Sun-Thu, 10am-11pm Fri & Sat; ⊖ Bond St; ♿

There are few more idyllically placed restaurants than this French brasserie in the courtyard of the Wallace Collection (p96), London's finest small gallery and virtually unknown to most Londoners. Michelin-starred chef Thierry Laborde's seasonal menus are a veritable *tour de France* and cost £32 to £36 for three courses.

EAT & TWO VEG Map p90   Vegetarian ££

☎ 7258 8595; www.eatandtwoveg.com; 50 Marylebone High St W1; mains £10-12; ⊖ Baker St

One of the best vegetarian experiences in London, Eat & Two Veg is bright and breezy with charming, friendly staff and a smart 21st-century American-diner look. The menu is international eclectic – Thai green curry, Lankawi hotpot – and the mock meat dishes ('sausage' and mash, cheeseburger and fries) would fool even carnivores. There's plenty on offer for vegans, too.

NATURAL KITCHEN Map p90   Organic £

☎ 7486 8065; 77-78 Marylebone High St W1; mains £8-10; ⊖ Bond St

This is a decent, practical place to drop in for a relaxing pit stop in between raiding the shops on Marylebone High Street. The organic shop – with fresh produce, butcher's, deli and wine – has a restaurant on the 1st floor. It offers good-value breakfasts (£3 to £5) of porridge, fruit and granola yoghurt, and eggs with soldiers (toast cut in strips to dip), and an all-day brunch (around £7), in addition to lunches.

GOLDEN HIND Map p90   Fish & Chips £

☎ 7486 3644; 73 Marylebone Lane W1; mains £6.90-10.60; ⊗ closed lunch Sat & all day Sun; ⊖ Bond St

This 90-year-old chippie has a classic interior, chunky wooden tables and builders sitting alongside suits. And from the vintage fryer comes some of the best cod and chips available in London.

Also recommended:

Ping Pong (Map p90; ☎ 7009 9600; www.ping pongdimsum.com; 10 Paddington St W1; dim sum from £3, set lunches £10-13; ⊖ Baker St) Marylebone branch of a trendy six-outlet chain that is a popular lunch and after-work dinner destination.

Le Pain Quotidien (Map p90; ☎ 7486 6154; www
.lepainquotidien.com; 72-75 Marylebone High St W1;
mains £6.25-10.50; ❻ Baker St) Simple, stripped-down
French-style cafe serves salads, soups and *tartines* (open-
face sandwiches; £7 to £10).

THE CITY

The financial heart of London perhaps unsurprisingly caters for a well-heeled crowd
and, with few exceptions, it can be a tough
place to find a meal at the weekend, if not on
a weekday evening. But with neighbouring
districts such as Shoreditch, Spitalfields and
Clerkenwell becoming ever more residential
there is now a good selection of eating options
in the square mile itself.

SWEETING'S Map p100   Seafood ££
☎ 7248 3062; 39 Queen Victoria St EC4; mains
£12.50-25; ❨ lunch Mon-Fri; ❻ Mansion House
Sweeting's is a City institution, having been
around since 1830. It hasn't changed much,
with its small sit-down restaurant area, mosaic floor and narrow counters, behind which
stand waiters in white aprons. Dishes include
wild smoked salmon, oysters (in season from
September to April), potted shrimps, eels and
Sweeting's famous fish pie (£12.50).

WHITE SWAN PUB & DINING ROOM
Map p100   Gastropub ££
☎ 7242 9696; www.thewhiteswanlondon.com;
108 New Fetter Lane EC4; pub mains £9.50-14;
❨ closed Sat & Sun; ❻ Chancery Lane
Despite looking like any other anonymous
City pub from the street, inside the White
Swan is anything but typical – a smart
downstairs bar that serves excellent pub
food (£10 for a main with a glass of wine)
under the watchful eyes of animal trophies
and an upstairs dining room with a classic, meaty British menu (two-/three-course
meal £24/29).

PATERNOSTER CHOP HOUSE
Map p100   British ££
☎ 7029 9400; www.paternosterchophouse.com;
Warwick Ct, Paternoster Sq EC4; mains £16.50-20;
❨ closed all day Sat & dinner Sun; ❻ St Paul's
Right next to St Paul's Cathedral, this
sprawling upmarket chophouse serves
delightfully British fare – from the 'beast of
the day' (£19) to a huge shellfish and grill
selection, and favourites such as bubble

and squeak (fried leftover veggies from a
roast dinner) and haggis. Sunday brunch
(noon to 4pm) features a carvery.

ROYAL EXCHANGE GRAND CAFÉ &
BAR Map p100   Modern European ££
☎ 7618 2480; www.danddlondon.com; Royal
Exchange Bank, Threadneedle St EC3; mains £10-19;
❨ 8am-11pm Mon-Fri; ❻ Bank
This cafe sits in the middle of the covered
courtyard of the beautiful Royal Exchange
Bank building. The food runs the gamut
from sandwiches to oysters (from £10.75 a
half-dozen), whole roast Dover Sole (£18)
and pork belly (from £12). It's the perfect
place for an informal business meeting.

WINE LIBRARY Map p100   Modern European ££
☎ 7481 0415; www.winelibrary.co.uk; 43 Trinity
Sq EC3; set meals £16.45; ❨ 11.30am-2.30pm
Mon-Fri, 5-8.30pm Tue; ❻ Tower Hill
This is a great place for a light but boozy
lunch in the City. Buy a bottle of wine at
retail price (no mark-up; £6.50 corkage fee)
from the large selection on offer at this
vaulted-cellar restaurant and then snack on
a set plate of delicious pâtés, cheeses and
salads for £16.45.

PLACE BELOW Map p100   Vegetarian £
☎ 7329 0789; www.theplacebelow.co.uk; St
Mary-le-Bow Church, Cheapside EC2; dishes £3-8;
❨ 7.30am-3pm Mon-Fri; ❻ Mansion House
This atmospheric vegetarian restaurant is in
the crypt of one of London's most famous
old churches. The menu is a daily changing
set of veggie dishes, from quiche to sourdough sandwiches.

THE SOUTH BANK

The revitalised South Bank, with the Tate
Modern, the replicated Globe Theatre and
the splendid Millennium Bridge its major
drawcards, now has an interesting array of
restaurants. Many, including the Oxo Tower
and Butler Wharf Chophouse, take full advantage of their riverine locations, offering
a titbit of romance as a prelude to the main
course. Borough and Bermondsey, historically
important but run-down and almost forgotten in modern times, are no longer just the
provinces of smoked and jellied eel; you're just
as likely to find yourself sitting in a Victorian
market pavilion and enjoying fresh oysters or
a perfectly grilled steak.

WATERLOO

OXO TOWER RESTAURANT & BRASSERIE Map p126   Modern International £££

☎ 7803 3888; www.harveynichols.com; 8th fl, Barge House St SE1; mains £17-33, brasserie 2-/3-course set lunch £21.50/24.50, restaurant 3-course set lunch £33.50; ⊖ Waterloo

The conversion of the old Oxo Tower on the South Bank into housing with this restaurant on the 8th floor helped spur much of the dining renaissance south of the river. In the stunning glassed-in terrace you have a front-row seat for the best view in London, and you pay for this (not the fusion food) handsomely in the brasserie and stratospherically in the restaurant. Fish dishes – confit sea bass with truffle gnocchi, black bream *escabèche* – usually comprise half the menu.

SKYLON Map p126   Modern International ££

☎ 7654 7800; www.skylonrestaurant.co.uk; 3rd fl, Royal Festival Hall, South Bank Centre, Belvedere Rd SE1; restaurant 2-/3-course meal £37.50/42.50, grillroom mains £11.50-16.50; ☾ grillroom noon-11pm, restaurant lunch daily, dinner to 10.30pm Mon-Sat; ⊖ Waterloo

This cavernous restaurant on the top of the refurbished Royal Festival Hall is divided into grillroom and fine-dining sections with a large bar (open 11am to 1am) separating the two. Floor-to-ceiling windows offer views of the Thames and the City, and the decor of muted colours and period chairs harkens back to the 1951 Festival of Britain, when the hall opened. Try the confit leg of duck or the sautéed rabbit loin. Weekday lunch is £21.50/26.50 for two/three courses.

ANCHOR & HOPE Map p126   Gastropub ££

☎ 7928 9898; 36 The Cut SE1; mains £11.50-16; ☾ closed lunch Mon & dinner Sun; ⊖ Southwark or Waterloo

The hope is that you'll get a table without waiting hours because you can't book at this quintessential gastropub, except for Sunday lunch at 2pm. The anchor is gutsy, unashamedly carnivorous British food. The critics love this place but, with dishes such as salt marsh lamb shoulder cooked for seven hours and soy-braised shin of beef, it's decidedly not for vegetarians. Its sister-restaurant, Great Queen Street (p239) in Covent Garden, is smaller, does not have a pub and takes reservations (which are, in fact, essential).

Also recommended:

Masters Super Fish (Map p126; ☎ 7928 6924; 191 Waterloo Rd SE1; mains £6.50-16; ☾ closed Sun; ⊖ Waterloo) Superlative fish (brought in fresh daily from Billingsgate Market and grilled rather than fried if desired) at this rather humble-looking institution.

Mesón Don Felipe (Map p126; ☎ 7928 3237; 53 The Cut SE1; tapas £3.75-6.25; ☾ closed Sun; ⊖ Southwark or Waterloo) Veritable Waterloo institution serves standard-issue tapas like *patatas bravas* (potatoes in tomato sauce) and *albondigas* (meatballs) around a central bar to punters turned away fromt the Anchor & Hope.

BOROUGH & BERMONDSEY

ROAST Map p126   Modern British ££

☎ 7940 1300; www.roast-restaurant.com; 1st fl, Floral Hall, Borough Market, Stoney St SE1; mains £14-25; ☾ closed dinner Sun; ⊖ London Bridge

The focal point at this unique restaurant and bar perched directly above Borough Market is the glassed-in kitchen with an open spit, where ribs of beef, suckling pigs, birds and game (no doubt sourced from the stalls below) are roasted. The emphasis is on roasted meats (featherblade of beef, lamb's kidneys) and seasonal vegetables, though there are lighter dishes from salads to grilled fish. The views below of Borough Market on trading days (Thursday to Saturday) are frenetic.

BUTLERS WHARF CHOP HOUSE

Map p126   Modern British ££

☎ 7403 3403; www.chophouse.co.uk; Butlers Wharf Bldg, 36e Shad Thames SE1; mains £15.50-22.50, 2-/3 course set lunch £19.50/24.50, dinner £22/26; ⊖ Tower Hill

A poster child for early Modern British cuisine, the Chop House continues to create upmarket variants on bangers and mash, bubble and squeak and fish pie, as well as 'new-old' arrivals like Old Spot pork from Gloucestershire and spatchcock chicken. A great view of Tower Bridge (which could be your main reason for visiting) is part of the deal but best enjoyed from an outdoor table.

MAGDALEN Map p126   Modern British ££

☎ 7403 1342; www.magdalenrestaurant.co.uk; 152 Tooley St SE1; mains £13.50-17, 2-/3-course set lunch £15.50/18.50; ☾ closed lunch Sat & all day Sun; ⊖ London Bridge

This stylish dining room on two levels seems somewhat out of place in hard-core

Tooley St but any port in a storm will do in these parts. The Modern British fare takes familiar dishes and puts a spin on them (roast pork loin with sage and lentils, smoked haddock choucroute). The welcome is warm and the service impeccable. A winner in its class and neighbourhood.

CHAMPOR-CHAMPOR
Map p126   Asian Fusion ££
☎ 7403 4600; www.champor-champor.com; 62-64 Weston St SE1; 2-/3-course set meal £25/29; ⏱ lunch Thu & Fri, dinner Mon-Sat; ⊖ London Bridge
Not surprisingly, a restaurant whose name means 'mix and match' in Malay serves up some unusual creations. East-west cuisine includes ostrich sausages in Sichuan pepper-and-peanut sauce, and pigeon-and-plum hotpot, as well as vegetarian options such as roast aubergine teriyaki. Some dishes are successful, others less so. The eclectic Asian decor is a delight.

APPLEBEE'S FISH CAFÉ   Map p126 Seafood ££
☎ 7407 5777; 5 Stoney St SE1; mains £12.50-19, 2-course set lunch £13.50; ⏱ closed Sun & Mon; ⊖ London Bridge
If you are tempted by the offerings of the fishmongers of Borough Market and must have a fix of iodine right then and there, head for this excellent fishmongers with a cafe-restaurant attached. You'll find all manner of fresher-than-fresh fish and shellfish dishes on the ever-changing chalkboard, but we always go for the meal-in-itself fish soup (£8.50).

GARRISON PUBLIC HOUSE
Map p126   Gastropub ££
☎ 7089 9355; www.thegarrison.co.uk; 99-101 Bermondsey St SE1; mains £11.50-16; ⏱ breakfast, lunch & dinner daily, brunch Sat & Sun; ⊖ London Bridge
The Garrison's traditional green-tiled exterior and rather distressed, beach-shack interior are both appealing, and it boasts an actual cinema in its basement, but it's the food – pressed ham-hock terrine, calf's liver with smoked bacon, lamb with rosemary and garlic – that lures the punters to this evergreen gastropub. If you don't fancy nearly bashing your neighbour's elbow every time you lift your fork, though, come for breakfast (8am to 11.30am weekdays) or weekend brunch (9am to 11.30am).

BERMONDSEY KITCHEN
Map p126   Modern European ££
☎ 7407 5719; www.bermondseykitchen.co.uk; 194 Bermondsey St SE1; mains £9.50-16.50; ⏱ closed dinner Sun; ⊖ London Bridge or Borough
As this is a great place to curl up on the sofas with the Sunday newspapers or enjoy brunch at the weekend, it's hardly surprising that many locals seem to have made BK their second living room. The Modern European food (with a nod towards the Mediterranean) that comes from the open grill is as homely and unpretentious as the butcher-block tables, and the refreshingly brief menu (six starters and as many mains) changes daily. Set lunch can cost below £10 on weekdays.

Also recommended:

Hartley (Map p126; ☎ 7394 7023; www.thehartley.com; 64 Tower Bridge Rd SE1; mains £8.50 14.50; ⏱ closed dinner Sun; ⊖ London Bridge) Fence-sitter of a pub/gastropub does rump steak burger (£6.50) and Sunday roast (£11.50), as well as more fanciful dishes like rabbit leg confit (£14.50).

Tsuru (Map p126; ☎ 7928 2228; www.tsuru-sushi .co.uk; 4 Canvey St SE1; dishes £4.95-7.95; ⏱ 11am-9pm Mon-Fri; ⊖ St Paul's, Southwark or London Bridge) Cheap and cheerful sushi by day and early evening, just behind the Tate Modern.

HYDE PARK TO CHELSEA
In the early 18th century, the influx of foreign migrants to London, already Europe's largest city, led to the expansion of the working-class areas to the east and the south while the more affluent high tailed it for the north and, to an even greater extent, the west. Quality tends to gravitate to where the money is, and you'll find some of London's finest establishments in the swanky hotels and ritzy mews of Chelsea, Belgravia and Knightsbridge. The king of them all, Gordon Ramsay, has three Michelin stars in its crown and resides in Chelsea. Chic and cosmopolitan South Kensington has always been reliable for pan-European options.

CHELSEA & BELGRAVIA
GORDON RAMSAY
Map pp136-7   Modern European £££
☎ 7352 4441; www.gordonramsay.com; 68 Royal Hospital Rd SW3; 3-course lunch/dinner £45/90; ⏱ lunch & dinner Mon-Fri; ⊖ Sloane Sq
One of Britain's finest restaurants and still the only one in the capital with three

Michelin stars, this is hallowed turf for those who worship at the altar of the stove, notwithstanding the hot water Mr Ramsay seems to get himself into regularly. It's true that it is a treat right from the taster to the truffles, but you won't get much time to savour it all. Bookings are made in specific sittings and you dare not linger; book as late as you can to avoid that rushed feeling. The blow-out tasting Menu Prestige (£120) is seven courses of absolute perfection.

CHEYNE WALK BRASSERIE

Map pp136-7   French £££

☎ 7376 8787; www.cheynewalkbrasserie.com; 50 Cheyne Walk SW3; mains £19.50-39.50, 2-/3-course set lunches £17/23, weekend brunch £27/33; ✆ closed dinner Sun & lunch Mon; ⊖ Sloane Sq

With a reputation for especially tender steaks, the focus of the food preparation at this brasserie is the large open grill in the centre of the ground-floor dining room. However, you might prefer something like sea bream with lemon and bay leaves with a salad of green beans, pistachio and mint. The belle époque decoration is just this side of kitsch, with turquoise banquettes, red leather chairs, chandeliers and crystal lamps topped with pink shades. The attractive salon upstairs offers stunning views of the Thames (in winter, in any case, when the trees are bare).

KNIGHTSBRIDGE, KENSINGTON & HYDE PARK

CAPITAL Map pp136-7   Modern European £££

☎ 7589 5171, 7591 1202; www.capitalhotel.co.uk; Capital Hotel, 22-23 Basil St SW3; 2-/3-course set lunch £27.50/33, dinner £55/63; ⊖ Knightsbridge

Of the eight restaurants in London to have been awarded two Michelin stars, the Capital behind Harrods is the least known, and so much the better. The modern yet warmth-inducing decor, welcoming and accommodating staff and chef Eric Chavot's award-winning dishes (roasted lobster with chilli and coconut broth, a saddle of rabbit seared calamari and tomato risotto) all remain our secret. And now yours. Tasting menu is £70 (add £55 for accompanying wines).

BIBENDUM Map pp136-7   Modern European £££

☎ 7581 5817, 7589 1480; www.bibendum.co.uk; Michelin House, 81 Fulham Rd SW3; mains £23-27, 2-/3-course set lunches £25/29; ⊖ South Kensington

top picks

TABLES WITH A VIEW

- Oxo Tower Restaurant & Brasserie (p246)
- Portrait (p238)
- Min Jiang (below)
- Butlers Wharf Chop House (p246)
- Roast (p246)

Located in listed art nouveau Michelin House (p142), Bibendum offers upstairs dining in a spacious and light room with stained-glass windows, where you can savour fabulous and creative food, and what, it must be said, is fairly ordinary service. The Bibendum Oyster Bar on the ground floor offers a front-row seat from which to admire the building's architectural finery while lapping up terrific native and rock oysters (per half-dozen £12; mains £7.50 to £10.50)

MIN JIANG Map pp136-7   Chinese £££

☎ 7361 1988; www.minjiang.co.uk; 10th fl, Royal Garden Hotel, 2-24 Kensington High St W8; mains £12-48; ⊖ Kensington High St

This stunner of a Chinese restaurant, perched on the top of a hotel owned by a Hong Kong–based group, offers million-dollar views of Kensington Palace and Gardens as well as arguably the best Peking duck (half/whole £25/48) in all of London. You'll consume everything from the skin and feet to the shredded meat and then get the bill. It's cooked in a wood-burning stove. There's excellent seafood here, too.

LAUNCESTON PLACE

Map pp136-7   Modern European ££

☎ 7937 6912; www.launcestonplace-restaurant .co.uk; 1a Launceston Pl W8; 3-course lunch/Sun lunch/dinner £18/24/42; ✆ closed lunch Mon; ⊖ Gloucester Rd or Kensington High St

This exceptionally handsome restaurant on a picture-postcard Kensington street of Edwardian houses is about the chic-est address in this part of town at the moment. The food, prepared by chef Tristan Welsh, a protégé of Marcus Wareing, tastes as divine as it looks. The adventurous (and flush) will go for the tasting menu (£52).

RACINE Map pp136-7 French ££

☎ 7584 4477; 239 Brompton Rd SW3; mains £12.50-26.25, 2-/3-course set lunch £17.50/19.50; ⊖ Knightsbridge or South Kensington
Regional French cooking is the vehicle at this brasserie that looks like it just stepped off the Eurostar. Expect the likes of *tête de veau* (the classic French veal dish; £16.50), grilled rabbit with mustard (£19.95), and veal kidneys with Fourme d'Ambert (a blue cheese from the Auvergne) and walnut butter. Being French and very classic, dishes might feel heavy to some, but the sauces and the desserts are all spot on.

AWANA Map pp136-7 Malaysian ££

☎ 7584 8880; www.awana.co.uk; 85 Sloane Ave SW3; mains £11.50-25, 2-/3-course set lunch £12.50/15; ⊖ South Kensington
London's only real fine-dining Malay restaurant, Awana has all our favourite dishes – beef *rendang*, laksa (coconut broth with prawns and rice noodles), *murtabak* (pancake with savoury fillings), *ikan bakar* (grilled butterfish wrapped in banana leaves with herbs and baked) in a stylish and minimalist 'New Asian' dining room. The uninitiated may want to consider the Malaysian Journey sampling menu at £45 (£40 for the vegetarian version). The Satay Bar serves delicious skewers of chicken, beef, lamb and prawns (£7.50 to £9.50) accompanied by the restaurant's own spicy peanut sauce. We'll be back.

ORIEL Map pp136-7 French ££

☎ 7730 2804, www.tragusholdings.com; 51 Sloane Sq SW1; mains £10.25-22.95; ⊖ Sloane Sq
With its comfortable wicker chairs and mirrors, and tables overlooking Sloane Sq, the Oriel makes the perfect place to meet before going shopping in the King's Rd or Sloane St. Expect all the usual French brasserie dishes like *confit de canard* (preserved duck), *foie de veau* (calf's liver) and *moules marinières* (mussels in white wine and cream).

LUCIO Map pp136-7 Italian ££

☎ 7823 3007; www.luciorestaurant.com; 257-259 Fulham Rd SW3; mains £18.50-20.50, 2-/3-course set lunch £15.50/19; ⊖ South Kensington
One of our favourite Italian eateries in London, Lucio is decidedly top end but not overly so. Try the exquisitely cooked pasta with clams, the crab ravioli or, when in sea-

son, the deep-fried zucchini. The surrounds are understatedly stylish, the clientele subdued and the service seamless.

OGNISKO Map pp136-7 Polish ££

☎ 7589 4635; www.ognisko.com; 55 Exhibition Rd SW7; mains £10.50-20.50; ⊖ South Kensington
This is Polish style of another world and time: a clubby baroque dining room filled with portraits, chandeliers and mirrors and overlooking a verdant square. But stick with the basics at 'The Hearth': *barszcz czwerwony* (beetroot soup) and *pierogi* (dumplings stuffed with meat or cheese and potatoes).

FRANKIE'S Map pp136-7 Italian ££

☎ 7590 9999; www.frankiesitalianbarandgrill .com; 3 Yeoman's Row, Brompton Rd SW3; mains £10.50-18.50; ⊖ Knightsbridge
Brainchild of jockey Frankie Dettori and seminal chef Marco Pierre White, Frankie's serves up good, solid, old-fashioned food (in this case, immigrant Italian) – and lots of it – in a basement bar and grill. The menu, popular with families, is top-heavy with steaks and fish, though burgers (£8.95) and pastas (£7.50 to £10.50) also figure.

ORANGERY Map pp136-7 Teahouse ££

☎ 0844 482 7777; www.hrp.org.uk; Kensington Palace, Kensington Gardens W8; mains £9.95-12.95, tea £13.50-28.50; ⏲ 10am-6pm Mar-Oct, to 5pm Nov-Feb; ⊖ Queensway, Notting Hill Gate or High St Kensington
The Orangery, housed in an 18th-century conservatory on the grounds of Kensington Palace, is a great place for lunch, especially in fine weather, but nothing beats this place for tea. Choose from several varieties, which start with a 'normal' tea (sandwiches, desserts and tea) and end with a champagne one (the same but with champagne)

top picks

DINING WITH KIDS

- Giraffe (p268)
- Frankie's (above)
- Frizzante@City Farm (p256)
- Nando's (p269)
- Pavilion Café at Victoria Park (p257)

at £28.50, which you're almost certain not to be able to finish.

DAQUISE Map pp136-7 — Polish £

☎ 7589 6117; 20 Thurloe St SW7; mains £6.50-13.50, set lunch £9.50; ⊖ South Kensington

This dinosaur – a loveable little tyrannosaurus indeed – is a rather dowdy Polish cafe-cum-diner, with a good range of vodkas and extremely reasonably priced dishes, including the oft-seen *bigos* (£8), a 'hunter's stew' of cabbage and pork, stuffed cabbage (£8.50) and ravioli-like *pierogi* (£6.50)

PIZZA ON THE PARK Map pp136-7 — Italian £

☎ 7235 7825; www.pizzaonthepark.co.uk; 11 Knightsbridge SW5; mains £7.80-11; ⊖ Hyde Park Corner

This place is as popular for its nightly jazz in the basement as for its pizza. There's also a spacious restaurant upstairs and, if you're lucky, a few tables overlooking Hyde Park. In addition to pizza and pasta there are more substantial grills and main dishes.

JAKOB'S Map pp136-7 — Middle Eastern £

☎ 7581 9292; 20 Gloucester Rd SW7; mains £7-10; ⊖ Gloucester Rd

This charismatic Armenian-owned restaurant serves delicious and wholesome (and sometimes organic) salads, vegetarian lasagne, filo pie, falafel and kebabs that you choose at the counter– after having laid claim to a table in the back. A plate of three/four choices is £7/10. Desserts are very good.

BYRON Map pp136-7 — Hamburgers £

☎ 7352 6040; www.byronhamburgers.com; 300 King's Rd SW3; mains £5.75-8; ⊖ Sloane Sq

A bit of a wasteland for affordable and acceptable food, the King's Rd can now boast a Byron, the place that serves up only 'proper hamburgers' (or so says its sign). The Classic – 6oz of Aberdeen Angus beef – and Classic Caesar (which just means traditional) was sufficiently impressive for the American in our group to come back for more.

Also recommended:

Tom's Kitchen (Map pp136–7; ☎ 7349 0202; www.tomskitchen.co.uk; 27 Cale St SW3; mains £12.50-29; ⊙ 7-10am & noon-3pm Mon-Fri, 10am-3pm Sat & Sun, plus 6-11pm Mon-Sun; ⊖ South Kensington) Celebrity

chef Tom Aikens, who runs a Michelin-starred restaurant around the corner, opened this less fussy eatery serving meals (including his award-winning breakfasts) throughout the day.

Sticky Fingers (Map p178; ☎ 7938 5338; 1 Phillimore Gardens W8; mains £9.50-14.50; ⊖ High St Kensington) Though Bill Wyman has sold his interests, Sticky Fingers remains a Rolling Stones–themed eatery with gold discs and other memorabilia and rather good burgers.

Serpentine Bar & Kitchen (Map pp136–7; ☎ 7706 8114; www.serpentinebarandkitchen.com; Serpentine Rd, Hyde Park W2; mains £7.50-9.75; ⊙ 8am-9pm; ⊖ Hyde Park Corner) This glass-enclosed cafe and bar is an excellent place for a drink or light meal while frolicking in Hyde Park.

VICTORIA & PIMLICO

ROUSSILLON Map pp136-7 — French £££

☎ 7730 5550; www.roussillon.co.uk; 16 St Barnabas St SW1; 3-course set lunch/dinner £35/55; ⊙ closed lunch Sat & all day Sun; ⊖ Sloane Sq

On a quiet side street off Pimlico Rd, Michelin-starred Roussillon offers such fine service, lovely muted decor and settings, and fresh English ingredients dexterously cooked à la française that we're almost hesitant to show off this sparkling gem to the world. There's no à la carte; choose from among four to six starters and main courses at lunch or dinner, or there's a more extravagant tasting menu (£48 to £58 at lunch, £75 at dinner) of eight courses. The Menu Légumes (£65) puts vegetarian cooking into the haute cuisine league.

LA POULE AU POT Map pp136-7 — French ££

☎ 7730 7763; 231 Ebury St SW1; mains £15.50-21, 2-/3-course set lunches £18.75/22.75; ⊖ Sloane Sq

Illuminated with candlelight even at lunch, the 'Chicken in the Pot' is a long-established country-style French restaurant that is long on romance and cosiness and somewhat shorter on the quality of what it serves. Still, the alfresco front terrace is a lovely spot in the warmer months. Expect dishes like onion *tarte,* rabbit casserole and roast guinea fowl.

OLIVO Map pp136-7 — Italian ££

☎ 7730 2505; 21 Eccleston St SW1; mains £13.75-17.50; ⊙ closed lunch Sat & Sun; ⊖ Victoria or Sloane Sq

This colourful restaurant specialises in the food and wine of Sardinia and Sicily, and

FARMERS MARKETS

For fresh fruit, vegetables, dairy products, meat and fish, bread and other foodstuffs that taste the way they did when you were a kid, head to one of the growing number of weekend farmers markets that have been springing up around London in the past decade or so. Here producers sell their own wares, the atmosphere is sociable and the produce is guaranteed fresh. The following are some of the best and most central; for a complete listing see www.lfm.org.uk.

Blackheath (Map p62; Blackheath train station, car park No 2, Blackheath SE10; 🕙 10am-2pm Sun; 🚇 Blackheath)

Clapham (off Map p190; Bonneville Primary School, Bonneville Gardens SW4; 🕙 10am-2pm Sun; ⊖ Clapham South)

Islington (Map p170; William Tyndale School, Upper St N1; 🕙 10am-2pm Sun; ⊖ Highbury & Islington or Angel)
London's original farmers market, this one (behind Islington Town Hall) sells organic produce and other foodstuffs grown or reared within a 50-mile radius of the capital.

Marylebone (Map p90; Cramer St car park, off Marylebone High St W1; 🕙 10am-2pm Sun; ⊖ Baker St or Bond St)
The largest farmers market in town, with some three dozen producers coming from within a 100-mile radius of the M25.

Notting Hill (Map p176; car park behind Waterstone's, Kensington Pl W8; 🕙 9am-1pm Sat; ⊖ Notting Hill Gate)

Pimlico Road (Map pp136–7; Orange Sq, cnr Pimlico Rd & Ebury St SW1; 🕙 9am-1pm Sat; ⊖ Sloane Sq)

South Kensington (Map pp136–7; Bute St, off Brompton Rd SW7; 🕙 9am-1pm Sat; ⊖ South Kensington)

Wimbledon Park (off Map p62; Wimbledon Park First School, Havana Rd SW19; 🕙 9am-1pm Sat; ⊖ Wimbledon Park)

has a dedicated clientele who, frankly, would rather keep it to themselves. Not surprising, really, because this place near Victoria station is a true gem. As a general rule, drink Sicilian and eat Sardinian. Excellent pasta dishes (£10.75 to £15.50).

JENNY LO'S TEA HOUSE
Map pp136-7   Chinese £
☎ 7259 0399; 14 Eccleston St SW1; mains £6.95-8.50; 🕙 lunch & dinner Mon-Fri; ⊖ Victoria
This is a good-value place in Victoria for rice and noodles. It was set up by the daughter of the late Chinese cookery-book author Kenneth Lo, who introduced the UK to Chinese food in the 1950s.

CLERKENWELL, SHOREDITCH & SPITALFIELDS

Shoreditch offers some of the best eating in London these days – the neighbourhood's creative flair has attracted similarly minded, independent restaurateurs and there seems to be a new opening every week. Clerkenwell has a more traditional feel, but continues to host some of London's most celebrated eateries, while Spitalfields is home to other gems including several of London's best-loved bagel bakeries and a slew of often rather lacklustre balti houses.

CLERKENWELL
LE CAFÉ DU MARCHÉ   Map p150   French ££
☎ 7608 1609; 22 Charterhouse Sq, Charterhouse Mews EC1; 3-course set menus £33.85; 🕙 closed Sat lunch & all day Sun; ⊖ Barbican
Tradition is a watchword at this quaint French bistro housed in an exposed-brick warehouse down a tiny alleyway near Smithfield Market. The food is mostly gutsy French fare – hearty steaks with garlic and rosemary flavours, fish soup with aioli – and there's piano playing and jazz upstairs. Meals are set menu only.

SMITHS OF SMITHFIELD
Map p150   Modern British ££
☎ 7251 7950, 7236 6666; www.smithsofsmithfield.co.uk; 67-77 Charterhouse St EC1; mains £10-27; 🕙 breakfast, lunch & dinner; ⊖ Farringdon
This Clerkenwell institution packs in a mixture of locals, city workers and clubbers for its rightly celebrated breakfast in the cavernous ground-floor canteen. Elsewhere in the building, the food quality and prices increase with each staircase: the wine rooms on the 1st floor (small plates and sandwiches); the brasserie on the 2nd floor; and the rooftop dining room above, which has great views of Smithfield Market and St Paul's Cathedral. The linking factor between them all is a focus on top-quality British meat and organic produce.

ST JOHN Map p150 British ££

☎ 7251 0848; www.stjohnrestaurant.co.uk; 26 St John St EC1; mains £12.50-22; ⏲ closed dinner Sun; ⊖ Farringdon

This London classic is wonderfully simple – its light bar and cafe area giving way to a surprisingly small dining room where 'nose to tail eating' is served up courtesy of celebrity chef Fergus Henderson. This was one of the places that launched Londoners on the quest to rediscover their culinary past, and it's a place for anyone who wants an off-piste eating experience. Don't miss the signature roast bone-marrow salad with parsley and follow it with one of the tasty daily specials – roast kid, fennel and green sauce, for example, or smoked eel with beetroot and horseradish. The traditional British puddings are similarly superb.

MORO Map p150 North African, Spanish ££

☎ 7833 8336; www.moro.co.uk; 34-36 Exmouth Market EC1; mains £15.50-18.50; ⊖ Farringdon or Angel

The best-known restaurant in Clerkenwell and still a frequent award winner a decade after it launched, Moro serves 'Moorish' cuisine, a fusion of Spanish, Portuguese and North African flavours. The restaurant doesn't look like anything special, though it's always full and buzzing, but the food is generally fabulous with such dishes on its constantly evolving menu as wood-roasted mackerel with sweet onion-and-oloroso sauce, and charcoal-grilled lamb with deep-fried aubergine. Reservations are essential.

QUALITY CHOP HOUSE Map p150 British ££

☎ 7837 5093; www.qualitychophouse.co.uk; 92-94 Farringdon Rd EC1; mains £10-18; ⏲ closed lunch Sat; ⊖ Farringdon

This place might be about as working class as the new media crowd that frequents its mockney (mock cockney) interior, but it's still a charmer, with vintage flooring, old church pews as seats and incongruously formal service for an establishment dubbing itself a 'progressive working class caterer'. The food is generally excellent, though – posh versions of British classics such as pork pies with piccalilli, eel and, of course, pork chops.

MEDCALF Map p150 British £-££

☎ 7833 3533; www.medcalfbar.co.uk; 40 Exmouth Market EC1; mains £8.50-19.50; ⏲ closed dinner Sun; ⊖ Farringdon or Angel

Medcalf is one of the best-value hangouts in Exmouth Market. Housed in a beautifully converted butcher shop dating back to 1912, it serves up innovative and well-realised British fare, such as handpicked Devon crab and Welsh rarebit.

EAGLE Map p150 Gastropub ££

☎ 7837 1353; 159 Farringdon Rd EC1; mains £8.50-13; ⏲ closed dinner Sun; ⊖ Farringdon

London's first gastropub may have seen its original owners move on, but it's still a great place for a bite to eat and a pint, especially at lunchtime, when it's relatively quiet and there's an alluring spread of its much-loved Mediterranean-led fare on the bar counter.

MODERN PANTRY Map p150 Fusion ££

☎ 7553 9210; www.themodernpantry.co.uk; 47-48 St John's Sq EC1; mains £12.50-18.50; ⏲ 8am-11pm Mon-Fri, 9am-11pm Sat, 10am-10pm Sun; ⊖ Farringdon

Currently one of London's most talked-about eateries, this three-floor Georgian townhouse in the heart of Clerkenwell has a cracking all-day menu, which gives almost as much pleasure to read as to eat from. Ingredients are combined sublimely into dishes such as grilled whole mackerel, aubergine, currant and coriander *harasume* noodles and sweet soy sauce. The breakfasts are great, too, though sadly portions can be on the small side. Reservations recommended for the evenings. There's also a small shop.

COACH & HORSES Map p150 Gastropub £

☎ 7278 8990; www.thecoachandhorses.com; 26-28 Ray St EC1; mains £4-11.50; ⊖ Farringdon

For our money this is Clerkenwell's best gastropub, which sacrifices none of its old-world pub charm in attracting a well-heeled foodie crowd for its range of great-value dishes (prices in increments of £2). The signature beer-battered cod, chips and mushy peas is well worth its £11.50 price tag.

AKI Map p150 Japanese £

☎ 7837 9281; www.akidemae.com; 182 Gray's Inn Rd WC1; mains £5-18; ⏲ closed Sat lunch & all day Sun; ⊖ Chancery Lane

This charmingly shabby *izakaya* ('sake bar with food' or Japanese-style bistro) is an excellent and very authentic place for noodles (£5), sushi (£1.70 to £3) or one of the excellent set lunch menus (£9.30). Friendly staff and a huge sake selection add to the attraction.

SHOREDITCH & HOXTON

EYRE BROTHERS
Map p150   Spanish, Portuguese £££
☎ 7613 5346; www.eyrebrothers.co.uk; 70 Leonard St EC2; mains £10-27; ☒ closed lunch Sat & all day Sun; ⊖ Old St

This sublime, elegant Shoreditch restaurant is well worth travelling to and making reservations for. Its cuisine is Iberian with a touch of African flair, courtesy of the eponymous brothers' upbringing in Mozambique, and it's every bit as exciting as it sounds. On a recent visit the Bacalhau (salt cod) was simply superb, while the rare acorn-fed Ibérico pork was similarly top notch.

BOUNDARY Map p150 Modern European £££
☎ 7729 1051; www.theboundary.co.uk; 2-4 Boundary St E2; mains £14-28; ☒ closed lunch Mon & dinner Sun; ⊖ Liverpool St

This is the extraordinary new venture for Sir Terence Conran, who was London's most prolific restaurateur until the recent sale of his portfolio of some 29 restaurants. Boundary marks his re-entry to the capital's eating scene – a combination of two eateries, a hotel and a fantastic rooftop terrace. The ground-floor cafe-cum-deli is great for a light meal (£3 to £6) or a posh cuppa, while the subterranean restaurant is the spot for a glamorous meal of French and British cooking, with a focus on seafood, cheese and charcuterie.

FIFTEEN Map p150   Italian ££
☎ 0871 330 1515, 7251 3909; www.fifteen.net; 15 Westland Pl N1; mains £14-21; ⊖ Old St

It would be easy to dismiss Jamie Oliver's nonprofit training restaurant as a gimmick, but on our latest visit the kitchen was in fine fettle. Here 15 young chefs from disadvantaged backgrounds (indicated by their black, as opposed to white, chef's hats) train with experienced professionals, creating an ambitious and interesting Italian menu. The ground-floor trattoria is a relaxed venue, while the more formal underground dining room has a set tasting menu. We found the gnocchi, veal ravioli and bream were all excellent, and the atmosphere was still as buzzing and exciting as ever. Reservations are usually essential.

HOXTON APPRENTICE
Map p150   Modern European ££
☎ 7749 2828; www.hoxtonapprentice.com; 16 Hoxton Sq N1; mains £4.50-14.50; ☒ closed all day Mon & dinner Sun; ⊖ Old St

This is another training restaurant where worthy applicants do their time at the stove. It may lack the glamour of Fifteen, but it's still a sleek establishment with bubble lighting and seating on two levels. It's tucked away and unknown to most people, on one of East London's trendiest squares. The menu is a range of classic dishes, such as fishcakes, Cumberland sausages with mash and Navarin of lamb.

FURNACE Map p150   Italian £
☎ 7613 0598; www.hoxtonfurnace.com; 1 Rufus St N1; mains £6.85-10; ☒ closed lunch Sat & all day Sun; ⊖ Old St

Furnace serves up the best pizza in Hoxton – what more do you need to know? If this isn't enough, it's got great staff, a good and affordable wine selection, a funky, buzzing feel within its brick walls and great pasta dishes, too. But go for the pizza – the suckling pig topping is unmissable.

SONG QUE   Vietnamese £
☎ 7613 3222; 134 Kingsland Rd E2; mains £5-7; ⊖ Old St/Liverpool St

With the kind of demand for seats that most London restaurants can only dream of, this perennial favourite in Hoxton's Vietnamese quarter always has a line of people waiting for a table. Service is frenetic and sometimes rude, but the food is great and good value.

CAY TRE Map p150   Vietnamese £
☎ 7729 8662; www.vietnamesekitchen.co.uk; 301 Old St EC1; mains £5-7; ⊖ Old St

This authentic place serves up classic Vietnamese beef noodle soup, *banh xeo* (a kind of pancake with prawns, chicken and vegetables) and wonderful pan-fried *basa* fish with lemongrass and shallots.

SPITALFIELDS

MESÓN LOS BARRILES Map p150 Spanish ££
☎ 7375 3136; 8a Lamb St E1; mains £10.50-17.50; ☒ closed Sat, dinner Sun; ⊖ Liverpool St

Avoid the chain-gang restaurants that now dominate the newly 'regenerated' (read sterile and corporate-friendly) Spitalfields market and stick to the old school with this long-established family restaurant. While the fresh fish here is great, the real draw is the excellent selection of tapas (£3.50 to £11.95). Sawdust on the floor and air-dried hams overhead add to the rustic market feel of the place.

GREEN & RED Map p150 Mexican ££
☎ 7749 9670; www.greenred.co.uk; 51 Bethnal Green Rd E1; mains £10.50-14.50; 🕑 closed lunch Sat & Sun; ⊖ Liverpool St

On a corner where Banglatown grinds up against Shoreditch, Green & Red stylishly showcases traditional Jaliscan cooking. While it offers up tacos and burritos at lunchtime, come the evening the menu features far more authentic dishes, such as slow-roasted pork belly with avocado salsa and stuffed chayote with cheese, pumpkin and chilli. In the bar downstairs choose your poison from among the more than 100 tequilas on offer.

ST JOHN BREAD & WINE Map p150 British ££
☎ 7251 0848; www.stjohnbreadandwine.com; 94-96 Commercial St E1; mains £6-15; 🕑 closed dinner Sun; ⊖ Liverpool St

Little sister to St John (p252), this place is cheaper and more relaxed but offers similar 'nose to tail' traditional fare (duck hearts on toast, jellied ham, salt lamb and turnips) in a simple, clean and bright space popular with Spitalfields creative types. It also has an excellent selection of British cheeses and puddings.

CANTEEN Map p150 British £
☎ 0845 686 1122; www.canteen.co.uk; 2 Crispin Pl E1; mains £7.50-12.50; 🕑 8am-11pm Mon-Fri, 9am-11pm Sat & Sun; ⊖ Liverpool St

Despite being part of the rather sterile-feeling 'new' Spitalfields, this popular place celebrates British food with a great menu catering to all tastes. Choose from freshly baked pies, roast chicken and the fish of the day, or just grab an outside table and a pork sandwich from the spit roast.

Also recommended:

Route Master (Map p150; ☎ 0791 238 9314; Ely Yard, off Hanbury St E2; mains £5.50-15; 🕑 noon-9.45pm; ⊖ Liverpool St) This excellent vegan restaurant is housed in a 1960s London Routemaster bus, which, while a quite a draw, seems incidental compared to its tasty and imaginative cooking.

Café 1001 (Map p150; ☎ 7247 9679; www.cafe1001 .co.uk; 91 Brick Lane E1; mains £2.50-6.50; 🕑 6am-midnight; ⊖ Liverpool St) Popular and huge cafe with

PIE 'N' MASH SHOPS

Those curious about how Londoners used to eat before everything went trendy, ethnic and nouvelle should sample a pie made from minced beef and 'mash' (mashed potatoes, often made from powder) available at any of the following establishments for £1.30 to £2.80. Jellied eels, mushy peas and 'liquor' (a green sauce made from parsley and vinegar) are optional extras. For a more comprehensive listing check out the website of the Pie & Mash Club (www.pie-n-mash .com). A slightly more modern take on this traditional staple is available at Humble Pie (p265) and the Square Pie Company (Map p150; ☎ 7377 1114; Spitalfields Market, 105c Commercial St E1; pies £3.50-4.50; 🕑 10.30am-4.30pm Mon-Sat, to 5.30pm Sun; ⊖ Liverpool St), which now has six outlets in London.

AJ Goddard (Map p182; ☎ 8692 3601; 203 Deptford High St SE8; 🕑 9.30am-3pm Mon-Fri, from 9am Sat; 🚉 Deptford, DLR Deptford Bridge)

Castle's (Map p170; ☎ 7485 2196; 229 Royal College St NW1; 🕑 10.30am-3.30pm Tue-Sat; ⊖ Camden Town, 🚉 Camden Rd)

Clark's (Map p150; ☎ 7837 1974; 46 Exmouth Market EC1; 🕑 10.30am-4pm Mon-Thu, to 5.30pm Fri & Sat; ⊖ Farringdon)

F Cooke (Map p150; ☎ 7729 7718; 150 Hoxton St N1; 🕑 10am-7pm Mon-Thu, 9.30am-8pm Fri & Sat; ⊖ Old St or Liverpool St)

G Kelly (Map p156; ☎ 8980 3165; 526 Roman Rd E3; 🕑 11am-3pm Mon, 10am-3pm Tue-Thu, 10am-7pm Fri, 10am-5.30pm Sat; ⊖ Mile End, 🚌 8)

Manze's Tower Bridge (Map p126; ☎ 7407 2985; 87 Tower Bridge Rd SE1; 🕑 10.30am-2pm Tue-Sat; ⊖ London Bridge); Deptford (Map p182; ☎ 8692 2375; 204 Deptford High St SE8; 🕑 9.30am-1.30pm Mon & Thu, to 3pm Tue, Wed, Fri & Sat; 🚉 Deptford, DLR Deptford Bridge)

grills and cakes, lounge seating upstairs and live music. This place is rammed at weekends.

Brick Lane Beigel Bake (Map p150; ☎ 7729 0616; 159 Brick Lane E2; filled bagels 70p-£2.90; ✸ 24hr; ⊖ Liverpool St) You won't find fresher (or cheaper) bagels anywhere in London than at this bakery and delicatessen; just ask any taxi driver (it's their favourite nosherie).

THE EAST END & DOCKLANDS

The changes that have occurred in the East End dining scene over the past decade have been nothing short of phenomenal, with upmarket gastropubs now standing cheek-by-jowl with budget ethnic eateries. And while the Docklands pretty much remains the land of expense accounts and quick lunches, you can now find some excellent Asian food there. In fact the East End's multiculturalism means its ethnic cuisine stretches pretty far, with everything from Vietnamese, vegetarian Thai and even Georgian available. But the best – by far – are its Indian and Pakistani offerings. If you fancy the real McCoy, head for the bare-bones subcontinental restaurants and caffs of Whitechapel – most of them BYO (bring your own) alcohol and all of them halal.

WHITECHAPEL

CAFÉ SPICE NAMASTE Map p156   Indian ££
☎ 7488 9242; www.cafespice.co.uk; 16 Prescot St E1; mains £13.75-19.50, 2-course set lunch £16.95; ✸ closed lunch Sat & all day Sun; ⊖ Tower Hill
Chef Cyrus Todiwala has taken an old magistrates court just a 10-minute walk from Tower Hill and decorated it in 'carnival' colours; the service and atmosphere are as bright as the walls. The Parsee and Goan menu is famous for its superlative *dhansaak* (lamb stew with rice and lentils; £14.95) but just as good are the spicy chicken *frango piri-piri* and the Goan king-prawn curry. Bonuses: they make their own chutneys here and there's a little garden behind the dining room open in the warmer months.

WHITECHAPEL GALLERY DINING ROOM Map p156   Modern European ££
☎ 7522 7888; www.whitechapelgallery.org; 77-82 Whitechapel High St E1; mains £13.50-17.75, 2-/3-course lunch £15/20; ✸ closed dinner Sun & all day Mon; ⊖ Aldgate East

The recently reopened gallery (p155), at the forefront of art in London with its seminal exhibitions of new work and retrospectives, has also put in place a small but perfectly formed dining room with high-profile chef Maria Elia at the helm. The menu is short but comprehensive with things like roast rabbit, grilled sea bream and inventive vegetarian dishes.

TAYYABS Map p156   Indian, Pakistani £
☎ 7247 9543; www.tayyabs.co.uk; 83-89 Fieldgate St E1; mains £6.20-13.80; ⊖ Whitechapel
This buzzing (OK, crowded) Punjabi restaurant is in another league to its Brick Lane equivalents. *Seekh* kebabs, *masala* fish and other starters served on sizzling hot plates are delicious, as are accompaniments such as dhal, naan and raita. But with Tayyabs now appearing regularly in guidebooks and the huge London Royal Hospital round the corner, you should expect to wait for a table.

MIRCH MASALA Map p156   Indian, Pakistani £
☎ 7377 0155; www.mirchmasalarestaurant .co.uk; 111-113 Commercial Rd E1; mains £4.50-10; ⊖ Whitechapel, 🚌 15 or 115
'Chilli and Spice', part of a small chain based in the epicentre of London subcontinental food, Southall, is a less hectic alternative to Tayyabs and the food is almost up the same level. Order the prawn tikka (£8) as a 'warmer' followed by the *masala karella* (£4.50), a curry-like dish made from bitter gourd, and a *karahi* meat dish.

KOLAPATA Map p156   Bangladeshi £
☎ 7377 1200; www.kolapata.co.uk; 222 Whitechapel Rd E1; mains £4.50-9.95; ⊖ Whitechapel
This modest restaurant in Whitechapel serves up what should be the yardstick of all Bangladeshi cuisine in London. Try the excellent starter *haleem* (lamb with lentils and spices) and the *sarisha elish* (Bangladeshi fish cooked with mustard seed, onion and green chilli).

BETHNAL GREEN & HACKNEY

LAXEIRO Map p156   Spanish ££
☎ 7729 1147; www.laxeiro.co.uk; 93 Columbia Rd E2; tapas £3.95-8.95, paella £19.50-23.50; ✸ closed dinner Sun & all day Monday; ⊖ Bethnal Green, 🚋 Cambridge Heath, 🚌 8 or 55
This homely place dead in the centre of Columbia Rd, the site of London's famous Sunday flower market, serves generous-sized

LOCAL VOICES: JOE COOKE

A resident of Chingford in northeast London, Joe Cooke owns F Cooke (p254), a pie-and-mash shop that's been on the same Hoxton street for more than a century.

Nice name in your trade. Local boy? It's got an 'e' at the end. Yeah, born in Clapton – that's with a 'p' – not Clacton with a 'c' – and I live in Chingford. My family has had a pie shop on this street since 1902 and the business has been in the family since 1862.

Don't people prefer pizza and fried chicken nowadays? Whither goest pie and mash? It's got nothing to do with preferring one over the other. Years ago a High Street had three places to eat in: a caff, a fish-and-chips place and pie-and-mash shop. Our portion of the take was one-third. Now every conceivable kind of food is available.

Who comes in? There's not a lot of passing trade, but we get all sorts: young and old, locals and tourists. You name it. Yanks, Afghans, Hindus (who are not always necessarily adhering to their dietary laws) and Japanese (who love to take pictures).

And what goes in? The same exact ingredients as when we first opened. Everything is done on the premises. We make all of our own dough, bone all the meat, grind all the parsley for the liquor and jelly the eels. The only big change in recent years is we now sell vegetable pies. Frankly lots of proper pie shops have disappeared because they're a lot of work.

Proper pie shops? If they serve gravy with their pies, it's not a real pie-and-mash shop.

Where do the ingredients come from? The meat's from Smithfield Market, the potatoes are Maris Pipers at the moment and the parsley is English. Eels are local until the season ends in late autumn. Then we get farmed ones from the Netherlands. We tried to import them from other places. Irish ones are the best but the New Zealand ones: ugh, they've got a skin on them like a donkey's foreskin. We've never changed any of the recipes.

Simple as that? Look, if you start off with cream ingredients you'll still have something good even if you balls it all up. Crap ingredients make crap dishes.

When I'm not behind the stove… I'm behind a pot of tea and a rum baba at Maison Bertaux (☎ 7437 6007; 28 Greek St W1; 🕒 8.30am-11pm Mon-Sat, to 7pm Sun; ⊖ Tottenham Court Rd).

Joe Cooke was interviewed by Steve Fallon

tapas (it prefers to call them *raciones*). Tapas change every two weeks but the *cochinillo* (tender suckling pig) is a constant. The handful of more ambitious dishes includes paella to be shared.

LITTLE GEORGIA Map p156 Georgian £

☎ 7739 8154; 87 Goldsmith's Row E2; mains £8-11; 🕒 closed dinner Mon; ⊖ Bethnal Green, 🚆 Cambridge Heath

A charming slice of the Caucasus in East London, this simple eatery on two floors is an excellent introduction to the cuisine of Georgia (as in Tbilisi, not Atlanta or midnight trains); try the mixed starter plate (£12) for two. The menu includes such classics as *nigziani* (red pepper or aubergine stuffed with walnuts, herbs and roast vegetables), chicken *satsivi* in walnut sauce and the staple *khachapuri* (cheese bread). The cafe is a good place for breakfast and does takeaway lunch (£4.50 to £7).

GREEN PAPAYA Map p156 Vietnamese £

☎ 8985 5486; www.greenpapaya.com; 191 Mare St E8; mains £5.50-8.50; 🕒 dinner Tue-Sun; 🚆 London Fields, 🚌 D6, 55 or 277

This oasis just south of the landmark Hackney Empire music hall serves Vietnamese food of very high quality and tends to put a 'modern' spin on many of the dishes. Try the *banh tom* (lightly fried strips of sweet potato and king prawns), the banana-flower salad and 'Mama's Pork', slow-cooked with mushrooms and vegetables. The staff are enthusiastic and helpful.

Also recommended:

Tas Firin (Map p156; ☎ 7729 6446; 160 Bethnal Green E2; mains £5-13.50; ⊖ Liverpool St) The 'Stone Oven' is just about as authentic a Turkish grill restaurant as you'll find in this neighbourhood.

Frizzante@City Farm (Map p156; ☎ 7739 2266, 0788 313 3451; www.frizzanteltd.co.uk; Hackney City Farm, 1 Goldsmith's Row E2; mains £5.25-7.50; 🕒 10am-4.30pm Tue-Sun, 7-10pm Thu; 🚆 Cambridge Heath; 🚌 55) Award-winning restaurant serving excellent Italian food next door to one of London's half-dozen city farms for children (p159) with a weekly *agroturismo* night with special country dishes (mains £10 to £12).

E Pellici (Map p156; ☎ 7739 4873; 332 Bethnal Green Rd E2; dishes £4.80-7.80; 🕒 6am-5pm Mon-Sat; ⊖ Bethnal Green, 🚌 8) Museum-quality art nouveau caff (1900) celebrated for its fry-ups, chips, simple Italian dishes and cacophonous clientele.

Taste of Bitter Love (Map p156; ☎ 0796 356 4095; www.tasteofbitterlove.com; 276 Hackney Rd E2; dishes £2.95-6.95; ⊙ 7.30am-4pm Mon-Fri, 10am-3pm Sun; ⊖ Bethnal Green, ⊞ Cambridge Heath; ⊟ 48 or 55) We visit this small but upbeat cafe as much for its name and award-winning coffee as for its soups, salads and cakes.

MILE END & VICTORIA PARK

FISH HOUSE Map p156   Seafood ££

☎ 8533 3327; www.fishouse.co.uk; 126-128 Lauriston Rd E9; mains £8.50-12.50; ⊖ Mile End, then ⊟ 277

This combination seafood restaurant and chippy is just the sort of place you wish you had in your own neighbourhood. The freshest of fresh fish and crustaceans are dispensed from both a busy takeaway section and a cheerful sit-down restaurant. The lobster bisque and Colchester oysters are always good, while the generous fish pie (£8.50) bursting with goodies from the briny deep is exceptional.

NAMO Map p156   Vietnamese £

☎ 8533 0639; www.namo.co.uk; 178 Victoria Park Rd E9; mains £6.50-9; ⊙ lunch Thu-Sun, dinner Tue-Sun; ⊖ Mile End, then ⊟ 277

This very bohemian place takes the Vietnamese dishes so characteristic of nearby Dalston and pulls them into the 21st century; expect things like chilli jam with your slow-cooked pork and a new take on *bun hue*, Vietnam's signature beef noodle soup. Seating is cramped, but the array of plants and flowers brings nearby Victoria Park even closer.

Also recommended:

Thai Garden (Map p156; ☎ 8981 5748; www.thethaigarden.co.uk; 249 Globe Rd E2; mains £5.50-11.95; ⊙ lunch Mon-Fri, dinner Mon-Sat; ⊖ Bethnal Green or ⊟ 8) This is a rare bird indeed – a mostly vegetarian (with some seafood dishes) Thai restaurant in Bethnal Green – and well worth the trip.

Pavilion Café at Victoria Park (Map p156; ☎ 8980 0030; www.the-pavilion-cafe.com; cnr Old Ford Rd & Grove Rd E3; mains £4.50-8; ⊙ 8.30am-5pm; ⊖ Mile End, ⓑ 277 or 425) Superb cafe overlooking ornamental lake in Victoria Park and serving breakfasts and lunches made with locally sourced ingredients.

Wild Cherry (Map p156; ☎ 8980 6678; www.wildcherrycafe.com; 241-245 Globe Rd E2; dishes £3.75-5.95;

⊙ 10.30am-7pm Mon-Fri, 10.30am-4pm Sat; ⊖ Bethnal Green, then ⊟ 8) In the London Buddhist Centre, this simple cafe with a delightful courtyard serving tasty and substantial vegetarian dishes, including shop-made cakes (£2.50 to £3.50).

WAPPING

IL BORDELLO Map p156   Italian ££

☎ 7481 9950; 75 Wapping High St E1; mains £7.75-16.50; ⊙ lunch Mon-Fri, dinner Mon-Sat; ⊖ Wapping

This boisterous – bordello also means 'chaos' or a 'mess' – neighbourhood eatery is always crammed with happy diners. If you're drinking at the Captain Kidd (p284) or Prospect of Whitby (p284), it's a convenient blotter stop for excellent pizzas (£7.95 to £9.95) and pasta (£7.75 to £12.45) as well as more ambitious meat and fish main courses.

DOCKLANDS

EL FARO Map p162   Spanish ££

☎ 7987 5511; www.el-faro.co.uk; 3 Turnberry Quay, Pepper St E14; mains £14.50-18.95; ⊙ closed dinner Sun; DLR Crossharbour

An E14 address rarely signifies a destination restaurant but hop on the DLR (a picturesque and worthwhile ride) and travel to the 'Lighthouse' for what are known as the best (and most inventive) tapas (£4.45 to £10.95) and Spanish dishes in town. The location on a basin in the Docklands is restful and within easy walking distance of Canary Wharf.

ROYAL CHINA RIVERSIDE
Map p162   Chinese ££

☎ 7719 0888; www.royalchinagroup.co.uk; 30 Westferry Circus E14; mains £8.50-25, set lunch £15; ⊖ /DLR Canary Wharf

Admittedly one of four outlets of a chain, including the Royal China Queensway (Map p176; ⊖ 7221 2535; 13 Queensway W2; ⊖ Bayswater), this is London's best Cantonese restaurant and excels in standard and unusual dim sum, available daily from noon (11am on Sunday) to 5pm. The Riverside branch has impressive views of the Thames, and in the warmer months tables are at the water's edge.

NORTH LONDON

North London is full of eating gems. From historic pubs to smart eateries catering for some of the capital's most sought-after residential neighbourhoods, this is not a place where you'll be left without options. While Islington is no longer London's foodie capital, it still has more than its fair share of excellent restaurants. Elsewhere you'll find a large choice running from Afghani and Greek to Russian and Turkish.

CAMDEN

ENGINEER Map p166   Gastropub ££
☎ 7722 0950; www.the-engineer.com; 65 Gloucester Ave NW1; mains £12.50-17; ⊖ Chalk Farm
One of London's original gastropubs, the Engineer serves up consistently good international cuisine – from simple but delicious burgers and grills to miso marinated sea bass with bok choi – and is hugely popular with impeccably styled North Londoners. The splendid walled garden is a highlight.

BAR GANSA Map p170   Spanish ££
☎ 7267 8909; www.bargansa.co.uk; 2 Inverness St NW1; mains £10-14.50; ⊖ Camden Town
Bar Gansa is a focal point of the Camden scene, has a late licence and is howlingly popular. The menus – mostly tapas (averaging £3) – are good value. Bigger specialities include traditional favourites such as Paella Valenciana. There's live flamenco on Monday evening.

MARKET Map p170   Modern British ££
☎ 7267 9700; 43 Parkway NW1; mains £10-14; ⊖ closed dinner Sun; ⊖ Camden Town
This much talked-about addition to Camden's reliable yet slow-changing eating scene is all about simple, good British food. The light and airy space reflects this simplicity, and the menu manages to make classic cookery memorable with delights such as Rose veal with anchovy butter, spinach and chilli, and whole plaice with caper butter and chips.

MANGO ROOM Map p170   Caribbean ££
☎ 7482 5065; www.mangoroom.co.uk; 10-12 Kentish Town Rd NW1; mains £10-13; ⊖ Camden Town
With delightful pastel decor and genteel service, Mango Room is a kind of decaf Caribbean experience, although there's no holding back with the food: grilled sea bass with coconut milk and sweet pepper sauce, salt fish with ackee (a yellow-skinned Jamaican fruit that has an uncanny resem-

blance to scrambled eggs), and curried goat with hot pepper and spices.

MANNA Map p166   Vegetarian ££
☎ 7722 8082; www.mannav.com; 4 Erskine Rd NW3; mains £9.50-13; ⊖ lunch Sat & Sun, dinner Tue-Sun; ⊖ Chalk Farm
Tucked away on a side street in Primrose Hill, London's most glamorous inner-city village, this little place does a brisk trade in inventive vegetarian cooking. The menu features such mouthwatering dishes as green korma, wild garlic and pea risotto cake and superb desserts. Reservations are usually essential.

TROJKA Map p166   Russian, Eastern European £
☎ 7483 3765; www.trojka.co.uk; 101 Regent's Park Rd NW1; mains £7.50-11; ⊖ Chalk Farm
If only the staff here were as charming as the richly painted red interior with stained-glass window, matryoshkas lining the walls and gold trim. Sadly the service – as if part of the Russian theme – is decidedly frosty, though this doesn't stop this cafe from being extremely popular. Its Eastern European food is delicious and filling, ranging from blini with caviar to *bigos* (a cabbage stew with mixed meats). Avoid the house wine by bringing your own (£3 corkage). There's live Russian music at the weekend.

MARINE ICES Map p166   Italian £
☎ 7482 9003; www.marineices.co.uk; 8 Haverstock Hill NW3; mains £6-13.50; ⊖ Chalk Farm
As its name suggests, this Chalk Farm institution started out as an ice-cream parlour (in fact, a Sicilian *gelateria*) but these days it does some savoury dishes as well, including pizzas and hearty pasta dishes. Be sure to try some of the excellent ice cream, which has its own menu – look for the long line out on the street on summer weekends!

Also recommended:

Belgo Noord (Map p166; ☎ 7267 0718; www.belgo-restaurants.com; 72 Chalk Farm Rd NW1; mains £8.95-15.95; ⊖ Chalk Farm) Branch of a Belgian restaurant chain; one of the few places in town that still serves *moules frites* (mussels and chips; £11.95).

Asakusa (Map p170; ☎ 7388 8533; 265 Eversholt St NW1; mains £3-8; ⊖ dinner Mon-Sat; ⊖ Mornington Cres) This somewhat scruffy but clean place has cheap sushi for £1.10 to £1.40 per piece, along with more elaborate set menus (£6 to £10).

TO MARKET, TO MARKET

At first glance, London's food markets may seem to have changed beyond recognition in recent years. Borough Market on the South Bank, equal to or even better than anything you'll find on the Continent, is now a top tourist attraction and Broadway Market caters to the capital's Gordon Ramsay and Nigella Lawson wannabes. But for those who still want to experience a traditional London market, where the oranges and lemons come from who knows where and the barrow boys and girls speak with cockney accents straight out of Central Casting, there's more than ample opportunity.

For information on farmers markets, which tend to sell much more local, organic and – inevitably – expensive produce, see the boxed text, p251.

Berwick Street Market (Map p66; Berwick St W1; ☒ 9am-5pm Mon-Sat; ⊖ Piccadilly Circus or Oxford Circus) South of Oxford St and running parallel to Wardour St, this fruit-and-vegetable market, the last of its breed in central London, has managed to hang onto its prime location since the 1840s. It's a great place to put together a picnic or shop for a prepared meal.

Billingsgate Fish Market (Map p162; Trafalgar Way E14; ☒ 5-8.30am Tue-Sat; DLR West India Quay) This wholesale fish market is open to the public, but you'll have to be up at the crack of dawn. People will tell you that you have to buy in bulk here, but most of the wise-crackin' vendors are prepared to do a deal.

Borough Market (Map p126; www.boroughmarket.org.uk; cnr Southwark & Stoney Sts SE1; ☒ 11am-5pm Thu, noon-6pm Fri, 9am-4pm Sat; ⊖ London Bridge) Located here in some form or another since the 13th century, 'London's Larder' has enjoyed an enormous renaissance in the past decade. Always overflowing with food lovers, both experienced and novices, this market has become quite a tourist destination. Along with a section devoted to quality fresh fruit, exotic vegetables and organic meat, there's a fine-foods retail market, with the likes of home-grown honey and homemade bread. Throughout, takeaway stalls allow you to sample a sizzling gourmet sausage or tuck into a quality burger. Shoppers queue at the excellent Monmouth Coffee Company, Neal's Yard Dairy, the Spanish deli Brindisa or butcher Ginger Pig, and generally bleed the local cash machines dry on Saturday.

Brixton Market (Map p190; Electric Ave, Pope's Rd & Brixton Station Rd SW9; ☒ 8am-6pm Mon, Tue & Thu-Sat, 8am-3pm Wed; ⊖ Brixton) This market is a heady, cosmopolitan mix with everything, from halal butchers and fishmongers touting tilapia, to yams, mangoes, okra, plantains and other produce on sale in the covered Brixton Village (formerly Granville Arcade).

Broadway Market (Map p156; ☒ 9am-5pm Sat; ☒ London Fields or Cambridge Heath, ☒ 48, 55, 106 or 394) Offering some serious competition to overextended Borough, this much more manageable market with almost a village feel, south of London Fields E8, has the choicest produce, dairy products, baked goods and coffees on offer.

Chapel Market (Map p170; Chapel Market N1; ☒ 9am-3.30pm Tue, Wed, Fri & Sat, 9am-1pm Thu & Sun; ⊖ Angel) This rough-and-ready all-day market sells mostly fruit and vegetables and some fish along an Islington street called Chapel Market, just off Liverpool Rd.

Leadenhall Market (Map p100; Whittington Ave EC1; ☒ 7am-4pm Mon-Fri; ⊖ Bank) This market serves food and drink to City folk and has a fishmonger, a butcher and a cheesemonger. The selection is excellent for an urban market, and the Victorian glass-and-iron market hall, designed by Horace Jones in 1881, is an architectural delight. It's off Gracechurch and Leadenhall Sts.

Ridley Road Market (Map p156; Ridley Rd E8; ☒ 9am-3pm Mon-Wed, 9am-noon Thu, 9am-5pm Fri & Sat; ⊖ Dalston Kingsland) In many ways this African Caribbean and Turkish market in the East End is more colourful than the one in Brixton, and it's certainly less touristed. You'll find more types of Turkish delight, Caribbean tubers and unidentified sea creatures than you'll know what to do with.

Roman Road Market (Map p156; Roman Rd E3; ☒ 9am-3.30pm Tue & Thu, 9am-5pm Sat; ⊖ Mile End, ☒ 8) This market along Roman Rd between St Stephen's and Parnell Rds has pretty standard fare on offer, though some people rave about the low prices.

Smithfield Market (Map p100; see also p105) London's last surviving meat market is still clinging on. While cattle were slaughtered here once, today this is the most modern of its kind in Europe and almost bloodless (though it would still be a vision of hell itself for vegetarians).

KING'S CROSS & EUSTON

MESTIZO Map p170   Mexican ££

☎ 7387 4064; www.mestizomx.com; 103 Hampstead Rd NW1; mains £9.80-19.50; ⊖ Warren St

If your idea of Mexican food is tacos and gluggy refried beans, think again. At this large and very attractive restaurant and tequila bar you'll find everything from quesadillas (cheese-filled pasties) to filled corn enchiladas. But go for the specials: *pozole*, a thick fresh corn soup with meat, and several different preparations of *mole*, chicken or pork cooked in a rich chocolate sauce.

ACORN HOUSE Map p170   Modern European ££

☎ 7812 1842; www.acornhouserestaurant.com; 69 Swinton St WC1; mains £12-18.50; ☾ closed Sun; ⊖ King's Cross St Pancras

We've enjoyed several top-notch meals at London's first 'totally ecofriendly' training restaurant – a venture of the Shoreditch Trust, but one that in no way feels like a charity. Fresh seasonal ingredients, an inventive modern British menu and a sleek, buzzing space make for an excellent lunch or dinner spot.

KONSTAM AT THE PRINCE ALBERT

Map p170   Modern British ££

☎ 7833 5045; www.konstam.co.uk; 2 Acton St WC1; mains £7-17; ☾ closed dinner Sun; ⊖ King's Cross

This unusual transformation of a King's Cross pub into a sleek dining space, complete with chains hanging from the ceiling in beautiful patterns, is a success, even if its lack of walk-by trade can sometimes leave it feeling rather less than buzzing. The unique selling point is Konstam's sourcing of 85% of its ingredients from areas covered by the London Underground – something that would feel gimmicky were the food not so good. The menu is always tempting – from roast belly of Amersham pork to pan-fried Waltham Abbey chicken.

CAMINO Map p170   Spanish £

☎ 7841 7331; www.barcamino.com; Regent Quarter, off Caledonian Rd N1; mains £6.75-18.50; ⊖ King's Cross St Pancras

This new venture in the Regent Quarter development in the heart of King's Cross is a much needed boost to the area's regeneration, serving up from a huge menu of tapas, main dishes, brunch and cocktails to

anyone who can find the place. It can feel rather large and impersonal, but the food is great and good value.

ADDIS Map p170   North African £

☎ 7278 0679; www.addisrestaurant.co.uk; 40-42 Caledonian Rd N1; mains £8-9; ⊖ King's Cross St Pancras

Cheery Addis serves pungent Ethiopian dishes such as *ye beg tib* (chunks of tender lamb cooked with onions and spices) and *doro wat* (chicken cooked with hot pepper and spices), which are eaten on a platter-sized piece of soft but slightly elastic *injera* bread. It's normally full of Ethiopian and Sudanese punters, which is always a good sign. The Addis Special Platter (£15.99) lets you sample all the highlights.

DIWANA BHEL POORI HOUSE

Map p170   Indian, Vegetarian, £

☎ 7387 5556; 121-123 Drummond St; mains £7-9; ⊖ Euston or Euston Sq

The first of its kind and arguably the best on this busy street, Diwana specialises in Bombay-style *bhel poori* (a sweet-and-sour, soft and crunchy 'party mix' snack) and dosas (filled pancakes made from rice flour). Thalis offering a selection of tasty treats are £6.75 to £8.50 and the all-you-can-eat lunchtime buffet (£6.95) is legendary.

RAVI SHANKAR Map p170   Indian £

☎ 7388 6458; 133-135 Drummond St NW1; mains £6-10; ⊖ Euston or Euston Sq

Another reliable *bhel poori* house on Drummond St, this place with the memorable name is a good second choice if you can't get a table at Diwana.

HAMPSTEAD & HIGHGATE

WOODLANDS Map p166   Vegetarian, Indian ££

☎ 7794 3080; www.woodlandsrestaurant.co.uk; 102 Heath St NW3; mains £6-18.50; ☾ lunch Fri & Sat, dinner Mon-Sat; ⊖ Hampstead

This South Indian vegetarian restaurant, whose rallying cry is 'Let Vegetation Feed the Nation', is determined to prove that South Indian vegetarian food can be as inventive as any meat-based cuisine and it does a pretty convincing job of it. Superb thalis and dosas are recommended highlights. There are three other branches around the capital.

BLACK & BLUE Map p166   British ££
☎ 7443 7744; www.blackandbluerestaurants
.com; 205-207 Haverstock Hill NW3; mains £8-26;
⊖ Belsize Park
This steakhouse chain might not merit a
mention elsewhere in London, but in the
desert of Belsize Park's eating choices it's
a reliable option, easily identifiable by the
life-size black plaster cow standing outside.
In addition to a panoply of steaks (£13 to
£26) there are also gourmet burgers (£8 to
£13) and a good grill selection.

WELLS TAVERN Map p166   Gastropub ££
☎ 7794 3785; www.thewellshampstead.co.uk; 30
Well Walk NW3; mains £10-16; ⊖ Hampstead
This popular gastropub, with a surprisingly
modern interior (given its traditional exterior), is a real blessing in good-restaurant
deprived Hampstead. The menu is proper
posh English pub grub – Cumberland sausages, mash and onion gravy, or just a full
roast with all the trimmings. At the weekends you'll need to fight to get a table.

BOMBAY BICYCLE CLUB   Indian ££
☎ 7435 3544; www.thebombaybicycleclub.co.uk;
3 Downshire Hill NW3; mains £10-15; 🕒 dinner;
⊖ Hampstead
One of three 'BBC' restaurants in London,
though there are also several delivery stations for this upmarket chain around the
capital. This Hampstead sidestreet space
is all scrubbed wooden floorboards and
starched white tablecloths, with an alluring
and interesting menu and plenty of veggie
choices.

LA GAFFE Map p166   Italian £
☎ 7435 8965; www.lagaffe.co.uk; 107-111 Heath
St NW3; mains £6-10; 🕒 lunch Thu-Sun, dinner
daily; ⊖ Hampstead
This Hampstead landmark is a comfortable,
family-run restaurant in an 18th-century
cottage that is now a hotel. It serves reliably
good Italian dishes, particularly the choice of
fresh pasta dishes, and you can upgrade their
size by adding £2 to the price. A three-course
set lunch (£12.50) is available weekdays.

ISLINGTON

METROGUSTO Map p170   Italian ££
☎ 7226 9400; www.metrogusto.co.uk; 13 The-
berton St N1; mains £15.50-18.50; 🕒 closed lunch
Mon-Thu & all day Sun; ⊖ Angel

This laid-back place with a selection of
interesting modern art on the walls serves
progressive, if somewhat pricey, Italian
cuisine. Typical dishes include Jerusalem artichoke ravioli in broad bean sauce or lamb
and veal meatballs with an almond dip.

MORGAN M Map p170   French £££
☎ 7609 3560; www.morganm.com; 489 Liverpool
Rd N1; set 2-/3-course lunch £22.50/26.50, set
3-course supper £39; 🕒 closed lunch Mon-Thu & all
day Sun; ⊖ Highbury & Islington
This new gourmet addition to Highbury's
eating options is a conversion of an old pub
into a very stylish French restaurant. Here
it's all about the set menus, which run from
a relatively restrained two courses at lunchtime to the full gastronomic blow out of
the six-course tasting menu in the evening.
It quickly became one of Islington's most
talked-about restaurants and is a real treat
for any lover of traditional French cooking.

DUKE OF CAMBRIDGE Map p170 Gastropub ££
☎ 7359 3066; www.dukeorganic.co.uk; 30 St
Peter's St N1; mains £12.50-18.50; ⊖ Angel
The UK's first certified organic pub is a
great place to avoid the crowds, as it's
tucked some way down a side street off
the Essex Rd where casual passers-by rarely
tread. There's a fantastic selection of beers
and ales on tap, a great wine list and an
interesting organic menu with a Mediterranean bent. You can eat in the pub proper
for a relaxed meal, or enjoy more formal
service in the restaurant at the back (reservations are a good idea in the evenings).

MASALA ZONE Map p170   Indian ££
☎ 7359 3399; www.masalazone.com; 80 Upper St
N1; mains £7-12; ⊖ Angel
This spacious place with outside seating set
back from Upper St in Islington is one of
the best budget Indian options in London.
Thoroughly modern in design, it serves up
meals centred on its famous thalis, as well
as tandoor and grilled dishes. There are
now several other branches throughout the
capital.

OTTOLENGHI Map p170   Italian ££
☎ 7288 1454; www.ottolenghi.co.uk; 287 Upper
St N1; mains £6.80-11.80; 🕒 8am-10pm Mon-Sat,
9am-7pm Sun; ⊖ Highbury & Islington or Angel
This is the pick of Upper Street's many
eating options – a brilliantly bright, white

space that's worth a trip to see the eye-poppingly beautiful cakes and bread in the front deli alone. But get a table at this temple to good food and you'll really appreciate it. At lunch you choose between the dishes spread out on the counter, while in the evening there's á la carte dining, too, though so fanatical about ingredient quality are the chefs that the menu is not confirmed until 5pm. Weekend brunch here is fabulous, though you'll usually have to wait for a table. Reservations are essential in the evenings.

BREAKFAST CLUB Map p170 — Cafe £
☎ 7226 5454; www.thebreakfastclubangel.com; 31 Camden Passage N1; dishes £3-9; ☽ 8am-10pm Mon-Fri, 9.30am-10pm Sat & Sun; ⊖ Angel
This bright and quirky oasis in Islington's Camden Passage follows in the footsteps of the Breakfast Club Soho (Map p66; ☎ 7434 2571; 33 D'Arbly St; ⊖ Oxford Circus) and has just spawned its third location with the Breakfast Club Hoxton (Map p150; ☎ 7729 5252; 2-4 Rufus St; ⊖ Old St). But, despite the name, breakfast (£3 to £8.30) is not the only game here: it also does sandwiches, salads and decent pies (£6 to £13). All venues are remarkable for their super-friendly staff and craaaazy decor.

GALLIPOLI Map p170 — Turkish £
☎ 7359 0630; www.gallipolicafe.com; 102 Upper St N1; mains £6.25-7.75; ⊖ Angel or Highbury & Islington
This popular Turkish restaurant crams its fans in both here and at nearby Gallipoli Again (Map p170; ☎ 7226 8099; 120 Upper St N1; ☽ closed lunch Mon-Thu & all day Sun), the over-spill premises. The draw here is decent Turkish dishes at low prices (by Islington standards, at least). The menu runs from a great selection of meze to a large range of kebabs.

LE MERCURY Map p170 — French £
☎ 7354 4088; www.lemercury.co.uk; 140a Upper St N1; mains £6.45; ⊖ Angel or Highbury & Islington
An excellent and wildly popular budget French eatery where the mains all cost the same very reasonable amount. Reservations are advised.

AFGHAN KITCHEN Map p170 — Afghani £
☎ 7359 8019; 35 Islington Green N1; mains £5.50-6.50; ☽ lunch & dinner Tue-Sat; ⊖ Angel

This minute two-floor gem serves up some of Islington's best-value and most interesting cuisine. It features traditional Afghan dishes such as *qurma suhzi gosht* (lamb cooked with spinach) and *qurma e mahi* (fish stew) alongside a generous vegetarian selection, including *borani kado* (pumpkin with yoghurt) and *moong dall* (lentil dhal). It's absolutely brilliant value, and rightly popular so book ahead for the evenings.

STOKE NEWINGTON

BLUE LÉGUME Map p62 — Vegetarian £
☎ 7923 1303; 101 Stoke Newington Church St N16; mains £5-12; ⧉ Stoke Newington, ⊟ 73
This lively Stokey mainstay has mosaic tables and rather hippie decor, with a bright conservatory at the back, and a scattering of tables outside on the street. The breakfasts are rightly popular – and there's a full Mediterranean menu ranging from lunches to a weekly paella night.

MANGAL OCAKBASI Map p156 — Turkish £
☎ 7275 8981; www.mangal1.com; 10 Arcola St E8; mains £5-11.50; ⧉ Dalston Kingsland
Mangal is the quintessential Turkish *ocakbasi* (open-hooded grill) restaurant: cramped and smoky and serving superb meze, grilled lamb chops, quail and *lahmacun* (Turkish 'pizza' topped with minced meat, onions and peppers). It's been here for almost 20 years and is always busy in the evenings. Takeaway is also available if you can't get a table.

RASA Map p62 — Vegetarian, Indian £
☎ 7249 0344; www.rasarestaurants.com; 55 Stoke Newington Church St N16; mains £4-8; ☽ lunch Sat & Sun, dinner daily; ⧉ Stoke Newington, then ⊟ 73
Flagship restaurant of the Rasa chain, this South Indian vegetarian eatery is Stoke Newington's best known restaurant and real destination dining for the capital. Friendly service, a calm atmosphere, jovial prices and outstanding food from the Indian state of Kerala are its distinctive features. If in doubt, don't bother with the menu and order the multicourse Keralan Feast (£16). Rasa Travancore (Map p62; ☎ 7249 1340; 56 Stoke Newington Church St N16) just across the road is more of the same, but with fish and meat.

WEST LONDON

The sheer variety on offer in multicultural West London means rich pickings for those seeking truly excellent restaurants. Notting Hill is the epicentre of this area and offers a superb range of eateries whatever the size of your belly or purse, from venerated chippies to fashionable fusion. Shepherd's Bush is constantly abuzz with new openings and revamps of old favourites, while Earl's Court offers a good range of cheaper options and some great people-watching. Hammersmith makes up for its lack of sights with some unique eateries, which are well worth travelling for. Both St John's Wood and Maida Vale also have interesting offerings that justify the trek out here.

ST JOHN'S WOOD & MAIDA VALE

BOATHOUSE Map p176   Modern European ££
☎ 7286 6752; www.boathouselondon.co.uk; Grand Union Canal, opposite 60 Blomfield Rd W9; mains £14-18.50; ☒ closed dinner Sun; ⊖ Warwick Ave
The Boathouse has cosy outside tables and a main dining room in a high wooden-ceilinged boathouse that feels almost alfresco. After a total overhaul and rebranding (it was for years a seafood restaurant called Jason's) it has moved away from fish to meatier climes, testifying to its Australian links. It's a great place for weekend lunch in fine weather.

MANDALAY Map p176   Burmese £
☎ 7258 3696; www.mandalayway.com; 444 Edgware Rd W2; mains £4.80-7.90; ☒ closed Sun; ⊖ Edgware Rd
Despite its unprepossessing appearance and location on a fairly grim part of Edgware Rd, Mandalay is actually one of the capital's most wonderful secrets, not to mention its only Burmese restaurant. The crispy *a-kyaw* fritters (£2.40) of vegetables and shrimps and the spicy bottle-gourd soup with noodles (£2.90) make great starters, while the twice-cooked fish curry with tamarind and lime (£6.90) is a scrumptious main course.

PADDINGTON & BAYSWATER

LE CAFÉ ANGLAIS
Map p176   Modern European £££
☎ 7221 1415; www.lecafeanglai.co.uk; 8 Porchester Gardens W2; mains £12.50-27, 2-/3-course

set lunch £16.50/19.50, weekday dinner £20/25; ⊖ Bayswater
After ditching Kensington Place (p264), Rowley Leigh opened this bustling restaurant with a very eclectic menu a short distance to the northeast. With beef hash and poached egg sitting comfortably with Thai green prawn curry and gigantic roasts that would feed a large family, this place means to please everyone; and, with such excellently priced set menus, it certainly does us.

PEARL LIANG Map p176   Chinese £££
☎ 7289 7000; www.pearlliang.co.uk; 8 Sheldon Sq W2; mains £7-28; ⊖ Paddington
Touted by many as London's best Chinese restaurant, this stylish eatery, incongruously wedged between Paddington train station and the Westway, serves up Chinese with a modern slant and the dim sum (£2.50 to £3.50) is out of this world. Love the decor, just this side of naff – water features, oversized abacus, plum blossoms.

COUSCOUS CAFÉ Map p176   North African ££
☎ 7727 6597; 7 Porchester Gardens W2; mains £9.95-15.95; ⊖ Bayswater
This cosy and vividly decorated basement place does a faultless line in familiar favourites from all over North Africa, but really excels with Moroccan-style couscous and *tagines* (spicy stews cooked in an earthenware dish), *pastillas* (filled savoury pastries) and slightly exaggerated service. Try the small/large mixed meze plate (£6.95/11.95). Alcohol is served but you can BYO (no corkage fee).

NOTTING HILL & PORTOBELLO

ELECTRIC BRASSERIE
Map p176   Modern British, European ££
☎ 7908 9696; www.electricbrasserie.com; 191 Portobello Rd W11; mains £9-32.50 ⊖ Ladbroke Grove or Notting Hill Gate
The name comes from the adjoining art deco cinema, but the place itself never seems to stop buzzing. Whether it's for breakfast (£5 to £10) or brunch over the weekend, a hearty lunch or a full dinner, the Electric certainly draws a trendy and wealthy Notting Hill crowd with its British/European Modern, which includes treats such as a jazzed-up chicken-and-leek pie, beetroot-and-goat's-cheese salad and – a personal favourite – lobster and chips (£32.50).

E&O Map p176   Asian Fusion ££
☎ 7229 5454; www.rickerrestaurants.com;
14 Blenheim Cres W11; mains £7.50-20.50;
✈ Ladbroke Grove

This Notting Hill hot spot presents fusion
fare, which usually starts with an Asian
base and then pirouettes into something
resembling Pacific Rim (eg green curry with
aubergine and lychee, or blackened cod
with miso and chilli tofu). The decor is stark
and minimalist – a 'cheaper and cooler version of Nobu' (p241), the tout. You can do dim
sum (£3.50 to £7) at the bar if no tables are
available in the evening.

COMMANDER PORTERHOUSE & OYSTER BAR Map p176   Seafood ££
☎ 7229 1503; www.thecommanderbar.co.uk; 47
Hereford Rd W2; mains £9.75-19.25, 2-/3-course set
lunch £12.95/15.95; ✈ Bayswater

This extravagant retro-style pub and eatery
does meat and fish with equal aplomb
but we usually steer clear of turf and go
straight for surf and the oysters. The seafood platter for two (from £44) is an easy
introduction to *fruits de mer* and the fish pie
with saffron, leeks and vermouth (£12.50) is
a showstopper.

KENSINGTON PLACE
Map p176   Modern European ££
☎ 7727 3184; www.kensingtonplace-restaurant
.co.uk; 201-209 Kensington Church St W8;
2-/3-course set lunch & dinner £16.50/19.50;
✈ Notting Hill Gate

Trailblazing chef Rowley Leigh has flown
the coop, leaving Kensington Place in the
hands of the successors to the Conran
chain. But that's not such a bad thing for
the budget-conscious, with identically
priced set meals served at lunch and dinner. The impressive glass frontage, de-
sign-driven interior and attached Fish Shop
(⏲ 9am-7pm Tue-Fri, to 5pm Sat), which is always
helpful for inspiration, remain in place.

GEALES Map p176   Fish & Chips ££
☎ 7727 7528; www.geales.com; 2 Farmer St
W8; fish & chips £9.75-17; ⏲ closed lunch Mon;
✈ Notting Hill Gate

Gregarious Geales, established in 1939
but, thankfully, made over since then, is a
popular fixture with locals and tourists alike
in Notting Hill. The menu now includes
fish pie and even sirloin steak. Geales is, of
course, more expensive than your everyday

chippie, but it's arguably the best in London. There's outside seating.

COW Map p176   Gastropub ££
☎ 7221 5400; www.thecowlondon.co.uk;
89 Westbourne Park Rd W2; mains £7.95-17;
✈ Westbourne Park or Royal Oak

Owned by Tom Conran, scion of celebrated
former restaurateur Sir Terence, this attractive boozer was one of London's original
gastropubs and the upstairs dining room is
so cool it creates its own ventilation. Name
of the game both upstairs and downstairs
at the main bar is seafood: Irish rock oysters, haddock fishcakes, pasta with cut-
tlefish and samphire. Despite its fair share
of trust-funded West Londoners, it's still a
great hangout.

MARKET THAI Map p176   Thai £
☎ 7460 8320; www.themarketthai.co.uk; 1st fl,
240 Portobello Rd W11; mains £4.95-13.95;
✈ Ladbroke Grove

Drippy white candles, carved arches and
wrought-iron chairs mark out the interior
of this delightful restaurant. It occupies the
1st floor of the Market Bar but is independent of it and feels way, way, way beyond
the market crowds. Hospitable staff and
fresh, delicately spiced Thai cuisine make
this place a little money very well spent.
Enter from Lancaster Rd.

COSTA'S FISH RESTAURANT
Map p176   Fish & Chips £
☎ 7229 3794, 7727 4310; 12-14 Hillgate St W8;
mains £5.50-8.50; ⏲ lunch & dinner Tue-Sat;
✈ Notting Hill Gate

This fondly regarded local puts a Cypriot
spin on the traditional chippy and has a
huge array of fresher-than-fresh fish dishes
at market prices, which many prefer to the
more upmarket Geales (left) nearby. Don't
confuse this place with Costa's Grill at No
18 on the same street.

TAQUERIA Map p176   Tex-Mex £
☎ 7229 4734; www.coolchiletaqueria.co.uk;
139-143 Westbourne Grove; tacos £5.50-7.50;
⏲ closed Sun; ✈ Bayswater or Notting Hill Gate

You won't find fresher, limper (they're not
supposed to be crispy!) tacos anywhere in
London and that's *seguro* (definite) because
the 'Tacory' (for lack of a better translation)
makes its own fresh corn tortillas next door –
as you'll see through the window. It's a small

casual place serving Mexico's favourite street food. The last time we visited, the Mexican embassy was having a party here.

Also recommended:

Churreria Española (Map p176; ☎ 7727 3444; 177-179 Queensway W2; mains £5.95-8.95; ⏱ 8am-8pm Mon-Fri, from 9am Sat & Sun; ◉ Bayswater) This extremely popular cafe with the open frontage serves a variety of cheap dishes, from English breakfasts to a range of Spanish tapas (£2.25 to £4.50).

Humble Pie (Map p176; ☎ 7243 5762; www.eathumble .com; 121 Portobello Rd W11; pies £3.45-4.45; ⏱ 11am-6pm Thu, from 8am Fri, from 6am Sat, 9.30am-2pm Sun; ◉ Notting Hill Gate or Ladbroke Grove) This excellent pie shop, years ahead of your traditional pie 'n' mash dive (lamb in shiraz or chicken with mango, anyone?), caters to happy market-goers on the Portobello Rd.

Arancina (Map p176; ☎ 7221 7776; www.arancina.co.uk; 19 Pembridge Rd, W11; dishes £2.70-5.20; ⏱ 7.30am-10pm; ◉ Notting Hill Gate) A fantastic place to indulge in Sicilian snacks. Try the *arancini* (fried balls of rice with fillings; £2), or the excellent pizza, and get hooked on the creamy desserts known as *cannoli siciliano*.

EARL'S COURT

MR WING Map p178 — Asian Fusion ££
☎ 7370 4450; www.mrwing.com; 242-244 Old Brompton Rd SW5; mains £14-33; ◉ Earl's Court or West Brompton
Mr Wing is a very smart, rather pricey Asian-fusion place offering the full spectrum of Chinese cuisine with some Thai and Japanese cooking – tom yum with prawns, sake clay pot with seafood – thrown in. To recommend it are a plush, dark interior filled with greenery and tropical aquariums, helpful staff and a basement where live jazz sessions are held Thursday to Saturday nights.

TENDIDO CERO Map p178 — Spanish £
☎ 7370 3685; www.cambiodetercio.co.uk; 174 Old Brompton Rd SW5; tapas £3-13; ◉ Gloucester Rd
This stylish (think clean lines in black and purple) place, limbo'd somewhere between South Kensington and Earl's Court, serves traditional tapas in just about the trendiest Spanish restaurant you've seen outside the Iberian Peninsula. It's popular and there are two sittings, so book ahead at all times.

KRUNGTAP Map p178 — Thai £
☎ 7259 2314; 227-229 Old Brompton Rd SW10; mains £5.75-12.95; ◉ Earl's Court or West Brompton

This friendly cafe-style undertaking with the unlikely name of 'Bangkok' (in Thai) serves good-value and relatively authentic Thai food.

SHEPHERD'S BUSH & HAMMERSMITH

RIVER CAFÉ Map p178 — Italian £££
☎ 7386 4200; www.rivercafe.co.uk; Thames Wharf, Rainville Rd W6; mains £29-32; ⏱ closed dinner Sun; ◉ Hammersmith
To the great relief of West Londoners and those further afield, the Thames-side restaurant that spawned the world-famous eponymous cookery books has reopened after another protracted refit. The simple, precise cooking showcases seasonal ingredients sourced with fanatical expertise; the menus change daily. Booking is essential, as it's still a favourite – yet again – of the Fulham set.

HARWOOD ARMS Map p178 — Modern British ££
☎ 7386 1847; www.harwoodarms.com; 27 Walham Grove SW6; mains £13.50-15.50; ◉ Fulham Broadway
A food-reviewer friend of ours with impeccable taste buds lists this gastropub as one of his favourite places to eat in London – sorry mate! – and returns not infrequently for the likes of game tea accompanied by venison sausage roll, grilled salted ox tongue with Jerusalem artichokes and/or Berkshire wood pigeon with Cumbrian air-dried ham. Carniphobes should hightail it west to the Gate (p266).

ESARN KHEAW Map p178 — Thai ££
☎ 8743 8930; www.esarnkheaw.com; 314 Uxbridge Rd W12; mains £6.95-16.50; ⏱ lunch Mon-Fri, dinner daily; ◉ Shepherd's Bush
Welcoming you back into the 1970s is the very green interior of this superb restaurant serving food from the Esarn (or Issan), the northeast of Thailand where people munch on chillies like chewing gum. The house-made Esarn Kheaw sausage and *som tom* (green papaya salad) are sublime. If you can handle it, the so-called Tiger's Cry (grilled strips of ox liver served with a fiery chilli sauce) is as authentic a northeastern dish as you'll find west of Nakhorn Ratchasima (or Korat, the capital of the Esarn).

PATIO Map p178 — Polish ££
☎ 8743 5194; 5 Goldhawk Rd W12; mains £8.50-14.90, set meal with glass of vodka £16.50; 🕑 lunch Mon-Fri, dinner daily; ⊖ Shepherd's Bush or Goldhawk Rd
This cosy restaurant is cluttered with curios and antiques and serves fairly authentic home-style Polish food. This cosy restaurant is cluttered with curios and antiques and is presided over by a kindly matriarch who knows and sees all. It serves fairly authentic home-style Polish food.

GATE Map p178 — Vegetarian ££
☎ 8748 6932; www.thegate.tv; 51 Queen Caroline St W6; mains £10.50-13.50; 🕑 lunch Mon-Fri, dinner Mon-Sat; ⊖ Hammersmith
Widely considered the best vegetarian restaurant in town, this destination eatery has a poor location behind the Hammersmith Apollo and is surrounded by flyovers, but the inventive dishes (aubergine teriyaki, shitake wonton and pumpkin laksa, rocket cannelloni), friendly and welcoming staff, and the relaxed atmosphere of the large, bright dining room overlooking a quiet courtyard make the trek here worthwhile. Surprisingly enough, it's the desserts, such as the orange and Cointreau cheesecake, that get recurring rave reviews, as do the simple but inspired starters and the fine wine list.

TATRA Map p178 — Polish £
☎ 8749 8193; www.tatrarestaurant.co.uk; 2 Goldhawk Rd W12; mains £8.90-12.90; ⊖ Goldhawk Rd
Despite the surfeit of Poles in West London, upmarket Polish eateries remain as scarce as hens' teeth. Tatra is one major exception, with its designer-driven decor and ever-so-cool waiting staff. The menu offers all the usual favourites as well as less familiar treats, such as *kaszanka* (grilled black pudding with toast and apple) and a risotto of *kasza* (buckwheat groats) and wild mushrooms.

BLAH BLAH BLAH Map p178 — Vegetarian £
☎ 8746 1337; www.gonumber.com/2524; 78 Goldhawk Rd W12; mains £7.95-9.95; 🕑 closed Sun; ⊖ Goldhawk Rd
This vegetarian institution has been packing them in for years with imaginative, well-realised food and informal and very upbeat surrounds. Dishes lean towards the Mediterranean, though not exclusively, with other offerings including Kashmiri curry and vegetarian fajitas. You can bring your own bottle (corkage £1.50 per person).

GREENWICH & SOUTHEAST LONDON

It's not that we've been lazy in compiling the following very brief section. It's just that Southeast London's culinary reputation is only starting to emerge, if at all. Even locals despair about where to eat in Greenwich; you'll pass plenty of eateries along the main street, but few places are really any good. Blackheath, across Greenwich Park to the south, has a couple of notable eateries and Dulwich (especially Dulwich Village) is starting to support a gastropub culture, but nothing that's really noteworthy has arrived yet.

GREENWICH

SE10 RESTAURANT & BAR
Map p182 — Modern European ££
☎ 8858 9764; www.se10restaurant.co.uk; 62 Thames St SE10; mains £13-19.50, 2-/3-course set lunch weekdays £11.75/14.95, weekend £17.95/21.95; 🕑 lunch & dinner Thu-Sun; DLR Cutty Sark
This outwardly scruffy restaurant and wine bar, west of the Cutty Sark DLR station, hides a light, airy and very warm interior of yellow and gold hues. There's a good concentration of fish dishes – though you'd hardly even know the Thames was at the back door – and traditional British dishes (though with only one mean vegetarian option). The desserts are pure comfort food, especially the sticky-toffee pudding. Sundays host both breakfast (£5.59 to £7.95) and lunch.

INSIDE Map p182 — Modern European ££
☎ 8265 5060; www.insiderestaurant.co.uk; 19 Greenwich South St SE10; mains £12.95-17.95, 2-/3-course set menu lunch £11.95/15.95, set menu early dinner £16.95/20.95; 🕑 closed dinner Sun & all day Mon; DLR/ 🚉 Greenwich
With stark white walls, modern art and linen tablecloths, Inside looks quite stuffy, but it's a pretty relaxed kind of place. The crisp food typically includes things like roast tomato soup with mascarpone, cod roasted with Spanish paprika, and desserts such as apple and rhubarb crumble.

ROYAL TEAS Map p182   Cafe £

☎ 8691 7240; 76 Royal Hill SE10; dishes £2.35-6.95; ⏲ 9.30am-5.30pm Mon-Fri, 10am-6pm Sat, 10.30am-6pm Sun; DLR/🚇 Greenwich

Royal Teas is not exactly vegetarian – you can get smoked salmon as part of a cream tea (£6.95) at lunchtime – but dishes are mostly comforting meatless things such as baked beans with melted cheese and Spanish-style eggs, and lots of baguettes and soups. We come for the ginger cake (£2.60) served with cream or ice cream.

Also recommended:

Spread Eagle (Map p182; ☎ 8853 2333; 1-2 Stockwell St SE10; mains £13.95-19.50, 2-/3-course set lunch £13.50/16.50, 3-course set dinner £22.50; ⏲ closed dinner Sun; DLR Cutty Sark) Smart, French-inspired restaurant opposite the Greenwich Theatre in what was once the terminus for the coach service to/from London.

Rivington Grill (Map p182; ☎ 8293 9270; www.rivingtongrill.co.uk; 178 Greenwich High Rd SE10; mains £9.75-27.50; DLR/🚇 Greenwich) Younger sister of the trendy bar and grill in Hoxton (☎ 7729 7053; 28-30 Rivington St EC2; 🚇 Old St) serves meals throughout the day.

SOUTH LONDON

The choice of restaurants in South London may not be as extensive as it is across the Thames, but the places that do exist are often stellar – Brixton has the best pizza in London and one of the city's sweetest cafes, plus a fantastic market. You'd actually travel here just to visit some of the restaurants in Battersea, Wandsworth and Clapham, while Kennington has one of the best Chinese restaurants in London.

BRIXTON

LOUNGE CAFÉ Map p190   Cafe £

☎ 7733; 56-58 Atlantic Rd SW9; mains £5.50-13.50; ⏲ closed dinner Sun; 🚇 Brixton

As much as a bar as a place to eat, this self-styled 'original urban retreat' has breakfast, day and evening menus with everything from vegetarian fry-ups and burgers to meze platters. It's an excellent place for a cocktail and a nosh, and there's live music.

FUJIYAMA Map p190   Japanese £

☎ 7737 6583; 5-7 Vining St SW9; mains £5.40-10.75; 🚇 Brixton

This deceptively small Japanese place behind Dogstar (p290), with its welcoming dark-red interior and communal benches, has a large choice of bento (meal) boxes, noodles, tempura, miso soups and sushi and sashimi on its lengthy menu.

ROSIE'S DELI CAFÉ Map p190   Cafe £

www.rosiesdelicafe.com; 14e Market Row SW9; mains £4-6; ⏲ 9.30am-5.30pm Mon-Sat; 🚇 Brixton

A much-loved Brixton cafe run by Rosie Lovell, a young cook hailed as 'the new Nigella'. She's certainly every bit as charming – and a real celebrity in Brixton Market and wider with her new recipe book, *Spooning With Rosie* – and she makes some fantastic cakes and biscuits, as well as quiches, wraps, sandwiches and salads that keep her loyal lunch customers coming back for more. It's a Brixton must.

FRANCO MANCA Map p190   Italian £

☎ 7738 3021; 4 Market Row SW9; mains £4-6; ⏲ noon-5pm Mon-Sat; 🚇 Brixton

Voted as the best pizza in London by literally everybody, Franco Manca is worth every minute (or hour, on Saturdays) spent waiting for a table or takeaway. Beat the queues by avoiding lunch hours and Saturday, and eat the incredible pizza in a relaxed atmosphere. The secret of pizza is always in the base, and this place only uses its own sourdough (all made in the upstairs bakery), with flour from a Neapolitan mill. There are six pizzas to choose from, and the source of every single ingredient is accounted for, and fantastically delicious – the vegetables are from a small London grocer, the organic olive oil brought from fincas in Spain and Sicily, the cheese is from Somerset, the tomatoes from Liguria in Italy and the meat from an independent London butcher. The beer and wine are organic (from Sussex and Piedmont, respectively) and the lemonade is homemade. The place itself is simple, and the pizza extraordinary (and so cheap!). Shame the opening times are so limiting.

ASMARA Map p190   North African £

☎ 7737 4144; 386 Coldharbour Lane SW9; mains £4-7.50, 6-/7-course set meals £25/27; ⏲ dinner daily; 🚇 Brixton

A rare Eritrean restaurant, Asmara serves spicy chicken, lamb and beef stews and vegetable dishes that you scoop up with *injera*, the flat, slightly spongy sourdough bread that is a national dish. Staff provide colour in their traditional costumes, while there's a

THE LONDON CHAIN GANG

While the usual bleak offerings of US-based chain restaurants are to be found all over the capital, London also boasts some excellent chains of inventive and interesting restaurants, which locals patronise frequently. Here are some of our favourites; check their websites for a full list of outlets.

ASK

Cheap and cheerful chain selling decent Italian fare, ASK has some 18 outlets that are usually quite large and conveniently located near major transport hubs, including the Paddington branch (Map p176; ☎ 7706 0707; www.askcentral.co.uk; 41-43 Spring St W2; ⊖ Paddington).

Carluccio's

Inventive and authentic, the Italian restaurants at this ever-expanding chain have a somewhat upmarket ambience, helped along by the open space created by the deli-counter at each of the almost two-dozen outlets, including the Fitzrovia branch (Map p66; ☎ 7636 2228; www.carluccios.com; 8 Market Pl W1; ⊖ Oxford Circus).

Giraffe

There's a kind of sunny Californian feel to family-friendly Giraffe, where the likes of coarse-cut chips (fries), burritos, vegetarian salad wraps and burgers are on the menu, and friendly service is a given. (In fact staff will just about serve you anything you ask for – within reason.) There are currently a dozen Central London outlets, including an Islington branch (Map p170; ☎ 7359 5999; www.giraffe.net; 29-31 Essex Rd N1; ⊖ Angel).

Gourmet Burger Kitchen

The burgers at GBK are the real deal, made from prime Scottish beef and enlivened by specially created sauces and superb chips. Vegetarian versions are also available. Of the two-dozen outlets, the Bayswater branch (Map p176; ☎ 7243 4344; www.gbkinfo.co.uk; 50 Westbourne Grove W2; ⊖ Royal Oak) is among the most useful.

Hamburger Union

Highly recommended, Hamburger Union delivers gourmet, calorific fast-food favourites to you in six smart and perennially packed central London locations, including a Soho branch (Map p66; ☎ 7437 6004; www.hamburgerunion.com; 22-25 Dean St W1; ⊖ Tottenham Court Rd). All meat is free of additives, and free range.

Le Pain Quotidien

Simple, stripped-down French-style cafes serve salads, soups, filled baguettes and excellent cakes from 12 outlets across London, including a South Bank branch (Map p126; www.lepainquotidien.com; ☎ 7486 6154; Upper Festival Walk, Royal Festival Hall SE1; ⊖ Embankment or Waterloo).

nod to the former colonial power, Italy, with four pasta dishes (£4 to £4.59) on the menu.

BATTERSEA & WANDSWORTH

CHEZ BRUCE Map p62 French £££
☎ 8672 0114; www.chezbruce.co.uk; 2 Bellevue Rd SW17; 3-4 course set menus £40-50; ⊛ Wandsworth Common
Though Michelin-starred, this feels more like a quality local than a flash restaurant. The rustic façade, beside leafy Wandsworth Common, belies its modern interior. The

fixed-price-only set-up means that there's fortunately no need to scrimp on desserts.

BUTCHER & GRILL Map p190 British ££
☎ 7924 3999; www.thebutcherandgrill.com; 39-41 Parkgate Rd SW11; mains £9-23; ⊛ closed dinner Sun; ⊖ Sloane Sq, then ☐ 19 or 319
This combination grill and butcher shop has made quite a slap south of the river, winning awards as fast as it sizzles T-bones. But while not everyone likes the idea of seeing their meat *au naturel* on entry, the quality of the ingredients, the wide choice

Nando's

If you must do real fast food, Nando's is one of the better options in London, offering chicken *a la portuguesa* by way of Africa and Brazil from as many as 65 outlets, including a Camden branch (Map p166; ☎ 7424 9040; www.nandos .co.uk; 57-58 Chalk Farm Rd NW1; ⊖ Camden Town). The decor is colourful and upbeat, the ambience laid-back and the signature *peri-peri* (chilli) sauce fiery.

Real Greek

This chain of Greek restaurants serving souvlaki (Greek kebab) and meze now counts eight outlets, including the original Hoxton branch (Map p150; ☎ 7739 8212; www.therealgreek.com; 14-15 Hoxton Market N1; ⊖ Old St), which is a work of art in itself.

Strada

A cut (and a slice) above when it come to chain pizzerias, Strada serves only what comes out of its wood-burning ovens at almost 30 outlets, including a Clerkenwell branch (Map p150; ☎ 7278 0800; www.strada.co.uk; 8-10 Exmouth Market EC1; ⊖ Farringdon). The pasta is also pretty good.

Tas

This is an established chain of very good Turkish restaurants with a roll call of stews and grills that will never disappoint loyal customers. There are eight outlets all together, spread out all over London, including a Waterloo branch (Map p126; ☎ 7928 1444; www.tasrestaurant.com; 33 The Cut SE1; ⊖ Waterloo). However, our favourite is easily Tas Pide (Map p126; ☎ 7928 3300; www.tasrestaurant.com; 20-22 New Globe Walk SE1; ⊖ London Bridge), which specialises in pide (Turkish 'pizza', for lack of a better word) and is excellently located opposite Shakespeare's Globe (p129) in Bankside.

Wagamama

There's nothing new or exciting about this chain of noodle bars, with almost 30 locations in London, including a Marylebone branch (Map p90; ☎ 7409 0111; www.wagamama.com; 101a Wigmore St W1; ⊖ Bond St); it's 'slurp, bam, thank you ma'am' and you're out. But the food's reliable and cheap (for London) and the bench seating excellent for solo travellers in search of 'dining companions'.

Yo! Sushi

London's original conveyer-belt sushi chain, Yo Sushi remains a fun place to visit. The original Soho branch (Map p66; ☎ 7287 0443; www.yosushi.com; 52 Poland St W1; ⊖ Tottenham Court Rd or Piccadilly Circus) is among 20 outlets spread across London.

of sauces and the views from the main dining room (all brickwork and exposed ducts) are more than compensation.

RANSOME'S DOCK Map p190   Modern British ££
☎ 7223 1611; www.ransomesdock.co.uk; 35-37 Parkgate Rd SW11; mains £14-22; ⏰ closed dinner Sun; ⊖ Sloane Sq, then 🚌 19 or 319
Diners flock to this restaurant not because it's trendy or on the dock of a bay (rather a narrow inlet of the Thames) but for fresh and very thoughtfully prepared food: smoked Lincolnshire eel fillets with buck-

wheat pancakes and crème fraîche; duck breast with apple sauce; and red cabbage organic lamb noisettes with roast root vegetables. Weekday two-course lunch is £15.

SANTA MARIA DEL SUR
Map p190   Argentine ££
☎ 7622 2088; www.santamariadelsur.co.uk; 129 Queenstown Rd SW8; mains £12-19; ⏰ lunch Sat & Sun, dinner daily; 🚉 Queenstown Rd or Battersea Park, 🚌 77, 137 or 345
The southern branch of the much-beloved Argentine steakhouse Santa Maria del Buen

Ayre (Map p156; ☎ 7275 9900; www.buenayre.co.uk; Broadway Market E8; ➔ Bethnal Green, ⓡ Cambridge Heath) in Hackney– hence the 'sur' (south) in the name – caters to carnivores south of the river with grilled meats and sausages. Go for one of the *parrilladas* (mixed grill; £16 to £25 per person) to share.

CLAPHAM KENNINGTON, OVAL & STOCKWELL

LOBSTER POT Map p189   Seafood ££
☎ 7582 5556; www.lobsterpotrestaurant.co.uk; 3 Kennington Lane SE11; mains £16-23; ◷ closed Mon; ➔ Kennington or Elephant & Castle
This charming French-owned restaurant hidden in the wastelands south of Elephant & Castle turns out excellently prepared fish and seafood dishes *à la française* (think lots of butter and garlic) to an appreciative local cognoscenti. An eight-course tasting menu with/without lobster is £50/45.

DRAGON CASTLE Map p189   Chinese ££
☎ 7277 3388; 100 Walworth Rd SE17; mains £7-20; ➔ Elephant & Castle
It's hard to imagine that what just might be the best nonchain Chinese restaurant in London is hidden within one of the brutalist buildings of deepest, darkest Kennington. But it's true, and even the incomparable food critic Fay Maschler of the *Evening Standard* concurs. The duck, pork and seafood (deep-fried crispy oysters; crab with black bean) are renowned – but come for the dim sum (£1.90 to £3), especially at weekend lunch.

GRAFTON HOUSE
Map p190   Modern International ££
☎ 7498 5559; www.graftonhouseuk.com; 13-19 Old Town SW4; mains £12.50-15.50, 2-/3-course set meals £22/27; ➔ Clapham Common
The A-listers of Clapham rub shoulders in this very stylish bar-restaurant with marble floors, tropical hardwood tables and curved leather sofas. The menu is modern international – simple but with that extra caress (pumpkin risotto, venison and plum burger; lobster, crab and salmon fishcake) – and brunch is a big deal here, served daily from noon to 4pm. There's live jazz on Sunday evenings.

KENNINGTON TANDOORI Map p189   Indian £
☎ 7735 9247; www.kenningtontandoori.co.uk; 313 Kennington Rd SE11; mains £6-13; ➔ Kennington

This local curry house is a favourite of MPs from across the river, including former Prime Minister John Major.

SOUTHWEST LONDON
Although not universally known for its cuisine, this area of London can lay claim to a number of decent gastronomic outposts, some of which are well worth crossing town for. If you're in Fulham, wander down Fulham Rd, up New King's Rd and along Wandsworth Bridge Rd for a good choice. In Putney, head down the High Street or the roads heading off it. In keeping with the high standard of living along the gentrified banks of the river, restaurants in places such as Richmond and Kew are usually exquisitely presented, featuring superlative food and wine lists.

FULHAM

BLUE ELEPHANT Map p196   Thai ££
☎ 7385 6595; www.blueelephant.com; 4-6 Fulham Broadway SW6; mains £15-22; ◷ lunch & dinner Sun-Fri, dinner Sat; ➔ Fulham Broadway
The sumptuous surroundings, attentive staff and excellent food of this Fulham institution with branches around the globe make dining at the Blue Elephant a memorable (if expensive) experience. The atmosphere is romantic, with candlelit tables, fountains and lush 'jungle' foliage, though the 'gift shop' at the front is a bit naff.

LOTS ROAD PUB & DINING ROOM
Map p196   Gastropub ££
☎ 7352 6645; www.lotsroadpub.com; 114 Lots Rd SW10; mains £9-14; ➔ Fulham Broadway
No one has a bad thing to say about this tucked-away gastropub, aside from the minor affectation of listing prices in hundreds of pence. Light floods through the windows into the high-ceilinged, wood-lined curved dining area and onto the black-and-chrome bar, where choice wines are sold by the glass. The regularly changing menu reads as pretty standard fare – roast pork, salmon, lamb – but it's all delicious and dependable. For dessert, try the sticky-toffee pudding or the honey-roasted figs.

HACHÉ Map p196   Hamburgers £
☎ 7823 3515; www.hacheburgers.com; 329-331 Fulham Rd SW10; mains £6.95-12.95; ◷ noon-

10.30pm Mon-Wed, to 11pm Thu, to 11.15pm Fri & Sat, to 10pm Sun; ⊖ Sloane Sq, then 🚍 19 or 319
This fancy Fulham burger joint with the French name (meaning 'mince') receives consistently ecstatic praise for its Scotch beefsteak burgers.

PUTNEY & BARNES

CHAKALAKA Map p196 South African ££
☎ 8789 5696; www.chakalakarestaurant.co.uk; 136 Upper Richmond Rd SW15; mains £10-25; 🕑 lunch Sat & Sun, dinner daily; ⊖ East Putney
This South African restaurant, done up in brash tiger patterns and colours, serves springbok and kudu (both types of antelope), ostrich, zebra and other creatures that are usually seen grazing – not being grazed on – and is probably best visited on a dare. It also has *bobotie* (£11), a very South African dish of spiced minced meat baked with a breadfruit-custard topping, on the menu. Good selection of South African wines.

CHOSAN Map p196 Japanese ££
☎ 8788 9626; 292 Upper Richmond Rd SW15; mains £4-17; 🕑 closed Mon; ⊖ Putney Bridge, 🚇 Putney
This little Japanese restaurant whose name means Korea in Korean (go figure) doesn't look like much from the outside – or the inside for that matter – but it does turn out excellent sushi and sashimi as well as tempura and *kushiage* (more deeply fried than tempura) dishes.

ENOTECA TURI Map p196 Italian ££
☎ 8785 4449; www.enotecaturi.com; 28 Putney High St SW15; mains £10-16, 3-course set lunches/dinners £15.50/25.50; 🕑 closed Sun; ⊖ Putney Bridge, 🚇 Putney
The atmosphere at this stylish place is serene, the service charming. Enoteca Turi devotes equal attention to the grape as to the food, which means that each dish, be it a shellfish *tagliolini* or saddle of new season lamb, comes recommended with a particular glass of wine (or you can pick from the enormous wine list if you have ideas of your own).

MA GOA Map p196 Indian ££
☎ 8780 1767; www.ma-goa.com; 242-244 Upper Richmond Rd SW15; mains £9-15; 🕑 dinner Tue-Sun; ⊖ Putney Bridge, 🚇 Putney

The speciality here is the subtle cuisine of Portugal's erstwhile colony on the west coast of India. Dishes include the homemade chorizo topped with a spicy onion sauce; and fish *caldin,* a sour-sweet coconut-based concoction.

OLÉ Map p196 Spanish £
☎ 8788 8009; www.olerestaurants.com; 240 Upper Richmond Rd SW15; tapas £2-8, mains £10-17; ⊖ Putney Bridge, 🚇 Putney
This very un-Spanish-looking restaurant in Putney has lots of light and blond-wood furniture and serves excellent tapas.

RICHMOND

PETERSHAM NURSERIES CAFÉ
Map p200 Modern European £££
☎ 8605 3627; www.petershamnurseries.com; Church Lane, off Petersham Rd TW10; mains £18-29, 2-/3-course menu Wed-Fri £23/28; 🕑 lunch Tue-Sun; ⊖ / 🚇 Richmond, then 🚍 65 or 371
In a greenhouse at the back of the gorgeously situated Petersham Nurseries is this award-winning cafe straight out of the pages of *The Secret Garden.* Well-heeled locals tuck into confidently executed food that often began life in the nursery gardens – organic vegetable dishes, such as artichokes braised with preserved lemon sage and black olives, feature alongside seasonal plates of, say, roasted quail with walnut sauce or white polenta with squid and sherry butter. Booking in advance is essential. There's also a teahouse (🕑 10am-4.30pm Tue-Sat, from 11am Sun) for sandwiches, tea and cakes.

Because of local residents and council concerns about traffic increasing with the cafe's popularity, patrons are asked to walk here via the picturesque river towpath or use public transport.

FISHWORKS Map p200 Seafood ££
☎ 8948 5965; www.fishworks.co.uk; 13-19 The Square, Old Market TW9; mains £10-25; 🕑 closed dinner Sun; ⊖ / 🚇 Richmond
This Bath-based chain was London's first truly French *poissonnerie* (fishmonger) with a restaurant attached, its entranceway counters piled high with shaved ice, crustaceans and fish. We return regularly, especially for the sublime Dartmouth crab eaten cold and the incomparable *zuppa del pescatore* (fisherman's soup; £19), a symphony of

delights from the deep. There is also a Marylebone branch (Map p90; ☎ 7935 9796; 89 Marylebone High St W1; ⊖ Bond St).

CHEZ LINDSAY Map p200   French ££
☎ 8948 7473; www.chezlindsay.co.uk; 11 Hill Rise TW10; mains £13-19, 2-/3-course set lunches £15/18 & dinners £19/22; ⊖ / 🚇 Richmond
Offering a slice of Brittany at the bottom of Richmond Hill, Chez Lindsay's simply furnished dining room draws visitors with its wholesome Breton cuisine, comfortable ambience and river views. The house specialities include galettes with myriad tasty fillings, washed down with a variety of hearty (and very dry) Breton ciders.

DON FERNANDO'S Map p200   Spanish £
☎ 8948 6447; www.donfernando.co.uk; 27f The Quadrant TW9; mains £9-12; ⊖ / 🚇 Richmond
The Izquierdo family have been serving superb cuisine from their native Andalucía for nigh on 20 years now, and their enthusiasm shows no signs of waning. With an exhaustive list of tapas (£5 to £8), Spanish beers, wines and culinary specialities, including (unusually) some vegetarian options along with cheerful service, this makes a great place for a good lunch or a slow supper.

KEW

GLASSHOUSE Map p62   Modern European ££
☎ 8940 6777; www.glasshouserestaurant.co.uk; 14 Station Pde TW9; mains £17-22; ⊖ / 🚇 Kew Gardens

A meal at this splendid restaurant is a great way to cap off a day spent at the botanical gardens (p199) in Kew. Its glass-fronted exterior reveals a delicately lit, low-key interior, whose unassuming decor ensures that the focus remains on the divinely cooked food. Punters choose from such mains as a rump of veal with caramelised calf's tongue and sweetbreads, or roast fillet of cod with creamed white polenta, which combine traditional English mainstays with modern European innovation. The Glasshouse is sister restaurant to Chez Bruce (p268) in Wandsworth.

NEWENS MAIDS OF HONOUR
Map p62   Cafe £
☎ 8940 2752; www.theoriginalmaidsofhonour .co.uk; 288 Kew Rd W9; set tea £6.50; 🕙 9.30am-1pm Mon, to 6pm Tue-Sat; ⊖ / 🚇 Kew Gardens
The name of this quirky Kew tearoom a short distance from the main entrance to Kew Gardens comes from its famed dessert (£3), supposedly created by Anne Boleyn, Henry VIII's ill-fated second wife. It is made of puff pastry, lemon, almonds and curd cheese, and anyone visiting should try it at least once .

KEW GREENHOUSE Map p62   Cafe £
☎ 8940 0183; 1 Station Pde TW9; mains £7-10; 🕙 8.30am-6.30pm; ⊖ / 🚇 Kew Gardens
This delightful botanically themed cafe will help set the mood for a visit to nearby Kew Gardens (p199). Food is all about simple staples, such as jacket potatoes and sandwiches, as well as a daily surprise. Perfect for a cup of tea and cake.

top picks

DRINKING

There's little Londoners like to do more than drink. From Hogarth's 18th-century *Gin Lane* prints to Boris Johnson's decision to ban all alcohol on public transport in 2008, the capital's history has been shot through with the population's desire to imbibe as much alcohol as possible, particularly when the powers that be attempt to discourage them. Until recently, this manifested itself in London's draconian licensing laws, under which only private clubs could sell booze after 11pm. Now liberalisation has come (though, beyond busy drinking strips, finding a pub open after 11pm can still be a challenge) and the pickings are richer than ever as Londoners have rediscovered their fantastic pub heritage.

The pub (public house) is of course at the heart of London's existence and is one of the capital's great social levellers. A pub's history is usually written on the walls and etched in the bloodshot faces of the regulars who prop up the bar. Virtually every Londoner has a 'local' and looking for your own and sampling a range of boozers (pubs) is one of the highlights of any visit to the capital.

Unfortunately, an increasing number of London's traditional boozers, known for their particular atmosphere of sticky carpets, prawn-cocktail crisps (potato chips) and jukebox music, have been converted into a range of different venues, from soulless chain bars to ever-in-demand housing. Avoid high-street chain pubs and head to one of the establishments below.

Aside from the bars we recommend, it's a great idea to check out a few drinking strips yourself, such as Islington's Upper St or Essex Rd; Shoreditch's Old or High Sts; Soho's Dean St or Greek St; West London's Portobello Rd; the Cut on the South Bank; Clapham High St and Borough High St in South London; or Parkway and Camden High St in Camden Town. We've provided information on many of *our* favourite drinking dens here, although there's no substitute for individual research – your liver's the only limit.

Opening Hours

Back in 2005 new licensing laws granted pubs and bars, at the discretion of local authorities, permission to stay open past the traditional 11pm closing-time gong. This has made it somewhat easier to get a late drink in central areas, though closing times still vary from place to place. Unless otherwise stated, all pubs and bars reviewed here open at 11am and close at 11pm from Monday to Saturday and at 10.30pm on Sunday.

THE WEST END

You have to do a bit of planning before you head out in the West End: most Londoners find it difficult to beat the crowds, get a table without a struggle and drink in bars that aren't mobbed by weekend visitors. The truth is that the West End, though the first port of call for most visitors, is no longer a prime drinking area for discerning Londoners. Yet Soho is still a wonderful place for a night out – Friday and Saturday nights are buzzing with excitement and decadence, and there are people, booze and rickshaws in the streets till the early hours.

SOHO & CHINATOWN

COACH & HORSES Map p66   Pub
☎ 7437 5920; 29 Greek St W1; ⊖ Leicester Sq
Famous as the place where *Spectator* columnist Jeffrey Bernard drank himself to death, this small, busy and thankfully unreconstructed boozer retains an old Soho bohemian atmosphere with a regular clientele of soaks, writers, hacks, tourists and those too pissed (drunk) to lift their heads off the counter. Pretension will be prosecuted.

ENDURANCE Map p66   Bar
☎ 7437 2944; 90 Berwick St W1; ⊖ Oxford Circus or Piccadilly Circus
A Soho favourite, especially for music lovers who comb the vinyl shops (p221) on this street before surrendering to the pull of the pint. The Endurance has a retro jukebox that's full of indie hits, there's good wine and draught ales to be savoured, and there's decent food too; Sundays are quiet and good for a long, newspaper-reading lunch. Often the crowds spill outside in the evenings, and daytime drinks afford good views of Berwick Street market (p259) buzz.

FRENCH HOUSE Map p66   Bar
☎ 7437 2799; 49 Dean St W1; ⊖ Leicester Sq
French House is Soho's legendary boho
boozer (with a good restaurant downstairs)
with a history to match: this was the meeting place of the Free French Forces during
WWII, and De Gaulle is said to have drunk
here often, while Dylan Thomas, Peter
O'Toole and Francis Bacon all frequently
ended up on the wooden floors. Come here
to sip on Ricard, French wine or Kronen-
bourg and check out the quirky locals.

JOHN SNOW Map p66   Pub
☎ 7437 1344; 39 Broadwick St W1; ⊖ Oxford
Circus or Piccadilly Circus
This is one of Soho's most popular pubs,
as attested by the crowds inside, in winter,
and outside, in spring and summer, on
almost any day of the week. The interior is
simple and quietly stylish, there's no music,
just plenty of chat and good own ale, lager,
bitter and stout from independent British
brewery Sam Smith's. You can also get
organic beer and cider, plus, for the sweet-
tooths, cherry beer.

MILK & HONEY Map p66   Cocktail Bar
☎ 7292 9949, 0700 655 469; www.mlkhny.com;
61 Poland St W1; ⊖ Leicester Sq or Tottenham
Court Rd
Milk & Honey's number one 'House Rule'
reads: 'No name-dropping, no star fucking', so prepare for a tight-lipped but
glamorous clientele at this cocktail bar. It's
a members' club that lets nonmembers
in on weeknights (though it's preferred if
the plebeians stick to the beginning of the
week), and you have to phone in advance
to reserve your own private booth for a
two-hour slot. Once you're there, you have
to ring the bell and whisper your name
into the buzzer, the speakeasy way. This
practice is heavenly if you like privacy and
great drinks, and hellish if you prefer a
more down-to-earth atmosphere. It's worth
sampling the vast and exquisite cocktail list.

PLAYER Map p66   Cocktail Bar
☎ 7494 9125; www.thplyr.com; 8 Broadwick St
W1; ☾ to midnight Mon-Wed, to 1am Thu-Sat,
closed Sun; ⊖ Oxford Circus
The Player was one of London's top cocktail
bars during the 1990s, when Dick Bradsell,
the Lenin of London's cocktail revolution,
started mixing his substantial and stylish

drinks behind the basement bar. He has
since moved on and, although the bar still
serves great drinks, the clientele is a lot less
suave than when the bar was at its best. A
cooler Soho crowd heads down after 9pm,
when you too should descend and sample
the cocktail list. Unfortunately, only members are admitted after 11pm.

TWO FLOORS Map p66   Bar
☎ 7439 1007; 3 Kingly St W1; ☾ to midnight Fri &
Sat, closed Sun; ⊖ Oxford Circus or Piccadilly Circus
It's amazing that Two Floors has managed
to keep its relaxed atmosphere when so
many bars in Soho have been mobbed by
drunken weekenders, but it might be to do
with the fact that it's hard to notice from
the outside, and this low profile has helped
maintain its cool personality. The punters
are young and bohemian, the bar staff
equally so, and the music is usually uber-
now. The distressed decor is leather sofas
and country-diner tables and chairs.

COVENT GARDEN & LEICESTER SQUARE

CROSS KEYS Map pp70-1   Pub
☎ 7836 5185; 31 Endell St WC2; ⊖ Covent Garden
Covered in ivy and frequented by loyal
locals who come here for pints of Young's
and spicy fry-ups, the Cross Keys is Covent
Garden's tourist-free local pub. Eccentric
landlord Brian shows off his pop purchases
as bar decorations (such as his £500 Elvis
Presley napkin); brass pots, kettles and
diving gear hang off the ceiling; and the
punters range from bar props and fruit-
machine (poker machine) devotees to Covent Garden professionals, all of whom spill
onto the pavement and outside tables on
summer days.

FREUD Map pp70-1   Bar, Cafe
☎ 7240 9933; 198 Shaftesbury Ave WC2; ☾ to
1am Thu, to 2am Fri, to 1am Sat; ⊖ Covent Garden
Make this the first stop on your crawl
because there's no way you'll make it down
the stairs (not much more than a ladder)
after a few bevvies (drinks). It's a small
basement bar-cafe-gallery with the sort of
beige walls that could look just plain dirty,
but purposefully arty pictures head off
close scrutiny. The decor and punters are
suitably scruffy and arty, and the cocktails

are fat and fancy, but beer is sadly only by
the bottle.

LAMB & FLAG Map pp70-1 — Pub
☎ 7497 9504; 33 Rose St WC2; ⊖ Covent Garden
or Leicester Sq
Good pubs can be hard to come by in over-
touristy Covent Garden, but the Lamb &
Flag makes up for any character or soul the
area has lost – the interior is more than 350
years old, with creaky wooden floors and
winding stairs, there's live jazz on Sunday
afternoons and, come sunshine or summer
evenings, it's a miracle if you can approach
the bar for all the people crowding outside.
Its setting is equally charming: the main
entrance is on top of a tiny cobbled street,
but you can also reach it from the backstreet donkey path that'll make you think of
Victorian England.

SALISBURY Map pp70-1 — Pub
☎ 7836 5863; 90 St Martin's Lane WC2; ☽ to
midnight Fri & Sat; ⊖ Leicester Sq
Facing off the superchic St Martin's Lane
Hotel, the Salisbury offers everything its
opposite number doesn't: warmth, centuries of history, and a glorious, traditionally
British pub interior. The Salisbury is packed
in the evenings by pre- and post-theatre
drinkers and, while it can be a little touristy,
it's still a true London gem.

HOLBORN & THE STRAND

GORDON'S WINE BAR Map pp70-1 — Bar
☎ 7930 1408; www.gordonswinebar.com; 47 Villiers St WC2; ⊖ Embankment or Charing Cross
We shouldn't really include Gordon's here –
it's already too crowded as soon as the
office hours are over – but it's simply too
good to leave out. It's cavernous and dark,
and the French and New World wines are
heady and reasonably priced; and you can
nibble on bread, cheese and olives.

POLSKI BAR Map pp70-1 — Bar
☎ 7831 9679; 11 Little Turnstile WC1; ☽ closed
Sun; ⊖ Holborn
Formerly known as Na Zdorowie ('cheers'
in Polish), Polski Bar changed its name
probably as a result of no one being able
to pronounce it before or after many a
flavoured vodka shot, but the spirit (no pun
intended) has remained: around 60 different types of vodka, from coffee to fruity

to wheat-flavoured, there's even kosher
vodka, or simple old Polish *slivowica* (plum
brandy). There's great Polish food here, too.

PRINCESS LOUISE Map pp70-1 — Pub
☎ 7405 8816; 208 High Holborn WC1; ⊖ Holborn
We might have used the word gem before, but we take all of the other instances
back. This late-19th-century Victorian pub
is spectacularly decorated with a riot of
fine tiles, etched mirrors, plasterwork and
a stunning central horseshoe bar. After an
eight-month renovation, it's looking even
better. The old tiles and plasterwork have
been scrubbed up, and Victorian wood
partitions have been reinstated, giving
punters nooks and alcoves to hide in. There
are Corinthian columns too, would you
believe? Beers are Sam Smith's only, and, at
£2 a pint, it's a wonder anyone ever leaves.

SEVEN STARS Map pp70-1 — Pub
☎ 7242 8521; 53-54 Carey St WC2; ⊖ Holborn or
Temple
Even though it's packed with lawyers in
the after-office booze rush hour, the tiny
Seven Stars is still a relative secret to many
Londoners. Sitting behind the Royal Courts of
Justice (p77) and originally a sailors' hangout,
this is a place overflowing with character,
great food, beer and wine. The eccentric landlady and chef, Roxy Beaujolais,
a former TV chef and raconteur, lets her
cat, Tom Paine, roam around the pub and
snooze on the window sills; the bar staff are
friendly and the game dishes ravishing.

BLOOMSBURY

KING'S BAR Map pp80-1 — Bar
☎ 7837 6470; Hotel Russell, Russell Sq WC1;
⊖ Russell Sq
Nestled behind the awesome Victorian
Gothic facade of the Hotel Russell, the King's
Bar is an oasis of booze in a neighbourhood
sorely lacking decent bars. The grand Edwardian decor, huge leather armchairs and
table service make the prices worthwhile.
There's a great selection of cocktails and
wines, and you're always guaranteed a seat.

LAMB Map pp80-1 — Pub
☎ 7405 0713; 94 Lamb's Conduit St WC1; ☽ to
midnight Mon-Sat, to 10.30pm Sun; ⊖ Russell Sq
The Lamb's central mahogany bar with
beautiful Victorian dividers has been its

pièce de résistance since 1729, when the screens used to hide the music stars from the punters' curious gaze. Just like three centuries ago, the pub is still wildly popular, so come early to bag a booth. It has a decent selection of Young's bitters and a genial atmosphere perfect for unwinding.

LORD JOHN RUSSELL Map pp80-1 Pub
☎ 7388 0500; 91 Marchmont St WC1; ⊖ Russell Sq
If you're pining for your student days or just want a cheap pint, head down to the Lord John Russell. Here you can blend in with the under- and post-grads who are escaping the local halls of residence. It's a traditional one-room bar where chatting is the norm, and the relaxed atmosphere is perfect for getting away from noisy Central London bars.

MUSEUM TAVERN Map pp80-1 Pub
☎ 7242 8987; 49 Great Russell St WC1; ⊖ Tottenham Court Rd or Holborn
This is where Karl Marx used to retire for a well-earned pint after a hard day's inventing communism in the British Museum Reading Room, and where George Orwell boozed after his literary musings. A lovely traditional pub set around a long bar, it has friendly staff and is popular with academics and students alike, and while tourists check in for the atmosphere, the place retains its loyal regulars.

QUEEN'S LARDER Map pp80-1 Pub
☎ 7837 5627; 1 Queen Sq WC1; ⊖ Russell Sq
In a lovely square southeast of Russell Sq, this pub is so called because Queen Charlotte, wife of 'Mad' King George III, rented part of the pub's cellar to store special foods for him while he was being treated nearby. There are benches outside for fair-weather fans and a good dining room upstairs.

FITZROVIA

BRADLEY'S SPANISH BAR Map p66 Bar
☎ 7636 0359; 42-44 Hanway St W1; ⊖ Tottenham Court Rd
Hanway St is home to several Spanish-style tapas-and-flamenco and speakeasy bars that open till dawn and serve beer from crates. Bradley's is vaguely Spanish in decor, though it's really Spanish in its

choice of booze: San Miguel, Cruzcampo and some decent wines. The punters are squeezed under low ceilings in the nooks of the basement, while a vintage vinyl jukebox plays out rock tunes of your choice.

NEWMAN ARMS Map p66 Pub
☎ 7636 1127; www.newmanarms.co.uk; 23 Rathbone St W1; ⊖ Goodge St or Tottenham Court Rd
A lovely local that is also one of the few family-run pubs in central London, Newman Arms is a one-tiny-room affair with a 100-year history, good music, great beer and loyal locals who mingle with the media types in the evening. George Orwell and Dylan Thomas were regulars in their day, and Michael Powell's *Peeping Tom* was filmed here in 1960. There's also an excellent pie room – the Famous Pie Room (pies from £7) – upstairs.

SOCIAL Map p66 Bar
☎ 7636 4992; www.thesocial.com; 5 Little Portland St W1; ☾ to 1am Thu-Sat, to midnight Mon-Thu, to 12.30am Sun, closed Sun; ⊖ Oxford Circus
The Social remains one of the best places for a good night out in Central London thanks to the fact that it steers well clear of catering to the regular West End crowd. You can have a lunch been of beans on toast or, indeed, spaghetti hoops on toast, and follow it up with a quiet drink in the stylish wood-panelled upstairs bar, or descend into the downstairs area, revel in live or DJ music and £6 cocktails until late.

MAYFAIR

GUINEA Map p90 Pub
☎ 7409 1728; 30 Bruton Pl W1; ⊖ Green Park or Bond St
Top-quality Young's beers, famous autographs on the toilet walls and the whiff of money define this quiet and out-of-the-way pub in London's most exclusive neighbourhood, Mayfair. There are very few places to sit, though, and it sometimes feels little more than a waiting room for the rear restaurant (renowned for its pies).

SALT WHISKY BAR Map p90 Bar
☎ 7402 1155; www.saltbar.com; 82 Seymour St W1; ☾ to 1am Mon-Sat, to 12.30am Sun; ⊖ Marble Arch
Two hundred whiskies and bourbons and a sleek, dark-wood interior make this friendly

bar and comfortable lounge a fab place for drinking. Staff are knowledgeable and keen to share their tips with customers.

THE CITY

Catering to bankers, dealers and other suits, the City generally does traditional pubs, most of which are only open Monday to Friday and are often deserted by 10pm. Despite this, the City has some magical places that positively ooze history and character.

BLACK FRIAR Map p100   Pub
☎ 7236 5474; 174 Queen Victoria St EC4;
🕑 to 11.30pm Thu & Fri; ⊖ Blackfriars
It may look like Friar Tuck just stepped out of this 'olde pubbe' just north of Blackfriars tube station, but the interior is actually an Arts and Crafts makeover dating back to 1905. Not surprisingly, the Black Friar is the preserve of City suits during the week, but they disappear at the weekend, leaving it to the rest of us. There's a good selection of ales and bitters here.

COUNTING HOUSE Map p100   Pub
☎ 7283 7123; 50 Cornhill EC3; 🕑 closed Sat & Sun; ⊖ Bank or Monument
They say that old banks – with their counters and basement vaults – make perfect homes for pubs, and this award-winner certainly looks and feels most comfortable in the former headquarters of NatWest with its domed skylight and beautifully appointed main bar. This is a City-boy favourite – they come for the good range of real ales (beer

brewed in the traditional way) and the specialty pies (£9 to £10).

EL VINO Map p100   Wine Bar
☎ 7353 6786; www.elvino.co.uk; 47 Fleet St EC4;
🕑 closed Sat & Sun; ⊖ Blackfriars or Temple
A venerable institution that plays host to barristers, solicitors and other legal types from the Royal Courts of Justice (p77) across the way, this wine bar (one of five in a small chain) has one of the better wine lists in the City and prices at the attached shops are reasonable. El Vino featured as the wine bar Pomeroys in the TV series Rumpole of the Bailey.

YE OLDE CHESHIRE CHEESE Map p100 Pub
☎ 7353 6170; Wine Office Ct, 145 Fleet St EC4;
🕑 to 5pm Sun; ⊖ Blackfriars
The entrance to this historic pub is via a narrow alley off Fleet St. Locals over its long history have included Dr Johnson, Thackeray and Dickens. Despite (or possibly because of) this, the Cheshire feels today like a bit of a museum piece, and a fairly shabby one at that, with sawdust on the floors and a not inconsiderable smell in its warren of bars now that the cigarette smoke has disappeared. Nevertheless, it's one of London's most famous pubs and it's well worth popping in for a pint.

YE OLDE WATLING Map p100   Pub
☎ 7653 9971; 29 Watling St EC4; 🕑 closed Sat & Sun; ⊖ Mansion House
This small strip back behind St Paul's has an almost villagelike feel to it, and the

---

BEER: THE NATIONAL TIPPLE

In a public house it is possible to order a glass of wine or even a simple cocktail. But the raison d'être of a 'pub' is first and foremost to serve beer – be it lager, ale or stout in a glass or a bottle. On draught (drawn from the cask) it is served by the pint (570mL) or half-pint (285mL). The alcohol percentage (minimum: 2%) can reach a lurching and staggering 8%.

Most beers are made from malted barley and flavoured with hops. The term lager refers to the amber-coloured bottom-fermented beverage found the world over. In general, lagers are highly carbonated, of medium hop flavour and drunk cool or cold. In London, the best known home brews are Tennent's and Carling, but there's nothing special about either of them.

Ale is a top-fermented beer whose flavours can run the gamut from subtle to robust; proponents of 'real ale' (ie beer made according to traditional recipes and methods) use the language of oenologists to describe them. Ales can be very slightly gassy or completely still, have a strong hop flavour, and are drunk at slightly above room temperature (seldom colder). Real ale is sometimes pulled from barrels. Among the multitude of ales on offer in London pubs, London Pride, Courage Best, Burton Ale, Adnam's, Theakston (in particular Old Peculiar) and Old Speckled Hen are among the best. If in doubt, just ask for 'a bitter' and you'll be served the house ale. Stout, the best known of which is Irish Guinness, is a slightly sweet, dark beer whose distinct flavour comes from malt that is roasted before fermentation.

centre of the village is definitely Ye Olde Watling, an old timer with a gorgeous wooden bar that is always busy from 5pm. Food is served and a there's a 'taste before you try' policy for the great selection of real ales.

THE SOUTH BANK

The South Bank is a strange hybrid when it comes to drinking. On the one hand, a large portion of the establishments here are good, down-to-earth boozers, which just happen to have been here for hundreds of years. These are complemented by modern bars – all neon and alcopops – patronised by a younger, trendier crowd. Most (but not all) are much of a muchness.

WATERLOO

BALTIC Map p126   Bar
☎ 7928 1111; www.balticrestaurant.co.uk; 74 Blackfriars Rd SE1; ⏱ noon to midnight Mon-Sat, to 10.30pm Sun; ⊖ Southwark
This very stylish bar at the front of an Eastern European restaurant specialises – not surprisingly – in vodkas; some 50-plus, including bar-infused concoctions, are on offer. The bright and airy, high-ceilinged dining room, with a glass roof and lovely amber wall, is just behind, should you need some blotter.

CONCRETE Map p126   Cafe-Bar
☎ 7928 4123; www.southbankcentre.co.uk; Hayward Gallery, Southbank Centre, Belvedere Rd SE1; 10am-6pm Sun & Mon, 10am-11pm Tue-Thu, to 1am Fri & Sat; ⊖ Waterloo
By day this outlet in the Hayward Gallery (p125) is a discreet cafe serving tea and cake to an earnest art-loving crowd. By night this Cinderella transforms into a wicked stepsister, with late-night bar, DJs and live music from Thursday to Saturday and neon-pink cement mixers as props.

KING'S ARMS Map p126   Pub
☎ 7928 4334; 25 Roupell St SE1; ⊖ Waterloo or Southwark
A relaxed and charming neighbourhood boozer at the corner of a terraced Waterloo backstreet, the award-winning King's Arms was a funeral parlour in a previous life, so show some respect. The large traditional bar area, serving up a good selection of

ales and bitters, gives way to a fantastically odd conservatory bedecked with junk-store eclectica of local interest, which has decent Thai food.

LAUGHING GRAVY Map p126   Bar
☎ 7721 7055; www.thelaughinggravy.co.uk; 154 Blackfriars Rd SE1; ⏱ noon-11pm Mon-Fri, from 7-11pm Sat; ⊖ Southwark
This casual bar fronting a sky-lit themed eatery (Laughing Gravy, which is the name of Laurel and Hardy's dog, is a colloquialism for whisky) has a delightful and almost louche atmosphere. With vintage advertising posters, paintings, potted plants and piano, it recalls a bohemian late-1940s living room.

SCOOTERWORKS Map p126   Cafe-Bar
☎ 7620 1421; www.scooterworks-uk.com; 132 Lower Marsh Rd SW1; ⏱ 10am-11pm Mon-Thu, to midnight Fri & Sat; ⊖ Waterloo
A real find in the elephants' graveyard we like to call Waterloo, this lovely cafe-bar does a sideline in vintage Vespas so you can scoop while you scoot. Opening hours have just been extended, giving you even more time to haggle over those two-wheelers.

BANKSIDE & SOUTHWARK

ANCHOR BANKSIDE Map p126   Pub
☎ 7407 1577; 34 Park St SE1; ⊖ London Bridge
This pub dating back to the early 17th century (but subsequently rebuilt after the Great Fire and again in the 19th century) has superb views across the Thames from its terrace and is the most central – and most popular – riverside boozer in London; expect a scrum at almost all times. Dictionary writer Samuel Johnson, whose brewer friend owned the joint, drank here as did diarist Samuel Pepys.

BAR BLUE Map p126   Cocktail Bar
☎ 7940 8333, 0870 899 8856; www.barblue vinopolis.com; 1 Bank End SE1; ⏱ 11am-11pm; ⊖ London Bridge
This stylish bar attached to Vinopolis (p130) and close to the Thames has floor-to-ceiling windows and a colour scheme supposedly derived from a bottle of Bombay Sapphire Gin. The stools, the bar, the ceiling – everything but the nearby river – are bluer than blue. It's a convenient place for a

cocktail before or after a performance at the nearby Shakespeare's Globe (p312).

BOROUGH & BERMONDSEY

GEORGE INN Map p126 — Pub
☎ 7407 2056; Talbot Yard, 77 Borough High St SE1;
↔ Borough

The always-popular George Inn is London's last surviving galleried coaching inn. It dates from 1676 and is mentioned in Dickens' *Little Dorrit*. No wonder it falls under the protection of the National Trust. It is on the site of the Tabard Inn (thus the Talbot Yard address), where the pilgrims in Chaucer's *Canterbury Tales* gathered before setting out (well lubricated, we suspect) on the road to Canterbury, Kent.

RAKE Map p126 — Pub
☎ 7407 0557; 14 Winchester Walk SE1; ☯ noon-11pm Mon-Fri, from 10am Sat; ↔ London Bridge

The place of superlatives – it's the only pub actually in Borough Market and supposedly the smallest boozer in London – the Rake has one of the best line-ups of bitters and real ales in town. The outside deck is a plus and has more than doubled the pub's seating capacity.

ROYAL OAK Map p126 — Pub
☎ 7357 7173; 44 Tabard St SE1; ☯ noon-11pm Mon-Sat, to 6pm Sun; ↔ Borough

This authentic Victorian place, owned by a small independent brewery in Sussex, is tucked away down a side street and is a mecca for serious beer drinkers. The literati might find their way here too; it's just a hop, skip and a handful of rice south of the Church of St George the Martyr, where Little Dorrit (aka Amy) got married in Dickens' eponymous novel.

WINE WHARF Map p126 — Wine Bar
☎ 7940 8335, 0870 899 8856; www.wine wharf.co.uk; Stoney St SE1; ☯ closed Sun; ↔ London Bridge

Located in an erstwhile Victorian warehouse close to the culinary joys of Borough Market, this very smart wine bar's selection will delight oenophiles as well as people just coming along for a drink. The range is truly enormous, and the staff is more than happy to advise and let you taste. There's live jazz on Monday evenings.

HYDE PARK TO CHELSEA

This is where high style and traditional pubs meet and coexist in surprising harmony. You can choose between the sultry lights of expensive cocktail bars, frequented by the deep-pocketed Knightsbridge and Chelsea dwellers, or join the area's ale lovers in some of the most beautiful of London's old pubs.

DRAYTON ARMS Map pp136-7 — Pub
☎ 7835 2301; 153 Old Brompton Rd SW5;
☯ noon-midnight; ↔ West Brompton or South Kensington, ▣ 430

This vast Victorian corner boozer is as delightful on the inside as out, with some bijou art nouveau features (sinuous tendrils and curlicues above the windows and the doors), interesting contemporary art on the walls and a fabulous coffered ceiling. The crowd is both hip and down-to-earth, young and been around a bit, in that relaxing sort of way. There's a good beer and wine selection.

GALVIN AT WINDOWS — Cocktail Bar
☎ 7208 4021; www.galvinatwindows.com;
London Hilton on Park Lane, 28th fl, 22 Park Lane W1; ☯ 10am-1am Mon-Wed, to 3am Thu-Sat, to 11pm Sun; ↔ Hyde Park Corner

This swish bar is a popular place for observing London from a great height: the 28th floor of the Hilton Hotel on the edge of Hyde Park. The cocktails are priced in the stratosphere (£12.75 to £14.95) and the 'live' band has a pre-recorded track but the leather seats are comfortable, the marble bar gorgeous and the views of the city breathtaking, particularly at dusk.

NAG'S HEAD Map pp136-7 — Pub
☎ 7235 1135; 53 Kinnerton St SW1;
↔ Hyde Park Corner

Located in a serene mews not far from bustling Knightsbridge, this gorgeously genteel early-19th-century drinking den has eccentric decor (think 19th-century cricket prints), a sunken bar and a 'no mobile phones' rule. A dreamy delight, this one.

QUEEN'S ARMS Map pp136-7 — Pub
☎ 7581 7741; 30 Queen's Gate Mews SW7;
↔ Gloucester Rd

The Queen's Arms wouldn't get much cover if elsewhere. But location, location, location, as they say: tucked down a quiet mews off

Queen's Gate, this place wins bouquets from the many students living in the area as well as from concert-goers heading for the Royal Albert Hall (p306), just around the corner. Add to that four hand pumps and a decent (mostly gastropub) menu.

CLERKENWELL, SHOREDITCH & SPITALFIELDS

If you want coolness that hurts, this is where you'll find it. Hoxton and Shoreditch remain the absolute centre of London's hipster scene, with Old St, Kingsland Rd, Shoreditch High St and Hoxton Sq all overflowing with busy bars. Spitalfields and Clerkenwell have slightly more comfortable scenes, and the odd killer pub. Whatever you're looking for in a drinking venue, this area will deliver.

CLERKENWELL

CHARTERHOUSE BAR Map p150   DJ Bar
☎ 7608 0858; www.charterhousebar.co.uk; 38 Charterhouse St EC1; ⏲ to midnight Mon-Wed, to 2am Thu, to 4am Fri & Sat; ⊖ Barbican or Farringdon
Charterhouse Bar is most people's pit stop before going on to Fabric (p296), so expect loud music on weekends, with a good preclub atmosphere. For those preferring something quieter, pop by for brunch – the food is great – and enjoy the wedge-shaped structure, a traditional Clerkenwell warehouse design. DJs are on every evening and entry is free at all times.

FILTHY MACNASTY'S Map p150   Pub
☎ 7837 6067; www.filthymacnastys.com; 68 Amwell St EC1; ⊖ Angel or Farringdon
The local of 'Amwell Village', tucked between Clerkenwell and Islington, is this stellar Irish music pub and whiskey bar that is every bit as cool as its name suggests. The two-room pub attracts an up-for-it young crowd who come for live bands in the back room, the great whiskey list and – we're assured – the best toilet graffiti In London.

JERUSALEM TAVERN Map p150   Pub
☎ 7490 4281; www.stpetersbrewery.co.uk; 55 Britton St EC1; ⏲ closed Sat & Sun; ⊖ Farringdon
Starting life as one of the first London coffee houses (founded in 1703), with the

18th-century decor of occasional tile mosaics still visible, the JT is an absolute stunner, though sadly it's both massively popular and tiny, so come early to get a seat. There's good lunch food and, this being the only London outlet of St Peter's Brewery (based in North Suffolk), it has a brilliant range of drinks: organic bitters; cream stouts; wheat and fruit beers – many of which are dispensed in green apothecary-style bottles.

SLAUGHTERED LAMB Map p150   Pub
☎ 7253 1516; www.theslaughteredlambpub.com; 34-35 Great Sutton St EC1; ⏲ noon-midnight Mon-Thu, noon-1am Fri & Sat, noon-10.30pm Sun; ⊖ Farringdon or Barbican
This Clerkenwell hipster outpost is unusually large for a pub – the main bar is very spacious, with flea-market furniture, large windows, wooden floors and motorised hand fans flapping away on the walls. The beer on offer Is good and the food is old England (fish and chips, fish fingers, sausage and mash etc). The black-wallpapered downstairs room hosts regular live music and open mic nights.

YE OLDE MITRE Map p150   Pub
☎ 7405 4751; 1 Ely Ct EC1; ⏲ closed Sat & Sun; ⊖ Chancery Lane or Farringdon
A delightfully cosy historic pub, tucked away in a backstreet off Hatton Garden, Ye Olde Mitre was built for the servants of Ely Palace. There's still a memento of Elizabeth I – the stump of a cherry tree around which she once danced. There's no music, so the rooms only echo to the sound of amiable chitchat.

SHOREDITCH

BAR KICK Map p150   Bar
☎ 7739 8700; 127 Shoreditch High St E1; ⏲ until midnight Thu-Sat; ⊖ Old St or Liverpool St
A much larger sister venue to Clerkenwell's Café Kick (☎ 7837 8077; 43 Exmouth Market, EC1; ⏲ noon-11pm Mon-Thu, until midnight Fri & Sat; ⊖ Farringdon or Angel), this place has a slightly edgier Shoreditch vibe. This time, too, there's some floor space left over after four footy tables were installed, so there are leather sofas and simple tables and chairs.

BRICKLAYERS ARMS Map p150   Pub
☎ 7739 5245; 63 Charlotte Rd EC2; ⊖ Old St
A determinedly down-to-earth stalwart of the Hoxton scene, the Bricklayers Arms

attracts an unpretentious but cool-looking crowd who spill out into the street in the summer months. This funky old-meets-new-style pub is friendly and unpretentious, and there's good Thai food on offer in the restaurant upstairs as well.

DREAMBAGSJAGUARSHOES

Map p150   DJ Bar

☎ 7729 5830; www.dreambagsjaguarshoes.com; 34-36 Kingsland Rd E2; ⏰ to 1am Tue-Sun, to midnight Mon; ⊖ Old St

The bar is named after the two shops whose space it now occupies, and this nonchalance is a typical example of the we-couldn't-care-less Shoreditch chic. The small interior is filled with sofas and formica-topped tables, a DJ plays in the corner, and art exhibitions deck the graffiti-covered walls.

FOUNDRY Map p150   Bar

☎ 7739 6900; www.foundry.tv; 84-86 Great Eastern St EC2; ⊖ Old St

Everything about the Foundry is refreshingly surreal. Let's start with the look: it's 'decorated' with genuinely shabby (not chic) furniture that clutters the space, the bar is made out of a plank of wood and propped by a yellowing old man, and the floor is icky. Art events (often in the loosest sense of the word) begin at 7pm each evening and they are always free. Downstairs is a live gig venue where anything can, and does, happen. It's so mad and unpredictable we love it.

GEORGE & DRAGON Map p150   DJ Bar, Pub

☎ 7012 1100; 2-4 Hackney Rd E2; ⊖ Old St

Once a scuzzy local pub, the George (as ye shall dub it if you value your Shoreditch High St cred) was taken over and decorated with the owner's grandma's antiques (antlers, racoon tails, old clocks), cardboard cut-outs of Cher and fairy lights, turning this one-room pub into what has remained the epicentre of the Hoxton scene for more than a decade. It's one of the most exciting places to go out, with a great jukebox, though it tends to get packed out at the weekends. Some of the best DJ nights in London are on offer here, with cabaret performances taking place on window sills. It's total fun and mindless hedonism. Definitely not a place for a quiet pint.

LOUNGELOVER Map p150   Cocktail Bar

☎ 7012 1234; www.lestroisgarcons.com; 1 Whitby St E1; ⏰ to midnight Sun-Thu, to 1am Fri & Sat; ⊖ / ▣ Liverpool St

The drinks and the look are both faultless at this Shoreditch institution, where it's all about the superb, expensive cocktails and the junk-shop chic of the decor. Sometimes it gets packed out with city suits, and service can be hit-and-miss, so it's always best to reserve a table, but despite these gripes this is a glamorous, camp place for a killer cocktail.

MACBETH Map p150   Pub

☎ 7739 5095; 70 Hoxton St N1; ⏰ until 2am Thu-Sun; ⊖ Old St

This enormous old boozer on this still-to-be-yuppified street just a short walk north of Hoxton Sq is a rough and ready addition to the ever-changing Hoxton scene. Run by musicians and providing a great platform for up-and-coming talent on its downstairs stage, Macbeth is a fantastic venue, with a second bar upstairs and a large roof terrace as well.

MOTHER BAR Map p150   DJ Bar

☎ 7739 5949; www.333mother.com; 333 Old St EC1; ⏰ to midnight Sun-Thu, to 2am Fri & Sat; ⊖ Old St

Where can you go dancing till late on a Sunday night, you may wonder? Come to Mother. Still one of the best bars in town, it's above Shoreditch's original hipster club, 333 (p295). Though it's mobbed at weekends, don't be put off – there's a lounge, a dance floor and a fun, up-for-it crowd.

OLD BLUE LAST Map p150   DJ Bar, Pub

☎ 7739 7033; www.oldbluelast.com; 38 Great Eastern Rd, EC2; ⏰ until midnight Mon-Wed, until 12.30am Thu & Sun, until 1.30am Fri & Sat; ⊖ Old St or Liverpool St

You might walk into this East End spit-and-sawdust pub expecting to find old geezers sitting at the bar, but instead you're greeted by a hip teenage-and-up crowd of Hoxtonites wearing hooded tops, fluorescent T-shirts and nylon caps. The seedy and trendy look is courtesy of Vice magazine, the hipster bible/global conglomerate and try-hard bad boy magazine that owns the place. It hosts some of the best Shoreditch parties, has a rocking jukebox and does a mean square pie to boot.

RED LION Map p150   DJ Pub

☎ 7729 7920; www.redlionhoxton.com; 41 Hoxton St N1; ⊙ to midnight Mon-Sat, to 11pm Sun; ⊖ Old St

Our favourite spot for pre-club drinks in Hoxton, this denizen of the scene is run by the team behind both 333 (p295) and Mother Bar (opposite). Despite being spitting distance from Hoxton Sq, it's well enough tucked away down a side street to avoid being overrun by the suburban crowd that now dominates the area at the weekends. Inside it's pure kitsch fun – eclectic DJs spin downstairs while the friendly crowd spills out onto the street with pints in their hands.

SPITALFIELDS

GOLDEN HEART Map p150   Pub

☎ 7247 2158; 110 Commercial St E1; ⊖ Liverpool St

It's an unsurprisingly trendy Hoxton crowd that mixes in the surprisingly untrendy interior of this brilliant Spitalfields boozer. While it's famous as the watering hole for the cream of London's art crowd, our favourite part about any visit is a chat with Sandra, the landlady-celebrity who talks to all comers and ensures that the bullshit never outstrips the fun.

TEN BELLS Map p150   Pub

☎ 7366 1721; 84 Commercial St E1; ⊖ Liverpool St

This landmark pub, opposite Spitalfields Market (p227) and next to the area's striking church, is famous for being one of Jack the Ripper's pick-up joints, although these days it's about as far from a museum piece as you can get. In fact, ask most of the young and hip crowd about the history, and few will have any idea that this beautifully decorated, airy and friendly place has anything sinister about its Victorian past.

VIBE BAR Map p150   DJ Bar

☎ 7247 3479; www.vibe-bar.co.uk; Old Truman Brewery, 91-95 Brick Lane E1; ⊙ until 11.30pm Sun-Thu, until late Fri & Sat; ⊖ Liverpool St or Aldgate East

Once the epicentre of the Hoxton scene, the Vibe is part bar, part club, part outdoor drinking arena complete with fast food stalls. While its '90s time in the sun is long past, it's still popular and good fun outside in the summer. There are live acts most nights, and DJs at other times in the spacious interior.

THE EAST END & DOCKLANDS

Once famous for gangster shoot-ups and Saturday night fights at drinking-up time, the pubs of the East End have come a long way in the past few years. There are still some fairly odious dives where only locals will feel comfortable, but the following places are just fine and welcome all. And some of the pubs in Hackney have become positively trendy.

THE EAST END
Whitechapel

URBAN BAR Map p156   Pub

☎ 7247 8978; 176 Whitechapel Rd E1; ⊙ 11am-11pm Mon-Wed, noon-1am Thu-Sat, noon-11.30pm Sun; ⊖ Whitechapel

You probably wouldn't travel far or wide for this boozer with its distinctive tiger-striped livery. But it's an unmissable (to say the least) and convivial Whitechapel landmark, just opposite the tube. Definitely a pub (with a good range of beers) but somehow reminiscent of a cafe, UB attracts students in the area (Queen Mary College is a short distance to the east) and the occasional white coat from the Royal London Hospital next door.

Bethnal Green & Hackney

BISTROTHEQUE Map p156   Bar, Cabaret Bar

☎ 8983 7900; www.bistrotheque.com; 23-27 Wadeston St E2; ⊙ 6pm-midnight Tue-Sat, 4-11pm Sun; ⊖ Bethnal Green, ▣ Cambridge Heath, ▣ 55

This place in a converted East End warehouse offers three things: drinking in the Napoleon bar, transvestite lip-synch cabaret in the Cabaret Room (9.30pm Friday and Saturday) on the ground floor and dining in its stylish white restaurant above. The bar is a moody, slightly decadent room with dark walls (the oak panels came from a stately home in Northumberland) and plush seating, the drinks are expertly mixed and the bar staff always friendly.

DOVE FREEHOUSE Map p156   Pub

☎ 7275 7617; www.belgianbars.com; 24 Broadway Market E8; ⊙ noon-11pm Mon-Thu, to midnight Fri & Sat; ▣ London Fields, ▣ 48, 55, 106 or 394

This pub attracts at any time with its rambling series of rooms and wide range – some

283

20 on draft – of Belgian Trappist, wheat and fruit-flavoured beers. But there's something about the dim back room, with its ethnic bohemian chic and decent gastropub menu, which makes this pub a great place to hunker down against the chill.

PRINCE ARTHUR Map p156   Pub
☎ 7249 9996; www.theprincearthurlondonfields.com; 95 Farm Rd E8; ☷ 4-11pm Mon-Thu, from noon Fri, from 10.30am Sat & Sun; ▣ London Fields, ▨ D6, 106 or 394
Though this somewhat made-over pub, just northeast of London Fields, touts itself as a retro gastropub, we come here to drink. It's named after Queen Victoria's third son (and supposedly favourite child). That's him in animal skins in the photographs hanging between the boar and wildcat trophies.

ROYAL OAK Map p156   Pub
☎ 7729 2220; 73 Columbia Rd E2; ☷ 5-11pm Mon, from noon Tue-Sun; ▣ Cambridge Heath, ▨ 8 or 55
Not to be confused with the similarly named pub south of the river, this traditional boozer was recently gentrified (at long last!) and has a good selection of bitter and a better-than-average wine list. It gets into its stride on Sunday when London's famous flower market is on just outside the door.

Mile End & Victoria Park
PALM TREE Map p156   Pub
☎ 8980 2918; 127 Grove Rd E3; ☷ noon-midnight Mon-Thu, to 2am Fri & Sat, to 1am Sun; ⊖ Mile End, ▨ 277
The Palm, the quintessential East End pub on the Grand Union Canal, soldiers on, with its comforting gold-flock wallpaper, photos of also-ran crooners and a handful of different guest ales to every week. There's jazz on Friday and Saturday from around 9.30pm.

ROYAL INN ON THE PARK Map p156   Pub
☎ 8985 3321; 111 Lauriston Rd E9; ⊖ Mile End, then ▨ 277
On the northern border of Victoria Park, this excellent place, once a poster pub for Transport for London, has a half-dozen real ales and Czech lagers on tap, outside seating to the front and an enclosed terrace in back. It's always lively and attracts a mixed boho/louche Hackney crowd.

Wapping
CAPTAIN KIDD Map p156   Pub
☎ 7480 5759; 108 Wapping High St E1; ⊖ Liverpool St or Tower Hill, then ▨ 100
With its large windows, fine beer garden and mock scaffold recalling the hanging nearby of the eponymous pirate in 1701, this is a favourite riverside pub in Wapping that only dates back to the 1980s. There's a restaurant predictably called the Gallows on the 1st floor.

DOCKLANDS
GRAPES Map p162   Pub
☎ 7987 4396; 76 Narrow St E14; DLR Westferry
One of Limehouse's renowned historic pubs – there's been a drinking house here since 1583, we're told – the Grapes is cosy and as narrow as the name of the street it's on. Actually, it's tiny, especially the riverside terrace, which can only really comfortably fit about a half-dozen close friends. But it continues to radiate olde-worlde charm, the choice of beer is good and they love dogs here.

PROSPECT OF WHITBY Map p156   Pub
☎ 7481 1095; 57 Wapping Wall E1; ⊖ Tower Hill then ▨ 100
Once known as the Devil's Tavern, the Whitby's said to date from 1520, making it the oldest riverside pub in London. It's firmly on the tourist trail now, but there's a small-ish terrace to the front and the side overlooking the Thames, a decent restaurant upstairs and open fires in winter. Check out the wonderful pewter bar – Samuel Pepys once sidled up to it to sup.

NORTH LONDON
Camden Town is one of North London's favoured drinking areas, with more bars and pubs pumping music than you can manage to crawl between. The hills of Hampstead are a real treat for old-pub aficionados, while painfully hip Dalston is currently London's coolest place to drink.

CAMDEN
BAR VINYL Map p170   DJ Bar
☎ 7482 5545; www.barvinyl.com; 6 Inverness St NW1; ☷ to midnight Sun-Wed, to 1am Thu-Sat; ⊖ Camden Town

Bar Vinyl is the epicentre for Camden's young and urban crowd, with cool kids behind the decks, a record shop downstairs and graffiti whirling along narrow walls. But it's superfriendly at the same time, and everyone's here to relax and enjoy the music rather than pose. Weekends are packed and buzzing, midweek nights are quieter, and the music is always good.

BARTOK Map p166   DJ Bar
☎ 7916 0595; www.bartokbar.com; 78-79 Chalk Farm Rd NW1; ✆ to 3am Sun-Thu, to 4am Fri & Sat; ⊖ Chalk Farm
Here's a true oasis: an elegant classical-music lounge-bar in the midst of grungy Camden. And not only is it an original find in this area, it's pretty unusual in the whole of London. Named after the Hungarian composer and pianist, Bartok specialises in classical concertos, live jazz or brilliant DJ sets blending jazz, classical, electro and world music. Sadly the beer choices are standard issue, though cocktails are good here – kick back on one of the low sofas and enjoy until the wee hours.

CROWN & GOOSE Map p170   Pub
☎ 7485 8008; www.crownandgoose.co.uk; 100 Arlington Rd NW1; ✆ to 12am Sun-Thu, to 2am Fri & Sat; ⊖ Camden Town
One of our favourite London pubs, this square room has a central wooden bar between British-racing-green walls studded with gilt-framed mirrors and illuminated by big shuttered windows. More importantly, it combines a friendly, quietly cool crowd, easy conviviality, great food and a good range of inexpensive beers.

EDINBORO CASTLE Map p170   Pub
☎ 7255 9651; www.edinborocastlepub.co.uk; 57 Mornington Tce NW1; ⊖ Camden Town
A reliable Camden boozer, the large and relaxed Edinboro actually has more of a refined Primrose Hill atmosphere. It boasts a full menu, gorgeous furniture designed for slumping, and a huge outdoor seating area that is perfect for summer evenings.

PROUD CAMDEN Map p166   DJ Bar
☎ 7482 3867; www.proudcamden.com; The Horse Hospital, Stables Market, Chalk Farm Rd NW1; ✆ to 1.30am Mon-Wed, to 2.30am Thu-Sat, to 12.30am Sun; ⊖ Chalk Farm

Just when Camden was beginning to look hopelessly old-hat, Proud opened as the art-performance-drinking venue London's been in need of for decades. Fantastic in summer, this former Horse Hospital has retained its stables, in which you can drink and play table football or pool, while live bands and DJs play in the large main room, and art exhibits deck the walls. Definitely our favourite bar in Camden right now.

QUEEN'S Map p166   Pub
☎ 7586 0408; 49 Regent's Park Rd NW1; ✆ to midnight Fri & Sat; ⊖ Camden Town or Chalk Farm
While the ghost of actress, royal 'friend' and former next-door neighbour Lillie Langtry is said to reside in the cellar of this spirited joint, the pub proper is haunted by contemporary beauties such as Jude Law and the other fashionistas of Primrose Hill. The food and drinks won't disappoint, and there's plenty to look at among the clientele.

KING'S CROSS

BIG CHILL HOUSE Map p170   DJ Bar
☎ 7427 2540; www.bigchill.net; 257-259 Pentonville Rd N1; ✆ until midnight Sun-Wed, until 1am Thu, until 3am Fri & Sat; ⊖ King's Cross St Pancras
It's been everything from a gay bar to an Egyptian belly-dancing club over the years, but now the owners of the Big Chill (a popular summer music festival) appear to have found this difficult venue's calling: hosting a young, friendly muso crowd in a smart, welcoming corner of King's Cross. Daily lunch for £5 is a great deal, and we love the large sundeck – a great place for a summer beer. Sister to the popular Big Chill bar (☎ 7392 9180; Dray Walk E1; ⊖ Liverpool St) off Brick Lane. There are also club nights here (see p295).

RUBY LOUNGE Map p170   DJ Bar
☎ 7837 9558; www.ruby.uk.com; 33 Caledonian Rd N1; ✆ to midnight Thu, to 2am Fri & Sat; ⊖ King's Cross St Pancras
King's Cross is being groomed slowly, so what was once an area frequented only by hardened clubbers, prostitutes and junkies is now turning into a three-Starbucks-per-square-metre neighbourhood. But the Ruby Lounge was around when the going was tough and is here to stay. It's a great place, with a warm interior, excellent DJs and an up-for-it preclubbing crowd.

HAMPSTEAD & HIGHGATE

BOOGALOO Map p166   Bar
☎ 8340 2928; www.theboogaloo.org; 312 Archway Rd N6; ⏰ to midnight Thu, to 1.30am Fri & Sat; ⊖ Highgate
'London's Number 1 Jukebox' is how Boogaloo flaunts itself and how it's been described in the local media: its celebrity-musician-fiddled-with jukebox playlists feature the favourite 10 songs of the likes of Nick Cave, Sinead O'Connor, Howie B and Bobbie Gillespie, to name but a few. There's plenty to boogie to, with live music on every night of the week. If you're into music in a big way, it's worth going out to Archway.

FLASK TAVERN Map p166   Pub
☎ 8348 7346; 77 Highgate West Hill N6; ⊖ Highgate
This weekend favourite is a brilliant place to end a walk in either Hampstead Heath or Highgate Wood. In the summer months it's all about its large courtyard where delicious burgers are served up along with pints. In the winter, huddle down in the cosy interior and enjoy its much-loved Sunday roast.

HOLLY BUSH Map p166   Pub
☎ 7435 2892; www.hollybushpub.com; 22 Holly Mount NW3; ⊖ Hampstead
A beautiful pub that makes you envy the privileged residents of Hampstead, the Holly Bush has an antique Victorian interior, a secluded hilltop location, open fires in winter and a knack for making you stay longer than you had intended. Set above Heath St, it's reached via the Holly Bush Steps.

SPANIARD'S INN Map p166   Pub
☎ 8731 6571; Spaniards Rd NW3; ⊖ Hampstead then 🚌 21
This marvellous tavern dates from 1585 and has more character than a West End musical. It was highwayman Dick Turpin's hangout between robbing escapades, but it's also served as a watering hole for more savoury characters, such as Dickens, Shelley, Keats and Byron. There's a big, blissful garden, though you might want to eat elsewhere.

ISLINGTON

25 CANONBURY LANE Map p170   Cocktail Bar
☎ 7226 0955; www.25canonburylane.com; 25 Canonbury Lane N1; ⏰ to midnight Sun-Thu, to 1am Fri & Sat; ⊖ Highbury & Islington

This somewhat quiet stretch of Islington has been in need of a good cocktail bar for years, and we love 25 Canonbury Lane for fulfilling this need perfectly – it's funky, friendly, the cocktail and wine lists are superb and the staff know their stuff. You can usually get a seat in the lovely interior, and there's a good food menu too.

ELK IN THE WOODS Map p170   Bar
☎ 7226 3535; www.the-elk-in-the-woods.co.uk; 39 Camden Passage N1; ⊖ Angel
A wonderful take on a stylish countryside hunters' pub, this comfy Islington bar is also equally notable for its good, simple food. With its large, rough oak-wood tables, old mirrors, stuffed deer head and friendly staff, this is a spot to savour – though, as ever, come early, as tables are always sought after and it's not the kind of bar you stand in.

EMBASSY Map p170   DJ Bar
☎ 7226 7901; www.embassybar.com; 119 Essex Rd N1; ⏰ to 1am Fri & Sat; ⊖ Angel
It's been around for years, but Embassy's reputation and appeal just keeps rising, so get there early on weekends and mingle with the cool music and media crowd and enjoy the good DJs. The darkened windows and black walls make it look secretive, but inside everyone's relaxing on the ubiquitous comfy sofas on the ground and basement floors. There are varying cover charges on weekends.

HOPE & ANCHOR Map p170   Pub
☎ 7354 1312; 207 Upper St N1; ⏰ to midnight; ⊖ Highbury & Islington
There is a scarcity of decent pubs in Islington, where the offerings are overwhelmingly cocktail lounges or DJ bars, but this rough-round-the-edges boozer with a famous musical past (U2, Dire Straits, Joy Division and, more recently, the Libertines have all played here) attracts a muso cross-section of the neighbourhood and is a lot of fun.

DALSTON

BAR 23   Bar
☎ 7241 2060; 23 Stoke Newington Rd N16; 🚇 Dalston Kingsland; ⏰ until 1am Sun-Thu, until 2am Fri & Sat; 🚌 67, 76, 149 or 243
Film stars bedeck the walls of this at first unremarkable Turkish-run bar on Dalston's

coolest stretch. But, come the evenings, the place is always full, DJs play and drinks are served up to the friendly crowd late into the evening.

DALSTON SUPERSTORE DJ Bar
☎ 7254 2273; 117 Kingsland Rd E8; ☽ to 2am; Ⓡ Dalston Kingsland; 🚍 67, 76, 149, 243
Confirming Dalston's pre-eminence as the area to hang out, the Dalston Superstore opened in 2009 and provided the cool kids with a base to work out of. This two-level industrial space is open all day and serves up sandwiches and light meals, though it really comes into its own after dark when there are club nights in the basement and DJs spinning upstairs. Get here early.

JAZZ BAR DALSTON Cocktail Bar
☎ 7254 9728; 4 Bradbury St N16; ☽ to 1am Mon-Thu, to 3am Fri & Sat, to midnight Sun; Ⓡ Dalston Kingsland
Jazz Bar is Dalston's most excellent and unexpected find, hidden just off the chaos of Dalston Junction. Housed within glass walls, it's not really a jazz bar but a cocktail place where the neighbourhood's hip and friendly inhabitants congregate at the weekends to party on to hip-hop, R&B and reggae.

MOUSTACHE BAR DJ Bar
58 Stoke Newington Rd N16; ☽ to 4am Fri & Sat, 8.30pm-midnight Sun-Wed; 🚍 73
Look for its signature moustache sign to find this local favourite – the Moustache packs them in at the weekends for sweaty and crowded drinking and dancing in its basement bar, or – equally crowded – on its makeshift smoking terrace. Drinks are cheap, and the cleverly decorated bar has some fascinating oddities on its walls (when you can see them).

STOKE NEWINGTON

AULD SHILLELAGH Pub
☎ 7249 5951; 105 Stoke Newington Church St N16; 🚍 73
The Auld Shillelagh is one of the best Irish pubs in London and full of old-style liver pounders. It's many things to many people: a theatre and a cosy room, centre stage and a sanctuary, a debating chamber and a place for silent contemplation. The staff are sharp, the Guinness is good, and the live entertainment is frequent and varied.

FOX REFORMED Bar
☎ 7254 5975; www.fox-reformed.co.uk; 176 Stoke Newington Church St N16; ☽ until midnight; Ⓡ Stoke Newington, 🚍 73
Stoke Newington's firm favourite for more than two decades, the Fox has all the qualities of a good local: a friendly landlord, loyal regulars, good food, wine and beer, and a cosy back garden. The quiet atmosphere and chess and backgammon boards for entertainment on relaxing afternoons always bring new converts to its charms.

WEST LONDON
The bars and pubs of the more down-to-earth areas of West London are restful, many with excellent river views. Shepherd's Bush is good for both pubs and wine bars, and Earl's Court attracts travellers, especially from Australia and South Africa. Maida Vale and St John's Wood have some London classics. West London's Portobello Rd draws a very mixed crowd of rich kids and a keeping-it-real crowd.

ST JOHN'S WOOD & MAIDA VALE

PRINCE ALFRED Map p176 Pub
☎ 7286 3287; 5a Formosa St W9; ⊖ Warwick Ave
Pubs don't really come much better than this charming place. Originally designed in Victorian times to separate the classes and sexes, the semicircular bar is divided into five gorgeous booths, each with its waist-high door. The pub is always busy with adoring locals, many of whom make their way up to the stunning Formosa Dining Room.

WARRINGTON Map p176 Pub
☎ 7286 2929; 93 Warrington Cres W9; ⊖ Warwick Ave or Maida Vale
This former hotel and brothel is now an ornate art nouveau pub with heaps of character. The huge saloon bar, dominated by a marble-topped hemispherical counter with a carved mahogany base and a huge stained-glass window by Tiffany, is a fabulous place to sample a range of four real ales. There's also outdoor seating. The rather bland-looking restaurant upstairs is in the Gordon Ramsay stable.

WATERWAY Map p176   Pub
☎ 7266 3557; www.frgroup.co.uk; 54 Formosa St W9; ✆ noon-1am; ⊖ Warwick Ave
Don't come here for the selection of beer or ales or the overly expensive nosh; this place, hard by the Grand Union Canal in Little Venice, is all about location and it's hard to imagine a better place short of a Thames-side pub to while away a weekend afternoon.

NOTTING HILL & WESTBOURNE GROVE

CHURCHILL ARMS Map p178   Pub
☎ 7792 1246; 119 Kensington Church St W8; ⊖ Notting Hill Gate
This traditional English pub is renowned for its Winston memorabilia, chamber pots, golf bags suspended from the ceiling and butterflies under glass. It's a favourite of both locals and tourists (what either group makes of the Winnie/lepidopterous connection is anyone's guess), and you'll have to fight your way through scrums of punters at the horseshoe-shaped bar for a pint. The attached conservatory has been serving excellent Thai food for two decades.

EARL OF LONSDALE Map p176   Pub
☎ 7727 6335; 277-281 Portobello Rd W11; ⊖ Notting Hill Gate or Westbourne Park
We love this place, especially when we've been schlepping around the market and need a nice cold drink. Despite being in the middle of the Portobello Road market, the Earl is peaceful during the day, with a mixture of old biddies and young hipsters inhabiting the reintroduced snugs. There are Samuel Smith's ales, and a fantastic backroom with sofas, banquettes and open fires as well as a recently extended beer garden.

GREYHOUND Map p178   Pub
☎ 7937 7140; 1 Kensington Square W8; ⊖ High St Kensington
The old dog certainly kennels in a pedigree neighbourhood, with a verdant square of blue-plaqued Georgians ('John Stuart Mill lived here'; see p142) opposite, and a turning nearby named Thackeray St after the satirist who (supposedly) imbibed here. With the *Daily Mail* and *Evening Standard* offices just a lurch and stagger away, the Greyhound's inky tradition lives on, and it's not a bad place for stories (both real and imagined).

LONSDALE Map p176   Cocktail Bar
☎ 7727 4080; www.thelonsdale.co.uk; 48 Lonsdale Rd W11; ✆ 6pm-midnight Mon-Thu, to 1am Fri & Sat, to 11.30pm Sun; ⊖ Notting Hill Gate or Westbourne Park
The place that humbly calls itself the 'epicentre of the cocktail world' retains its somewhat tired space-age walls suffused in purple light and other sci-fi kitsch. But the exceptional cocktails, listed over 20 pages and created from some 200 different spirits, are what people come here for.

TWELFTH HOUSE Map p176   Bar, Cafe
☎ 7727 9620; www.twelfth-house.co.uk; 35 Pembridge Rd W11; ✆ 10am-11pm Mon-Sat, to 10.30pm Sun; ⊖ Notting Hill Gate
This is a lovely Notting Hill coffee house with a kooky edge. The bar is dominated by an amazing astrological clock and the owner will work out your astrological chart (£5) or read your 'tarot card of the day' (£3).

WINDSOR CASTLE Map p178   Pub
☎ 7243 9551; 114 Campden Hill Rd W8; ⊖ Notting Hill Gate
A wonderful, relatively out-of-the-way tavern between Notting Hill and Kensington High St, this place has history, nooks and charm on tap. It's worth the search for its historic interior, roaring fire (in winter), delightful beer garden (in summer) and friendly regulars (most always).

EARL'S COURT

ATLAS Map p178   Pub
☎ 7385 9129; www.theatlaspub.co.uk; 16 Seagrave Rd SW6; ✆ from noon Mon-Sat; ⊖ West Brompton
This cosy Victorian-era pub attracts a younger local crowd with its real ales, excellent food, and a lovely side courtyard. The gastropub menu features essentially Mediterranean-inspired dishes.

SCARSDALE ARMS Map p178   Pub
☎ 7937 1811; 23a Edwardes Sq W8; ⊖ High St Kensington or Earl's Court
Not the easiest pub in London to find, this historic and verdant Georgian space south of Kensington High St and just off Earl's Court Rd was (so they say) originally built as quarters for the officers of Napoleon's conquering army. Dream on, Bonaparte. Today it's an attractive and stylish pub with

prints and oils in gilt frames, heavy drapes at the windows and stained-glass snob screens. Fuller ales are on tap and there's a fully fledged restaurant behind.

TROUBADOUR Map p178   Bar, Cafe
☎ 7370 1434; www.troubadour.co.uk; 265 Old Brompton Rd SW5; ☽ 9am-midnight; ⊖ Earl's Court or West Brompton
Bob Dylan and John Lennon have performed here and this friendly cafe-bar remains a wonderfully relaxed boho hangout decades later. There's still live music (folk, blues) most nights and a large, pleasant garden open in summer.

SHEPHERD'S BUSH & HAMMERSMITH

ALBERTINE WINE BAR Map p178   Wine Bar
☎ 8743 9593; 1 Wood Lane W12; ☽ 10am-11pm Mon-Thu, to midnight Fri; 6.30pm-midnight Sat; ⊖ Shepherd's Bush
A Shepherd's Bush mainstay (some would say oasis) for two decades, Albertine's is a relaxed wine bar that takes its drink seriously but lets bottles go at affordable prices. The food is wine-bar fare but excellent. A nice night away from the pub.

DOVE Map p196   Pub
☎ 8748 9474; 19 Upper Mall W6; ⊖ Hammersmith or Ravenscourt Park
A 17th-century coffee house-cum-pub, the Dove has many claims to fame, namely that it was in the *Guinness Book of Records* in 1989 for having the smallest bar in England (though there are larger areas, including a terrace, lounge and conservatory). It was Graham Greene's local and Hemingway drank here too; William Morris lived next door. There are good river views from the charming dark-wood interior, but if the sun is shining, fight for a place in the garden.

OLD SHIP Map p196   Pub
☎ 8748 2593; 25 Upper Mall W6; ⊖ Hammersmith or Ravenscourt Park
This restful towpath pub is the prime stop-off for families and couples on their walks by the Thames. It looks south across the lazy bend of the river to Putney, and it's popular during the rest of the week, especially on spring and summer days, thanks to its outdoor dining area, terrace and 1st-floor balcony.

GREENWICH & SOUTHEAST LONDON
If you're looking for old school pubs, this part of London can oblige – and will throw in some wonderful views to boot. We'd steer clear of the new bars in the area looking to accommodate recent arrivals – stick to traditional boozers and you can't go wrong. Of course there are always exceptions and we include at least one here.

GREENWICH

CUTTY SARK TAVERN Map p182   Pub
☎ 8858 3146; 4-6 Ballast Quay SE10; DLR Cutty Sark, 🚍 177 or 180
Housed in a delightful Georgian building directly on the Thames, the Cutty Sark is one of the few independent pubs left in Greenwich. There are half a dozen ales on tap and a wonderful sitting-out area along the river just opposite. Count on about a 15-minute walk from the DLR station or hop a bus along Trafalgar Rd and walk north.

GREENWICH UNION Map p182   Pub
☎ 8692 6258; www.greenwichunion.com; 56 Royal Hill SE10; DLR Cutty Sark
South of the river and a gimmicky 0° 0' 36" west of the meridian, this award-winning pub offers a range of six or seven beers produced by a local microbrewery, including raspberry and wheat varieties. It's a handsome place, serving good food and attracting locals, especially families at the weekend.

INC BAR Map p182   Cocktail Bar
☎ 8858 6721; www.incbar.com; 7a College Approach SE10; ☽ 6pm-1.30am Wed & Thu, 7pm-3am Fri & Sat, 5pm-midnight Sun; DLR Cutty Sark
The newest arrival to Greenwich Market and the talk of the village is this bar with a seemingly endless list of cocktails. Among them is one they call *tatanka* (buffalo in Polish), which is Zubrowka vodka and apple juice – a match made in heaven.

MAYFLOWER Map p182   Pub
☎ 7237 4088; 117 Rotherhithe St SE16; ⊖ Rotherhithe
Northwest of Deptford in Rotherhithe, this 15th-century pub, originally called the Shippe but rebuilt and renamed the Spread Eagle in the 18th century, is now named after the vessel that took the pilgrims to

America in 1620; US visitors might want to make their own pilgrimage here. The ship set sail from Rotherhithe, and Captain Christopher Jones supposedly charted out its course here while supping schooners. There's seating on a small back terrace, from which you can view the Thames.

TRAFALGAR TAVERN Map p182   Pub
☎ 8858 2437; www.trafalgartavern.co.uk; 6 Park Row SE10; ☻ noon-11pm Mon-Thu, to midnight Fri & Sat, to 10.30pm Sun; DLR Cutty Sark
This cavernous pub with big windows looking onto the Thames and the O2 (the erstwhile Millennium Dome) is steeped in history and you can see some of it illustrated in the prints on the walls. Dickens apparently knocked back a few here – and used it as the setting for the wedding breakfast scene in *Our Mutual Friend* – and prime ministers Gladstone and Disraeli used to dine on the pub's celebrated whitebait, when the start of the season was so keenly anticipated that Parliament would suspend sitting for a day.

SOUTH LONDON

Brixton pub regulars turn up their noses at all the pretentious posing that goes on in many of London's neighbourhoods *du jour*, but nearby Battersea and Clapham have a stylish bar or two and there's even a decent riverside pub in Wandsworth. Brixton remains one of the most vibrant and exciting places to go out drinking in South London, though.

BRIXTON

BABALOU Map p190   Bar
☎ 7738 3366; www.babalou.net; St Matthew's Church, Brixton Hill SW2; ☻ 7pm-2am Wed & Thu, to 5am Fri & Sat; ☻ Brixton
The Bug Bar in the crypt of a Methodist church has turned into a bar-lounge-club called Babalou with fabulous cocktails and parties. The neogothic architecture stays but there are now North African touches and discreet little 'snugs' (OK, booths) in red velvet.

BRIXTON BAR & GRILL Map p190   Cocktail Bar
☎ 7737 6777; www.bbag.me.uk; 15 Atlantic Rd SW9; ☻ 4.30pm-midnight Tue & Wed, to 1am Thu, to 2am Fri & Sat, to 11pm Sun; ☻ Brixton
This stylish bar under the railway arches is a superb choice for 'slinky' (their word) cocktails and listening to live music. It also

has an interesting menu of small and large 'plates' as well as tapas.

DOGSTAR Map p190   Bar
☎ 7733 7515; 389 Coldharbour Lane SW9; ☻ 4pm-2am Mon-Fri, noon-4am Sat, 11am-2am Sun; ☻ Brixton
Downstairs this long-running local institution has a cavernous DJ bar, always mobbed with a young South London crowd. The main bar is as casual as you'd expect from a converted pub – comfortable sofas, big wooden tables – so dressing to kill is not obligatory.

EFFRA Map p190   Pub
☎ 7274 4180; 38A Kellet Rd SW2; ☻ Brixton
A lovely old boozer that will bring you closer to the heart of the Brixton Caribbean vibe than any other pub in the area, thanks to the spicy Jamaican menu, lively local characters who stay loyal to the Effra year after year and live jazz in the evenings. There's a lovely garden for outdoor drinking, while the interior is all shabby and charming Victorian splendour.

WHITE HORSE Map p190   Bar
☎ 8678 6666; www.whitehorsebrixton.com; 94 Brixton Hill SW2; ☻ 5pm-1am Mon-Thu, 2pm-3am Fri, noon-3am Sat, noon-1am Sun; ☻ Brixton
This mixed bag of a pub-bar-club might seem to house some people for the weekend. It consists of just one big room decorated with modern art against the long bar, but it's lots of fun. We usually play pool here.

BATTERSEA & WANDSWORTH

LOST SOCIETY Map p190   Bar
☎ 7652 6526; www.lostsociety.co.uk; 697 Wandsworth Rd SW8; ☻ 5pm-midnight Mon-Wed, to 1am Thu & Sun, to 2am Fri & Sat; ☻ Wandsworth Rd, Battersea Park or Queenstown Rd
A fantastic bar whose six rooms are dedicated to delightful decadence, it's all 1920s glamour and aristocratic glitz in Wandsworth these days. There's a garden at the back where many a summer drinking session goes on, DJs take over on weekends and create a good party atmosphere.

CLAPHAM

PRINCE OF WALES Map p190   Pub
☎ 7622 3530; 38 Old Town SW4; ☻ 5-11pm Mon-Wed, 5pm-midnight Thu, 5pm-1am Fri, 1pm-1am Sat, 1-11pm Sun; ☻ Clapham Common

While pubs that hang eclectic kitsch from their ceilings in a bid to seem quirky can be tedious, the Prince of Wales is still a very pleasant Clapham hangout, and its decor, unlike that of most pubs of the genre, is genuinely collected rather than supplied en masse. Real ales appear regularly.

SO.UK Map p190 — Bar

☎ 7622 4004; www.soukclapham.co.uk; 165 Clapham High St SW4; ⏰ 5pm-2am Mon-Wed, to 3am Thu-Sat, to 1am Sun; ⊖ Clapham Common

So.uk is a stylish Moroccan-themed bar that's light and airy and serves unusual cocktails (Twisted Mojito, anyone?) and shooters. It's extremely popular, with the chance to spot a few well-known faces among the Clapham professionals on the pull.

TIM BOBBIN Map p190 — Pub

☎ 7738 8953; 1-3 Lillieshall Rd SW4; ⏰ to midnight Thu-Sat; ⊖ Clapham Common

This charming boozer, a short walk from Clapham Common, is worth seeking out if you're trying to avoid Cla'am boys and girls on the piss. It's decorated with copies of its namesake caricaturist's rather rude 18th-century sketches, there are some decent ales on tap and a garden and brick conservatory with open kitchen in the back.

WHITE HOUSE Map p190 — Cocktail Bar

☎ 7498 3388; www.thewhitehouselondon.co.uk; 65 Clapham Park Rd SW4; ⏰ 5.30pm-5am Tue, Wed & Fri, 6.30pm-5am Sat, 5pm-2am Sun; ⊖ Clapham Common

Attracting Clapham's beautiful people with its stylish low-lit interior – tan sofas, small square tables, expansive bar and polished wooden floors – this chic bar on three floors also boasts a decent restaurant serving dim sum and a fantastic roof terrace for summer.

SOUTHWEST LONDON

Going out in Fulham is mainly about cheesy nights with lots of drinking, dancing on tables and generally behaving badly. Don't head to this part of town if you want a classy evening. Putney, Chiswick and Richmond offer an altogether more sedate and neighbourhood experience – so unlike the anonymous pubs of central London, where the transience of both staff and punters is a major theme. Often centuries old, many of the best pubs in this area overlook the river and make a great place to stop for a drink at any time of day.

FULHAM

MITRE Map p196 — Pub

☎ 7386 8877; www.fulhammitre.com; 81 Dawes Rd; ⊖ Fulham Broadway

A beautiful, light-filled and airy pub with a large semicircular bar and walled courtyard at the back, the award-winning Mitre gets very crowded in the evenings and at the weekends, especially at lunchtime.

WHITE HORSE Map p196 — Pub

☎ 7736 2115; 1-3 Parson's Green; ⏰ to midnight Mon-Sat, to 11pm Sun; ⊖ Parsons Green

Directly on Parsons Green, the White Horse is an inviting pub with a diverse clientele. Come here for the good hearty fare, barbecues during summer, the warm and friendly atmosphere and – most important – the extensive range of beers (draught ales, Belgian Trappist beers). There's pleasant outside seating at the front.

PUTNEY & BARNES

COAT & BADGE Map p196 — Pub

☎ 8788 4900; www.geronimo-inns.co.uk; 8 Lacy Rd SW15; ⏰ to midnight Fri & Sat; ⊖ Putney Bridge or ⊕ Putney

The Coat & Badge has gone for a tried and tested lounge-room approach (large sofas, second-hand books on shelves, standard lamps, sport on the telly), which seems to please the local clientele. It has a short but excellent menu and a fantastic large terrace out the front.

JOLLY GARDENERS Map p196 — Pub

☎ 8780 8921; 61-63 Lacy Rd SW15; ⊖ Putney Bridge or ⊕ Putney

Our favourite pub in Putney, the JG has been lovingly and eclectically kitted out; you'd never guess that Victorian oak cabinets went quite so well with Art Deco lamps. The pub plays host to amiable 30-somethings and boasts excellent wine and food menus. Its large terrace fronts a quiet road.

SHIP Map p196 — Pub

☎ 8870 9667; www.theship.co.uk; 41 Jew's Row SW18; ⏰ to midnight daily; ⊕ Wandsworth Town

Though the Ship is right by the Thames, the views aren't really spectacular along this stretch of the river – unless you're partial to retail parks and workaday bridges (which the owners freely admit). Still, the outside area is large, the barbecues in fine weather a real treat and the conservatory bar fun in any weather.

YE WHITE HART Map p62   Pub
☎ 8876 5177; The Terrace SW13; ☾ to midnight daily; ⊠ Barnes Bridge
This riverside Young's pub in Barnes has a lovely terrace that is somewhat marred by the busy road outside. Housed in a one-time Masonic lodge, the place is huge, but if you've been to a Young's pub before, you know exactly what the interior looks like: swirly carpets, fruit machines and an old man supping a pint at the bar. It's old and charming and the way pubs used to be.

CHISWICK

BOLLO Map p62   Pub
☎ 8994 6037; 13-15 Bollo Lane W4; ☾ from noon daily; ⊖ Chiswick Park
Out of the way even by Chiswick's standards, this backstreet gastropub has been a huge success, run by local restaurateurs who redeveloped it from a simple local. It's best at the weekend when it is at its busiest, catering to a well-heeled, older crowd looking for a pub and dining room rolled into one.

CITY BARGE Map p62   Pub
☎ 8994 2148; 27 Strand on the Green W4; ⊖ Gunnersbury
The Barge, perched dramatically close to – but not on – the Thames, has been operating as a pub since the Middle Ages (1484, to be exact). It is split into two bars (go for the downstairs one) and there is a small waterside terrace. Little known fact: a scene from the Beatles' film *Help!* was shot here.

RICHMOND

CRICKETERS Map p200   Pub
☎ 8940 4372; The Green TW9; ☾ from noon; ⊖ / ⊠ Richmond
Facing Richmond Green from its southern side (where its very own team bats and bowls), the Cricketers is a friendly and comfortable, themed (guess what) pub with a decent selection of ales and a mixed clientele.

DYSART ARMS Map p200   Pub
☎ 8940 8005; www.thedysartarms.co.uk; 135 Petersham Rd TW10; ⊖ / ⊠ Richmond, then ▣ 65

This wonderful, almost churchlike place with stone walls and an open fire is a great family pub facing Richmond Park's Petersham entrance. It succeeds on all fronts: families are made to feel welcome, the food is very good, and the large terrace is packed on a warm afternoon. Best of all there are musical evenings – jazz and classical – twice a week (usually Thursday and Saturday).

WHITE CROSS Map p200   Pub
8940 6844; Water Lane TW9; ☾ to midnight Mon-Sat; ⊖ Richmond
The riverside location, good food and fine ales make this pub on the site of a former monastery a winner. There are entrances for low and high tides, but when the river is at its highest, Cholmondeley Walk running along the Thames floods and the pub is out of bounds to those not willing to wade.

TWICKENHAM

BARMY ARMS Map p62   Pub
☎ 8892 0863; The Embankment TW1; ⊠ Twickenham
This is a popular Twickenham pub that gets packed to capacity on international match days; it claims to welcome *all* rugby fans. It's just by Eel Pie Island, a once-funky hippy hangout that still attracts the alternative crowd, despite its heyday having long passed. It also has decent pub food and a charming beer garden to recommend it.

LONDON APPRENTICE Map p62   Pub
☎ 8560 1915; 62 Church St TW7; ⊠ Isleworth
If you're really into sunning along the Thames, you may want to venture north of Twickenham to Isleworth and this riverside pub dating back to the early 17th century. Henry VIII is believed to have dallied with wife-to-be No 5, Catherine Howard, at an earlier tavern on the site.

WHITE SWAN Map p62   Pub
☎ 8892 2166; Riverside TW1; ⊠ Twickenham
This traditional pub in Twickenham overlooks a quiet stretch of the Thames from what must be one of the most English-looking streets in London. It boasts a fantastic riverside location, a great selection of beer and a loyal crowd of locals. Even if you are not in Twickenham, the White Swan is worth a detour.

NIGHTLIFE

top picks

What's your recommendation? www.lonelyplanet.com/london

You could live in London for 100 years and still not be able to 'do' all the nightlife. It's no wonder, then, that Londoners can get a bit overwhelmed with all that's on offer: clubs, live music, comedy, cabaret, and within all of those, hundreds of subsections catering to all kinds of tastes and preferences.

You'll probably come here knowing what you want to experience (it might be big clubs such as Fabric, or sweaty shoebox clubs with the latest DJ talent), but there's plenty to tempt you to branch out from your usual tastes and try something new.

There are clubs across town (though East London is the top area for cutting-edge clubs), with house, electro, glam, indie or rave nights. If clubbing is not your thing, try out the stand-up comedy scene and see if you can heckle without being singled out for the next joke (dangerous if you go for front-row seating).

London's live-music scene is still rocking, jazzing, folking and booming, so you'll be able to hear as many established or up-and-coming artists as your ears desire. Prepare to cough up for the pleasure of seeing big bands live in mega venues, or revel in the pleasure of a tiny club in East London or Camden Town where you can witness a performance by the latest scandal-clad indie superstar.

CLUBBING

When it comes to clubbing, London's where it's at, and anyone who can get here on a Friday or Saturday night, be it from zone 2, the suburbs or a Ryanair flight, wants a night in London's clubs. Whether you're a lover of thumping techno, rock, nu rave, Latin, ska, pop, country, grime, minimal electro, hip hop or 1950s lindy hopping, there's something going on every night. Thursdays are loved by those who want to have their fun before the office workers mob the streets on Friday; Saturdays are the busiest and best if you're a serious clubber, and Sundays often have surprisingly good events across town.

93 FEET EAST Map p150

☎ 7247 3293; www.93feeteast.co.uk; 150 Brick Lane E2; ⏰ 5-11pm Mon-Thu, 5pm-1am Fri, noon-1am Sat, noon-10.30pm Sun; ⊖ Liverpool St or Aldgate East

Brick Lane's hot spot is evident by the long queue outside. This great venue has a courtyard, three big rooms and an outdoor terrace that gets crowded on sunny afternoons, and it's packed with a cool East London crowd.

TIPS FOR CLUBBERS

- Where to go? Most Londoners start their nights in a bar before moving on to clubs and gig venues, gravitating from Soho towards Shoreditch and Hoxton – the location of the majority of London's cutting-edge bars and clubs. Notting Hill also has some excellent clubs, while Brixton is top for hip hop, R&B, reggae and grime venues.
- What does it cost? Clubbing can be an expensive pastime, but not always. Midweek prices are reasonable, and there are plenty of student nights or those oriented to a budget crowd. Search through the listing magazines during your visit. If you want to go to big clubs such as Fabric (p296) or Matter (p297) on a Saturday night (*the* night for clubbing), expect to pay at least £20 for the pleasure.
- Will I get in? Exclusivity is not such an issue as it is in, say, New York or Moscow – very few people are turned away from London clubs, but queuing in the cold while the gorgeous and connected jump out of cabs and straight into the warmth of the club can be a humiliating experience. As ever, get there early and try to get advance (or 'queue-jump') tickets for bigger events if you can't bear being left in door-whore limbo.
- What to wear? Dress codes vary widely, but London's clubs are generally relaxed and you won't need to worry about being turned away from clubs for your appearance – it's more about whether you care to blend in with a particular venue's crowd. Generally, the 'posh' clubs will want a glam look – which can include trainers and jeans – and the more alternative venues will be full of skinny jeans worn hip-hop style (bums on display), mad haircuts and baggy shirts.
- What's on where? Check the weekly listings in *Time Out* or the *Evening Standard* – part of the charm of London's nightlife is that it's always changing and new venues and club nights sprout up every week, so keep your eyes peeled!

There are some excellent nights, such as the superpopular Slipped Disco on Friday. Relaxed Sunday afternoon Fuse Party sessions are free and see tonnes of DJs sizzling inside, while a barbecue's smokin' in the courtyard. It's worth getting tickets in advance through the website to beat the queue.

333 Map p150

☎ 7739 5949; www.333mother.com; 333 Old St EC1; ☽ 10pm-5am Fri, 10pm-4am Sat & Sun; ⊖ Old St

Hoxton's true old-timer, 333's stripped-down manner doesn't bow to Shoreditch's silly cool and just keeps going, despite not being what it once was in terms of pulling power. The club still hosts great nights that are simultaneously scruffy and innovative and is a key player on the electro-glam and indie rave scene.

AQUARIUM Map p150

☎ 7253 3558; www.clubaquarium.co.uk; 256-264 Old St EC1; ☽ 10pm-3am Sat, 10pm-4am Sun; O Old St

The Saturday-night hitch-up between '70s disco evening Carwash and this converted gym seems like a great match: clubbers dressed in sexy, retro gear – compulsory, but disco wigs not allowed – now mingle around the huge pool or in the trendy bar. Trainers are not welcome here.

BAR RUMBA Map p66

☎ 7287 2715; www.barrumba.co.uk; 36 Shaftesbury Ave W1; ☽ 10.30pm-3am Mon & Wed, 8.30pm-3am Tue, Thu & Fri, 9pm-5am Sat, 8pm-1.30am Sun; ⊖ Piccadilly Circus

A small club just off Piccadilly with a loyal following and fab DJs, specialising in hip hop, Latin, and drum and bass. It was relaunched in 2008, and has once again reasserted its appeal with drum and bass and hip-hop lovers. Movement is all about jungle, every other Thursday, while salsa and Latin urban dance parties are on at Barrio Latino on Tuesday.

BETHNAL GREEN WORKING MEN'S CLUB Map p156

☎ 7739 2727; www.workersplaytime.net; 42-44 Pollard Row E2; ☽ hr vary; ⊖ Bethnal Green

This is a true rags-to-riches story: BGWMC was on the brink of bankruptcy, its working men about to become destitute and pintless, until a clever promoter spread the news of trashy burlesque nights taking place in the club's main hall – sticky carpets, shimmery stage set 'n' all – and (literally) overnight, half of London stormed the venue, making it one of the most successful and popular clubs in the capital. There are regular burlesque bonanzas in addition to tassel-twirling contests, alternative Eurovision nights and many more sweet selections. Check the website for what's on when you're around.

BIG CHILL HOUSE Map p170

☎ 7427 2540; www.bigchill.net; 257-259 Pentonville Rd N1; ☽ noon-midnight Mon-Wed & Sun, noon-1am Thu, noon-3am Fri & Sat, 10.30pm-4am Sun; ⊖ King's Cross St Pancras

A three-floor space with a good selection of live music and DJs, and a great terrace for hanging out on, Big Chill also hosts a popular festival, and runs a record label. The music choice is always varied and international, the sound system is fantastic, plus entry is free most nights.

BURLESQUE-TASTIC!

After years of low-profile parties with high-glitter gowns, the burlesque scene burst onto the mainstream, showering London with nipple tassels, top hats, sexy lingerie and some of the best parties in town. Young Londoners caught the dressing-up bug with such a frenzy that many grandmas' wardrobes were looted for frocks. Subsequently, the 'alternative' burlesque scene became overwhelmingly mainstream, and club-night organisers, passionately dedicated to dressing up and taking fun seriously, raised prices in many of the venues in order to ward off those who wouldn't buck up and dress up. So prepare to pay an average of £25 for some (but not all) of the city's best burlesque nights, and make sure you look like a million dollars. Best burlesque venues are Bethnal Green Working Men's Club (above), where you can find anything from male burlesque contests to girls on roller skates hosting tea parties, and Volupté (p298), a tiny but elegant cabaret club with some excellent nights, such as Wednesday's Cabaret Salon and once-monthly Black Cotton Club.

Outstanding nights are Flash Monkey (www.theflashmonkey.biz), whose parties are always a sell-out, and The Last Tuesday Society's (www.thelasttuesdaysociety.org), whose fantastic masked balls are not to be missed. The long-running Lady Luck night (www.myspace.com/theladyluckclub) is the city's top for rockabilly and old jazz, while the old-timer, Rakehell's Revels, hosts 'secret' nights (just Google it) at various venues.

BLACK GARDENIA Map p66

☎ 7494 4955; www.myspace.com/blackgardenia93;
93 Dean St; ☽ from 8pm Fri & Sat; ⊖ Tottenham
Court Rd

A fantastic Soho dive, Black Gardenia is tiny,
red-walled, shabby and underground. Run
by rockabillies and people with tattoos and
1950s dress sense, it offers a variety of gigs,
from lesbian bands, to rock'n'roll bonanzas
and schmoozy piano music accompanied by
a crooning, middle-aged Soho character.

CARGO Map p150

☎ 7739 3440; www.cargo-london.com; 83 Rivington
St EC2; ☽ noon-1am Mon-Thu, noon-3am Fri, 6pm-
3am Sat, noon-midnight Sun; ⊖ Old St or Liverpool St

Cargo is one of London's most eclectic clubs.
It has three different spaces – a dance-floor
room, bar and lounge, and a little diner –
under brick railway arches. The music policy
is innovative, with plenty of Latin House, nu-
jazz, funk, groove and soul, DJs, global or up-
and-coming bands, demos and rare grooves.
Some of its nights have included the dark
burlesque Torture Gardens annual party, African music festival, Balkan brass bands and
Cuban ska. There's also an excellent bar.

CATCH Map p150

☎ 7729 6097; www.myspace.com/thecatchbar;
22 Kingsland Rd E2; ☽ 6pm-midnight Mon-Wed,
6pm-2am Thu-Sat, 6pm-1am Sun; ⊖ Old St

It doesn't look like much, but Catch is one of
the best nights out in Shoreditch. Upstairs,
every other Saturday, you can hear Get Rude,
hosted by DJ duo Zombie Disco Squad,
which mixes bass, tropical and electro music.
Downstairs you get a big house-party vibe
with DJs who mix up pretty much anything
from '90s Euro disco to chart hits to electro
and techno. It's free, open late and great fun.

DOGSTAR Map p190

☎ 7733 7515; 389 Coldharbour Lane SW9;
☽ 9pm-3am Fri & Sat; ⊖ Brixton

You'll have to push your way through
the huge downstairs bar (see p290) of this
converted pub to get to the house-music
club upstairs, but that's what all the Brixton
clubbers do.

EAST VILLAGE Map p150

☎ 7739 5173; www.eastvillageclub.com; 89 Great
Eastern St EC2; ☽ 5pm-1am Mon & Tue, 5pm-
3.30am Wed-Sun; ⊖ Old St

The old Medicine Bar's popularity flagged
so much that it was only a matter of time
before someone snapped up the fine location and did something worthwhile with
it. Well, finally the space has been transformed into a club that has seen house lovers flocking from all over London. There's a
wide array of quality DJs on the program,
though our favourite is the New York–style
disco punk night, Sweatshop.

EGG Map p170

☎ 7428 7574; www.egglondon.net; 5-13 Vale
Royal N1; ☽ 10pm-4am Fri, 10pm-5am Sat;
⊖ King's Cross St Pancras

Egg has the most superb layout with three
exposed concrete rooms (across three
floors), a garden and two gorgeous tropical roof terraces (relieving the edgy, exiled
smokers). Some say it would fit perfectly in
New York's meat-packing district thanks to
its design, but it's ours and we're keeping it
because it rocks. Located off York Way, the
club hosts 'omnisexual' nights, with a mix
of electro, minimal and house. At weekends, a free shuttle bus runs here, every
30 minutes between 10pm and 2am, from
outside American Carwash on York Way.

FABRIC Map p150

☎ 7336 8898, 7490 0444; www.fabriclondon.com;
77a Charterhouse St EC1; ☽ 9.30pm-5am Fri &
Sun, 10pm-7am Sat; ⊖ Farringdon

This most impressive of superclubs is still the
first stop on the London scene for many international clubbers, as the lengthy queues
attest (worst from about 9pm to 11pm).
A warren of three floors, three bars, many
walkways and unisex toilets, it has a kidney-
shaking 'sonic boom' dance floor. The crowd
is hip and well dressed without overkill, and
the music – mainly electro, house, drum and
bass, and breakbeat – is as superb as you'd
expect from London's top-rated club. Superstar DJs often sell out Friday-night's Fabric
Live when big names such as Goldie, DJ
Diplo, Plump DJ or DJ Hype take over.

FAVELA CHIC Map p150

☎ 7613 5228; www.favelachic.com; 91 Great
Eastern St E1; ☽ 6pm-late Tue-Sun; ⊖ Old St

Smaller sister of the original Paris club, this
place profits from 'slum chic' just like the
producers of Havaiana flip-flops did. It's a
one-room bar-club with permanently long
queues on Friday and Saturday and innova-

tive music nights. The decor is very much about the vintage, distressed and flea-market pieces, though markedly self-consciously so, but if you can endure the long wait and get past the high 'n' mighty door whores, you'll have a good night.

HERBAL Map p150

☎ 7613 4462; 10-14 Kingsland Rd E2; ⏱ 9pm-2am Wed, Thu & Sun, to 3am Fri, 10pm-3am Sat; ⊖ Old St

You'll recognise Herbal by all the plastic grass stapled to its front wall. Inside is a two-level bar-club. The laid-back, grown-up loft upstairs has a small dance floor, seating and a window overlooking Shoreditch. Downstairs is more minimalist and can get very sweaty. There's a mix of drum and bass, house, funk-house and hip hop, interspersed with live shows.

KOKO Map p170

☎ 0870 432 5527; www.koko.uk.com; 1a Camden High St NW1, ⏱ 10pm-2.30am Tue, 10pm-6am Fri & Sat; ⊖ Mornington Cres

Once the legendary Camden Palace, where Charlie Chaplin, the Goons, the Sex Pistols and Madonna have all performed in the past, Koko is keeping its reputation as one of London's better gig venues – Madonna played a Confessions on a Dance Floor gig here in 2006 and Prince gave a surprise gig in 2007. The theatre has a dance floor and decadent balconies, and attracts an indie crowd with Club NME on Friday. There are live bands almost every night of the week.

LAST DAYS OF DECADENCE Map p150

☎ 7033 0085; www.thelastdaysofdecadence.com; 145 Shoreditch High St E1; ⏱ 8pm-2.30am Thu, Fri & Sat, 8pm-midnight Sun-Wed; ⊖ Old St

A brand new club that opened in the height of the recession, this is a place that celebrates the 1930s through its heady, abandon-fuelled parties and through its Great Depression–inspired name. Not that it sticks to 1930s music, however – you'll find regular nights hosting DJs such as the out-there trannie DJ Jodie Harsh on Fridays' Circus, and Last Days of Decadence's eponymous night that mixes up D&B, nu-rave and jungle. On a quieter note, there are free jazz gigs on Tuesdays, and Monday nights are life-drawing classes – £10 a go.

MADAME JO JO'S Map p66

☎ 7734 2473; www.madamejojos.com; 8 Brewer St W1; ⏱ 10.30pm-3am Wed-Fri, from 9.30pm Thu, cabaret 7-10pm & club 10pm-3am Sat; ⊖ Leicester Sq or Piccadilly Circus

The renowned subterranean crimson cabaret bar and all its sleazy fun kitsch comes into its own with London Burlesque Social Club on the first Thursday of the month, and there's Kitsch Cabaret on Saturday. Keb Darge's Deep Funk night on Friday is legendary, attracting a cool crew of breakers, jazz dancers and people just out to have a good time.

MATTER Map p182

☎ 7549 6686; www.matterlondon.com; O2 Arena, Peninsula Sq SE10; ⊖ North Greenwich

This is London's greatest new club, in all senses of the adjective – it's massive (therefore great), with a 2600 capacity, underneath O2 (formerly called the Millenium Dome), though its real greatness lies in the fact that it's the larger appendage to the best club in town, Fabric (opposite). You get all the same fantastic names here as there, only with the enhancements of a state-of-the-art sound system, 3D visuals on interlocking screens, and lots of bars and toilets (so no tiresome queuing). It's a bit of a trek from other parts of town, but Thames Clipper boats run half-hourly to Waterloo from

NEW BEGINNINGS AT KING'S CROSS

Recent years have seen nearly all the clubs in the area around King's Cross close down. The Cross, The Key and Canvas all went down in 2008 to make way for a huge redevelopment of the run-down neighbourhood. The old clubs inhabited industrial buildings along dodgy streets and getting to them could be as much of an experience as the club itself, but that's all looking to change with the promise of 15 new arts and music venues, courtesy of University of the Arts London. Historic buildings will be incorporated in the redevelopment, and there will apparently be theatres, independent cinemas, galleries, pubs, restaurants and bars. King's Place (www.kingsplace.co.uk) is a beautiful new building on York Way that might signal the look of things to come – it houses the *Guardian* and *Observer* newspapers, and is home to the London Sinfonietta and the Orchestra of the Age of Enlightenment, as well as being the venue for live music and spoken word. The arts redevelopment area should be ready for action by the time you read this, and we're hoping some of the old clubs might return. Check it out in any case.

6am (last boat from Waterloo at 12.45am), a great journey home at dawn.

MINISTRY OF SOUND Map p189

☎ 7378 6528; www.minstryofsound.com; 103 Gaunt St SE1; ⊗ 10.30pm-6am Fri, midnight-9am Sat; ⊖ Elephant & Castle

This legendary club-cum-enormous-global-brand suffered from a loss of 'edge' in the early naughties, but after pumping in top DJs the Ministry has firmly rejoined the top club ranks. Fridays is Gallery trance night, while Saturday Sessions offers the *crème de la crème* of house, electro and techno DJs.

NOTTING HILL ARTS CLUB Map p176

☎ 7460 4459; www.nottinghillartsclub.com; 21 Notting Hill Gate W11; ⊗ 6pm-1am Tue-Sat, 6pm-2am Fri & Sat, 4-11pm Sun; ⊖ Notting Hill Gate

London simply wouldn't be what it is without places like NHAC. There's a night for everyone in this small basement club, from knitting societies to country folk, house nights and Eastern European punk. The famous monthly Thursday Yo-Yo night, where singer Lily Allen and producer Mark Ronson met, is one of the best nights for R&B, '80s boogies, hip hop, ragga and diverse live sets, while the bimonthly Sunday Radio Gagarin features 'experiments in Sunday Socialism'.

ON THE ROCKS Map p150

25 Kingsland Rd E2; ⊗ 10.30pm-2am Fri, 9pm-2am Sat; ⊖ Old St

If a place could ever be described as a den, this is it: small, dark, sweaty and in a category of its own, On The Rocks caters to a mixed crowd of trendsters, trashy youngsters and a lost soul or two, all of whom are pretty much only interested in carrying on the party.

PASSING CLOUDS Map p156

☎ 7168 7146; www.passingclouds.com; Richmond Rd E8; ⊗ 10pm-4am Fri & Sat, hr vary Mon-Fri; ⊖ Old St or ⊚ Dalston Kingsland, 🚌 243, 55 or 76

One of those little flickers of nightlife brilliance, Passing Clouds is a 'members club' that actually hosts massive parties open to everyone (admission around £8) and go on until the early hours of the morning. The music is predominantly world oriented, with a lot of African influence and regular Afrobeat bands; the parties are a healthy mix of DJs and live music with a multicultural crowd that really makes you feel you're in London. The decor is makeshift

bar, colourful lanterns and tropical titbits, and the atmosphere is just exhilarating. Well worth checking out.

PLASTIC PEOPLE Map p150

☎ 7739 6471; www.plasticpeople.co.uk; 147-149 Curtain Rd EC2; ⊗ 10pm-2am Thu, 10pm-3am Fri & Sat; ⊖ Old St

This is a tiny club with just a dance floor and bar and a booming sound system that experts say easily kicks the butt of bigger clubs. It's also a venue that features the most progressive club nights, which fearlessly introduces new or controversial music. Head here on Friday for And Did We Mention Our Disco with Rory Phillips (of ex-Trash, current Durrr DJ), and Saturday for Balance, with a healthy mix of Latin, jazz, hip hop, house and techno. Ben Watt hosts occasional Sunday nights at Buzzin' Fly, while once a month Thursday's Forward has filthy grime sounds ripping the dance floor. Highly recommended.

PROUD CAMDEN Map p166

☎ 7482 3867; www.proudcamden.com; Horse Hospital, Stables Market, Chalk Farm Rd NW1; ⊗ 7.30pm-1am Mon-Wed, 7.30pm-2am Thu-Sat, 7.30pm-midnight Sun; ⊖ Camden Town or Chalk Farm

It's very trendy indeed at Proud, with gorgeous Camdenites heading to the sunset-watching terrace for outdoor gigs in summer or indoor booths in winter. Proud is a great venue in North London that combines live music and exhibitions, and it's really best in summer, when the terrace is open. Also see p285.

SCALA Map p150

☎ 7833 2022; www.scala-london.co.uk; 275 Pentonville Rd N1; ⊗ 10pm-5am Fri & Sat; ⊖ King's Cross

On Friday this multilevel former cinema hosts Popstarz, a laid-back gay/mixed potpourri of indie, alternative and kitsch among other, more eclectic nights. On Saturday it's UK garage night Cookies and Cream. The venue is expansive but excellent, with a glass bar at its centre overlooking the stage but insulated from the noise.

VOLUPTÉ Map p100

☎ 7831 1622; www.volupte-lounge.com; 7-9 Norwich St EC4; ⊗ from 11.30am Tue-Fri, from 7.30pm Sat; ⊖ Chancery Lane

A gorgeous little cabaret venue in a small street off Fleet St, Volupté is where all of London's lindy hop dancers come to practice their moves on weekend evenings. The once-monthly Black Cotton Club is a harkback to the 1920s in terms of dress code and music choice. Saturday afternoon's Afternoon Tease is a fab mix of, well, yes, afternoon tea and burlesque performances.

COMEDY

You might not think Londoners are a cheerful lot when they growl at you on the tube, but actually they love a good chuckle. This is evident in the fact that despite the winter gloom and drizzly rain (or perhaps because of it), you can roll up at any one of the 20-plus major comedy clubs or countless other venues (including pubs) and warm your heart and exercise your lungs with laughter.

Most comedy acts gravitate around the Edinburgh Festival season: April to July new acts are being tried out on audiences; August is the cruellest month for comedy in London, because everyone's shifted up north for the festival itself; winter has the comedians doing the stuff that went down well at the festival. Check Edinburgh Festival Awards for the new bright stars.

Some of the world's most famous comedians hail from, or made their names in, London. To whet your appetite, a quick roll call from recent decades might include Peter Sellers, Peter Cook, Spike Milligan, Dudley Moore, Tommy Cooper, Dawn French, Jennifer Saunders, Ruby Wax, Lenny Henry, Ben Elton, Alexei Sayle, Harry Enfield, Victoria Wood, Julian Clary, Rowan Atkinson, Reeves & Mortimer, Eddie Izzard, Jo Brand, Sacha Baron Cohen (aka Ali G, Borat and Brüno), Ricky Gervais, Matt Lucas and David Walliams.

Recent years have unearthed Russell Brand, one of the UK's most loved and prolific comedians, and stars such as young but sharp Josie Long, Paul Sinha, Tiernan Douieb and Russell Howard. We don't have space to name

LOCAL VOICES: LYDIA FULTON

An Off-Beat Literary Night

I discovered the Wapping Project Bookshop (☎ 7680 2080; www.thewappingproject.com; Wapping Wall E1) some six months after it opened, on a late winter day. It doesn't really look like a bookshop at first – it's inside a glasshouse and the books sit in cages (though not enclosed) – but with all the natural light and a cosy and quiet atmosphere, it's pretty much the perfect bookshop.

I got talking to Lydia, the lovely manager, whose passion for art, design, fashion and photography titles is well combined with fiction and poetry. She runs a popular literary evening at the bookshop on Thursdays, when punters pop their bums on cushions scattered on the shop floor, hear readings, and ask questions of well-established and new writers. Check out the Wapping Project Bookshop at its website; details of readings can be found on Lydia's website at http://lydiafulton.co.uk.

So, tell me about the literary evenings. The weekly readings started in January 2009 as a way of having a regular focus to brighten the endless winter nights. The readings are very intimate, for only a lucky few people, and the idea is to keep them that way, so that the reader and the audience interact in a manner that wouldn't usually be possible.

How do you choose the writers? I select writers who inspire me, or who have great character. We've had people from the top of the literary tree to emerging names who are creating a storm. My favourite so far was Edna O'Brien. It was wonderful to see a writer of her stature humbly sharing her writing, talking about her achievements and her drinking sessions with everyone from Ted Hughes to Samuel Beckett. And all inside a tiny bookshop no bigger than the average family's sitting room.

What's the audience like? There are a couple Wapping locals who tend to come to every other readings or so, but usually the audience is very different and reflects the diversity of the readers. A gentleman and his daughter once travelled all the way from Aberdeen to come hear their favourite author, Nigerian writer Helen Oyeyemi, read.

What it is like to work in a glasshouse year-round? The bookshop really changes throughout the year. In the wintertime we light the wood burner and the smell of wood fills the bookshop, and the smoke plumes signal that the shop is open to all around. In the summer the shop is covered with bamboo and the doors open out into the garden. Customers read their books on cushions among the dandelions.

And what do you do on quiet days? I was an art student so I always have a notebook with me to draw the outline of an interesting building or the view from the window. I transfer some of these drawings onto tea plates and tea cups to add a touch of fun and beauty to tea time. I am also working on my first novel, based on fact, set in 1920s Somerset.

Lydia Fulton, Manager of Wapping Project Bookshop, was interviewed by Vesna Maric

all the comedians on this jolly circuit, but do look out for the fantastic London-based American comedian Rich Hall; Geordie sonic-waffler Ross Noble; musician, poet and Luton-towner John Hegley; controversial and politically minded Mark Thomas; and dead-pan and dirty Jimmy Carr. Other brilliant comedians are Alan Carr, Omid Djalili, Gina Yashere, Lee Hurst, Simon Amstell, Jenny Eclair, Arthur Smith, Richard Herring, Bill Bailey, Daniel Kitson and Simon Munnery, and they can all be seen on London's stages.

Many of London's established comedians get together to goof around at inventive co-median Robin Ince's legendary Book Club night (www.myspace.com/bookclublive) at various locations in town; Union Chapel (p304) is a wonderful venue that hosts a monthly Live at the Chapel (http://liveat thechapel.co.uk) with big names and live music.

AMUSED MOOSE SOHO Map p66
☎ 7287 3727; www.amusedmoose.com; Moon-lighting, 17 Greek St W1; ⊖ Tottenham Court Rd
One of the city's best clubs, Soho's Amused Moose is popular with audiences and comedians alike, perhaps helped along by the fact that heckling is 'unacceptable' and all of the acts are 'first date friendly' in that they're unlikely to humiliate the front row.

CHUCKLE CLUB Map pp70-1
☎ 7476 1672; www.chuckleclub.com; Three Tuns Bar, London School of Economics, Houghton St WC2; admission £5-15; ⏱ Sat; ⊖ Holborn or Temple
The comedian's favourite, this club has a great atmosphere thanks to comedy stal-wart, resident host and all-round lovely bloke Eugene Cheese, who begins every night with the Chuckle Club warm-up song.

COMEDY CAFÉ Map p150
☎ 7739 5706; www.comedycafe.co.uk; 66-68 Rivington St EC2; admission free Wed, up to £15 Sat; ⏱ Wed-Sat; ⊖ Old St or Liverpool St
A major venue, the Comedy Café is purpose-built for, well, comedy, hosting some good comedians. It can be a little too try-hard and wacky, but it's worth seeing the Wednesday-night try-out spots for some wincing entertainment.

COMEDY CAMP Map p66
☎ 7483 2960; www.comedycamp.co.uk; 3-4 Archer St W1; admission £10; ⏱ 8.30pm Tue; ⊖ Piccadilly Circus

This gay (but very straight-friendly) com-edy club, hosted by Simon Happily, has become one of Soho's favourites. It's held in the basement area of one of Soho's more enjoyable gay bars, Barcode (p325). Comedy Camp features both up-and-coming queer comedy acts as well as more established gay and lesbian comics.

COMEDY STORE Map p66
☎ 7344 4444; www.thecomedystore.co.uk; Hay-market House, 1a Oxendon St SW1; admission from £13-18; ⏱ Tue-Sun; ⊖ Piccadilly Circus
This was one of the first (and is still one of the best) comedy clubs in London. It was established down the road in Soho in 1979, the year Margaret Thatcher came to power, which we're sure was no coincidence. Al-though it's a bit like conveyor-belt comedy, it gets some of the biggest names. Wednes-day and Sunday night's Comedy Store Play-ers is the most famous improv outfit in town with the wonderful Josie Lawrence; while Thursday's, Friday's and Saturday's brilliant The Best in Stand Up features (you guessed it) the best on London's comedy circuit.

DOWNSTAIRS AT THE KING'S HEAD Map p62
☎ 8340 1028; www.downstairsatthekingshead .com; 2 Crouch End Hill N8; ⏱ Sat & Sun; ⊖ Finsbury Park then 🚌 W7
A club that hails from the 1980s, with suc-cess stories of launching the careers of Eddie Izzard and Mark Lamarr in its busy and intimate room. It hosts newbies and biggies in equal proportions. Check the website for the different nights and admission prices.

HEADLINERS Map p62
☎ 8566 4067; www.headlinerscomedy.com; George IV, 185 Chiswick High Rd W4; admission £12; ⏱ Fri & Sat; ⊖ Turnham Green
The first purpose-built venue in West Lon-don, Headliners is comfortable and has a traditional shape in that the compere intro-duces the act then scarpers, try-outs open the night and the best is saved until last.

JONGLEURS Map p166
☎ 0870 787 0707; www.jongleurs.com; Dingwalls, 11 East Yard, Camden Lock NW1; admission from £16; ⏱ Fri & Sat; ⊖ Camden Town
This is something like a Starbucks-size international chain that serves comedy in-stead of coffee. There's eating, drinking and

laughing (probably all at the same, choke-risking time). Friday and Saturday nights normally feature one big-name comedian and a couple of guys on unicycles (or thereabouts) and the shows are so popular, you usually have to book in advance. There are other venues in Battersea (Map p190; ☎ 0844 499 4060; 49 Lavender Gardens SW11) and Bow (Map p156; ☎ 0844 499 4062; 221 Grove Rd E3).

LOWDOWN AT THE ALBANY Map p166
☎ 7387 5706; www.lowdownatthealbany.com; 240 Great Portland St W1; admission £7-10; ✆ Regent's Park
A shabby basement venue that is programmed together with the Hen and Chickens Theatre (☎ 7704 2001; 109 St Pauls Rd N1; ✆ Highbury & Islington). The two venues host stand-up and sketch sets, Edinburgh previews and theatre. The Hen and Chickens, in particular, is a good place to see solo shows.

SOHO THEATRE Map p66
☎ 7470 0100, www.sohotheatre.com; 21 Dean St W1; admission £10-18; ✆ Tottenham Court Rd
Soho Theatre has developed into a quality comedy venue and hosts some of the top names of both stand up or sketch-based comedy. Hilarious US comics (such as Louis CK and Kirsten Schaal) frequently come here to perform.

UP THE CREEK Map p182
☎ 8858 4581; www.up-the-creek.com; 302 Creek Rd SE10; admission £10-15; Fri & Sat; Greenwich, DLR Cutty Sark
Bizarrely enough, the hecklers can be funnier than the acts at this great club. Up the Creek was established and is still living in the spirit of the legendary Malcolm Hardee. Hardee, who was the patron sinner of British comedy, famously stole Freddie Mercury's 40th birthday cake and donated it to his local old folks home. Mischief, rowdiness and excellent comedy are the norm.

JAZZ CLUBS
London's jazz scene was always hot and smoky (though with the smoking ban, it's now just hot) and great jazz names play regularly on the circuit. Particularly good times of the year for jazz are: November, when the 10-day London Jazz Festival (www.serious.org.uk) takes place in venues across central London; July, with a week of Jazz

on the Streets (www.jazzonthestreets.co.uk) mainly gravitating around Soho, while Ealing Jazz Festival (www.ealing.gov.uk) in Walpole Park goes over five evenings; and September, the month for Riverfront Jazz Festival (www.riverfrontjazz.co.uk) in Greenwich, with gigs over the whole month.

100 CLUB Map p66
☎ 7636 0933; www.the100club.co.uk; 100 Oxford St W1; ✆ Tottenham Court Rd
This legendary London venue has always concentrated on jazz, but it's also spreading its wings to swing and rock nowadays. It once showcased Chris Barber, BB King and the Stones, and was at the centre of the punk revolution as well as the '90s indie scene. It hosts dancing swing gigs and local jazz musicians, as well as the occasional big name.

606 CLUB Map p196
☎ 7352 5953; www.606club.co.uk; 90 Lots Rd SW10; ✆ Fulham Broadway or Earl's Court
A lovely but slightly out-of-the-way basement jazz club and restaurant that gives centre stage to contemporary British-based jazz musicians nightly. The club frequently opens until 2am, although at weekends you have to dine to gain admission (booking is advised). There is no entry charge, but a music fee (£8 during the week, £12 Friday and Saturday, £10 Sunday) will be added to your food/drink bill at the end of the evening.

BULL'S HEAD Map p62
☎ 8076 5241; www.thebullshead.com; 373 Lonsdale Rd SW13; Barnes Bridge
This traditional pub dates from Tudor times and has hosted modern jazz concerts in its Jazz Room since 1959. It continues to offer some of the best British jazz nightly and at Sunday lunchtime.

JAZZ CAFÉ Map p170
☎ 7916 6060; www.jazzcafe.co.uk; 5 Parkway NW1; ✆ Camden Town
Though its name would have you think that jazz is this club's main staple, its real speciality is the crossover of jazz into the mainstream. It's a trendy industrial-style restaurant with jazz gigs around once a week, while the rest of the month is filled with Afro, funk, hip hop, R&B and soul styles with big-name acts and a faithful bohemian Camden crowd.

PIZZA EXPRESS JAZZ CLUB Map p66

☎ 7439 8722; www.pizzaexpress.co.uk/jazz.htm; 10 Dean St W1; ◒ Tottenham Court Rd

Believe it or not, this is one of the most consistently popular and good jazz venues in London. It's a bit of a strange arrangement, having a small basement venue beneath the main chain restaurant, but it seems to work well. Patrons listen attentively to modern jazz, and lots of big names perform here.

RONNIE SCOTT'S Map p66

☎ 7439 0747; www.ronniescotts.co.uk; 47 Frith St W1; ◒ Leicester Sq

Ronnie Scott originally opened his jazz club on Gerrard St in 1959 under a Chinese gambling den. The club moved to its current location six years later and became widely known as Britain's best jazz club. It was the only place the British public could listen to modern jazz – luminaries such as Miles Davis, Charlie Parker, Thelonious Monk, plus Ella Fitzgerald, Count Basie and Sarah Vaughan. Even rock bands such as The Who played here. Over the years the club has survived a roller coaster of uncertainty over its existence and overcome the death of its saxophonist owner in 1996. It continues to build upon its formidable reputation by hosting a range of big names and new talent. The atmosphere is great, but talking during music is a big no-no. Door staff can be terribly rude and the service slow, but that's how it's always been. Gigs are nightly and usually last until 2am.

VORTEX JAZZ CLUB Map p170

☎ 7254 4097; www.vortexjazz.co.uk; 11 Gillet St N16; 🚌 73 or 🚇 Dalston Kingsland

The Vortex has a good program of musicians from the UK, US and Europe, and hosts jazz musicians, singers and songwriters.

ROCK & POP

Everybody who likes pop knows Blur, Oasis, Suede, Pulp, Garbage, Elastica and Radiohead, and remembers the golden age of London's live music – the 1990s and Britpop – when the British capital produced more cutting-edge bands than you could keep up with and play on your stereo. The 21st century, however, found the scene all washed up and London not so hip any more, and the lull lasted until the sun shone on the capital's music scene once again and London's bands were jamming the iPods of pop lovers worldwide – Coldplay, Bloc Party and Razorlight or Amy Winehouse, Adele and Lily Allen are all London's babies.

All major artists continue to consider London an essential place to tour, so prepare to find the biggies (from Bob Dylan to Björk) to the new kids on the block. Multitalented Cargo (p296) spices up its club nights with performances from up-and-coming bands or visiting cult bands from overseas. The new band scene is particularly blossoming, and with MySpace it's easier than ever to keep up with your favourite unsigned band and alternative venue. Together, these musicians keep London's wide range of rock and pop venues – from the aircraft hangar–sized Earl's Court Exhibition Centre (opposite), Wembley Arena (p304) and the O2 (opposite) to the tiny Borderline (below) or Barfly (below) – humming and full.

BARDENS BOUDOIR Map p62

☎ 7249 9557; www.bardensbar.co.uk; 36-44 Stoke Newington Rd N16; 🚇 Dalston Kingsland, then 🚌 243, 55 or 76

The Dalston music scene is on the rise, and Bardens Boudoir is firmly at the forefront, hosting some fantastic nights. There are live gigs and DJ nights, so check the website for all the listings.

BARFLY@THE MONARCH Map p166

☎ 7691 4244, 7691 4245; www.barflyclub.com; Monarch, 49 Chalk Farm Rd NW1; ◒ Chalk Farm or Camden Town

Barfly, Charles Bukowski, lounge lizards – you get the picture. This typically grungy, indie-rock Camden venue is full of small-time artists looking for their big break. The focus is on rock from the US and UK, with alternative-music radio station Xfm hosting regular nights. There's a new sister venue, the Fly (Map pp70–1; 36-38 New Oxford St WC1; ◒ Tottenham Court Rd), with a similar set up.

BORDERLINE Map p66

☎ 7734 2095; www.mamagroup.co.uk/borderline; Orange Yard W1; ◒ Tottenham Court Rd

Through the Tex-Mex entrance off Orange Yard and down into the basement you'll find a packed, 275-capacity venue that really punches above its weight. Read the writing on the walls (literally, there's a gig list): Crowded House, REM, Blur, Counting Crows, PJ Harvey, Lenny Kravitz, Debbie Harry, plus many anonymous indie outfits, have all played here. The crowd's equally

City Festivals

Many of the music festivals that have sprung up in the city take place during the summer. Groove Armada's Lovebox Weekender (www.lovebox.net) is excellent (2009 had Duran Duran!). It takes place in Victoria Park in mid-July, while Hyde Park hosts the Wireless Festival (www.o2wirelessfestival.co.uk) in mid-June; both festivals have big names and up-and-coming acts. Somerset House (p76) has its Summer Series that sees open-air gigs held in its beautiful courtyard, with names like Grace Jones, Lily Allen and Bat For Lashes in recent years. The best festival of all has to be the Southbank Centre's (p307) Meltdown, where one musician each year is selected to choose and bring those who influenced them and whom they admire. Previous Meltdown artists included David Bowie, Massive Attack and Ornette Coleman.

If you love live music, summer is increasingly the time to be in London these days. For info on other London festivals, see p16.

diverse but full of music journos and talent-spotting record-company A&Rs.

BULL & GATE Map p166

☎ 7485 5358; www.bullandgate.co.uk; 389 Kentish Town Rd NW5; ⊖ Kentish Town
The best place to see unsigned-but-promising talent, the legendary Bull & Gate's old-school music venue still pulls in the punters eager to see guitar bands that might just turn out to be the next big thing.

CAFÉ OTO Map p156

www.cafeoto.co.uk; 18-22 Ashwin St E8; ⊖ Old St, then 🚍 55, 242, 243
Café Oto is one of London's most idiosyncratic and interesting music venues. Set in a converted print warehouse and run by a Japanese-British couple, this place dedicates itself to promoting experimental and off-mainstream international musicians. You'll find lots of Japanese stars of experimental, jazz and pop music, as well as legendary 1960s folk and rock stars. During the day it's a lovely cafe.

EARL'S COURT EXHIBITION CENTRE
Map p170

☎ 7385 1200, 0870 903 9033; Warwick Rd SW5; ⊖ Earl's Court
The kind of large, soulless venue that gave stadium rock its bad name, Earl's Court was where Justin Timberlake was famously photographed pawing Kylie Minogue's bum and where most of the gigs you'll see will be by massively expensive, high-flying stars, whose faces will be a dot in the distance.

FORUM Map p166

☎ 0870 534 4444; www.meanfiddler.com; 9-17 Highgate Rd NW5; ⊖ Kentish Town
You can find your way to the Forum – once the famous Town & Country Club – by the

ticket touts that line the way from Kentish Town tube. It's a really popular venue for seeing new big bands, and the medium-sized hall, with stalls and a mezzanine, is spacious enough and perfectly intimate.

LUMINAIRE Map p62

☎ 7372 7123; www.theluminaire.co.uk; 311 High Rd NW6; ⊖ Kilburn
The Luminaire is one of London's best small music venues. Compact but not crowded, it has a big emphasis on friendly service and silence while music is playing – but what's really impressive is the list of people who've played here: Babyshambles, Bat For Lashes, Colleen, Editors, Dirty Pretty Things, Hanne Hukkelberg and Mark Eitzel of American Music Club are just a few.

O2 Map p182

☎ 0871 984 0002; www.theo2.co.uk; Peninsula Sq SE10; ⊖ North Greenwich
Formerly the doomed Millennium Dome, this pricey fiasco has now reinvented itself as one of the city's major concert venues, hosting all the biggies – the Rolling Stones, Prince, Elton John, Scissor Sisters and many others, inside the 20,000 capacity stadium. Ticket prices start at £25. This was also the venue where Michael Jackson was meant to appear for his marathon tour, just before his untimely death.

O2 ACADEMY BRIXTON Map p190

☎ box office 0844 477 2000; www.o2academybrixton.co.uk; 211 Stockwell Rd SW9; ⊖ Brixton
It's hard to have a bad night at the Brixton Academy, even if you leave with your soles sticky with beer, as this cavernous former theatre (holding 5000) always thrums with bonhomie. There's a properly raked floor for good views, as well as plenty of bars. You can catch international acts of the ilk of Madonna

(once), but more likely artists are Amy Winehouse, Basement Jaxx or DJ Shadow.

O2 ACADEMY ISLINGTON Map p170
☎ box office 0844 477 2000; www.o2academyislington.co.uk; N1 Centre, 16 Parkfield St N1; ✈ Angel
Many complain about Islington Academy's lack of atmosphere – it is, after all, set in a shopping centre – but all agree that the artists' line-up is pretty top class: Franz Ferdinand, Kings of Leon and even Tom Jones have played here. The acoustics are excellent and the discerning crowd is serious about its music. The adjacent Bar Academy hosts up-and-coming groups and can be a great place to see new talent.

RHYTHM FACTORY Map p156
☎ 7247 9386; www.rhythmfactory.co.uk; 16-18 Whitechapel Rd E1; ⏰ to 3am Sun-Thu, to 5am Fri & Sat; ✈ Aldgate East
Perennially hip and popular, the Rhythm Factory is a relaxed and friendly coffee shop with a Thai lunch and dinner menu during the day, but come the evening it opens up the large back room, and tonnes of bands and DJs of all genres keep the up-for-it crowd happy until late.

ROUNDHOUSE Map p166
☎ 7424 9991; www.roundhouse.org.uk; Chalk Farm Rd NW1; ✈ Chalk Farm
The Roundhouse was once home to 1960s avant garde theatre, then a rock venue, then it fell into oblivion for a while before reopening a few years back to hold great gigs and theatre performances. It hosted a series of come-back gigs for Grace Jones in 2009 (all sold out), as well as Pete(r) Doherty and Bat For Lashes. The building was once a railway turntable shed and the (round) interior is impressive.

ROYAL FESTIVAL HALL Map p126
☎ 7960 4242; www.southbankcentre.co.uk; Belvedere Rd SE1; admission £6-60; ✈ Waterloo
The Royal Festival Hall is one of the best places for catching world-music artists and hosts the fantastic Meltdown festival (see p303). It reopened in Summer 2007 after two years of renovations. Allies and Morrison architects worked on the £91-million renovations by using the existing 1950s materials – concrete, leather and wood – to superb effect. The sound is fantastic, the programming

impeccable and there are frequent free gigs in the wonderfully expansive foyer.

O2 SHEPHERD'S BUSH EMPIRE Map p178
☎ box office 0844 477 2000; www.o2shepherdsbushempire.co.uk; Shepherd's Bush Green W12; ✈ Shepherd's Bush
Top musicians perform in this midsized venue, such as PJ Harvey or Antony and the Johnsons, and there's always something interesting going on. The downers are the fact that the floor doesn't slope, so if you're not so tall it can be impossible to see from up the back in the stalls – it's worth paying for the balcony – and the avalanche of security and 'safety regulations' within the venue, which can considerably spoil the fun.

UNDERWORLD Map p170
☎ 7482 1932; www.theunderworldcamden.co.uk; 174 Camden High St NW1; ✈ Camden Town
Hear ye, all ye metal heads out there! The Underworld awaits! Metallica, Black Sabbath, Sepultura and other skull-clad screamers have made their appearance either live or as a DJ's choice in this underground warren beneath the World's End pub. It's got plenty of nooks and crannies for ritual head-banging, but it does also host some 'softer' musicians such as KT Tunstall and Radiohead.

UNION CHAPEL Map p170
☎ 7226 1686; www.unionchapel.org.uk; Compton Tce N1; ✈ Highbury & Islington
One of London's most atmospheric and individual music venues, the Union Chapel is an old church that still holds services, and concerts – mainly acoustic – in between. It was here that Björk performed one of her most memorable concerts to a candlelit audience. The chapel hosts a monthly comedy night (see p300).

WEMBLEY ARENA Map p62
☎ 0870 060 0870; www.whatsonwembley.com; Empire Way, Wembley; ✈ Wembley Park
Some years and £30 million later, the Wembley Arena has been vastly improved, though its size will never make you feel 'at one' with the artist. It's the place to come and see big names such as Gwen Stefani, vintage artists such as Lionel Richie, or dance and scream to Girls Aloud. Tickets can be massively overpriced (up to £100 for really big names).

THE ARTS

top picks

London's cultural life is the richest and most varied in the English-speaking world. Its theatre has the longest history and is the most diverse in the world, from Shakespeare's classics performed in the traditional manner, to innovative productions that involve Harlem transvestites and gangstas. There's a wealth of new writing and acting talent and, after many decades, politically provocative plays are making headlines again; Caryl Churchill's *Seven Jewish Children: A Play for Gaza* performed at the Royal Court in early 2009 is a stunning example. In fact, theatre in London is taken so seriously that many deem performing in the West End to be the only way to earn respect among their peers. Even Hollywood stars are abandoning their pampered lives for a season treading the boards in London.

But it's not all high drama. In fact, one of the most popular forms of entertainment in the capital is the American-style musical. The 1980s revival put *Dirty Dancing* into musical form, making it one of the most successful shows around. Today you can catch everything from *Grease* and *Hairspray* to *The Lion King* and *La Cage aux Folles*. Dance is another much-loved art form here, with performances ranging from classical ballet to modern dance, many of which are held in wonderful venues such as the renovated Sadler's Wells and Laban.

The Royal Opera House stages classical opera and ballet in a grandiose building in the heart of Covent Garden, while the English National Opera takes more risks (and always in English). Classical music aficionados won't know where to start, from high-profile BBC Proms to fantastic lunchtime concerts at Wigmore Hall.

London's a fantastic place for catching up on film and cinema seasons that celebrate the independents and the classics, though if you like a blockbuster, fret not, as there are many (overpriced) cinemas offering Hollywood flicks. Huge multiplexes give you endless screens and mega-sound systems, and smaller, independent cinemas offer the delight of a sofa for two, with a glass of wine at your side. The refurbished and expanded British Film Institute (BFI) is a temple to film.

CLASSICAL MUSIC

London is a major classical-music capital, with four world-class symphony orchestras, two opera companies, various smaller ensembles, brilliant venues, reasonable prices and high standards of performance. On any night of the year the choice will range from traditional crowd-pleasers to new music and 'difficult' composers.

BARBICAN Map p100

☎ information 7638 4141, bookings 7638 8891; www.barbican.org.uk; Silk St EC2; admission £8-45; ⊖ Moorgate or Barbican

The Barbican is home to the wonderful London Symphony Orchestra, but scores of leading international musicians also perform here every year. The lesser-known BBC Symphony Orchestra and English Chamber Orchestra are also regulars and the City of London Symphonia plays occasionally.

KENWOOD HOUSE Map p166

☎ information 0845 658 6960, bookings 0870 154 4040; www.picnicconcerts.com; Hampstead Lane

NW3; admission £23.50-39; ⊖ Archway or Golders Green, then 🚌 210

Attending an outdoor concert in the grounds of Hampstead's Kenwood House has been a highlight of any good summer in London for years. These days the so-called Picnic Concerts sponsored by English Heritage focus as much on jazz (Ray Davies, Gypsy Kings, Jools Holland) and pop (Simply Red) as they do classical music and opera but the Summer Prom here does at least one of each. Concerts take place on Saturday evenings from late June to late August; the last concert concludes with a massive fireworks display.

ROYAL ALBERT HALL Map pp136-7

☎ information 7589 3203, bookings 7589 8212, www.royalalberthall.com; Kensington Gore SW7; admission £5-150, Proms admission £5-75; ⊖ South Kensington

This splendid Victorian concert hall hosts many classical-music, rock and other performances, but it is most famous as the venue for the BBC-sponsored Proms – one of the world's biggest classical-music festivals. Booking is possible, but from mid-July to mid-September Proms punters also queue for £5 standing (or 'promenading') tickets that go on sale one hour before curtain up. Otherwise, the box office and prepaid ticket collection counter are both through door 12 on the south side of the hall.

SOUTHBANK CENTRE Map p126
☎ 0871 663 2500; www.southbankcentre.co.uk; Belvedere Rd SE1; admission £8-45; ⊖ Waterloo
The Royal Festival Hall, which reopened in 2007 after an extensive two-year overhaul, is London's premier concert venue and seats 3000 in a now acoustic amphitheatre. You can see music and dance performances here and more eclectic gigs at the smaller Queen Elizabeth Hall and Purcell Room.

WIGMORE HALL Map p90
☎ 7935 2141; www.wigmore-hall.org.uk; 36 Wigmore St W1; admission £6-50; ⊖ Bond St
This is one of the best concert venues in town, not only because of its fantastic acoustics, beautiful art nouveau hall and great variety of concerts and recitals, but also because of the sheer standard of the performances. Built in 1901 as the recital hall for Bechstein Pianos, it has remained one of the top places in the world for chamber music. The Sunday-morning coffee concerts (adult/concession £12/10) and the lunchtime concerts at 1pm on Monday (adult/senior £12/10) are both excellent value.

DANCE

London is home to five major dance companies and a host of small and experimental ones. The Royal Ballet (www.royalballet.co.uk), the best classical-ballet company in the land, is based at the Royal Opera House in Covent Garden. The English National Ballet (www.ballet.org.uk) often performs at the London Coliseum (p310) especially at Christmas and in summer.

The annual contemporary dance event in London is Dance Umbrella (p17; www.danceumbrella.co.uk). For more information about dance in the capital, visit the website of London Dance (www.londondance.com).

BARBICAN Map p100
☎ information 7638 4141, bookings 7638 8891; www.barbican.org.uk; Silk St EC2; admission £6.50-30, student half-price Wed; ⊖ Moorgate or Barbican
The Barbican centre stages dance performances within its eclectic program. Its multi-disciplinary festival called Barbican International Theatre Events (bite; www.barbican.org.uk/theatre/about-bite), which runs year-round, has great dance performances.

LABAN Map p182
☎ information 8691 8600, bookings 8469 9500; www.laban.org; Creekside SE8; admission £3-12; ▣ Deptford Bridge, DLR Greenwich
This is an independent dance training school, which also presents student performances, graduation shows and regular

CHURCH VENUES

Many of London's churches host evening concerts or lunchtime recitals year-round or during the summer months. Sometimes they are free (with a suggested donation requested); at other times there is a quoted admission. A few of the city's redundant churches now serve as concert halls.

- **St James's Piccadilly** (Map p66; ☎ 7734 4511; www.st-james-piccadilly.org; 197 Piccadilly W1; lunchtime suggested donation £3, evenings £10-30; ⊖ Piccadilly Circus) Concerts at 1.10pm on Monday, Wednesday and Friday. Evening concerts at 7.30pm (days vary).
- **St John's, Smith Square** (Map pp84–5; ☎ 7222 1061; www.sjss.org.uk; Smith Sq SW1; lunchtime £7, evenings £5-17; ⊖ Westminster or St James's Park) Lunchtime concerts at 1pm on Thursday, evening concerts (days vary) are at 7.30pm.
- **St Martin-in-the-Fields** (Map pp70–1; ☎ 7766 1100; www.stmartin-in-the-fields.org; Trafalgar Sq WC2; lunchtime suggested donation £3.50, evening £6-25; ⊖ Charing Cross) Concerts at 1pm on Monday, Tuesday and Friday. Evening concerts at 7.30pm or 8pm (days vary).
- **St Paul's Cathedral** (Map p100; ☎ 7236 4128; www.stpauls.co.uk; New Change EC4; organ recitals £7; ⊖ St Paul's) Free organ recitals at 4.45pm on Sunday. Evensong is usually at 5pm Monday to Saturday and at 3.15pm Sunday (special events permitting).
- **Southwark Cathedral** (Map p126; ☎ 7367 6700; www.southwark.anglican.org/cathedral; Montague Close SE1; ⊖ London Bridge) Organ recitals at 1pm on Monday free; other concerts vary (eg at 3.15pm on Tuesday). Evensong at 5.30pm on Tuesday, Thursday and Friday, at 4pm on Saturday and at 3pm (choral) on Sunday.
- **Westminster Abbey** (Map pp84–5; ☎ 7222 5152; www.westminster-abbey.org; Dean's Yard SW1; tickets usually £6-18; ⊖ Westminster) Free organ recitals at 5.45pm on Sunday (and certain other days). Evensong on weekdays at 5pm (excluding Wednesday) and at 3pm on Saturday and Sunday. Ring or check the website for details of the summer organ festival, usually held in July.

pieces by the resident troupe, Transitions Dance Company, as well as other assorted dance, music and physical performances. Its stunning £23 million home was designed by Herzog & de Meuron, the same people who built the Tate Modern (see p128).

PLACE Map pp80-1
☎ 7387 0031; www.theplace.org.uk; 17 Duke's Rd WC1; admission £5-15; ⊖ Euston Square
One of the most exciting modern dance venues, the Place was the birthplace of modern British dance. It concentrates on challenging, contemporary and experimental choreography. Behind the late-Victorian facade you'll find a 300-seat theatre, an arty, creative cafe atmosphere and six training studios. The Place sponsors an annual dance award, 'Place Prize', which strives to seek out and award new and outstanding dance talent.

ROYAL OPERA HOUSE Map pp70-1
☎ 7304 4000; www.roh.org.uk; Royal Opera House, Bow St WC2; admission £4-120; ⊖ Covent Garden
Although the Royal Ballet's program has been fluffed up by modern influences, classical ballet is still its bread and butter. This is where to head if you want to see traditional performances such as *Giselle* or *Romeo*

& Juliet (or *The Nutcracker* at Christmas). Restricted-view seats cost £4 to £5. There are same-day tickets, one per customer available to the first 67 people in the queue, from 10am for £8 to £40. Half-price stand-by tickets are very occasionally available.

SADLER'S WELLS Map p150
☎ 7863 8000; www.sadlers-wells.com; Rosebery Ave EC1; admission £10-60; ⊖ Angel
The theatre site dates from 1683 but was complete rebuilt in 1998; today it is the most eclectic and modern dance venue in town, with experimental dance shows (anyone for the Mahabharata on the boards?), hip-hop conventions and an annual flamenco festival in March. The Lilian Baylis Studio stages smaller productions while the Peacock Theatre (Map pp70–1; ☎ 7863 8222; www.sadlers-wells.com; Portugal St WC2; ⊖ Holborn) is a kind of West End branch, hosting smaller dance and music performances.

SOUTHBANK CENTRE Map p126
☎ 0871 663 2500; www.southbankcentre.co.uk; Belvedere Rd SE1; admission £6-75; ⊖ Waterloo
The Royal Festival Hall, Queen Elizabeth Hall and Purcell Room are regular venues for the Dance Umbrella citywide festival, as well as hosting independent dance productions year-round.

FILM

Londoners love their film. That's why the city has so many fabulous independent cinemas, where you can put your feet up (often literally), sip a drink and feel at home. Aside from general releases, there are monthly seasons and premieres, plus directors and actors talking about their films. If you're in town in the second half of October, try to attend at least one screening at the Times BFI London Film Festival (www .bfi.org.uk), Europe's largest, with plenty of previews, debates, talks and film-star spotting.

Latest Hollywood blockbusters play at the various first-run cinemas; be prepared to pay up to an astonishing £18 (compared to around £6 to £9 at most arthouse cinemas). Many major premieres are held in Leicester Sq, which is a bit of an eyesore but always buzzy.

If your tastes are a little more eclectic, try one of the following cinemas. Most art-house or mainstream cinemas offer price discounts all day Monday and for most weekday afternoon screenings (before 5pm).

BARBICAN Map p100
☎ info 7382 7000, bookings 7638 8891; www.barbican.org.uk; Silk St EC2; ⊖ Moorgate or Barbican
The three screens at the Barbican pull the crowds with great programming, regular film seasons, and talks by directors and stars. It's a dream to watch a film here, with brilliant sloping seating that ensures full-screen view wherever you sit and generous legroom.

BFI SOUTHBANK Map p126
☎ information 7633 0274, bookings 7928 3232; www.bfi.org.uk; Belvedere Rd SE1; ⊖ Waterloo
Tucked almost out of sight under the arches of Waterloo Bridge is the British Film Institute, containing four cinemas that screen thousands of films each year, a gallery devoted to the moving image and the Mediatheque (☎ 7928 3535; admission free; ⏰ 1-8pm Tue, 11am-8pm Wed-Sun), where you watch film and TV highlights from the BFI National Archive. There's also a gallery space with shows relating to film, a well-stocked film- and bookshop, a restaurant and a gorgeous cafe. The BFI is largely a repertory or art-house theatre, runs regular retrospectives and is the major venue for the Times BFI London Film Festival, which screens 300 films from 60 countries in the second half of October.

CINÉ LUMIÈRE Map pp136-7
☎ 7073 1350; www.institut-francais.org.uk; 17 Queensberry Pl SW7; ⊖ South Kensington
Ciné Lumière is attached South Kensington's French Institute, and its large art deco salle (cinema) screens great international seasons and French and other foreign films subtitled in English. The London Spanish Film Festival takes place here in September/October.

CORONET Map p176
☎ 7727 6705; www.coronet.org; 103 Notting Hill Gate W8; ⊖ Notting Hill Gate
This fin de siècle (1898) stunner with two screens is one of London's most atmospheric places to watch a film. Indeed, a lovesick Hugh Grant munches popcorn here while watching Julia Roberts on the big screen in Notting Hill. The wonderful Edwardian interior, including a gorgeous balcony and even boxes, recalls the glory days of cinema, when filling a 400-seat house for every showing was easy. The other hall seats 150.

CURZON SOHO Map p66
☎ info 7734 2255, bookings 0870 756 4620; www.curzoncinemas.com; 99 Shaftesbury Ave W1; ⊖ Leicester Sq or Piccadilly Circus
Curzon Soho is London's best cinema. It has fantastic programming with the best of British, European, world and American indie films; regular Q&As with directors; shorts and minifestivals; a Konditor & Cook cafe (p224) upstairs with tea and cakes to die for, and an ultracomfortable bar.

ELECTRIC CINEMA Map p176
☎ 7908 9696; www.electriccinema.co.uk; 191 Portobello Rd W1; ⊖ Ladbroke Grove or Notting Hill Gate
If you've got a date who's hard to impress, head here for certain success. This is the UK's oldest cinema, updated with luxurious leather armchairs, footstools, tables for food and drink in the auditorium, and the upmarket Electric Brasserie (p263) next door. Seeing a flick at this Edwardian building is, of course, slightly pricier than elsewhere; on full-price nights the seats are £12.50 to £14.50, or £30 for a two-seater sofa.

EVERYMAN HAMPSTEAD Map p166
☎ 0870 066 4777; www.everymancinema.com; 5 Holly Bush Vale NW3; ⊖ Hampstead
Ever dream of having your own private cinema? For the next best thing, go to the

Everyman. The two auditoriums have comfy armchairs and sofas where you can sprawl out and watch a film with your cup of tea or glass of wine. The program has a wide range of films, from *Singing in the Rain* and opera on film to current blockbusters.

GATE PICTUREHOUSE Map p176
☎ 0871 704 2058; www.picturehouses.co.uk; 87 Notting Hill Gate W1; ⊖ Notting Hill Gate
The Gate's single screen has one of London's most charming art deco cinema interiors – although the bar area is pretty cramped. Despite its retro-cutesy name, this cinema takes its programming seriously, introducing new art-house and independent films.

ICA CINEMA Map pp84-5
☎ information 7930 6393, bookings 7930 3647; www.ica.org.uk; Nash House, The Mall SW1; ⊖ Charing Cross or Piccadilly Circus
The Institute of Contemporary Arts (ICA) is a treasure for all lovers of indie cinema – its program always has material no-one else is showing, such as the latest American independents, odd seasons, all-night screenings and rare documentaries. The two screens are quite small, but comfortable enough.

PRINCE CHARLES Map p66
☎ 0870 811 2559; www.princecharlescinema.com; Leicester Pl WC2; ⊖ Leicester Sq
You'd be right to think that ticket prices at Leicester Sq cinemas are daylight robbery, so wait until the first-runs have finished and moved to central London's cheapest cinema (members £3.50 to £7.50, nonmembers £4 to £9.50). There are also minifestivals and Q&As with film directors. Famously, the cinema also transformed *The Sound of Music* into a phenomenal – and very camp – sing-a-long hit.

RIO CINEMA Map p156
☎ 7241 9410; www.riocinema.org; 107 Kingsland High St E8; 🚊 Dalston Kingsland
The Rio is Dalston's neighbourhood art-house, classic and new-release cinema, and *the* venue for offbeat festivals, such as the East End Film Festival in April and the Turkish Film Festival in December. Despite its major renovation in the late '90s, you can still see traces of the lovely art deco theatre in the auditorium.

RITZY PICTUREHOUSE Map p190
☎ 0871 704 2065; www.picturehouses.co.uk; Brixton Oval, Coldharbour Lane SW2; ⊖ Brixton
Despite fears that making the Ritzy a multiplex would kill its cool style and community feeling (four new screens were added to this 1911 building in the late '90s, making it London's biggest independent cinema), this is still one of London's favourites, screening a good mix of mainstream and indie films. The Ritzy is an off–West End screen during the Times BFI London Film Festival, and alternative gigs are often held inside the large original auditorium. The funky bar-cafe upstairs is a gathering spot for arty locals.

RIVERSIDE STUDIOS Map p196
☎ 8237 1111; www.riversidestudios.co.uk; Crisp Rd W6; ⊖ Hammersmith
Once a film and TV studio, where such classics as *Dr Who* and *Hancock's Half-Hour* were shot, the cinema at the Riverside now shows classic art-house flicks and those you might have missed a few months back. Much emphasis these days is on Eastern European film.

OPERA

It's not just the classics that get staged in London's opera houses. Apart from the traditional Verdi tragedies or Mozart's comedies, you'll also find innovative productions that bring modern-day events to the bellowing music form. Be prepared for a costly evening, though. Opera is expensive to produce and consequently tickets are very pricey.

KORN/FERRY OPERA HOLLAND PARK Map p178
☎ 0845 230 9769; www.operahollandpark.com; Holland Park W8; admission £10-54; ⊖ High St Kensington
This is Ye Olde Englande, with picnics on the grass, opera on stage and frightfully posh surroundings. Sit under the 800-seat canopy, which is temporarily erected every summer for a nine-week season in the middle of Holland Park, and enjoy the fabulous setting and good performances. The program mixes crowd pleasers like Verdi and Humperdinck with rare (even obscure) works and attracts a diverse audience.

LONDON COLISEUM Map pp70-1

☎ info 7632 8300, bookings 0870 145 0200; www.eno.org; Coliseum, St Martin's Lane WC2; admission £10-85; ⊖ Leicester Sq or Charing Cross

The Coliseum is home to the English National Opera (ENO), celebrated for making opera modern and relevant; all operas here are sung in English. After several years in the wasteland, the ENO has been receiving better reviews and welcoming much bigger audiences since the arrival of music director Edward Gardner. The building, built in 1904 and lovingly restored 100 years later, is very impressive. Five hundred £10-and-under tickets are available for all weekday performances.

ROYAL OPERA HOUSE Map pp70-1

☎ 7304 4000; www.royaloperahouse.org; Bow St WC2; admission £7-195; ⊖ Covent Garden

The Royal Opera House has been doing its best to ward off the stuffy, exclusive image it was accused of having some years ago, and is attracting a younger, wealthy audience. Its £210 million redevelopment for the millennium gave the classic a fantastic setting, and coming here for a night is a sumptuous prospect. Midweek matinees are usually much cheaper than evening performances and restricted-view seats cost as little as £7. Half-price stand-by tickets are available if the performance isn't selling very well. This, apparently, doesn't happen very often, but it might be worth a try.

THEATRE

Don't even think about leaving London without a night at the theatre. This is the epicentre of English-language theatre and, as much as we love it, it's not just about Portia telling Shylock that 'The quality of mercy is not strained/It droppeth as the gentle rain from heaven' in *The Merchant of Venice*. London is also the centre of theatrical innovation and great new writing. Spend a night at the National or the Old Vic, go for a good old-fashioned (and usually intimate) performance at a pub-theatre or take in a West End show.

Every summer the West End theatres unveil a new crop of plays and musicals, but some performances really do run and run. Examples of seemingly immortal musicals are *Mamma Mia*, *Phantom of the Opera*, *Chicago* and *Les Misérables*, though new shows such as *Wicked*,

Jersey Boys and *Billy Elliot* are looking to become new classics.

Consult London's weekly 'what's on' bible *Time Out* for current offerings. You'll find the same information as well as addresses and box-office phone numbers of individual theatres on the website of the London Theatre Guide (www.londontheatre.co.uk).

BARBICAN Map p100

☎ information 7638 4141, bookings 7638 8891; www.barbican.org.uk; Silk St EC2; admission £7-50, Pit £15, student half-price Wed; ⊖ Moorgate or Barbican

Now approaching its third decade in show-biz the Barbican is looking – and feeling – as great as ever. Barbican International Theatre Events (bite) continues to find exciting overseas drama companies, alongside local fringe-theatre troupes; among its recent outstanding performances were Complicite's Shun-Kin with an all-Japanese cast and Chekhov's *Three Sisters*, staged in Russian by Cheek by Jowl.

NATIONAL THEATRE Map p126

☎ 7452 3000; www.nationaltheatre.org.uk; South Bank SE1; admission £10-41; ⊖ Waterloo

England's flagship theatre showcases a mix of classic and contemporary plays performed by excellent casts. Its outstanding artistic director, Nicholas Hytner, is not only using exciting stagings and plays to attract new audiences but has also slashed ticket prices. The powerful *War Horse* with its life-sized equine puppets, *Phèdre* with the incomparable Helen Mirren and Lee Hall's tough look at art, class and politics in *The Pitmen Painters* – each season seems to bring new surprises. Travelex tickets costing just £10 are available to certain performances during the peak period; otherwise, stand-by tickets (usually £20) are sometimes available 90 minutes before the performance. Students must wait until just 45 minutes before the curtain goes up to purchase £10 stand-by tickets. Sell-out performances allow for some standing room (£5).

ROYAL COURT THEATRE Map pp136-7

☎ 7565 5000; www.royalcourttheatre.com; Sloane Sq SW1; admission free-£25; ⊖ Sloane Sq

Equally renowned for staging innovative new plays and old classics, the Royal Court is among London's most progressive theatres. Starting with its inaugural piece in 1956, John Osborne's *Look Back In Anger*, now considered the starting point of modern British theatre, under its inspirational artistic director Dominic Cooke (opposite) it has continued to discover major writing talent across the UK. Recent triumphs were a star-studded performance of *The Seagull,* a sassy new musical about drag queens and a retrospective of plays by American actor and playwright Wallace Shawn.

Tickets for concessions are £6 to £10, and £10 for everyone on Monday. At the same time, under 25s can get into selected performances at the Jerwood Theatre Downstairs for free. Stand-by tickets are sold an hour before the performance, but normally at full price.

SHAKESPEARE'S GLOBE Map p126
☎ information 7902 1400, bookings 7401 9919; www.shakespeares-globe.org; 21 New Globe Walk SE1; adult £15-33, concession £12-30, standing £5; ⊖ St Paul's or London Bridge
If you love Shakespeare and the theatre, the Globe will knock you off your feet. This is authentic Shakespearean theatre, and a near-perfect replica of the building the Bard worked in from 1598 to 1611, that follows Elizabethan staging practices. The building is a wooden O without a roof over the central stage area, and although there

are covered wooden bench seats in tiers around the stage, many people (there's room for 700) like to do as the 17th-century 'groundlings' did, and stand in front of the stage, shouting and heckling. Because the building is quite open to the elements, you may have to wrap up. No umbrellas are allowed, but cheap rain coats are on sale.

The theatre season runs from late April to mid-October and includes works by Shakespeare and his contemporaries such as Christopher Marlowe. The theatre's artistic director, Dominic Dromgoole, has decided to introduce a couple of new plays each season and we can't help but think that Will would have liked it that way.

A warning: two pillars holding up the stage canopy (the so-called Heavens) obscure much of the view in section D; you'd almost do better to stand.

OFF–WEST END & FRINGE
Held in smaller theatres, this is where most of the really creative and innovative drama happens in the capital – thanks to new writing that can be experimental, amazing or even downright ridiculous. We've included some of the better venues here.

SPOKEN WORD
Londoners treat their literati like glitterati. And it's not just home-grown talent that get all the attention. Along with the likes of Monica Ali, Louis de Bernieres, Zadie Smith, Tony Parsons and Will Self, international writers such as Bill Bryson, Douglas Coupland and Jonathan Safran Foer go on promotional tours.

The best place to see both established and budding authors is the once-monthly Book Slam (www.bookslam.com) held at Tabernacle (☎ 7221 9700; 34-35 Powis Sq W11; admission £6-8; ☽ 6pm last Thu of the month), and hosted by founder/author Patrick Neate. It's had guests such as Nick Hornby, Hari Kunzru and Mil Millington, and hosts readings, slam poetry, live music and DJs; the literary fun can go on until late at night.

A weekly writers' Express Excess (www.expressexcess.co.uk) session is held at Enterprise (Map p166; ☎ 7485 2659; 2 Haverstock Hill NW3; ☽ 8pm Wed; ⊖ Chalk Farm). From small beginnings in 1996, the Express Excess evening has since managed to attract top names in British writing (John Cooper Clarke, John Hegley, Will Self and Murray Lachlan Young) to its cosy room at the top of a typically grungy Camden pub.

The Institute of Contemporary Arts (ICA; ☎ information 7930 6393, bookings 7930 3647; www.ica.org.uk; Nash House, the Mall SW1; ⊖ Charing Cross or Piccadilly Circus) has excellent talks every month, with well-known writers from all spectrums, from the hip to the seriously academic. The best events are those in the wonderful, high-ceilinged Nash Room upstairs.

Covent Garden's Poetry Café (Map pp70–1; ☎ 7420 9888; www.poetrysociety.org.uk; 22 Betterton St WC2; ⊖ Covent Garden) is a favourite for lovers of verse. It has almost daily readings and performances by established poets, open-mic evenings and writing workshops.

Additionally, bookshops, particularly Waterstone's (p216) and Foyle's (p215), often have readings. Some major authors now appear at the Southbank Centre (p307). As they tend to rely on the author's availability, many of these readings are organised on an ad-hoc basis, so if you're interested it's best to keep an eye on the listings in *Time Out* or any of the weekend newspaper supplements, including *The Guardian Guide* distributed with the Saturday edition of that paper.

LOCAL VOICES: DOMINIC COOKE

Born in Wimbledon and raised North London, Dominic Cooke has been artistic director of the Royal Court (p311) since 2007, a theatre celebrated for its new writing and internationalism.

'I'd say that most of the interesting changes and shifts of British theatre in the last half century have come from Europe.

'When George Devine set up the English Stage Company here at the Royal Court in 1956, he was very influenced by the aesthetics and values of European theatre. And it was here that writers like Brecht, Ionesco and Beckett were first staged in the UK.

'The visit of the Berlin Ensemble to Britain in the 1950s had a massive effect on theatre here. They introduced the very German idea of the theatre as a moral institution, where ideas are debated.

'In Britain we have a writer-based theatre tradition – the director is an interpretive artist, who realises the writing on stage. In most European theatre it's the director who is the primary artist; the text is just a starting point and they use it to explore their own vision. We have a lot to learn from European directing traditions but it can become solipsistic because so much depends on the director. As a result, some European countries have a very a stultified new writing culture.

'Someone once said that if you're thinking about the audience when you put on a piece, that's showbiz. If you base it on the artist's ideas then it's theatre. Here we start with the writer and the play and try to discover what they are trying to communicate.

'Britain is not conservative in its taste in theatre and things move quickly here. In the 1990s plays were much more about individual experience; there was the notion that everyone was apathetic, dumbed down by *The X Factor* and shopping. Now when we put on plays that really tackle issues people come in large numbers. People seem to want to engage with what is going on in the world. But that will change too. What people might want to watch five years from now is hard to say. I suspect they might favour more escapism.

'I love going to musicals and films too but because most of my job is indoors my ideal day out is spent in Richmond or Regent's Park. London is great for open spaces. There's such a range. I miss them when I'm away from home but I miss irony and the unique local sense of humour and London's mix of peoples too. This is one of the most truly multicultural cities in the world. It's not perfect but people generally live alongside one another quite well here compared to other parts of the world.'

Dominic Cooke was interviewed by Steve Fallon

ALMEIDA THEATRE Map p170
☎ 7359 4404; www.almeida.co.uk; Almeida St N1; ✆ Angel or Highbury & Islington
A plush venue that can be relied on to provide the city with an essential program of imaginative theatre, the Almeida, under its creative artistic director, Michael Attenborough, attracts directors such as Richard Eyre and Rufus Norris, and stages plays such as *The Mercy Seat* and the acclaimed *Duet for One*.

ARCOLA THEATRE Map p156
☎ 7503 1646; www.arcolatheatre.com; 27 Arcola St E8; ✆ Dalston Kingsland
The Arcola's location in Dalston in the East End makes it a bit of a trek, but many still flock to this innovative theatre whose director Mehmet Ergen has been staging adventurous and eclectic programs since founding the theatre in 2000. The program focuses on cutting-edge, international productions (such as work by young Turkish, Swedish and Austrian playwrights) and a unique annual feature is Grimeborn, a music

and opera festival in August/September diametrically opposed to the posh Glyndebourne opera festival near Lewes in Sussex.

BATTERSEA ARTS CENTRE Map p190
☎ 7223 2223; www.bac.org.uk; Lavender Hill SW11; ✆ Clapham Common, ✆ Clapham Junction, ✆ 77, 77A or 345
This is a friendly, down-to-earth community theatre where staff chat to you and the actors mingle in the bar with the audience after the show. Playwrights see it as a valuable nurturer and crucible of new plays and talent. Artistic director David Jubb's famous 'Scratch' program is an excellent exercise in learning about the writing process: a developing play is shown to ever-increasing audiences until it's finished.

BUSH THEATRE Map p178
☎ information 8743 3584, bookings 8743 5050; www.bushtheatre.co.uk; Shepherd's Bush Green W12; ✆ Shepherd's Bush
For what is essentially a pub-theatre, the Bush is exceptionally good and encourages

new writing. Its success over the past three decades is down to strong writing from the likes of Jonathan Harvey, Conor McPherson, Stephen Poliakoff and Mark Ravenhill.

DONMAR WAREHOUSE Map pp70-1
☎ 0870 060 6624; www.donmarwarehouse.com; 41 Earlham St WC2; ⊖ Covent Garden
The small Donmar Warehouse, the 'thinking man's theatre' in London, has taken a step back from the days when Nicole Kidman administered 'theatrical Viagra' nightly by peeling off her clothes in Sam Mendes' production of *The Blue Room* and Zoë Wanamaker really did Gothic Southern as Amanda Wakefield in Tennessee Williams' *The Glass Menagerie*. Still, artistic director Michael Grandage stages interesting and somewhat inventive productions such as Ibsen's *A Doll's House* with Gillian Anderson and *Hamlet* with the blue-eyed Jude Law.

HACKNEY EMPIRE Map p156
☎ 8985 2424; www.hackneyempire.co.uk; 291 Mare St E8; ⑧ Hackney Central, ⊞ 38, 106, 277 or 394
Theatre in the East End has undergone something of a renaissance with the top-to-tail renovation of this Edwardian music hall (1901). The programming is eclectic to say the least and defines 'something for everyone' – from hard-edged political theatre (*The Hounding of David Oluwale*) to opera (*Aida*) and comedy (Jo Brand). What's more, the Empire has become Pantomime Central at Christmas. There's comedy at the lively Marie Lloyd Bar below on Monday and live music on Thursday. Theatre as it was meant to be.

HAMPSTEAD THEATRE Map p166
☎ 7722 9301; www.hampsteadtheatre.com; Eton Ave NW3; ⊖ Swiss Cottage
Not only is this Ewan McGregor's favourite London theatre, the Hampstead is famed for putting on new writing and taking on emerging directors. It staged Harold Pinter's new work way back in the 1960s, which shows it knows a good thing when it sees one. The theatre is housed in a purpose-built building (2003), with a main auditorium seating 325 and the Michael Frayn Space seating 80.

KING'S HEAD Map p170
☎ information 7226 8561, bookings 0844 209; www.kingsheadtheatre.org; 115 Upper St N1; ⊖ Angel

This stalwart pub-theatre in the heart of the Islington party district has in the past staged some of the most memorable theatre in North London. Nowadays it's a bit hit or miss, with tribute mini-musicals to the likes of Dorothy Fields (she wrote songs like 'I'm In The Mood For Love' and 'If My Friends Could See Me Now') and Sophie Tucker and provocative cabaret like *Naked Boys Singing!* (yes, for real). It might not be fun for the whole family, but you might like it.

LITTLE ANGEL THEATRE Map p170
☎ 7226 1787; www.littleangeltheatre.com; 14 Dagmar Passage N1; ⊖ Angel or Highbury & Islington
It might sound like kids' stuff but this puppet theatre down an alleyway in Islington has programs for grownups, including the adults-only Puppet Grinder Cabaret. Especially memorable was their staged version of Shakespeare's lengthy poem, Venus and Adonis. We'd never seen marionette birds before (or puppets in the throes of, err, passion, for that matter).

LYRIC HAMMERSMITH Map p178
☎ 0871 221 1729; www.lyric.co.uk; Lyric Sq, King St W6; ⊖ Hammersmith
The Lyric is a great venue that turns classics on their head, staging Greek tragedies through mixed media, with film projection, dance and music. A modern glass entrance takes you to the historic 19th-century auditorium seating 550, and a smaller 110-seat studio.

MENIER CHOCOLATE FACTORY Map p126
☎ 7907 7060; www.menierchocolatefactory.com; 53 Southwark St SE1; ⊖ London Bridge
Theatre and chocolate, two of many Londoners' major passions, have never been as gloriously paired up as they have here – a theatre inside a gorgeous conversion of a 19th-century chocolate factory. To make matters better, the theatre's superb restaurant makes for great combination deals (from around £24 per person for a two-course dinner and a ticket).

OLD VIC Map p126
☎ 0870 060 6628; www.oldvictheatre.com; Waterloo Rd SE1; ⊖ Waterloo
Never has there been a London theatre with a more famous artistic director.

American actor Kevin Spacey looks after this glorious theatre's program and he just keeps going from strength to strength, with such recent pickings as Brian Friel's *Dancing at Lughnasa* with singer Andrea Corr (who knew?) and a new version of Chekhov's *Cherry Orchard* by Tom Stoppard and directed by ex-Donmar Warehouse honcho Sam Mendes. Breathtaking.

SOHO THEATRE Map p66

☎ information 7478 0100, bookings 0870 429 6883; www.sohotheatre.com; 21 Dean St W1; ⊖ Tottenham Court Rd

The Soho Theatre Company dedicates itself to the noble task of finding new writing talent, having put on hundreds of new plays since it started operating from its smart Dean St premises in 2000. Indeed its staging of Polish playwright Dorota Maslowska's *A Couple Of Poor, Polish-Speaking Romanians* in 2008 was one of the most memorable pieces of theatre in recent memory in a decade. It has innovative workshops to support and develop new writing, and also showcases comedy. This is the place to see where London drama is heading.

TRICYCLE THEATRE Map p62

☎ information 7372 6611, bookings 7328 1000; www.tricycle.co.uk; 269 Kilburn High Rd NW6; ⊖ Kilburn

If political theatre is on your shopping list, the Tricycle delivers. This small theatre has made a name for itself in recent years as the theatre-world's conscience, with plays that draw on world events (conflicts in Iraq, the Middle East and especially Afghanistan, with 2009's memorable *The Great Game*) in intelligent and provocative ways. There's a nice cinema and bar on site as well.

YOUNG VIC Map p126

☎ 7922 2922; www.youngvic.org; 66 The Cut SE1; ⊖ Waterloo

One of the capital's most respected theatre troupes – bold, brave and talented – the Young Vic grabs audiences with arresting plays such as *Vernon God Little* (as adapted from DBC Pierre's novel) and the English Touring Theatre's foot-stompin' soul-funk musical *Been So Long*. There's a lovely two-level bar-restaurant with an open-air terrace upstairs.

SPORTS & ACTIVITIES

top picks

London's a great place for sport lovers, be it those who love to play or just sit back and watch a game, and for a place that's traditionally associated with cold and bad weather, you'll be surprised at the number of outdoor swimming options. Those of you who like to get sweaty and pump some 'aayron' (Arnie-style) will find gleaming state-of-the-art gyms and community sports centres to work out in, while those of you who prefer something a little more sedate have tons of pampering spas to choose from.

Needless to say that lovers of football, rugby, horse racing, tennis or cricket have come to the right place to see great matches and tournaments. Just prepare to queue for those tickets.

HEALTH & FITNESS

London loves to sweat on the dance floor and on the treadmill. And if you too love a good workout, there are so many gyms and swimming pools in the city, you'll always be in the vicinity of a chance to burn those calories. Gyms are either local authority–run places at the bottom end of the market or private enterprises at the top, with the latter often coming in large chains. Like most other things in London, keeping fit in the capital can be expensive and riddled with snobbery – the gym you're a member of says a lot about you.

Opening hours vary hugely even within certain leisure centres, where some facilities open or close before others. As a rule, most gyms open very early, mostly from 6.30am, to ensure early-risers get their workout on time. Equally, they are open until at least 9pm. However, it's best to call ahead.

GYMS

CENTRAL YMCA Map p66
☎ 7343 1700; www.centralymca.org.uk; 112 Great Russell St WC1; membership per day/week £15/50; ⊖ Tottenham Court Rd
The gym at London's YMCA is popular and busy. Membership gives you the chance to use the pool. The YMCA compares favourably with many of the more expensive and elitist London gyms, and of course it's very friendly.

FITNESS FIRST
☎ 01202-845000; www.fitnessfirst.co.uk
The largest health club in the UK as well as the whole of Europe, this pan-London organisation has a reputation as a good middle-range gym chain. Handily, you can use any Fitness First club, no matter where

you joined up. With branches all over the city, this chain is very popular with short-term visitors to London.

GYMBOX
☎ 7395 0270; www.gymbox.co.uk
With two big gyms in the West End (one is inside an old cinema), Gymbox is presently the most popular gym chain in town. It's got an array of innovative classes and facilities, including an Olympic-size boxing ring and Latino hip-hop workout/dance classes.

LA FITNESS
☎ 7366 8080; www.lafitness.co.uk
With more than 20 gyms in all areas of London, from Victoria to the City, LA Fitness is another big player on the scene. Its gyms are modern and well equipped, and the membership packages are extremely flexible.

QUEEN MOTHER SPORTS CENTRE
Map pp136-7
☎ 7630 5522; www.courtneys.co.uk; 223 Vauxhall Bridge Rd SW1; membership per month from £30; ⊖ Victoria
This place is another reliable, central London gym, named after the Queen's late mum. It features three pools and comprehensive sporting facilities.

SEYMOUR LEISURE CENTRE Map p90
☎ 7723 8019; www.courtneys.co.uk; Seymour Pl W1; membership per month £30, pool visit £4.25; ⊖ Marble Arch or Edgware Rd
The Seymour is a bit of a shabby but long-standing London leisure centre. Its main advantage is the central location and reasonable prices, which means it's always quite busy.

THIRD SPACE Map p66

☎ 7439 6333; www.thethirdspace.com; 13 Sherwood St W1; membership per month £118; ⊖ Piccadilly Circus

London's most chic gym provides everything necessary for busy Soho media execs to relax in or work up a sweat on, at a hefty price.

VIRGIN ACTIVE

☎ 0845 130 4747; www.virginactive.co.uk

Virgin Active is the biggest chain in the UK, and is the best of the top-end gym chains in terms of quality and services. It has masses of facilities (pools, classes etc) and offers options for families and children.

SWIMMING

London has something of a love affair with its lovely 'lidos'. They are what most people simply call swimming pools, though the term historically denotes an open-air establishment. There are some lovely 1930s Art Deco lidos and most neighbourhoods have at least one.

BROCKWELL PARK LIDO Map p190

☎ 7274 3088; www.brockwell-lido.com; Dulwich Rd SE24; adult/child £3.10/5.20; ☽ 6.45am-7pm mid-Jun–Aug, weather dependent rest of year; ⊖ Brixton, ☒ Herne Hill

A beautifully designed 1930s lido, Brockwell is one of London's best, as witnessed by the multitudes that descend in the summer months.

HAMPSTEAD HEATH PONDS Map p166

Hampstead Heath, Gordon House Rd NW5; adult/concession £2/1; ☒ Gospel Oak or Hampstead Heath, ☒ 214, C2 or 24

Set in the midst of the gorgeous heath, the three ponds offer a slightly chilly dip surrounded by wild shrubbery; the men's pond is a bit of a gay cruising area (but it's also a fantastic, beautiful place for a swim), the secluded women's pond is less cruisy. The mixed pond can sometimes get rather crowded and isn't so scenically located.

IRONMONGER BATHS Map p150

☎ 7253 4011; www.aquaterra.org; Ironmonger Row EC1; per swim £3.70; ⊖ Old St

The Ironmonger Baths is a local authority–run gym and pool complex which is popular but not too crowded, and has a great pool and friendly atmosphere. There are

wonderful Turkish baths downstairs (£10 per day).

OASIS Map pp70-1

☎ 7831 1804; 32 Endell St WC2; adult/child £3.90/1; ⊖ Tottenham Court Rd or Covent Garden

A brilliant heated open-air pool has to be the best thing to find right in the heart of London. At such bargain prices, it often gets very crowded. There's an indoor pool for fresher London days.

PARLIAMENT HILL LIDO Map p166

☎ 7485 3873; Hampstead Heath, Gordon House Rd NW5; adult/concession £2/1; ☒ Gospel Oak, ☒ 214 or C2

This classic lido on Hampstead Heath is a wonderful place to come for a bracing morning swim during the summer months. It attracts a friendly but dedicated bunch of locals and boasts a children's paddling pool and sunbathing area.

PORCHESTER BATHS Map p176

☎ 7792 2919; Porchester Centre, Queensway W2; admission £5; ⊖ Bayswater or Royal Oak

The lovely Porchester Baths pool has had its 1930s art deco beauty fully restored and is loved by those wishing to swim in atmospheric surroundings.

SERPENTINE LIDO Map pp136-7

☎ 7298 2100; Hyde Park W2; ⊖ Hyde Park Corner or Knightsbridge

Perhaps the ultimate London pool inside the Serpentine lake, this fabulous lido is usually open in July and August. Admission prices and opening times are always subject to change, so it's essential to call ahead.

TOOTING BEC LIDO Map p62

☎ 8871 7198; Tooting Bec Rd SW17; adult/under 5yr/concession £4.75/free/£3.15; ☽ May-Sep; ⊖ Tooting Bec

The first-ever public lido in London, Tooting Bec was built in 1906 and remains one of the largest in Europe at 90m by 36m. There are Jacuzzis and saunas.

YOGA & PILATES

TRIYOGA

☎ 7483 3344; www.triyoga.co.uk

One of London's first yoga centres and still its most prestigious, Triyoga has three venues (Primrose Hill, Soho and Covent Garden), first-class teachers and classes of all types of yoga, as well as pilates. Classes cost £12, and courses start at £60.

ACTIVITIES

If you love spending a day being pampered with hot towels, heated pebbles and facials, and pummelled with hands covered in aromatic oils, and at the end swimming in heated pools and lying in wonderfully relaxing spaces for hours on end, London's spas will provide you with many joyous hours.

SPAS

ELEMIS DAY SPA Map p90
☎ 8909 5060; www.elemis.com/dayspa.html; 2-3 Lancashire Ct; ⊖ Bond St
This incredible Mayfair spa is almost ridiculously elaborate and features themed suites: Balinese, Moroccan, the purple room and the emerald room. Upmarket and offering a huge range of services, this is one hell of a place to treat yourself. Book ahead.

K SPA Map p178
☎ 0870 027 4343; www.k-west.co.uk; Richmond Way W12; ⊖ Shepherd's Bush
The K Spa is an important part of the K West hotel (p352), and has a good range of facilities: a Jacuzzi, eucalyptus steam room, sauna and two gyms. Alternatively, you can choose from a range of exotic treatments, facials and massages. It's one of the best complexes in West London.

SANCTUARY Map pp70-1
☎ 0870 770 3350; www.thesanctuary.co.uk; 12 Floral St WC2; ⊖ Covent Garden
A women's-only spa, the Sanctuary lives up to its name. With heated and exercise pools, saunas, Jacuzzis, masses of treatments, quiet rooms for napping, a cafe and a relaxing and friendly atmosphere, it's a haven to escape the chaos of the West End.

SPECTATOR SPORTS

As capital of a sports-mad nation, you can expect London to be brimming over with sporting spectacles throughout the year. The entertainment weekly Time Out (www.timeout.com) is the best source of information on fixtures, times, venues and ticket prices.

FOOTBALL

There are a dozen league teams in London, and usually around five or six play in the Premier League, meaning that on any weekend of the season – from August to mid-May – top-quality football is just a tube or train ride away. If you really want to see a match, you might consider dropping a division and going to see one of the first-division teams, for which you can normally just rock up on the day.

Wembley Stadium (Map p62; www.wembleystadium .com), in northwest London, has been the city's premier national stadium since it was built in 1923. It's where England traditionally plays its international matches and where the FA Cup final is contested in mid-May. Its greatest moment came when the victorious England captain, Bobby Moore, held the World Cup trophy aloft in 1966. Controversially, the great stadium and its two landmark towers were demolished in 2001, and even more controversially, the new 90,000-capacity, state-of-the-art Norman Foster–designed complex, due to open in 2003, hosted its first game four years late: the FA Cup final in 2007. Even though it was abysmally late and cost twice the original budget (at £798 million, one of the most expensive stadium ever built), Wembley is one of the world's most significant football landmarks.

On the other hand, Arsenal Emirates Stadium (www.arsenal.com), opened on time in July 2006, and although quite a bit smaller (60,400 capacity), it is still the third largest in London. It's located in Ashburton Grove, Highbury, and was named after the project's biggest sponsor, the airline Emirates. Many were sorry to see the old stadium go, with its old tea ladies and working-class atmosphere, and the new construction was met with objections from the unhappy locals whose houses and businesses were cleared for the stadium. Most have learned to love it, however.

CRICKET

If you're hot and bothered from seeing the sights, you could do a lot worse than packing up a picnic and spending a day enjoying the thwack of leather on willow and savouring the atmosphere of this most English of sports. Although the game was invented here, the English team has mostly struggled on the international stage.

The English Cricket Board (☎ 0870 533 8833; www .ecb.co.uk) has full details of match schedules and tickets, which cost between £20 and £50

CLUBS IN THE CAPITAL

Football is at the very heart of English culture, and attending a game is one of the highlights of any visit to London. At the time of writing, Arsenal, Chelsea, Fulham, Tottenham Hotspur and West Ham were all in the Premiership League (www.premierleague.com). For more on football in London, see opposite.

Arsenal (Map p62; ☎ 7704 4040; www.arsenal.com; Avenell Rd N5; admission £33-66; ❷ Arsenal)

Charlton Athletic (Map p62; ☎ 8333 4010; www.cafc.co.uk; The Valley, Floyd Rd SE7; admission £20-40; ⊞ Charlton)

Chelsea (Map p178; ☎ 0870 300 1212, 7915 2222, tickets 7915 2951; www.chelseafc.com; Stamford Bridge Stadium, Fulham Rd SW6; admission £40-65; ❷ Fulham Broadway)

Crystal Palace (Off Map p62; ☎ 0871 200 0071; www.cpfc.co.uk; Selhurst Park, Whitehorse Lane SE25; admission £25-35; ⊞ Selhurst)

Fulham (Map p196; ☎ 0870 442 1234; www.fulhamfc.com; Craven Cottage, Stevenage Rd SW6; admission £25-55; ❷ Putney Bridge)

Leyton Orient (Map p62; ☎ 8926 1111; www.leytonorient.com; Matchroom Stadium, Brisbane Rd E10; admission £20-35; ❷ Leyton)

Millwall (Map p182; ☎ 7232 1222; www.millwallfc.co.uk; The Den, Zampa Rd SE16; admission £16-25; ⊞ South Bermondsey)

Queens Park Rangers (Map p62; ☎ 0870 112 1967; www.qpr.co.uk; Loftus Rd W12; admission £20-35; ❷ White City)

Tottenham Hotspur (Map p62; ☎ 0870 420 5000; www.spurs.co.uk; White Hart Lane N17; admission £37-49; ⊞ White Hart Lane)

West Ham United (Map p62; ☎ 0870 112 2700; www.westhamunited.co.uk; Boleyn Ground, Green St E13; admission £35-63; ❷ Upton Park)

and can be difficult to get. Test matches are regularly played at the venerable Lord's and Oval grounds. Tickets (between £10 and £20) are a lot easier to come by for county games; county teams compete in four-day, one-day and 20-over matches between April and September.

BRIT OVAL Map p189
☎ 7582 7764; www.surreycricket.com; Kennington Oval SE11; ❷ Oval
County side Surrey plays at the Oval, known for its distinctive gasholders. It's also famous as the place where cricket-lover John Major went immediately after losing the election to Tony Blair in 1997. For more on the Brit Oval, see p193.

LORD'S Map p166
☎ tours 7616 8585, switchboard 7616 8500; www.lords.org; St John's Wood Rd NW8; ❷ St John's Wood
The 'home of cricket,' a trip to Lord's is often as much a pilgrimage as anything else. As well as being home to Middlesex County Cricket Club, the ground hosts test matches, one-day internationals and domestic finals. For more on Lord's see p168.

RUGBY UNION & RUGBY LEAGUE

Between January and March, England competes against Scotland, Wales, Ireland, France and Italy in the Six Nations Championship. Three games take place at Twickenham Stadium.

Union fans should head to Southwest London, where mighty teams including the Harlequins (☎ 8410 6000; www.quins.co.uk; Stoop Memorial Ground, Langhorn Dr, Twickenham TW2; admission £15-30; ⊞ Twickenham) and Wasps (☎ 8993 8298; www.wasps.co.uk; Adams Park, High Wycombe W3; admission £15-45; ⊞ High Wycombe) play from August to May. London Irish (☎ 01932-783034; www.london-irish.com; Bennet Rd, Reading; admission £20-30; ⊞ Reading) and Saracens (☎ 01923-475222; www.saracens.com; Vicarage Rd, Watford; admission £20-60; ⊞ Watford High St) are also in the Premiership. Most matches are played on Saturday and Sunday afternoons. Tickets are for sale on each of the websites or at the stadiums.

LONDON BRONCOS STADIUM Map p62
☎ 8853 8001; www.londonbroncos.co.uk; The Valley, Floyd Rd SE7; ⊞ Charlton
The only place in southern England to see rugby league.

TWICKENHAM RUGBY STADIUM

☎ 8892 2000; www.rfu.com; Rugby Rd, Twickenham TW1; ⊖ Hounslow East, then 🚌 281, 🚉 Twickenham

The home of English rugby union. There is a museum here that showcases old matches in the video theatre and has a collection of 10,000 items of rugby memorabilia. You can go on a guided tour of the stadium and museum (adult/child/family £14/8/40) at 10.30am, noon, 1.30pm and 3pm Tuesday to Saturday and at 1pm and 3pm on Sunday. There are no tours on match days and the museum is closed on Mondays.

TENNIS

Tennis and Wimbledon, in Southeast London, are almost synonymous, and SW19 suddenly becomes the centre of the sporting universe for a fortnight in June/July when the world-famous tennis tournament takes place.

WIMBLEDON Off Map p62

☎ 8944 1066, 8946 2244; www.wimbledon.org; Church Rd SW19; ⊖ Wimbledon, then 🚌 493

The All England Lawn Tennis Championships have been taking place here in late June/early July since 1877. Most tickets for the Centre and Number One courts are distributed by ballot, applications for which must be made the preceding year. Try your luck by sending a stamped self-addressed envelope to the All England Lawn Tennis Club (PO Box 98, Church Rd, Wimbledon SW19 5AE). Limited tickets go on sale on the day of play, though queues are painfully long. The nearer to the finals, the higher the prices. Prices for outside courts are under £15, reduced after 5pm. You might be better off going to the men's warm-up tournament at Queen's Club (Map p178; ☎ 7385 3421; www.queensclub.co.uk; Palliser Rd, Hammersmith W14; admission per day £12; ⊖ Barons Ct), which takes place a couple of weeks before Wimbledon.

ATHLETICS

England – and London in particular – has a rich history in athletics and continues to produce world champions. There are major international meets each summer at the grand old venue of Crystal Palace in Southeast London, which has been the site of many magical

moments in recent years and where every major international athlete has competed.

CRYSTAL PALACE NATIONAL SPORTS CENTRE Off Map p62

☎ 8778 0131; www.crystalpalace.co.uk; Ledrington Rd SE19; 🚉 Crystal Palace

Athletics and swimming meetings attracting major international and domestic stars take place here regularly throughout the summer. Tickets available on the website or at the venue itself.

HORSE RACING

There are several racecourses within striking distance of London for those wanting to have a flutter. The flat racing runs from April to September, while you can see the gee-gees jumping fences from October to April.

ASCOT

☎ 01344-622211; www.ascot.co.uk; Berkshire; admission from £8; 🚉 Ascot

Best known for the fashion circus of Royal Ascot in June.

EPSOM

☎ 01372-470047; www.epsomderby.co.uk; Epsom, Surrey; admission from £7; 🚉 Epsom Downs

With much more racing credibility than Ascot, this famous racetrack's star turn is Derby Day in June, but it has meets all year.

KEMPTON PARK

☎ 01932-782292; www.kemptonpark.co.uk; Staines Rd East, Sunbury-on-Thames, Middlesex; admission from £8; 🚉 Kempton Park

Of its all-year meetings, summer-evening events are best.

ROYAL WINDSOR RACECOURSE

☎ 01753-865234; www.windsor-racecourse.co.uk; Maidenhead Rd, Windsor, Berkshire; admission from £8; 🚉 Windsor

An idyllic spot beside the castle.

SANDOWN PARK

☎ 01372-463072; www.sandown.co.uk; Portsmouth Rd, Esher, Surrey; admission from £14; 🚉 Esher

Generally considered the southeast's finest racecourse.

GAY & LESBIAN LONDON

top picks

- Duckie (p326)
- Circus (p326)
- Joiners Arms (p327)
- Gay's the Word (p324)
- Barcode (p325)
- Heaven (p325)
- Ghetto (p327)
- G Spot (p325)
- Orange (p328)
- XXL (p326)

What's your recommendation? www.lonelyplanet.com/london

The city of Oscar Wilde, Quentin Crisp and Elton John does not disappoint its queer visitors, proffering a fantastic mix of brash, camp, loud and edgy parties, bars, clubs and events all year round. A world capital of gaydom on par with New York and San Francisco, London is home to enormous gay and lesbian communities that fan out throughout the city. There's also a superb film festival (p16), one of the world's largest annual gay pride events (see p17) and a simmering activist movement to boot.

Things have improved immeasurably in the past decade for gay and lesbian rights and recognition: protection from discrimination is now enshrined in law, and civil partnerships now allow gay couples the same rights as straight couples, even with respect to adoption. That's not to say homophobia doesn't exist – outside the bubble of Soho, abuse on the street at public displays of affection is still not unusual and sadly it's always best to assess the area you're in before walking hand in hand down the street.

The long-established gay village of Soho, once so central to any gay experience of London, has somewhat lost its pre-eminence in a city where redevelopment and high rents have pushed people out to cheaper neighbourhoods. Soho retains the largest number of gay bars and pubs; walk down Old Compton St at any time and you'll notice omnipresent gay and lesbian life – but many of the city's better clubs and venues are now to be found elsewhere. The alternative two focuses of the city's gay life are in Vauxhall, south of the river, and Shoreditch, in London's east. Vauxhall, once a bleak concrete jungle, is now home to London's mainstream muscle boys, who party from Thursday to Tuesday without break. Fashionable Shoreditch is home to London's more alternative gay scene, often very well mixed in with local straight people; here you'll find arty parties and the hipper bars and clubs, where the muscle boys fear to tread.

The lesbian scene in London is far less visible than the flamboyant gay one, though there are still a couple of excellent lesbian bars in Soho and plenty going on elsewhere around the city. Certain areas of the capital are well known to have thriving lesbian communities and are worth a visit in their own right – particularly Stoke Newington and Hackney in northeast London. Check out the excellent lesbian London website www.gingerbeer.co.uk for the full lowdown on events, club nights and bars.

SHOPPING

PROWLER   Map p66   Accessories

☎ 7734 4031; www.prowler-stores.co.uk; 5-7 Brewer St W1; ⏰ 11am-10pm Mon-Fri, 10am-10pm Sat, noon-8pm Sun; ⊖ Piccadilly Circus
Prowler's flagship Soho store is a gay shopping mecca selling books, magazines, clothes and 'lifestyle accessories'. There's also a discreet 'adult' section with the usual array of DVDs and magazines, but the overall feel is of a respectable gay department store.

GAY'S THE WORD   Map pp80-1   Books

☎ 7278 7654; http://freespace.virgin.net/gays .theword/; 66 Marchmont St WC1; ⏰ 10am-6.30pm Mon-Sat, 2-6pm Sun; ⊖ Russell Sq or King's Cross
This London gay institution has been selling books nobody else stocks for three decades now, and still has a great range of gay- and lesbian-interest books and magazines as well as a real community spirit.

DRINKING & NIGHTLIFE

The queer drinking scene in London is wonderfully varied: whether you fancy a quiet pint in a traditional boozer that just happens to be gay or want a place to wet your whistle before going out dancing, you'll be spoiled for choice. Following are our favourite bars and clubs, although there are plenty more; check the gay press for comprehensive listings.

London has some of the most exciting and varied gay clubbing in the world, but it's a moveable feast, as the clubbing scene is about club nights rather than venues, meaning a club that was fantastic and full of drag queens one night might well be straight and full of Goths the next. Whether it's drug-addled muscle boys, fetish clubs or skinny punk-rock guys and girls you're after, look no further – London has it all. The few exclusively gay clubs are listed here, while most big nights are held in straight clubs that put on a gay night or two each week. The gay press and the Gay & Lesbian section in weekly listings magazine *Time Out* are the best places to check for up-to-date club listings, as things change weekly.

THE WEST END

BARCODE Map p66 — Bar

☎ 7734 3342; www.bar-code.co.uk; 3-4 Archer St W1; ⊗ 4pm-1am Mon-Sat, to 11pm Sun; ⊖ Piccadilly Circus

Tucked away down a Soho side street is this fun gay bar, full of a diverse range of people enjoying a pint or two and some evening cruising. There are frequent club nights in the downstairs area, including the very popular gay comedy night, Comedy Camp (p300), every Tuesday. There's a second, clubbier venue, Barcode Vauxhall (☎ 7582 4180; Arch 69, Albert Embankment SE11; ⊗ until 1am, until 4am Fri & Sat; ⊖ Vauxhall) south of the river.

CANDY BAR Map p66 — Bar

☎ 7494 4041; 4 Carlise St W1; ⊗ to midnight Sun-Thu, to 2am Fri-Sat; ⊖ Tottenham Court Rd

This brilliant bar has been the centre of London's small but fun lesbian scene for years and is showing no signs of waning. Busy most nights of the week, this is very much a girls space (one male guest per two women are allowed though) and this should definitely be your first port of call on the London lesbian scene.

EDGE Map p66 — Bar

☎ 7439 1313; 11 Soho Sq W1; ⊗ to 1am Mon-Sat; ⊖ Tottenham Court Rd

Overlooking Soho Sq in all its four-storey glory, the Edge is London's largest gay bar and heaves from the early evening until the early hours with preclubbing revellers fuelling up for the night ahead. There's a heavy straight presence, as it's so close to Oxford St, but it's still a fun place to start the evening.

FREEDOM Map p66 — Cafe-Bar

☎ 7734 0071; www.freedombarsoho.com; 66 Wardour St W1; ⊗ to 3am Mon-Sat, 11.30pm Sun; ⊖ Piccadilly Circus

Freedom, once Soho's coolest bar back in the 90s, is back and better than ever. Its total design rethink has given it a fantastically glamorous feel, whether it be upstairs in the main cafe-bar area, or downstairs in its dark underground club venue, which plays host to cool midweeker Hot Pink on Tuesdays.

FRIENDLY SOCIETY Map p66 — Bar

☎ 7434 3805; 79 Wardour St W1; ⊗ 6-11pm Mon-Thu, to midnight Fri & Sat, to 10.30pm Sun; ⊖ Piccadilly Circus

Definitely one of Soho's friendliest and more relaxed gay bars, and thankfully one of the few fashionable queer drinking establishments that hasn't initiated a dubious door policy or membership scheme to ensure that only the rich and beautiful arrive. A fun and up-for-it crowd assemble in the early evening, drink beer under S&M Barbie and Ken, and chill out to live DJs all evening.

G SPOT Map pp70-71 — Bar

www.gspotgirlbar.com; 10 Adelaide St WC2; ⊗ 6pm-late Fri & Sat; ⊖ Charing Cross

This racily-named bar offers gay girls a great venue to call their own in this basement bar off the Strand. Sadly it's only open two nights a week, but when it is, this place is always a great place to spend an evening with a mixed crowd of up-for-it girls.

HEAVEN Map pp70-1 — Club

☎ 7930 2020; www.heavennightclub-london.com; Villiers St WC2; ⊗ 10.30pm-3am Mon, 10pm-3am Thu & Fri, 10pm-5am Sat; ⊖ Embankment or Charing Cross

This long-standing and perennially popular gay club, under the arches beneath Charing Cross station, has always been host to good club nights, but after languishing rather in the past few years it has been rejuvenated by the arrival of G-A-Y here, doing nights on Thursday (G-A-Y Porn Idol), Friday (G-A-Y Camp Attack) and Saturday (plain ol' G-A-Y). Also check out Monday's Latin-themed cheap night out, Popcorn.

KU BAR Map pp70-1 — Bar

☎ 7437 4303; www.ku-bar.co.uk; 30 Lisle St WC2; ⊗ 5pm-midnight Sun-Thu, to 3am Fri & Sat; ⊖ Leicester Sq

The Ku Bar now runs a small Soho empire, consisting of two bars and a club. All three venues are very popular – the former pub on Lisle St is always rammed with teens warming up for the evening with the Ku Klub downstairs hosting a range of fun nights throughout the week, while the new Ku Bar Frith St (Map p66; 25 Frith St; ⊗ until midnight Fri & Sat; ⊖ Leicester Sq) is popular with a slightly older, smarter crowd.

SHADOW LOUNGE Map p66   Bar

☎ 7287 7988; www.theshadowlounge.co.uk; 5 Brewer St W1; ⌚ 10pm-3am Mon-Sat; ⊖ Piccadilly Circus

This home from home for the Soho glitterati is a stylish basement bar with plenty of comfortable coves to hang out in as well as a dance floor complete with pole for dirty dancing. The door policy is a little erratic: at quiet times you're usually fine although there's generally a £5 to £10 entry charge; other times you'll need to be with a

BEST GAY CLUB NIGHTS

Monday

- Popcorn (Heaven, p325) A fun and cheap night out, Popcorn is an 'Ibiza-style club night' with a great selection of music on offer and refreshingly priced drinks offers.

Tuesday

- Hot Pink (Freedom, p325) London's gayest, pinkest midweek party is in the basement at Soho old-timer Freedom – a glamorous event run by the ubiquitous Jodie Harsh where those in hot pink enter for free.

Wednesday

- Shinky Shonky (Ku Bar, p325) If you need any proof that the London gays are every bit as quirky and idiosyncratic as the rest of the country, this is it. Boogaloo Stu hosts an unforgettably mad night based around audience participation and out-there performance.

Thursday

- Industri (Barcode Vauxhall, p325) The hottest warm-up night for the weekend, this Vauxhall social is the place to befriend the DJs, door whores and gogo boys who will be entertaining you for the next couple of nights.

Friday

- A:M (Fire, p328) One of the fiercest and most popular gay nights in Vauxhall, A:M packs in a beautiful crowd of serious clubbers for an incredible 12-hour stretch. The music features some of the best techno and electro DJs on the London scene.
- Popstarz (www.popstarz.org; Den, 18 West Central St WC1; ⊖ Holborn) This grand dame of gay indie has been revitalised by a recent transfer to the heart of the West End. It's popular with a studenty, friendly, mixed crowd. There are three rooms of great indie pop.

Saturday

- Duckie (Royal Vauxhall Tavern, p328) Get here by 10.30pm to avoid a massive queue because Duckie, hosted by the marvellous Amy Lamé, is the perfect antidote to pretension on the gay scene. Great indie tunes and some of the most unusual cabaret in London await you here.
- Circus (Last Days of Decadence, p297) Jodie Harsh, the tranny whose fame now actually exceeds that of the person she impersonates (model Jodie Marsh), hosts this hyper-fashionable gay night. This is the place to meet the glamorous Hoxton crowd on their own territory – lots of fun.
- G-A-Y (Heaven, p325) Love it or hate it, G-A-Y is a centre of gravity for the gay scene and seemingly where half of Soho is headed on a Saturday night. Its new home at Heaven has helped the ageing club to get a new lease on life. Bring your tight T-shirt!
- XXL (Map p126; www.xxl-london.com; 51/53 Southwark St, London Bridge SE1; ⌚ 10pm-6am Sat) The world's biggest club for bears (hairy, stocky gay men) and their admirers is a real event. A very friendly crowd is spread out over a wonderfully quirky space, with two dance floors and a 'recreational maze'.

Sunday

- Horsemeat Disco (Eagle, opposite) This funky end of weekend night brings together both mainstream and alternative Vauxhall scenes with great thumping electro and a chilled-out, but sexy, vibe.

member or a Soho 'face' to make it past the gorillas on the door.

YARD Map p66 Bar

☎ 7437 2652; www.yardbar.co.uk; 57 Rupert St W1; 🕐 1-11pm Mon-Sat, 1-10.30pm Sun; ⊖ Piccadilly Circus

This old Soho favourite attracts a great cross-section of the great and the good. It's a pretty attitude-free place, perfect for preclub drinks or just an evening out. There are DJs upstairs in the Loft most nights as well as a friendly crowd in the eponymous courtyard downstairs.

CLERKENWELL, SHOREDITCH & SPITALFIELDS

GHETTO Map p150 Club

☎ 7287 3726; www.ghetto-london.co.uk; 58 Old St EC1; 🕐 5.30pm-1am Mon-Tue, to 3am Wed & Thu, to 5am Fri & Sat, to 2am Sun; ⊖ Barbican or Old St

Having moved out of Soho, the Ghetto is now the biggest and smartest gay venue around Shoreditch, London's most sizzlingly alternative and creative neighbourhood. The two-floor bar and club contains the wood-panelled Trash Palace (www.trashpalace.co.uk) upstairs, a haven of self-styled 'odd glamour' where you can also get free or discounted entry tickets to the Ghetto proper, the downstairs club. This is a friendly, pioneering venue with plenty of interesting nights, not least pop-classic night Wigout, on Saturday.

THE EAST END & DOCKLANDS

JOINERS ARMS Map p156 Pub

☎ 7739 9854; 116 Hackney Rd E2; 🕐 6pm-2am Fri & Sat; ⊖ Shoreditch or Old St

Determinedly rundown and cheesy, the Joiners is Hoxton's only totally gay pub-club (perhaps reflecting the degree to which such distinctions are blurred around E2). It's a crowded, funky old boozer where hip gay boys and a smattering of celebrities hang out at the bar, dance and watch people play pool all night.

WHITE SWAN Map p156 Club

☎ 7780 9870; www.bjswhiteswan.com; 556 Commercial Rd E14; 🕐 9pm-2am Tue-Thu, 9pm-4am Fri & Sat, 6pm-midnight Sun; DLR Limehouse

The White Swan is a fun East End kind of place, with a large dance floor as well as a more relaxed pub area. Its legendary amateur strip night has sadly disappeared, but there's still plenty of flesh on stage on Saturday. Club classics and cheesy pop predominate.

NORTH LONDON

BLACK CAP Map p170 Bar

☎ 7485 0538; www.theblackcap.com; 171 Camden High St NW1; 🕐 noon-2am Mon-Thu, to 3am Fri & Sat, to 1am Sun; ⊖ Camden Town

This friendly, sprawling place is Camden's premier gay venue, and attracts people from all over North London for its great outdoor terrace, the pleasantly pub-like upstairs Shufflewick bar and the downstairs club, where you'll find plenty of hilarious camp cabaret as well as decent dance music.

GREEN Map p170 Bar

☎ 7226 8895; www.thegreenislington.co.uk; 74 Upper St N1; 🕐 noon-11pm Mon-Thu, to 1am Fri & Sat, to midnight Sun; ⊖ Angel

A much-needed modern addition to the gay pubs in and around Islington, the Green is a funky, friendly two-floor place where the young of N1 hang out, meet friends and warm up for a night out. There's usually a cover charge after 11pm.

SOUTH LONDON

AREA Map p189 Club

www.areaclublondon.com; 67-68 Albert Embankment SE1; 🕐 10.30pm-6am Sat; ⊖ Vauxhall

Home from home for circuit party boys but still very welcoming to all, Area describes itself as 'polysexual' and hosts some of the most inventive nights in town, including monthly Queer Kandi and Saturday-nighter Evolve.

EAGLE Map p189 Club

☎ 7793 0903; www.eaglelondon.com; 349 Kennington La SE11; 🕐 9pm-2am Mon-Thu, until 3am Fri & Sun, until 4am Sat; ⊖ Vauxhall

This fantastic place is a haven of alternative queer goings on in muscle-bound Vauxhall. Open nightly with a different feel throughout the week, we love Thursday night's Berlin, which takes its inspiration from both the electrobeats and the sleazy feel of the German capital and Sunday night's legendary Horse Meat Disco.

FIRE Map p189 Club

☎ 0790 503 5682; www.fireclub.co.uk; South Lambeth Rd SW8; ⏰ 10pm-4am; ◉ Vauxhall

Sealing Vauxhall's reputation as the new gay nightlife centre of London, Fire is another expansive, smart space under the railway arches, hosting the centrepieces of the Vauxhall weekend A:M (p326) on Friday, Beyond on Saturday, and Sunday all-nighter Orange.

HOIST Map p189 Club

☎ 7735 9972; www.thehoist.co.uk; Arches 47B & 47C, South Lambeth Rd SW8; ⏰ 10pm-3am Thu, Fri & Sun, 10pm-4am Sat; ◉ Vauxhall

One of Europe's most famous fetish clubs, the Hoist is a one-stop shop for guys into leather and uniforms. The dress code is very strict – everyone has to wear boots, and rubber, leather or uniform. Check out the array of fetish nights on the website.

ROYAL VAUXHALL TAVERN Map p189 Club

☎ 7820 1222; www.theroyalvauxhalltavern.co.uk; 372 Kennington Lane SE11; ⏰ 7pm-midnight Mon-Thu, 7pm-4am Fri, 7pm-2am Sat, 2pm-midnight Sun; ◉ Vauxhall

Rough around the edges to say the least, this is the perfect antidote to the gleaming new wave of gay venues now crowding Vauxhall's gay village. Saturday's Duckie, a wonderful indie performance night hosted by Amy Lamé, is rightly considered to be one of the best club nights in London. Also check out S.L.A.G.S. on Sundays, and keep an eye out on the website for other upcoming events – from cabaret nights to previews for the Edinburgh Fringe.

TWO BREWERS Map p190 Bar

☎ 7819 9539; www.the2brewers.com; 114 Clapham High St SW4; ⏰ noon-2am Sun-Thu, noon-4am Fri & Sat; ◉ Clapham Common or Clapham North

LOCAL VOICES: TOMMY TURNTABLES

Tommy Turntables is a club and music events producer and promoter of Popstarz and The Ghetto.

How long have you been out on London's gay scene and what are your early memories of it? I've been on the scene, working and clubbing for 12 years. My earliest memories are of dodgy, smelly, smoky Soho bars, none of which exist any more. Instead they've all been gentrified and are now owned by big corporations with 'glamorous' fixtures and 'tasteful' fittings. I prefer the old smelly bars.

Twenty-four hours in London – where should a gay visitor go and what should they do? See all of London and not just the traditional gay haunts of Soho and Old Compton St. Head south to Vauxhall for Duckie (p326) and the Eagle (p327) and go east to the Ghetto (p327), the George & Dragon (p282) and Dalston Superstore (p287); the venues are excellent even if the surrounding area looks a little like Beirut in the '80s…

Gay Shame or Gay Pride? Gay Shame, definitely. Although sadly this year's alternative gay pride party was the last one. In general I always try to go to the alternative clubs rather than the mainstream ones – London has a first-class underground scene that dates back decades.

The best thing about gay London? The diversity of the people and the clubs is the best thing – there's something for everyone: gay book clubs, gay jazz clubs and even gay choirs. But more importantly the gay scene (particularly the more alternative side of it) manages not to ghettoize itself too much – everyone remains welcome.

…and the worst? The gentrification of traditional gay places such as Soho is sad to see, as are the high prices in some bars and the nonacceptance of women and straight people in some more mainstream gay bars and clubs.

And how does the lesbian scene fit into that? It's strange – for years lesbians kept themselves very separate from the male gay scene and then the two began to converge much more, which was a welcome breath of fresh air. But these days there are so many great lesbian nights and events that they seem to be branching off again which I think is a shame but still represents progress for the London lesbian scene.

Is the future in Soho, Vauxhall or Shoreditch? All of them! London has enough gay residents and tourists to keep the three gay villages it now has teeming with people.

Why is London so unique as a destination for gay travellers? It's due to its diversity, originality and quirkiness – all things that both the city and its people have in bucket loads. Historically there's nowhere like London on the planet, it's been a hub for travellers, entrepreneurs and weirdoes since time immemorial. Gay travellers are drawn to places like that; it's iconic, something else that seems to appeal to gay sensitivities. If Madonna was a city she'd be London.

Tommy Turntables was interviewed by Tom Masters.

Clapham may have a rather suburban feel in general, and the High Street in particular, but the Two Brewers endures as one of the best London gay bars outside the gay villages. Here there's a friendly, laid-back, local crowd who come for a quiet drink during the week and some madcap cabaret and dancing in the club at weekends.

FURTHER RESOURCES

London has a lively free gay press documenting the ever-changing scene. You can pick up these publications at any gay venue and it's always a good idea to do so as the listings are the most up-to-date and wide-ranging available. The mainstays are the tabloids *Boyz* (www.boyz.co.uk) and *QX* (www.qxmagazine.com), and the more serious and newsy *Pink Paper* (www.pinkpaper.com). They all include weekly listings for clubs, bars and other events, and often contain flyers that grant discounted entry to various venues. Magazines on sale at most London newsagents include *Gay Times* (www.gaytimes .co.uk), *Diva* (www.divamag.co.uk), *Attitude* (www.attitude.co.uk) and *AXM* (www.axm -mag.com), although some less enlightened proprietors still place them on the top shelf next to the pornography.

Check out the following listings, personal websites and activist groups:

Gaydar (www.gaydar.co.uk or gaydargirls.co.uk)

Ginger Beer (www.gingerbeer.co.uk)

Time Out (www.timeout.com/london/gay)

Visit London (www.visitlondon.com/people/gay)

London Lesbian & Gay Switchboard (☎ 7837 7324; www.llgs.org.uk) Provides free advice, counselling and other help to anyone who needs a sympathetic ear.

Stonewall (www.stonewall.co.uk)

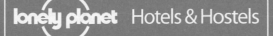

lonely planet Hotels & Hostels

Want more sleeping recommendations than we could ever pack into this little ol' book? Craving more detail – including extended reviews and photographs? Want to read reviews by other travellers and be able to post your own? Just make your way over to **lonelyplanet.com/hotels** and check out our thorough list of independent reviews, then reserve your room simply and securely.

SLEEPING

top picks

SLEEPING

Accommodation in London is among the world's most expensive and wherever you stay is going to take a great wad out of your budget. Demand can outstrip supply – especially at the bottom end of the market – so it's worth booking at least a few nights' accommodation before arriving, particularly during holiday periods and in summer.

Another problem here can be quality – even at the midrange level. A large part of readers' letters sent to us about London are complaints about the quality and cleanliness of hostels, guesthouses and some B&Bs, 'fauna' in the rooms and the rudeness of staff. The descriptions in this chapter will help you make your choice.

It's not all bad news, though. A slew of upmarket boutique hotels have brought a real sense of style to the city's digs, and scores of midrange hotels and B&Bs are following suit. At the other end of the spectrum, some places have begun providing boringly functional but affordable rooms. A very exciting trend has been the convergence of these two extremes in a new crop of 'budget boutique' hotels, with a bit of chic at reasonable prices.

ACCOMMODATION STYLES & COSTS

London has a superb range of deluxe hotels (from £350 per double) and you'll be spoiled for choice with old classics that combine the best in traditional atmosphere and modern comforts. There's also good variety in the top-end category (anything from £180 upwards), which offers superior comforts without the prestige. Also in this bracket you'll find many of the boutique and style hotels that have sprung up in recent years. Below £180 there's a bit of a slide in quality and choice. Although there's an increasing number of terrific places to rest your head without haemorrhaging your budget, it's still not enough. And if you were expecting to spend less than £100 a night on a double room during the week, your lodgings probably won't provide the most cherished memories of your trip. (On the other hand, there are some good weekend deals for that price.) In London, cheap means less than £80 for an en suite double. After B&Bs, the cheapest forms of accommodation are hostels, both the official Youth Hostel Association (YHA) ones, of which there are seven in cen-

tral London, and the (usually) hipper, more party-orientated independent ones, which are growing in number.

Hotel rooms in the UK are subject to 'value-added tax' or VAT (currently at 15%). Many hotels quote rates inclusive of VAT, while others do not, so it always pays to ask if you are uncertain. Remember, though, that many hotels – especially deluxe ones – regularly offer promotional deals on the internet that are much lower than their published rates. Unless otherwise indicated, accommodation prices quoted in this book include breakfast.

The accommodation options in this guide are listed by area and then by price, from most to least expensive. See the Price Guide boxed text, below, for more information on accommodation prices.

LONGER-TERM RENTALS
Apartments & Serviced Apartments

If you are visiting London for a few weeks or several months, staying in a short-term or serviced apartment is the best way to get a sense of living in the city. Many agencies in *Loot* (p389) advertise less-than-salubrious properties; ask to see rooms first. London Craig's List (http://london.craigslist.co.uk) is always worth checking for rental properties. Some better agencies and their daily rates are listed here.

196 BISHOPSGATE
☎ 7621 8788; www.196bishopsgate.com; studio/
1-bedroom apt from £193/230, cheaper after 6
nights

PRICE GUIDE

The symbols below indicate the cost per night of a standard double room in high season.

£££	over £180
££	£80-180
£	under £80

Luxury serviced apartments in the City opposite Liverpool St tube and train station. Has longer-stay properties.

CITADINES APART'HOTEL
☎ 0800 376 3898; www.citadines.com; 2-person studio £105-150, cheaper after 6 nights
Ever-popular, ever-expanding French chain has four apartment blocks in London, including a Holborn-Covent Garden branch (Map pp70–1; ☎ 7395 8800; 94-99 High Holborn WC1; ⊖ Holborn).

ASTON'S APARTMENTS
☎ 7590 6000; www.astons-apartments.com; s/d/tr/f from £74/101/141/187, weekly rates 5% less
Has three Victorian town houses on a quiet street in South Kensington divided into serviced apartments of varying sizes.

Rooms & Flats
Most newcomers to the city still find renting expensive (note that almost all rented accommodation in London is furnished). At the very bottom end, bedsits (£300 to £500 per month) are single furnished rooms, usually with a shared bathroom and kitchen, and they are always pretty grim. A step up is a self-contained studio (from £600), which normally has a separate bathroom and kitchen. You'll rarely get a two-bedroom flat for less than £1000 even in far-flung locations. Shared accommodation offers the best value, at £350 and upwards for a room in a flat or a house with several bedrooms. Most landlords demand a security deposit (normally one month's rent) plus a month's rent in advance.

To get abreast of current prices, consult the classifieds in publications such as *Loot*, *TNT*, *Time Out* and the *Evening Standard*'s Wednesday supplement *Homes & Property* (www.homesandproperty.co.uk). Some of the better websites are Gumtree (www.gumtree.com), Move Flat (www.moveflat.com), and the gay and lesbian Outlet (www.outlet4homes.com).

RESERVATIONS & BOOKINGS
The London tourist organisation Visit London (☎ 0870 156 6366; www.visitlondon.com) offers a free booking service with a wide range of accommodation options and always has special deals; see its website. There's also the British Hotel Reservation Centre (☎ 7592 3055; www.bhrconline.com), which has desks at Gatwick, Heathrow and Stansted airports and Paddington, Victoria and St Pancras International train stations that charge a booking fee. Other good sources for hotel bookings and discounts are Hotels of London (☎ 7096 0313; www.hotelsoflondon.co.uk), LondonTown (☎ 7437 4370; www.londontown.com) and London Lodging (☎ 870 042 9292; www.londonlodging.co.uk).

You can book a hostel through the YHA central reservations system (☎ 0870 770 6113; www.yha.org.uk). If you want to stay in a B&B or private home, reservations can be made through the following agencies. See the boxed text on p342 for details on booking rooms in student dorms and halls of residence during university holidays.

UPTOWN RESERVATIONS
☎ 7937 2001; www.uptownres.co.uk; s/d/tr/q £80/105/135/145
Offers well reviewed B&B accommodation in stylish private homes, mostly around the West End, Kensington, Belgravia, Chelsea and Knightsbridge.

AT HOME IN LONDON
☎ 8748 1943; www.athomeinlondon.co.uk; s/d/tr from £50/70/92
This is worth looking at if you're considering staying one week to a month as some properties have minimum stays.

LONDON BED & BREAKFAST AGENCY
☎ 7586 2768; www.londonbb.com; s/d from £47/70
Offering spare rooms in London homes. Properties are concentrated for the most part in central and northern London.

LONDON HOMESTEAD SERVICES
☎ 7286 5115; www.lhslondon.com; per person £18-40
Small family-run business offering B&B rooms in private homes across London.

WHERE TO STAY
Where you choose to stay in London will also have a big effect on the kind of time you have here. Base yourself anywhere in the West End and you'll soon get into the throbbing rhythm of London at play (though stay in Hoxton, Clerkenwell or Shoreditch and you'll be even closer to the cutting edge). If your idea of the capital is one of stately Georgian houses,

Regency crescents and private parks in the centre of leafy squares, book a place in Chelsea or Mayfair. You want ethnic London? Stay in Notting Hill or Whitechapel. Culture vultures and/or those with literary aspirations should choose a place in Bloomsbury, Kensington or even Fitzrovia. If you want to feel how most Londoners live, you might hang out in Camden or Stoke Newington. If you prefer to hang out with your 'mites', Earl's Court (aka Kangaroo Valley) or Shepherd's Bush is for you.

THE WEST END

You're really at the hub of London life in the West End, where you won't have to worry about running for the last tube home. The city's major theatres, as well some of its best dining and drinking, is right on your doorstep, as are many major attractions. Of course such a privilege doesn't come cheaply. Moderately priced hotels in the centre are as scarce as hen's teeth. Having said that Bloomsbury is a haven of B&Bs and guesthouses, and tucked away in leafy Cartwright Gardens, north of Russell Sq and within easy walking distance of the West End, you'll find some of central London's best-value small hotels. At the other end of the accommodation spectrum Mayfair boasts hotels so grand that many of them are tourist attractions in their own right.

SOHO & CHINATOWN

COURTHOUSE HOTEL KEMPINSKI
Map p66   International Hotel £££
☎ 7297 5555; www.courthouse-hotel.com;
19-21 Great Marlborough St W1; r £300-400,
ste from £550; ⊖ Oxford Circus; ⊠ ⊛ ⊛
Oscar Wilde, John Lennon and Mick Jagger all made appearances at this former magistrate's court, now a 112-room luxury hotel just south of Oxford St. Special features include a spa and pool as well as a bar whose tables sit within original prison cells – authentic iron bars cordon off the lounge area.

SOHO HOTEL Map p66   Hotel £££
☎ 7559 3000; www.sohohotel.com; 4 Richmond Mews W1; d £280-350, ste from £385-3000;
⊖ Tottenham Court Rd; ⊠
One of London's hippest hotels, the Soho is in a reconverted car park just off Dean St. All the hallmarks of the eclectically chic hoteliers and designers Tim and Kit Kemp

have been writ large over 91 individually designed rooms, the colours lean towards the raspberries and puces, and there's a stunning black cat Botero sculpture at the entrance.

HAZLITT'S Map p66   Hotel £££
☎ 7434 1771; www.hazlittshotel.com;
6 Frith St W1; s £175, d & tw £210-265, ste £400;
⊖ Tottenham Court Rd; ⊠
Built in 1718 and comprising three original Georgian houses, this is the one-time home of essayist William Hazlitt (1778–1830), and all 23 rooms are named after former residents or visitors to the house. Bedrooms boast a wealth of seductive details, including mahogany four-poster beds, Victorian claw-foot tubs, sumptuous fabrics and genuine antiques. It's a listed building so there is no lift.

PICCADILLY BACKPACKERS
Map p66   Hostel £
☎ 7434 9009; www.piccadillyhotel.net;
12 Sherwood St W1; dm £12-19, s/d £40/60;
⊖ Piccadilly Circus
The most centrally located budget accommodation in London, Piccadilly Backpackers has more than 700 beds spread over five floors, with dormitory rooms containing anything from four to 10 beds. Rooms are bright and clean, and we especially like the pod dorms with wooden bunk beds in their own little compartments.

YHA OXFORD ST Map p66   Hostel £
☎ 7734 1618; www.yha.org.uk; 3rd fl,
14 Noel St W1; dm £19-25; ⊖ Oxford Circus or Tottenham Court Rd
The most central of London's seven YHA hostels is basic, clean, loud and not particularly all that welcoming. Most of the 76 beds are in twin rooms, though there are dormitories with three and four beds. There is a large kitchen, but no meals are served apart from a packed breakfast.

COVENT GARDEN & LEICESTER SQUARE

ST MARTIN'S LANE Map pp70-1   Hotel £££
☎ 7300 5500; www.stmartinslane.com;
45 St Martin's Lane; standard s & d £220-270,
garden r £310, ste from £600; ⊖ Covent Garden or Leicester Sq; ⊠ ⊛

A slice of New York urban chic just a stone's throw from Covent Garden, this Philippe Starck–designed hotel is so cool you'd hardly notice it was there. ('What, in that glass box?!?') Its 204 rooms have floor-to-ceiling windows with sweeping West End views, the public rooms are bustling meeting points and everything (and everyone) is beautiful. The overwhelmingly yellow reception area plays havoc with some complexions, though.

HAYMARKET Map pp70-1   Boutique Hotel £££
☎ 7470 4000; www.haymarkethotel.com; 1 Suffolk Pl SW1; r from £260-340, ste from £410; ✪ Piccadilly Circus; ⌧ ⬜
Named by *Condé Nast Traveller* as one of the world's finest hotels *before* it opened, the 50-room Haymarket in a John Nash building next to the Theatre Royal is further proof that London is becoming the epicentre of stylish boutique hotels. It's the progeny of Tim and Kit Kemp and it shows – from the hand-painted Gournay wallpaper to the 18m pool with funky drawing room.

COVENT GARDEN HOTEL
Map pp70-1   Boutique Hotel £££
☎ 7806 1000; www.coventgardenhotel.co.uk; 10 Monmouth St WC2; s/d from £230/310, ste from £410; ✪ Covent Garden or Tottenham Court Rd; ⌧
As fresh as the morning but in a stylishly reserved British sort of way, this 58-room boutique hotel housed in an old French hospital and dispensary uses antiques (don't miss the beautiful marquetry desk in the drawing room), gorgeous fabrics and quirky bric-a-brac to stake out its individuality. There's an excellent bar-restaurant called Brasserie Max just off the lobby.

TRAFALGAR Map pp70-1   International Hotel £££
☎ 7870 2900; www.thetrafalgar.com; 2 Spring Gardens SW1; s & d from £200, ste from £375; ✪ Charing Cross or Embankment; ⌧ ⬜
The demand for designer digs has become so strong in London that even the Hilton got in on the act with this tastefully minimalist hotel on the south side of Trafalgar Sq. Now it's become the capital's 'first unbranded Hilton property' (meaning no logo), though the stylish 129 rooms, jaw-dropping roof terrace and the two-tier Rockwell bar, with the largest selection of bourbon outside the USA, are all still in place.

KINGSWAY HALL Map pp70-1   Hotel £££
☎ 7309 0909; www.kingswayhall.co.uk; Great Queen St WC2; s & d £130-190, ste from £330, breakfast £15-30; ✪ Holborn; ⌧ ⬜
Tipping its cap fairly determinedly at the professional traveller, Kingsway nonetheless manages to provide 170 smart, comfortable and very central rooms for anyone with less business and more play on their mind. The atmosphere is more relaxed on the weekend, when rates are considerably cheaper.

SEVEN DIALS HOTEL Map pp70-1   Hotel ££
☎ 7240 0823; www.sevendialshotellondon.com; 7 Monmouth St WC2; s/d/tw/tr £80/95/105/120; ✪ Covent Garden or Tottenham Court Rd; ⌧
The Seven Dials is a clean and comfortable budget/midrange option in a very central location. The 18 rooms come in a number of varieties – from single with shared facilities to triple with bathroom – and half face onto charming Monmouth St. Just don't expect the Ritz at this kind of money.

FIELDING HOTEL Map pp70-1   Hotel ££
☎ 7836 8305; www.the-fielding-hotel.co.uk; 4 Broad Ct, Bow St WC2; s/d £90/115; ✪ Covent Garden
You can almost feel the pulse of the West End – and the odd high C from the Royal Opera House a block away – at this 24-room hotel, located in a pedestrianised court in the heart of Covent Garden. It's named after the novelist Henry Fielding (1707–54), who lived on the street. Space is at a premium, but you can't beat the location at this price.

HOLBORN & THE STRAND
SAVOY Map pp70-1   Hotel £££
☎ 7836 4343; www.fairmont.com/savoy; The Strand WC2; s/d/ste from £389/409/589; ✪ Charing Cross; ⌧
The £100 million face-lift was still going on at the time of writing, and the legendary hotel should be open by the time you read this. Built on the site of the old Savoy Palace in 1889, the Savoy has welcomed the high, the mighty and the not untalented, including a certain Monsieur Monet who immortalised the views from the 'river rooms' on canvas. Fun fact: the Savoy's forecourt is the only street in the British Isles where motorists must drive on the right.

ONE ALDWYCH Map pp70-1 Hotel £££

☎ 7300 1000; www.onealdwych.co.uk;
1 Aldwych WC2; d £230-550, ste from £600,
weekend rates from £200; ⊖ Covent Garden or
Charing Cross; ✲ ✲ ✲

Housed in what were once art nouveau
newspaper offices (1907), One Aldwych is
a merry and upbeat hotel with 105 rooms
and modern art everywhere (we love the
bronze of a rower in the lobby). The spacious and stylish rooms are replete with
raw silk curtains, natural tones and bath-
tubs with room for two; the health club has
an 18m-long swimming pool.

WALDORF HILTON

Map pp70-1 International Hotel £££

☎ 7836 2400; www.hilton.co.uk/waldorf;
Aldwych WC2; r from £350, breakfast £25, weekend
package from £300; ⊖ Temple, Covent Garden or
Charing Cross; ✲

The glorious Edwardian splendour of this
renovated old pile still lives on in the
heritage-listed Palm Court. So thorough is
the break from the past elsewhere, however, that the 299 rooms are now divided
into either just 'contemporary' or 'design'
(the latter is slightly trendier and more
minimalist).

BLOOMSBURY

MYHOTEL BLOOMSBURY

Map p66 Boutique Hotel £££

☎ 7667 6000; www.myhotels.com; 11-13 Bayley St
WC1; s £120-205, d & tw £205-250, ste from £355,
weekend rates from £130; ⊖ Tottenham Court Rd
or Goodge St; ✲

Its less-than-inspired name notwithstanding, this stylish Conran-designed hotel was
one of London's first boutique hotels and
still bears the classic boutique combination of colours (blacks, greys and reds) in
its 78 guestrooms. The library is a welcome
retreat for chilling. The quirkier Myhotel Chelsea (Map pp136–7; ☎ 7225 7500; 35 Ixworth Pl SW3;
⊖ South Kensington) has 45 rooms.

GRANGE BLOOMS HOTEL

Map pp80-1 Hotel ££

☎ 7323 1717; www.grangehotels.com;
7 Montague St WC1; s/d from £150/180;
⊖ Tottenham Court Rd or Russell Sq

This elegant and airy 18th-century town
house has the feel of a country home,
which belies its position in the heart of

London (in what used to be the grounds
of the British Museum). Think floral prints,
classical music, portraits on the walls of
the 36 guestrooms and a delightful terrace
garden at the back.

AMBASSADORS BLOOMSBURY

Map pp80-1 Hotel ££

☎ 7693 5400; www.ambassadors.co.uk;
12 Upper Woburn WC1; r £99-155; ⊖ Euston; ✲

This 100-room hotel in a gem of a belle
époque building just south of Euston
Rd has been beautifully renovated. The
emphasis here is on comfort, the style is
contemporary and the attached Number
12 bar a welcome addition to the area.
Weekend rates are cheaper and worth
checking.

ACADEMY HOTEL Map pp80-1 Boutique Hotel ££

☎ 7631 4115; www.theetoncollection.com;
21 Gower St WC1; s/d £120-205, weekend rate incl
breakfast from £150; ⊖ Goodge St; ✲

This terribly English 49-room hotel is set
across five Georgian town houses but has
a slight Regency feel. Quality rooms are kitted out with fluffy duvets, plump cushions
and bolster pillows. There's a conservatory
overlooking a leafy back garden with fish
pond, and a contemporary-looking bar in
blue tones called the Library.

MORGAN HOTEL Map pp80-1 Hotel ££

☎ 7636 3735; www.morganhotel.co.uk;
24 Bloomsbury St WC1; s/d from £80/110,
ste £135-220; ⊖ Tottenham Court Rd

In a row of 18th-century Georgian houses
alongside the British Museum, this is one
of the best midpriced hotels in London.
With 20 guestrooms at its disposal, the
warmth and hospitality more than make
up for the slightly cramped quarters. The
larger suites are well worth the extra
money.

HARLINGFORD HOTEL Map pp80-1 Hotel ££

☎ 7387 1551; www.harlingfordhotel.com;
61-63 Cartwright Gardens WC1; s/d/tr/q
£85/110/125/135; ⊖ Russell Sq

With its 'H' logo proudly sewn on your
bedroom cushion, and a modern interior
design with lots of lavender and mauve
and green-tiled bathrooms, this stylish
Georgian hotel with 43 rooms is arguably
the best on the street. You'll recognise it
from all the ivy at the front.

ARRAN HOUSE HOTEL Map pp80-1 Hotel ££

☎ 7636 2186; www.arranhotel-london.com; 77-79 Gower St WC1; dm £23-27, s/d/tr/q £65/105/123/127, with shared bathroom £55/82/100/106; ⊖ Goodge St

This welcoming place in Bloomsbury provides excellent value for the location and even has a garden. The 28 rooms range from basic dormitory-style accommodation to bright well-furnished doubles with bathrooms. The lounge is pleasant, guests can cook for themselves and there are laundry facilities.

CRESCENT HOTEL Map pp80-1 Hotel ££

☎ 7387 1515; www.crescenthoteloflondon.com; 49-50 Cartwright Gardens WC1; s £55-83, d/tr/q £100/115/123, s with shared bathroom £50; ⊖ Russell Sq

In the middle of academic London, this friendly, family-owned hotel built in 1810 overlooks a private square flanked by student residences. While the 27 rooms range from pokey singles without facilities to relatively spacious doubles with bathrooms, all are comfortable and maintained at a very high standard.

HOTEL CAVENDISH Map pp80-1 Hotel ££

☎ 7636 9079; www.hotelcavendish.com; 75 Gower St WC1; s/d/tr/q £75/90/120/140; ⊖ Goodge St

Run by an amiable family, this hotel has 32 en suite rooms and a lovely walled garden. The rooms are small but comfortable and the welcome here's always warm. Try booking online for cheaper rates.

JENKINS HOTEL Map pp80-1 Hotel ££

☎ 7387 2067; www.jenkinshotel.demon.co.uk; 45 Cartwright Gardens WC1; s £52-72, d/tr £95/110; ⊖ Russell Sq

Close to the British Museum, this hotel in business since the 1920s has 14 comfortable rooms and a friendly welcome. Cheaper singles have shared bathrooms. Enter from Burton Pl. Guests get to use the tennis courts in the gardens across the road.

JESMOND HOTEL Map pp80-1 B&B £

☎ 7636 3199; www.jesmondhotel.org.uk; 63 Gower St WC1; s/d/tr/q/f £50/75/95/110/120, with shared bathroom £40/60/80/100/110; ⊖ Goodge St; 📶

We've received more than a few letters from readers singing the praises of this B&B in Bloomsbury. The 16 guestrooms – a dozen with bathroom – are basic but clean and cheerful, and it's a good choice if you're travelling in a small group. There's laundry service and internet's free, but wi-fi is £10 flat rate.

AROSFA Map pp80-1 Hotel £

☎ 7636 2115; www.arosfalondon.com; 83 Gower St WC1; s/d/tr/q £60/90/102/145; ⊖ Euston Sq or Goodge St

The new owners have really spanked up old Arosfa, decking out the lounge with Philippe Starck furniture, blow-ups of the Manhattan skyline on the wall and a generally modern look. The rooms are less lavish, however, with cabin-like bathrooms in each that the owners say they are going to change and update. It's good value, in any case, though watch out for the tiny singles.

RIDGEMOUNT HOTEL Map pp80-1 Hotel £

☎ 7636 1141; www.ridgemounthotel.co.uk; 65-67 Gower St WC1; s/d/tr/q £54/75/93/104, with shared bathroom £42/58//78/92; ⊖ Goodge St

This old-fashioned hotel offers its guests a warmth and consideration that you don't come across very often in the city these days. About half of its 30 utilitarian rooms have bathrooms. It also has a laundry service.

GENERATOR Map pp80-1 Hostel £

☎ 7388 7655; www.generatorhostels.com; Compton Pl, opp 37 Tavistock Pl WC1; dm £15-17, s/tw/tr/q £5/50/60/£80; ⊖ Russell Sq

With its industrial decor, blue neon lights and throbbing techno, the huge Generator is one of the grooviest budget places in central London and not for the fainthearted. The bar stays open until 2am and there are frequent drinking competitions. Along with 214 rooms, which have dorm rooms of between four and 14 beds, there are pool tables, safe-deposit boxes and a large eating area, but no kitchen.

FITZROVIA

SANDERSON Map p66 Boutique Hotel £££

☎ 7300 1400; www.sandersonlondon.com; 50 Berners St W1; d from £235, loft ste £600; ⊖ Oxford Circus

Don't be deterred by the white aluminium and grey-green glass facade of a 1960s-era corporate HQ: this uberdesigned 'urban spa' – recognise Philippe Starck's hand, by any chance? – comes with a lush bamboo-filled garden, artworks and installations, bed sheets with a 450-thread count and a jumble of personality furniture, including a Dalí 'lips' sofa and swan-shaped armchairs. It's a quirky, almost surreal place, with 150 rooms, and decadent enough to die for.

CHARLOTTE STREET HOTEL
Map p66   Boutique Hotel £££
☎ 7806 2000; www.charlottestreethotel.com; 15-17 Charlotte St W1; s/d from £220/310, ste from £375; ⊖ Tottenham Court Rd; ✲ ৬
This wonderful 52-room hotel, where Laura Ashley goes postmodern and comes up smelling of roses, is a favourite of visiting media types. The bar buzzes by night, while the Oscar restaurant is a delightful spot any time of day, but particularly for afternoon tea.

GRANGE LANGHAM COURT HOTEL
Map p66   Hotel ££
☎ 7436 6622; www.grangehotels.co.uk; 31-35 Langham St W1; s/d from £150/170; ⊖ Oxford Circus
This 60-room hotel has a lovely black-and-white tile exterior but rather ordinary guestrooms and public areas (who chose the tartan armchairs and that diamond-patterned carpet?). But it's in a great location just north of Oxford St and Soho.

ST JAMES'S

41 Map pp84-5   Hotel £££
☎ 7300 0041; www.41hotel.com; 41 Buckingham Palace Rd SW1; s & d from £230, ste from £395; ⊖ Victoria; ✲ ☐ ৬
This hotel, situated in a lovely old town house opposite Buckingham Palace's Royal Mews, almost feels like you're staying in a private club. There are valets working around the clock, 30 classically designed black-and-white rooms and a large skylit lobby. Reception is on the 5th floor.

WELLINGTON Map pp84-5   Hotel £
☎ 7834 4740; www.the-wellington.co.uk; 71 Vincent Sq SW1; s/d/tr/q with shared bathroom £55/70/95/125; ⊖ Victoria; ☐
As welcoming as an icy winter and as clean as a used whistle, this place overlooking a leafy square is a former student residence with 91 rooms. It's easily reached on foot from the Victoria train and coach stations and close to the Tate Britain.

RITZ Map p66   Hotel £££
☎ 7493 8181; www.theritzlondon.com; 150 Piccadilly W1; s/d from £400/500, ste from £730; ⊖ Green Park; ✲
What can you say about a hotel that has lent its name to the English lexicon? Arguably London's most celebrated hotel, this 136-room caravanserai has a spectacular position overlooking Green Park and is supposedly the royal family's 'home away from home'. The Long Gallery and Palm Court restaurant have Louis XVI themes; book weeks ahead if you want to sample afternoon tea (£37). A planned extension on Arlington St just east will add 45 rooms.

METROPOLITAN Map pp84-5   Hotel £££
☎ 7647 1000; www.metropolitan.co.uk; 19 Old Park Lane W1; r £375-475, ste £650-3200; ⊖ Hyde Park Corner; ✲ ৬
In the same stable as the Halkin (p343), the 155-room Metropolitan is another minimalist hotel – 'stripped of nonessentials' (as they say) and decorated in shades of cream and burlwood. It attracts a super trendy, well-heeled crowd (more rock star than royal, really). The hotel's Japanese restaurant, Nobu (p241), is outstanding.

SANCTUARY HOUSE HOTEL
Map pp84-5   Hotel ££
☎ 7799 4044; www.fullershotels.com; 33 Tothill St SW1; s & d £160-195; ⊖ St James's Park; ৬
A cut above your average pub hotel, the 34-room Sanctuary lives up to its name, although it's just a few minutes' walk from Westminster Abbey and the Houses of Parliament. The style is very much cosy English country cottage and some of the refurbished superior rooms even contain four-poster beds. Rates don't include breakfast.

MAYFAIR

BROWN'S Map p66   Hotel £££
☎ 7493 6020; www.brownshotel.com; 30 Albemarle St W1; s & d from £340, ste from £800; ⊖ Green Park; ✲ ৬
A stunner of a five-star number, this 117-room hotel was created in 1837 from 11 houses joined together. Some traditional features retained from an earlier refurbishment of the public areas include stained-glass windows, Edwardian oak panelling, working fireplaces and gilt mirrors. The 117

updated rooms have soft colours and works by young English artists.

CLARIDGE'S Map p90   Hotel £££
☎ 7629 8860; www.claridges.co.uk;
55 Brook St W1; r from £500, ste from £740,
breakfast £21-28; ⊖ Bond St; 🔀
Claridge's, with 203 rooms, is one of the greatest of London's five-star hotels, a cherished reminder of a bygone era. Many of the art deco features of the public areas and suites were designed in the late 1920s, and some of the 1930s-vintage furniture once graced the staterooms of the decommissioned SS *Normandie*. Celebrity chef Gordon Ramsay reigns over the kitchen (see p243).

DORCHESTER Map p90   Hotel £££
☎ 7629 8888; www.dorchesterhotel.com;
Park Lane W1; s/d from £400/570, ste from £710,
breakfast £25; ⊖ Hyde Park Corner; 🔀 ♿
This opulent *tour de force* has been the hotel of choice for movie stars, fashionistas and those with a wallop of cash to spend and an image to cultivate since it opened for business in 1931. The lobby is possibly the most lavish in London and the enormous ballroom with its sparkling mirrored walls remains one of the most grand today. In the 250 guestrooms a mixture of antique and individual furniture, four-poster beds, chaise lounges and roaring fireplaces evoke an English country-house feel.

CHESTERFIELD Map p90   Hotel £££
☎ 7491 2622; www.redcarnationhotels.com;
35 Charles St W1; s £145-225, d & tw £170-305, ste from £325, breakfast £17.50-19.50; ⊖ Green Park; 🔀
Just a block west of Berkeley Sq, the 110-room Chesterfield comprises five floors of refinement and lustre hidden behind a fairly plain Georgian town house. It has ceilings with mouldings, marble floors and period-style furnishings as you'd expect from one of the grand dames of London digs. We love the four themed suites (Music, Garden, Theatre and Study).

NUMBER 5 MADDOX STREET
Map p66   Hotel £££
☎ 7647 0200; www.5maddoxstreet.com; 5 Maddox St W1; ste £270-750; ⊖ Oxford Circus; 🔀
This all-suite hotel with a dozen units aims to provide a 'contemporary, urban sanctuary' and succeeds, making you feel more like you're 'super styling' in your own rented pad than staying in a hotel. On show are Eastern themes, natural tones and an exquisite eye for detail, along with all the technical facilities the contemporary traveller could require. Reception is on the 1st floor.

MARYLEBONE
DORSET SQUARE HOTEL
Map p90   Hotel £££
☎ 7723 7874; www.dorsetsquare.co.uk; 39 Dorset Sq NW1; d from £240, ste from £350; ⊖ Baker St
Two combined Regency town houses contain this enchanting 37-room hotel overlooking leafy Dorset Sq, where the very first cricket ground was laid in 1814 (which explains the cricket memorabilia in glass cases in the lobby). Guestrooms are small but almost dreamily decorated with a blend of antiques, sumptuous fabrics and crown-canopied or four-poster beds.

MANDEVILLE Map p90   Hotel £££
☎ 7935 5599; www.mandeville.co.uk;
Mandeville Pl W1; s/d £290/316, ste from £440;
⊖ Bond St; 🔀 ♿
This wonderful deluxe hotel, within listening distance of the Wigmore Hall and within view of the Wallace Collection, has 142 luxuriously appointed guestrooms designed by Stephen Ryan. What we find unforgettable are the explosively coloured DeVigne Bar (another Ryan creation) and the view from the roof terrace of the Penthouse Suite (£880).

CUMBERLAND HOTEL Map p90   Hotel ££
☎ 0870 333 9280; www.thecumberland.co.uk;
Great Cumberland Pl W1; s £100-295, d £120-370;
⊖ Marble Arch; 🔀 ♿
You'll be forgiven for thinking you've accidentally stumbled into a contemporary art gallery in the hangar-sized lobby with larger-than-life sculptures and backlit perspex columns. Some of the more than 1000 guestrooms have views of nearby Hyde Park. Celebrity chef Gary Rhodes is in charge of the in-house brasserie-bar called Rhodes W1.

DURRANTS HOTEL Map p90   Hotel £££
☎ 7935 8131; www.durrantshotel.co.uk; George St W1; s £125-155, d/f £250/265, ste £295-425;
⊖ Bond St; 🔀
This sprawling 92-room hotel, just behind the Wallace Collection and excellently placed for Oxford St shopping, was once a

country inn and still retains something of the feel of a gentleman's club. The same family has owned it since 1921.

LEONARD HOTEL Map p90   Hotel ££
☎ 7935 2010; www.theleonard.com; 15 Seymour St W1; s £80-125, d £170-180; ⊖ Marble Arch
Originally four separate town houses and later a hospital, the Leonard has 46 guestrooms that are somewhat conservative in appearance but elegant and very comfortable nonetheless. Eschew the standard rooms if you can; they're on the 5th floor and the lift finishes at the 4th.

HOTEL LA PLACE Map p90   Hotel ££
☎ 7486 2323; www.hotellaplace.com; 11 Nottingham Pl W1; s £99-130, d £139-145, f £164-179, ste £139-160; ⊖ Baker St
The 18 rooms here are very much in the traditional mode, but impeccably cared for, and some have updated bathrooms. The friendly family management has installed a 24-hour wine bar downstairs, with comfy – and stylishly colourful – modern lounge chairs.

SUMNER HOTEL Map p90   Hotel ££
☎ 7723 2244; www.thesumner.com; 54 Upper Berkeley St W1; r £155-193; ⊖ Marble Arch; 🖳
This five-star town house hotel just north of Oxford St and west of Portman Sq offers incomparable value for such a central location. The 20 rooms are contemporary, comfortable and of a good size, but the focal point of the hotel is the sitting room with an original fireplace and hardwood flooring.

EDWARD LEAR HOTEL Map p90   Hotel £
☎ 7402 5401; www.edlear.com; 28-30 Seymour St W1; s £72-91, d & tw £89-113, f £115-145, with shared bathroom s £52-60, d & tw £60-74, f £89-113; ⊖ Marble Arch
Once the home of a Victorian painter and poet (well, composer of limericks), the 31 rooms of this flower-bedecked terrace hotel offer basic accommodation at spectacular prices. Indeed, never undersold, the management claims that 'if you can find a hotel as close to Oxford St that quotes a lower price, we will match it'.

GLYNNE COURT HOTEL Map p90   Hotel ££
☎ 7258 1010; www.glynne-court-hotel.com; 41 Great Cumberland Pl W1; s/d/tr/f £55/90/95/110; ⊖ Marble Arch

Fairly typical for this price range and location, the Glynne Court has 15 rooms housed in an historic listed building dating back to the late 18th century. The owners are eager to please and will be happy to tell you about the colourful history of 41 Cumberland Pl. Watch out for dark basement singles.

THE CITY

Staying in the Square Mile gives you the chance to see another side of this area – after the workers have left for the suburbs or during its eerily quiet weekends, the City is pretty much all yours to enjoy. This is a great way to avoid the crowds, yet with easy access to such attractions as the Tower of London and the restaurants and bars of Shoreditch.

THREADNEEDLES
Map p100   Boutique Hotel £££
☎ 7657 8080; www.theetoncollection.com; 5 Threadneedle St EC2; s & d £282-558, ste from £480; ⊖ Bank; 🖳 📶
You have to know this place is here. It's wonderfully anonymous, though once through the doorway the grand circular lobby, which is furnished in a vaguely art deco style and covered with a hand-painted glass dome, comes into view. The 69 rooms here may not be cutting edge, but they're very pleasantly done, all with high ceilings, free wi-fi and dark, sleek furnishings.

ANDAZ LIVERPOOL STREET
Map p100   Hotel £££
☎ 7961 1234; www.andaz.com; 40 Liverpool St EC2; r from £115-230, ste from £260; ⊖ Liverpool St; 🖳 ♿ 📶
Another discreet choice, the former loud and proud Great Eastern Hotel is now a Hyatt branded property, the London flagship for its youth-oriented Andaz chain. There's no reception here, just black-clad staff who check you in on mini laptops. Rooms are cool and spacious, with free nonalcoholic drinks, wi-fi and local calls. On top of this there are five restaurants and a subterranean Masonic Temple discovered during the hotel's refit in the '90s. This is a solid choice, well located, and a good compromise between business and boutique.

YHA LONDON ST PAUL'S Map p100 Hostel £

☎ 0845 371 9012; www.yha.org.uk; 36 Carter Lane
EC4; 11-bed dm £15.95-28.95, s £18.95-35.95,
d £38.95-71.95, tr £58.95-107.95; ✈ St Paul's
This excellent 193-bed hostel stands in the
very shadow of St Paul's Cathedral and opposite the Tate Modern. Most rooms have
two, three or four beds, though 19 rooms
have five to 11 beds. There's a licensed
cafeteria but no kitchen. Check out the
building's gorgeous facade in Carter St
while you're here!

CITY YMCA EC1 Map p150 Hostel £

☎ 7614 5000; www.cityymca.org; 8 Errol St EC1;
s with shared bathroom £35, tw £64; ✈ Barbican
Much nicer than its nearby Barbican
counterpart, this 112-room budget hotel
on four floors has better bathrooms, and
bedrooms with TV and phone for incoming
calls. There are also four single rooms. It's
very handy for Shoreditch, and as such you
should book about a month ahead. There
are also weekly rates (single/twin including
all meals £215/370) and free internet access
from terminals downstairs.

THE SOUTH BANK

With this once-neglected riverbank now one
of the city's most vibrant stretches, the South
Bank has become an increasingly good and useful base. Restaurant and bar pickings are slim-
mer than in the West End, but who wouldn't
be tempted to stay near the Tate Modern or
Borough Market and all its epicurean offerings?
Further westwards you'll find yourself near the
London Eye and the multitude of attractions
within the London County Hall.

WATERLOO

LONDON MARRIOTT COUNTY HALL
Map p126 Hotel £££
☎ 7928 5200; www.marriott.co.uk/lonch;
Westminster Bridge Rd SE1; r from £240, with river
views from £270, breakfast £18.95-20.95;
✈ Westminster; 🐾 🖴 🐕 🕭
This elegant 200-room hotel is famed for
its fabulous close-up views of the Thames
and the Houses of Parliament. It was
formerly the headquarters of the Greater
London Council; the atmosphere in the
traditional rooms remains somewhat stuffy
in a wood-panelled kind of way. There's
a well-equipped fitness centre on the

5th floor and a 25m-long pool on the 6th
floor.

BANKSIDE & SOUTHWARK

SOUTHWARK ROSE HOTEL
Map p126 Boutique Hotel ££
☎ 7015 1480; www.southwarkrosehotel.co.uk;
47 Southwark Bridge Rd SW1; d & tw £125-190,
breakfast £9-13, weekend rate incl breakfast £95;
✈ London Bridge; 🐾 🖴 🕭
Billed as London's first 'budget boutique'
hotel, this 84-room place just minutes
from the Thames is very versatile. Service
is good, prices are reasonable and while
the rooms are compact, they're stylish in
a vaguely minimalist way, with plum-col-
oured headboards, white fluffy duvets and
silver lampshades. There's a great penthouse lounge bar on the 6th floor.

MAD HATTER Map p126 Hotel ££
☎ 7401 9222; www.madhatterhotel.com;
3-7 Stamford St SE1; r £145-165, breakfast £7.50-11,
weekend rate incl breakfast £90-100;
✈ Southwark; 🐾 🖴 🕭
Its 30 rooms across three floors are quite
generic, but the Mad Hatter feels slightly
homier than most chain hotels – it belongs
to the Fuller's brewery group – thanks to
its traditionally styled reception area and
(surprise, surprise) an adjacent pub with
the same name.

BOROUGH & BERMONDSEY

BERMONDSEY SQUARE HOTEL
Map p126 Boutique Hotel ££
☎ 0870 111 2525, 0774 884 3350; www.bermond
seysquarehotel.co.uk; Bermondsey Sq, Tower Bridge
Rd SE1; r £119-299; ✈ London Bridge; 🐾 🖴 🕭
Just the ticket for this up-and-coming area
of South London crying out for quality
accommodation is this stunner of a purpose-built boutique hotel with 79 rooms.
The smallish standard rooms make good
use of space with an excellent work area
and Apple TVs that link with your laptop
and iPod, a rainforest of a shower and great
modern art on the walls. Our favourites,
though, are at the top: four themed loft
rooms with '60s music names like 'Ruby'
and 'Lucy' and views all the way to...no,
not the Eiffel Tower but the top of Crystal
Palace. Below, London's most famous flea
market (p227) takes place on Fridays.

ST CHRISTOPHER'S VILLAGE

Map p126   Hostel £

☎ 7407 1856; www.st-christophers.co.uk; 161-163 Borough High St SE1; dm £12.50-21, d & tw £46-56; ✆ Borough or London Bridge; 🖳

This 185-bed place is the flagship of a hostel chain with basic, but cheap and clean accommodation totalling eight properties across London. There's a roof garden with bar, barbecue and excellent views of the Thames, as well as a cinema and Belushi's bar below for serious partying to 2am weekdays and 4am at the weekend. Dorms have four to 14 beds. Its two nearby branches (same contact details) are St Christopher's Inn (Map p126; 121 Borough High St SE1), with 50 beds, another pub below and a small veranda, and the Orient Espresso (Map p126; 59-61 Borough High St SE1), with 40 beds, a laundry, cafe, and dormitory for women only.

DOVER CASTLE HOSTEL Map p126   Hostel £

☎ 7403 7773; www.dovercastlehostel.co.uk; 6a Great Dover St SE1; dm £12-19.50, per week £80; ✆ Borough; 🖳

This 80-bed hostel in a four-storey Victorian terrace house has a welcoming bar below it as well as lounge with TV, kitchen facilities, luggage storage and laundry (£5). It's a somewhat frayed but friendly place to stay. Dorms have between three and

12 beds. It also organises flat shares from single/double £119/150 per week including bills.

HYDE PARK TO CHELSEA

Gracious Chelsea and Kensington present London at its elegant best, though count on very little in the midrange and budget categories. Accommodation is more modest in Victoria and Pimlico. The former may not be the most attractive part of London, but you'll be very close to major transport links and the hotels in this area are better value than those in Earl's Court. Pimlico is more residential, though convenient for the Tate Britain at Millbank.

CHELSEA & BELGRAVIA

B+B BELGRAVIA Map pp136-7   B&B ££

☎ 7259 8570; www.bb-belgravia.com; 64-66 Ebury St SW1; s/d/tw/tr/q £99/120/130/150/160; ✆ Victoria; 🖳 ♿

This B&B, stunningly remodelled in contemporary style, boasts a chic black-and-white lounge where you can relax before a fire or watch a DVD, and 17 earth-toned rooms that aren't enormous but have flat-screen TV. There's a lovely back garden and guests get to use hotel bicycles for free.

STUDENT DIGS

During university holidays (generally mid-March to late April, late June to September and mid-December to mid-January), student dorms and halls of residence are open to paying visitors. Accommodation might not be in the luxury class, but it certainly will be clean and cheap.

Try LSE Vacations (☎ 7955 7575; www.lsevacations.co.uk; s/tw/tr/q £53/75/99/110, s with shared bathroom £43), the agent for the London School of Economics, whose eight halls include the 800-bed Bankside House (Map p126; ☎ 7107 5750; 24 Sumner St SE1; ✆ Southwark), just behind the Tate Modern on the South Bank; the 281-bed Butler's Wharf Residence (Map p126; ☎ 7107 5798; 11 Gainsford St SE1; ✆ Tower Hill or London Bridge), almost at the foot of Tower Bridge in Shad Thames; and High Holborn Residence (Map pp70–1; ☎ 7107 5737; 178 High Holborn WC1; ✆ Holborn), with 495 beds near Covent Garden. Open school holidays.

Halls administered by King's College Conference & Vacation Bureau (☎ 7248 1700; www.kcl.ac.uk/kcvb; s £30-40, d £52-60) include the Great Dover St Apartments (Map p126; ☎ 7407 0068; 165 Great Dover St SE1; ✆ Borough), with 716 rooms in a big brick pile in Borough, and the Stamford St Apartments (Map p126; ☎ 7633 2182; 127 Stamford St SE1; ✆ Waterloo), with 535 rooms near Waterloo. Open late June to September.

Other options worth trying:

International Students' House (Map p90; ☎ 7631 8310; www.ish.org.uk; 229 Great Portland St W1; dm £13-19, s/d/tr from £38/60/78; ✆ Great Portland St) Unusual for a hall of residence, this 700-bed place near Regent's Park has rooms available all year.

Finsbury Residences (Map p150; ☎ 7040 8811; www.city.ac.uk/ems; 15 Bastwick St EC1; s with shared bathroom £19-21; ✆ Barbican) These residences between Islington and the City comprise two modern halls with 320 rooms belonging to City University London. Open mid-July to August.

KNIGHTSBRIDGE, KENSINGTON & HYDE PARK

HALKIN Map pp136-7   Hotel £££

☎ 7333 1000; www.halkin.como.bz; Halkin St SW1; r from £390, ste from £600, breakfast £20-25; ✷ Hyde Park Corner; ☒ ▣

The chichi Halkin is for business travellers of a minimalist bent. Bedroom doors are hidden within curved wooden hallways, and the 41 rooms are filled with natural light, cream walls, burlwood panelling and large all-marble bathrooms. Gratefully they are as stylishly uncluttered as the staff, who wear Armani-designed uniforms.

LANESBOROUGH Map pp136-7   Hotel £££

☎ 7259 5599; www.lanesborough.com; Hyde Park Corner; s £355-415, d £475-575, ste from £675; ✷ Hyde Park Corner; ☒ ▣ ♿

This is where visiting divas doze and Regency opulence meets state-of-the-art technology. The 95 guestrooms are lavishly appointed, including the three-bedroom Royal Suite which, at £7500, is among the most expensive digs in town. The staff, as you might expect, are impeccably dressed in bowler hats and morning suits and are insufferably correct.

BLAKES Map pp136-7   Hotel £££

☎ 7370 6701; www.blakeshotels.com; 33 Roland Gardens SW7; s £175, d £225-375, ste from £565, breakfast £17.50-25; ✷ Gloucester Rd; ☒ ▣

For classic style (and celebrity spotting), one of your first choices in London should be Blakes: five Victorian houses cobbled into one hotel, painted an authoritative, very serious dark green and designed by the incomparable Anouska Hempel of the Hempel Hotel (p348). Its 41 guestrooms are elegantly decked out with four-poster beds (with and without canopies), rich fabrics and antiques set on bleached hardwood floors. It has a pretty but postage-stamp-sized courtyard.

KNIGHTSBRIDGE HOTEL
Map pp136-7   Hotel £££

☎ 7584 6300; www.knightsbridgehotel.com; 10 Beaufort Gardens SW3; s £170-185, d & tw £210-295, ste £345, breakfast £16-17.50; ✷ Knightsbridge; ☒ ▣

The lovely Knightsbridge occupies a 200-year-old house just around the corner from

Harrods (p224) on a quiet, tree-lined street and has elegant and beautiful interiors done in a sumptuous, subtle and modern English style. Some of the 44 rooms, although beautifully furnished, are very small for the price, though the oak-and-granite bathrooms are great.

CADOGAN HOTEL Map pp136-7   Hotel ££

☎ 7235 7141; 75 Sloane St SW1; r £180-335, ste from £395, breakfast £20-25; ✷ Sloane Sq; ☒ ▣ ♿

This 64-room hotel is a wonderful hybrid, with two lower floors contemporary in style and the recently refurbished top two a wonderful vestige from Edwardian times, filled with polished oak panels, wing chairs, rich heavy fabrics and a refined drawing room for afternoon tea. Not surprisingly, the two rooms that are the most indulgent (and coveted) are No 118 where Oscar Wilde was arrested for 'Indecent acts' in 1895 and the Lillie Langtry room (No 109) – all rose wallpaper, feather boas and pink lace – where the eponymous actress (and mistress to Edward VII) once laid her head.

GORE Map pp136-7   Hotel ££

☎ 7584 6601; www.gorehotel.com; 190 Queen's Gate SW7; s £140-180, d £180-280, ste from £440, breakfast £12.95-16.95; ✷ Gloucester Rd or High St Kensington; ☒ ▣

Charismatically kooky, this splendid 50-room hotel is a veritable palace of polished mahogany, oriental carpets, antique-style bathrooms, potted aspidistras, and portraits and prints (some 4500, in fact) covering every square centimetre of wall space. The attached Bistrot One Ninety Queen's Gate is a fine place for brunch or a pre- or post-concert drink for the nearby Royal Albert Hall. A two-/three-course lunch is £21.50/23.50.

NUMBER SIXTEEN
Map pp136-7   Boutique Hotel ££

☎ 7589 5232; www.numbersixteenhotel.co.uk; 16 Sumner Pl SW7; s £120, d £165-270, breakfast £16-17.50; ✷ South Kensington; ☒ ▣

With cool grey muted colours, tasteful clarity and choice art throughout, Number Sixteen is a stunning place to stay, with 42 individually designed rooms, a cosy drawing room and fully stocked library. And wait till you see the idyllic back garden set around a fishpond with a few cosy snugs, or have breakfast in the conservatory.

ASTER HOUSE Map pp136-7   B&B ££

☎ 7581 5888; www.asterhouse.com; 3 Sumner Pl SW7; s £100-120, d & tw £145-250; ⊖ South Kensington; ⊠ ▣

What has made this Singaporean-run property the winner of Visit London's best B&B award not just once but three times? No doubt the quintessential English aura, the welcoming staff, the comfortable rooms with good-quality furnishings and sparkling bathrooms, and the reasonable price all had something to do with it. Oh, and that's not to mention the lovely garden and the delightful plant-filled Orangerie where breakfast is served on the 1st floor.

VICARAGE HOTEL Map p178   Hotel ££

☎ 7229 4030; www.londonvicaragehotel.com; 10 Vicarage Gate W8; s/d/tr/q £93/122/156/172, with shared bathroom £55/93/117/128; ⊖ High St Kensington; ▣

Gilt mirrors, sconces, chandeliers and striped red-and-gold wallpaper – this former Victorian home is about as close as you will get to staying in a living, breathing Linley Sambourne House (p175). The 17 rooms are less lavish, but atmospherically olde-worlde English all the same and slightly larger than usual. The 3rd- and 4th-floor rooms have shared bathrooms.

MEININGER Map pp136-7   Hostel £

☎ 7590 6910; www.meininger-hostels.com; 65-67 Queen's Gate SW7; dm £15-27, s/d/tr from £69/90/99; ⊖ Gloucester Rd or South Kensington; ⊠ ▣

Now tenanted in Baden Powell House, London HQ of the Scout Association and next to the Natural History Museum, this German-run 'city hostel & hotel' has 47 spotlessly clean rooms, three dozen of which are dorms with between four and 12 beds. The 11 private rooms all have bathrooms and have a good-size working area. The service here is efficient and correct, and there's a bar in-house and a great roof terrace that hosts barbecues in warm weather.

ASTOR HYDE PARK Map pp136-7   Hostel £

☎ 7581 0103; 191 Queen's Gate SW7; www .astorhostels.co.uk; dm £20-31, tw £70-80, d £80-90; ⊖ Gloucester Rd or High St Kensington; ▣

It's fairly unlikely you've ever seen a hostel like this one, with its wood-panelled walls, bay windows with leaded lights, 19th-century vibe and ever-so-posh address just over from the Royal Albert Hall. It has 150 beds in rooms over five floors (no lift), including dorms with three to 12 beds, and a fabulous kitchen complete with incongruous pool tables. Its sister property, the Astor Kensington (Map pp136–7; ☎ 7373 5138; www.astorhostels.co.uk; 138 Cromwell Rd SW7; dm £13-23, d £60; ⊖ Gloucester Rd), a kilometre or so to the southwest, is every bit as nice but in a modern, upbeat sort of way, and is closer to the action and a tube stop. It's got 120 beds (dorm rooms in bright primary colours have four to 10 beds), a huge and bright modern kitchen, and (joy of joys) a lift.

YHA HOLLAND HOUSE Map p178   Hostel £

☎ 7937 0748; www.yha.org.uk; Holland Walk W8; dm £20.95-27.50; ⊖ High St Kensington; ▣

Built into the Jacobean wing of Holland House (1607) in the middle of Holland Park, this hostel has 201 beds in large rooms with between six and 20 beds. It's large, always busy and rather institutional, but the position is unbeatable. There's a cafe and kitchen.

VICTORIA & PIMLICO

WINDERMERE HOTEL Map pp136-7   Hotel ££

☎ 7834 5163; www.windermere-hotel.co.uk; 142-144 Warwick Way SW1; s £99, d & tw £124-155, f £169; ⊖ Victoria; ▣

The attractive (and award-winning) Windermere has 20 small but individually designed and spotless rooms in a sparkling white mid-Victorian town house. There's a

top picks

GARDENS & COURTYARDS

- Garden Court Hotel (p349)
- Hempel (p348)
- Barmy Badger Backpackers (p352)
- Ace Hotel (p351)
- Academy Hotelp336

top picks

B&BS

- B+B Belgravia (p342)
- Guesthouse West (p350)
- Aster House (opposite)
- Gate Hotel (p350)
- Number 16 St Alfege's (p352)

reliable and reasonably priced restaurant (mains £9.95 to £15.95) on site called the Pimlico Room.

MORGAN HOUSE Map pp136-7   Hotel ££
☎ 7730 2384; www.morganhouse.co.uk; 120 Ebury St SW1; d/tr/f £92/112/132, s/d/tr with shared bathroom £52/72/92; ↔ Victoria; 🖳
The 11-room Morgan House might be humble but it knows how to do pretty, with small bunches of fresh flowers placed in rooms. The options range from a compact but liveable single with shared facilities to a large family room with en suite. The best rooms in the house are the two doubles in the back: No 2 with shared facilities and No 8 with a bathroom.

LUNA SIMONE HOTEL Map pp136-7   Hotel £
☎ 7834 5897; www.lunasimonehotel.com; 47-49 Belgrave Rd SW1; s £60-70, d £85-100, tr £105-120, q £130-150; ↔ Victoria or Pimlico; 🖳
If all of London's budget hotels were like this central, welcoming and spotlessly clean and comfortable 35-room place, we'd all be happy campers. Modern art and some partially slate-tiled bathrooms provide some focal points to the refurbished rooms, and there are free storage facilities if you want to leave bags while travelling; no lift.

ASTOR VICTORIA Map pp136-7   Hostel £
☎ 7834 3077; www.astorhostels.com; 71 Belgrave Rd SW1; dm £17-25, d & tw £50-75; ↔ Pimlico
Mother ship of the Astor group of five hostels (p343), this central place has 180 beds so it is busy without being too impersonal. It is staffed by travellers who are between trips and are a font of information. Dorms have between four and eight beds and there's a handful of twins and doubles.

CLERKENWELL, SHOREDITCH & SPITALFIELDS

Clerkenwell, Spitalfields and especially Shoreditch, with its northern extension Hoxton, are very popular neighbourhoods, and there are a few good places to stay here. Accommodation choices are, for the most part, at the top end, with the exception of the superb value Hoxton Hotel, for which you should book as far ahead as possible!

ROOKERY Map p150   Hotel £££
☎ 7336 0931; www.rookeryhotel.com; Peter's Lane, Cowcross St EC1; s £200, d & tw £240-340, ste £570; ↔ Farringdon; 🐾 🛜
This absolute charmer is a warren of 33 rooms that has been built within a row of 18th-century Georgian houses and fitted out with antique furniture (including a museum-piece collection of Victorian baths, showers and toilets), original wood panelling, statues in the bathrooms and art works selected personally by the owner. There's a small courtyard garden and a wonderfully private and whimsical feel to the whole place.

MALMAISON Map p150   Hotel £££
☎ 7012 3700; www.malmaison-london.com; 18-21 Charterhouse Sq EC1; r only £145-250, ste from £395; ↔ Farringdon; 🐾 🧏 🛜
Facing a picture-postcard leafy square in Clerkenwell, this conservatively chic 97-room hotel feels more like a dangerously expensive cocktail bar when you enter its lobby. Public areas are moodily low-lit, with the exception of the luminous subterranean restaurant; rooms are glamorous, if a little on the small side at this price.

ZETTER Map p150   Boutique Hotel ££
☎ 7324 4444; www.thezetter.com; 86-88 Clerkenwell Rd EC1; r only £170-270, ste from £276; ↔ Farringdon; 🐾 🛜
The Zetter is a special place – a temple of cool with an overlay of kitsch on Clerkenwell's titular street. Its rooms are small but perfectly formed, with Penguin Classics on the bookshelves and hi-tech flat screens and air-conditioning (using water from the hotel's very own bore hole). It's worth investigating the superb weekend deals,

which make some rooms available for as little as £99. The Italian restaurant is also superb.

true
false

HOXTON HOTEL Map p150 — Hotel ££

☎ 7550 1000; www.hoxtonhotels.com; 81 Great Eastern St EC2; r £1-199; ⊖ Old St; 🔲 🔲 🔲

This is hands down the best hotel deal in London. In the heart of Shoreditch, this sleek 205-room hotel aims to make its money by being full each night, rather than ripping its guests off. Nearly all phone calls are free, there's free wi-fi, free computer terminal access in the lobby, free printing and free breakfast at a nearby Prêt à Manger. Rooms are small but stylish, with flat-screen TV, desk and fridge with complimentary bottled water and milk. Best of all is the price – while you have to be very lucky to get one of the £1 rooms, it's quite normal to find a room for £59 or £79 – still excellent deals for this level of comfort.

THE EAST END & DOCKLANDS

RCA CITY HOTEL Map p156 — Hotel ££

☎ 7247 3313; www.cityhotellondon.co.uk; 12 Osborn St E1; s/d/tr/f £150/160/170/200; ⊖ Aldgate East; 🔲 🔲 🔲

This 109-room place is hardly no-frills, but it's got a long way to go before it features in *Wallpaper* magazine. Still, it's at the southernmost end of Brick Lane so is well suited for those with business in the City or out on the town in Shoreditch. An extension that went upward (forming a 6th floor) rather than alongside has increased the room numbers by a quarter and added a bar and restaurant.

OLD SHIP Map p156 — Hotel ££

☎ 8986 1641; www.urbaninns.co.uk; 2 Sylvester Path E8; s £70-80, d £80-100; 🚇 Hackney Central; 🚌 38, 106, 277 or 394; 🔲

This tiny 10-room place facing Mare St two doors down from the landmark Hackney Empire (p311) has 10 surprisingly cheerful rooms and public areas – bold floral wallpaper, TVs screens in gilded frames – that can almost be called 'boutique'. The gastropub of the same name below serves, among other things, excellent English 'tapas' and pies. Hackney is not in the centre of London but

it's a convivial neighbourhood and easily accessible by bus or train.

40 WINKS Map p156 — Guesthouse ££

☎ 7790 0259; www.40winks.org; 109 Mile End Rd E1; s £60-80, d £95-100; ⊖ Stepney Green

Short on space but not on style, this two-room boutique guesthouse in less-than-desirable Stepney Green oozes charm and chotchkies. It is housed in an early-18th-century town house owned by a successful designer and has been used as a location for a number of fashion shoots. The rooms (the single is quite compact) contain most everything you'll need, everything else – shops, cinema, the tube – is five minutes away.

NORTH LONDON

If you wish to base yourself away from the main tourist areas, North London possesses a couple of decent options in several neighbourhoods, including King's Cross, Camden and Hampstead, the latter being one of the city's leafiest and most sought-after residential areas.

CAMDEN

66 CAMDEN SQUARE Map p170 — B&B ££

☎ 7485 4622; rodgerdavis@btinternet.com; 66 Camden Sq NW1; B&B per person £50-60; ⊖ Camden Town; 🔲

This unusual glass-and-teak contemporary space offers great value and the chance to base yourself off a quiet North London square not far from Camden Town and Regent's Park. The owners are fans of things Japanese and the whole house is attractively minimalist – apart from the occasionally noisy macaw. Rooms must be booked in advance.

ST CHRISTOPHER'S INN CAMDEN Map p170 — Hostel £

☎ 7388 1012, 7407 1856; www.st-christophers .co.uk; 48-50 Camden High St NW1; dm £12.90-21, tw £26-50; ⊖ Camden Town or Mornington Cres; 🔲 🔲

This 54-bed branch of the popular hostel chain is five minutes from Camden Town tube station along the High Street, atop the very busy Belushi's bar, which has a 2am licence. Staff are very friendly, there's no curfew, and the lodgings are nice and

true

clean, although some of the private rooms are very small. Dorms have between six and 10 beds. Wi-fi is free, and there's access from terminals costing £1 per 20 minutes.

KING'S CROSS & EUSTON

YHA ST PANCRAS INTERNATIONAL
Map p170   Hostel £

☎ 0845 371 9344; www.yha.org.uk; 79-81 Euston Rd NW1; dm from £21.95, tw £60-70; ✆ King's Cross/St Pancras or Euston; ♿ 🖥 📶
This 185-bed hostel is one of the best in town – well located for the sights even if it is on a busy road, and with a full renovation completed in 2009 the rooms are now

modern, airy and clean, sleeping four to six in dorms (nearly all with private facilities) and with private rooms available, too. There's also air-con in some rooms, free wi-fi, a coin-op laundry, and a good bar and cafe, although there are no self-catering facilities.

CLINK Map p170   Hostel £
☎ 7183 9400 www.clinkhostel.com; 78 King's Cross Rd WC1; dm from £9-26, s £40-70, tw from £50, tr £70-90; ✆ King's Cross/St Pancras; ♿ 🖥 📶
This fantastic 350-bed hostel is housed in a 19th-century magistrates courthouse where Dickens once worked as a scribe and

CHAINS WITHOUT FRILLS

London counts several discount hotel chains that offer clean and modern – if somewhat institutional – accommodation for reasonable rates.

easyHotel (www.easyhotel.com) uses the same pricing model to get bods on bed as its sister airline easyJet does to get bums on seats. It's a functional hotel that offers the best deals to early birds, with rates from £25 up to £60 per room. Each of the garishly orange plastic-moulded rooms contains a bed next to a sink and a shower and toilet unit that could fit on an airplane. There are no phones in the rooms, TV is an optional extra (as is cleaning and fresh linen at £10 a pop) and some rooms have no windows. There are currently four branches in London, including easyHotel Earl's Court (Map p178; 44-48 West Cromwell Rd SW5; ✆ Gloucester Rd), easyHotel Victoria (Map pp136–7; 36-40 Belgrave Rd SW1; ✆ Victoria) and easyHotel Paddington (Map p176; 10 Norfolk Pl W2; ✆ Paddington), which is convenient for the Heathrow Express.

Express by Holiday Inn (☎ 0800 434 040; www.hiexpress.co.uk) is the most upmarket of the chains listed here, and is most notable for its clever locations. Of the two dozen or so properties in central London, for example, is the so-called London City branch (Map p150; ☎ 7300 4300; 275 Old St EC1; ✆ Old St) in the heart of the Shoreditch nightlife area; the Limehouse branch (Map p156; ☎ 7791 3850; 469-475 The Highway E1; ✆ Shadwell, DLR Limehouse) in the East End; and the Southwark branch (Map p126; ☎ 7401 2525; 103-109 Southwark St SE1; ✆ Southwark or London Bridge) behind the Tate Modern. Rates vary wildly but start at about £115/70 for a double during the week/weekend.

Premier Inn (☎ 0870 242 8000; www.premierinn.com) is London's original cheap chain, herding them in and out of mostly converted older buildings at 26 different properties. Hotels are fairly bare-bones, beds are soft, the second bed is a pull-out sofa and there are a lot of 'do nots', but from £110 a night per room on weekdays (£99 at weekends), few guests complain. The original property, London County Hall (Map p126; ☎ 0870 238 3300; Belvedere Rd SE1; ✆ Waterloo), is near the London Eye but doesn't have river views; the Southwark branch (Map p126; ☎ 0870 990 6402; 34 Park St SE1; ✆ London Bridge) is directly behind Shakespeare's Globe. The Euston branch (Map p170; ☎ 0870 238 3301; 1 Duke's Rd WC1; ✆ Euston or King's Cross/St Pancras) is handy to the train stations but is on a very busy street.

Travelodge (☎ 0871 984 8484; www.travelodge.co.uk) charges £75 to £105. Here you get a nicer room, but few public facilities; there's usually no lounge, the reception areas are small and service can be rather cavalier. Of the 16 properties in central London, among the best positioned are the Liverpool Street branch (Map p100; ☎ 0871 984 6190; 1 Harrow Pl E1; ✆ Aldgate), just west of Petticoat Lane, and the Covent Garden branch (Map pp70–1; ☎ 0871 984 6245; 10 Drury Lane WC2; ✆ Holborn or Covent Garden).

Among the best value is the Days Hotel (☎ 0800 028 0400; www.daysinn.co.uk) group, part of the Days Inn chain but with little extras and rooms between £69 and £125. Though the chain is expected to grow, there are just two properties in central London at present, including the new Shoreditch branch (Map p156; ☎ 7613 6500; 419-437 Hackney Rd E2; ✆ Bethnal Green, 🚈 Cambridge Heath, 🚌 48 or 55), which is actually some distance from the trendy neighbourhood in its name but easily accessible by bus, and the Waterloo branch (Map p189; ☎ 7922 1331; 54 Kennington Rd SE1; ✆ Lambeth North), which is really in Lambeth south of Waterloo. But what's in a name?

members of the Clash made an appearance in 1978; some parts of it, including seven tiny cells converted to bedrooms and a pair of wood-panelled court rooms used as a cafe and an internet room, are listed. Rooms feature pod beds (including storage space) in the coloured-coded dormitories (four to 16 beds) and about a third of the 128 rooms have their own bathroom. There's a superb kitchen and a bar in the basement, and the staff are some of the friendliest we've met.

ASHLEE HOUSE Map p170   Hostel £

☎ 7833 9400; www.ashleehouse.co.uk; 261-265 Gray's Inn Rd WC1; dm £14-23, s £45-60, tw £50-60, tr £63-69; ⊖ King's Cross/St Pancras; 🖳 🛜
Run by the same team responsible for the excellent Clink (above), Ashlee House is a friendly and well-run place, though it's pretty shabby compared to its neighbour, with flaking paint and damp in the bathrooms. The large dorms are quite crowded, but generally fine, containing a total of 170 beds. There is a TV lounge in the basement, plus a laundry, decent-sized kitchen, free left-luggage room, free secure lockers and charged internet access.

HAMPSTEAD & HIGHGATE

LA GAFFE Map p166   Hotel ££

☎ 7435 8965; www.lagaffe.co.uk; 107-111 Heath St NW3; s £70, d & tw £85-95, tr £125; ⊖ Hampstead
Perched above a popular Italian restaurant of the same name (see p261), La Gaffe is an eccentric but nonetheless comfortable and cheery 18-room hotel in a 200-year-old cottage located in an affluent and very residential area.

HAMPSTEAD VILLAGE GUEST HOUSE
Map p166   Guesthouse ££

☎ 7435 8679; www.hampsteadguesthouse.com; 2 Kemplay Rd NW3; s/d £75/95, with shared bathroom s £55-65, d £80, studio apt s/d/tr/f £100/125/145/160, breakfast £7; ⊖ Hampstead
This lovely nine-room guesthouse with a quirky character, rustic and antique decor and furnishings, comfy beds and a delightful back garden makes for a great place to stay. There's also a studio apartment that can accommodate up to five people and the hosts are very welcoming – you're even able to invite nonguests round to join you for breakfast!

REGENT'S PARK

MELIÃ WHITE HOUSE Map p166   Hotel ££

☎ 7391 3000; www.solmelia.com; Albany St NW1; r £99-265; ⊖ Great Portland St; 🏷 🛗 🖳 🛜
This enormous 545-room hotel in a stylish white-tile art deco building is unsurprisingly popular with groups, and its rooms are rather on the flouncy side. But the location, just west of Regent's Park and within easy walking distance of Soho and three Underground stations, and the reasonable price make it a great option.

WEST LONDON

From the style hotels of Notting Hill to the hostels of Earl's Court and Shepherd's Bush, West London has traditionally offered a broad range of accommodation options. Bayswater is an extremely convenient location, though some of the streets immediately to the west of Queensway can be run-down and depressing. Parts of Paddington are pretty seedy, too, but there are lots of budget and midrange hotels and it's a good transit location; you can reach Heathrow in 15 minutes via the Heathrow Express. St John's Wood and Maida Vale are quiet, leafy neighbourhoods with very few (but some attractive) accommodation offerings.

ST JOHN'S WOOD & MAIDA VALE

COLONNADE Map p176   Hotel ££

☎ 7286 1052; www.theetoncollection.com; 2 Warrington Cres W9; s £99-130, d £105-150, ste from £155, breakfast £8.50-16; ⊖ Warwick Ave; 🏷 🖳
A charmer in lovely Little Venice, the Colonnade is the handsome Victorian structure where Sigmund Freud sheltered after he fled Vienna in June 1938. Apart from the three in the basement, the 43 guestrooms are light, spacious and relaxing, and just up from the Grand Union Canal.

PADDINGTON & BAYSWATER

HEMPEL Map p176   Boutique Hotel £££

☎ 7298 9000; www.the-hempel.co.uk; 31-35 Craven Hill Gardens W2; d from £189, ste from £499; ⊖ Lancaster Gate or Queensway; 🏷 🖳
This stunner of a boutique hotel, designer Anouska Hempel's minimalist symphony in white and natural tones, still has the ability to impress a dozen years on. The 50 rooms

and studios are effortlessly beautiful, comfortable and unique (the Lioness Den even contains a bed within a cage suspended over a living area!), and the Japanese-style garden opposite is a restful oasis.

HOTEL INDIGO Map p176   Boutique Hotel ££
☎ 7706 4444; www.hipaddington.com; 16 London St W2; s £140, d £155-190; ↔ Paddington;
A magnificent new addition to the Paddington accommodation stable is this 64-room property, part of the boutique division of the huge US InterContinental group of hotels. No dummy this filly, the Indigo takes its inspiration from the 13th-century Fibonacci sequence of numbers (ie pi) that apparently produces shapes in nature. You'll find them throughout – on the glass staircase, at reception, in the carpet, on the bed board – and each of the four floors has its own colour scheme. It's textual and textural; it feels great and we've learned something!

VANCOUVER STUDIOS Map p176   Hotel ££
☎ 7243 1270; www.vancouverstudios.co.uk; 30 Prince's Sq W2; s £89, d & tw £130-160, tr £170, 3-bedroom apt £350; ↔ Bayswater;
Everyone will feel at home in this lovely terrace of 45 stylish and very affordable studios. Rooms all contain kitchenettes but otherwise differ wildly – ranging from a tiny but well-equipped single to a generously sized family room with balcony, and embracing all styles of decoration from faux-mink throws to Japanese to gingham. There's even a walled garden with small fountain.

PARKWOOD HOTEL Map p176   Hotel ££
☎ 7402 2241; www.parkwoodhotel.com; 4 Stanhope Pl W2; s/d/tr/f £75/89/99/115, with shared bathroom s/d/tr £49.50/68.50/79; ↔ Marble Arch
You certainly get value for money at this small hotel. The 16 refurbished rooms are pretty in pink and yellow with candy-striped spreads, crown canopies and potted plants. All but four guestrooms have bathrooms, although they could stand with some updating.

GARDEN COURT HOTEL Map p176   Hotel ££
☎ 7229 2553; www.gardencourthotel.co.uk; 30-31 Kensington Gardens Sq W2; s/d/tr/f

£72/115/150/170, s/d with shared bathroom £48/75; ↔ Bayswater;
Noteworthy for its Beefeater statue grasping a battleaxe in the lobby, the spotless Garden Court is truly a cut above most classic English properties in this price range. While the decor retains a few restrained traditional twirls, there are some discreet designer touches in its 32 guestrooms and the bathrooms are modern. A bonus: guests have access both to the hotel garden and the leafy square across the street.

PAVILION HOTEL Map p176   Hotel ££
☎ 7262 0905; www.pavilionhoteluk.com; 34-36 Sussex Gardens W2; s £60-85, d/tw/tr/f £100/100/120/130; ↔ Paddington
The quirky Pavilion boasts 30 individually themed rooms: Honky Tonky Afro has a 1970s theme, Casablanca a Moorish one and Goldfinger a James Bond theme, while Enter the Dragon conjures up Shanghai nights and Indian Summer is a tribute to Bollywood. They're meant to reflect the hotel's slogan – 'Fashion, Glam & Rock 'n' Roll' – and are both good fun and good value.

CARDIFF HOTEL Map p176   Hotel ££
☎ 7723 9068; www.cardiff-hotel.com; 5-9 Norfolk Sq W2; s £49-65, d/tr/q £95/110/125; ↔ Paddington;
Run by the same family for half a century, the Cardiff overlooks lovely Norfolk Sq, a positive oasis in the warmer months. The 61 guestrooms are of standard size and level of decor but offer one of the best mid-range deals around. The cheapest singles have shower but no toilet.

STYLOTEL Map p176   Hotel ££
☎ 7723 1026; www.stylotel.com; 160-162 Sussex Gardens W2; s/d/tr/q £60/85/105/120, studio ste £149,1-bed ste £179; ↔ Paddington;
The industrial design – scored aluminium treads, opaque green glass, lots of stainless steel – of this 47-room hotel is as self-conscious as the name and the motto ('Not just a hotel, a machine for living in'). But it's a real joy to get such a clean, sleek and contemporary look at these prices and the eight new suites (studios and one-bedroom) around the corner on London St are a big plus for longer-stayers and families.

top picks

BOUTIQUE HOTELS

- Hotel Indigo (p349)
- Bermondsey Square Hotel p341
- Number Sixteen p343
- Mayflower (opposite)
- Rockwell (opposite)

LANCASTER HALL HOTEL

Map p176   Hotel ££

☎ 7723 9276; www.lancaster-hall-hotel.co.uk; 35 Craven Terrace W2; s/tw £65/85, s/d/tr/q with shared bathroom £30/48/60/80; ⊖ Lancaster Gate
A short walk from Kensington Gardens, Lancaster Hall comes in two parts: 80 en-suite rooms in a standard hotel offering all the usual amenities at a midrange price and a recently refurbished 'youth wing' that counts 22 guestrooms with washbasins and shared bathrooms in the corridor,

ELYSEE HOTEL Map p176   Hotel £

☎ 7402 7633; www.hotelelysee.co.uk; 25 Craven Tce W2; s £65-89, d £79-120; ⊖ Lancaster Gate; ✿ 🖳
This budget-category hotel on a quiet street on the north side of Kensington Gardens offers excellent value for its location and class (three stars). A new lift offers a less stressful access to the 55 guestrooms, and the flower-bedecked front facade is welcoming.

OXFORD HOTEL LONDON Map p176   Hotel £

☎ 7402 6860; www.oxfordhotellondon.co.uk; 13-14 Craven Tce W2; s £50-60, d/tr/q £68/83/98; ⊖ Lancaster Gate
For a humble establishment, the 21-room Oxford sure tries hard with its sunny yellow walls and blue-checked bedspreads, although the swirly carpets in the breakfast room and dodgy stairs are a reminder of how tired things can get here. Reception is always welcoming.

NOTTING HILL & PORTOBELLO

PORTOBELLO HOTEL Map p176   Hotel £££

☎ 7727 2777; www.portobello-hotel.co.uk; 22 Stanley Gardens W11; s £150-195, d £ 200-255, tw £225-285, ste from £265; ⊖ Notting Hill Gate; ✿ 🖳

This beautifully appointed 21-room property is in a great location and has been a firm favourite with rock and rollers and movie stars down the years. Rooms and furnishings are done up in a stylish colonial decor and have an exclusive feel to them. There's an in-house restaurant and 24-hour bar to fuel guests on their merry way.

GUESTHOUSE WEST Map p176   B&B ££

☎ 7792 9800; www.guesthousewest.com; 163-165 Westbourne Grove W11; s & d £165-195; ⊖ Westbourne Park or Royal Oak; ✿ 🖳
Dubbing itself as 'Notting Hill's chic reinvention of the traditional bed and breakfast', this lovely guesthouse in a three-storey town house features 20 refreshingly bare and simple yet chic guestrooms with modern four-poster beds, flat-screen TVs, shiny kettles and cream mosaic-tiled bathrooms. The breezy terrace rooms on the ground floor have French doors leading onto a communal wooden terrace and modern artwork hangs in the communal lounge. Cheaper rates (singles and doubles £150 to £180) can be obtained on Sundays to Tuesdays.

MILLER'S RESIDENCE Map p176   B&B ££

☎ 7243 1024; www.millersuk.com; 111a Westbourne Grove W2; s & d £150-195, ste £230; ⊖ Bayswater or Notting Hill Gate; ✿ 🖳
More a five-star B&B than a hotel, this 18th-century rooming house is chock-a-block with curiosities and antique furnishings, and quite literally brimming with personality and objets d'art. The eight rooms come in all shapes, sizes and shades of antique opulence and are tailor-made for a romantic sojourn. The Victorian-style drawing room has to be seen to be believed (preferably by candlelight). Enter from Hereford Rd.

GATE HOTEL Map p176   B&B ££

☎ 7221 0707; www.gatehotel.co.uk; 6 Portobello Rd W11; s £60-70, d £80-100, tr £105-125; ⊖ Notting Hill Gate; 🖳
The half-dozen guestrooms in this old town house with classic frilly English decor and flowery front facade all have private facilities. The management is very welcoming and helpful, and you're as close as you're going to get to the buying and selling of Portobello Rd at a midrange price.

PORTOBELLO GOLD Map p176   Guesthouse £

☎ 7460 4910; www.portobellogold.com; 95-97 Portobello Rd W11; r from £65, apt from £120; ⊖ Notting Hill Gate; 🖳
This homely guesthouse above a pleasant restaurant and pub has seven rooms of varying sizes and quality of furnishings. There are several small doubles and the so-called Large Modern Suite has antique furnishings, a four-poster bed and open-hearth fireplace. The Roof Terrace studio is more up to date and has a galley kitchen and exclusive access to the roof.

EARL'S COURT

ROCKWELL
Map p178   Boutique Hotel ££

☎ 7244 2000; www.therockwell.com; 181-183 Cromwell Rd SW5; s £120, d £160-180, ste from £200; ⊖ Earl's Court; ▤ 🖳
A very welcome and friendly addition to the greater Earl's Court neighbourhood, the 40-room Rockwell is a 'budget boutique' hotel par excellence, carved out of two town houses. The decor puts a contemporary spin on English traditional and the three rooms (LG1, 2 and 3) giving on to the garden are particularly fine.

BASE2STAY Map p178   Hotel ££

☎ 7244 2255, 0845 262 8000; www.base2stay.com; 25 Courtfield Gardens SW5; s £91-96, d & tw £103-199; ⊖ Earl's Court or Gloucester Rd; ▤ 🖳 ♿
base2stay has endeavoured to filter out all the 'unnecessary' extras most hotels offer and concentrate on the 'important' things like communications facilities, music systems and kitchenettes. The result is a pared-down but extremely comfortable 67-room hotel. The cheapest twin has bunk beds.

MAYFLOWER Map p178   Boutique Hotel ££

☎ 7370 0991; www.mayflowerhotel.co.uk; 26-28 Trebovir Rd SW5; s £85-90, d £99-165, tr/f £145/169; ⊖ Earl's Court; 🖳
One of London's cheaper boutique hotels, the 46-room Mayflower has chosen an updated colonial style, with wooden carvings from India, ceiling fans and black-tiled bathrooms. The deluxe doubles all have private balconies and individual furnishings such as a carved double bed. Sister hotels in West London include the nearby Twenty Nevern Square (Map p178; ☎ 7565 9555; 20 Nevern Sq SW5; s £99-120, d £110-140; ⊖ Earl's Court),

with 20 rooms also done up in colonial style, although with a little less black tile and a lot more carved wood that seems to whisper Batavia rather than Bombay, and the 51-room New Linden Hotel (Map p176; ☎ 7221 4312; 58-60 Leinster Sq W2; s £65-79, d £89-139, tr £140-170; ⊖ Notting Hill Gate) between Westbourne Grove and Notting Hill.

RUSHMORE Map p178   Hotel ££

☎ 7370 3839; www.rushmore-hotel.co.uk; 11 Trebovir Rd SW5; s £69-79, d £89-99, tr & q £115-139; ⊖ Earl's Court; 🖳 ♿
The soft pastel colours, draped fabrics and simple-yet-elegant designs of this modest hotel create a cheery, welcoming atmosphere. All 22 guestrooms, which have renovated bathrooms, are of a decent size. Four rooms on the 1st floor have balconies: Nos 11 and 12 face the street and Nos 14 and 15 the courtyard.

MERLYN COURT HOTEL Map p178   Hotel £

☎ 7370 1640; www.merlyncourthotel.com; 2 Barkston Gardens SW5; s/d/tr/f from £56/80/90/95, s/d with shared bathroom £50/70; ⊖ Earl's Court
The Merlyn Court's 18 humble but partly refurbished rooms are unremarkable, but the atmosphere is wonderful, the welcome always warm and it's on a quiet street very close to the Earl's Court tube station. A budget category winner, this one.

ACE HOTEL Map p178   Hostel ££

☎ 7602 6600; www.ace-hotel.co.uk; 16-22 Gunterstone Rd W14; dm £19-29, d £105, d with shared bathroom £56-60; ⊖ Barons Court; 🖳 ♿
Squeaky clean and on a quiet residential street west of Earl's Court (so a bit in the middle of nowhere but close to the tube), this 163-bed place has a contemporary, upbeat feel to it and a fabulous back garden, complete with hot tub. Accommodation is in dorms with between three and eight bunk beds, and there is private accommodation in four double rooms with bathroom, all of which give on to a patio overlooking the garden.

YHA EARL'S COURT Map p178   Hostel £

☎ 7373 7083; www.yha.org.uk; 38 Bolton Gardens SW5; dm £17.50-28.50, tw £44-72; ⊖ Earl's Court; 🖳
The Earl's Court YHA hostel had a remake after a fire a few years ago and, despite

new surrounds, the great atmosphere in this big Victorian pile remains. The place is cheerful but basic: most accommodation (186 beds) is in dormitories of between four and 10 bunk beds. There's a good-sized kitchen, a bright and modern cafe, and a courtyard garden at the back.

BARMY BADGER BACKPACKERS
Map p178   Hostel £

☎ 7370 5213; www.barmybadger.com; 17 Longridge Rd SW5; dm £17-21, d & tw £42; ⊖ Earl's Court; 🖳

Smack bang in the middle of a residential area, this Victorian-town-house-turned-backpackers haven is smaller than many other hostels in town, giving it a homely feel. As a result, some guests settle in for the long haul, attracted no doubt by the lovely back garden and even more attractive weekly rates (from £96 in a six-bed dorm). There's a small kitchen, laundry and 42 beds in 14 rooms. Dorms have four or six beds and there are five twins (three with bathroom).

BARKSTON HOSTEL Map p178   Hostel £

☎ 7373 4322; youthhostel1@yahoo.com; 1 Barkston Gardens SW5; dm £11-14, s/d/tr/q £25/34/45/52; ⊖ Earl's Court; 🖳

A positively enormous place with 315 beds in rooms strewn throughout three Victorian buildings (some of which retain original features such as stained glass), this rather institutional hostel is as cheap a place as you'll find to lay your head in Earl's Court. Dorms count six to eight beds (No 120 looks onto a delightful leafy square) and there are private rooms with shared facilities.

SHEPHERD'S BUSH & HAMMERSMITH

K WEST Map p178   Hotel ££

☎ 7674 1000; www.k-west.co.uk; Richmond Way W14; s £79-119, d £100-159, ste from £450, breakfast £11.50-17; ⊖ Shepherd's Bush; 🐾 🖳 ♿

This very stylish 220-room place hard by Shepherd's Bush Green doesn't look like much from the outside but step inside and you'll encounter a world where dark wood and suede happily coexist with stainless steel and sandblasted glass. Many people come to stay here to take advantage of the indulgent pampering at the K Spa and

there's a buzzy restaurant called (what else?) Kanteen.

ST CHRISTOPHER'S SHEPHERD'S BUSH Map p178   Hostel £

☎ 7407 1856; www.st-christophers.co.uk; 13-15 Shepherd's Bush Green; dm £12.50-21, tw £46-56; ⊖ Shepherd's Bush

Just around the corner from Westfield London, the largest shopping mall in Europe with 265 outlets and 50 eateries, St Christopher's Shepherd's Bush property is right in the middle of the action with no curfew and the tube and a sprawling pub right on the doorstep. The accommodation is rather cramped, but special offers can often mean beds at under £10 per night.

GREENWICH & SOUTHEAST LONDON

Away from the hustle and bustle across the Thames, Greenwich often feels more like a village than most other London neighbourhoods and you may think you've gone and moved to provincial England if you stay out here. It's ideal for those who fancy getting up early to go for a jog through Greenwich Park, complete with great river views, or anyone going to a concert or gig at the O2, the erstwhile Millennium Dome. Night revellers will find it less attractive as (a) there ain't a whole lot happening here and (b) it's difficult to return to from more happening neighbourhoods late at night.

GREENWICH
HARBOUR MASTER'S HOUSE
Map p182   Apartment ££

☎ 8293 9597; http://website.lineone.net/~harbourmaster; 20 Ballast Quay SE10; s & d £75-85, tr & q £85-95; 🚆 Greenwich, DLR Cutty Sark

This self-contained three-room basement apartment is right on the river in a Grade II heritage-listed Georgian building dating to 1855. It combines such mod cons as heated towel rails and full kitchen with the charm of vaulted white-brick ceilings and a vague maritime feel. As it's quite compact, it's likely to work best for couples.

NUMBER 16 ST ALFEGE'S Map p182   B&B £

☎ 8853 4337; www.st-alfeges.co.uk; 16 St Alfege's Passage SE10; s/d £75/90; 🚆 Greenwich, DLR Cutty Sark

Just about the most coveted address in Greenwich ever since it appeared on Channel 5's Hotel Inspector, this gay-owned B&B in the heart of Greenwich has two well-appointed doubles and a single, individually decorated in shades of blue, green or yellow and all with bathroom. The owners do their best to make everyone, gay or straight, feel at home, with chats and cups of tea. For such a central location, the immediate neighbourhood is quiet. Turn the corner into Roan St to find the main door.

YHA LONDON THAMESIDE
Map p182   Hostel £

☎ 7232 2114; www.yha.org.uk; 20 Salter Rd SE16; dm £16-27, tw £39-67; ⊖ Canada Water or Rotherhithe; ▣ ⏃

Facilities at this large flagship YHA hostel are very good, but the location is a bit remote. There's a bar, a restaurant, kitchen facilities and a laundry. Dorm rooms have from four to 10 beds; the 20 twins have bathrooms.

ST CHRISTOPHER'S INN GREENWICH
Map p182   Hostel £

☎ 8858 3591; www.st-christophers.co.uk; 189 Greenwich High Rd SE10; dm £8-25, tw £45-50; ⊖ Greenwich, ▣ Greenwich

The Greenwich branch of this successful chain of hostels has 55 beds and is quieter than some of its more centrally located sister properties (though it stands cheek-by-jowl to Greenwich train station). Dorms have six to eight beds, there's just two twin rooms and there's a pub on site.

NEW CROSS INN Map p182   Hostel £

☎ 8691 7222; www.newcrossinn.co.uk; 323a New Cross Rd SE14; dm £10-16, d & tw £60-72; ▣ New Cross Gate or New Cross

Sister property to the Dover Castle Hostel (p342) in Borough, this 75-bed hostel is in far-flung New Cross, which is southwest of Greenwich. Basic rooms have basin and fridge, there are two kitchens and there's a pub attached. Reach here most easily by train from London Bridge station in about six minutes, though it's also convenient to the newly reopened New Cross Gate station on the overground line. Dorms have four to eight beds.

top picks
HOSTELS

- Astor Hyde Park (p344)
- Clink p347
- Meininger (p344)
- Generator p337)
- St Christopher's Village (p342)

SOUTHWEST LONDON

Suburban Southwest London is not an obvious place to base yourself for a trip to London – it's quite a slog to the centre and more expensive than other parts of suburbia. However, anyone wanting to stay in a quieter, more-refined part of London will be right at home here – near greenery and within reach of the river.

PETERSHAM Map p200   Hotel ££

☎ 8940 0061; www.petershamhotel.co.uk; Nightingale Lane TW10; s £135-160, d £170-235, ste £300, weekend rate s £95-120, d £150; ⊖ Richmond, ▣ Richmond then bus 65

Neatly perched on the slope down Richmond Hill leading across Petersham Meadows towards the Thames, the Petersham offers stunning, Arcadian views at every turn. And its restaurant, with its large windows gazing down to the river, has the very best of these. The 60 rooms are classically styled and offer a wonderful escape from the city.

RICHMOND PARK HOTEL
Map p200   Hotel ££

☎ 8948 4666; www.therichmondparkhotel.com; 3 Petersham Rd TW10; s £87-90, d £99; ⊖ Richmond, ▣ Richmond

This hotel at the bottom of Richmond Hill is a pleasant midrange place for anyone wanting to be right in the centre of Richmond. All 22 rooms have private facilities and are comfortably furnished. While continental breakfast is included, the owners will do a full calorific English slap-up for £5.

EXCURSIONS

EXCURSIONS

No matter how much you love London, getting out of the city is the only way to appreciate just how different the capital is from the rest of the country. Forget – for the most part – ethnic and religious diversity, urban chaos and architectural variety, you're up for a whole different experience, a classic England that's about fish and chips, thatched roofs, cream teas and pubs that close at 11pm. That's not to say there isn't quality outside London – you'll find some fantastic places to eat in the provinces, and the alfresco culture that's taken over London is spreading outward too. If you're here in the summer and head for the coast, you may even get to swim in the sea.

As England is a relatively small country and its transport systems generally fan out from London, almost nowhere is impossibly far away from the capital. However, there are several places within a 60-mile radius of the capital that can be easily visited on a day trip.

CLASSIC TOWNS

If you want to immerse yourself in the historical and academic, the classic towns of Oxford (right) and Cambridge (p361) offer both a serene and intellectual day out. Just over an hour away from London, both have quarters that have remained largely unchanged for some eight centuries. Majestic Canterbury Cathedral (p369) may also take your fancy.

SEASIDE

If you like the seaside and come from the Continent (or America or Australia or just about anywhere), prepare for something completely different. The weather is invariably unreliable, the 'beach' is made up of small stones, and the sea is not so much for swimming, but for gazing at while battling to save your chips from being blown away by gale-force winds. The coastal towns are usually more working-class, with fish-and-chip and kebab shops, kitsch

game halls and B&Bs cheek-by-jowl. Brighton (p363) is the most vivacious of the seaside places, its rapid gentrification having made it almost an extension of London, with cool bars, restaurants and some wonderful places to stay the night. But the real charm is in the classic English seaside towns such as nostalgic Broadstairs, kitschy Margate or oyster-rich Whitstable (for all three, see p367). Medieval Rye (p367) is a great combination of the seaside with a historic town latticed with quaint streets. Romney Marsh and Dungeness (p367) near Rye are some of the weirdest coastal areas you'll ever see.

CASTLES

Over the centuries, successive kings, queens, princes, dukes and barons have tried to outdo each other by building the country's finest country house – and more than one have succeeded. Windsor (p371), official residence of Queen Elizabeth, is the oldest inhabited castle in the world (and while you're out this way you can delve into the gastronomic delights on offer at nearby Bray, see p371). Hever Castle (p372), the childhood home of Henry VIII's second wife, Anne Boleyn, has lovely landscaped gardens while fairytale-like Leeds Castle (p372), set on two lakes in Kent, has been called 'the loveliest castle in the world'. Sissinghurst Castle (p373) is home to one of the planet's most famous contemporary gardens.

OXFORD
☎ 01865

The Victorian poet Matthew Arnold described Oxford, England's first university town, as 'that sweet city with her dreaming spires'. These days the spires coexist with a flourishing commercial city that has some typical

---

WHY NOT WALK?

A great way to get out of London for the day is to join an organised country walk. A good-value, quality and fun option is English Country Walks (www.englishcountrywalks.com; per person incl lunch, transportation & admission £40-80), which takes small groups rambling through farm fields, exploring castles such as Leeds (p372) in Kent or takes you teetering along the Seven Sisters chalk cliffs high above the English Channel. You get the added delight of relaxing (with a beer usually) at one of the traditional pubs along the way. The charming guide is full of informative and entertaining stories about local history, and the excursions start and finish at major London terminals.

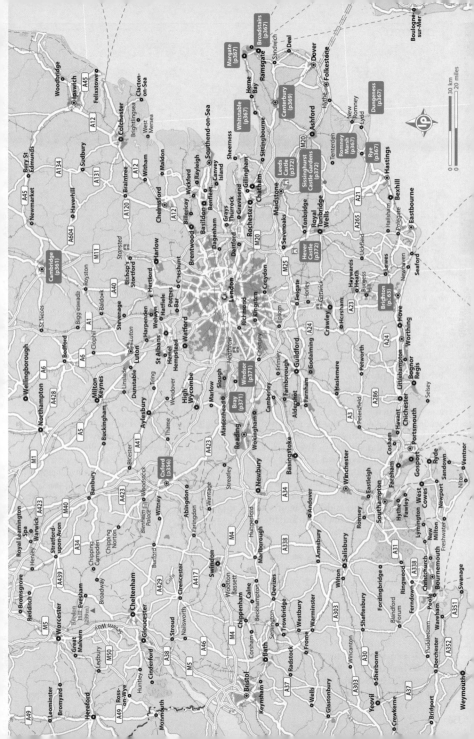

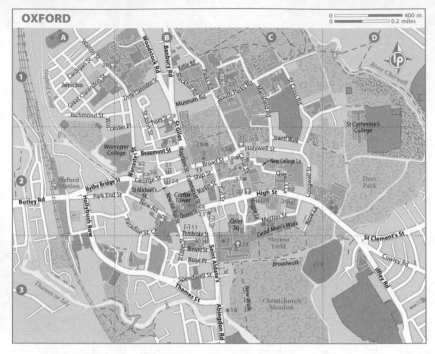

OXFORD

0 _____ 400 m
0 _____ 0.2 miles

urban social problems, including more than its share of street beggars in summer. But for visitors the superb architecture and the unique atmosphere of the colleges – synonymous with academic excellence – and their courtyards and gardens remain major attractions.

The town dates back to the early 12th century (having developed from an earlier Saxon village) and in the intervening period has been responsible for educating more than two dozen British prime ministers, including Margaret Thatcher and Tony Blair. Other alumni include Osama bin Laden and former US president Bill Clinton.

A central and useful landmark is Carfax Tower (☎ 792653; cnr Queen & Cornmarket Sts; adult/child £2/1; ♥ 10am-5.30pm Apr-Sep, to 4.30pm Oct, to 3.30pm Nov-Mar), part of the medieval Church of St Martin demolished in 1896. There's a great view from the top (99 steps). The 'quarter boys' beneath the clock strike the bells every quarter-hour.

Oxford's 38 colleges are scattered around the city. The grandest is Christ Church College (☎ 286573; www.chch.ox.ac.uk; St Aldate's; adult/concession/family £6/4.50/12; ♥ 9am-5pm Mon-Sat, 2-5pm Sun), founded in 1525 and now massively popular with Harry Potter fans, having appeared

in several of the films. The main entrance to the college is below Tom Tower (1682), designed by Christopher Wren and containing Great Tom, a 6.35-tonne bell. Visitors should enter farther down St Aldate's via the wrought-iron gates of the War Memorial Gardens and Broadwalk. The college chapel is Oxford Cathedral, the smallest in the country.

Merton College (☎ 276310; www.merton.ox.ac.uk; Merton St; admission free; ♥ 2-4pm Mon-Fri, 10am-4pm Sat & Sun), founded in 1264, sits just north of Dead Man's Walk. The 14th-century Old Library in Mob Quad is the oldest medieval one still in use in the UK. JRR Tolkien, author of *Lord of the Rings*, taught English at Merton from 1945 until his retirement in 1959.

Stunning Magdalen College (☎ 276000; www.magd .ox.ac.uk; adult/concession £4/3; ♥ noon-6pm Jul-Sep, 1-6pm Oct-Jun), pronounced *maud-lin*, has huge grounds along the River Cherwell, including a deer park. On 1 May it's traditional for students to leap off Magdalen Bridge, although low water levels and recent injuries have led authorities to ban the practice (to no avail). Just opposite are the University Botanic Gardens (☎ 286690; www.botanic-garden.ox.ac.uk; Rose Lane; adult/child/concession £4/free/2.50; ♥ 9am-6pm May-Aug, to 5pm

OXFORD

Mar, Apr, Sep & Oct, to 4.30pm Nov-Feb) established in 1631 and Britain's oldest botanic gardens.

Trinity College (☎ 279900; www.trinity.ox.ac.uk; Broad St; adult/concession £1.50/0.75; 🕑 10am-noon & 2-4pm Mon-Fri, 2-4pm Sat & Sun), one of the smallest colleges in terms of enrolment, was founded in 1555. Next door is **Balliol College** (☎ 277777; www.balliol .ox.ac.uk; cnr Broad & Magdalen Sts; adult/concession £1/0.50) founded in 1263 and though to be the oldest college in Oxford. The huge Gothic wooden doors between the inner and outer quadrangles bear scorch marks from when four Protestant clerics were burned at the stake here in the mid-16th century.

The **University Church of St Mary the Virgin** (☎ 279111; www.university-church.ox.ac.uk; tower adult/ concession/family £3/2.50/10; 🕑 9am-6pm Mon-Sat, noon-6pm Sun Jul & Aug, 9am-5pm Mon-Sat, noon-5pm Sun Sep-Jun) has a 14th-century tower that can be climbed

(124 steps) for a fantastic view of the town's 'dreaming spires'.

The Palladian-style **Radcliffe Camera** (1749) functions as a reading room for the **Bodleian Library** (☎ 277224; www.bodley.ox.ac.uk; Catte St; tours £6; 🕑 9am-5pm Mon-Fri, to 4.30pm Sat, tours 10.30am, 11.30am, 2pm & 3pm) and boasts Britain's third-largest dome. Check out the **Bridge of Sighs**, a 1914 copy of the famous Venice bridge, spanning New College Lane just east of the library. To the north is the brutalist **New Bodleian Library** (☎ 277162; cnr Broad St & Parks Rd) designed in 1938 by Sir Giles Gilbert Scott, the architect responsible for the Battersea Power Station (p192) and the iconic red telephone box (booth). Wren's first major work, the 1669 **Sheldonian Theatre** (☎ 277299; www.sheldon.ox.ac.uk; adult/concession £2/1; 🕑 10am-12.30pm & 2-4.30pm Mon-Sat Mar-Oct, to 3.30pm Mon-Sat Nov-Feb), is where matriculations, graduations and occasional concerts take place.

Oxford has some excellent (free) museums, among them the **University Museum of Natural History** (☎ 272950, www.oum.ox.ac.uk; Parks Rd; admission free; 🕑 10am-5pm), famous for its dinosaur and dodo skeletons, and the attached (and incomparable) **Pitt Rivers Museum** (☎ 270927; www.prm .ox.ac.uk; Parks Rd; admission free; 🕑 noon-4.30pm Mon, 1-4.30pm Tue-Sun), an Aladdin's cave spread over three floors and crammed with such things as voodoo dolls and shrunken heads from the Caribbean and Pacific. Visitors are given torches (flashlights) to 'explore' the lower Court Gallery and are allowed to open all the drawers. Great stuff.

The **Ashmolean Museum** (☎ 278000; www.ashmolean .org; Beaumont St; admission free; 🕑 10am-5pm Tue-Sat, 2-5pm Sun), which opened in 1683 and is Britain's oldest, houses a stunning collection of antiquities as well as European and British art (Rembrandt, Michelangelo, Turner, Picasso etc). The museum was closed at the time of research while a stunning new building, designed by architect Rick Mather, was being completed to replace all but the original Cockerell Building (1845). It will provide some 39 new galleries and 100% more display space than the former building.

Modern Art Oxford (☎ 722733; www.modernartoxford .org.uk; 30 Pembroke St; admission free; 🕑 10am-5pm Tue-Sat, noon-5pm Sun) has established itself as the best contemporary art museum outside London – both inside and out; a recent exhibition saw the building's facade transformed into a colourful wall festooned with political slogans. Guided tours depart at 1pm Tuesday and Thursday and at 11am or 3pm on Saturday.

The Museum of Oxford (☎ 252761; www.museum ofoxford.org; cnr St Aldate's & Blue Boar St; admission free, audioguide adult/concession/family £4/3.50/12; ☺ 10am-5pm Tue-Fri, noon-5pm Sat & Sun) housed in the wedding-cake Victorian Oxford Town Hall (check out the ornate Central Hall on the 1st floor) offers an easy introduction to the city's long history, from prehistoric creatures to modern times, and includes re-created shops and flats.

A great way to soak up Oxford's atmosphere is to take to the Isis (the name of the Thames in these parts) in a punt. These can be hired from the Magdalen Bridge Boathouse (☎ 202643; www.oxfordpunting.com; Magdalen Bridge; punting max 5 people per hr £14, deposit £30, chauffeured boat max 4 people per 30 min £20, with bottle of wine £25; ☺ 9.30am-9pm Mar-Oct) just below the northeast end of Magdalen Bridge, and Salters Boat Hire (☎ 243421; www.salterssteamers.co.ok; St Aldate's; punting/rowing boat max 5/4 people per hr £20, deposit £20; ☺ 10am-5pm Mar-Oct) next to the Head of the River pub on Folly Bridge. Salters also offer a 40-minute river steamer cruise (adult/child £6.50/3.50).

INFORMATION

Carfax Tower is just under a kilometre southeast of the train station and about half that distance from the bus station in grassless Gloucester Green.

Tourist office (☎ 252200; www.visitoxford.org; 15-16 Broad St; ☺ 9.30am-5pm Mon-Sat, 10am-4pm Sun) Staff can book accommodation; regular 1½-hour themed (CS Lewis & JRR Tolkien, Harry Potter, Tudor Oxford etc) walking tours (adult £7.50-10.50, child £3.50-6.50, concession £6.50-10.50) leave the tourist office at 11am, 1.30pm (themed tour) and 2pm daily with additional tours at 10.30am and 1pm in peak seasons.

EATING & DRINKING

In addition to the following, there are plenty of ethnic eateries – Indian, Chinese, Thai and so on – along Cowley Rd, off High St southeast of Magdalen College.

Quod (☎ 202505; www.quod.co.uk; 92-94 High St; mains £10-15.95; ☺ 7am-11pm Mon-Sat, to 10.30pm Sun) Perennially popular for its smart surroundings, as well as for its grills, fish and pasta, this is the place Oxford students drag the rich uncle when he's in town. Try its afternoon tea (£5.95 to £15.50; from 3pm to 5.30pm).

Jamie's Italian (☎ 838383; www.jamiesitalian.com; 24-26 George St; mains £9.95-15.95) The first of celebrity chef Jamie Oliver's ever-expanding affordable Italian chain, this open-plan and very central restaurant serves rustic and unfussy dishes with ingredients sourced both in Italy and the UK.

Grand Café (☎ 204463; 84 High St; teas £7.50-16.50; ☺ 9am-11pm Mon-Sat, to 6pm Sun) This museum piece of a cafe done up in the Regency style – it's really more Brighton than Oxford – is on the site of England's first coffee house (1650), with great cream teas in the afternoon.

Chutneys (☎ 724241; 36 St Michael's St; mains £7.95-11.95) A mostly vegetarian south Indian brasserie a curry whiff away from the bus station, Chutneys attracts customers as much by its brightly coloured exterior as its affordable *idlis* (fermented rice cakes eaten with chutney) and *dosa*s (filled rice-flour pancakes). Express lunch is just £7.50.

G&D's (☎ 245952; 94 St Aldate's; 1/2 scoops £2.15/3.15; ☺ 8am-midnight) One of three outlets of Oxford's own mini ice cream chain, this branch will satisfy a craving for frozen lactose till the (almost) wee hours.

TRANSPORT: OXFORD

Distance from London 57 miles

Direction Northwest

Travel time 1½ hours by bus, about 1¼ by train.

Bus Oxford Tube (☎ 772250; www.oxfordtube.com) and Oxford Express (☎ 785400; www.oxfordbus.co.uk) buses depart every 12 to 30 minutes round the clock from Victoria coach station (single £13, return £16) and can be boarded at various other points in London too, including Marble Arch, Notting Hill Gate and Shepherd's Bush.

Car The M40 provides access from London, but Oxford has a serious traffic problem and parking is a nightmare. We highly recommend that you don't drive. If you do, use the Park & Ride system – as you approach the city follow the signs for the car parks.

Train There are two trains (☎ 0845 748 4950; www.nationalrail.co.uk) per hour from London's Paddington train station (adult same-day return £20).

PUNTING FOR PUNTERS

Punting looks fairly straightforward, but we've landed in the drink, heels (and other bits) over head, enough times to say unequivocally that it ain't. Still, that shouldn't deter anyone who isn't afraid of getting a wee bit wet.

Here are a half-dozen basic tips on how to move the punt forward and, in doing so, not fall in the water:

- Standing at the end of the punt, lift the pole out of the water at the side of the punt.
- Allow the pole to slide through your hands and touch the bottom of the river.
- Tilt the pole forward (ie in the direction you're headed) and push down to propel the punt forward.
- Twist the pole to free the end from the mud at the bottom of the river.
- Let the pole float up and trail behind the punt (you can then use it as a rudder to steer with).
- If you've not fallen in (yet), raise the pole out of the water and into the vertical position to begin the cycle again.

Freud (☎ 311171; 119 Walton St; ⏲ 10.30am-2am Mon-Sat, to midnight Sun) A boho hangout in a crumbling desanctified church, with distressed pews, stained-glass windows and modern art on the walls, this cerebrally named venue is especially popular with students.

Eagle & Child (☎ 302925; 49 St Giles) The so-called Rabbit Room of this atmospheric old pub, with its snugs and Ganymede-like 'Bird & Baby' pub sign, is where JRR Tolkien, CS Lewis and other members of the Inklings literary society met for lunch on Tuesdays.

King's Arms (☎ 242369; 40 Hollywell St) This sprawling place with its nooks and crannies and photographs on the walls of famous guests (including the Queen Mum pulling herself a pint) is the place to get lost in on a chilly winter's afternoon.

CAMBRIDGE

☎ 01223

Even though Oxford students wouldn't like to admit it, Cambridge beats Oxford as the quintessential English university town. Whereas Oxford has a solid record in educating political grandees, Cambridge's reputation lies more in the technological sphere. Past names to have worked and studied here range from Isaac Newton and Charles Darwin to the discoverers of DNA, James Watson and Francis Crick, and renowned physicist Stephen Hawking. In some senses it's the mother of English scientific ideas. And even though you may think all those medieval and neo-Gothic buildings look serious, Cambridge was where English humour was nurtured, producing John Cleese, Michael Palin and others of the Monty Python team.

Founded in the 13th century, contemporary Cambridge is less touristy and more manageable than its competitor. However, note that during exam time – mid-April to late June – its colleges are often shut to the public.

The centre of town lies in a wide bend of the River Cam. The best-known section of riverbank is the mile-long Backs, which combines lush scenery with superb views of half a dozen colleges (the other 25 colleges are scattered throughout the city).

The Round Church (Church of the Holy Sepulchre; ☎ 311602; www.christianheritageuk.org.uk; cnr Round Church & Bridge Sts; adult/child £2/free; ⏲ 10am-5pm Tue-Sat, 1-5pm Sun) was built in 1130 to commemorate its namesake in Jerusalem. Nearby is St John's College (☎ 338600; www.joh.cam.ac.uk; St John's St; adult/seniors & child 12-17 years/under 12 years £3/2/free; ⏲ 10am-5pm Mon-Fri, 9.30am-5pm Sat & Sun Mar-Oct, 9.30am-5pm Sat & Sun Nov-Feb), with a 16th-century gatehouse and three beautiful courtyards, two of which date from the 17th century. From the third court, the picturesque Bridge of Sighs spans the Cam. Stand in the centre and watch the punts float by.

Just south of St John's, Trinity College (☎ 338400; www.trin.cam.ac.uk; Trinity Lane; adult/child 12-17 years/under 12 years £3/1/free; ⏲ 10am-5pm) is one of the largest, wealthiest and most attractive colleges. It was established in 1546 by Henry VIII, whose statue peers out from the top niche of the great gateway (he's holding a chair leg instead of the royal sceptre, the result of a student prank). Check the website for frequent free entry periods. The Great Court, the largest in either Cambridge or Oxford, incorporates some fine 15th-century buildings. Beyond the Great Court are the cloisters of Nevile's Court and the dignified Wren Library (⏲ noon-2pm Mon-Fri & 10.30am-12.30pm Sat during term), built by Sir Christopher in the 1680s.

Next come Gonville and Caius (pronounced keys) College and King's College (☎ 331100; www.kings.cam.ac.uk; King's Pde; adult/concession £5/3.50; ⏲ 9.30am-3.30pm Mon-Fri, 9.30am-3.15pm Sat, 1.15-2.15pm Sun term time, 9.30am-4.30pm Mon-Sat, 10am-5pm Sun university holidays), one of the most sublime buildings in Europe and Cambridge's

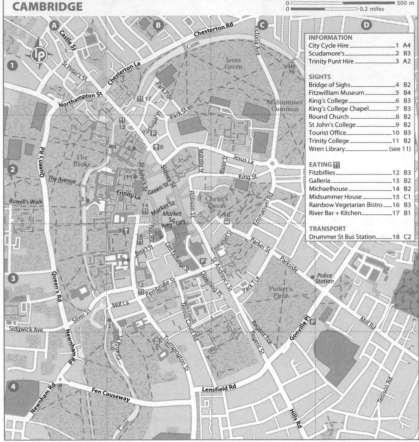

INFORMATION
City Cycle Hire.................................1 A4
Scudamore's....................................2 B3
Trinity Punt Hire...........................3 A2

SIGHTS
Bridge of Sighs...............................4 B2
Fitzwilliam Museum......................5 B4
King's College.................................6 B3
King's College Chapel..................7 B3
Round Church.................................8 B2
St John's College...........................9 B2
Tourist Office...............................10 B3
Trinity College.............................11 B2
Wren Library............................(see 11)

EATING 🍴
Fitzbillies.......................................12 B3
Galleria..13 B2
Michaelhouse...............................14 B2
Midsummer House........................15 C1
Rainbow Vegetarian Bistro......16 B3
River Bar + Kitchen.....................17 B1

TRANSPORT
Drummer St Bus Station...........18 C2

foremost tourist attraction. The chapel was begun in 1446 by Henry VI and completed around 1516. Henry VI's successors, notably Henry VIII, added the intricate fan vaulting and elaborate wood-and-stone carvings of the interior. The chapel comes alive when the choir sings and there are services during term and in July (phone for performance times).

The Fitzwilliam Museum (☎ 332900; www.fitz museum.cam.ac.uk; Trumpington St; admission free, tours £3; 🕑 10am-5pm Tue-Sat, noon-5pm Sun, guided tours 2.45pm Sun), otherwise known as 'The Fitz', was one of the first art museums in the UK. It houses Egyptian sarcophagi, Greek and Roman art, Chinese ceramics and English glass in the lower galleries, while the upper galleries have paintings by Titian, Leonardo, Rubens, Rembrandt and Picasso, among others.

Taking a punt along the Backs is great fun, but can also be a wet and hectic experience. The secret to propelling these flat-bottomed boats is to push gently on the pole to get the punt moving and then to use the pole as a rudder to keep on course. See p361 for tips. In Cambridge, as opposed to Oxford, the tradition is to punt from the flat, decked end of the boat.

INFORMATION

City Cycle Hire (☎ 365629; www.citycyclehire.com; 61 Newnham Rd; bikes half-day/day/24 hr from £5/8/10 plus a £40 deposit; 🕑 9am-5.30pm Mon-Fri year round, 9am-5pm Sat Apr-Sep)

Scudamore's (☎ 359750; www.scudamores.com; Granta Pl, Mill La; per hr £16-18, 45-min chauffeured rides £14 per person) Has punts for hire and chauffeured rides.

Tourist office (☎ 0871 226 8006; www.visitcambridge
.org; Old Library, Wheeler St; ⏱ 10am-5pm Mon-Sat,
11am-3pm Sun May-Sep, 10am-5.30pm Mon-Sat Oct-Apr)
Just south of Market Sq. Staff can arrange accommodation
and two-hour walking tours (adult/child including entry
to King's College £10/8.50), leaving at 1.30pm year-round,
with more departures during summer.

Trinity Punt Hire (☎ 338800; www.trin.cam.ac.uk; Trinity St, Trinity College; punts per hr £12) Has punts for hire
and chauffeured rides.

EATING

In addition to the places listed below, cheap
Indian and Chinese eateries can be found
where Lensfield Rd meets Regent St towards
the train station.

Midsummer House (☎ 369299; www.midsummerhouse
.co.uk; Midsummer Common; set lunch £24, 3-course dinner
£65; ⏱ Mon-Sat) Two Michelin stars adorn this
fantastic modern French restaurant, which
has one of the best lunch offers around. It's a
formal affair, with the restaurant's two floors
sitting on the corner of the common, near the
river. Book ahead.

River Bar + Kitchen (☎ 307030; www.riverbarkitchen
.co.uk; Quayside, off Bridge St; mains £10-15) Conran-
designed, light and modern, this is a two-
storey riverside brasserie that attracts a smart
young crowd with its modern Mediterranean
cuisine.

Galleria (☎ 362054; www.galleriacambridge.co.uk; 33
Bridge St; mains £8-17, 2-course set lunch £19.95) If you
didn't manage the punting, watch others try
from this Continental-style cafe overlooking
the Cam that serves good French and Mediterranean cuisine.

TRANSPORT: CAMBRIDGE

Distance from London 54 miles

Direction North

Travel time Two hours by bus, 55 minutes by train.

Bus National Express (☎ 0870 580 8080; www
.nationalexpress.com) runs hourly shuttle buses (day
return from £8, 2 hrs 10 mins).

Car The M11 connects the London Orbital Motorway
(M25) to Cambridge. Take Exit 13 onto A1303 (Mad-
ingley Rd) and follow it towards the city centre.

Train There are trains (☎ 0845 748 4950; www
.nationalrail.co.uk) every 30 minutes from both
King's Cross and Liverpool St stations (day return
from £20, 45 minutes to one hour).

Rainbow Vegetarian Bistro (☎ 321551; www.rainbow
cafe.co.uk; 9a King's Pde; mains £8-10; ⏱ 10am-9.30pm Tue-
Sat, 10am-4pm Sun & Mon) We love this massively
popular cafe, as do Cambridge's carnivores
and herbivores alike who head down the small
passageway opposite King's College to try experimental vegetarian and vegan food, such
as Latvian potato bake, Libyan couscous and
spicy Indonesian gado gado.

Michaelhouse (☎ 309167; Trinity St; mains £4-6.50;
⏱ 9.30am-5.30pm Mon-Fri) A beautifully converted
church, this stylish cafe has fair-trade coffee and sandwiches, which can be eaten in
a pew amid impressive medieval arches. A
top choice.

Fitzbillies (☎ 352500; www.fitzbillies.co.uk; 52 Trumpington St; pastries & cakes from £2) Cambridge's much-
loved, oldest bakery is famous for its super
sticky Chelsea buns and cakes, but it serves
as a restaurant in the evenings.

BRIGHTON
☎ 01273

With its heady mix of seediness and sophistication, Brighton is London's favourite seaside
resort. Owing to its university and language
schools, it has a young cosmopolitan population as well as atmospheric cafes, excellent restaurants and a varied nightlife. And Brighton
caters to everyone. Despite its rapid gentrification, Brighton hasn't lost its working-class
soul, with the tacky but charming Brighton
Pier and beach seafood huts still extant. Just
northeast of the pier is Kemp Town (dubbed
Camp Town), home to one of Britain's most
vibrant gay scenes.

The town's character essentially dates from
the mid-1780s when the dissolute, music-loving
Prince Regent (later King George IV) built
his outrageous summer palace, the Royal Pavilion, here in the 18th century as a venue for
lavish parties by the sea. And that charmingly
seedy, 'great-place-for-a-dirty-weekend' vibe
lasted throughout the gang-ridden 1930s of
Graham Greene's novel *Brighton Rock* and the
mods-versus-rockers rivalry of the 1960s.

Any visit to Brighton is essentially about
life's simple pleasures – shopping in the trendy
boutiques in the narrow streets called 'The
Lanes' or in the separate 'North Laine', eating,
and hanging out and buying a stick of hard
'Brighton rock' candy among the tacky stalls
and amusement rides on Brighton Pier (☎ 609361;
www.brightonpier.co.uk; Madeira Dr; admission free). Just
north of the pier is the very up-to-date Brighton

BRIGHTON

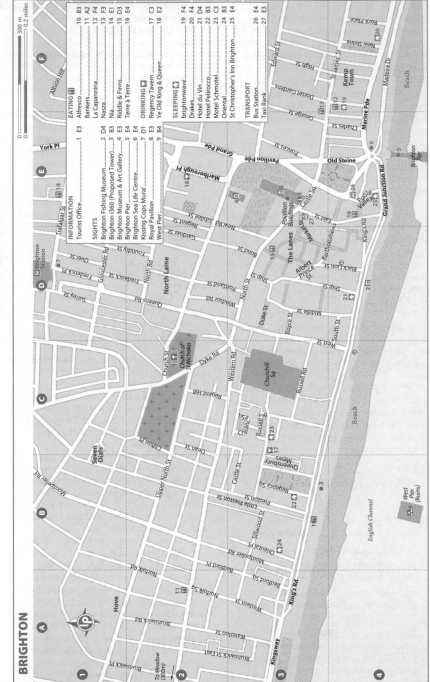

INFORMATION		
Tourist Office......................	1	E3

SIGHTS		
Brighton Fishing Museum........	2	D4
Brighton i360 (Proposed Tower)...	3	B3
Brighton Museum & Art Gallery...	4	E3
Brighton Pier........................	5	E4
Brighton Sea Life Centre........	6	E4
Kissing Cops Mural................	7	D1
Royal Pavilion......................	8	E3
West Pier............................	9	B4

EATING		
Alfresco..............................	10	B3
Bankers..............................	11	A2
La Capannina......................	12	F4
Nasza................................	13	F3
Nia....................................	14	E1
Riddle & Finns......................	15	D3
Terre à Terre........................	16	E4

DRINKING		
Regency Tavern....................	17	C3
Ye Old King & Queen............	18	E2

SLEEPING		
brightonwave......................	19	F4
Drakes................................	20	F4
Hotel du Vin........................	21	D4
Hotel Pelirocco....................	22	B3
Motel Schmotel....................	23	C3
Oriental..............................	24	B3
St Christopher's Inn Brighton...	25	E4

TRANSPORT		
Bus Station..........................	26	E4
Taxi Rank............................	27	E3

Sea Life Centre (☎ 604234; www.sealife.co.uk; Marine Pde; adult/child/concession/family £14.50/10/12.50/40; ⏰ 10am-6pm Mar-Sep, to 5pm Oct Feb), the world's oldest operating aquarium, with some 150 species in almost five dozen tanks and pools, as well as a walk-though tunnel.

Brighton's primary attraction, the Royal Pavilion (☎ 290900; www.royalpavilion.org.uk; Royal Pavilion Gdns; adult/child/concession/family £8.80/5.10/6.90/22.70; ⏰ 9.30am-5.45pm Apr-Sep, 10am-5.15pm Oct-Mar), is an extraordinary folly – Indian palace on the outside and over-the-top chinoiserie inside. The first pavilion, built in 1787, was a classical villa. It wasn't until the early 19th century, when things Asian became all the rage, that the current confection began to take shape under the direction of John Nash, architect of Regent's Park and its surrounding crescents. The entire over-the-top edifice, which Queen Victoria – who found Brighton 'far too crowded' – sold to the town in 1850, is not to be missed, but of the dozen or so rooms, described in a concise, self-paced audioguide tour, have an especially good look on the ground floor at the Long Gallery with its metal bamboo staircases, the Banqueting Room (especially the domed and painted ceiling and the rococo furnishings), the superb Great Kitchen and the restored Music Room with its nine lotus-shaped chandeliers and Chinese murals in vermilion and gold. Not to be missed on the 1st floor are the South Galleries and Queen Victoria's Apartments (including her water closet). Also keep an eye out for Rex Whistler's humorous painting *HRH The Prince Regent Awakening the Spirit of Brighton* (1944)

in which the overweight (and all-but-naked) prince is rousing a nubile 'Brighton' with a lascivious look in his eye. It's just before the entrance to the tearoom.

Across the Royal Pavilion Gardens is the surprisingly captivating Brighton Museum & Art Gallery (☎ 290900; www.virtualmuseum.info; Royal Pavilion Gdns; admission free; ⏰ 10am-7pm Tue, 10am-5pm Wed-Sat, 2-5pm Sun). Of the half-dozen galleries here our favourites are World Art, which effectively displays the spoils and souvenirs brought home by 19th-century colonialists; the excellent Brighton History gallery, with its 'naughty-but-nice' displays; and the new Ancient Egypt collection. Other galleries show ceramics, fashion and costumes and fine arts from the 15th to 20th centuries.

The historic West Pier (www.westpier.co.uk), which closed in 1975, began to collapse into the sea in December 2002 and, having since caught fire twice, is just a dark shadow on the water. It's still quite an arresting, beautiful sight and many visitors – including thousands of starlings in November and December – flock to see it. There are plans to mark the spot on shore with a controversial 176m-tall observation mast called the Brighton i360 designed by the same husband-and-wife team of architects behind the London Eye. For details, see the West Pier website or visit the quirky Brighton Fishing Museum (☎ 723064; 201 King's Rd Arches; admission free; ⏰ 9am-5pm) on the seafront.

Check out the Kissing Cops mural (Frederick Pl) by guerrilla artist Banksy just south of the train station.

INFORMATION

Tourist office (☎ 0906 711 2255; www.visitbrighton .com; 4-5 Pavilion Buildings; ⏰ 9am-5.30pm Mar-Oct, 10am-5pm Nov-Feb)

EATING & DRINKING

Brighton and the contiguous town of Hove to the west have more restaurants per head of population than anywhere in the UK outside London. For a snack pick up little tubs of seafood (from £2) from the little stands lining the beach.

Alfresco (☎ 206523; Milkmaid Pavilion, King's Rd Arches; mains £11.95-19.95) Housed in a glassed-in pavilion both on and above the beach, this is the place to enjoy Italian specialities like lobster linguine while enjoying uninterrupted seafront views. Pizzas are £9.95 to £13.95.

TRANSPORT: BRIGHTON

Distance from London 51 miles

Direction South

Travel time One hour 50 minutes by bus, 50 minutes by fast train.

Bus National Express (☎ 0871 781 8181; www .nationalexpress.com; return from £10.20, promotional fares online).

Car The M23/A23 runs straight into Brighton town centre.

Train There are about 40 fast trains (☎ 0845 748 4950; www.nationalrail.co.uk) each day from London's Victoria station (return £20.90), and slightly slower ones from Blackfriars, London Bridge and King's Cross (return £17).

Riddle & Fins (☎ 323008; www.riddleandfinns.co.uk; 11 Meeting House Lane; mains £12.95-17.50) We're told that Gordon Ramsay called the fare served in this elegant oyster bar hidden in The Lanes 'seafood as it should be'. We don't care about that, but we'll come back for our favourite bivalves (from £10 a half-dozen) and more bubbly.

Meadow (☎ 721182; www.themeadowrestaurant.co.uk; 64 Western Rd; mains £10-16.50; ☯ closed Mon & dinner Sun) Arguably the area's finest restaurant, this elegant but relaxed eatery in Hove serves 'new British' cuisine, with meat, fish and produce sourced in Sussex and Kent.

Terre à Terre (☎ 729051; www.terreaterre.co.uk; 71 East St; mains £10.50-14.60) A gourmet vegetarian restaurant is not an oxymoron; we discovered some of the most inventive meatless dishes we've ever had at this very popular and stylish eatery.

La Capannina (☎ 680839; 15 Madeira Pl; main £9.95-17) Many people say this is the best homestyle Italian restaurant in Brighton and we tend to agree. Pizzas (£5.75 to £8.80) are baked in a wood-burning stove and the gnocchi and raviolis are made in-house.

Nia (☎ 671371; www.nia-brighton.co.uk; 87-88 Trafalgar St; mains £8.95-14.50; ☯ 9am-5pm Sun & Mon, to 9.30pm Tue-Thu, to 10.30pm Fri & Sat) Rustic but chic, with solid wood tables, large windows and a chalkboard menu, Nia is one of the loveliest cafes in a town not at a loss for same. Set lunch starts at £7.25.

Nasza (☎ 622770; 22 St James St; mains £5.95-11.50) This friendly Polish eatery called 'Our' serves some of our favourite comfort food, including *pierogi* (dumplings stuffed with meat or cheese and potatoes), *bigos*, a 'hunter's stew' of cabbage and pork, and *golabki* (stuffed cabbage).

Bankers (☎ 328267; www.bankersrestaurant.com; 116a Western Rd; mains £2.95-4.95; ☯ 11.30am-10pm) While Brighton's beloved chippie has a fancy restaurant attached, we always come for some of the best takeaway fish and chips on the south coast.

Regency Tavern (☎ 325652; 32-34 Russell Sq) This unprepossessing place from the outside hides what looks like a room from the Royal Pavilion: striped wallpaper, cameo portraits and brass palm trees.

Ye Old King & Queen (☎ 607207; 13-17 Marlborough Pl; ☯ to midnight) Cobbled together from an 18th-century farmhouse, a nobleman's hall and the former Brighton Corn Exchange, this cavernous boozer is a convenient place to sup a pint after visiting the Royal Pavilion.

SLEEPING

Most places have a minimum two-night stay on weekends. You should book ahead for weekends in summer and during the Brighton Festival in May and Brighton Pride in late July/early August.

Hotel du Vin (☎ 718588; www.hotelduvin.com; Ship St; d/ste from £170/275; ☒ ☐) Located in a former wine merchant's home, this award-winning hotel has an ornate double helix staircase, a wonderful Tudor entrance, an excellent wine bar and 49 elegant rooms named after wine producers.

Drakes (☎ 696394; www.drakesofbrighton.com; 44 Marine Pde; s/d from £100/130; ☒ ☐) Classy atmosphere, fantastic sea views from many of its 20 rooms, obliging staff, and beautiful 'feature rooms' (£155 to £325) with clawfoot baths in front of a massive bay window overlooking the sea (try room 104). It's our favourite in Brighton.

brightonwave (☎ 676794; www.brightonwave.co.uk; 10 Madeira Pl; s £60-65, d £90-175; ☒ ☐ ☒) Combining the cool, muted design of a boutique hotel with the warm welcome of a small B&B, the eight-room brightonwave offers great value, service and style. Fantastic (late) breakfasts, too.

Hotel Pelirocco (☎ 327055; www.hotelpelirocco.co.uk; s/d from £50/90; ☐) Still crazy after all these years, Brighton's original punk 'n' fashion hotel has 19 brilliant (as in colour and name) rooms – choose from Durex Play, Betty's Boudoir, Soul Supreme and the evocatively named Pussy (among others).

Oriental (☎ 205050; www.orientalbrighton.co.uk; 9 Oriental Pl; s £50-75, d £75-200; ☐) Stylishly decorated in luscious plums and teals, this renovated nine-room boho hotel has aromatherapy lights, spa baths in its superior rooms and organic breakfasts.

Motel Schmotel (☎ 326129; www.motelschmotel.co.uk; 37 Russel Sq; s £45-65, d £55-110, tr £90-140; ☐) We'll come back to this minimalist and very affordable nine-room B&B just round the corner from chichi Regency Sq as much for the name as the great breakfasts and attention to guests' needs (daily weather displayed on a chalkboard, useful lists of recommended restaurants etc).

St Christopher's Inn Brighton (☎ 202035; www.st-christophers.co.uk; dm £17-22, d £46-110; ☐) This new kid in town down from London, where they've got digs in Borough and four other locations, offers both hostel and budget accommodation in a very central location with 116 beds above a popular, very busy bar called Belushi's.

BROADSTAIRS, MARGATE & WHITSTABLE

Each of these seaside towns has distinct character and bags of charm. Broadstairs is a nostalgic place with a patina of both Victorian and postwar history. Slightly dilapidated Margate is the archetypal kitsch English seaside resort, now forever associated with homegirl Tracey Emin, the Brit artist. Increasingly gentrified Whitstable is the best place for fresh, locally farmed oysters. It's been nicknamed 'Islington-on-Sea' since arty and wealthy Londoners began buying up the gorgeous fishermen's huts as second homes.

People mostly head to Broadstairs to soak up the atmosphere, swim (in good weather) and just hang around. Stroll along the Broadstairs Promenade, or take the cliffside walkway from Viking Bay to secluded Louisa Bay. The Dickens House Museum (☎ 01843-861232; www.dickensfellowship.org, 2 Victoria Pde, Broadstairs; adult/concession £2.50/1.40; ☼ 10am-4.30pm) commemorates the writer's love of, and association with, Broadstairs; there's also a Dickens festival in the middle of June.

Alternatively, you could visit Margate's unusual Shell Grotto (☎ 01843-220008; www.shellgrotto.co.uk; Grotto Hill, Margate; adult/child £3/1.50; ☼ 10am-5pm Apr-Oct, 11am-4pm Sat & Sun Nov-Apr), a mysterious underground temple dating from pagan times. It's off Northdown Rd. The 1000-year-old Margate Caves (1 Northdown Rd, Cliftonville) are closed due to subsidence, but keep an eye out for them reopening. There is a church, smugglers' refuge, dungeon, cave paintings and some witty (if not 100% proven) historical explanations.

Check out the summer huts on the beach in Whitstable, the traditional working-class summer weekend hangouts, painted in a rainbow of colours and given affectionate names. The annual Whitstable Oyster Festival (www.whitstableoysterfestival.co.uk) is held in the third week of July.

INFORMATION

Broadstairs tourist office (☎ 01843-577671; www.visitthanet.co.uk; 6b High St; ☼ 9.15am-4.45pm Mon-Fri year-round, 10am-4pm Sat & Sun Apr-Sep, 10am-4.45pm Sat Oct-Mar)

Margate tourist office (☎ 01843-577671; www.visitthanet.co.uk; 12-13 The Parade; ☼ 9.15am-4.45pm Mon-Fri year-round, 10am-4pm Sat & Sun Apr-Sep, 10am-4.45pm Sat Oct-Mar)

Whitstable tourist office (☎ 01227-378100; www.canterbury.co.uk; 57 Harbour St; ☼ 10am-5pm Mon-Sat Jul & Aug, 10am-4pm Mon-Sat Sep-Jun)

EATING

Wheelers Oyster Bar (☎ 01227-273311; 8 High St, Whitstable; mains £8-20; ☼ Thu-Tue) This tiny place is a favourite with locals, with delicious fresh Whitstable oysters.

Whitstable Oyster Fishery Company (☎ 01227-276856; www.oysterfishery.co.uk; Royal Native Oyster Stores, Horsbridge, Whitstable; mains £13-28; ☼ lunch & dinner Tue-Sat, lunch Sun) Enjoy all kinds of seafood in the refurbished company HQ with great sea views. Have your oysters with champagne, of course.

RYE, ROMNEY MARSH & DUNGENESS

☎ 01797

The impossibly picturesque medieval town of Rye looks like it has been preserved in historical formaldehyde. Not even the most talented Hollywood set-designers could have come up with a better representation of a Ye Olde English

---

TRANSPORT: BROADSTAIRS, MARGATE & WHITSTABLE

Distance from London Whitstable 58 miles, Margate 74 miles, Broadstairs 78 miles

Direction East

Travel time 1¼ to 2¾ hours

Bus Five daily departures to Ramsgate stop at all three towns (outward 10.30am to 8.30pm, return 8.05am to 5.55pm). Same-day returns are £13.40 to Whitstable, and £14.20 to Broadstairs or Margate.

Car Follow the M2; at the Margate/Ramsgate sign, follow the Thanet Way.

Train Trains (☎ 0845 748 4950; www.nationalrail.co.uk) from London's Victoria station to Ramsgate leave every 30 minutes (1¼ to two hours); a day return is £20.10 to Whitstable, and £25.30 to Margate, Broadstairs and Ramsgate.

Village: the half-timbered Tudor buildings, Georgian town houses, winding cobbled streets, abundant flowerpots and strong literary associations should be enough to temper even the most hard-bitten cynic's weariness of the made-for-tourism look. (All the same, such cynics should avoid crowded summer weekends.)

The town is easily covered on foot. Around the corner from the tourist office, in Strand Quay, are a number of antique shops selling all kinds of wonderful junk. From here walk up cobbled Mermaid St, with its timber-framed houses dating from the 15th century.

Turn right at the T-junction for the Georgian Lamb House (☎ 224982; www.nationaltrust.org.uk; West St, Rye; adult/child £3.80/2; ☼ 2-6pm Wed & Sat Apr-Oct), mostly dating from 1722. It was the home of American writer Henry James from 1898 to 1916 (he wrote *The Wings of the Dove* here). Continue around the dog-leg until you come out at gorgeous Church Sq. The Church of St Mary the Virgin (tower views adult/child £2.20/1.20; ☼ 9am-4pm winter, 9am-6pm rest of the year) incorporates several styles. The turret clock (1561) is the oldest in England and still works with its original pendulum mechanism. There are great views from the church tower. Turn right at the square's east corner for Ypres Tower & Castle Museum (☎ 226728; www.ryemuseum.co.uk; 3 East Rye St, Rye; tower only adult/child £3/2.50; ☼ 10.30am-1pm & 2-5pm Thu-Mon Apr-Oct, tower only 10.30am-3.30pm Nov-Mar), variously pronounced yeeps or wipers, part of Rye's former fortifications.

The town celebrates its medieval heritage with a two-day festival each August, and in September there is the two-week Festival of Music & the Arts.

East of Rye lie Romney Marsh and Dungeness, England's most otherworldly coast, pic-tured in Derek Jarman's film *The Garden*. The vast, flat Romney Marsh has a unique ecology, with unusual flora and fauna, and was once a favourite place for smuggling. Dotted across Romney Marsh is also a collection of tiny medieval churches – start with St Augustine's in Brookland. Desolate, barren Dungeness is the world's largest expanse of shingle and home to an unlikely combination of an old lighthouse (☎ 232 1300; tower views adult/child £3/2; ☼ 10.30am-5pm Jul-mid-Sep, 11am-5pm Sat & Sun mid-Sep-Jun), a nuclear power station and the Dungeness Royal Society for the Protection of Birds Nature Reserve (RSPB; ☎ 320588; www.rspb.org.uk/reserves/Dungeness; Dungeness Rd, Lydd; adult/child/concession £3/1/2; ☼ reserve 9am-dusk, visitors centre 10am-5pm Apr-Oct, 10am-4pm Nov-Mar). Jarman's famous garden can still be seen on the road to the old lighthouse, although the new owner of the black cottage has a sign out asking you to respect their privacy, so please do.

INFORMATION

Hythe Visitors Centre (Red Lion Sq; ☼ 9am-5pm Mon-Sat) Can book accommodation and offer information on Dungeness; open to personal callers only.

Romney Marsh Countryside Project (☎ 367974; www.rmcp.co.uk) This project has a useful website and organises all sorts of interesting guided walks across the marsh.

Rye Hire (☎ 223033; Cyprus Pl; bicycles per day £15) There is a cycle path to Lydd, followed by a road down to Dungeness.

Rye tourist office (☎ 226696; www.visitrye.co.uk; Strand Quay; ☼ 10am-5pm Apr-Oct, 10am-4pm Mon-Sat Nov-Mar) Gives out a free guide to the town and offers audio tours (adult/child/concession £2.50/1/1.50). Can also help with basic information on Dungeness.

TRANSPORT: RYE, ROMNEY MARSH & DUNGENESS

Distance from London 54 miles

Direction Southeast

Travel time One to two hours

Bus To Dungeness, catch the hourly 711 from Rye train station to the Ship pub at New Romney, from where you can take the Romney, Hythe and Dymchurch Railway. Alternatively, get a bus to Romney and carry on down on the world's smallest railway, the Romney, Hyde and Dymchurch Railway (www.rhdr.org.uk; tickets from New Romney to Dungeness £7.70) which covers 13.5 miles from Hythe via Romney to Dungeness, on old-fashioned locomotives and cranky carriages. The service thins out at the end of the year, so check the timetable.

Car Follow the M2, M20 then A20.

Train Trains (☎ 0845 748 4950; www.nationalrail.co.uk) head to Rye from Charing Cross station via Ashford International or Hastings, where you will have to change. Two trains leave every hour, but both leave about the same time (day return £24.10).

EATING

George in Rye (☎ 222114; www.thegeorgeinrye.com; 98 High St, Rye; mains £13-16) Probably the hottest place to eat in Rye, thanks to its chef Rod Grossmann, formerly of Moro (p252) in London. It's also a smart hotel.

Fish Café (☎ 222226; www.thefishcafe.com; 17 Tower St, Rye; mains £7-12; ☻ 10am-11pm) Inside a renovated antiques warehouse with simple and delicious locally sourced seafood and fish dishes.

Old Borough Arms (☎ 222128; The Strand, Rye) For a proper old pub, head to this 300-year-old former smugglers' inn with a truly lovely guesthouse and an excellent cafe.

CANTERBURY
☎ 01227

Canterbury's greatest treasure is its majestic cathedral (☎ 762862; www.canterbury-cathedral.org; Sun St; adult/concession £7.50/6.50; ☻ 9am-6pm Mon-Sat, 9am-2pm & 4.30-5.30pm Sun Apr-Oct, 9am-4.30pm Mon-Sat, 10am-2pm & 4.30-5.30pm Sun Nov-Mar, access may be restricted for services 9am-12.30pm Sun). Yet, despite the impressive 66m Bell Harry Tower lording it over the surrounding countryside, it's the assassination of archbishop Thomas Becket in 1170 inside that made the building famous, turning it into the site of one of Europe's most important medieval pilgrimages, as immortalised by Geoffrey Chaucer in *The Canterbury Tales*.

Becket clashed with Henry II over tax and then over the coronation of Henry's son. Hearing Henry mutter 'who will rid me of this turbulent priest?', four knights dispatched themselves to Canterbury, where they scalped the archbishop and amputated his limbs in the late afternoon of 29 December. The murder caused indignation throughout Europe, and Henry was forced to do penance at Becket's tomb, which was later said to be the site of many miracles.

The traditional approach to the cathedral, which dates from 1070, is along narrow Mercery Lane to Christ Church Gate. The main entrance is through the southwest porch, built in 1415 to commemorate the English victory at Agincourt. You'll pass a visitors centre before this, where you can pick up free leaflets, ask for information or book tours. One-hour guided tours (adult/concession £4/3) leave at 10.30am, noon and 2.30pm Monday to Saturday Easter to September, and noon and 2pm Monday to Saturday October to Easter. A 30-minute audioguide tour costs £2.95/1.95 per adult/child.

TRANSPORT: CANTERBURY

Distance from London 56 miles

Direction Southeast

Travel time One hour 50 minutes by bus, 1¾ hours by train.

Bus National Express (☎ 08717 818181; www.nationalexpress.com) has 16 daily shuttle buses (day return £14.20).

Train Canterbury East train station is accessible from London's Victoria station, and Canterbury West from Charing Cross and Waterloo stations. Trains (☎ 0845 748 4950; www.nationalrail.co.uk) leave regularly (up to every 10 minutes); same day return is £21.90.

The perpendicular-style nave (1405) into which you enter is famous for its intricate ribbed vaulting, and there's more fabulous vaulting under the Bell Harry Tower. To your right (east) is the pulpitum screen that separates the nave from the quire.

Thomas Becket is believed to have been murdered in the northwest transept (before you reach the pulpitum); the modern Altar of the Sword's Point marks the spot. On the south side of the nave, you can descend into the Romanesque crypt, the main survivor of an earlier cathedral built by St Augustine in 597 to help convert the post-Roman English to Christianity.

Continuing eastwards through the pulpitum into the quire, you'll come to St Augustine's chair, the seat of the Archbishop of Canterbury. Behind this, in Trinity Chapel, a burning candle and a brass inscription mark the site of the former Tomb of St Thomas, which was destroyed on Henry VIII's orders during the Reformation. The chapel's stained glass is mostly 13th century, celebrating the life of St Thomas Becket.

Also in the chapel you'll find the magnificent Tomb of the Black Prince (Edward, Prince of Wales, 1330–76), with its famous effigy that includes the prince's shield, gauntlets and sword. The Corona once contained the slightly macabre relic of the part of Thomas' skull that was sliced off during his murder.

Outside, walk around the eastern end of the cathedral and turn right into Green Court. In the northwestern corner (far left) is the much celebrated Norman Staircase (1151).

Canterbury's other attractions are very much epilogues to the main act. The Museum of Canterbury (☎ 452747; www.canterbury-museums.co.uk; Stour St; adult/child/£3.30/2.20; ☻ 10.30am-5pm Mon-Sat

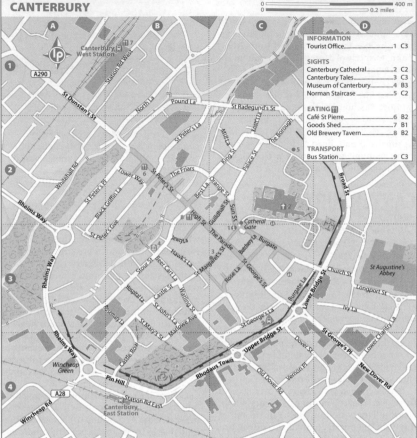

CANTERBURY

| | 0 | 400 m |
| 0 | 0.2 miles |

year-round, 1.30-5pm Sun Jun-Sep) has been given a thorough revamp, and is particularly aimed at children and families. New hands-on exhibits include a medieval discovery gallery (where you can look at medieval poo under the microscope) and a 'whodunnit' on the mysterious death of playwright Christopher Marlowe (originally a Canterbury lad). Children's cartoon characters Rupert Bear, Bagpuss and the Clangers also appear.

If you're really keen to acquaint or reacquaint yourself with Chaucer's famous stories, head to Canterbury Tales (☎ 454888, 479227; www.canterburytales.org .uk; St Margaret's St; adult/child £7.75/5.75; ⏰ 9.30am-5.30pm Jul & Aug, 10am-5pm Mar-Jun, Sep & Oct, 10am-4.30pm Nov-Feb), where, armed with a storytelling audioguide, you pass puppets re-creating various scenes. It might be better to just buy the book, though, to read on the train back to London.

INFORMATION

Tourist office (☎ 766567, 767744; www.canterbury .co.uk; 34 St Margaret's St; ⏰ 9.30am-5.30pm Mon- Sat, 10am-4pm Sun Apr-Oct, 9.30am-5pm Mon-Sat, 10am-4pm Sun Nov & Dec, 9.30am-5pm Mon-Sat Jan-Mar)

EATING

Old Brewery Tavern (☎ 826682; www.michaelcaines .com; 30-33 High St; mains £19-23) Somewhere between a local boozer and a posh eatery (which, admittedly, is a large margin), this is Michelin-starred chef Michael Caines' place, which has sprinkled a glittering of gastronomic stardom onto Canterbury. It's a good place for an elaborate and rich lunch or dinner.

Goods Shed (☎ 459153; Station Rd West; mains £10-18; ⏰ lunch & dinner Tue-Sat, lunch Sun) A fantastic place overlooking a farmers market, Good Shed is, unsurprisingly, in a converted railway shed, with high ceilings, huge windows and exposed brick. The changing French country menu uses fresh produce inventively.

Café St Pierre (☎ 456791; 40 St Peter's St; pastries £2-3.50) The perfect place for breakfast or an afternoon break, with delicious pastries, pavement seats and a shady back garden.

WINDSOR & BRAY
☎ 01753

British monarchs have inhabited Windsor Castle (☎ 831118, 020-7766 7304; www.royalcollection.org.uk; adult/child 5-16 years/senior & student/family £15.50/9/14/41, when State Apartments are closed £8.50/5.50/7.50/22.50; ☼ 9.45am-5.15pm Mar-Oct, 9.45am-4.15pm Nov-Feb, last entry 1¼ hours before closing) for more than 900 years and it is well known to be the Queen's favourite residence and the place she calls home after a hard day's cutting ribbons. A disastrous fire here in 1992 nearly wiped out this incredible piece of English cultural heritage, luckily damage, though severe, was limited and a £37 million restoration, completed in 1998, has restored the state apartments to their former glory. Windsor town hit the spotlight in 2005 when Prince Charles and Camilla Parker-Bowles were married in a civil ceremony (shock, horror!) in Windsor's Guildhall in 2005 (a ceremony his mother, the Queen, did not attend).

Starting out as a wooden castle erected in 1070 by William the Conqueror, and rebuilt in stone in 1165, this is one of the world's greatest surviving medieval castles, and its longevity and easy accessibility from London guarantee its popularity (indeed, it crawls with tourists all year round). However, it's not the only attrac-tion in the area. Across the River Thames lies Eton College, while the gastronomic hotspot of Bray is a short bus ride away.

Inside the castle the first thing you'll see are the queues that form in front of the impossibly intricate Queen Mary's Dolls' House, the work of architect Sir Edwin Lutyens. Built in 1923 on a 1:12 scale, it took 1500 craftsmen three years to finish and it's complete in every detail, right down to electric lights and flushing toilets.

The State Apartments – open to the public at certain times – reverberate with history, including the impossibly opulent Grand Staircase and extraordinary St George's Hall, the structure most affected by the 1992 fire but now gloriously restored.

After the Waterloo Chamber, created to commemorate the Battle of Waterloo and still used for formal meals, and the Garter Throne Room, you move to the King's Rooms and Queen's Rooms. These are lessons in how the other half lives, with opulent furniture, tapestries and paintings by Canaletto, Dürer, Gainsborough, Van Dyck, Hogarth, Holbein, Rembrandt and Rubens.

One of Britain's finest examples of early English architecture, the castle's St George's Chapel (begun in 1475, but not completed until 1528) has a superb nave in perpendicular style, with gorgeous fan vaulting arching out from the pillars. The chapel contains royal tombs, including those of George V and Queen Mary, George VI, Edward IV and the Queen Mother.

Do not miss the beautiful Windsor Great Park (☎ 860222; admission free; ☼ 8am-dusk) for a walk if the weather is good. This 1920-hectare park, where in 1999 Elizabeth II's husband, Prince Philip, had an avenue of ancient trees beheaded because they got in the way of his horse and buggy, extends from behind the castle almost as far as Ascot.

TRANSPORT: WINDSOR & BRAY

Distance from London 23 miles

Direction West

Travel time One hour by bus, 55 minutes by train.

Bus Green line buses (www.greenline.co.uk) depart Victoria Central station to Windsor between eight and 12 times per day (day return £11); bus 6 operated by Courtney Coaches (☎ 01344-482200) leaves for Bray outside Barclays Bank on Windsor High St (return £4.50, 35 minutes, hourly 7am to 6pm).

Train Trains (☎ 0845 748 4950; www.nationalrail.co.uk) from Waterloo station go to Windsor Riverside station every 30 minutes, or hourly on Sunday (day return, from £9, 50 minutes). Trains from Paddington go via Slough to Eton and Central station (day return from £8.50, 45 minutes). Alternatively, to go straight to Bray, catch a Maidenhead train (day return from £9.50, 40 minutes) from Paddington station and take a taxi for the last five minutes of the journey.

In Windsor itself have a look at the central columns in the Guildhall (☎ 743900; High St; admission free; ☺ 10am-2pm Mon, except bank holidays) beside Castle Hill: they don't actually touch the ceiling. The council of the day, in 1686, insisted upon them, but Sir Christopher Wren was convinced they weren't necessary and left a few centimetres of clear space to prove his point.

Cross the River Thames by the pedestrian Windsor Bridge to reach Eton College (☎ 671177; www.etoncollege.com; Baldwins Shore; adult/child £5/3.50; ☺ 2-4.30pm term time, 10.30am-4.30pm Easter & summer holidays). This famous public (ie private) school has educated no fewer than 18 prime ministers, and several buildings date from the mid-15th century. One-hour tours are held at 2.15pm and 3.15pm.

The nearby village of Bray is home to some excellent restaurants (see below).

INFORMATION

French Brothers (☎ 851900; www.boat-trips.co.uk; Clewer Court Rd; adult/child/senior/family £5/2.50/4.75/12.50) Runs a range of cruises, including 35-minute boat trips from Windsor to Boveney Lock (hourly 11am to 4pm mid-February to mid-March and Saturday and Sunday November to mid-December, half-hourly 10am to 5pm mid-March to October).

Tourist office (☎ 743900; www.windsor.gov.uk; Old Booking Hall, Windsor Royal Shopping, Thames St; ☺ 10am-5pm Mon-Sat, 10am-4.30pm Sun Apr-Jun, Sep & Oct, 9.30am-6pm Jul & Aug, 10am-4pm Nov-Mar)

EATING

In Windsor, Peascod St and its extension, St Leonard's Rd, are full of restaurants, although most are pretty touristy. Bray is where to head for a once-in-a-lifetime gastronomic blow-out.

Fat Duck (☎ 01628-580333; www.fatduck.co.uk; 1 High St, Bray; tasting menu £130; ☺ lunch Tue-Sun, dinner Tue-Sat) The Fat Duck is the baby of self-taught chef, Heston Blumenthal, and regularly tops various polls of the best restaurants in the world, so eating here is an experience to be cherished, even despite a brief closure in 2009 following a mystery outbreak of illness among diners there (nothing amiss was found with the food). Blumenthal's fascination with the science of taste means menus include incredible (and sometimes insane) combinations, experimenting with nitrogen (in nitro-green tea and lime mousse) and bizarre taste combinations such as sardine on toast sorbet, oysters and pas-

sionfruit, salmon poached with liquorice and smoked bacon and egg ice cream. It's all delicious and mind-boggling, and the atmosphere is refreshingly relaxed. You will need to book up to two months ahead, and can do so only by phone – email reservations are not accepted.

Waterside Inn (☎ 01628-620691; www.waterside-inn.co.uk; Ferry Rd, Bray; mains £47.50-68; ☺ lunch & dinner Wed-Sun except Jan, plus dinner Tue in summer) Also voted among the world's top 50 restaurants, this Michel Roux establishment serves French haute cuisine in a rustic riverside environment.

Riverside Brasserie (☎ 01628-780553; www.riversidebrasserie.co.uk; Bray Marina, Monkey Island Lane, Bray; mains £18-25; ☺ lunch & dinner Apr-Sep) This is Blumenthal's pitch to the less adventurous (and possibly less loaded) diner, with a more conventionally British menu, though this is still a real experience. Tuck into pork belly, its most famous dish, while overlooking the river, secure in the knowledge that every reservation covers a table inside as well as one by the river, for those unpredictable English downpours. Note that the Brasserie is closed for six months of the year, and booking is advised for the six months it is open.

KENT CASTLES

Castle buffs can enjoy a fabulous day in each of the three Kentish castles and stately homes. Perhaps the world's most romantic, Leeds Castle (☎ 01622-765400, 0870 600 8880; www.leeds-castle.com; Maidstone, Kent; castle & gardens adult/child/concession £16.50/9.50/13.50; ☺ 10am-7pm, last entry 5pm Mar-Oct, 10am-5pm, last entry 3.30pm Nov-Feb) is spectacularly located on two small islands in the middle of a lake, provoking oohs and aahs from visitors. Surrounded by rolling wooded hills, it was colloquially known as 'Ladies Castle', being home to many queens over the centuries, including Catherine de Valois, Catherine of Aragon and even Elizabeth I, who was imprisoned here before she took the throne. The grounds are particularly striking, from the glorious moat to the gardens and a maze with an underground grotto. There is also an aviary, with more than 100 endangered bird species; a museum of dog collars; and interesting, avian-inspired wallpaper and other decorative features in the castle interior.

The gardens at the small but sweet Hever Castle (☎ 01732-865224; www.hevercastle.co.uk; Hever, Kent; castle & gardens adult/concession/child £12/10/6.50, gardens only £9/8/6.20; ☺ gardens 11am-6pm Mar-Oct, 11am-4pm Nov, castle opens 1hr later), the childhood home of Henry VIII's second wife, Anne Boleyn,

TRANSPORT: KENT CASTLES

Hever Castle

Distance from London 33 miles

Direction Southeast

Travel time Forty minutes by car, 40 minutes (Monday to Friday) to 1½ hours (Saturday and Sunday) by train plus 10 minutes by taxi.

Car Take the M25, turning off at Junction 5 or 6 and following the signs south to Edenbridge and the castle.

Train Catch a train from London Bridge to Edenbridge Town (£9 day return, via east Croydon), then take a taxi (3 miles). Alternatively, the castle is a 1-mile walk from Hever station. On Sundays services terminate one stop down the line at East Grinstead; a taxi from East Grinstead to Hever will cost £10.

Leeds Castle

Distance from London 44 miles

Direction Southeast

Travel time One and a half hours by car, 1½ hours by bus, one hour 10 minutes by train.

Bus National Express (☎ 08717 818181; www.nationalexpress.com; adult/child combined bus & entry ticket £13.60/6.80) runs to Leeds Castle, with services leaving Victoria Central station in the morning and returning to Victoria around 2pm to 3pm, Monday to Friday.

Car Take the M20 southeast of London, turning off at Junction 8 and following the signs to the nearby castle.

Train Trains (☎ 0845 748 4950; www.nationalrail.co.uk) from London's Victoria station go to Bearsted station (day return £16), from where you can catch the connecting coach to Leeds Castle.

Sissinghurst Castle Garden

Distance from London 46 miles

Direction Southeast

Travel time One and a half hours by car, one hour by train plus 15 minutes by castle bus.

Bus From Staplehurst train station, there's a special link to Sissinghurst Castle Garden on Tuesdays, Sundays and bank holiday Mondays May to mid-September, leaving at 11.40am and 1.45pm Tuesday, returning 3.35 and 5.30pm; 10.40am and 1.40pm Sunday and holidays, returning 3.15 and 5.15pm (15 minutes, £4 return). Phone ☎ 01580-710700 for exact times.

Car Exit the M20 at Junction 5 or 6 and follow the A229 to the A262.

Train Head from Charing Cross station to Staplehurst station (day return £15) and catch the special castle bus (see Bus above) or a taxi (5½ miles).

are equally spectacular. They include roses, bluebells, rhododendrons, topiary, rockeries, Italian sculptures, fountains, lakes and a yew maze, and also combine several of the last two in a water maze, which is extremely popular with children. The castle is, however, a little tricky to get to (see transport details, above).

Sissinghurst Castle Garden (☎ 01580-710 700; www .nationaltrust.org.uk/sissinghurst; Sissinghurst, Cranbrook, Kent; adult/concession/family £8.80/4.40/22; 11am-6.30pm, last entry 5.30pm Mon, Tue & Fri, 10am-6.30pm, last entry 5.30pm Sat & Sun mid-Mar–Nov) is one of the most famous 20th-century gardens in the world, legendary among writers and the green-fingered. The creation of poet Vita Sackville-West and husband Harold Nicolson, it innovatively grouped similarly coloured plants to create 10 distinct garden 'rooms'. The famous White Garden, with its shades of white, grey and green, was a source of inspiration for Sackville-West as she gazed upon it from her study, also open to visitors.

INFORMATION

A useful source of information is the Visit Kent (www.visitkent.co.uk) website .

AIR

Check any of the websites below for good deals on airline tickets.

www.cheapflights.co.uk

www.ebookers.com

www.lastminute.com

www.opodo.co.uk

www.skyscanner.net

Airlines

London is served by nearly every international airline, most with offices in the city. The major airlines include:

Aer Lingus (☎ 0870 876 5000; www.aerlingus.com)

Aeroflot (☎ 7355 2233; www.aeroflot.co.uk)

Air Berlin (☎ 0871 500 0737; www.airberlin.com)

Air Canada (☎ 0871 220 1111; www.aircanada.com)

Air France (☎ 0871 663 3777; www.airfrance.com/uk)

Air New Zealand (☎ 0800 028 4149; www.airnew zealand.co.uk)

Alitalia (☎ 0870 225 5000; www.alitalia.com)

American Airlines (☎ 7365 0777; www.americanairlines .co.uk)

BMI (☎ 0870 607 0555; www.flybmi.com)

British Airways (☎ 0844 493 0787; www.britishairways .com)

Brussels Airlines (☎ 0905 609 5609; www.brusselsair lines.com)

Cathay Pacific (☎ 8834 8888; www.cathaypacific.com)

Continental Airlines (☎ 0845 607 6760; www.continen tal.com)

THINGS CHANGE...

The information in this chapter is particularly vulnerable to change. Check directly with the airline or a travel agent to make sure you understand how a fare (and ticket you may buy) works and be aware of the security requirements for international travel. Shop carefully. The details given in this chapter should be regarded as pointers and are not a substitute for your own careful, up-to-date research.

Delta Air Lines (☎ 0845 600 0950; www.delta.com/ uk)

easyJet (☎ 0905 560 7777; www.easyjet.com) Calls cost £1 per minute.

El Al (☎ 7121 1400; www.elal.com)

Emirates (☎ 0870 243 2222; www.emirates.com/uk)

Flybe (British European; ☎ 0871 522 6100, 0871 700 2000; www.flybe.com)

Iberia (☎ 0870 609 0500; www.iberia.com)

Icelandair (☎ 870 787 4020; www.icelandair.net)

KLM (☎ 0870 507 4074; www.klm.com)

Lufthansa (☎ 0845 773 7747; www.lufthansa.co.uk)

Olympic Airlines (☎ 0870 606 0460; www.olympicair lines.com)

Qantas Airlines (☎ 0845 774 7767; www.qantas.co .uk)

Ryanair (☎ 0871 246 0000; www.ryanair.com)

Scandinavian Airlines (SAS; ☎ 8990 7000; www .scandinavian.net)

Singapore Airlines (☎ 0844 800 2380; www.singapore air.com)

South African Airways (☎ 0871 722 1111; www.flysaa .com)

TAP Air Portugal (☎ 0845 601 0932; www.flytap.com/uk)

Thai Airways International (☎ 0870 606 0911; www .thaiair.com)

Thomas Cook Airlines (☎ 0871 895 0055; www.thomas cook.com/flights)

Turkish Airlines (☎ 7766 9333; www.thy.com)

United Airlines (☎ 0845 844 4777; www.unitedairlines .co.uk)

US Airways (☎ 0845 600 3300; www.usairways.com)

Virgin Atlantic (☎ 0870 574 7747; www.virgin-atlantic .com)

Wizz Air (☎ 0904 475 9500; www.wizzair.com) Calls cost 65p per minute.

Airports

London is served by five major airports: Heathrow, which is the largest, to the west; Gatwick to the south; Stansted to the east; Luton to the north; and London City.

HEATHROW AIRPORT

Some 15 miles west of central London, Heathrow (LHR; off Map p62; ☎ 0844 335 1801; www.heathrowairport.com) is the world's busiest international airport and now counts five terminals. For information call the relevant terminal during the times listed:

Terminal 1 (☎ 8745 5301; ☾ 6am-11pm)

Terminal 2 (☎ 8897 9541; ☾ 6am-10.30pm)

Terminal 3 (☎ 8759 3344; ☾ 5.30am-10.30pm)

Terminal 4 (☎ 8897 6874; ☾ 5.30am-11pm)

Terminal 5 (☎ 8283 5073; ☾ 5.30am-11pm)

Each terminal has currency-exchange facilities, information counters and accommodation desks. Three Piccadilly line tube stations serve the airport: one for Terminals 1, 2 and 3, another for Terminal 4 and a third for Terminal 5. There are also left-luggage facilities in each terminal. The charge is £8 per item for 24 hours (or part thereof), up to a maximum of 90 days. All branches can forward baggage.

There are three international hotels that can be reached on foot from the terminals at Heathrow and another 20 or so nearby should you be arriving or leaving particularly early or late. To reach them from Heathrow Terminals 1, 2, 3 or 5, take the Heathrow Hotel Hoppa bus (adult/child three to 15 years £4/50p), which departs every 15 to 30 minutes from about 4.30am to midnight. Terminal 4 passengers can take the free Heathrow Express rail link to/from Terminal 3.

Here are options for getting to/from Heathrow Airport:

Black cab A metered trip to/from central London will cost between £45 and £65 (£55 from Oxford St) and takes 45 minutes to an hour depending on your departure point.

Heathrow Connect (☎ 0845 678 6975; www.heathrowconnect.com) Travelling between Heathrow and Paddington station, this modern passenger train service (one way £7.40, 25 minutes, every 30 minutes) makes five stops en route at places like Southall and Ealing Broadway. The first trains leave Heathrow at about 5.20am (6am Sunday) and the last service is around midnight. From Paddington, services leave between approximately 4.30am (6am Sunday) and 11pm.

Heathrow Express (☎ 0845 600 1515; www.heathrowexpress.com) This ultramodern train (one way/return £16.50/32, 15 minutes, every 15 minutes) whisks passengers from Heathrow Central station (serving Terminals 1, 2 and 3) and Terminal 5 to Paddington. Terminal 4 passengers should take the free shuttle train available to Heathrow Central and board the Heathrow Express there. Trains run approximately from just after 5am in both directions to between 11.45pm (from Paddington) and just after midnight (from the airport).

National Express (☎ 0871 781 8181; www.nationalexpress.com) Coaches (one way/return from £5/9, tickets valid three months, 45 minutes to 90 minutes, every 30 minutes to one hour) link the new Heathrow Central Bus Station with Victoria coach station (164 Buckingham Palace Rd SW1; ⊖ Victoria) about 45 times per day. The first bus leaves the Heathrow Central Bus station (at Terminals 1, 2 and 3) at 5.25am with the last departure at 9.40pm. The first bus leaves Victoria at 7.15am, the last at 11.30pm.

CLIMATE CHANGE & TRAVEL

Climate change is a serious threat to the ecosystems that humans rely upon, and air travel is the fastest-growing contributor to the problem. Lonely Planet regards travel, overall, as a global benefit, but believes we all have a responsibility to limit our personal impact on global warming.

Flying & Climate Change

Pretty much every form of motor transport generates CO_2 (the main cause of human-induced climate change) but planes are far and away the worst offenders, not just because of the sheer distances they allow us to travel, but because they release greenhouse gases high into the atmosphere. The statistics are frightening: two people taking a return flight between Europe and the US will contribute as much to climate change as an average household's gas and electricity consumption over a whole year.

Carbon Offset Schemes

Climatecare.org and other websites use 'carbon calculators' that allow jetsetters to offset the greenhouse gases they are responsible for with contributions to energy-saving projects and other climate-friendly initiatives in the developing world – including projects in India, Honduras, Kazakhstan and Uganda.

Lonely Planet, together with Rough Guides and other concerned partners in the travel industry, supports the carbon offset scheme run by climatecare.org. Lonely Planet offsets all of its staff and author travel.

For more information check out our website: www.lonelyplanet.com.

Underground (☎ 7222 1234; www.tfl.gov.uk) The tube (one way £4, from central London one hour, every five to nine minutes) is the cheapest way of getting to Heathrow. It runs from just after 5/5.45am from/to the airport (5.50/7am Sunday) to 11.45/12.30am (11.30pm Sunday in both directions). You can buy tickets from machines in the baggage reclaim areas of the Heathrow terminals or in the station. At night the N9 bus connects Heathrow with central London.

GATWICK AIRPORT

Located some 30 miles south of central London, Gatwick (LGW; off Map p62; ☎ 0844 335 1802; www.gatwickairport.com) is smaller and better organised than Heathrow. The North and South Terminals are linked by an efficient rail service, with the journey time about three minutes. For information, call the relevant terminal:

North Terminal (☎ 01293-502013; ☽ 5am-9pm)

South Terminal (☎ 01293-502014; ☽ 24hr)

Gatwick has left-luggage facilities in both terminals. The charge is £8 per item for 24 hours (or part thereof), up to a maximum of 90 days' storage.

Here are options for getting to/from Gatwick Airport:

Black cab A metered trip to/from central London costs about £85 and takes just over an hour.

easyBus (☎ 0870 141 7217; www.easybus.co.uk) This budget outfit runs 19-seater minibuses (one way £10, from £2 online, 70 minutes, every 20 minutes) from Fulham Broadway tube station on the District line to the North terminal from 6.40am to 11pm daily. Departures from Gatwick are between 6am and 10pm. Tickets can be purchased from the driver and there are ticket outlets at the airport in both the North and South Terminals.

First Capital Connect (☎ 0845 748 4950; www.firstcapitalconnect.co.uk) This rail service (one way/return £9.80/12.70, one hour to 70 minutes) runs through East Croydon, London Bridge, Blackfriars and St Pancras International.

Gatwick Express (☎ 0845 850 1530; www.gatwickexpress.com) Trains (one way/return £16.90/28.80, 30 minutes, every 15 minutes) link the station near the South Terminal with Victoria station. From the airport, there are services between about 4.30am and 1.35am. From Victoria, they leave between 5am and 12.30am.

National Express (☎ 0871 781 8181; www.nationalexpress.com) Coaches (one way/return £7.30/15.10, tickets valid three months, 65 minutes to 90 minutes) run from Gatwick to Victoria coach station about 18 times per day. Services leave the airport at least once an hour between 5.15am and 9.45pm and operate hourly on the hour from Victoria between 7am and 10pm, with extra ones at 11.30pm and a very early service at 3.30am.

Southern Trains (☎ 0845 748 4950; www.southernrailway.com) This rail service (one way/return from £9.80/12.70, 30 to 50 minutes, every 15 to 30 minutes, every hour from midnight to 4am) runs from Victoria station to both terminals.

STANSTED AIRPORT

London's third-busiest international gateway, Stansted (STN; off Map p62; ☎ 0844 335 1803; www.stanstedairport.com) is 35 miles northeast of central London, heading towards Cambridge. It's become Europe's fastest-growing airport thanks to no-frills carriers easyJet and Ryanair, which use it as a hub.

Options for getting to/from Stansted Airport:

Black cab A metered trip to/from central London costs between £85 and £100.

easyBus (☎ 0870 141 7217; www.easybus.co.uk) Minibuses (one way £10, from £2 online, 90 minutes, every 20 to 30 minutes) from Victoria coach station to Stansted via Gloucester Pl W1 at the Baker St tube station go from 3am to 10.20pm daily. Departures from Stansted are between 7am and just after 1am.

National Express (☎ 0871 781 8181; www.nationalexpress.com) Coaches run around the clock, offering some 120 services per day. The A6 runs to Victoria coach station (one way/return £10.50/18, 85 to 110 minutes, every 10 to 20 minutes) via North London. The A9 runs to Stratford (£8.50/16, 45 minutes to one hour, every 30 minutes), from where you can catch a Jubilee line tube (20 minutes) into central London.

Stansted Express (☎ 0845 850 0150; www.standstedexpress.com) This rail service (one way/return £19/28.80, £18/26.80 online, 45 minutes, every 15 to 30 minutes) links the airport and Liverpool St station. From the airport the first train leaves at 5.30am, the last just before midnight. Trains depart Liverpool St station from 4.10am to just before 11.30pm. If you need to connect with the tube, change at Tottenham Hale (one way/return £17/26.60) for the Victoria line or stay on to Liverpool St station for the Central line. Some early services do not stop at Tottenham Hale.

Terravision (☎ 1279 680 028; www.terravision.eu/london.html) Coaches (one way/return £9/14) link Stansted to both Liverpool St rail station (bus A51; 55 minutes) and Victoria coach station (bus A50; 75 minutes) every 20 to 40 minutes between 7.15am and 1am. Services from Victoria run between 2.40am and just after 11pm. Services to Liverpool St are between 6am and 1am; from Liverpool St they run from 3am to 11.30pm.

LONDON CITY AIRPORT

Its proximity to central London, which is just six miles to its west, as well as to the commercial district of the Docklands, means London City Airport (LCY; Map p62; ☎ 7646 0000; www .londoncityairport.com) is predominantly a gateway airport for business travellers, although it does also serve holidaymakers with its two dozen Continental European and seven national destinations.

Here are options for getting to/from London City Airport:

Black cab A metered trip to or from the City/Covent Garden/Oxford St costs about £20/25/30.

Docklands Light Railway (DLR; ☎ 7363 9700; www .tfl.gov.uk/dlr) The Docklands Light Railway stops at the London City Airport station (one way £4, with an Oyster card £2.20-2.70). The journey to Bank takes just over 20 minutes, and trains go every eight to 15 minutes from 5.30am to 12.30am Monday to Saturday, and 7am to 11.30pm Sunday.

LUTON AIRPORT

A smallish airport 32 miles north of London, Luton (LTN; off Map p62; ☎ 01582-405100; www .london-luton.co.uk) caters mainly for cheap charter flights, though the discount airline easyJet operates scheduled services from here.

Here are options for getting to/from Luton Airport:

Black cab A metered trip to/from central London costs about £80.

easyBus (☎ 0870 141 7217; www.easybus.co.uk) Minibuses (one way £10, from £2 online, 80 minutes, every 30 minutes) from Victoria coach station to Luton via Marble Arch, Baker St and Finchley Rd tube stations every half-hour round the clock, with the same frequencies coming from the airport.

Green Line bus 757 (☎ 0844 801 7261; www.greenline .co.uk) Buses to Luton (one way/return £13/14.15, tickets valid three months, one hour) run from Buckingham Palace Rd just south of Victoria station, leaving approximately every half-hour round the clock.

First Capital Connect (☎ 0845 748 4950; www.first capitalconnect.co.uk) Trains (off-peak one way/return £11.90/21.40, 30 to 40 minutes, every six to 15 minutes 7am to 10pm) run from London Bridge, Blackfriars and St Pancras International stations to Luton Airport Parkway station, from where an airport shuttle bus will take you to the airport in eight minutes.

Terravision (☎ 1279 680 028; www.terravision.eu/ london.html) Coaches (one way/return £13/16) from Luton to Victoria coach station and vice versa go every 20 to 40 minutes round the clock.

BICYCLE

Cycling along London's canals or along the South Bank is delightful, but heading through the heavy traffic, with its aggressive drivers and noxious fumes, can be pretty grim. So not only should you always wear a helmet and have lights on the front and back of your bike if cycling after dusk, you might also want to join the many Londoners who also wear facemasks to filter out pollution.

The London Cycling Campaign (LCC; ☎ 7234 9310; www.lcc.org.uk) is working towards improving conditions throughout the city, campaigning to establish a comprehensive London cycle network. Also, City Hall and the current mayor are very pro-cycling and its popularity has sky-rocketed in recent years.

In conjunction with the LCC, Transport for London (www.tfl.gov.uk) publishes the free London Cycle Guides, which are in effect 14 maps of London cycle routes. Order them via the web through either group or call the 24-hour TfL information line (☎ 7222 1234). The maps are also available online at www.londoncyclenetwork .org.uk.

Bicycles on Public Transport

Bicycles can be taken only on the Circle, District, Hammersmith & City and Metropolitan tube lines, though not during peak times (7.30am to 9.30am and 4pm to 7pm Monday to Friday). Folding bikes can be taken on any line at any time, however. Bicycles can also travel on the Overground (p382) but not on the DLR.

Restrictions on taking a bike on suburban and mainline trains vary from company to company but many now have carriages with very generous handicapped sections that cyclists can take advantage of when not in use. For details call ☎ 0845 748 4950.

Hire

London Bicycle Tour Company (Map p126; ☎ 7928 6838; www.londonbicycle.com; 1a Gabriel's Wharf, 56 Upper Ground SE1; ✆ Waterloo or Blackfriars) Rentals cost £4 per hour or £19 for the first day, £9 for days two and three, £6 for days four and five, £49 for the first week and £10 for second week. It also offers 3½-hour bike tours of London daily at 10.30am for £15.95 and at noon and 2.30pm (£18.95 each) on weekends. For an extra £5 you get to keep the bike for 24 hours after the tour. Routes are on its website. You will need to provide credit card details as a deposit and must show ID.

On Your Bike (Map p126; ☎ 7378 6669; www.onyour bike.com; 52-54 Tooley St SE1; ✆ 7.30am-7.30pm Mon-

Fri,10am-6pm Sat,11am-5pm Sun; ✆ London Bridge) Rentals cost £12.50 for the first day, £8 for subsequent days, £35 per week. Prices include hire of a helmet. A deposit of £150 (via credit card) is necessary and you will be required to show ID.

Pedicabs

Three-wheeled cycle rickshaws, seating two or three passengers, have been a regular, if much-cursed, part of the Soho scene in the past 10 years. They're less a mode of transport than a gimmick for tourists and the occasional drunk on a Saturday night. Expect to pay about £5 for a trip across Soho. For more information visit www.londonpedicabs.com.

BOAT

With the drive to make use of London's often overlooked 'liquid artery', companies running boats on the river have been sprouting up in recent years. Only the Thames Clippers (✆ 0870 781 5049; www.thamesclippers.com) really offers commuter services, however. Running from 6am to just after 1am, the services (adult/child single £5/2.50 half-price, roughly every 20 minutes to 30 minutes) give you access to lots of the river sights. Boats run from Embankment to Woolwich Arsenal Piers, passing the Tate Modern, Shakespeare's Globe, Tower Bridge, Canary Wharf, Greenwich and the O2. For sightseeing tours, see p380. For more on cruising the Thames, see p109.

BUS

London's iconic double-decker Routemaster was phased out in 2005 except for two 'heritage routes' (Nos 9 and 15) but will soon reappear in a new, sleeker form; the reintroduction of the Routemaster was a campaign promise made by Mayor Boris Johnson in 2008. Even getting on today's modern double-deckers, you see more of the city than while below ground on the tube. Just beware that the going can be slow, thanks to traffic jams and the more than four million commuters that get on and off the buses every day.

Fares

Any single-journey adult bus ticket within London costs £2 (or £1 with an Oyster card; see opposite) Children under 11 travel free; those aged 11 to 18 years do as well but require an Oyster photocard. Travelcards (p383) are valid on all buses, including night buses. Be advised that

at some central London bus stops (where signs have a yellow background), drivers no longer sell tickets and you must buy before you board from the machines provided. Annoyingly, even when these work they do not give change, so you'll need the exact number of coins. However, they do sell daily bus passes (see below).

TRAVEL PASSES & DISCOUNT FARES

If you plan to use only buses during your stay in London, you can buy a one-day bus pass valid throughout London for adult/child £3.30/1.65; if using an Oyster card that is the daily price cap on buses and trams. Unlike Travelcards (or Oyster price cap) for the tube, DLR and London Overground, these are valid before 9.30am on weekdays. Weekly or monthly bus passes cost adult/child £13.80/6.90 or £53/26.50.

You should definitely get an Oyster card (opposite) even if you're here only for a weekend. Otherwise you'll be paying double the fare.

Information

Maps, which divide the city into five sections are available from most transport travel information centres or from www.tfl.gov.uk/buses. For general information on London buses call ✆ 7222 1234 (24 hours).

Night Buses

More than 50 night bus routes (which are prefixed with the letter 'N') run from midnight to 4.30am, when the tube shuts down and the daytime buses return to the barn. Oxford Circus, Tottenham Court Rd and Trafalgar Sq are the main hubs, but check bus-stop information boards to familiarise yourself with routes. Night buses can be infrequent and stop only on request, meaning you must signal clearly to the driver to stop.

Another 60 or so routes are also '24-hour buses', which means that they are different from night buses because they are the same bus you'd take during the day, though their frequency thins out during the night. Check the bus timetable for frequency details.

Within the UK & to Europe

National Express (✆ 0871 781 8181; www.nationalexpress .com) and, to a lesser extent, low-cost Megabus (✆ 0900 160 0900 per min 60p; www.megabus.com) are the main national operators. Megabus operates a no-frills airline-style of seat pricing, where some tickets go for as little as £1. National Express has dropped its fares considerably in order to compete. Another competitor on main UK routes is Green Line (☎ 0844 801 7261; www.greenline.co.uk; Bulleid Way Sw1; ⊖ Victoria).

Eurolines (☎ 0871 781 8177; www.eurolines.com; 52 Grosvenor Gardens SW1) has National Express–operated buses to Continental Europe leaving from Victoria coach station (Map pp136–7; 164 Buckingham Palace Rd SW1; ⊖ Victoria).

CAR & MOTORCYCLE

To drive in London is to learn the true meaning of road rage: traffic jams are common, parking space is at an extortionate premium and the congestion charge (right) adds to the general expense, including the high price of petrol, currently at £1 a litre. Traffic wardens and wheel clampers operate with extreme efficiency and if your vehicle is clamped it will cost you about £240 to have it released. If this happens call the number on the ticket; this varies across different London boroughs. If the car has been removed, ring the 'cutely' named free 24-hour service called TRACE (Tow-away Removal & Clamping Enquires; ☎ 7747 4747). It will cost you at least £200 to get your vehicle back on the road.

Driving
ROAD RULES

We don't recommend driving in London. However, if you insist, you should first obtain the *Highway Code,* which is available at Automobile Association (AA) and Royal Automobile Club (RAC) outlets, as well as some bookshops and tourist offices. A foreign driving licence is valid in Britain for up to 12 months from the time of your last entry into the country. If you bring a car from Europe make sure you're adequately insured. All drivers and passengers must wear seatbelts and motorcyclists must wear a helmet.

CONGESTION CHARGE

London was the world's first major city to introduce a congestion charge to reduce the flow of traffic into its centre from Monday to Friday. While the traffic entering the 'congestion zone' has fallen as a result, driving in London can still be very slow work.

The original congestion charge zone (Euston Rd, Pentonville Rd, Tower Bridge, Elephant & Castle, Vauxhall Bridge Rd, Park Lane and Marylebone Rd) has been extended to encompass Bayswater, Notting Hill, High St Kensington, North and South Kensington, Knightsbridge, Chelsea, Belgravia and Pimlico.

As you enter the zone, you will see a large letter 'C' in a red circle. If you enter the zone between 7am and 6pm Monday to Friday (excluding public holidays), you must pay the £8 charge on the same day (or £10 on the first charging day after travel) to avoid receiving a £120 fine. You can pay online, at newsagents, petrol stations or any shop displaying the 'C' sign, by telephone on ☎ 0845 900 1234 and even by text message/SMS once you've registered online. For full details log on to www.tfl.gov.uk/roadusers/congestioncharging.

Hire

Although driving in London is expensive and often slow, there is no shortage of rental agencies. Competition is fierce, with easyCar (www.easycar.com) having significantly undersold many of the other more traditional companies such as Avis (www.avis.com) and Hertz (www.hertz.com) over the past few years, forcing down prices. You should always book in advance as early as possible as cars are often in short supply, especially at weekends.

A godsend for those who need a car for just a couple of couple of hours or half a day is the

---

OYSTER CARD

The credit-card style Oyster card is the London commuter's best friend, and tannoy/loud speaker reminders to 'touch in and touch out' have become as common as the warning to 'mind the gap' at stations. You pay a £3 refundable deposit for the card, which soon pays for itself.

The Oyster card is a smart card on which you can store either credit towards so-called 'prepay' fares, a Travelcard or both. When entering the tube or boarding a bus, you need to touch your card on a reader (which has a yellow circle with the image of an Oyster card on them) at the tube gates or near the driver to register your journey. The system will then deduct the appropriate amount of credit from your card as necessary. The benefit lies in the fact that fares for Oyster-users are lower than the normal ones. If you are making many journeys during the day, you will never pay more than the appropriate Travelcard (peak or off peak) once the daily 'price cap' has been reached.

When leaving tube stations, you must also touch the card on a reader, so the system knows your journey was only, say, a zone 1 and 2 journey. Regular commuters can also store weekly or monthly Travelcards on their Oyster cards.

self-service pay-as-you-go scheme called Streetcar (☎ 0845 644 8475; www.streetcar.co.uk). After registering and paying the £59.50 annual membership, you locate the closest available Streetcar vehicle to where you are staying, unlock the car with your membership card, release the key with a PIN and drive on. Prices start at £3.95/39.50 per hour/day and you get 30 miles of free petrol.

ORGANISED TOURS

Although they're not particularly cool, organised tours provide a decent means of seeing the main sights while allowing you to return to certain areas for more in-depth exploration on your own; the 'jump-on, jump-off' services are particularly good for this. Also, for anyone with very limited time, it is (just about) possible to see the major landmarks of the British capital in one day. And they don't have to be your standard 'on your right you'll see Big Ben' variety; a huge number of companies offer countless wacky options.

Air

Adventure Balloons (☎ 01252-844222; www.adventureballoons.co.uk; Winchfield Park, London Rd, Hartley Wintney, Hampshire) Weather permitting, there are London flights (£185 per person) every Tuesday, Wednesday and Thursday morning shortly after dawn from late April to mid-August. The flight lasts one hour, but allow four hours including take-off, landing and recovery.

Cabair Helicopters (☎ 8953 4411; www.cabair.com; Elstree Aerodrome, Borehamwood, Hertfordshire) Thirty-minute flights over London twice a month on Saturday or Sunday for £150. Call for schedule details.

Boat

Travelcard holders (p383) get one-third off all boating fares listed here.

Circular Cruise (☎ 7936 2033; www.crownriver.com; adult/5-15yr/student & senior/family £8.70/4.40/7.70/28; ☽ tours every 30 min 11am-6.30pm late May-early Sep, every 40 min 11am-5pm early Apr-late May & early Sep-Oct, hourly 11am-3pm Nov-early Apr) Vessels travel east from Westminster Pier to St Katharine's Pier near the Tower of London and back, calling at Embankment, Festival, Bankside and London Bridge Piers. Fares are cheaper if travelling just one way (eg adult £6.90) or between just two stages (eg Bankside to/from London Bridge costs adult/child £3/1.50).

London Waterbus Company (Map p166; ☎ information 7482 2660, bookings 7482 2550; www.londonwaterbus.co.uk; 2 Middle Yard, Camden Lock NW1; adult/child one way £6.50/5.20, return £9.30/7.40; ☽ hourly 10am-5pm Apr-Sep, every 2hr 10am-4pm Thu & Fri, hourly 10am-5pm

Sat & Sun Oct, every 2hr 10am-3pm Sat & Sun Nov-Mar; ⊖ Camden Town) Runs 90-minute trips on Regent's Canal in an enclosed barge between Camden Lock and Little Venice, passing through Regent's Park and London Zoo.

RIB London Voyages (Map p126; ☎ 7928 8933; www.londonribvoyages.com; Boarding Gate 1, London Eye, Waterloo Millennium Pier, Westminster Bridge Rd SE1; adult/child £32.50/19.50; ☽ hourly 11am-4pm daily May-Oct, 11am-4pm Fri-Sun Nov-Mar) Feel like James Bond on this high-speed inflatable boat that flies down the Thames at 30 to 35 knots. They also do a Captain Kidd–themed one between the London Eye and Canary Wharf at the same price.

Thames River Services (Map pp84–5; ☎ 7930 4097; www.westminsterpier.co.uk; Westminster Pier, Victoria Embankment SW1; adult/child one way £8.40/4.20, return £11/5.50, family £28; ☽ tours every 30min 10am-4pm or 5pm Apr-Oct) These cruise boats leave Westminster Pier for Greenwich, stopping at the Tower of London. Every second service continues on from Greenwich to the Thames Barrier (one way adult/child £10.40/5.20, return £12.80/6.40, hourly 11.30am-3.30pm) but does not land there, passing the O2 along the way. From Westminster it's a three-hour round trip; from Greenwich it takes just one hour. From November to March there's a reduced service from Westminster, with eight daily departures between 10.40am and 3.20pm

Westminster Passenger Services Association (Map pp84–5; ☎ 7930 2062; www.wpsa.co.uk; Westminster Pier, Victoria Embankment SW1; Kew adult/child/senior/family one way £10.50/5.25/7/26.25, return £16.50/8.25/11/41.25, Hampton Court adult/child/senior/family one way £13.50/6.75/9/33.75, return £19.50/9.75/13/48.75; ☽ 10.30am, 11am, noon & 2pm daily Apr-Oct) These boats go upriver from Westminster Pier to the Royal Botanic Gardens at Kew (1½ hours) and on to Hampton Court Palace (another 1½ hours). It's possible to get off the boats at Richmond but it depends on the tides; check before you sail.

Bus

The following companies offer commentary and the chance to get off at each sight and rejoin the tour on a later bus. Tickets are valid for 24 hours.

Big Bus Tours (☎ 7233 9533; www.bigbustours.com; adult/child/family £25/10/60; ☽ every 15 mins 8.30am-6pm)

Original Tour (☎ 8877 1722; www.theoriginaltour.com; adult/child/family £22/10/69; ☽ every 15 mins 8.30am-6pm)

Specialist

Black Taxi Tours of London (☎ 7935 9363; www.blacktaxitours.co.uk; 2hr for up to 5 passengers £100; ☽ 8am-midnight) Hire your own black cab with a trained tour guide at the wheel (although you are likely to hear equally amusing tales from any other cabbie in the city). Fares are £10 to £15 higher after 6pm and at the weekend.

London Duck Tours (Map p126; ☎ 7928 3132; www .londonducktours.co.uk; adult/child/concession/family from £20/14/16/58; ☉ Westminster) Amphibious craft based on D-Day landing vehicles depart from outside County Hall and cruise the streets of central London before making a dramatic descent into the Thames at Vauxhall. Tour lasts 80 minutes.

Open House (☎ 7383 2131; www.londonopenhouse .org; Bldg Centre, 26 Store St WC; adult/student £18.50/13; ☑ 10am Sat; ☉ Tottenham Court Rd or Goodge St) Along with the annual Open House London (p208) weekend event in September, when more than 700 buildings are open to the public, this architectural charity sponsors talks and architectural tours to one of four different areas (Square Mile, Bankside, the West End or Docklands) weekly. The tours include lively, well-informed commentary.

Walking

Association of Professional Tourist Guides (APTG; ☎ 7611 2545; www.touristguides.org.uk; half/full day £120/190) Hire a prestigious Blue Badge Guide, know-it-all guides who have studied for two years and passed written exams to do their job.

GLIAS (☎ 01689 852186; www.glias.org.uk; membership adult/family £10/12) If you really want to scratch below the surface (sometimes literally) of London, join the Greater London Industrial Archaeology Society, which arranges scores of walks and lectures (free or at a nominal fee) each month related to London's industrial history.

London Walks (☎ 7624 3978; www.walks.com; adult/ concession £7/5) A huge array of walks, including Jack the Ripper tours at 7.30pm daily and 3pm Saturday, Beatles tours at 11.20am Tuesday and Saturday and a Sherlock Holmes tour at 2pm Friday.

London Mystery Walks (☎ 0795 738 8280; www.tour guides.org.uk; adult/child/family £9/7.50/25; ☉ Aldgate) Tour Jack the Ripper's old haunts at 7pm on Wednesday, Friday and Sunday, and visit Haunted London at 7pm on Tuesday. Meet outside Aldgate tube station.

TAXI
Black Cabs

The London black cab (www.londonblackcabs.co.uk) is as much a feature of the cityscape as the red bus double-decker bus. Licensed black-cab drivers have 'The Knowledge' acquired after rigorous training and a series of exams. They are supposed to know every central London street and the 100 most visited spots of the moment, including sights, clubs and restaurants.

Cabs are available for hire when the yellow sign above the windscreen is lit; just stick your arm out to signal one. Fares are metered, with the flag-fall charge of £2.20 (covering the first 336m during a weekday), rising by increments of 20p for each subsequent 168m. Fares are more expensive in the evenings and overnight. You can tip taxi drivers up to 10% but few Londoners do, simply rounding up to the nearest pound.

Do not expect to hail a taxi in popular nightlife areas of London such as Soho late at night (and especially after 11pm when the majority of pubs still close). If you do find yourself in any of those areas, signal all taxis – even those with their lights off – and act sober. Many drivers are very choosy about their fares at this time of night. To order a cab by phone try Computer Cabs (☎ cash 7908 0207, credit card 7432 1432; www.comcablondon.com); it charges a £2 booking fee and what it cost to get to you in addition to your actual fare.

Zingo Taxi (☎ 0870 070 0700; http://pda.london-taxi .co.uk) uses GPS to connect your mobile phone to that of the nearest free black-cab driver – after which you can explain to the cabbie exactly where you are. This service costs only £2, which is included in the final price of the taxi; you will also be charged what it cost the cab to reach you (maximum £3.80). It's a good idea late at night, when it's notoriously difficult to find a free cab.

Minicabs

Minicabs, which are now licensed, are (usually) cheaper freelance competitors of black cabs. However, minicab drivers are often untrained and far less sure of the way than black-cab drivers; it's not unusual for Londoners to have to direct the driver. Minicabs cannot legally be hailed on the street; they must be hired by phone or directly from one of the minicab offices (every high street has at least one). Minicab drivers seeking fares might approach you; it's best to decline their offer, as they will certainly be underinsured. There have been allegations of rape made against some unlicensed cab drivers.

Minicabs don't have meters, so it's essential to fix a price before you start. Most don't bargain – there's usually a fare set by the dispatcher – but it never hurts to try. It's not usual to tip minicab drivers.

Ask a local for the name of a reputable minicab company in the neighbourhood (every Londoner has a regular he or she uses) or phone a large 24-hour operator such as

Addison Lee (☎ 7387 8888) or GLH Express (☎ 7272 3322). Women travelling alone at night can choose Lady Cabs (☎ 7272 3800), which has women drivers. Liberty Cars (☎ 0800 600 006) caters for the gay and lesbian market (though gay couples are extremely unlikely to experience open homophobia from drivers of black cabs).

TRAIN
Docklands Light Railway

The driverless Docklands Light Railway (DLR; ☎ 7363 9700; www.tfl.gov.uk/dlr) is basically an adjunct to the Underground. It links the City at Bank and Tower Hill Gateway stations with Beckton and Stratford to the east and northeast, the Docklands (as far as Island Gardens at the southern end of the Isle of Dogs), Greenwich and Lewisham and to the south and Woolwich via London City Airport to the southeast. The DLR runs from 5.30am to 12.30am Monday to Saturday and from 7am to 11.30pm Sunday. Fares are adult/child £1.60/80p, or £1.10/55p with an Oyster card. There's also a Rail & River Rover ticket (adult/5-15yr/family £12/6/28) unique to the DLR which allows you to jump on and off certain riverboats as well as the DLR.

London Overground & Suburban Trains

Several other rail lines are of some (though limited) use to visitors. What most Londoners still call the Silverlink (or North London line), a railway through the inner suburbs of North London from Richmond in the west to Stratford in the east via Kew, West Hampstead, Camden Rd and Highbury & Islington, now joins five other lines to form the commuter rail service known as the London Overground (☎ 7222 1234; www.tfl.gov.uk). These include the East London Railway, once the Underground's East London line but now extended by four stations (Shoreditch High St, Hoxton, Haggerston and Dalston Junction) to link up with the Silverlink at Highbury & Islington by 2011

First Capital Connect (www.firstcapitalconnect.co.uk) currently runs the crowded service still known to most people as Thameslink from Elephant & Castle and London Bridge and suburbs farther afield in the south through the City to King's Cross and as far north as Luton. Most lines connect with the Underground system at some point, and Travelcards can be used on them. Note, however,

that Oyster prepay are accepted at selected train stations only.

If you're staying long term in Southeast London, where suburban trains are usually much more useful than the tube, it's worth buying a one-year Network Railcard (£25), available at most stations This card offers one-third off most rail fares in southeast England and on one-day off-peak Travelcards for all six zones.

Most of the large mainline London stations have left-luggage facilities available, although due to the perceived terrorist threat, baggage lockers no longer exist. Excess Baggage (☎ 0800 783 1085; www.left-baggage.co.uk) has services costing £8 per bag for the first 24 hours (or part thereof) and £4 for each additional day. These services operate from eight stations: St Pancras, Paddington, Euston, Victoria, Waterloo, King's Cross, Liverpool St and Charing Cross.

Within the UK & to Europe

Main national rail routes are served by Inter-City trains, which can travel up to 225km/h. However, with the national inability to keep any moving conveyance in motion (including lifts and escalators), don't be surprised by – nay, expect – delays. Same-day returns and one-week advance purchases (available from mainline train stations) are the cheapest tickets for those without rail passes. National Rail Enquiries (☎ 0845 748 4950; www.nationalrail.co.uk) has timetables and fares.

The high-speed passenger rail service Eurostar (☎ 0870 518 6186; www.eurostar.com) links St Pancras International station with Gare du Nord in Paris, making the journey in just two hours and 15 minutes with up to two dozen daily departures. (The trip to Brussels, on any of a dozen daily trains, now takes just one hour and 50 minutes.) Fares vary enormously. To Paris/Brussels, for example, costs run between £59 for a cheap midweek return (with an overnight required) to £309 for a fully flexible return.

Eurotunnel (☎ 0870 535 3535; www.eurotunnel.com) transports motor vehicles and bicycles between Folkestone in England and Coquelles (near Calais) in France. Services run up to every 15 minutes during the day (but hourly 1am to 6am). Booking online is cheapest, where day/overnight return fares start at £44 and a two- to five-day excursion fare is from £150. All prices include a car and passengers.

For other European train enquiries contact Rail Europe (☎ 0844 848 5848; www.raileurope.co.uk).

TRANSPORT TRAIN

TRAM

South London has a small network called London Tramlink (☎ 7222 1234; www.tfl.gov.uk). There are three routes running along 28km of track, including Wimbledon to Elmers End via Croydon; Croydon to Beckenham; and Croydon to New Addington. Single tickets cost £2 (£1 with an Oyster card). Bus passes are valid on trams.

UNDERGROUND

Despite the long-overdue (Victorian times, anyone?) renovations and the frequent threat of strikes, the London Underground, or 'the tube', is overall the quickest and easiest way of getting around the city. It is expensive, however: compare the cheapest one-way fare in central London (Oyster/no Oyster £1.60/4) with those charged on the Paris metro and New York subway and you'll see how much Londoners pay over the odds.

Fares

The Underground divides London into six concentric zones. Fares for the more central zones are more expensive than for those zones further out. Oyster peak/Oyster off-peak/non-Oyster adult fares are listed below. Children aged 11 to 15 years pay a uniform 55p with an Oyster card and £2 without one.

Zone 1 only adult £1.60/£1.60/4

Zones 1 & 2 adult £2.20/1.60/4

Zones 1-3 adult £2.70/2.20/4

Zones 1-4 adult £2.80/2.20/4

Zones 1-5 adult £3.70/2.20/4

Zones 1-6 adult £3.80/2.20/4

If you're caught on the Underground without a valid ticket (and that includes crossing into a zone that your ticket doesn't cover) you're liable for an on-the-spot fine of £50. It's your call, but if you do decide to ride 'black' (without a valid ticket) and get nabbed, do us all a favour and just pay up.

TRAVEL PASSES & DISCOUNT FARES

If you're travelling only by tube, bus, tram or DLR, Oyster is your best bet and cheaper than a Day Travelcard. But if you're using the National Rail, your Oyster will not be accepted at certain stations, so go for the Day Travelcard (peak/off peak zones 1 and 2 £7.20/5.60; zones 1 to 6 £14.80/7.50).

The three-day Travelcard for zones 1 and 2 (£18.40) is valid all day; the one for zones 1 to 6 is available for use anytime (£42.40) or off-peak hours (£21.20). Off-peak travel is permitted only after 9.30am Monday to Friday and at any time on Saturday and Sunday

If you're here for a longer period, and are using the tube every day, get either a weekly (adult/child zones 1 and 2 £25.80/12.90) or monthly (£99.10/49.60) Travelcard for zones 1 and 2.

Information

Underground travel info centres sell tickets and provide free maps. There are centres at Heathrow 1,2,3 Underground station as well as Euston, Liverpool St, Piccadilly Circus and Victoria tube and mainline train stations. There is also an information office in Camden Town Hall at 27 Argyle Street WC1 opposite King's Cross St Pancras station. For general information on the tube, buses, the DLR or trains within London ring ☎ 7222 1234 or visit www.tfl.gov.uk.

Network

Greater London is served by 11 tube lines, along with the independent (though linked) and privately owned DLR, the London Overground system and an interconnected rail network. The first tube train operates around 5.30am Monday to Saturday and 7am Sunday; the last train leaves between 11.30pm and 12.30am depending on the day, the station and the line.

Tube lines vary in their reliability, and the Circle Line, which links most of the main-line stations and is therefore much used by tourists, has one of the worst track records. However, when it does work, this line is very fast. Other lines low in the league tables are the Northern line (though improving) and the Hammersmith & City (often referred to as the 'Hammersmith & Shitty') line. The Piccadilly line to/from Heathrow is usually pretty good, as are the Victoria line, linking the station with Oxford Circus and King's Cross, and the Jubilee line, linking London Bridge, Southwark and Waterloo with Baker St.

Remember that, although a design icon, the London Underground map is a graphical representation of the actual tunnels. Some stations, most famously Leicester Sq and Covent Garden, are much closer in real life than they appear on the map. Often, as between those two stations, it's quicker to walk the distance. The distances are marked on some maps.

BUSINESS HOURS

London is a world business hub, and doing business here (not including the media and new technology industries) is as formal as you would expect from the English. Looking smart at all times is still seen as a key indicator of professionalism, along with punctuality and politeness. Business cards are commonplace.

While the City of London continues to work a very traditional Monday to Friday 9am to 5pm routine (the Square Mile is deserted at weekends), business hours elsewhere in the city are extremely flexible. Larger shops and chain stores are usually open until 7pm Monday to Friday, as well as until at least 5pm Saturday and Sunday. Thursday, or sometimes Wednesday and more often Friday, there's late-night shopping. For more details, see p214.

Banks in central London are open until 5pm, although counter transactions after 3.30pm are usually not processed until the next working day. Post offices vary in their opening times, but most are open from 9am to 5.30pm Monday to Saturday.

Traditionally, pubs and bars have been open from 11am until 11pm. The licensing laws were changed in 2005 to allow pubs and bars to apply for licences to stay open later, which means that some pubs are now open until midnight or later on weeknights and until 1am or 2am on weekends.

Restaurants are usually open for lunch from noon until 2.30pm or 3pm, and dinner from 6pm or 7pm until 11pm (with last orders by 10pm).

CHILDREN

London offers a wealth of sights and museums that appeal to children. It's a city with many green spaces, often including safe areas for children to play, and swings and slides.

There is nearly always a special child's entry rate to paying attractions, although ages of eligibility may vary. Children also travel more cheaply on public transport (bus travel is free for all under-16s, and under-18s in full-time education).

The only places where children are traditionally not accepted are pubs, although many now have a family area, a garden or a restaurant where kids are welcome. For more information on life on the road with the little ones, see Lonely Planet's *Travel with Children*.

Babysitting

All the top-range hotels offer in-house babysitting services. Prices vary enormously from hotel to hotel, so enquire with your concierge. You might also like to try Sitters (☎ bookings 0800 389 0038; www.sitters.co.uk). A quarterly registration fee costs £12.75 and prices vary between £5.75 and £6.85 per hour, with an additional £4 booking charge per session. Two other recommended babysitting services are Top Notch Nannies (☎ 7244 6053; www.topnotchnannies.com; babysitters & nannies per hr from £8) and, in West London only, Nick's Babysitting (☎ 07853 981917; www .nicksbabysittingservice.co.uk; per hr from £10).

CLIMATE

Many who live in London would swear that global warming has added a twist to the city's unpredictable climatic conditions. While locals used to complain about the frequent, but still somehow always unforeseen, arrival of rain, now they find themselves faced with sudden outbreaks of sunshine and heat instead. Recent summers have seen record temperatures approaching 40°C. As the tube turns into the Black Hole of Calcutta and traffic fumes become choking, London is particularly ill-equipped to cope with such heat.

However, meteorologists point out that recent statistics don't represent anything terribly out of the ordinary yet for such a naturally variable climate. The average maximum temperature for July, the hottest month, is still only about 23°C. In spring and autumn

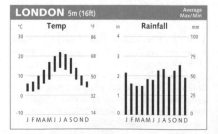

temperatures drop to between 13°C and 17°C. In winter the average daily maximum is 8°C, the overnight minimum 2°C. Despite the appearance of snow in the past few years, it still rarely freezes in London.

What weather forecasters do predict in the long term, as a result of climate change in London, is drier summers, wetter and stormier winters and more flash floods. Meanwhile, for more immediately useful reports on actual and imminent conditions in Greater London, contact Weathercall (☎ 09068 500 401; www.weathercall .co.uk; calls cost per min 60p) or visit www.bbc.lon don.co.uk/weather for a five-day forecast.

See also p16 to help you decide on the best time to go.

COURSES

London is a centre of learning, and boasts countless colleges, universities and other educational institutions. The jewel in its crown is the University of London, whose worldrenowned colleges include King's, University and Imperial Colleges, as well as the London School of Economics.

Many people come to London to study English as a foreign language – walk down Oxford St and you're likely to be handed a flyer on the subject. The British Council (Map pp70–1; ☎ 7930 8466; www.britishcouncil.org; 10 Spring Gardens SW1; ⊖ Charing Cross) publishes a free list of accredited colleges whose facilities and teaching reach the required standards. It can also advise foreign students on educational opportunities in the UK.

Thousands of London courses, from needlework to Nietzsche, photography to politics, are listed in the annual Floodlight (www.floodlight .co.uk) and the quarterly Hotcourses (www.hotcourses .com), both available from larger newsagents and bookshops. For more vocational courses, try the free Careers Advice (☎ 0800 100 900; www .careersadvice.direct.gov.uk).

CUSTOMS REGULATIONS

Like other nations belonging to the EU, the UK has a two-tier customs system: one for goods bought duty-free and one for goods bought in another EU country where taxes and duties have already been paid.

Duty-Free

For goods purchased at airports or on ferries outside the EU, you are allowed to import 200 cigarettes, 50 cigars or 250g of tobacco; 4L of still wine plus 1L of spirits over 22% or 2L of wine (sparkling or otherwise); 60ml of perfume; and other duty-free goods to the value of £300.

Tax & Duty Paid

Although you can no longer bring in dutyfree goods from another EU country, you can bring in duty-paid goods that cost less than you'd pay for the same items in your destination country. The items are supposed to be for individual consumption but a thriving business has developed, with many Londoners making day trips to France to load up their cars with cheap grog and smokes.

If you purchase from a normal retail outlet on the Continent, customs uses the following maximum quantities as a guide to distinguish personal imports from those on a commercial scale: 3200 cigarettes, 200 cigars, 3kg of tobacco, 10L of spirits, 20L of fortified wine, 90L of wine (of which not more than 60L is sparkling) and 110L of beer.

DISCOUNT CARDS

Students studying full time in London are eligible for discounted travel on all London public transport. However, it takes some time to receive your discount card, as it needs to be sent by post for processing and you need a stamp from your university; ask for a form to fill out at any tube station.

For details on Travelcards offering discounts on public transport, see p383.

Possibly of most interest to visitors who want to take in lots of sights is the London Pass (www .londonpass.com). Passes start at £14.50 per day (for six days), although they can be altered to include use of the Underground and buses. They offer free entry and queue-jumping to all major attractions; check the website for details.

ELECTRICITY

The standard voltage throughout the UK is 230/240V AC, 50Hz. Plugs have three square pins and can look rather curious to nonBrits. Adapters for European, Australasian and American electrical items are available at any electrical store. Check www.kropla.com for useful info on electricity and adaptors.

EMBASSIES

It's important to realise what your own embassy can and cannot do to help you if you get into trouble. Generally, it won't be much help if the trouble you're in is remotely your own fault. Remember that while in London you are bound by British law.

In genuine emergencies you might get some assistance, but only if other channels have been exhausted. The embassy will expect you to have insurance for any unpredictable costs. If you have all your money and documents stolen, it might assist with getting a new passport but a loan for onward travel is almost always out of the question.

The following is a list of selected foreign representative offices in London. For a more complete list check under 'Embassies & Consulates' in the central London Yellow Pages (www .yell.co.uk).

Australia (Map pp70–1; ☎ 7379 4334; www.australia .org.uk; Australia House, The Strand WC2; ⊖ Holborn or Temple)

Belgium (Map pp136–7; ☎ 7470 3700; www.diplomatie .be/london; 17 Grosvenor Cres SW1; ⊖ Victoria)

Canada Embassy (Map pp70–1; ☎ 7258 6476; www .canada.org.uk; Canada House, Trafalgar Sq SW1; ⊖ Charing Cross); Consulate (Map p90; ☎ 7258 6600; 1 Grosvenor Square, W1; ⊖ Bond St)

France (Map pp136–7; ☎ 7073 1000; www.ambafrance -uk.org; 58 Knightsbridge SW1; ⊖ Knightsbridge)

Germany (Map pp136–7; ☎ 7824 1300; www.london .diplo.de; 23 Belgrave Sq SW1; ⊖ Hyde Park Corner)

Ireland (Map pp136–7; ☎ 7235 2171; www.embassyof ireland.co.uk; 17 Grosvenor Pl SW1; ⊖ Hyde Park Corner)

Netherlands (Map pp136–7; ☎ 7590 3200; www.nether lands-embassy.org.uk; 38 Hyde Park Gate SW7; ⊖ Gloucester Rd)

New Zealand (Map p66; ☎ 7930 8422; www.nzembassy .com; New Zealand House, 80 Haymarket SW1; ⊖ Piccadilly Circus)

South Africa (Map pp70–1; ☎ 7451 7299; www.south africahouse.com; South Africa House, Trafalgar Sq WC2; ⊖ Charing Cross)

Spain (Map pp136–7; ☎ 7235 5555; www.conspalon.org; 39 Chesham Pl SW1; ⊖ Hyde Park Corner); Consulate (Map pp136–7; ☎ 7589 8989; 20 Draycott Pl, SW3; ⊖ Sloane Sq)

USA (Map p90; ☎ 7499 9000; www.usembassy.org.uk; 5 Upper Grosvenor St W1; ⊖ Bond St)

EMERGENCY

Dial ☎ 999 to call the police, fire brigade or ambulance in an emergency. For hospitals with 24-hour accident and emergency departments, see opposite.

HOLIDAYS

With typically four to five weeks' annual leave, Britons get fewer holidays than their European compatriots, but more than their American friends.

Public Holidays

Most attractions and businesses close for a couple of days over Christmas, and those places that normally shut on Sunday will probably also do so on bank holiday Mondays.

New Year's Day 1 January

Good Friday/Easter Monday Late March/April

May Day Holiday First Monday in May

Spring Bank Holiday Last Monday in May

Summer Bank Holiday Last Monday in August

Christmas Day 25 December

Boxing Day 26 December

For details of the many festivals London hosts throughout the year, see p16.

School Holidays

These change from year to year and often from school to school. Moreover, public (ie private) school holidays tend to differ from those of state schools. As a general rule, however:

Spring half term One week in mid-February.

Easter holidays Two weeks either side of Easter Sunday.

Summer half term One week during end of May/early June.

Summer holiday Late July to early September.

Autumn half term Last week of Octobe.r

Christmas holidays Roughly 20 December to 6 January.

INTERNET ACCESS

Logging onto the internet shouldn't be a problem: if you have your own laptop you can go online with ease from most hotel rooms (though, sadly, expect to pay in most places), and if you don't you can drop into any internet cafe or library throughout the capital. For internet cafe locations, visit www.cybercafes .com. The most readily available internet cafe chain in London is easyInternetcafe (www.easyinter netcafe.com) with branches throughout the city. Prices vary depending on the time of day, but start at £1 per hour.

Wireless access is improving. The City of London is one big wifi zone (see www.the

cloud.net), which is free for the first month you use it and then you have to pay; Islington's Upper St is a 'technology mile' of free wifi access, and Leicester Sq has free wifi access (that you can even get inside Starbucks!). Most major train stations and airport terminals, as well as Starbucks, have wifi access, but it can be quite pricey. Many cafes and public spaces offer wifi, although you usually have to ask for the password and sometimes pay. For more info on wifi spots, go to www .wi-fihotspotlist.com.

LEGAL MATTERS

Should you face any legal difficulties while in London, visit any one of the Citizens Advice Bureaux (www.citizensadvice.org.uk) listed under 'Counselling & Advice' in the Yellow Pages, or contact the Community Legal Services Directory (☎ 0845 345 4345; www.clsdirect.org.uk).

Driving Offences

The laws against drink-driving are very strict and are treated seriously. Currently the limit is 80mg of alcohol in 100mL of blood. The safest approach is not to drink anything at all if you're planning to drive.

Drugs

Illegal drugs of every type are widely available in London, especially in clubs. Nonetheless, all the usual drug warnings apply. Cannabis was reclassified as a Class C drug in 2004, removing the risk of arrest for the possession of small quantities, but then later reclassified as a Class B drug in 2009 following new studies that prompted a government rethink. If you're caught with pot today, you're likely to be arrested. Possession of harder drugs, including heroin and cocaine, is always treated seriously. Searches on entering clubs are common.

Fines

In general you rarely have to cough up on the spot for an offence. The exceptions are trains, the tube and buses, where people who can't produce a valid ticket for the journey when asked to by an inspector can be fined there and then. No excuses are accepted, though if you can't pay, you'll be able to register your details (if you have ID with you) and sent a fine in the post.

Britain has 'Anti-Social Behaviour Orders' (ASBOs), allowing police to issue fixed penalty notices for antisocial behaviour. These run from £50 for minors attempting to buy alcohol to £100 for being drunk and disorderly, making false ☎ 999 calls or wasting police time.

MAPS

The *London A-Z* series produces a range of excellent maps and hand-held street atlases. All areas of London mapped on this system can be accessed at www.streetmap.co.uk, one of London's most invaluable websites.

Lonely Planet also publishes a *London City Map*.

Bookshops with a wide selection of maps include Stanford's (p216), Foyle's (p215), Waterstone's (p216) and Daunt Books (p215).

MEDICAL SERVICES

Reciprocal arrangements with the UK allow Australian residents, New Zealand nationals, and residents and nationals of several other countries to receive free emergency medical treatment and subsidised dental care through the National Health Service (NHS; ☎ 0845 4647; www .nhsdirect.nhs.uk). They can use hospital emergency departments, GPs and dentists (check the Yellow Pages). Visitors staying 12 months or longer, with the proper documentation, will receive care under the NHS by registering with a specific practice near their residence.

EU nationals can obtain free emergency treatment on presentation of a European Health Insurance card.

Travel insurance, however, is advisable as it offers greater flexibility over where and how you're treated and covers expenses for an ambulance and repatriation that won't be picked up by the NHS.

Dental Services

For emergency dental care, call into UCL Eastman Dental Hospital (Map p150; ☎ 7915 1000; www.eastman.ucl .ac.uk; 256 Gray's Inn Rd WC1; ⊖ King's Cross).

Hospitals

The following hospitals have 24-hour accident and emergency departments. However, in an emergency just call ☎ 999 and an ambulance will normally be dispatched from the hospital nearest to you.

Charing Cross Hospital (Map p178; ☎ 8846 1234; Fulham Palace Rd W6; ⊖ Hammersmith)

Chelsea & Westminster Hospital (Map p196; ☎ 8746 8000; 369 Fulham Rd SW10; ⊖ South Kensington, then 🚌 14 or 211)

Guy's Hospital (Map p126; ☎ 7188 7188; St Thomas St SE1; ⊖ London Bridge)

Homerton Hospital (Map p156; ☎ 8510 5555; Homerton Row E9; 🚉 Homerton)

Royal Free Hospital (Map p166; ☎ 7794 0500; Pond St NW3; ⊖ Belsize Park)

Royal London Hospital (Map p156; ☎ 7377 7000; Whitechapel Rd E1; ⊖ Whitechapel)

University College Hospital (Map pp80–1; ☎ 0845 1555 000; 253 Euston Rd NW1; ⊖ Euston Sq)

Pharmacies

There's always one neighbourhood chemist that's open 24 hours; check the Yellow Pages for one near you.

Most people will be instantly struck by the almost total monopoly enjoyed by Boots, which has one of its most centrally located outlets at Piccadilly Circus (Map p66; ☎ 7734 6126; 44-46 Regent St; 🕙 9am-8pm Mon-Sat, noon-6pm Sun; ⊖ Piccadilly Circus). The Superdrug chain is the only potential rival. Both chains are extremely well supplied.

METRIC SYSTEM

People in London use both the metric and imperial systems interchangeably. Some older people will not readily comprehend metric measurements and, similarly, some younger people will not readily understand imperial. See the inside front cover for conversions.

MONEY

Despite being a member of the EU, the UK has not signed up to the euro and has retained the pound sterling (£) as its unit of currency. One pound sterling is made up of 100 pence (called 'pee', colloquially). Notes come in denominations of £5, £10, £20 and £50, while coins are 1p, 2p, 5p, 10p, 20p, 50p, £1 and £2. Unless otherwise noted, all prices in this book are in pounds sterling. See p18 for an idea of the cost of living in London.

ATMs

ATMs are a way of life in London, as the huge queues by them on Saturday nights in the West End attest. There is no area in London unserved by them, and they accept cards from any bank in the world that is tied into the Visa, MasterCard, Cirrus or Maestro systems, as well as more obscure ones. After a national campaign, most banks now allow their cardholders to withdraw money from other banks' ATMs without charge. However, those without UK high-street bank cards should be warned that there is nearly always a transaction surcharge for cash withdrawals. You should contact your bank to find out how much this is before using ATMs too freely. There are nonbank-run ATMs that charge £1.50 to £2 per transaction. These are normally found inside shops and are particularly expensive for foreign bank card holders. The ATM does warn you before you take money out that it'll charge you so you don't get any surprises on your bank statement.

Also, always beware of suspicious-looking devices attached to ATMs. Many London ATMs have now been made tamperproof, but certain fraudsters' devices are capable of sucking your card into the machine, allowing the fraudsters to release it when you have given up and left.

Changing Money

The best place to change money is in any local post office branch, where no commission is charged. You can also change money in most high-street banks and some travel-agent chains, as well as at the numerous bureaux de change throughout the city. Compare rates and watch for the commission that is not always mentioned. The trick is to ask how many pounds you'll receive in all before committing – you'll lose nothing by shopping around.

Credit & Debit Cards

Credit and debit cards are accepted almost universally in London, from restaurants and bars to shops and even some taxis. American Express and Diner's Club are less widely used than Visa and MasterCard, while most Londoners simply live off their Switch debit cards, which can also be used to get 'cash back' from supermarkets, saving a trip to an ATM if you are low on cash.

NEWSPAPERS & MAGAZINES

Newspapers

For a good selection of foreign-language newspapers, try the newsstands in the Victoria Pl shopping centre at Victoria train station, along Charing Cross Rd, in Old Compton St and along Queensway. See p329 for details of gay and lesbian publications.

DAILY PAPERS

Daily Express Midlevel tabloid.

Daily Mail This is often called the voice of middle England, and is a centre-right publication well known for its stance on immigrants and its obsession with house prices.

Daily Star Very low-brow tabloid with wacky tales that often beggar belief.

Daily Telegraph Dubbed the 'Torygraph', this is the unofficial Conservative party paper, whose reputation has grown enormously in the wake of its disclosure and scrutiny of MPs' expenses in 2009.

Evening Standard London's main daily paper has introduced a free *London Lite* to compete with the giveaway *Metro*. Most useful on Thursday for its listings magazine *Metro Life*, it was recently bought by Russian former KGB agent Alexander Lebedev.

Financial Times Heavyweight business paper with a great travel section in its weekend edition.

Guardian Liberal and middle-class, the *Guardian* has good reporting and an award-winning website. An entertainment supplement, the *Guide,* comes with Saturday's paper.

Independent Not aligned with any political party, the *Independent* is a left-leaning serious-minded tabloid with opinion columns and a good culture supplement.

London Lite A free paper launched in autumn 2006, Lite really is the right word when it comes to the substance and quality of this celebrity-fad-obsessed trashy publication.

Metro This free morning paper from the *Daily Mail* stable litters tube stations and seats, giving you an extra excuse to ignore your fellow passengers. It's as lightweight as it is thin.

Mirror This is the country's second most famous tabloid, a working class, Old Labour paper best known these days for its celebrity gossip pages.

Sun The UK's bestseller, this gossip-loving tabloid is owner Rupert Murdoch's entrée to power here. Legendary for its clever (and sometimes offensive) headlines, it supported the Tories during their 1980s glory years, before switching to New Labour. It's now leaning back to the Tories though.

Times The first to follow the *Independent* in downsizing to a smaller format, this stalwart of the British press is part of the Murdoch stable too. It's a decent read with a wide range of articles and good foreign reporting.

SUNDAY PAPERS

Mail on Sunday Similar in style and tone to its weekly sister paper.

News of the World Sister to the *Sun,* this is the ultimate scandal mag, with an enormous readership. It has a passion for kiss-and-tell stories and campaigns.

Observer Sunday-only paper similar in tone and style to the *Guardian,* which owns it, with a great Sunday arts supplement (the *Review*).

Sunday Telegraph As serious as its weekly sister.

Sunday Times Full of scandal and fashion. Probably destroys at least one rainforest per issue, but most of it can be arguably tossed in the recycling bin upon purchase.

Magazines

Dazed & Confused The heady days when Rankin made his name as a photographer are long gone, but Jefferson Hack (father of Kate Moss' daughter) has managed to keep his style magazine going many years.

Economist In-depth global news stories come with an unsurprising but unobtrusive financial bent in this quietly successful weekly magazine (or, as the proprietors insist, 'newspaper'). It's the one people say they read to create an aura of substance.

Heat This phenomenally successful celebrity mag created a whole new genre, as rivals raced to imitate its weekly dose of iconoclasm and sycophancy.

i-D This ubercool London fashion/music gospel is possibly too hip for its own good, but it's still turning out its trademark winking covers every month.

Loaded The original lads mag (as opposed to a men's magazine such as the market-leading *FHM*), *Loaded* reinvented itself as a 'new lads' mag, throwing some investigative journalism, real-life stories and an 'arty' black-and-white centrefold section into the mix.

London Review of Books Shunning the general trend for lifestyle journalism, this literary criticism magazine sticks to academic-style essays.

Loot (www.loot.com) This paper appears five times per week and is made up of classified ads placed free by sellers. You can find everything from kitchen sinks to cars, as well as an extensive selection of flat- and house-share ads.

New Statesman This left-wing intellectual news magazine was given a new lease of life in 2005 by editor John Kampfner after a difficult period, returning to its 'heritage of radical politics'. In 2008, its new editor Jason Cowley pledged to make it more internationalist in its coverage.

Private Eye (see p54) This brilliant satirical weekly was established by comedian Peter Cook and is edited by Ian Hislop. Its twist on the news often borders on the surreal; check its always-hilarious front page.

Spectator Tory voters love this right-wing weekly, but its witty articles are often loved by left-wingers too. It claims to be Britain's oldest running magazine.

Time Out (www.timeout.com) The London going-out bible is published every Tuesday, providing a complete listing of what's on and where.

POST

The Royal Mail has suffered somewhat in its speed and accuracy since privatisation, though it's still generally very reliable. For general postal enquiries ring ☎ 08457 740 740, or visit www.royalmail.co.uk.

Postal Rates

Domestic 1st-class mail is quicker (next working day) but more expensive (39p per letter under 100g) than 2nd class (30p per letter under 100g, taking three working days).

Postcards and letters up to 20g cost 56p to anywhere in Europe; to almost everywhere else, including the Americas and Australasia, it's 62/90p up to 10/20g. Parcels up to 100/250g cost £1.28/1.62 to Europe and £1.69/2.82 to the Americas and Australasia. They must be taken to the post office for weighing.

Airmail letters to the USA or Canada generally take three to five days; to Australia or New Zealand, allow five days to a week.

Postcodes

The unusual London postal code system dates back to WWI. The whole city is divided up into districts denoted by a letter (or letters) and a number. For example, W1, the Mayfair and Soho postcode, stands for 'West London, district 1'. EC1, on the other hand, stands for 'East Central London, district 1'. The number a district is assigned has nothing to do with its geographic location, but rather its alphabetical listing in that area. For example, in north London N1 and N16 are right next to each other. While in West London W2 is very central indeed, W3 is further out.

RADIO

For a taste of London on the airwaves, tune into:

BBC London Live (94.9 FM) Talk station focusing on London.

Capital FM (95.8 FM) The commercial equivalent of the BBC's national Radio 1 and the most popular pop station in the city.

Capital Gold (1548AM) Plays oldies from the '60s, '70s and '80s.

Choice FM (96.9 FM) Soul station.

Jazz FM (102.2 FM) Smooth jazz and cheesy tunes.

Kiss 100 (100 FM) Dance music.

LBC (1152AM) A talkback channel.

Magic FM (105.4 FM) Mainstream oldies.

News Direct (97.3 FM) An all-news station with full reports every 20 minutes.

Talk Sport (1089AM) Self-explanatory!

Virgin (105.8 FM) Pop station.

Xfm (104.9 FM) An alternative radio station playing indie music.

RELOCATING

If you're moving to London and you come from outside the EU, make sure you have a valid residence and work visa; see p393 and p394. Those of you looking for accommodation, check the Loot (www.loot.com) newspaper or web page, or see the brilliant Gumtree (www.gumtree.com), where you can look for flats and jobs. See p332 for more on longer term rentals in London.

If you're looking for areas to hang out with expats, try West London (Earl's Court, Fulham and Shepherd's Bush) for Aussie, US and Kiwi communities; there's a big concentration of South Africans in Putney. Poles are scattered over much of the city, but Balham and Hammersmith have Polish community centres and churches; the Spanish are traditionally around the Portobello area, while the Portuguese are in Stockwell. Cypriot and Turkish communities are found in Dalston, Stoke Newington and along Green Lanes. Edgware Rd is a bustling Arab area; Dalston is known as the Caribbean core, together with Brixton.

Check the weekly freebies *TNT Magazine*, *Southern Cross* or *SA Times*, with Australasian and South African news and sports results. They are also useful for their entertainment listings, travel sections and classified ads for jobs, cheap tickets, shipping services and accommodation, and can be found outside most tube stations.

SAFETY

London's a fairly safe city considering its size, so exercising common sense should keep you safe.

If you're getting a cab after a night's clubbing, makes sure you go for a black cab or a licensed minicab firm. Many of the touts operating outside clubs and bars are unlicensed and can therefore be unsafe. The areas where you should try hard to avoid wandering around alone at night are King's Cross, Dalston and Peckham, though sticking to the main roads offers a certain degree of safety. Pickpocketing does happen in London, so keep your handbag closed and any obvious pocket empty or buttoned up, especially in crowded areas, most particularly in the West End and within the Underground.

TAXES & REFUNDS

Value-added tax (VAT) is normally a 17.5% sales tax levied on most goods and services except food, books and children's clothing. In December 2008 it was lowered to 15% to help boost the languishing economy in the wake of the economic downturn, though it may change back in the lifetime of this book. Restaurants must, by law, include VAT in their menu prices.

It's sometimes possible for visitors to claim a refund of VAT paid on goods, resulting in considerable savings. You're eligible if you have spent fewer than 365 days out of the two years prior to making the purchase living in the UK, and if you're leaving the EU within three months of making the purchase.

Not all shops participate in the VAT refund scheme, called the Retail Export Scheme or Tax-Free Shopping, and different shops will have different minimum purchase conditions (normally around £75 in any one shop). On request, participating shops will give you a special form (VAT 407). This must be presented with the goods and receipts to customs when you depart the country (VAT-free goods can't be posted or shipped home). After customs has certified the form, it should be returned to the shop for a refund (minus an administration or handling fee), which takes about eight to 10 weeks to come through.

TELEPHONE

British Telecom's (BT's) famous red phone boxes survive in conservation areas only (notably Westminster), and in the mobile-phone age the company is even lobbying to get rid of its more modern glass cubicles.

Some phones still accept coins, but most take phonecards or credit cards. BT's £5, £10 and £20 phonecards are widely available from retailers, including most post offices and some newsagents. A digital display on the telephone indicates how much credit is left on the card.

The following are some important telephone numbers and codes (some numbers are charged calls):

Directory enquiries, international (☎ 118 661/118 505)

Directory enquiries, local & national (☎ 118 118/118 500)

International dialling code (☎ 00)

Operator, international (☎ 155)

Operator, local & national (☎ 100)

Reverse charge/collect calls (☎ 155)

Time (☎ 123)

Weathercall (☎ 0906 654 3268) Covers the Greater London area.

Following are some special phone codes worth knowing:

Local call rate applies (☎ 08457)

National call rate applies (☎ 0870/0871)

Premium rate applies (☎ 09) From 60p per minute.

Toll-free (☎ 0800)

Calling London

London's area code is ☎ 020, followed by an eight-digit number beginning with 7 (central London) or 8 (Greater London). You only need to dial the ☎ 020 when you are calling London from elsewhere in the UK.

To call London from abroad, dial your country's international access code, then 44 (the UK's country code), then 20 (dropping the initial 0), followed by the eight-digit phone number.

International Calls & Rates

International direct dialling (IDD) calls to almost anywhere can be made from nearly all public telephones. Direct dialling is cheaper than making a reverse-charge (collect) call through the international operator (☎ 155).

Many private firms offer cheaper international calls than British Telecom (BT). In such shops you phone from a metered booth and then pay the bill. Some cybercafes and internet access shops also offer cheap rates for international calls.

It's also possible to undercut BT international call rates by buying a special card (usually denominated £5, £10 or £20) with a PIN that you use from any phone, even a home phone, by dialling a special access number. These cards are available at most corner shops.

Local & National Call Rates

Local calls are charged by time alone; regional and national calls are charged by both time and distance. Daytime rates apply from 6am to 6pm Monday to Friday; the cheap rate applies from 6pm to 6am Monday to Friday; and the cheap weekend rate applies from 6pm Friday to 6am Monday.

Mobile Phones

The UK uses the GSM 900 network, which covers Europe, Australia and New Zealand, but is not compatible with the North American GSM 1900 or the totally different system in Japan (though many North Americans have GSM 1900/900 phones that do work in the UK). If you have a GSM phone, check with your service provider about using it in the UK, and beware of calls being routed internationally. It's usually most convenient to buy a local SIM card from any mobile phone shop, though in order to do that you must ensure your handset is unlocked before you leave home – contact your home cell provider before you travel.

TELEVISION

Five free-to-air analogue stations exist, along with digital channels that can be viewed through a Freeview box (free viewing after purchasing the box) or cable/satellite providers. The UK is gradually phasing out analogue broadcasts though – by 2012 only digital televisions will be able to receive programmes. See www.digitaltelevision.gov.uk for more information.

The main UK channels available to anyone at present are BBC1, BBC2, ITV, Channel 4 and Five.

TIME

Wherever you are in the world, the time on your watch is measured in relation to the time at Greenwich in London – Greenwich Mean Time (GMT). British Summer Time, the UK's form of daylight-saving time, muddies the water so that even London is ahead of GMT from late March to late October. To give you an idea, San Francisco is usually eight hours and New York five hours behind GMT, while Sydney is 10 hours ahead of GMT. Phone the international operator on ☎ 155 to find out the exact difference.

TIPPING

Many restaurants now add a 'discretionary' service charge to your bill, but in places that don't you are expected to leave a 10% to 15%

tip unless the service was unsatisfactory. Waiting staff are often paid poorly. It's legal for restaurants to include a service charge in the bill but this should be clearly advertised. You never tip to have your pint pulled in a pub but staff at bars often return change in a little metal dish, hoping some of the coins will glue themselves to the bottom.

If you take a boat trip on the Thames you'll find some guides and/or drivers importuning for a tip in return for their commentary. Whether you pay is up to you. You can tip taxi drivers up to 10% but most people round up to the nearest pound.

TOILETS

Train stations, bus terminals and attractions generally have good facilities, providing also for people with disabilities and those with young children. At train and bus stations you usually have to pay 20p to use the facilities.

It's an offence to urinate in the streets, although arrests are rare. However, with the streets of Soho so frequently stinking of urine, Westminster council has pioneered an excellent scheme whereby public urinals are set up on the streets at weekends for those who can't make it to the next bar without relieving themselves. These can be found on Soho Sq, Wardour St, off Oxford St and on The Strand, among other locations. The street urinals are obviously only useable by men so women will need to cross their legs until they find somewhere they can go.

For information on toilets for the disabled, see opposite.

TOURIST INFORMATION

London is a major travel centre, so along with information on London, tourist offices can help with England, Scotland, Wales, Ireland and most countries worldwide.

Tourist Offices

Visit London (☎ 7234 5800, 0870 156 6366; www.visit london.com), formerly the London Tourist Board, can fill you in on everything from tourist attractions and events (such as the Changing of the Guard) to river trips and tours, accommodation, eating, theatre, shopping, children's London, and gay and lesbian venues.

London's main tourist office is the Britain Visitor Centre (Map p66; 1 Regent St SW1; ☯ 9.30am-6pm Mon, 9am-6.30pm Tue-Fri, 10am-4pm Sat & Sun, to 5pm Sat

Jun-Sep; ⊖ Piccadilly Circus). It has comprehensive information in eight languages, not just on London, but on Wales, Scotland, Northern Ireland, the Irish Republic and Jersey too. It can arrange accommodation, tours, and train, air and car travel. It also has a theatre ticket agency, a bureau de change, international telephones and a few computer terminals for accessing tourist information on the web. The centre deals with walk-in enquiries only, so if you're not in the area, contact the British Tourist Authority (☎ 8846 9000; www.visitbritain.com).

Other useful tourist offices include the London Visitor Centre (Map p126; Arrivals Hall, Waterloo International Terminal; ☾ 8.30am-10.30pm), Heathrow Airport TIC (Terminal 1, 2 & 3 Underground station; ☾ 8am-6pm) and Liverpool Street tourist office (Map p100; Liverpool St Underground station; ☾ 8am-6pm). Hotel booking offices are also found in the halls of Paddington train station, Victoria train station (☾ 8am-8pm Mon-Sat, 8am-6pm Sun Apr-Oct, 8am-6pm Mon-Sat, 9am-4pm Sun Nov-Mar) and Victoria coach station. There are also accommodation booking services at other London airports.

A few London boroughs and neighbourhoods have their own tourist offices. These include:

City Information Centre (Map p100; ☎ 7332 1456; www.cityoflondon.gov.uk; St Paul's Churchyard EC4; ☾ 9.30am-5pm Apr-Sep, 9.30am-5pm Mon-Fri, 9.30am-12.30pm Sat Oct-Mar; ⊖ St Paul's) Opposite St Paul's Cathedral.

Greenwich Tourist Office (Map p182; ☎ 0870 608 2000; www.greenwich.gov.uk; Pepys House, 2 Cutty Sark Gardens SW10; ☾ 10am-5pm; DLR Cutty Sark)

Richmond Tourist Office (Map p200; ☎ 8940 9125; www.visitrichmond.co.uk; Old Town Hall, Whittaker Ave, Richmond, Surrey TW9 1TP; ☾ 10am-5pm Mon-Sat, plus 10.30am-1pm Sun May-Sep; ☒ Richmond)

Southwark Tourist Office (Map p126; ☎ 7357 9168; www.southwark.gov.uk; Vinopolis, 1 Bank End SE1; ☾ 10am-6pm Tue-Sun; ⊖ London Bridge)

TRAVELLERS WITH DISABILITIES

For disabled travellers London is an odd mix of user-friendliness and downright disinterest. New hotels and modern tourist attractions are legally required to be accessible to people in wheelchairs, but many B&Bs and guesthouses are in older buildings, which are hard (if not impossible) to adapt. This means that travellers who have mobility problems may end up paying more for accommodation.

It's a similar story with public transport. Access to the tube is limited. However, some of the newer trains and buses have steps that lower for easier access, and there are two dedicated bus services with automatic ramps offering disabled access: the 205 and the 705. The 205 runs from Paddington to Whitechapel every 10 to 12 minutes. The 705 runs between Victoria, Waterloo and London Bridge half-hourly. Both services operate approximately from 6am to midnight.

Transport for London's Access & Mobility for Disabled Passengers (☎ 7222 1234, textphone 7918 3015; Windsor House, 42/50 Victoria St, London SW1 9TN) can give you detailed advice and it publishes *Access to the Underground*, which indicates which tube stations have ramps and lifts (all DLR stations do).

The Royal Association for Disability & Rehabilitation (Radar; ☎ 7250 3222; www.radar.org.uk; Unit 12, City Forum, 250 City Rd, London EC1V 8AF) is an umbrella organisation for voluntary groups for people with disabilities. Many disabled-user toilets across London can be opened only with a special key, which can be obtained from tourist offices or for £3.50 (plus a brief statement of your disability) via the Radar website.

The Royal National Institute for the Blind (☎ 7388 1266; www.rnib.org.uk; 105 Judd St, London WC1) can also be contacted via its confidential helpline (☎ 0303 123 9999; ☾ 9am-5pm Mon-Fri, to 4pm Wed) and is the best point of initial contact for sight-impaired visitors to London. The Royal National Institute for Deaf People (☎ freephone 0808 808 0123, freephone/textphone 0808 808 9000; www.rnid.org.uk; 19-23 Featherstone St, London EC1) is a similar organisation for the deaf and hard of hearing. Many ticket offices and banks are fitted with hearing loops to help the hearing-impaired; look for the ear symbol.

VISAS

Citizens of Australia, Canada, New Zealand, South Africa and the USA are given, at their point of arrival, 'leave to enter' the UK for up to six months but are prohibited from working without a work permit. If you're a citizen of the EU, you don't need a visa to enter the country and may live and work here freely for as long as you like.

Visa regulations are always subject to change, so check at www.ukvisas.gov.uk or with your local British embassy before leaving home.

Immigration authorities in the UK are tough: dress neatly and be able to prove that you have sufficient funds to support yourself. A credit card and/or an onward ticket will help.

Student Visas

Nationals of EU countries can enter the country to study without formalities. Otherwise you need to be enrolled in a full-time course of at least 15 hours per week of weekday, daytime study at a single educational institution to be allowed to remain as a student. For more details, consult the British embassy, high commission or consulate in your own country.

Visa Extensions

Tourist visas can only be extended in clear emergencies (eg an accident, death of a relative). Otherwise you'll have to leave the UK (perhaps going to Ireland or France) and apply for a fresh one, although this tactic will arouse suspicion after the second or third visa. To extend (or attempt to extend) your stay in the UK, ring the Visa & Passport Information Line (☎ 0870 606 7766, 8649 7878; the Home Office's Immigration & Nationality Directorate, Lunar House, 40 Wellesley Rd, Croydon CR9 2BY; ☼ 10am-noon & 2-4pm Mon-Fri; ⓐ East Croydon) before your current visa expires. The process takes a few days in France/Ireland. Trying to extend within the UK takes a lot longer.

WOMEN TRAVELLERS

In general, London is a fairly laid-back place, and you're unlikely to have too many problems provided you take the usual city precautions. Apart from the occasional wolf whistle and unwelcome body contact on the tube, women will find male Londoners reasonably enlightened. Going into pubs alone may not always be a comfortable experience even in central London, though it's in no way out of the ordinary. Women travelling alone at night can choose Archway-based Ladycabs (☎ 7272 3300), which has women drivers.

Information & Organisations

Marie Stopes International (Map pp80–1; ☎ 0845 300 8090; www.mariestopes.org.uk; 108 Whitfield St W1; ☼ 8.30am-5pm Mon, Wed & Fri, 9.30am-6pm Tue & Thu, 9am-4pm Sat; ⊖ Warren St) Provides contraception, sexual health checks and abortions.

Rape & Sexual Abuse Helpline (☎ 8239 1122; ☼ noon-2.30pm & 7-9.30pm Mon-Fri, 2.30-5pm Sat & Sun)

Safety Precautions

Solo women travellers should have few problems, although common-sense caution should be observed, especially at night. It's particularly unwise to get into an Underground carriage with no-one else in it or with just one or two men. If you feel unsafe, you should hang the expense and take a taxi.

WORK

Even if you're unskilled, you'll almost certainly find work in London, but you have to be prepared to work long hours at menial jobs for low pay. Without skills it's difficult to find a job that pays well enough to save money.

Traditionally, unskilled visitors have worked in pubs and restaurants and as nannies. A minimum wage (£5.73 per hour; £4.77 for those aged 18 to 21) exists, but if you're working illegally no-one's obliged to pay you even that.

Accountants, health professionals, journalists, computer programmers, lawyers, teachers, bankers and clerical workers with computer experience stand a better chance of finding well-paid work. Don't forget copies of your qualifications, references (which will probably be checked) and a CV (résumé).

Teachers should contact the individual London borough councils, which have separate education departments, although some schools recruit directly.

To work as a trained nurse or midwife you have to apply to the UK Nursing & Midwifery Council (☎ 7333 9333; www.nmc-uk.org). Write to the Overseas Registration Department, UKNMC, 23 Portland Pl, London W1N 4JT. If you aren't registered then you can still work as an auxiliary nurse.

The free *TNT Magazine* is a good starting point for jobs and agencies aimed at travellers. For au pair and nanny work, buy the quaintly titled *The Lady*. Also check the *Evening Standard*, the national newspapers and government-operated Jobcentres, which are scattered throughout London and listed under 'Employment Services' in the phone directory. It's worth registering with a few temporary agencies.

If you play a musical instrument or have other artistic talents, busking will make you some pocket money. However, to perform in

Underground stations, you have to go through a rigorous process taking several months. After signing up at www.tfl.gov.uk, you will have to go through an audition and get police security clearance (£10) before being granted a licence to perform and then getting yourself on a rota of marked pitches. Buskers also need to have a permit to work at top tourist attractions and popular areas such as Covent Garden and Leicester Sq. Contact the local borough council for details.

Tax

As an official employee, you'll find income tax and National Insurance are automatically deducted from your weekly pay packet. However, the deductions will be calculated on the assumption that you're working for the entire financial year (which runs from 6 April to 5 April). If you don't work as long as that, you may be eligible for a refund. Visit the website of the Inland Revenue (www.inlandrevenue.org.uk) to locate your nearest tax office, or use one of the agencies that advertise in *TNT Magazine* (but check their fee or percentage charge first).

Work Permits

EU and Swiss nationals don't need a work permit to work in London but everyone else does.

If you're a citizen of a Commonwealth country and aged between 17 and 30, you may apply for a Working Holiday Entry Certificate, which allows you to spend up to two years in the UK and take 12 months' work 'incidental' to your holiday. You're not allowed to set up your own business or work as a professional sportsperson. You must apply to your country's British consulate or high commission before departure – Working Holiday Entry Certificates are not granted on arrival in Britain. It is not possible to switch from being a visitor to a working holiday-maker, nor can you claim back any time spent out of the UK during the two-year period. When you apply, you must satisfy the authorities that you have the means to pay for a return or onward journey and that you will be able to maintain yourself without recourse to public funds.

If you're a Commonwealth citizen and have a parent born in the UK, you may be eligible for a Certificate of Entitlement to the Right of Abode (or indeed a British passport), which means you can live and work in Britain free of immigration control.

If you're a Commonwealth citizen with a grandparent born in the UK, or if the grandparent was born before 31 March 1922 in what is now the Republic of Ireland, you may qualify for a UK Ancestry Employment Certificate, which means you can work in the UK full time for up to four years.

Students from the US who are at least 18 years old and studying full time at a college or university can get a Blue Card permit for US$250, allowing them to work in the UK for six months. It's available through the British Universities North America Club (Bunac; ☎ 203 264 0901; wib@bunacusa.com; PO Box 430, Southbury CT 06488). Once in the UK, Bunac can help Blue Card holders find jobs and accommodation; it also runs programmes for Australians, Canadians and New Zealanders but you must apply before leaving home. For more details visit www.bunac.org.

Most other travellers wishing to work and not fitting into any of the aforementioned categories will need a work permit and to be sponsored by a British company. See www.ukvisas.gov.uk for more details.

If you have any queries once you're in the UK, contact the Home Office (☎ 0870 000 1585).

BEHIND THE SCENES

THIS BOOK

This 7th edition of *London* was researched and written by Tom Masters, Steve Fallon and Vesna Maric, all of whom also worked on the 6th edition. Sarah Johnstone and Tom Masters wrote the 5th edition. Martin Hughes, Sarah Johnstone and Tom Masters wrote the 4th edition. Steve Fallon wrote the 2nd and 3rd edition. Pat Yale wrote the 1st edition. The guide was commissioned in Lonely Planet's London office and produced by the following:

Commissioning Editor Clifton Wilkinson

Coordinating Editors Holly Alexander, Carly Hall, Charlotte Orr

Coordinating Cartographer Jolyon Philcox

Coordinating Layout Designer Margaret Jung

Senior Editor Helen Christinis

Managing Cartographer Herman So

Managing Layout Designer Laura Jane

Assisting Editors Janice Bird, Stephanie Pearson

Assisting Cartographers Birgit Jordan, Tadhgh Knaggs

Cover research Marika Mercer, lonelyplanetimages.com

Internal image research Aude Vauconsant

Project Managers Glenn van der Knijff, Bronwyn Hicks

Thanks to Lucy Birchley, David Carroll, Daniel Corbett, Melanie Dankel, Sally Darmody, Ryan Evans, Joshua Geoghegan, Jane Hart, Ross Macaw, Darren O'Connell, Trent Paton, Malisa Plesa, Cara Smith, Lyahna Spencer, Juan Winata

Cover photographs Houses of Parliament at dusk, Radius Images/Photolibrary (top); Man reading next to telephone box in Smithfield Market, Ludovic Maisant/Hemis/Corbis (bottom).

Internal photographs by Lonely Planet Images: p114 (right) Glenn Beanland; p12 (#2 top) Paul Bigland; p8 (#2) James Braund; p9 (#1 bottom), p11 (#1 and #2 top), p12 (#3 top, #1 bottom), p110 (right), p116, p210 (right) Juliet Coombe; p9 (#2 top) Elliot Daniel; p7 (#1 and #2), p10 (#2 top), p11 (#2 bottom), p207 (top left and bottom) Travis Drever; p3 Krzysztof Dydyński; p208 Rocco Fasano; p206 Lee Foster; p6 (#2, #3), p8 (#1), p9 (#1 top, #1 and #2 bottom), p110 (left and right), p111, p115 Orien Harvey; p8 (#3) Charlotte Hindle; p7 (#3) Richard I'Anson; p9 (#3 top), p11 (#1 bottom), p12 (#3 bottom), p109, p209, p210 (left), p211, p212 Doug McKinlay; p12 (#2 bottom) Guy Moberly; p6 (#1), p9 (#2 bottom), p10 (#1 top), p12 (#1 top), p112 (left), p114 (left), p205, p207 (right) Neil Setchfield; p2, p113 David Tomlinson; p7 (#4) Wayne Walton.

All images are copyright of the photographer unless otherwise indicated. Many of the images in this guide are available for licensing from Lonely Planet Images: lonelyplanetimages.com.

THANKS
TOM MASTERS

Thanks enormously to Mike Christie who lent me his home as a base for my research. Thanks also to Steve Fallon and Vesna Maric for all their excellent hard work carving up a city as immense as London with me. Thanks to Clifton Wilkinson in the London office for commissioning me again, and as always, to James Bridle whose love of all things London has always been infective. Thanks also to Tommy Moss, Gabriel Gatehouse, Stephen Dorling, Zeeba Carroll, Gray Jordan, Chris Mackay, Leila Rejali, Stephen Billington and Etienne Gilfillan for their company and help while researching this book.

STEVE FALLON

I frequently enter the Underground at Bethnal Green, where 173 people (over a third of them children) were killed during an air raid in March 1943, the highest loss of civilian life in a single incident in London during WWII. The Blitz is thus not a 'foreign country' for me but in my own backyard. It is largely due to the more than 30,000 civilians – grannies and brothers and daughters and lovers – killed in the defence of London 1939–45 that you and I can enjoy London's past, present and future. Remember them.

It was fun working with co-authors Tom Masters and Vesna Maric again, though we passed like proverbial Thames barges in the night.

As always, I'd like to state my admiration, gratitude and great love for my partner, Michael Rothschild.

VESNA MARIC

Thanks to my co-authors Tom Masters and Steve Fallon, a pleasure, as always. Also thanks to Clifton Wilkinson, our CE, for giving me a chance to work on this book for the second time. Thanks to everyone who's accompanied me on my research, including Nicoline Gatehouse, Arijana Gurdon, Rafael Estefania and Gabriel Gatehouse.

OUR READERS

Many thanks to the travellers who used the last edition and wrote to us with helpful hints, useful advice and interesting anecdotes:

Ana Anastasijevic, Olaf G Apel, Alex Aristy, Tom Bartolomei, Riccardo Belletti, Tammy Botsford, Andrew Breitenbach, Dina Bullivant, Chuck Burdick, Linda Cahill, Alessio Cazzola, Ting-Hsu Chen, Evangeline Christie, Christian Dahl, Beren-gere Darsonval, Sally Davis, Tim Dierkes, Caroline Elliker, Rodney Fleming, Claire Fragonas, Nicky Fullmoon, Milind Gadgil, Lynne Grabar, Andrea Groll, Abheek Gupta, Miriam Harris, Michael Hayes, Laurel Herold, Roz Jones, Naeem Kapadia, Joy Kennedy, Judy Kenny, Peter Kim, Guy Kruger, Bernard Lazarus, Nicole Leggett, Anne Leroy, Kaung Chiau Lew, Ulrike Loehrer, Margot Helene Loeken, Barbara Mackney, Kevin P Mccarthy, Erin Mcdougall, Andrew Methven, Saddique Miah, Syarizan Adzlinda Mohd Zin, Heather Monell, Robert Moore, Edith Neele, Krystina Nellis, Guri Norstrøm, David O'Shell, Gerald Olsen, Funda Ozan, Marcus Paauwe, George Padova, Vilija Pauliukonis, Matt Pepe, Demian Perry, Tom Plattenberger, Jo Anne Post, Giovanna Procaccini, David Rhodes, Liesbeth Rijpma, M Roach, Tom Rooke, Veronica Ryan, Marcin Sadurski, David Salter, Aditya Sarkar, Lynden Schofield, Andrea Schulten, Howie Schuman, Anne Shaw, Itay Sidar, David Sojka, Stacey Spooner, Joy Stephens, Melissa Sullivan, Bronwyn Sutton, Stephen Thurlow, Marin Tomic, Lori Rae Tomlinson, Wim Vandenbussche, Marc Vauclair, Per Vinther, Stephanie Warren, Manuele Zunelli

SEND US YOUR FEEDBACK

We love to hear from travellers – your comments keep us on our toes and help make our books better. Our well-travelled team reads every word on what you loved or loathed about this book. Although we cannot reply individually to postal submissions, we always guarantee that your feedback goes straight to the appropriate authors, in time for the next edition. Each person who sends us information is thanked in the next edition and the most useful submissions are rewarded with a free book.

To send us your updates – and find out about Lonely Planet events, newsletters and travel news – visit our award-winning website: lonelyplanet.com/contact.

Note: We may edit, reproduce and incorporate your comments in Lonely Planet products such as guidebooks, websites and digital products, so let us know if you don't want your comments reproduced or your name acknowledged. For a copy of our privacy policy visit lonelyplanet.com/privacy.

ACKNOWLEDGMENTS

Many thanks to the following for the use of their content: London Underground Map © Transport for London 2009. The Central London Bus Map and Tourist Attractions Map © Transport for London 2009.

Notes

30 St Mary Axe 106-7,
212, **212**

A

accommodation 332-54,
see also Sleeping
subindex, individual
neighbourhoods
Ackroyd, Peter 37
activities 318-22,
see also Sports &
Activities subindex
Aikens, Tom 250
air travel 374-7
airlines 374
airports 374-7
to/from Gatwick Airport
376
to/from Heathrow 375-6
to/from London City 377
to/from Luton 377
to/from Stansted Airport
376
tours 380-1
ambulance 386
antiques 232
apartments 332-3
architecture 206-12
area codes, see inside front
cover
arts 34-48, 306-16, see also
Arts subindex
festivals 16, 17
athletics 322
ATMs 388

000 map pages
000 photographs

B

B&Bs, see Sleeping
subindex
babysitters 384
Bacon, Francis 44
Bank 105-17
Bankside 128-30
Barbican 107, **7**
Barnes 195-7
bars, see Drinking
subindex
bathrooms 392
Battersea 192, **190**
Battersea Power Station
192, **12**
BBC 27, 53-4, 97
BBC Promenade Concerts
(The Proms) 17
Beatles, The 30
Bedlam 188, **12**
beer 278
Belgravia 135-8
Bermondsey 130-3
Bethnal Green 158
Bexleyheath 186
bicycle travel 377-8
Big Ben 92, **3**
Black Death 22
Blair, Tony 32
Blitz, the 28
Bloomsbury 79-82, **80-1**
Blue Plaques Scheme 142
boat travel 109-16, 361, 378
tours 380, 381
body snatchers 29
Booker Prize 38
books 36, see also Shopping
subindex
Borough 130-3
boutique hotels, see
Sleeping subindex
Bray 371-2
Brentford 199-201
Brick Lane 152, **9**
Brighton 363-6, **364**
Britart 44-5
British cuisine 234-5
British Library 168-9, **211**
British Museum 79, 83, **6**
Brixton 191-2, **190**
walking tour 193-4, **194**

Brixton Market 193, 226,
259, **12**
Broadstairs 367
BT Tower 210, **210**
Buckingham Palace 86
burlesque 295
bus travel 378-9
to/from Europe 378-9
within UK 378-9
tours 380
business hours 214, 235,
384, see also inside front
cover

C

cabaret, see Drinking
subindex
cafes, see Drinking
subindex
Cambridge 361-3, **362**
Camden 168, **170**
Canterbury 369-70, **370**
car travel 379-80
congestion charge 379
hire 379-80
road rules 379
cathedrals, see Sights
subindex
cell phones 392
cemeteries, see Sights
subindex
changing of the guard 87
Charing Cross Station
111, **110**
Charles I 24
Charlton 183-4
Chelsea 135-47, **136-7**
accommodation 342-5
drinking 280-1
food 247-51
shopping 224-5
Chelsea flower show 17
chemists 388
children, travel with 384
attractions 82, 95-6,
132, 158
Chinatown 63-9
Chiswick 197
churches, see Sights
subindex
Churchill, Winston 94-5
cinema 46-7

cinemas 309-10, see
also Arts subindex
City Hall 115, 212, **114**
City, the 99-123, **100**
accommodation 340-1
drinking 278-9
food 245
shopping 223
walking tour 122-3, **122**
Clapham 192-3, **190**
classical music 306-7
Clerkenwell 148-54, **150**
accommodation 345-6
drinking 281-3
food 251-5
gay & lesbian 327
shopping 225-9
climate 384-5
clothing sizes 215
clubs 294-9
cockney 164
cocktail bars, see Drinking
subindex
comedy 299-301
congestion charge 49, 379
consulates 385-6
Cooke, Dominic 313
costs 18-19
accommodation 332
discount cards 385
eating out 235
taxes 391
tipping 392
County Hall 111, 125, **110**
courses 385
Covent Garden 69-76, **70-1**
credit cards 388
cricket 320-1, see
also Sports & Activities
subindex
Crouch End 173
customs regulations 385
cycling 377-8

D

dance 17, 48, 307-8
Dance Umbrella 17
Defoe, Daniel 34-5
department stores, see
Shopping subindex
Deptford walking tour
186-7, **187**